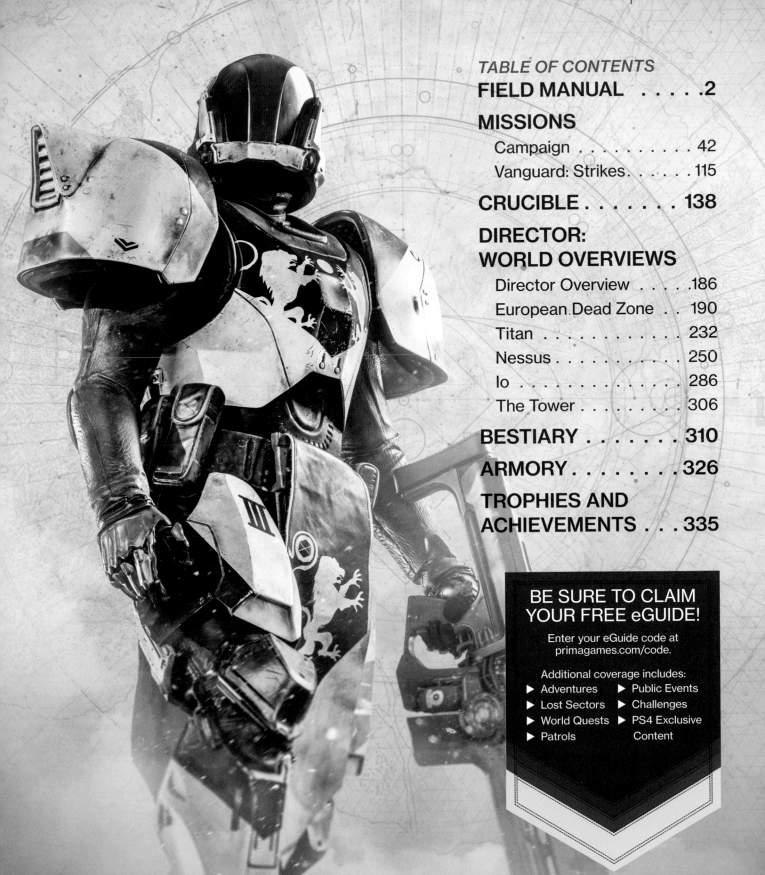

DESTINY 2

TABLE OF CONTENTS

BE SURE TO CLAIM YOUR FREE eGUIDE!

Enter your eGuide code at primagames.com/code.

Additional coverage includes:

- Adventures
- Lost Sectors
- World Quests
- Patrols
- Public Events
- Challenges
- PS4 Exclusive Content

Field Manual

Introduction and Overview

Welcome to training, Guardian! It seems Earth is in need of you more than ever, so it's important to learn exactly what is expected of you, and how to maximize your time for fun and profit. To help you progress, this guide includes a number of helpful chapters. Here's how all this information breaks down:

FIELD MANUAL: A complete overview covering everything from basic actions to Subclasses, Abilities, weapons, armor, gear, navigation, and character progression.

MISSIONS AND ACTIVITIES: An extensive series of chapters detailing the optimal methods for completing all the major missions and Quests. This includes the sprawling Campaign and Strikes. For information on Adventures, World Quests, and general information on Lost Sectors, Patrols, Public Events, and Challenges, consult the online component of this guide, free with the purchase of the book you are holding.

BE SURE TO CLAIM YOUR FREE eGUIDE!

Enter your eGuide code at primagames.com/code.

Additional coverage includes:

- Adventures
- Lost Sectors
- World Quests
- Patrols
- Public Events
- Challenges
- PS4 Exclusive Content

CRUCIBLE: Make Lord Shaxx proud by dominating in the Crucible. This chapter details all maps available at launch, including strategies for the different game modes, and how to better other Guardians in combat.

DIRECTOR: An extensive chapter detailing every Sector available to you at launch from across the four World Regions (European Dead Zone, Titan, Nessus, and Io). It includes enemy clusters, locations of chests and other collectibles, vendors, and extremely detailed maps.

BESTIARY: An overview of the enemies in the game, with visual representations of each, and how best to thwart them in combat.

ARMORY: A look at the available and most interesting (not to mention the rarest) weapons, armor, and other gear, as well as other pertinent data.

Guardian Creation

While returning players have the option to import existing characters, new players (or those looking for a fresh start) must build their first Guardian from the ground up.

Guardian Class

If you're creating a new Guardian, the first thing you must do is select one of three distinct Classes.

Titan

Disciplined and proud, **Titans** are capable of both aggressive assaults and stalwart defenses. Their Class Ability is Barricade, an energy barrier to reinforce a position for your fireteam. They are seen as the "tanks" of *Destiny*—geared to absorb or deflect damage that might otherwise harm their allies. They use punching in melee combat. Through armor specifically designed for Titans, expect to have impressive Resilience, at the cost of Mobility. This is a good choice for both the beginner and seasoned player. Their Guardian Mentor is Commander Zavala.

Hunter

With a specialization in agility, **Hunters** are quick on their feet and to battle. Their strong sense of wanderlust means they never stop exploring. Their Class Ability is Dodge, avoiding enemy attacks with nimble skill. If you prioritize Mobility over Resilience and Recovery, then choose this Guardian. They use knives in melee combat, and through use of Abilities, they attempt to perfect stealthy short- and long-range attacks to take down foes. Their Guardian Mentor is Cayde-6.

Warlock

Warlocks weaponized the mysteries of the universe to sustain themselves and devastate their foes. Their Class Ability is Rift, allowing you to summon Columns of Light that strengthen allies within. They melee strike with a push and tend to favor Recovery over Mobility or Resilience. They're capable of outstanding group support, but they're formidable warriors in their own right. Their Movement Modes are the most difficult to time correctly, but arguably give the most maneuverability once mastered. Their Guardian Mentor is Ikora Rey.

All Access: Multiple Characters

All Guardians have additional Subclasses that are unlocked later into your adventure, as well as a host of Abilities and different types of grenades. It is worth learning about these before committing to a particular Class and Subclass, as perfecting a Guardian is a lengthy process. Of course, you can start a new game with a different Class, and even store items in your vault for your subsequent characters to access.

Guardian Races

You then pick your race and gender. These have no impact on your performance, but they do determine your cosmetic options and your Guardian's default emotes. You can change your face (along with skin, mouth, and eye color), change your hair (or head feature, with color change), and add markings to your character.

Human

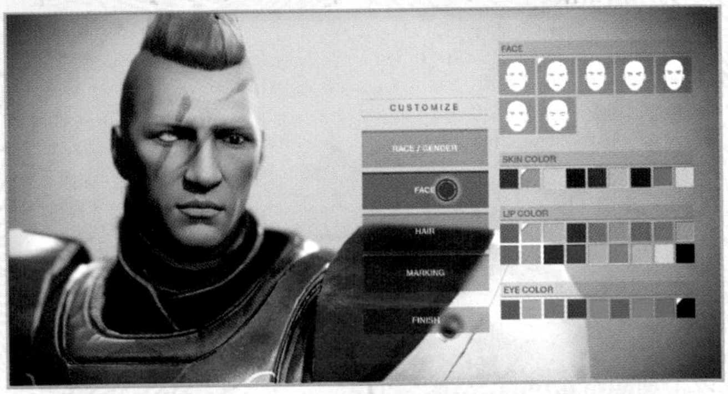

Once casualties of the Collapse, Human Guardians now stand determined to retake the solar system.

Awoken

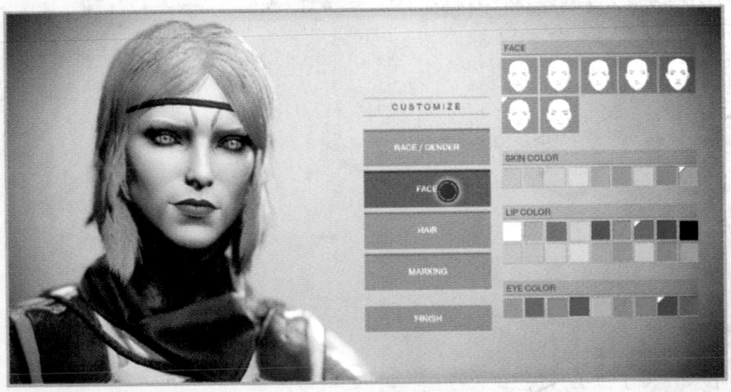

Humans who fled into deep space were forever changed. They're aloof and odd, but ready to fight for all of humanity.

Exo

Exo Guardians are self-aware war machines built for a long-forgotten struggle.

Main Menus

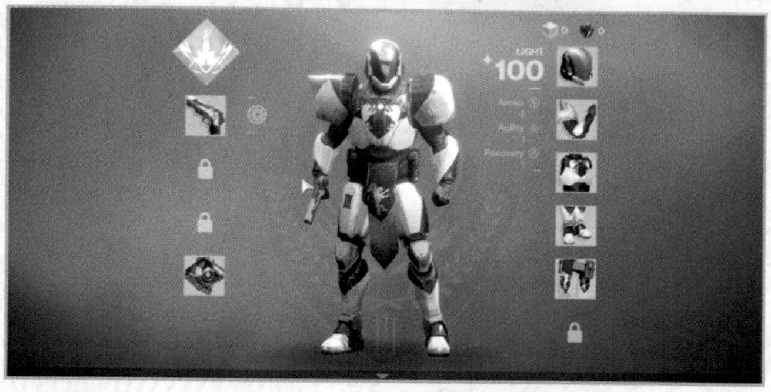

Once your character is created, you can cycle through the five main menus available to you. Here's a brief description of each menu:

CLAN: This menu allows you to create or join a clan if you want to be social, help newer Guardians find their feet, or plan Campaign Missions, Strikes, or other activities with groups of like-minded individuals.

CHARACTER: Used with the most frequency, this menu shows your level, Subclass, your weaponry (Kinetic, Energy, and Power weapons), your Ghost, your Power Level, any funds you have, your armor sections, any Emotes, and vehicles. Click any of the boxes for additional details.

INVENTORY: This shows the entire collection of items you have stored in a vault (found in either of the Social Sectors), which can be shared between your characters.

SETTINGS: Tweak with any and all game features here. Note that one of them allows you to wear a helmet at all times. If you need to fiddle with your sound, controls, visual elements, or accessibility settings, head here.

At this point, you begin your first three Campaign Missions. Once the true threat of the Cabal Red Legion has been assessed, you begin anew as part of Earth's resistance. You have one overriding goal: to build up your Guardian to become the very pinnacle of battle-hardened prowess.

Know Your Enemy

Do you know the differences between a base unit, an Elite, a Sub-Boss, and a Boss? Can you confidently explain the weaponry changes between types of Fallen Captains? If you're still learning what enemies there are and how to kill them, you'd do well to investigate the Bestiary chapter of this guide. It gives you a complete run-down of the strengths, weaknesses, and types of enemies you'll encounter.

Basic Actions

This section details the most basic actions and how to perfect them. It is assumed that you know how to move your character forward and backward. The following actions are listed in the likely order you attempt them.

Firing a Weapon

Fire your weapon until your foes fall down and repeat this until everything is dispatched. Generally, this is the plan of attack. But surviving the multitude of enemy threats requires much greater tactical planning than this. To start with, ensure that you know your weapon's statistics (detailed later in this chapter), its strengths and weaknesses (whether it can cut through Energy Shields or has a massive spread at longer ranges, for example), and how it handles.Then figure out which part of the enemy is vulnerable to Precision Damage. It's either the head or a white glowing "Juice Box" (in the case of some Vex).

Aiming Down Sights

Use this technique to more accurately aim at your foe's weak spots (usually the heads of enemy infantry) more easily, and to help contain your weapons' spread patterns. Note that the target reticle of your weapon usually turns red during this aiming, which is the best time to fire. You can attempt this with all bullet- or projectile-based weapons from all three types (Kinetic, Energy, and Power). Obviously, some weapons like sniper rifles are built for this function. When aiming down sights, expect to deal more damage more accurately, with a loss of peripheral vision.

Precision Kills

Your kill count is being checked at the end of each mission, activity, and Crucible match. Along with your regular kills, there are Precision Kills totals to understand. This is when you defeat an enemy with a killing blow to their weak spot. Look for the yellow (not white) damage numbers that indicate Precision hits—finish an enemy off with one of those shots, and you've earned yourself a Precision Kill.

Melee Attack

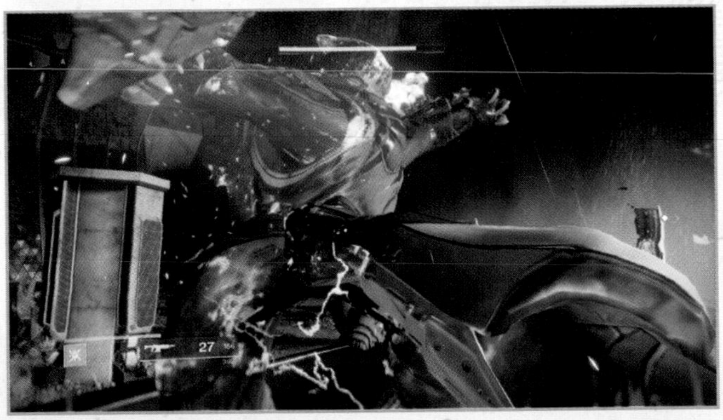

Melee attacks are extremely useful at close quarters, when the enemy is in danger of really hurting you. Make a swift and vicious strike, which can usually bring down a lesser infantry foe (like a Legionary or Dreg) with a single hit.

Position yourself properly before a melee attack, and you automatically complete a small charge and deliver a little more damage. Swipe again afterward if you miss or if the enemy still lives. Melee attacks are helpful if you want to start them a few feet away from a foe so you automatically sprint in and strike. They are also useful after you "soften up" a foe with gunfire and need to save ammunition or take down another enemy instead of reloading. Finally, note that Titans, Hunters, and Warlocks have different methods of inflicting melee damage (a punch, a knife strike, and a forceful push, respectively).

Throwing Grenades

Lobbing an explosive projectile is a great way to defeat or soften up groups of enemies or one larger foe you're having trouble with. Note the grenade icon that appears in the bottom-left corner of your HUD. This slowly refills as you continue, meaning you can only lob one grenade at a time, and only when the icon is full. The Campaign and Strike walkthroughs will let you know opportune moments to lob grenades, but feel free to try this at any time. Note that your Guardian Subclass has three different types of grenades, but the other two are Abilities that are unlocked later.

It is worth learning the arc and inertia of the grenade you throw. Some enemies tend to strafe or flee from grenades before they land, so lobbing "sticky" variants or dropping grenades in front, behind, or in small areas usually yields more damage. If a foe can use a jetpack, expect them to maneuver away from grenades. Careful use in more confined spaces, along with suppressing fire to stop foes from moving away from grenade explosions, is a good idea.

Jumping

Jumping is an integral part of your maneuvering, allowing you to cover gaps across bottomless terrain and leap across both obstacles and enemies. Note that you don't need to land on a location you're jumping to. If you reach the edge of a walkway, gantry, or other destination, your Guardian pulls themselves up and onto it. This is done automatically. In the future, if you want to land on an upper ledge or roof, aim so your torso hits the edge of the area you want to climb on so you don't miss the jump and fall.

Sprinting

Moving more quickly is obviously a help under most circumstances, as it allows you to reach cover, cross long corridors, and maneuver through areas more competently. However, you can't reload or fire your weapon when you sprint (though you can jump).

Ghost Flashlight

When exploring darkened chambers, you must rely on your Ghost to provide flashlight-like illumination. This is always done automatically.

Switching Weapons

A simple tap of the weapon switch button or key alternates between your Kinetic and Energy weapon (assuming you have one). You can easily see which weapon you're carrying in the bottom-left corner of your HUD (the Energy weapon has an Arc, Solar, or Void icon next to it). Switch weapons when you need to remove shields of a foe, you're low on ammunition for one weapon, or you want to finish off a group of foes without waiting to reload. Note that to switch to a Power weapon, you hold down the weapon switch button or key.

Crouching and Sliding

When you're exploring spaces that are too compact to stand in, you simply need to crouch. If you're sprinting when you reach such a location and hold down the crouch button, you'll slide. This is more than just a way to show off; you can quickly slide into cover during firefights. When crouching behind low cover, you can aim down sights to quickly pop up; then release your aim to automatically drop back down into cover.

The easiest way to come out of a crouch is to sprint.

Super Ability

Depending on your Guardian type, you have a Super that has been charging since the start of the mission. Though it was ready to use previously, the Campaign and Strike mission walkthroughs give you optimal conditions regarding when to activate it. Usually used on a cluster of foes to clear them out in seconds, Supers are sharp shocks of mayhem that can turn the tide of battle in your favor before slowly recharging to be used again. Try to take out three, four, or even five lesser foes with a single Super strike. Correct use of Supers can turn the tide of battle, especially against more dangerous Elite or Boss opponents, and knowing when and where to employ Supers is a key to victory.

Each Guardian Subclass has a different Super Ability. These are detailed later in the Guardian Abilities part of this training chapter.

ADVANCED JUMPING: MOVEMENT MODES

Experienced Guardians have access to a selection of Class-specific movement options that serve to extend or augment a standard jump. The basics are simple – jump while in the air to activate your selected Movement Mode.

While Movement Modes vary, most fall into one of three Class-based categories:

LIFT (Titan): Engage thrusters for a brief but impressive midair boost. Activate mid-jump for maximum effect.

JUMP (Hunter): Use your natural agility to extend your hang time with a midair jump. Activate at the height of your jump for maximum effect.

GLIDE (Warlock): Focus your Light while in midair to defy gravity's pull. Activate immediately after leaving the ground for maximum effect.

Different Movement Modes feature different effects. Some offer an initial boost of speed, some allow for superior directional control, and (in most cases) you'll find an option that balances these effects.

It's also worth noting that Titans and Warlocks can deactivate their Movement Modes mid use, allowing them to cut lengthy jumps short. In these cases, a canceled Movement Mode can be reactivated (once!) to slow a fall or make last minute adjustments.

A depleted Movement Mode is automatically recharged each time the Guardian touches down on solid ground.

Motion Tracker

It's important to use the radar in the top-left corner of your HUD, which can help you out during more chaotic combat situations. By now, you should have realized that the diamond-shaped waypoint icons point you in the way you need to go. But with places filled with foes, be sure to learn that the red glowing segments of the radar give the direction an enemy location or attack is coming from. If the center of the radar circle glows, an enemy is very close. If a marked enemy or objective is above or below you, an arrow within the waypoint icon indicates this. Learn these radar cues; they could save your life!

It's wise to check your motion tracker every few seconds, but make sure you do so whenever you hear an odd noise, spot signs of movement, or notice any other environmental cues that might indicate a nearby threat.

Buff/Debuff Notifications

By the end of the first Campaign Mission, you should be familiar seeing information periodically appear on the left side of your HUD. These are warnings or congratulatory messages, depending on the actions you are currently completing. Step in fire, and you'll receive a "Burning" warning message, for example. Defeat two or more foes in quick succession, and the "On a Roll" positive message appears.

Entering a Restricted Zone

Respawning Restricted! If you rely on your Ghost to resurrect you during combat so you can instantly begin to battle where you left off, restricted areas (also known as Restricted Zones) remove the possibility of this plan. Should you die in such an area, you are still resurrected, but usually at a location prior to engaging the enemies, meaning you need to complete some fighting again. For this reason, it's worth taking extra precautions when you're forewarned. Take your time, execute more accurate shots, pick weaponry you're comfortable using, don't take unnecessary chances, and use Energy weapons with the same energy as the shields of the foes you're about to face.

Ghost Interactions

Your Ghost can interact with a variety of objects, such as doors, computer terminals, and scannable objects. If a context-sensitive prompt appears on your HUD, access it as soon as it is safe to do so. Remember that your Ghost can also scan areas, which helps locate both enemies and scannable objects (which are bathed in the scan light for a few seconds as the scan expands through the nearby scenery).

Enemy Health and Armor

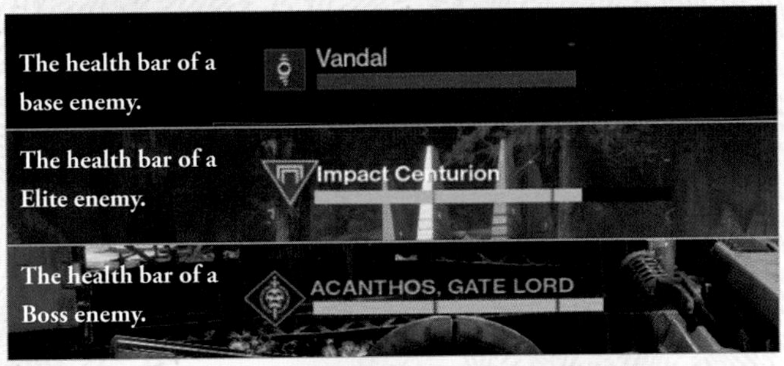
The health bar of a base enemy.
Vandal
The health bar of a Elite enemy.
Impact Centurion
The health bar of a Boss enemy.
ACANTHOS, GATE LORD

It is important to discern the different types of health bars that enemies possess. Regular enemies have a red health bar, which is whittled down using any offensive capabilities you may have.

If a foe has a light-orange health bar, this is usually an Elite version of a particular infantry foe, such as a "Quantum" Vex enemy.

If a foe has a yellow health bar, this is usually a Sub-Boss or Boss and is much tougher to tackle.

Enemies range from lowly Legionary grunts to massive hulking Boss Hobgoblins.

Finally, if a foe has a thin white line under its health bar, this indicates an active shield, which is always removed more easily if you use an Energy weapon with the matching energy type (Arc, Solar, or Void). Focus on completely removing the shield, and then defeating the enemy; these shields recharge, leaving a partly damaged foe with full shields if you become preoccupied with other fighting.

Guardian Subclasses and Abilities

Ability Basics

Each Class offers three Subclasses, and while each Subclass contains its own unique mix of Abilities, they all feature a shared format.

SUPER ABILITY: Every Subclass has a unique Super Ability.

GRENADE: Every Subclass offers three Grenade Abilities. Specific offerings are unique to each Subclass, but many share similar traits. Only one grenade can be active at a time.

MOVEMENT MODE: Every Subclass features three Movement Modes that serve to enhance a Guardian's jump. Specific offerings are generally (but not always) consistent across all three of a Guardian's Subclasses. Only one Movement Mode can be active at a time.

CLASS ABILITY: Every Guardian Class features two variations of a signature Class Ability. These offerings are consistent among all three of a Guardian's Subclasses. Only one Class Ability can be active at a time.

MELEE AND ABILITY ENHANCEMENTS: A Subclass' remaining Abilities are divided between two Ability clusters, or "paths." Each path features four Abilities: a Melee Ability and three Abilities that provide unique benefits. Only one path can be active at a time.

Using Abilities

Super Abilities

Supers are powerful Abilities that can turn the tide of battle. Using one requires a full charge of Super energy. Super energy builds slowly over time, but additional Super energy is earned each time you defeat an enemy or collect an Orb of Light.

Most Supers result in instant kills on all but the most durable enemies. Activating a Super also grants the Guardian increased damage mitigation, making them considerably more durable for the duration of the effect.

Orbs of Light

Orbs of Light are generated by Super Abilities, usually upon activation or after killing blows. Specifics vary between Supers, and some Abilities allow Supers to generate additional orbs.

A Guardian cannot collect any orbs produced by their Super Ability. They're reserved for (and visible only to) nearby allies. If you spot one of these glowing spheres, it's yours for the taking – and unless your Super energy is at capacity, an orb will be collected the moment you touch it.

Grenades

Grenades feature a variety of effects, but using one always requires a full charge of grenade energy. This energy builds slowly over time, and you can often accelerate the process via Ability enhancements or armor mods.

While each Grenade Ability is unique, most fall into one of five basic categories:

- **Seeker** grenades produce one or more projectiles that home in on nearby enemies, reducing the need for accuracy or line of sight.
- **Persistent** grenades produce damaging fields or other lasting effects. In most cases, the effects are fairly brief, but they serve to limit (or punish) enemy movements through affected areas.
- **Blast** grenades are no-frills damage dealers that explode shortly after they're thrown.
- **Sticky** grenades attach to enemies, ensuring that your target is unable to escape the blast.
- **Status** grenades inflict negative effects for a short time. Grenades of this type are less common and are typically used to gain a tactical edge in heated battles.

Movement Modes

Movement Modes are essentially jumps, allowing a Guardian to reach greater heights and distances. These jump Abilities automatically recharge each time a Guardian touches down on solid ground.

Class Abilities

Class Abilities vary between Guardian Classes, but each use triggers a moderate cooldown period. In some cases, you can accelerate these cooldowns via Abilities or armor mods.

Melee Abilities

Melee Abilities serve to enhance or augment melee attacks, and using one requires a full charge of melee energy. This energy builds slowly over time, but the process can usually be accelerated via Ability enhancements or armor mods. Melee energy is not required to perform standard melee attacks.

Unlocking Subclasses and Abilities

Your first true Subclass unlocks once you've completed Campaign Mission: Spark. It features the Subclass' Super Ability, one default Grenade Ability, and one default Movement Mode. The remaining Abilities are locked.

To gain access to a locked Ability, you'll need to invest an Upgrade Point. Some Abilities have additional requirements related to character level or prerequisite Abilities, but unlocking a new Ability always requires an Upgrade Point.

Earning Upgrade Points

An Upgrade Point is rewarded each time you gain a character level (or each time you fill the Experience bar after reaching Level 20). Upgrade Points are also granted as rewards for completing specific activities.

Let There Be Light: Artifacts and Subclasses

The initial Guardian Subclass is unlocked once you complete Campaign Mission: Spark. In order to unlock the other two Subclasses, you must find a (randomly looted) Artifact from a chest and complete Campaign Mission: Spark – Pt. 2. This must be completed twice (to unlock your Guardian's two remaining Subclasses, for a total of three). Naturally, you must complete the previous series of tasks two more times if you want to see all nine Guardian Subclasses (three for Titan, three for Hunter, and three for Warlock).

Before you can unlock your second (and third) Subclass, you'll need to find a Subclass-specific Artifact. While there's an element of luck to finding an Artifact, the chances of finding an Artifact grow as your character level increases:

- At Level 7, you have a small chance of finding a Subclass Artifact each time you loot a chest. The chances of finding one are significantly higher while looting chests related to Public Events and Lost Sectors. As your character level increases, the likelihood of looting an Artifact grows.
- At Level 14, you have a chance to find another Subclass Artifact each time you loot a chest. Again, Public Events and Lost Sectors provide the best chances of finding an Artifact—and again, those chances grow as your character level increases.

Once you collect an Artifact, you must charge it by defeating enemies. Any successful kill will progress your task, but kills earned during Public Events accelerate the process.

When an Artifact is fully charged, you're free to complete the indicated Quest and claim your next Subclass. It's important to note that Subclasses are unlocked in a specific order that varies based on Class type.

Subclass Unlocks

Class	Subclass 1	Subclass 2	Subclass 3
Titan	Sentinel (Void)	Striker (Arc)	Sunbreaker (Solar)
Hunter	Arcstrider (Arc)	Gunslinger (Solar)	Nightstalker (Void)
Warlock	Dawnblade (Solar)	Voidwalker (Void)	Stormcaller (Arc)

As you unlock new Subclasses, you'll need more Upgrade Points to unlock the Abilities they offer. It's also worth noting that Upgrade Points are placed in a common pool, so spending a point in one Subclass means one less point for another. While you'll eventually earn enough points to fully unlock all of your Abilities, it's best to invest in priority Abilities early on.

Titan Abilities

Sentinel (Void)

The Sentinel is a defensive powerhouse and an outstanding support Subclass, but it's also a formidable damage dealer. Offering an impressive mix of barriers, Overshields, and status effects, the Sentinel is a great frontline soldier with one of the most versatile Supers available to any Class.

The Sentinel Subclass is automatically unlocked when you complete Campaign Mission: Spark.

Super Ability: Sentinel Shield

Once activated, you can use Sentinel Shield in three very distinct ways:

- Aim down sights to eflect incoming attacks. Effective blocks generate Orbs of Light.
- Perform a Shield Throw (the Grenade button) to toss the shield straight ahead of you. Thanks to a nice ricochet effect, this attack is capable of hitting multiple targets. Like your grenade, the Shield Throw is a recharging ability that can only be used when the related energy gauge is at capacity.
- Use standard attacks to lunge forward for a powerful short-range attack. Each lunge you perform consumes a bit of your remaining Super energy.

Grenade

The Sentinel has a choice between a **sticky** grenade, a **persistent** grenade, and an outstanding **status** grenade.

Sentinel Grenade Abilities

Ability Name	Description	Prerequisites
Magnetic Grenade	A grenade that attaches to enemies and explodes twice.	Default Ability
Voidwall Grenade	A grenade that creates a horizontal wall of burning Void Light.	Upgrade Point/ Level 3
Suppressor Grenade	An explosive grenade that prevents enemies from using Abilities for a short time.	Upgrade Point/ Level 3

Movement Mode

All Titan Subclasses feature the same selection of jump enhancements.

Sentinel Movement Modes

Ability Name	Description	Prerequisites
High Lift	Jump while airborne to activate Lift and launch into the air at greater heights.	Default Ability
Strafe Lift	Jump while airborne to activate Lift and launch into the air with strong directional control.	Upgrade Point/ Level 4
Catapult Lift	Jump while airborne to activate Lift and launch into the air with a strong initial burst of momentum.	Upgrade Point/ Level 4

Class Ability

All Titan Subclasses feature the same Class Ability options.

Sentinel Class Abilities

Ability Name	Description	Prerequisites
Towering Barricade	Press and hold the Crouch button to create a large barrier that can be used to reinforce a position with cover from enemy fire.	Upgrade Point/ Level 7
Rally Barricade	Press and hold the Crouch button to create a small barrier that allows you to peek over it while aiming down sights and instantly reloads your equipped weapon when you take cover.	Upgrade Point/ Level 7

CLASS ABILITY: BARRICADE

The Titan is renowned for its Resilience. While its Subclasses allow for a variety of builds, the available Class Abilities ensure that even the most reckless Titan can provide their allies with some defensive support.

Towering Barricade generates a large barrier that serves as useful cover. It also damages enemies that dare to pass through it, making it a great tool for blocking chokepoints and controlling enemy movements.

Rally Barricade generates a waist-high barrier. While crouching behind it, aim down sights to pop up and fire away. Release your aim to drop into cover and instantly reload your weapon. Like its larger counterpart, Rally Barricade damages enemies that pass through it.

Melee and Ability Enhancements

The Sentinel's remaining Abilities support two distinct playstyles:

Code of the Protector features a heavy focus on survivability and support. While this path can be useful in any situation, it's a particularly good option for Titans who prefer close combat and team-focused content.

Ward of Dawn is worth a special mention: this iconic Titan Ability provides yet another way to use your Super energy.

Code of the Aggressor is more of an offensive path. The featured Melee Ability works well with Mobility-heavy builds. Also, its focus on grenades (not to mention an extra Shield Throw charge) makes it a good option for Sentinels who prefer to attack their enemies both up close and from range.

Upper Path: Code of the Protector

Ability Name	Description	Prerequisites
Defensive Strike	Kill an enemy with this Melee Ability to create an Overshield around you and nearby allies.	Upgrade Point
Rallying Force	Melee kills restore health for you and nearby allies.	Upgrade Point/ Defensive Strike
Turn the Tide	Your Overshield from Defensive Strike lasts longer and increases your melee damage and reload speed.	Upgrade Point/ Rallying Force
Ward of Dawn	When Super energy is full, press and hold the Super button(s) to create an indestructible dome to protect you and your allies.	Upgrade Point/ Turn the Tide

Lower Path: Code of the Aggressor

Ability Name	Description	Prerequisites
Shield Bash	After sprinting for a short time, use this Melee Ability to unleash a devastating Shield Bash that disorients enemies.	Upgrade Point
Superior Arsenal	Grenade kills recharge your grenade energy.	Upgrade Point/ Shield Bash
In the Trenches	Kills while surrounded by enemies reduce the cooldown of your Super.	Upgrade Point/ Superior Arsenal
Second Shield	Gain an additional Shield Throw charge while Sentinel Shield is active.	Upgrade Point/ In the Trenches

Striker (Arc)

The Striker excels at charging around the battlefield, blasting groups of enemies with Arc damage before dashing off to the next encounter. This Subclass supports aggressive playstyles, and it's a great choice for Titans who favor Mobility-based armor.

The Striker is the Titan's second available Subclass. It unlocks only after you've collected the required Artifact and completed the resulting mission.

Super Ability: Fists of Havoc

While active, Fists of Havoc offers two distinct attacks:

- Pressing the Fire button produces a lunging ground slam capable of dealing heavy damage to multiple enemies. This attack consumes a fair amount of Super energy.
- Pressing the Melee button initiates powerful Shoulder Charge. It deals heavy damage to a single target in exchange for a smaller amount of Super energy.

Grenade

The Striker has a choice between a **status** grenade and two **persistent** grenades.

Striker Grenade Abilities

Ability Name	Description	Prerequisites
Flashbang Grenade	An explosive grenade that disorients enemies it damages.	Default Ability
Pulse Grenade	A grenade that periodically damages enemies inside its explosion radius.	Upgrade Point
Lightning Grenade	A grenade that sticks to any surface and emits bolts of lightning.	Upgrade Point

Movement Mode

All Titan Subclasses feature the same selection of jump enhancements.

Striker Movement Modes

Ability Name	Description	Prerequisites
High Lift	A second jump that launches you into the air to greater heights.	Default Ability
Strafe Lift	A second jump that launches you into the air and grants strong directional control.	Upgrade Point
Catapult Lift	A second jump that has a strong initial burst of momentum.	Upgrade Point

Class Ability

All Titan Subclasses feature the same Class Ability options.

Striker Class Abilities

Ability Name	Description	Prerequisites
Towering Barricade	Press and hold the Crouch button to create a large barrier that can be used to reinforce a position with cover from enemy fire.	Upgrade Point/ Level 7
Rally Barricade	Press and hold the Crouch button to create a small barrier that allows you to peek over it while aiming down sights and instantly reloads your equipped weapon when you take cover.	Upgrade Point/ Level 7

Melee and Ability Enhancements

The Striker's remaining Abilities support two distinct playstyles:

Code of the Earthshaker features an increased focus on multi-target damage—even the featured Melee Ability can affect multiple enemies with a single blow. It's a good option for Strikers who want to double down on their area-of-effect damage.

Code of the Juggernaut supports more efficient weapon/melee attack combinations and prolonged Super use. Essentially, it's a good choice for aggressive Strikers looking to overwhelm their opponents by stringing together a barrage of attacks.

Upper Path: Code of the Earthshaker

Ability Name	Description	Prerequisites
Seismic Strike	While sprinting, activate this Melee Ability to slam shoulder-first into your target and release an Arc explosion on impact.	Upgrade Point
Aftershocks	Damaging enemies with Seismic Strike recharges your grenade.	Upgrade Point/ Seismic Strike
Magnitude	Gain an additional grenade charge. Increases the duration of grenade effects.	Upgrade Point/ Aftershocks
Terminal Velocity	Fists of Havoc's ground slam attack leaves a damage-dealing field in its wake and deals more damage the longer it's in the air.	Upgrade Point/ Magnitude

Lower Path: Code of the Juggernaut

Ability Name	Description	Prerequisites
Frontal Assault	Strike an enemy with this Melee Ability to reload your weapon and increase your weapon stability.	Upgrade Point
Reversal	Melee kills immediately trigger health regeneration.	Upgrade Point/ Frontal Assault
Knockout	Critically wounding an enemy or breaking their shields increases your melee range and damage.	Upgrade Point/ Reversal
Trample	Killing enemies with Fists of Havoc extends its duration.	Upgrade Point/ Knockout

Sunbreaker (Solar)

The Sunbreaker is a versatile damage dealer. It offers a solid mix of long-range attacks, splash damage, and burning damage, with a bit of utility thrown in for good measure. It's an explosive Titan that can be very effective at any range.

The Sunbreaker is the Titan's third available Subclass. It unlocks only after you've collected the required Artifact and completed the resulting mission.

Super Ability: Hammer of Sol

Once activated, you can use Hammer of Sol to hurl flaming projectiles across the battlefield. Each toss consumes a fair amount of Super energy, but every hammer that finds its mark deals serious damage.

Grenade

The Sunbreaker has a choice between a **blast** grenade, a **persistent** grenade, and a **sticky** grenade, all of which are capable of burning affected enemies.

Sunbreaker Grenade Abilities

Ability Name	Description	Prerequisites
Incendiary Grenade	A grenade whose explosion catches enemies on fire.	Default Ability
Thermite Grenade	A grenade that sends forward a burning line of fire.	Upgrade Point
Fusion Grenade	An explosive grenade that burns enemies when it attaches to targets.	Upgrade Point

Movement Mode

All Titan Subclasses feature the same selection of jump enhancements.

Sunbreaker Movement Modes

Ability Name	Description	Prerequisites
High Lift	A second jump that launches you into the air to greater heights.	Default Ability
Strafe Lift	A second jump that launches you into the air and grants strong directional control.	Upgrade Point
Catapult Lift	A second jump that has a strong initial burst of momentum.	Upgrade Point

Class Ability

All Titan Subclasses feature the same Class Ability options.

Sunbreaker Class Abilities

Ability Name	Description	Prerequisites
Towering Barricade	Press and hold the Crouch button to create a large barrier that can be used to reinforce a position with cover from enemy fire.	Upgrade Point
Rally Barricade	Press and hold the Crouch button to create a small barrier that allows you to peek over it while aiming down sights and instantly reloads your equipped weapon when you take cover.	Upgrade Point

Melee and Ability Enhancements

The Sunbreaker's remaining Abilities support two distinct playstyles:

Code of the Fire-Forged is a good fit for mobile playstyles. The featured Melee Ability is a sprinting charge but the real draw for Mobility-minded players is the option for a speed-boosting group buff. Of course, the included Super enhancements make it that much easier to deal massive damage on the run.

Code of the Siegebreaker supports a more stationary playstyle. Its most notable effects involve Sunspots that can both damage enemies and empower the Sunbreaker. It's an ideal choice for Titans who enjoy claiming and holding strategically advantageous locations.

Upper Path: Code of the Fire-Forged

Ability Name	Description	Prerequisites
Hammer Strike	While sprinting, use this Melee Ability to unleash a blazing Hammer strike that weakens enemies.	Upgrade Point
Tempered Metal	Solar Ability kills grant you and nearby allies bonus movement and reload speed.	Upgrade Point/ Hammer Strike
Battle-Forge	Enemies killed by Hammer of Sol explode.	Upgrade Point/ Tempered Metal
Vulcan's Rage	Hammers shatter into explosive molten embers on impact.	Upgrade Point/ Battle-Forge

Lower Path: Code of the Siegebreaker

Ability Name	Description	Prerequisites
Mortar Blast	Strike an enemy with this Melee Ability to release a Solar explosion, setting nearby enemies on fire.	Upgrade Point
Sun Warrior	Solar Ability kills restore your health. Grenade and Melee Ability kills leave a deadly Sunspot in their wake.	Upgrade Point/ Mortar Blast
Rings of Fire	While standing in a Sunspot, your Solar Abilities recharge faster and your Super lasts longer.	Upgrade Point/ Sun Warrior
Solar Siege	Hammers create a Sunspot on impact. While standing in Sunspots, you throw hammers faster.	Upgrade Point/ Rings of Fire

Hunter Abilities

CLASS ABILITY: DODGE

While its Subclasses contain some nice support Abilities, the Hunter's focus on Mobility makes it well-suited to lone-wolf playstyles. Hunters make valuable allies, no doubt, but their Class Abilities focus on self-preservation and combat proficiency.

Marksman's Dodge is an evasive maneuver that gives the Hunter a chance to avoid damage while automatically reloading the equipped weapon. As the name implies, this is a common choice for Hunters who prefer to keep their enemies at range.

Gambler's Dodge is an evasive maneuver that fully recharges the Hunter's Melee Ability when performed near enemies. It's a common choice for Hunters who prefer to stay in the thick of the action.

Effective Dodging

An effective Dodge is more a matter of prediction than reaction. The idea is to dart out of your opponent's line of fire, forcing them to adjust their aim or risk missing their shot. Once a shot has been fired, you have little chance of avoiding the attack.

Arcstrider (Arc)

The Arcstrider is a close-quarters specialist who thrives in group combat. It features some nice area-of-effect options and heavy focus on melee attacks. Relying on speed for survivability, the Arcstrider is well-suited to aggressive playstyles.

The Arcstrider Subclass is automatically unlocked when you complete Campaign Mission: Spark.

Super Ability: Arc Staff

Once activated, Arc Staff features two distinct attacks (one initiated by the Fire button and one initiated by the melee button) that can be chained together (on the ground and in the air) for a variety of sweeping short-range combos. Notable examples include:

- Melee button x3 (Three secondary melee attacks in quick succession)
- Melee button x2, Fire button (Two secondary melee attacks, followed by a primary attack)
- Fire button while airborne (One primary attack while airborne)
- Melee button x2 while airborne (Two secondary melee attacks while airborne)

Grenade

The Arcstrider can choose between two very different **seeker** grenades and a **sticky** grenade.

Arcstrider Grenade Abilities

Ability Name	Description	Prerequisites
Skip Grenade	A grenade that splits upon impact, creating multiple projectiles that seek enemies.	Default Ability
Flux Grenade	An explosive grenade that deals additional damage when attached to enemies.	Upgrade Point./ Level 3
Arcbolt Grenade	A grenade that chains bolts of lightning to nearby enemies.	Upgrade Point/ Level 3

Movement Mode

All Hunter Subclasses feature the same selection of jump enhancements.

Arcstrider Movement Modes

Ability Name	Description	Prerequisites
High Jump	While airborne, jump a second time to reach greater heights.	Default Ability
Strafe Jump	While airborne, jump a second time with strong directional control.	Upgrade Point/ Level 4
Triple Jump	While airborne, sustain your air control with a second or third jump.	Upgrade Point/ Level 4

Class Ability

All Hunter Subclasses feature the same Class Ability options.

Arcstrider Class Abilities

Ability Name	Description	Prerequisites
Marksman's Dodge	Dodge to perform an evasive maneuver with a steady hand. Dodging automatically reloads your weapon.	Upgrade Point/ Level 7
Gambler's Dodge	Dodge to perform a nimble tumble, avoiding enemy attacks. Dodging near enemies fully recharges your Melee Ability.	Upgrade Point/ Level 7

Melee and Ability Enhancements

The Arcstrider's remaining Abilities support two distinct playstyles:

Way of the Warrior has a heavy focus on melee attacks, making it essential when short-range damage is a priority. It's worth noting that this group of Abilities is most effective when Gambler's Dodge is selected. Among other benefits, this combination allows each Dodge to recharge your Melee Ability, while each Melee Kill recharges your Dodge.

Way of the Wind has an overall focus on survivability through utility. With Abilities that disorient enemies, increase sprinting speed, support Ability use, and improve evasion, it's a good path for those who favor versatility.

Upper Path: Way of the Warrior

Ability Name	Description	Prerequisites
Combination Blow	Kill an enemy with this Melee Ability to trigger health regeneration and increase your melee damage temporarily.	Upgrade Point
Combat Flow	Melee kills recharge your Dodge Ability.	Upgrade Point/ Combination Blow
Deadly Reach	Dodging increases your melee range, allowing you to lurch farther to strike enemies.	Upgrade Point/ Combat Flow
Lethal Current	After dodging, each Arc Staff hit creates a damaging lightning aftershock.	Upgrade Point/ Deadly Reach

Lower Path: Way of the Wind

Ability Name	Description	Prerequisites
Disorienting Blow	Strike an enemy with this Melee Ability to disorient your target and nearby enemies.	Upgrade Point
Focused Breathing	Sprinting recharges your Dodge Ability. Increases maximum sprint speed.	Upgrade Point/ Disorienting Blow
Combat Meditation	While you are critically wounded, melee and grenades recharge drastically faster.	Upgrade Point/ Focused Breathing
Lightning Reflexes	You are harder to kill while dodging.	Upgrade Point/ Combat Meditation

Gunslinger (Solar)

The Gunslinger is a devastating ranged fighter with a heavy focus on direct damage. It favors accuracy and finesse over raw aggression, but its damage potential makes the Gunslinger an appealing option for any Hunter.

The Gunslinger is the Hunter's second available Subclass. It unlocks only after you've collected the required Artifact and completed the resulting mission.

Super Ability: Golden Gun

By default, you can use Golden Gun to fire up to three high-damage projectiles. It's a straightforward Super, but it takes a cool head and a steady hand to put Golden Gun to good use.

Grenade

The Gunslinger can choose between a **blast** grenade, a **seeker** grenade, and something of an anomaly: the Tripmine Grenade. This grenade is best used as a damaging trap, but its trigger is visible enough to make it an effective deterrent (assuming your enemies are unable to shoot it).

Gunslinger Grenade Abilities

Ability Name	Description	Prerequisites
Incendiary Grenade	A grenade whose explosion catches enemies on fire.	Default Ability
Swarm Grenade	A grenade that detonates on impact, releasing multiple drones that seek nearby enemies.	Upgrade Point
Tripmine Grenade	An explosive grenade that sticks to surfaces and detonates when enemies pass through its laser trigger.	Upgrade Point

Movement Mode

All Hunter Subclasses feature the same selection of jump enhancements.

Gunslinger Movement Modes

Ability Name	Description	Prerequisites
High Jump	While airborne, jump a second time to reach greater heights.	Default Ability
Strafe Jump	While airborne, jump a second time with strong directional control.	Upgrade Point
Triple Jump	While airborne, sustain your air control with a second or third jump.	Upgrade Point

Class Ability

All Hunter Subclasses feature the same Class Ability options.

Gunslinger Class Abilities

Ability Name	Description	Prerequisites
Marksman's Dodge	Dodge to perform an evasive maneuver with a steady hand. Dodging automatically reloads your weapon.	Upgrade Point/ Level 7
Gambler's Dodge	Dodge to perform a nimble tumble, avoiding enemy attacks. Dodging near enemies fully recharges your Melee Ability.	Upgrade Point/ Level 7

Melee and Ability Enhancements

The Gunslinger's remaining Abilities support two distinct playstyles:

Way of the Outlaw allows for wilder playstyles, making it a good choice for those who enjoy mixing it up on the front lines. It features an explosive Melee Ability and some great utility, but its most notable effects involve the Gunslinger's Super. When this path is selected, Golden Gun not only features a more forgiving aim, it can also be used to fire up to six shots, though the Super's duration is noticeably shorter.

Way of the Sharpshooter focuses heavily on precision, making it a good fit for more disciplined playstyles. From its Melee Ability to its Super enhancements, it's a path that encourages a steady hand. Most notably, it allows for (and rewards) precision damage when using Golden Gun.

Upper Path: Way of the Outlaw

Ability Name	Description	Prerequisites
Explosive Knife	Throw a Knife from a distance that explodes shortly after impact.	Upgrade Point
Chains of Woe	Precision kills increase weapon reload speed for you and your nearby allies.	Upgrade Point/ Explosive Knife
Deadshot	Significantly improves your ability to hit with Golden Gun.	Upgrade Point/ Chains of Woe
Six-Shooter	Golden Gun can be fired quickly up to six times but has a shorter duration.	Upgrade Point/ Deadshot

Lower Path: Way of the Sharphooter

Ability Name	Description	Prerequisites
Knife-Juggler	Throw a knife from a distance. Precision knife kills immediately recharge your Melee Ability.	Upgrade Point
Practice Makes Perfect	Enter a trance with each precision hit, reducing the cooldown of your Super.	Upgrade Point/ Knife-Juggler
Crowd-Pleaser	Enables precision damage with Golden Gun. Precision hits with Golden Gun generate Orbs of Light.	Upgrade Point/ Practice Makes Perfect
Line 'Em Up	Precision hits with Golden Gun increase its damage and extend its duration.	Upgrade Point/ Crowd-Pleaser

Nightstalker (Void)

The Nightstalker favors deception over aggression. With a selection of Abilities that disorient, suppress, slow, and weaken enemies, this Subclass offers a great many support options.

The Nightstalker is the Hunter's third available Subclass. It unlocks only after you've collected the required Artifact and completed the resulting mission.

Super Ability: Shadowshot

By default, Shadowshot is a non-lethal Super that stands as one of the best support Abilities available to any Class. Activating this Super fires a Void Anchor that slows affected enemies, causes them to take more damage, and prevents them from using Abilities. However, it's worth noting that the Nightstalker has access to Abilities that turn Shadowshot into a very powerful attack.

Grenade

The Nightstalker can choose between three distinctly different **persistent** grenades.

Nightstalker Grenade Abilities

Ability Name	Description	Prerequisites
Vortex Grenade	A grenade that creates a vortex that continually damages enemies trapped inside.	Default Ability
Spike Grenade	A grenade that attaches to any surface and emits a torrent of damaging Void Light.	Upgrade Point
Voidwall Grenade	A grenade that creates a horizontal wall of burning Void Light.	Upgrade Point

Movement Mode

All Hunter Subclasses feature the same selection of jump enhancements.

Nightstalker Movement Modes

Ability Name	Description	Prerequisites
High Jump	While airborne, jump a second time to reach greater heights.	Default Ability
Strafe Jump	While airborne, jump a second time with strong directional control.	Upgrade Point
Triple Jump	While airborne, sustain your air control with a second or third jump.	Upgrade Point

Class Ability

All Hunter Subclasses feature the same Class Ability options.

Nightstalker Class Abilities

Ability Name	Description	Prerequisites
Marksman's Dodge	Dodge to perform an evasive maneuver with a steady hand. Dodging automatically reloads your weapon.	Upgrade Point
Gambler's Dodge	Dodge to perform a nimble tumble, avoiding enemy attacks. Dodging near enemies fully recharges your Melee Ability.	Upgrade Point

Melee and Ability Enhancements

The Nightstalker's remaining Abilities support two distinct playstyles:

Way of the Trapper focuses on survivability through utility. It turns the Nightstalker's Super and Melee Abilities into proximity-triggered traps.

Other highlights include a nice boost to sprint/sneak speed, the ability to vanish after dodging, and multiple status effects.

Way of the Pathfinder offers plenty of utility, but it includes a much greater focus on damage—particularly in the damage done by the Super Ability. With Moebius Quiver, the Nightstalker can fire Shadowshot multiple times per use, dealing massive damage to tethered enemies.

Upper Path: Way of the Trapper

Ability Name	Description	Prerequisites
Snare Bomb	Throw a smoke bomb trap from a distance with this Melee Ability. The smoke bomb sticks to surfaces and detonates when enemies are near, slowing and disorienting them.	Upgrade Point
Keen Scout	Sprint and sneak faster, and gain an enhanced tracker. Tethered enemies are marked for easy tracking.	Upgrade Point/ Snare Bomb
Deadfall	The Void Anchors fired from Shadowshot become traps and wait for prey. Void Anchors have increased range and last longer.	Upgrade Point/ Keen Scout
Vanishing Step	Dodging makes you vanish from sight for a short time.	Upgrade Point/ Deadfall

Lower Path: Way of the Pathfinder

Ability Name	Description	Prerequisites
Vanish in Smoke	Throw a smoke bomb explosive from a distance with this Melee Ability. The smoke bomb creates a cloud that makes you and nearby allies invisible.	Upgrade Point
Lockdown	Grenade and smoke effects last twice as long, allowing for strong territorial control and increased damage potential.	Upgrade Point/ Vanish in Smoke
Heart of the Pack	Killing tethered enemies creates Orbs of Light and increases Mobility, Recovery, and Resilience for you and nearby allies.	Upgrade Point/ Lockdown
Moebius Quiver	Fire Shadowshot multiple times in rapid succession. Shadowshot deals massive damage against tethered enemies.	Upgrade Point/ Heart of the Pack

Warlock Abilities

CLASS ABILITY: RIFT

Due to the Warlock's affinity for Recovery, it understands the fluid nature of give and take, gain and loss. The Warlock's Class Ability generates a Rift that grants bonuses to all allies within it. While both variations can be extremely useful, each Warlock must sacrifice one effect for the other, and anyone hoping to gain the selected bonus must be willing to stand wherever the Rift is summoned.

As the name implies, **Healing Rift** provides sustained healing for the Warlock and any allies within its border. It's a straightforward but extremely useful support Ability.

Empowering Rift gives the Warlock's Class Ability a decidedly offensive bent, boosting the damage of the caster and any allies who remain within its border.

Dawnblade (Solar)

The Dawnblade is a high-damage Subclass uniquely well-suited to aerial combat. It offers a bit of utility, but setting enemies ablaze is most definitely the Dawnblade's focus.

The Dawnblade Subclass is automatically unlocked when you complete Campaign Mission: Spark.

Super Ability: Daybreak

While active, Daybreak allows the Dawnblade to hurl flaming projectiles. It can be used both on the ground and in the air. It's a powerful attack in either case, but few things can match the spectacle of an airborne Dawnblade raining fire down upon its enemies.

Grenade

The Dawnblade can choose between a **persistent** grenade, a **seeker** grenade, and a **sticky** grenade.

Dawnblade Grenade Abilities

Ability Name	Description	Prerequisites
Solar Grenade	A grenade that creates a flare of Solar Light that continually damages enemies trapped inside.	Default Ability
Firebolt Grenade	A grenade that unleashes bolts of Solar Light on nearby enemies.	Upgrade Point/ Level 3
Fusion Grenade	An explosive grenade that burns enemies when it attaches to a target.	Upgrade Point/ Level 3

Movement Mode

The Dawnblade offers a typical selection of jump enhancements: directional control, a burst of speed, or a balance of speed and control.

Dawnblade Movement Modes

Ability Name	Description	Prerequisites
Strafe Glide	Jump while airborne to activate Glide and start an airborne drift with strong directional control.	Default Ability
Burst Glide	Jump while airborne to activate Glide and start an airborne drift with a strong initial burst of speed.	Upgrade Point/ Level 4
Balanced Glide	Jump while airborne to activate Glide and start an airborne drift with both moderate speed and directional control.	Upgrade Point/ Level 4

Class Ability

All Warlock Subclasses feature the same Class Ability options.

Dawnblade Class Abilities

Ability Name	Description	Prerequisites
Healing Rift	Press and hold the Crouch button to conjure a well of light that continually heals those inside it.	Upgrade Point/ Level 7
Empowering Rift	Press and hold the Crouch button to conjure a well of light that increases weapon damage for those inside it.	Upgrade Point/ Level 7

Melee and Ability Enhancements

The Dawnblade's remaining Abilities support two distinct playstyles:

Attunement of Sky features an undeniable focus on aerial combat. It allows for weapons and grenades to be used without breaking Glide, it unlocks a midair Dodge, and it rewards airborne kills with additional grenade and melee energy. Due to the inherent risks that come with aerial combat (like the noticeable lack of cover options), this path is best suited to aggressive, Mobility-focused playstyles.

Attunement of Flame also encourages high-flying antics, but it does so via Super enhancements. It adds multiple effects to Daybreak projectiles, and it serves to prolong the duration of an active Super. One of the most notable Abilities allows the Dawnblade to drop down mid-jump, regaining health based on the length of the fall and (if Daybreak is active) delivering damage upon landing. However, because Daybreak can also be used on the ground, this path is a good fit for more conservative playstyle

Upper Path: Attunement of Sky

Ability Name	Description	Prerequisites
Swift Strike	Strike an enemy with this Melee Ability to burn your target and temporarily increase your movement and reload speed.	Upgrade Point
Winged Sun	Engage your enemies mid-flight. Fire weapons and throw grenades while gliding.	Upgrade Point/ Swift Strike
Heat Rises	Airborne kills recharge your grenade and melee energy. Casting Daybreak instantly refills all your Ability energy.	Upgrade Point/ Winged Sun
Icarus Dash	Press the Crouch button twice in midair to dodge.	Upgrade Point/ Heat Rises

Lower Path: Attunement of Flame

Ability Name	Description	Prerequisites
Igniting Touch	Strike an enemy with this Melee Ability to burn them and cause them to explode when killed.	Upgrade Point
Fated for the Flame	Daybreak projectiles seek targets as they travel and launch a streak of deadly flames upon impact.	Upgrade Point/ Igniting Touch
Everlasting Fire	Killing an enemy with Daybreak extends its duration.	Upgrade Point/ Fated for the Flame
Phoenix Dive	Hold the Crouch button while in the air to quickly descend and restore your health. While Daybreak is active, descending causes explosive damage.	Upgrade Point/ Everlasting Fire

Voidwalker (Void)

The Voidwalker is an explosive combatant who typically favors hit-and-run tactics. As a Subclass, it offers impressive versatility, particularly when it comes to grenade use. Depending on the selected Abilities, a Voidwalker can consume grenade energy to regain health or sacrifice Super energy to use uniquely powerful grenade attacks. In either case, the Voidwalker allows for some very effective Ability rotations.

The Voidwalker is the Warlock's second available Subclass. It unlocks only after you've collected the required Artifact and completed the resulting mission.

Super Ability: Nova Bomb

In its simplest form, Nova Bomb is a powerful projectile that delivers a massive explosion on impact. However, available Abilities significantly change the nature of this Super, ensuring that a fully developed Voidwalker has some interesting strategic options.

Grenade

By default, Voidwalkers can choose between what amounts to a **persistent** grenade, a **seeker** grenade, and a **blast** grenade. However, the available Chaos Accelerant Ability can be used to enhance these offerings, most notably by adding a **seeker** effect to the otherwise straightforward Scatter Grenade.

Voidwalker Grenade Abilities

Ability Name	Description	Prerequisites
Vortex Grenade	A grenade that creates a vortex that continually damages enemies trapped inside.	Default Ability
Axion Bolt	A bolt of Void Light that forks into smaller bolts on impact, which seek enemies.	Upgrade Point
Scatter Grenade	A grenade that splits into many submunitions and covers a large area with multiple explosions.	Upgrade Point

Movement Mode

The Voidwalker features two standard jump enhancements in Strafe Glide and Burst Glide, but Blink is unique to this Subclass. This Movement Mode converts your jump into a short-range teleport. It takes some practice to use, but Blink serves as a very useful evasive maneuver.

Voidwalker Movement Modes

Ability Name	Description	Prerequisites
Strafe Glide	Jump while airborne to activate Glide and start an airborne drift with strong directional control.	Default Ability
Blink	Jump while airborne to teleport a short distance.	Upgrade Point
Burst Glide	Jump while airborne to activate Glide and start an airborne drift with a strong initial boost of speed.	Upgrade Point

Class Ability

All Warlock Subclasses feature the same Class Ability options.

Voidwalker Class Abilities

Ability Name	Description	Prerequisites
Healing Rift	Press and hold the Crouch button to conjure a well of light that continually heals those inside it.	Upgrade Point/ Level 7
Empowering Rift	Press and hold the Crouch button to conjure a well of light that increases weapon damage for those inside it.	Upgrade Point/ Level 7

Melee and Ability Enhancements

The Voidwalker's remaining Abilities support two distinct playstyles:

Attunement of Chaos focuses on improved multi-target damage, particularly through grenade use. Chaos Accelerant allows the Voidwalker to overcharge an equipped grenade to make it much more effective when thrown. As a nice bonus, the featured Melee Ability allows for more frequent grenade attacks. Along with the other bundled effects, this path is a good choice for damage-focused Voidwalkers.

Attunement of Hunger features a heavy focus on survivability. The most intriguing effect allows a Voidwalker to consume its grenade energy for a full heal, along with a brief heal-over-time benefit. This effect is also granted after Melee Ability kills. In both cases, subsequent kills can prolong the healing effect while recharging grenade energy.

Upper Path: Attunement of Chaos

Ability Name	Description	Prerequisites
Entropic Pull	Strike an enemy with this Melee Ability to drain your enemy's life force and use it to recharge your grenade.	Upgrade Point
Chaos Accelerant	Hold the Grenade button to draw power from your Super to overcharge your grenade, making it deadly and more effective.	Upgrade Point/ Entropic Pull
Bloom	Void Ability kills cause enemies to explode.	Upgrade Point/ Chaos Accelerant
Cataclysm	Nova Bomb travels slowly and seeks enemies. Detonations shatter into smaller seeker projectiles. Fire your weapon at the Nova Bomb to detonate it early.	Upgrade Point/ Bloom

Lower Path: Attunement of Hunger

Ability Name	Description	Prerequisites
Devour	Kill an enemy with this Melee Ability to fully regenerate your health. For a short time afterward, kills restore additional health.	Upgrade Point
Feed the Void	Hold the Grenade button to consume your grenade energy to regenerate your health. Grants the Devour effect.	Upgrade Point/ Devour
Insatiable	While the Devour effect is active, killing enemies refreshes its duration and recharges your grenade.	Upgrade Point/ Feed the Void
Vortex	Nova Bomb creates a singularity that continually damages enemies trapped inside.	Upgrade Point/ Insatiable

Stormcaller (Arc)

When it comes to multi-target damage, the Stormcaller is a terror on the battlefield. It lends itself to some very aggressive playstyles, but it also features some outstanding support Abilities. In the end, the Stormcaller is a great choice for Warlocks who like to charge into the fray, with or without their allies.

The Stormcaller is the Warlock's third available Subclass. It unlocks only after you've collected the required Artifact and completed the resulting mission.

Super Ability: Stormtrance

While active, Stormtrance allows a Stormcaller to float across the battlefield, electrocuting and disintegrating foe after foe. It has a fairly short range, but Stormtrance is a high-damage Super capable of tearing through an impressive number of enemies.

Grenade

The Stormcaller can choose between a **seeker** grenade, a **persistent** grenade, and a **blast** grenade.

Stormcaller Grenade Abilities

Ability Name	Description	Prerequisites
Arcbolt Grenade	A grenade that chains bolts of lightning to nearby enemies.	Default Ability
Pulse Grenade	A grenade that periodically damages enemies inside its explosion radius.	Upgrade Point
Storm Grenade	A grenade that calls down a focused lightning storm.	Upgrade Point

Movement Mode

The Stormcaller offers a typical selection of jump enhancements: directional control, a burst of speed, or a balance of speed and control.

Stormcaller Movement Modes

Ability Name	Description	Prerequisites
Strafe Glide	Jump while airborne to activate Glide and start an airborne drift with strong directional control.	Default Ability
Burst Glide	Jump while airborne to activate Glide and start an airborne drift with a strong initial boost of speed.	Upgrade Point
Balanced Glide	Jump while airborne to activate Glide and start an airborne drift with both moderate speed and directional control.	Upgrade Point

Class Ability

All Warlock Subclasses feature the same Class Ability options.

Stormcaller Class Abilities

Ability Name	Description	Prerequisites
Healing Rift	Press and hold the Crouch button to conjure a well of light that continually heals those inside it.	Upgrade Point
Empowering Rift	Press and hold the Crouch button to conjure a well of light that increases weapon damage for those inside it.	Upgrade Point

Melee and Ability Enhancements

The Stormcaller's remaining Abilities support two distinct playstyles:

Attunement of Ions features several improvements to multi-target damage. It offers chain-damage effects for Melee and Grenade Abilities, but it also includes some very useful Super enhancements. Overall, this path is a good fit for self-sufficient Stormcallers who favor aggressive tactics.

Attunement of the Elements features great utilities paired with a heavy focus on team play. When this path is selected, sticking close to allies increases the charge rate of the Stormcaller's chosen Class Ability. It also improves the assigned Rift by granting an auto-firing Arc Soul to any allies who pass through it.

Upper Path: Attunement of Ions

Ability Name	Description	Prerequisites
Chain Lightning	Deliver an electrocuting Arc melee strike at extended range that chains from the struck target to another enemy nearby.	Upgrade Point
Transcendence	When cast with full grenade and melee energy, Stormtrance lasts longer and fully restores health.	Upgrade Point/ Chain Lightning
Arc Web	Enemies damaged by your grenades chain deadly lightning to nearby enemies.	Upgrade Point/ Transcendence
Ionic Blink	Press the Sprint button to teleport during Stormtrance.	Upgrade Point/ Arc Web

Lower Path: Attunement of the Elements

Ability Name	Description	Prerequisites
Gale Force	This electrocuting Melee Ability hits at extended range and recharges your Super, grenade, and melee energy.	Upgrade Point
Landfall	On casting Stormtrance, fire a bolt of lightning into the ground, creating a devastating shockwave under you.	Upgrade Point/ Gale Force
Rising Storm	Your Rift charges faster when allies are near.	Upgrade Point/ Landfall
Arc Soul	Your Rift now grants you or any ally who uses it an Arc Soul to aid in battle.	Upgrade Point/ Rising Storm

Weaponry

This section is devoted to an overview of the various types of guns and other armaments that are not Guardian Abilities. If you want to know the difference between a sidearm and a sniper rifle, you've come to the right part of the training.

How to Obtain Weapons

Weapons are gathered in several ways. You can find them in the form of **engrams from the bodies of foes that you've killed, or in chests you have uncovered.** They are given as **rewards** when you complete a wide variety of tasks, such as finishing a mission or a Strike. You can **gift weapons to your other characters using your vault.**

Weapons that you carry are sorted out in your Character Menu based on the class of weapon you have found. So, an auto rifle that fires Kinetic ammunition is automatically placed in your Kinetic weapons inventory. Similarly, an auto rifle that fires Energy ammunition is placed in your Energy weapons inventory. You can have up to nine weapons for each Class slot, and therefore carry up to 27 extra weapons at a time (nine Kinetic, nine Energy, and nine Power).

Carrying Costs: Hoarding and Dismantling

If you pick up a weapon and your inventory slots are full, you cannot carry it until a slot is freed up. This is achieved by dismantling (at the Character Menu) an existing weapon into parts, which you can then trade to a Gunsmith for new and possibly more impressive weaponry. Alternately, you can visit a Postmaster and claim the weapon you couldn't carry. With this in mind, it's worth either hoarding or dismantling a number of weapons of a lower Attack rating, compared to the selection that you use. Consider keeping at least a few slots free to gather new equipment between hoarding or dismantling sessions.

Also, try to carry Arc, Solar, and Void Energy weapons (at least one of each type) so you're ready to take out enemy shields no matter what the situation.

Naturally, some weapons that you pick up require you to be a particular level. Save this equipment, only returning to grab it from your vault when you're about to increase your Experience to the appropriate level.

Weapon Classes

As you progress through the Campaign, you begin to accumulate a variety of weapons. These are accessible (and swappable) from your Character Menu. To begin with, it's worth learning what the three types of weapons are and how they differ.

Kinetic Weapons

A **Kinetic weapon** fires ammunition based on its type that damages in the usual manner (via physical impact to a foe) and is useful in almost every combat situation. Pick up **white ammunition boxes** to replenish the magazine of this weapon.

Energy Weapons

An **Energy weapon** fires ammunition based on its type that damages in one of three distinct ways: Arc (electrical damage), Solar (ignition-based damage), or Void (gravitational damage). Pick up **green ammunition boxes** to replenish the magazine of this weapon.

You can use any weapon type as often as you want. In fact, it's a great idea to switch between your Kinetic and Energy weapons instead of reloading.

Power Weapons

A **Power weapon** can inflict physical or energy damage and is generally a more damaging but possibly slower-firing weapon type. Shotguns, sniper rifles, and grenade launchers (as well as melee-only swords) fit into this category. Pick up **purple ammunition boxes** to replenish the magazine of this weapon.

Energy Weapon and Enemy Shields

Energy weapons only become more useful than their "Kinetic cousins" when the enemy is using one of three Energy Shield types:

Fire a Kinetic weapon at a foe using an Energy Shield, and only some of the damage goes through. It takes a lot longer for the Energy Shield to dissipate, and therefore, it takes much longer to kill the enemy.

Fire an Energy weapon at a foe with an energy shield and your weapon hits inflict much more damage. If you match the weapon energy type to the shield, destroying the shield deals bonus explosive damage to the target and any enemy units within the blast radius.

An enemy with an Arc Energy Shield.

An enemy with a Void Energy Shield.

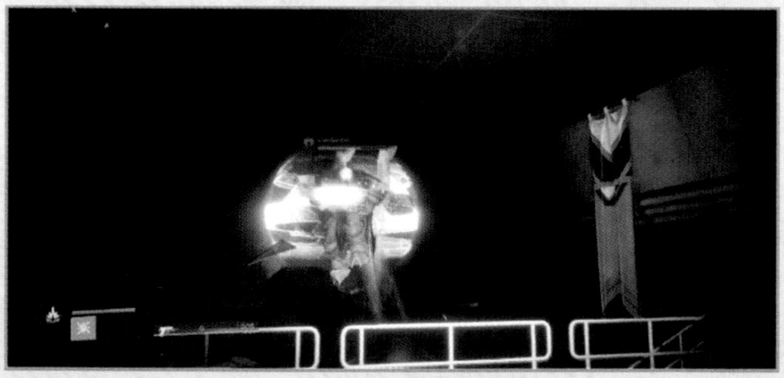

An enemy with a Solar Energy Shield.

But how do you tell which Energy weapon is best for a specific situation? You get a visual of the shield the enemy is utilizing (light blue for Arc, purple for Void, and orange for Solar).

I Don't Have the Energy

If you don't have an Energy weapon that matches a target's shield, take heart that any form of Energy Damage will cut through a shield (you'll just forgo the explosive bonus that comes from matching energy types), and a Kinetic weapon is always a viable option. It just takes a bit more time and ammunition.

Weapon Types

Every one of your weapons fits into one of the three previously listed classes. But what are the different types of weapons you can carry? These are all listed below. It's worth comparing statistics of weaponry of the same type, but when comparing stats between types (say, a shotgun to an auto rifle), the statistics may not be as relative, though you can get a good overview.

Nothing's Ever Good Enough

There's nothing better than battle-testing each and every weapon you pick up, as some guns may just feel right to you. This is especially true if you experiment with available Perk/Mod combinations, even if the base version of that weapon doesn't have the best statistics.

Auto Rifle

Class: Kinetic and Energy

An **auto rifle** may have a problem with stability (these weapons tend to have pronounced recoil), but they are fully automatic, enabling you to hold down the trigger and pump bullets into a foe while giving your trigger finger a rest. They are well-suited to mid-range combat.

Fusion Rifle

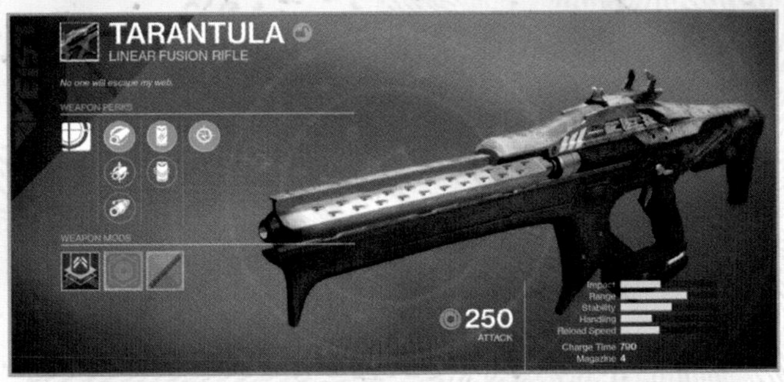

Class: Power

A typical **fusion rifle** offers good mid-range and closer-range takedown opportunities with an almost instant bolt of energy after a short charge-up. The timing is a little different because shots are not instantaneous, so practice and become more predictive with your firing tactics. A **linear fusion** rifle generally features much greater range and lower per-shot damage.

Hand Cannon

Class: Kinetic and Energy

A **hand cannon** is a revolver-like handgun designed to inflict single high-damaging shots in quick succession, firing as quickly (or as slowly) as you can manually pull the trigger. Expect a relatively short range and lengthy reload times.

Pulse Rifle

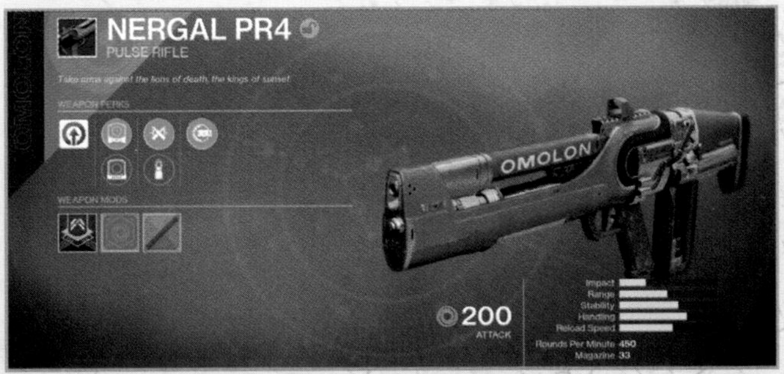

Class: Kinetic and Energy

A **pulse rifle** is best at medium-to-long range, allowing for multiple and accurate takedowns with a series of burst-fire blasts. If you favor short, sharp shocks of fire and extreme accuracy, this should be on your shortlist.

Grenade Launcher

Class: Power

A typical **grenade launcher** allows for (and requires) indirect fire. At maximum range, the weapon must be aimed well above the target area. Like the grenades that you have as a Guardian Ability, a grenade fired from one of these weapons can have different energy effects. Most grenades can bounce, so punt them to where the enemy will be, rather than where they are when you fire. Watch for grenades bouncing back at you!

Rocket Launcher

Class: Power

A **rocket launcher** hits a single foe and the area immediately around them with a massive amount of splash damage. The radius of the damage is the largest of all weapons. However, don't expect rapid firing or more than three rockets to fire before a reload.

The Scorch Cannon

Seen by some as a type of rocket launcher, this specialized weapon is used by Fallen Captains and is sometimes accessible during missions and Public Events. It isn't part of your inventory, has a timed use, and allows you to point, fire, and cause massive burning damage to multiple foes or a larger target. You can also hold the Fire button to charge an attack for even greater damage.

Scout Rifle

Class: Kinetic and Energy

A **scout rifle** generally offers a good balance of impact and firing rate, and it really shines in long-range combat. Some models feature automatic fire, but manual fire is far more common.

Shotgun

Class: Power

A **shotgun** is great for striking multiple impact points into a close-range target with a single blast. It can topple tougher foes and annoyances like Taken Blight pylons, though the reloading comes sooner than you think.

Sidearm

Class: Kinetic and Energy

A **sidearm** may be overlooked, but at your peril. These are practically useless at mid to long range because of their low impact and tendency to kick back. However, the incredible rate of fire means you can shave off a foe's shields and energy at closer ranges in less time than an auto rifle.

Sniper Rifle

Class: Power

A **sniper rifle** is one of the few weapons that must be aimed to be used effectively (though you can fire without the scope during chaotic close-combat if you're panicked). At all other times, this inflicts catastrophic damage on a single target from long range.

Submachine Gun

Class: Kinetic and Energy

A **submachine gun** combines a large capacity magazine, impressive damage, and a spectacular rate of fire. It's excellent for short-range combat and crowd control, though the ammunition expenditure can be severe.

Sword

Class: Power

A **sword** is a rarely seen weapon, usually rewarded for completing a lengthy and difficult mission. It inflicts exceptional damage when aimed at a single foe, and it can also be used to block incoming enemy damage. Your perspective changes to a third-person view when you're wielding one.

Weapon Rarity

As you continue to complete missions and gather weaponry (and armor), you may notice that the weapon has a Rarity rating and an associated background color. Weapons of any quality can be given as rewards, found in chests, dropped by enemies (often as engrams), and purchased from vendors. As your character level grows, you can expect an increased frequency of high-quality drops, rewards, and vendor items.

A weapon is more than just the sum of its parts, but in general:

Common (white) weapons are no-frills offerings designed to get the job done, but little else. They can serve as useful upgrades during early levels, but most Guardians outgrow them fairly quickly.

Uncommon (green) weapons drop more frequently as character level increases, serving as useful upgrades for low- to mid-level Guardians.

Rare (blue) weapons sometimes drop for novice players, but they drop more frequently as Guardians approach max-level. They tend to be exceptional upgrades throughout the leveling process.

Legendary (purple) weapons are considered "endgame" gear, typically serving as upgrades (and equal-level "sidegrades") to max-level Guardians.

Exotic (gold) weapons are exceptional, highly coveted pieces of gear. They feature uniquely powerful Perks. A Guardian can never equip more than one Exotic weapon at a time.

They're most commonly acquired during endgame (Level 20) content, and they can be purchased from an elusive vendor (Xur), but they're occasionally recovered during engram decryption.

A weapon's Rarity rating isn't just tied to scarcity or effectiveness. It usually indicates three specific qualities:

- The number of Perks the weapon features
- The customization options the weapon supports
- The item(s) gained from dismantling the weapon

Rarity Ratings: Weapons

Rarity Rating	Perks					Mods Slots	Dismantling Yield
	Intrinsic	Slot 1	Slot 2	Slot 3 (Trait)	Slot 4		
Common (white)	Fixed	Fixed	–	–	–	–	Glimmer (25)
Uncommon (green)	Fixed	Variable	Fixed	–	–	–	Glimmer (50)
Rare (blue)	Fixed	Variable	Fixed	Fixed	–	Energy (if applicable), Shader	Glimmer (100), Weapon parts (1)
Legendary (purple)	Fixed	Variable	Variable	Fixed	–	Energy (if applicable), Shader	Legendary Shards (2), Weapon parts (3)
Exotic (gold)	Fixed	Fixed	Fixed	Fixed	Fixed	Weapon Ornament (if applicable)	Legendary Shards (10), Experimental parts (1)

Some Exceptions May Apply

While weapons of the same Rarity generally share the same number of Perks and Mod slots, there's an exception to every rule. Occasionally, you can expect to find a weapon that deviates from established norms.

Weapon Statistics

Every single weapon has a set of associated statistics. These are likely to change (sometimes significantly) after game launch, but a basic understanding of what each statistic means and how to compare it with other weapons of the same (and different) type is important. Here is an overview.

ATTACK: This is an often misunderstood statistic, which indicates the basic damage a weapon inflicts, but in comparison to enemies and weapons of lower, similar, or higher levels. It is a damage rating modifier for the Impact statistic, determining how much Impact damage (see below) the weapon actually inflicts based on an enemy's level. The higher the value, the higher the level of foes you can strike with more damage.

Are you attempting Campaign or Strike Missions (for example) with a lower-level Guardian compared to what the game recommends (on the screen when you die)? Then your Attack modifier will be lower, resulting in more ammo expenditure to take down any enemy you face.

Are you choosing between weapons? Pick the one you're happiest using, and then compare the Attack rating: the higher, the better. Of course, higher Attack rated weapons may not be accessible to you until you level up, so choose a weapon with the highest Attack rating that you can actually use.

IMPACT: Think of this as the damage rating for the weapon: the higher, the better. This is the amount of hurting a single projectile (such as a bullet, slug, or sword swing) inflicts on a foe. Remember to take into consideration the Rounds Per Minute rating, as two high-powered shots per second may not be as lethal as 20 low-powered shots per second. Usually, slower-firing weapons (like pistols, shotguns, and sniper rifles) have higher Impact ratings.

RANGE: This is how effective the weapon is over distance. A weapon may have a spread of fire that decays the farther away you are from a target, leading to around half the damage being inflicted outside of the weapon's capable range. Note that aiming down your weapon sight helps with any range issues your weapon may have. Certain weapons with long ranges include fusion and sniper rifles. Weapons with poor range include shotguns. Want consistent and accurate headshots at any range? Choose a weapon with a high Range statistic.

STABILITY: The higher this rating, the more stable the weapon is under repeated firing in quick succession. With a highly stable weapon, you receive less of a "kick" and can fire more accurately and repeatedly at a target.

Weapons with low stability sway back and forth (causing inaccuracies) and usually fire larger (and sometimes area-of-effect) projectiles. You can mitigate this by aiming down the sights. Want consistent and accurate headshots with constant firing? Choose a highly stable weapon.

HANDLING: This gives a general idea of how quickly you can bring this weapon to bear, from the moment you bring the weapon up, raise and aim it, and then lower it afterward. The higher the stat, the quicker it can be employed. Light weapons like pistols have a high Handling rating. Grenade launchers are unwieldly, with a low rating. Need to get your shot in first? Pick a great-handling gun.

RELOAD SPEED: The higher this rating is, the faster you can reload the weapon (among weapons of the same type). Any rating you see should only be compared to the same type of weapon. Need a quick reload between blasting foes when using a sidearm? Compare the Reload Speed rating of all the sidearms you own. To check the reload speed of each weapon type, just use them during missions, or fire them at walls and see how long each reload lasts.

ROUNDS PER MINUTE: This is how fast the weapon fires, and the higher the number, the more projectiles are expended. This statistic is related to Impact damage. Remember that weapons that fire automatically or multiple times in a second (in a burst) may have a significantly lower Impact rating compared to, say, a hand cannon. But that doesn't mean they are less effective— the amount of damage they inflict over an amount of time may be greater as more projectiles are fired. Conversely, sniper rifles have low RPM ratings, but a single shot is all you usually need.

MAGAZINE: This shows you the number of shots the weapon holds in a chamber before it requires reloading. If you're constantly reloading, you may want to find a weapon with a higher magazine capacity. It's obviously more helpful to compare Magazine ratings between weapons of the same or a similar type. Don't ignore shotguns because they have a small magazine size; the devastation that they can enact is astounding.

Weapon Comparisons

Remember to compare your equipped weapon to other weapons of the same type that you pick up (in your Character Menu) so you can quickly determine which one is more suitable to your needs. For example, a newly acquired auto rifle should only be compared to another auto rifle (in terms of stats, at least).

Also, note the additional (and sometimes unique) abilities that some weapons can have. They're listed at the bottom of each weapon box under the statistics, along with any modifications the weapon may have.

Armor

The slots down the right side of your initial Character Menu are devoted to the different pieces of armor your Guardian wears, which are protective sections of your overall ensemble. This part of the training gives an overview of the different armor options available.

Armor Slots

There are five armor slots, divided into different body parts. Each slot can have up to nine different types of armor in it before it becomes full and additional armor pieces are sent to the Postmaster. Free up space by either dismantling items or storing them in a vault. These are the available slots:

HELMET: Armor protecting the head. This is not worn in Social Sectors, but you can change this in your Settings Menu.

GAUNTLETS: Armor protecting the hands and lower arms.

CHEST: Armor protecting the upper arms, torso, and abdomen.

LEGS: Armor encasing the legs and feet.

CLASS: This is a unique accoutrement that augments your Titan (a mark), Hunter (a cloak), or Warlock (a bond).

Armor Abilities

Armor has a set of statistics you can check, and these are related to one of three Attributes (detailed below).

DEFENSE RATING: Helps determine your Power Level (a rough average of Attack/Defense values of all equipped gear). Power Level determines the amount of damage you take and inflict while battling high-level enemies.

RESILIENCE: Increases the amount of damage you can take before dying.

MOBILITY: Increases your movement speed and maximum jump height.

RECOVERY: Increases the speed at which you regain lost health.

PERK OR MOD: If a Perk or Mod related to this piece of armor is available, it is listed under the statistical data.

Armor Differences

The previous pictures show how dissimilar a Guardian can look: The Titan, Hunter, and Warlock all have distinctly different sets of armor, and armor purchased or rewarded is always the type your Class wears. This means that you can't effectively share armor with a second character unless you're both of the same Class.

Though armor might look bulkier on a Titan and more flowing on a Warlock, it is important to look at substance over style. Check the statistical rating of an armor piece and whether it has a Perk that affects other functionality (such as giving you more grenades to throw or increasing the effectiveness of a weapon type).

Armor Rarity

Like weapons, armor pieces feature color-coded Rarity ratings. Armor of any quality can be offered as rewards, found in chests, dropped by enemies (often as engrams), and purchased from vendors. As your character level grows, you can expect an increased frequency of high-quality drops, rewards, and vendor items.

While you're free to use whatever bits of armor you choose, generally:

Common (white) armor pieces are as simple as it gets. They can serve as useful upgrades during early levels, but they're rarely used beyond that.

Uncommon (green) armor pieces drop more frequently as character level increases, serving as useful upgrades for low- to mid-level Guardians.

Rare (blue) armor pieces occasionally appear early on, but they drop more frequently as a Guardian approaches max-level. They tend to be exceptional upgrades throughout the leveling process.

Legendary (purple) armor pieces are considered "endgame" gear, typically serving as upgrades (and "sidegrades") to max-level Guardians.

Exotic (gold) armor pieces are exceptional Class-specific items that feature uniquely powerful Intrinsic Perks, many of which enhance one or more Abilities found within a specific Guardian Subclass. In many cases, Guardians will adjust their entire playstyle to make use of a recently acquired piece of Exotic armor. A Guardian can only equip one Exotic armor piece at a time. They're most commonly acquired during endgame (Level 20) content, and they can be purchased from Xur, but they're occasionally recovered during engram decryption.

As with weapons, the Rarity rating assigned to a piece of armor isn't just tied to scarcity. It also indicates three specific qualities:

- The number/types of Perks featured on the armor piece
- The customization options supported by the armor piece
- The item(s) gained from dismantling the armor piece

Rarity Ratings: Armor

Rarity Rating	Perks		Mod Slots			Dismantling Yield
	Intrinsic	Trait	Slot 1	Slot 2	Shader	
Common (white)	–	–	–	–	–	Glimmer (25)
Uncommon (green)	–	–	–	–	–	Glimmer (50)
Rare (blue)	Fixed	–	–	Available	Available	Glimmer (100), Armor materials (1)
Legendary (purple)	Fixed	Variable (2 options)	Fixed	Available	Available	Legendary Shards (2), Armor materials (3)
Exotic (gold)	Fixed	Fixed	Fixed	–	Available	Legendary Shards (10), Advanced materials (1)

Make an Exception

While armor pieces of the same Rarity generally share the same number of available Perks and Mod slots, you can expect to find the occasional outlier.

Other Gear and Vehicles

You've already received a briefing on a Guardian's Abilities, weapons, and armor. Now, it's time to check in with the secondary gear you can accrue for your Titan, Hunter, or Warlock, as well as customizable options and the vehicles you're able to control.

Armor and Weapon Perks and Mods

We've established that a gear piece's Rarity rating typically indicates the number of Perks and Mod slots it offers. Now, you will learn what Perks and Mods do.

Perks

Perks are existing qualities that help define a weapon or piece of armor. They cannot be removed, but some Perks on high-level gear can be adjusted to grant different benefits.

Weapon Perks

Every weapon that you find features at least one Perk. It might be a boost to range or stability—of course, it might cause your enemies to explode each time you execute a Precision Kill. A high-quality weapon usually features at least one variable Perk that you can use to adjust performance. Essentially, Perks define what makes a weapon the right (or wrong) fit for your playstyle.

Aside from those found on Exotic items, weapon Perks typically fall into one of the following categories:

INTRINSIC: This Perk is generally determined by a weapon's frame. It can't be changed, and its effects are automatically factored into the weapon's stats. Essentially, it's used to convey a weapon's basic performance at a glance. For example, the **Aggressive Frame** Perk indicates a high-damage, high-recoil weapon. However, each Exotic weapon features an Intrinsic Perk that grants one or more unique effects.

SIGHT/SCOPE: These Perks generally affect stats like range, handling, and zoom.

BARREL: These Perks typically affect stats like stability, handling, and range.

MAGAZINE: These Perks can affect nearly any weapon stat. Magazine size is obviously a common option, but reload speed, ammo capacity, and rate of fire are also frequent offerings. They can also add special properties to each bullet fired.

BATTERY: These Perks generally appear on fusion rifles. Like their ballistic counterparts, Battery Perks can affect nearly any weapon stat—magazine size, reload speed, stability, and so on.

TRAIT: These Perks typically provide a weapon with special bonuses that aren't directly related to stats. For example, **Snapshot Sights** allows for a quick transition between hip firing and aiming down sights, whereas **Firmly Planted** increases accuracy, stability, and handling when the wielder is crouched. Of course, Exotic Traits offer some especially potent effects.

Armor Perks

In contrast to weapon Perks, armor Perks are fairly straightforward. These only appear on higher-quality armor pieces. Essentially, they determine your balance of Resilience, Mobility, and Recovery. These Perks generally fall into one of two categories:

INTRINSIC: These Perks determine an armor piece's base Attributes. Each Class-specific variant offers a different combination of Resilience, Mobility, and Recovery.

TRAIT: These Perks further enhance an armor piece's Attributes. They're almost always variable, allowing for basic adjustments to individual armor pieces.

Mods

Mods can be used to change or enhance the qualities of most high-level gear items. Some Mods are purely cosmetic, but many provide benefits that can significantly improve your combat proficiency.

Weapon Mods

Weapon Mods only come in three varieties: Mods that change the damage type (Arc/Solar/Void) of high-quality Energy and Power weapons, Shaders that change a weapon's color scheme, and item-specific Weapon Ornaments that can be used to change the appearance of the related Exotic weapons.

Armor Mods

While weapon modification can be very useful, armor Mods play a far more noticeable role in combat.

Most of the armor Mods you acquire will come from decrypting Bright engrams or trading with Banshee-44, and you'd do well to hang on to as many as possible.

Armor Mods can affect everything from how often you can use various Abilities to how well your weapon performs in the field.

Of course, high-quality armor pieces also support Shaders, allowing you to mix and match your way to that perfect look.

Shaders

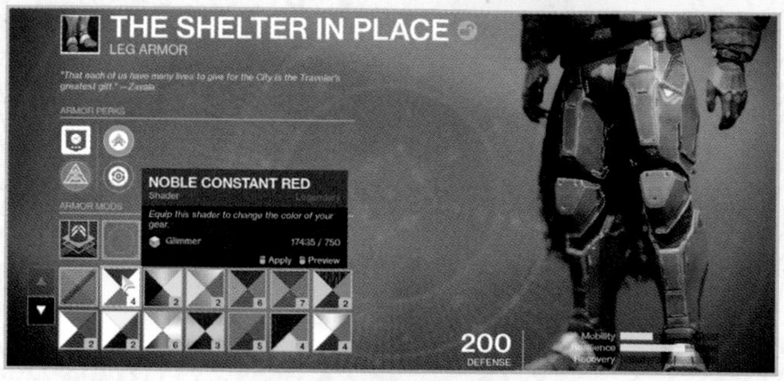

Found in chests, given as rewards, and traded by vendors, these items change the color scheme of your visible equipment, though the exact equipment parts that change color will vary. This is an optional activity. When you find a Shader that pleases you, select it to preview what colors it will change your equipment to. Then, you can create more uniform looks, eventually color-coding all of your weapons, armor, and vehicles. Or, you can shade each piece of equipment differently; it is entirely up to you.

Currency: Glimmer

This cube-like matter is the official currency and used in almost all purchases. You earn it by defeating particularly troublesome enemy types (Elites and Bosses), trading with vendors, inspecting loot caches, winning Crucible matches, harvesting resource materials, and completing certain missions and activities. Start finding Glimmer at the earliest possible moment; it's needed to buy gear as you level up.

Currency: Legendary Shard

Salvaged from Legendary or Exotic gear, the Legendary Shard is quite the commodity. While new uses are sure to be revealed in the future, for now, Legendary Shards are primarily used to purchase Exotic gear from Xur.

Currency: Bright Dust

Obtained by dismantling items acquired via Bright engrams, Bright Dust is an Eververse-specific currency.

Emotes

Emotes are actions that you can perform to denote a particular emotion, useful when attempting to convey a message to a teammate when talking isn't an option. Your Guardian has three Emotes to try out, and more can be purchased or awarded after the game launch. Check your Settings Menu to find out how to perform an Emote.

Ghosts

Though your Ghost is your permanent companion, this small floating drone with a flashlight and scanning capabilities can also be outfitted with different shells (as seen in your Character Menu). Such items can be more than cosmetic (and can be further changed with Shaders); some Ghost shells may grant perks or additional rewards for completing certain activities.

Ships

Known also as jumpships, these space vehicles allow transportation between the Orbital Regions of the solar system. To engage your ship, access this menu, locate the Region you want to visit, and check the overview map for the nearest Landing Zone (or "LZ") to your target Sector. Additional Landing Zones become available as you complete more Campaign Missions. Ships can be color-coded to your liking using Shaders. You can purchase additional ship types from Amanda Holliday at the Tower after you complete the Campaign.

Sparrows

Sparrows are land vehicles designed for quicker access between Sectors, which become accessible once you complete the Campaign. They have no offensive capabilities (aside from ramming enemies) and can be flipped over if you're driving erratically. They have a boost to enable even quicker travel. They can be color-coded using Shaders. Once you complete the Campaign, you can purchase additional Sparrow types from Amanda Holliday at the Tower.

Other Vehicles

In addition to your ship and Sparrow, there are other vehicles you're able to drive or pilot during the course of your exploration. These are as follows:

PIKES: Fallen land vehicles piloted by a Dreg. Pike Gangs are found randomly in some Public Sectors as part of a Secret Public Event. Remove the Dreg from the Pike to use it (and its forward-firing cannons) yourself.

INTERCEPTOR: Cabal land vehicle piloted by a Psion. Interceptors are found randomly in some Cabal-dominated Public Sectors as part of a Secret Public Event. Defeat the Psion, and hop on the Interceptor. It has a tougher armor than a Pike but is a little bulkier. You're able to drive an Interceptor during an Adventure, too.

CONSTRUCTION APC: A yellow personnel carrier found on Titan and used during Campaign Mission: Utopia. Consult that mission for further information.

DRAKE TANK: A heavy tank dropped into play during Campaign Mission: Payback. Consult that mission for further information.

Navigation

Exploring the Regions of the European Dead Zone, Titan, Nessus, and Io requires you to observe and investigate the world around you. Therefore, it is important to know all of the different environmental factors before you start investigating them. Pay particular attention to the available Loot Caches (AKA chests) and strange scannable lore objects that Ghost can interact with.

Know Your Environment

Aside from perfecting your running, sprinting, and jumping (as well as driving), you should also be aware of the main environmental areas of interest and hazards. This section details the most important ones.

SECTORS: Each World or Region is divided into different Sectors. The largest of these are Public Sectors, but there are a few other types.

PUBLIC SECTOR: A large Sector that is completely accessible to all Guardians. Expect most, if not all, activities to be available here. These offer roads to adjacent Sectors and are high-traffic areas.

LOST SECTOR: A small subterranean dungeon-like Sector with a few enemy clusters to fight and a Elite to face. Slay the Elite, and they drop a key to a specific chest contained within these Sectors (and only these Sectors). Occasionally, Lost Sectors link to other Public Sectors, but they are mainly dead ends.

ACTIVITY SECTOR: A medium-to-small sized Sector that may be partially or completely inaccessible during normal "social" circumstances. This Sector opens up during a particular mission or activity, so consult the Director to find out when this is.

SOCIAL SECTOR: The Farm and the Tower are the only two Social Sectors, where you have a large number of friendly Guardians and vendors, and your camera switches from first to third person. Head here to preen, fiddle, and tweak your Guardian, as well as access your vault and trading equipment.

Each Sector may link to another via one or more roads, or via a Landing Zone if they are self-contained. Certain Sectors are accessible all the time, while others are partially or fully inaccessible unless a mission or activity is occurring. A wide variety of activities take place within each Sector. The Director chapter details all of them.

VAULTS: Vaults are located in both of the Social Sectors. As you might expect, they store items or equipment that you don't want to currently use. Store items in a vault if you aren't high enough level to use it yet and want to free up an item slot in your Character Menu. Keep items that you don't want to dismantle but are saving for other purposes. Share items with your other Guardians (that you yourself create). Don't ignore vaults; they are extremely handy.

GHOST INTERACTIONS: If a bridge needs extending or a light switch needs fiddling with, Ghost is here to help.

Simply step up to any device (be it a transmat or a computer terminal), and if a context-sensitive prompt appears, use Ghost to access it.

Unless the prompt tells you explicitly not to press a button, press it every time! However, you may want to survey an area or replenish your Abilities beforehand.

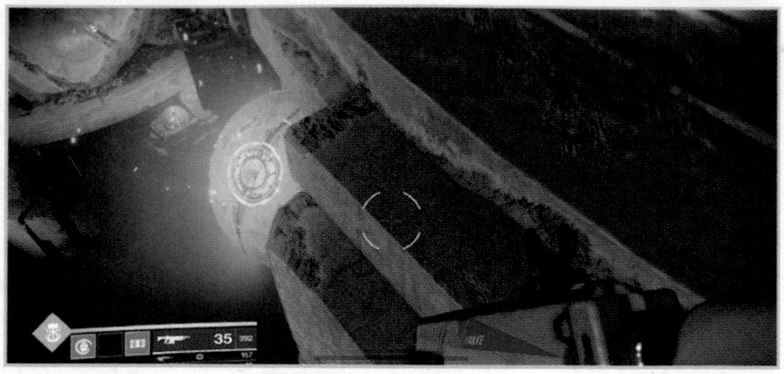

ENERGY CATAPULTS: The planetoid of Nessus has glowing embedded globes that bounce you from lower to upper areas that are too high to jump to. Look out for these, and land on them to first activate them.

LAUNCHERS: If you spot strange glowing rings floating in the air, these are strange Vex cannons that propel you in a roughly horizontal boost across a Sector. They are always used as part of a Secret Public Event (flagged in the Director chapter).

BARRELS AND CANISTERS: Be on the lookout for red barrels with a glowing light on them, as well as larger yellow canisters. These are explosive, and you can shoot them to cause area-of-effect damage after they detonate. This helps soften up enemies before you finish them with other attacks. Of course, this can also harm you, so clear an area of these if you're thinking of hiding near one.

LASER TRAPS: Mainly part of the Fallen's repertoire of defenses, these are laser beams emanating from an explosive tube, positioned at one end of the trap. Simply look for the tube, and shoot it. Be wary of setting off a chain reaction, and keep away from the clusters of traps so you aren't caught in the explosion. Walk into one of these lasers, and the trap triggers, wounding you.

MOTION TRAPS: Both the Fallen and the Taken have occasional motion traps. Placed in the ground, these orbs are activated by your nearby movement. They lift up and explode into a large globe-like trap that can wound and slow you down if you step near or into it. Avoid it, or shoot the trap before the globe is triggered.

HIVE TRAPS: Sometimes known as "anchor" traps, these nasty devices litter certain parts of Titan, and they slow you down and wound you if you step into one. Shoot them from range to neutralize them.

RESOURCE MATERIALS: Each of the four World Regions has a specific resource that you can gather. Simply approach the "node," which is usually a strange mineral or plant growing across the Public Sectors, Lost Sectors, or Activity Sectors. Harvest the material from it, along with a small amount of Glimmer. Each Region has the following material type:

EDZ: Dusklight Shard

Nessus: Microphasic Datalattice

Titan: Alkane Dust

Io: Phaseglass Needle

These raw materials are prized by local vendors, so try to collect every resource you find. When you visit an interested vendor, hand the materials over to gain Reputation and (eventually) a suitable reward for all of your hard work.

Rare Materials

Keep an eye out for Rare resource materials. They look fairly similar to their standard counterparts, but redeeming a Rare resource yields twice the Reputation.

RADIOLARIAN FLUID: The white fluid found across the Nessus Region, from the waterfalls to the lakes and streams, is dangerous to the touch and should not be stood on. This is Radiolarian Fluid, the by-product and lifeblood of the Vex. Avoid it.

BARRIERS: Throughout the Director chapter of this guide, whenever a Sector has an area that cannot be explored during normal circumstances (i.e., outside of a mission), expect it to be sealed with a barrier, usually a blue energy wall. There are also other types of barriers, but each serves the same purpose: it prevents you from exploring areas that are designated as mission-specific.

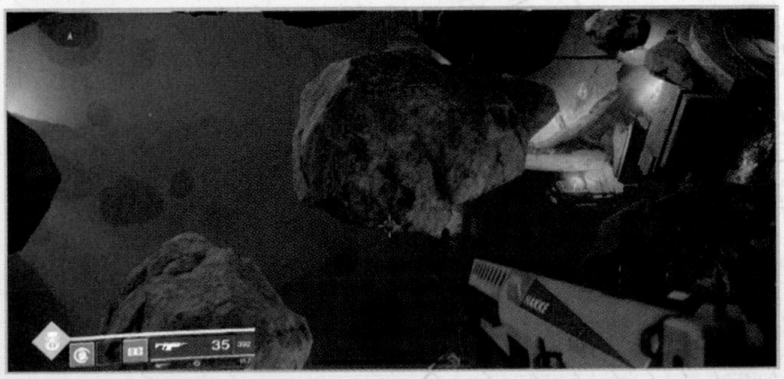

SHEER DROPS: Peer down between solid platform gaps. Can you see the ground below? Or is it a vague mist, a sea of methane, or an inky void of darkness? Those areas are sheer drops; don't fall down those.

CORES AND CORE GATHERING: At certain points during missions, you may be called upon to grab an orb-like core and then deposit it in a nearby receptacle. Note that your view changes to third-person perspective. You're slightly tougher during this time because you cannot fire weapons (the core requires both hands to carry). Plan your route ahead of time, and bring friends to cover you, if possible.

Loot Caches (Chests)

One of the key ways of improving your Guardian is the looting of equipment from chests that you find by different means. Expect to gather Glimmer, engrams, weapons and armor, and other items and equipment when you find one of these. Here are the different types of Loot Caches (AKA chests).

ENEMY CHEST: These chests are the most plentiful across the four World Regions. They are stashes collected by a particular enemy, so a cache may have a particular look to it (examples of Fallen and Hive chests are shown). The guide's Director chapter tracks the expected location of all Enemy Chests. However, only very few of these are active at any one time, so they won't appear in every location. A single Enemy Chest also becomes active and is awarded as a prize once you complete a Patrol. Enemy Chest locations are tracked in the Director chapter of this guide.

REGION CHEST: These gold-colored chests are scattered across every Public Sector, hidden away cunningly and requiring a modicum of searching to find. Expect higher-value items (compared to a Enemy Chest) when you open one. They can only be accessed once by your Guardian. If you need some additional equipment, this is a quick and easy way to find some. Region Chest locations are tracked in the Director chapter of this guide.

LOST SECTOR CHEST: These locked chests are specifically located inside a Lost Sector. To open one, you must first defeat the Elite enemy (and optionally, his minions) within the Lost Sector. After that, the key is looted, and you can open the chest. They can be looted multiple times (if you complete a foe removal sweep of the Lost Sector), though the quality of the items isn't as valuable after the first looting. Expect weekly resetting loots for this chest type. Lost Sector Chest locations are tracked in the Director chapter of this guide.

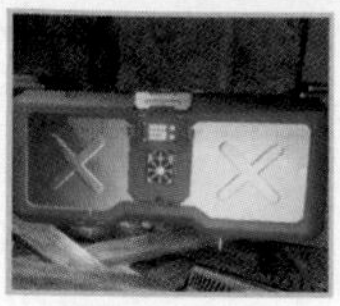

ELITE (AND BOSS) CHEST: Some Majors that periodically appear in Public Sectors (due to a Secret Public Event) drop a Loot Cache. These hold valuable items, which you can grab at the conclusion of the event. This type of chest also appears when you've slain a particularly troublesome foe, usually at the end of a mission (like an Adventure or a Strike). Grab what you can from it before the mission concludes.

TREASURE CHEST: Once you've completed the Campaign Missions and have obtained access to the Tower, you can visit Cayde-6. Under certain conditions, he offers you treasure maps to a number of chest locations within a Region. There are multiple chest locations, and each is static. The number of chests that you receive from Cayde-6 depends on what Bungie allows. Find a chest through the clues Cayde-6 gives you, and return with the items. This is endgame content, which is self-explanatory when you speak to Cayde-6 and is not included in this guide.

Scannable Objects (Lore Objects)

Across every Public Sector and some Activity Sectors in every Region (and both Social Sectors) are a wide variety of interesting, odd, and downright weird objects. Some look like scenery, while others appear to be out-of-place floating rift orbs. These are lore objects, also called scannable objects, and you use Ghost to interact with them to "find" each one. There are dozens of these to find. Use your Ghost to scan an area, and any of these objects are highlighted in the static. Be sure to do this everywhere you are exploring. Clues to the whereabouts of scannable objects are mentioned in the Director chapter of this guide.

Object Searching: Laying Down the Lore

Scannable objects are located in Sectors that are accessible both during and after missions are completed. This means that you don't have to worry about turning over every crate and searching every nook and cranny as you finish a mission. Instead, find these lore items when you are exploring between missions, with other Guardians.

Progression

This section details the optimal ways to gain levels and power for your Guardian. An explanation of the available vendors is given. An overview of engram collecting and decoding is revealed. In addition, a list of mission types, activities, and Milestones is explained. Lastly, an example Guardian (the Exo known as PR-1M4) is taken from inception to endgame.

Gaining Levels and Power

Character Level

Your character level determines the gear you can equip, the Subclasses and Abilities you can unlock, and the activities in which you can participate.

Each mission you fulfill, activity you complete, and enemy you defeat serves to fill your Experience bar. Fill the bar to capacity, and three things happen:

- Your character level increases by 1.
- You receive an Upgrade Point that you can use to unlock a latent Ability.
- Your Experience bar resets.

Of course, this is only true until you reach max level. At character level 20, filling your Experience bar yields an Upgrade Point and provides a chance for additional rewards.

There's no real shortcut to increasing your character level; it's an indication of your growth as a Guardian, so you should expect to put in a fair amount of effort. However, you can ensure that you make the most of your time.

Grinding away in an enemy hotspot can add up over time, but defeating enemies as you work toward completing an activity yields much better results. If you've run out of missions, pick a planet and clear out some Lost Sectors; run a series of Patrols as you look for Public Events to join. Head to the Crucible and hone your skills as you work toward rewards, or better yet, as you work toward completing Challenges and Milestones.

Completing activities is the best way to increase your character level, and as luck would have it, it's the best way to raise your Power Level.

This might seem obvious (considering that it's determined by Attack and Defense values), but it's important to remember that your Power Level is an average of *all* equipped items—including the weapons you aren't currently using.

If, for example, you're firing away with your Kinetic weapon, your Energy weapon, Power weapon, and all of your armor pieces help determine the damage you're able to inflict. An outdated piece of armor can reduce the effectiveness of your attacks, and a low-quality backup weapon can increase the amount of damage you take.

Luckily, increasing your Power Level is simply a matter of acquiring better gear. Once again, activities serve as your best option. Complete available missions. Prioritize Adventures that grant gear items. Spend some time in the Crucible, or work to gain Reputation rewards with your preferred vendor. Virtually everything you can do out in the field has a chance to yield a upgrade, so get out there and put your Power Level to good use.

Power Level

In essence, your Power Level represents the average **Attack** and **Defense** values of your equipped gear items. The higher those values, the higher your Power Level.

In practice, your Power Level is much more than gear summary. It determines how much damage you'll deal and suffer when squaring off against high-level enemies.

THE CLIMB TO POWER LEVEL 300

From activities to engrams, virtually every source of gear can provide a steady stream of incremental upgrades – until you reach Power Level 260, that is.

Early on, you'll notice that rewards typically feature slightly higher Attack or Defense ratings than your currently slotted option. A new chest piece might be a point or two higher than the chest piece you're wearing, even if your overall Power Level is noticeably lower.

These incremental upgrades are fairly common as your Power Level grows, but at Power Level 260, you'll notice that what used to be a reliable source of upgrades now yields only *sidegrades*. And while an equal-level piece of gear might be a better fit for your playstyle, it won't do anything for your Power Level.

What's a Guardian to do?

In a word: *Milestones*. Weekly Milestones are the best (and currently only) answer for the Power Level 260 plateau. If you want to keep gaining Power, you'll need to open the Director and get busy clearing those weekly Milestones.

See that **Flashpoint**? Go rustle up some Public Events. **Call to Arms**? Go start some trouble in the Crucible. If you've yet to finish any of the available Milestones, pick one from the list, and get to work. Then, check in the following week, and do it all over again.

Clans

If you're in the market for a few new allies, a clan might be just what you're looking for. No pressure! Joining a clan is extremely helpful, but it's entirely optional. You can still look for likeminded Guardians out in the wild, or queue up to be matched with other lone wolves. But if you're willing to take the plunge, you're sure to find that joining (or starting) a clan can be an enjoyable and very rewarding experience. If you're already running with a group of friends, there's no reason you shouldn't get together and form a clan of your own.

Aside from the obvious benefits of forging new alliances, clan benefits include:

A CLAN BANNER: If you join a clan, you'll finally have something to put in that final gear slot. Assist your clan to unlock special Clan Banner Perks for your Guardian.

CLAN REWARDS: If your clan members complete a specified endgame activity (such as a Nightfall Strike), every member of the clan receives an engram. Just head to Hawthorne and claim your not-so-hard-earned reward.

A WEEKLY MILESTONE: Not ready to tackle endgame content? You don't need to be the best to be an asset. Experience earned by every member goes toward unlocking new Clan Banner Perks, and every member receives a new Milestone encouraging them to do so.

GUIDED GAMES: Lead interested Guardians through endgame content. Success will boost your Clan's Oathkeeper's Score.

Of course, you can expect clan-related features and benefits to evolve over time. For now, it's important to note some things:

- You can't start a clan in the game. Would-be founders can visit Bungie.net to establish their clans and set member permissions.
- You can issue clan invites in the game. Assuming you have the required permissions, you can use the Roster to invite prospective members.
- You can only be a member of one clan at any given time, and membership is account-wide (all characters). There's no penalty for leaving a clan, but if you join a new one right away, you won't be eligible for Clan Rewards until the weekly activities reset.
- Unlocked Clan Banner Perks only last until the end of the season. At that point, all clans receive a new selection of Perks to unlock.
- Before you can lead a Guided Game, you must take a Guardian's Oath—basically, you agree to be friendly and helpful and see the activity through to the end. Failing to honor your oath lowers your Clan's Oathkeeper's Score and temporarily bars you from leading another Guided Game. This penalty is waived if the fireteam votes to surrender, but the failure is still factored into your Clan's Oathkeeper's Score.

Vendors

Redeem a Token at a vendor to gain Reputation with them so you can obtain unique items and greater-value equipment.

Vendors are an integral part of your continued survival and progression as a Guardian. The majority of these traders reside in the Social Sectors, though each Region has its own vendor, as well. The following table lists all available vendors:

Vendor Name	Location	Type
Darbi 55-30	The Farm	Postmaster
Kadi 55-30	The Tower	Postmaster
Tess Everis	The Farm, The Tower	Eververse Promoter
Tyra Karn	The Farm	Cryptarch Archivist
Master Rahool	The Tower	Cryptarch Archivist
Suraya Hawthorne	The Farm, The Tower	Farm Overseer
Lord Shaxx	The Farm, The Tower	Crucible Overseer
Arcite 99-40	The Farm	Gunsmith
Banshee-44	The Tower	Gunsmith
Cayde-6	The Farm, The Tower	Vanguard (Hunter)
Ikora Rey	The Farm, The Tower	Vanguard (Warlock)
Zavala	The Farm, The Tower	Vanguard (Titan)
Devrim Key	Trostland (EDZ)	Overseer
Sloane	Siren's Watch (Titan)	Overseer
Failsafe	Exodus Black (Nessus)	Overseer
Asher Mir	The Rupture (Io)	Overseer
Xur	All four Regions (Varies)	Special
Amanda Holliday	The Tower	Hangar Overseer

Redeemable Tokens and Reputation

Overseers, Gunsmiths, and some Vanguards have a Reputation rating that you need to earn with them. After you complete tasks in a particular area (by checking in first to see if they have a Reputation you need to improve with them), you can return and hand in these circular Tokens. In return, your Reputation increases with them. Continue to gain favor with a vendor, and you're soon able to purchase the specific items they sell, gain better items from them, and claim rewards.

For example, Devrim Kay, who is sniping from the steeple of the church in Trostland, requires that you provide him with EDZ Tokens. Keep giving him these (which are found as loot in the vicinity Sectors of his location), and you're eventually given access to a random offering of EDZ weapons and/or armor.

Redemption and Random Rewards

Each time you fill a vendor's Reputation bar, you receive a reward pack featuring one or more randomly selected items. The Reputation bar then resets, and you're free to start working toward your next reward.

Postmasters

Check the Postmaster at the Farm or the Tower for items you failed to pick up during your adventuring that are of a Rare quality or better. Additional loot, such as items like pre-order bonuses and gifts from Bungie, as also available here.

Cryptarch Archivists

Engrams are decoded by Cryptarchs, and there are two available: Tyra Karn (an Archivist on the Farm) and the infamous Master Rahool at the Tower. Provided you have the funds, bring them any engrams you have gathered, and they are turned into random items for you.

Eververse Promotions

Tess Everis runs this company, which shifts from the Farm to the Tower when you do. She offers certain promotional items (usually engrams), along with purchasable goods that cost Bright Dust or Silver bought with real-world funds.

Overseers

This general category of vendor covers each trader in a particular Region and various vendors in either Social Sector. Gain Reputation, and purchase unique equipment from them. Certain Overseers may have additional functionality; speak to them to find this out.

Gunsmiths

Gain Reputation with either Gunsmith, but especially Banshee-44 at the Tower. When you bring him a collection of dismantled weapon and armor elements, he grants you more powerful items in return. Continue endgame activities by gradually raising the quality of the random loot he trades you until you start to receive Legendary equipment.

Vanguards

Your Guardian Mentors have their own particular equipment for you to obtain once you gain Reputation with them. Additionally, Cayde-6 and Ikora have particular activities you can help them out with.

Xur, Agent of the Nine

Xur is a strange vendor who randomly appears in a Public Sector in each of the four Worlds, depending on planetary alignments and Bungie's whim. Xur sells Exotic equipment and only takes Legendary Shards in exchange for them.

Engrams and Decoding

Engrams are crystal-like items encoded with the properties of randomly determined weapons, armor, Perks, Mods, and other items. They are dropped by foes, found after defeating particularly hardy enemies (Elites and Bosses), located in chests, and given as rewards for completing Milestones and other activities. They are also bought from the Eververse vendor or Cryptarch vendors, although some other vendors may have them or gift them to you in exchange for Tokens. They are decoded by Tyra Karn or Master Rahool, the Archivists listed previously.

Engrams can be colored white (Encoded), green (Encrypted), blue (Decoherent), purple (Legendary), or gold (Exotic). The color of the engram, like the weapons and armor you collect, signifies the quality of the expected items you receive once the engrams are decoded.

Activities and Milestones

What is there to keep a Guardian occupied as the fires of humanity are rekindled? Quite a lot, actually.

Missions and Quests

There is a wealth of missions and quests to complete.

CAMPAIGN (16 missions): This single-player set of story missions is the key to unlocking all of the different Regions in the solar system. Complete the Campaign, and you can return to Ikora to "meditate" and play through these missions again, with a fireteam if you so desire. This unlocks Tokens and Reputation with her so you can purchase her equipment, including the best Guardian weapons and armor used before Ghaul's invasion.

ADVENTURE (29 missions): These are smaller missions that begin in a Public Sector across all of the four Regions. They drift into adjacent Sectors, and they take an hour or two to complete. Replay them at your leisure.

WORLD QUEST (4 quests): Each of the four Regions has a single World Quest that involves the Region's vendor and requires you to explore much of the Region and complete multiple sub-missions within the quest. These are done once.

STRIKES (5): These are high-level fireteam missions where you visit Activity Sectors and deal with a large number of enemy forces, including unique and powerful Elite and Boss foes. Expect to be tested.

Activities

CRUCIBLE: A series of PvP competitions under the watchful gaze of Lord Shaxx. Compete to win Tokens, other loot, and unique prizes. An entire chapter is devoted to this activity.

PATROLS: Small tasks to complete in each Public Sector after finishing all Campaign Missions on Io and visiting Cayde-6.

PUBLIC EVENTS: Enemy incursions in Public Sectors that occur randomly and are designed so that Guardians can work together to deal with threats.

LOST SECTORS: Most Public Sectors have a hidden subterranean Lost Sector where you can find additional foes and a special chest.

CHEST HUNTS: There are resource materials to harvest and Enemy Chests scattered across most Public and Lost Sectors. Grab them, and visit Cayde-6 at the Farm or the Tower for scout reports, giving you positions of a few of these chests.

SCANNABLE OBJECTS: Try to find scannable lore objects that give you insights, courtesy of Ghost.

CHALLENGES: A selection of activity-specific tasks that reset daily (or weekly, in the case of weekly activities). They give you rewards when you complete them, either in Public Sectors or during Crucible matches.

TREASURE HUNTS: Once you find him at the Tower, Cayde-6 has a number of treasure chests to hunt for. Bring the odd contents back to him.

Milestones

Milestones are time-sensitive tasks to complete that Bungie has decided are particularly useful for your continued Guardian advancement. These tasks change weekly, giving you a stream of new and exciting content to discover and complete. The previous picture details all of the general available Milestones. Below is a general description of some common Milestones:

THE CRUCIBLE AND CALL TO ARMS: Amazingly, some Guardians may not have completed the first few Campaign Missions and then spoken to Shaxx at the Farm in order to access the Crucible PvP content. This is an easy Milestone to accomplish and grants you Crucible access (both from the Social Sector and the Director Menu). Afterward, expect frequent Crucible Milestones (with a 100 percent total to reach) to be set for special gear and other prizes.

FLASHPOINTS: These are requests to complete Public Events in specific Regions. For example, you might be asked to find and finish Public Events on Io, continuing with this task until the percentage rating reaches 100. Success is likely to yield high quality gear.

NIGHTFALL: Bungie usually allows access to a different Nightfall Strike on a weekly basis. This is a toughened version of a regular Strike, with certain modifiers to make the mission even tougher. Access this from the Strikes section of the Director Menu. Success is likely to yield high quality gear.

DAILY MILESTONES: These daily tasks ask you to complete challenges related to a given activity. Doing so yields a large stack of redeemable Tokens.

Iconic Imagery

Remember to note the icons for each Milestone. These appear on your Director map (which shows the solar system) near a Region associated with a Milestone that is active. That way, you can easily navigate into the orbit of that location to begin a Milestone completion.

Grinding and Gear

Reaching character level 20 is a noteworthy achievement and one that should be celebrated, but a Guardian's work is never done. There are always more lives to be saved, more threats to be ended, and more bits of gear to be collected. In fact, reaching max-level doesn't necessarily mean that you're ready for endgame content. Boosting your Power Level should be your top priority.

Make the Most of Milestones

If you're aiming to power up as quickly as possible, try to complete every Milestone you can manage. Remember, once you reach Power Level 260, Milestone rewards are likely to be your only source of gear upgrades. The weekly Flashpoint is a good place to start, and it's always worth heeding the call of the Crucible.

Compete in the Crucible

The Crucible is one of the best options an under-geared Guardian could hope for. Level advantages are disabled during all standard contests, making it the closest thing to a fair fight you're likely to find. It's a great place to hone your skills, and it offers the chance to complete another Milestone. Win or lose, you're guaranteed to get at least one piece of equipment each time you complete a match. While these rewards aren't likely to boost your Power Level, you might find a new weapon or armor piece that suits you.

Worst case, you'll amass a nice collection of gear to dismantle—just make sure you hang on to those weapon parts and armor materials.

Collect (and Hoard) Tokens

If you've spent some time window shopping with vendors, it's likely that at least a few items have caught your eye—but now is not the time.

Remember: Milestone rewards are your most reliable source for gear upgrades. The Tokens you spend will likely yield an equal-level replacement for one of your currently equipped gear items. Even if you were to get a long-desired item, you'd be sure to outgrow it eventually.

Instead, take a look at what every vendor has to offer, find something you like, and then go about earning as many of the related Tokens as you can while you continue improving your Power Level. By the time you reach Power Level 300, you should have a nice stack of Tokens to redeem. If you're lucky, you'll get the item you want at the highest possible level, ensuring that it will be put to good use for a long time to come.

Set New Goals

Once you reach Power Level 300, every piece of gear you get should be a suitable option. Go ahead and grind away for anything that catches your fancy, then go about collecting new Mods for your gear.

Or don't! If you're happy with your gear, focus on completing challenging content. Join and support a clan. Make a name for yourself in the Crucible. Unlock your remaining Abilities and experiment with your various Subclasses, or create a new Guardian and do it all again.

You'll never run out of things to do, and new challenges are sure to be introduced in the future.

FROM ZERO TO HERO: PR-1M4

STEP 1: The Exo Guardian PR-1M4 is online! This section charts the activities, antics, and upgrades chosen as this sample Guardian gained in power and Experience. To begin with, PR-1M4 was created as an Exo Titan.

STEP 2 (Level 2): After checking all weapons, armor, and Ghost, PR-1M4 completed the initial set of Campaign Missions and accessed the Farm (Social Sector) for the first time. Leveling gear was compared when speaking with Hawthorne, and equipment scavenging began. Missed items were picked up from the Postmaster. Eververse promotions were gladly accepted. Extra items were stored in the Farm vault.

STEP 3 (Level 3): A key ally and vendor Devrim Kay was met in the church tower of Trostland Sector. EDZ Tokens (a redeemable object found in chests, rewarded after events, and given after killing random enemies) began to be gathered to raise PR-1M4's Reputation with Devrim.

An Adventure was undertaken and completed. Adjacent Sectors were explored in the vicinity of Trostland. A Public Event was taken part in. PR-1M4 explored a Lost Sector and gathered up contents from a chest inside. Region Chests, Enemy Chests, and scannable lore objects were hunted for and accessed. Glimmer accumulation began in earnest.

PR-1M4 returned to Devrim to purchase some weaponry and armor with statistics improved compared to the rags initially worn.

STEP 4 (Level 4): Campaign Mission: Combustion was completed, and the second Region of Titan was unlocked. Further activities in the EDZ commenced, and a new weapon (the Sand Wasp-3AU Auto Rifle) was obtained. Perks were tweaked in the weapon's menu, and a Shader was applied. Returning to the Farm, PR-1M4 started to find amusing side activities to complete. Lord Shaxx was met, his high-level equipment inspected, and PR-1M4 embarrassed himself in the PvP arena.

PR-1M4 visited Arcite 99-40 at the Farm and began dismantling some of his unused and lower-level equipment and starting his collection of Energy weapons (Arc, Solar, and Void). He now had 2-3 of each weapon type. He revisited the Gunsmith after each Campaign Mission from this point onward.

STEP 5 (Level 6): With further Campaign Missions under his belt on Titan, PR-1M4 returned to the Farm and took all his engrams to Tyra Karn to be decoded; he wished he'd done this earlier! The resulting weapons, armor, and other equipment was compared to his inventory and swapped, dismantled, or stored in the vault. Titan Subclass Abilities had been unlocked and upgraded as Abilities were awarded for each level up. PR-1M4's first Emote was unlocked: time for a Cheer!

STEP 6 (Level 10): Glimmer gathering, material node harvesting, and the completion of Campaign Mission: Six on Nessus was deemed a success. A strange Artifact was found in a Loot Cache, enabling PR-1M4 to complete a tough mission to unlock an additional Subclass. Different Kinetic, Energy, and Power weapons were collected, compared, and utilized extensively. Activities were undertaken planet-wide on EDZ, Titan, and Nessus. Dead Zone Lush Shader was applied to PR-1M4's equipment for a more cohesive and pleasing appearance.

STEP 7 (Level 15): After finishing up Campaign Missions on Io, Cayde-6 became available to visit at the Farm. Patrols and scout reports were now active. Rare equipment became more accessible from loot, foes, and vendors. Weapons and armor were further honed as Perks and Mods were applied. A full complement of shotguns, sniper rifles, rocket launchers, and even a sword was gathered in the Power weapon slot. The Campaign on EDZ was completed: Zavala and Ikora appeared at the Farm.

STEP 8 (Level 20): Guardian's Call: After finishing the Campaign entirely, a host of new activities and powerful enemies awaited PR-1M4 on every World. Legendary and Exotic weapons and armor became available. A clan was formed and joined.

STEP 9 (Level 20+): With the Tower (Social Sector) now available, PR-1M4 found a new best friend: Banshee-44. Gaining Reputation with this Gunsmith and with countless equipment dismantling, better and better gear (including Legendary items, Perks, Shaders, and Mods) began to be traded. Amanda Holliday was visited, and PR-1M4's Sparrow and ship were upgraded and even given a proper "white and red" Shader. Cayde-6 was visited, and one of his infamous treasure chest maps was purchased. Other vendors gave PR-1M4 small task-specific missions for Exotic weapon rewards. Master Rahool begrudgingly decoded the many engrams collected. PR-1M4's new vault in the Tower was getting full.

STEP 10 (Level 20+): Equipment was constantly tweaked and upgraded, with the Noble Constant Red Shader applied to it. Exotic equipment was added to the ensemble. Rookie Guardians were guided through previously played missions as part of clan activities. All vendors at the Tower were visited and their tasks completed. Milestones were met. Strikes were completed with clan mates. Nightfall Strikes were attempted. Countless Crucible matches were attempted.

Overview

The Campaign Missions represent the first major and continuous conflict that you and your fellow Guardians become part of. The Campaign is (initially) played using a single Guardian, and it's the key to unlocking all other mission types, locations, and activities across the four worlds of the Director. Continue to complete Campaign Missions to obtain looted engrams and items, the ability to unlock all the previously mentioned content, and more. Need to find Devrim Kay? Want to see Hawthorne on the Farm? Hoping to talk to Cayde-6? Want a full range of Guardian abilities? Once certain missions are concluded, the Campaign Missions hold the key to revealing all of this.

Ikora Rey's Campaign Meditation

Perhaps you only just scraped through a Campaign Mission, or you were hoping to replay a mission with a fireteam of like-minded individuals. Fortunately, after you've completed the Campaign once, you can visit Ikora Rey at the Tower and access available Campaign content. This is an excellent way to up your Reputation with Ikora so you can obtain the specific weapons and armor she possesses.

Campaign Content

This guide has recommended and optimal tactics for completing every Campaign Mission. As you read through each mission, you'll notice a number of references. Here's what everything means.

1 **Recommended Level and Power:** Missions have Requirements and Recommendations.

Requirements: This is the minimum Level the player must be to launch the mission. The most important Requirements for Campaign are Riptide (your first time on Titan, which requires Level 4), Looped (First time on Nessus, requires level 7), Sacrilege (First time on Io, requires level 11), and Payback (first mission back in EDZ after Vanguard re-unites, requires level 15)

Post-campaign requirements change from Level to Power.

Recommended Power is what is displayed once a player has access to a mission. Playing the mission under this recommended power is harder: enemies are harder to kill and deal more damage to the player.

2 **Objectives:** This lists the expected objectives you need to fulfill throughout the mission in question.

3 **Enemies Encountered:** This lists the expected enemies in each map Sector, arranged by combatant and then in the order of appearance. Consult the Bestiary for takedown tactics.

4 **New Actions to Learn:** The first time you are expected to complete a new action (all of which are detailed in this guide's Field Manual chapter), it is listed here.

5 **Important Allies:** The first time you meet a new and important ally is flagged here.

6 **Maps:** Each part of the mission is divided into specific Sectors, with a map showing pertinent information (usually waypoints that are called out in the main text).

7 **Super, Grenades, and Warnings:** "Super" and "Grenades" are the times when it is recommended to use these Guardian abilities. This helps you learn about optimal times so you don't waste a Super needlessly or use it just before you really need to. "Warnings" indicate whether the location you're about to enter is a Restricted Zone, where respawning is limited.

Campaign Missions Chart

The following table lists the available Campaign Missions:

Mission # and Name	Overview Objective	World Location
01 Homecoming	Defend your Home	Earth
02 Adieu	Follow your vision	EDZ
03 Spark – Pt. 1, Pt. 2	Go to the Traveler's Shard	EDZ
04 Combustion	Restore power to the mine elevator	EDZ
05 Hope	Rendezvous with Hawthorne	Titan
06 Riptide	Restore the shipyard power	Titan
07 Utopia	Retrieve a Golden Age CPU from the Festering Halls	Titan
08 Looped	Find Cayde-6	Nessus
09 Six	Rescue Cayde-6	Nessus
10 Sacrilege	Discover what the Red Legion are doing on Io	Io
11 Fury	Find the Warmind Vault to scan the Almighty	Io
12 Payback	Prevent the Cabal Carrier from taking off	EDZ
13 Unbroken	Get the key code for Thumos the Unbroken's ship	EDZ
14 Larceny	Steal Thumos's ship	EDZ
15 1AU	Disable the Almighty's weapon	The Almighty
16 Chosen	Retake the Last City from the Red Legion Save the Traveler, Get the city back	Earth

Homecoming

Recommended Level: None
Recommended Power: 10

Earth is under attack and the Vanguard, your Guardian mentors, are starting to scatter. While under heavy fire from the Cabal Red Legion, you must battle forth to find Cayde-6, Zavala, and Ikora. Although the Tower is lost, humanity cannot afford to fail. A gesture of resolve is needed; you are tasked with boarding the Cabal's command ship and crippling it. Along the way, you should be learning some basic maneuvering actions and methods of taking down various Cabal foes, as there are a whole lot more of them to come.

Tower Watch

The Last City, Earth

Enemies Encountered

CABAL: Legionary

Important Allies

Cayde-6
Lord Shaxx

Objectives

Defend your home.
Find Zavala.
Gear up for the fight.
Find Zavala (continued).

New Actions to Learn

Aiming Down Sights
Melee Attack
Weapon Classes and Types
Throwing Grenades
Sprinting
Jumping

1 Corridors

Super: Not available **Grenades:** Not available

After the two Cabal Legionaries break through the wall, aim for their heads. Round the corner and **aim down your sights** to more accurately deal with the two additional Legionaries charging you. Back up as you fire, if necessary. Weave along the corridor until a Legionary ambushes you at close quarters. Execute him with a **melee attack** before encountering **Cayde-6,** who vanishes as quickly as he appears.

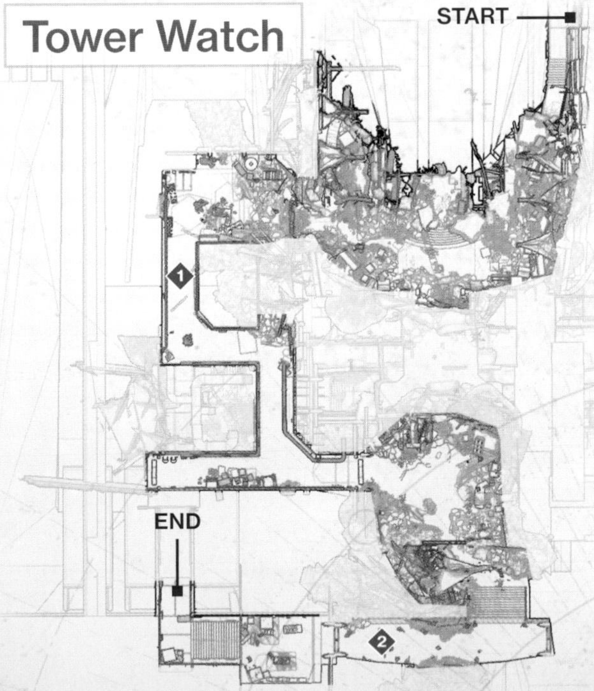

Additional Enemy Takedown Tactics

Every time you encounter a new enemy during the Campaign, consult the guide's Bestiary for more in-depth takedown knowledge.

Important Ally:

Cayde-6

"I've got a date with whoever's behind this. It'll be a short date."

Cayde-6 is an Exo and Hunter Vanguard, and he's a key ally for your cause. His dexterous and formidable combat prowess is matched only by his wit. Unfortunately, he's headed elsewhere to fight the Red Legion.

New Actions

To ensure that you fully understand all the new actions you're able to perform, check the list at the start of each section of this mission. Then, consult the guide's Field Manual chapter for in-depth tactical knowledge on all those actions.

2 Upper Corridors and Bay 04

Super: Not available **Grenades:** Recommended

Ascend the steps, and encounter **Lord Shaxx** tending to the citizens of the Tower. Enter his armory and grab a weapon. Descend the steps, and at the broken railing platform, **throw a grenade** down at two incoming Legionaries. Attempt to catch them both with a single explosion, then finish them off using your newly acquired Auto Rifle. Then, **sprint** along the corridor, passing the burning debris. Once in Bay 04, climb the metal steps, **jumping** the gap and grabbing the upper walkway, then pulling yourself up. Continue up and into the Tower hangar.

Additional Weapons Data

Learning about the differences between Kinetic and Energy weapons and how to remove enemy shields is critical to your success as a Guardian. Consult the Field Manual chapter for a complete overview of weapon classes and types, as well as information on weapon statistics, such as Impact, Range, Stability, Handling, Reload, RPM, and Magazine information.

Important Ally:

Lord Shaxx

"If the Cabal want war, give them war!"

A mighty veteran commander of the Last City's forces, decorated battle hero, and close friend of Zavala, Lord Shaxx is an imposing figure. Prior to this Red Legion attack, he ran the Crucible activities.

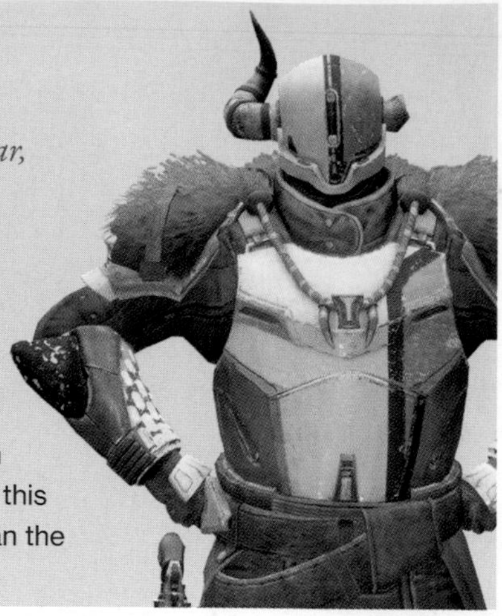

Tower Hangar

The Last City, Earth

Enemies Encountered

CABAL: Legionaries, Centurions

Objectives

Find Zavala (continued).

New Actions to Learn

Ghost Flashlight
Switching Weapons
Class-Specific Jumping
Crouching and Sliding

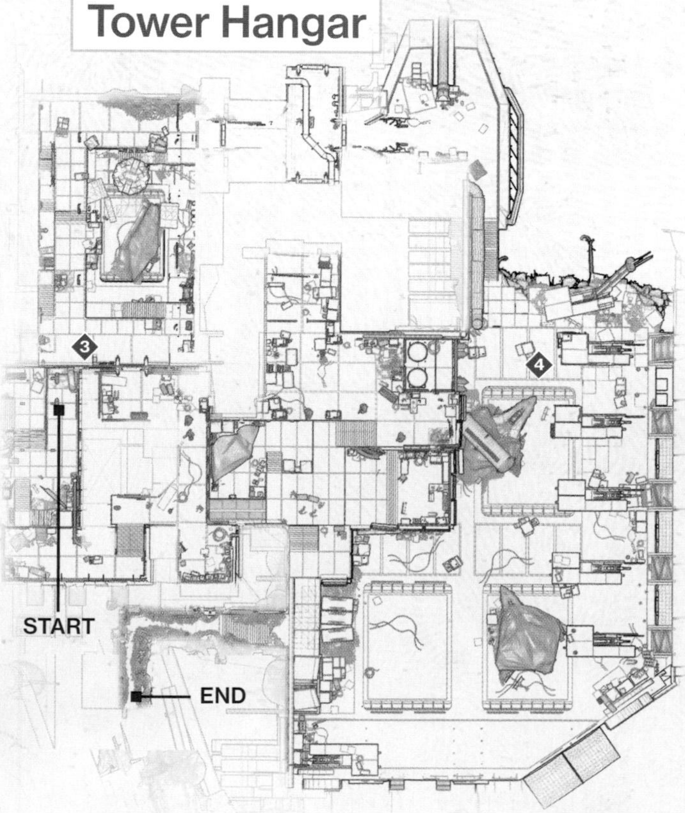

3 Storage Hangar

Super: Not available **Grenades:** Optional

As the battle rages on, **switch your weapons** (to the Energy weapon) and drop two Legionaries using it or melee attacks. After your **Ghost illuminates** the dark storage hangar, enter this gantry. Here, you're greeted by a Cabal **Centurion** and a Cabal drop pod with Legionaries to deal with. Remain on the gantry, concentrate on removing the Centurion's Solar Shield with your Energy weapon (as your Kinetic weapon is much less damaging to the enemy's shield), and finish him off with headshots from either of your armaments. Headshots usually result in quicker precision hits and kills. You can easily drop the Legionaries as they slowly jet around the room if you're still on the upper gantry. Down the sight aiming and melee strikes to finish them are also excellent. Note the second Centurion and a couple more Legionaries as you reach the storage hangar exit.

4 Main Hangar

Super: Optional **Grenades:** Recommended

Head past the Cabal's command ship and into the large open hangar. Repel a force of Legionaries, and start to try out your Movement Mode (learning to both fire down on foes and reach higher gantry areas). Watch your accuracy while airborne though; your weapons aren't as stable, even when aiming (until certain Guardian types learn the Angel of Light Perk later). Use cover, especially because there are two Centurions to defeat. If Legionaries are leaping at you with their swords drawn, shoot them and strike them with a melee blow as they land, before their swords can damage you. Once the fracas is over, attempt a powerful **class-specific jump (Movement Mode)** to the exit gantry.

Head into a half-demolished corridor. Here, you'll need to **crouch** (and optionally **slide**), maneuvering through the fire and sheared-off concrete into a hole and out to the Tower Plaza itself.

Dropping while Jumping

While learning the finer points of your Movement Mode (detailed in the Field Manual chapter), you may find that your second jump sends you floating across chambers and into roof beams, or far beyond where you want to land. Titans combat this by simply tapping the jump button one more time, starting their descent immediately, but other classes (like Warlocks) may increase their height with additional taps. Be sure to read up on jumping in the Field Manual: chapter. Titans have the most trouble over-jumping.

Tower Plaza

The Last City, Earth

Enemies Encountered

CABAL: Legionaries

Important Allies

Commander Zavala

Objectives

Find Zavala (continued).

Defend the Tower (repel three assaults).

Leave the plaza and find the Speaker.

New Actions to Learn

Super Attack

Radar Markers

Environmental Information

5 Repelling Three Assaults

Super: Recommended **Grenades:** Recommended

Head up into the plaza, where **Zavala** is bravely fending off a Cabal Red Legion bombardment. Your objective immediately updates to defending the Tower with Zavala, and chaos descends. You must now engage the Cabal forces for a protracted battle. You must destroy more than **30 Legionaries** in waves of four or five, while also facing periodic vicious bombardments from the carrier fleet in the skies above the earth.

Start by attacking the forces encroaching on Zavala's position by executing them with headshots from the side before you reach the Vanguard leader. As soon as you've neutralized assault wave one, head to Zavala.

The waves of foes arrive both via jet-packing down from the ships and via drop pods. It's less important to know where foes are landing; instead, concentrate on defeating them before they reach Zavala's position.

- The **first assault** wave consists of around nine Legionaries.
- The **second assault** wave consists of around 15 Legionaries.
- The **third and final assault** wave consists of about 15 Legionaries.

If you're feeling overwhelmed or close to death, it's likely because you're standing or moving slowly, getting hit by the enemy ordnance. Instead, use the ruined pillars, your Movement Mode, the walls and roof of the main kiosk, balconies, upper ground, and the rubble to vary your position so foes can't get a good targeting aim on you.

As soon as you hear Zavala shouting for you to get behind his protective shield (which he does twice during the battle), oblige him, or face heavy damage from a rocket bombardment from the Cabal ship. Stand inside Zavala's protective shield until the bombardment subsides.

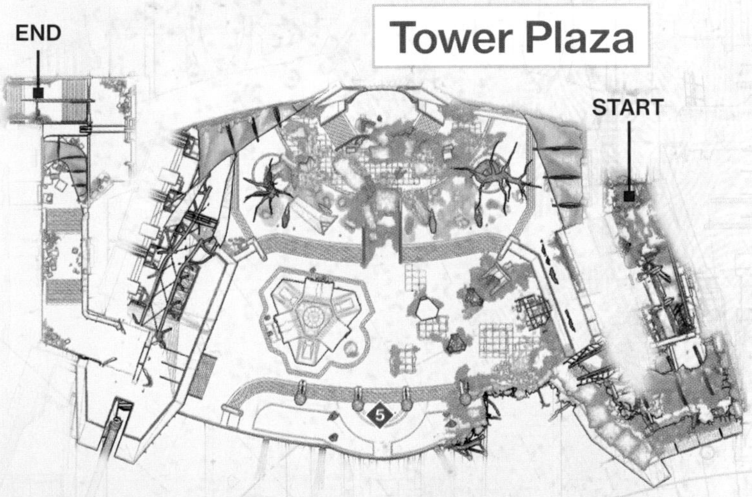

After this, remain here to tag a few Legionaries in the head before moving out to engage the larger numbers in the subsequent waves. Note that Zavala drops Orbs of Power each time he casts his Ward of Dawn shield; these help power up your Super, and should be gathered immediately.

To continue, you should move to the far right side of the plaza near the entrance to the Tower Boulevard where the Speaker resides.

Your weapon of choice here is the Kinetic Auto Rifle; it fires rapidly and gets the job done. Switch to a Sidearm, if you want. Grenades are also recommended, if you have one. The best time to throw one is just as a group of Legionaries is emerging from a drop pod, is landing, or is close to Zavala.

You can also launch your **Super**, usually for the first time. The Super you have depends on the Guardian class you chose for your character.

Once you've successfully defeated the third wave, you must rendezvous with Ikora in the northern part of the Tower. However, you can optionally cull more than a dozen Legionaries before you leave.

Head into the thoroughfare that leads to the northern part of the Tower, passing a Sweeperbot along the way.

Important Ally:

Commander Zavala

"The Red Legion are well-trained, but we are better. We will hold this line!"

A stern and by-the-book Titan Vanguard, Zavala has an iron will and a determination to succeed that impresses both friend and foe alike. However, he isn't prone to moments of levity, especially at times like these.

Tower North

The Last City, Earth

Enemies Encountered

CABAL: Legionaries, Incendiors, Centurions

Objectives

Leave the plaza and find the Speaker (continued).
Board the command ship.

Important Allies

Ikora Rey

Amanda Holliday

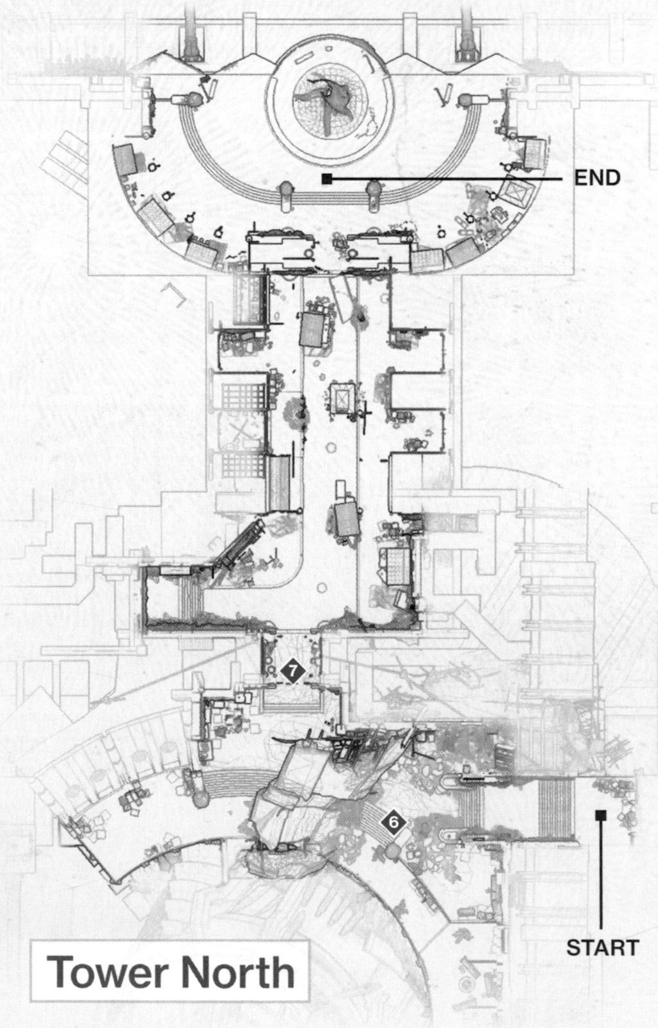

6 Ikora Encounter

Super: Not recommended **Grenades:** Recommended

Enter the Tower North area, where an angry **Ikora** lays waste to a group of Legionaries before revealing some startling news about the Speaker. She leaps atop a Cabal Thresher ship, forcing you into the boulevard area. A drop pod lands ahead of you. Lob in a grenade, or quickly tag the heads of the three Legionaries appearing.

7 Tower Boulevard

Super: Recommended **Grenades:** Recommended

The boulevard doors open, revealing a new threat: the **Incendior**—a Cabal shock trooper armed with a flame-thrower. Back up, drop him in a fiery explosion by aiming at his fuel tanks, and repeat this tactic to take down two more Incendiors and a cluster of Legionaries. Enemies may have different weak-spots where precision hits and kills can be administered.

The action ends at a large tiled plaza balcony with a burning tree, a couple of Legionaries, an Incendior, and a Centurion. Tackle the Incendior before you reach the open door into this area.

Only the Centurion should give you pause. Either use the Energy Sidearm you gathered to whittle down the foe's shield, or use your recharged Super attack to demolish him, along with a grenade. Then, board **Holliday's** ship.

The Right Energy For The Job

Using an Energy weapon is the optimal way to burn down an enemy shield. Any damage type will do nicely. However, matching damage types against enemy shields will create a powerful explosion that causes area-of-effect damage to surrounding enemy groups.

Start to plan ahead for which types of weapons you want to carry into different encounters, and try to wait for optimal times to burst enemy shields to get the best damage output on surrounding targets.

Important Ally:

Amanda Holliday

"All right, Guardian! Time to kick 'em where it hurts!"

An exceptional mechanic and even better pilot, Holliday is a skilled shipwright who is diligently helping with the hopeless task of defending the Tower. She proves invaluable in delivering you into the Cabal's command ship.

Important Ally:

Ikora Rey

"Red Legion! You will take no more from us! And you will find no mercy from me!"

Though blunt to a fault and without patience to suffer fools gladly, Ikora is a powerful Warlock Vanguard, with a penchant for solo infiltration missions. Her knowledge of enemy threat patterns should come in handy right about now.

The Chosen

Red Legion Command Ship

Objectives

Disable the shields.
Reach the shield generator.
Overload the generator.
Escape the command ship.

New Actions

Ghost: Interactions
Enemy Damage
Slowing Your Descent

Enemies Encountered

CABAL:	Legionaries, Incendiors, Sub-Boss: Pashk the Searing Will, Psions
CABAL: SUB-BOSSES:	Brann the Unbent Blade, Sub-Boss: Kreth the Living Skyfire

8 Drop Pod Bay and Upper Deck

Super: Not recommended **Grenades:** Optional

Leap up and over the chute that's dispensing Cabal drop pods, and enter the inside of the command ship. Immediately look slightly up and right so you can aim and drop the three Legionaries on the **loading bay** above you. Use your Ghost to access the schematics at the **hologram terminal**, which updates your objective and allows access as the opening to the exterior unseals.

Enter the **deck interior,** where two Legionaries and an Incendior are guarding. As shown in the previous picture, instead of just raking the area with gunfire (which is still a viable option), you can wait for the closest Legionary to walk toward his two brethren. Then, shoot the fuel tank of the Incendior, causing it to explode and dispatching (or badly damaging) all three enemies at once. It's this kind of **lateral thinking** that can save you ammunition and keep you safe when faced with overwhelming odds.

Sub-Boss: Step around the corner, immediately switching to your Energy weapon, and target the much more imposing Incendior with the Solar Shield. This is **Pashk the Searing Will**, and he has the same attacks as an Incendior, though he's tougher and uses a Void Shield. Make him a **priority target**. With the shield removed, shoot his head or fuel tanks. Once Pashk is down, finish the Legionaries.

Sub-Boss Strategies

As you progress, you will start to encounter toughened variants of many foe types. Generally, they are dispatched in the same manner as their lesser brethren, but some may use Energy Shields, employ different weapons, or have new offensive maneuvers. Check this guide's Bestiary to ensure that you know how to adjust for these eventualities.

The Chosen

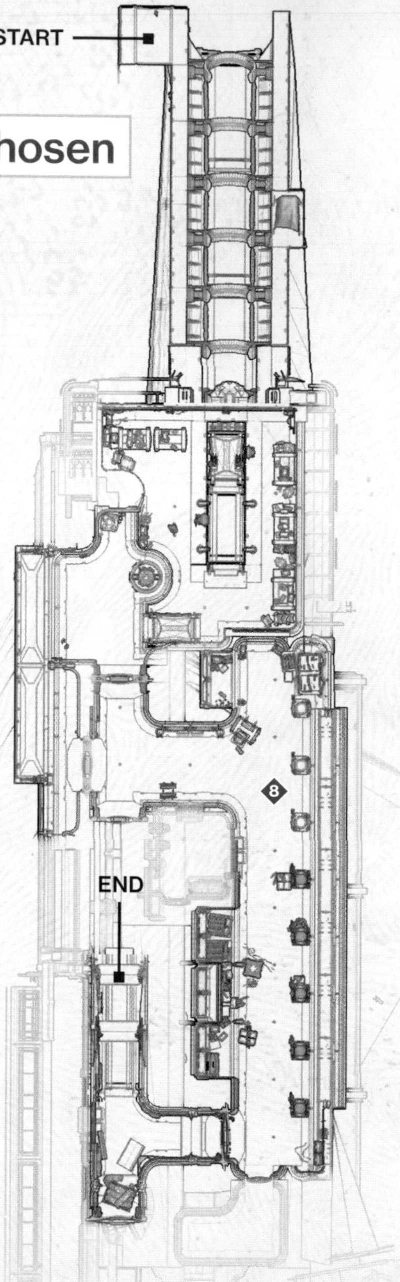

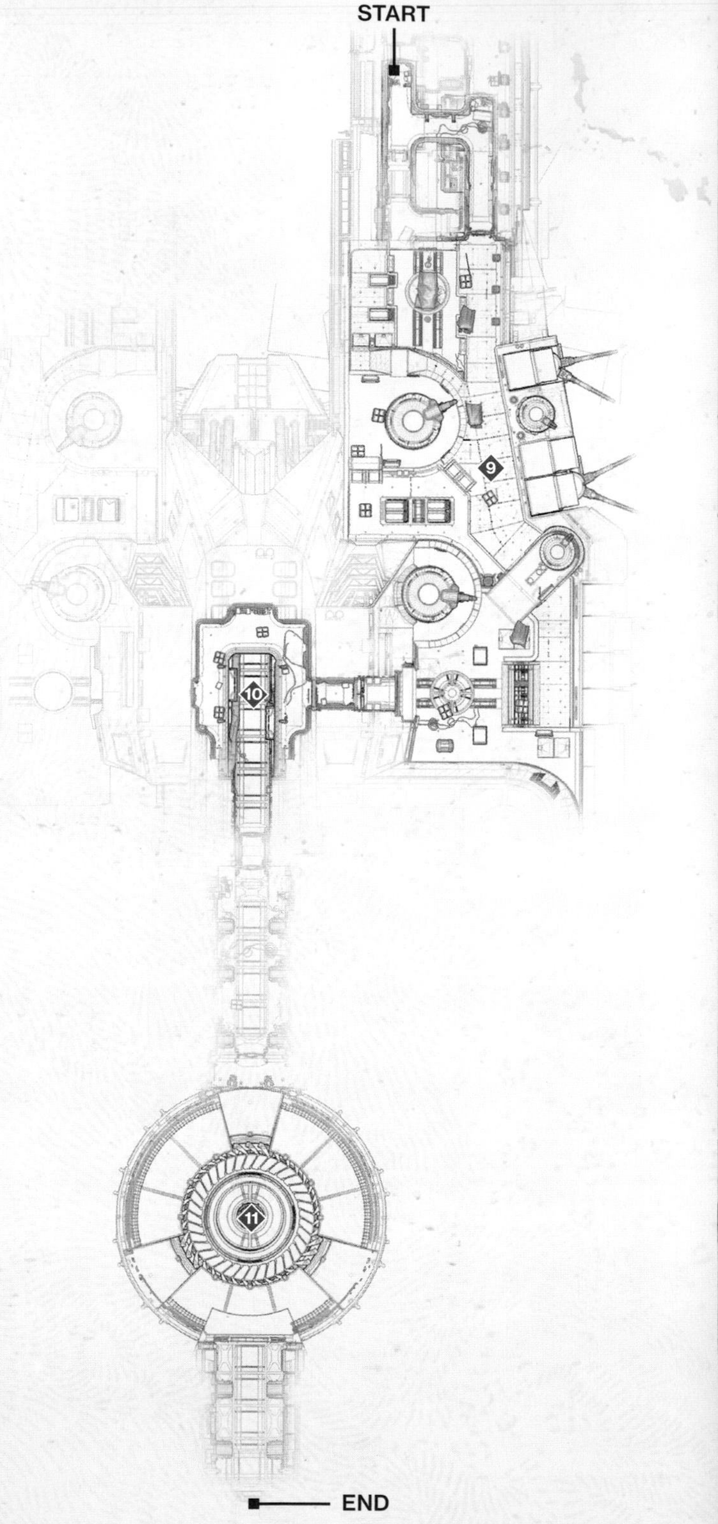

9 Main Exterior Deck

Super: Recommended **Grenades:** Recommended

Step out into the main exterior deck, and prepare for an elongated firefight with Cabal forces. This begins with dodging the shots of three **Psions**, the first time you've encountered this type of foe.

Focus on ridding the area of them first so you're not shot at range with their highly damaging weapons as you continue farther along the super-structure. Use your radar to keep track of these initial foes to ensure that they're defeated. Melee strikes and headshots are key, as well as advancing along the crates to use as cover.

The main deck concourse continues ahead, but to the right is a **large domed casement** for one of the many giant gun emplacements on the ship. This is a good place to head: there's cover, the third Psion is usually here and easily melee-attacked, and you can use the height advantage to deal with the three Legionaries. The narrow circular interior of the domed casement also affords you cover. You could also advance in the open, but you're much more exposed.

Sub-Boss: Instead, remain in and around the casement dome, dropping an Incendior and more Legionaries. Then, tag a Psion on the second casement ahead of you. By now, you should have noticed a **Sub-Boss Centurion: Brann the Unbent Blade**. He should be a priority target. He usually starts atop a small metal tunnel structure, which you can sprint into for cover. Alternately, you can fight him in the open or from the second casement dome, depending on your **Guardian's Super**. This is a good time to launch it. Then finish him as you would a normal Centurion. Then, mop up around nine more Legionaries (feel free to lob in a grenade as a few of them head up from the corridor tunnel). Head back into the ship's interior via the wide corridor tunnel ahead and right.

Flying the Unfriendly Skies

This open area is your second opportunity to start honing your maneuvering talents. Try your Guardian's Movement Mode jumping. While aiming down the sites (hitting foes as you fall) isn't the best plan due to airborne inaccuracy, you can still remove threats in this manner.

Warlock Guardians should perfect the extra height they gain on their jumps; double-tap as rapidly as possible).

10 Cargo Bay Descent

Super: Not recommended **Grenades:** Not recommended

Ahead of you down the corridor are two Psions and an Incendior on the opposite side of a **cargo ledge** chamber. You have plenty of room (and cover on the edges of the corridor) to avoid the Psion's ranged attacks. This allows you to either tag them at range or (better yet) shoot at the Incendior standing between them so he explodes, catches, and defeats both Psions in the explosion. You can perform this "**Cabal bomb**" maneuver throughout the following cargo bay descent.

There's an Incendior on a ledge ahead and above you. Tag him after removing threats ahead of you, but don't step too far because foes below will begin to battle you. Now, move around to where the two Psions were standing (in case one survived the explosion and is hiding behind one of the large crates dotted around), and gather any ammo you need, if any have dropped from your previous kills. Look out and down at the ledge below the entrance you arrived from, and execute another Incendior and Psion. There are three final enemies (two Psions and an Incendior) directly below the first trio. You can jump down and attack, tag them from an upper ledge, or lob a grenade down and finish them. Long-range Auto-Rifle fire is a good idea as you can tactically remove enemies through the 'Cabal Bomb' technique, though you can try dropping in and melee attacking too. Finally, drop to the cargo bay floor itself, **slowing your descent** so you aren't severely damaged by the fall.

A Slow, Not a Swift Descent

Hitting your jump button during falls is imperative if you don't want to die after lengthy plummets. It's also useful because it allows you to steer yourself onto lower platforms. Make a point of jumping across this cargo bay a few times to get the hang of this technique, as you need to perfect it. Learn how much of a fall you can take before you're damaged.

11 Shield Generator and Exit

Super: Recommended **Grenades:** Recommended

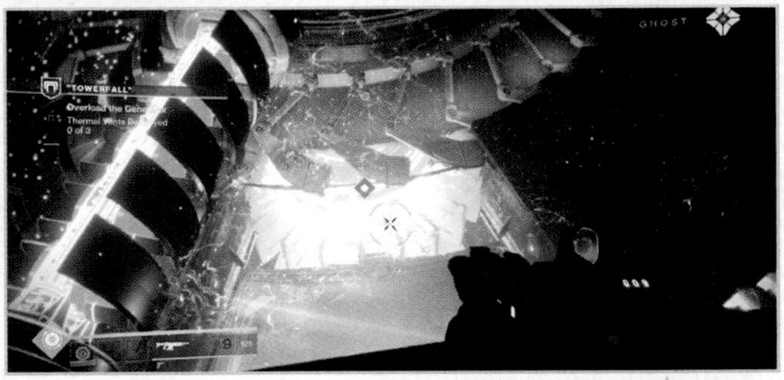

Sub-Boss: At the bottom of the cargo bay, **retreat back** as you reach the door so you can quickly dispatch an Incendior waiting to attack you at melee range (or use melee attacks yourself). Then, head down the huge cargo corridor a few feet before **sidestepping** to either side and tagging the six Psions that are present all the way down the corridor. They are joined by a couple of Legionaries and an Incendior. As you advance and engage these troops, the door to the shield generator room slides open, and a named Legionary saunters out. **Kreth the Living Skyfire** is an Elite-tiered Legionary with an Arc Shield, but not for long! Prioritize this target; you have the room, the cover, and a grenade to make short work of him. Once his shield is removed, treat him to multiple headshots.

Step through the door Kreth the Living Skyfire was guarding, and remain on the upper lip so you can study the massive **shield generator chamber** itself. Your plan is to overload **three thermal vents**, ideally without being struck by one of the three massive rotating arms. Scan the area with your Ghost if you're unsure what to shoot at; you're aiming for the glowing **white vent turbines**, one of which is directly ahead and below you. Shoot it or drop a grenade in.

Then, time a slowed fall onto the edge of the generator chamber, sprint either clockwise or counterclockwise, and drop down so you're under the rotating arms at the next thermal vent. Blast it until the vent explodes. Jump up and out of the vent area (just as an arm passes overhead), sprint to the next thermal vent, and drop down before the next arm catches and kills you. Destroy the third thermal vent, crippling the carrier.

With the generator overloaded, you must **now escape the ship**, which is achieved by leaping out of this chamber and back into a cargo bay corridor. This tests your jumping ability, and Warlocks may need to practice their jumping or land on one of the now-motionless arms first. Wind your way to the edge of the command ship, where you face the violent grievances of the Cabal leader himself.

Adieu

Recommended Level: 1
Recommended Power: 10

Even though the situation appears lost, and your body is damaged almost beyond repair, you must stagger on, finding your lost Ghost and escaping the war-torn city. A journey of discovery can then begin and a rebirth of sorts can occur once you meet a predestined group of resistance members led by Hawthorne.

Escaping the Last City

The Ruins of Humanity

Enemies Encountered

CABAL: War Beasts, Legionary

Important Allies

Hawthorne
Louis

Objectives

Follow your vision.

New Actions to Learn

Weapon Bullet Spread
Precision Kills
Postmaster Items
Archivist Engrams
Reputation
Vendors
Vaults

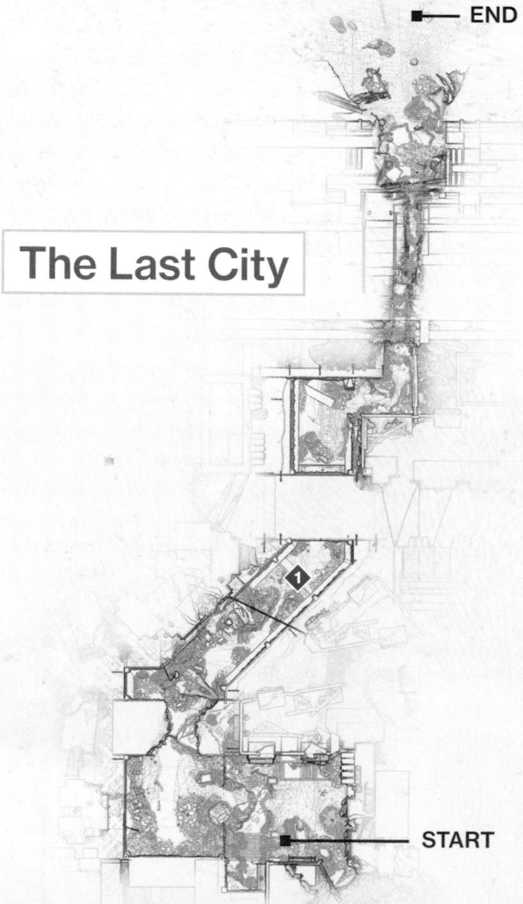

1 The Last City

Super: Not available **Grenades:** Not available
Warning: Restricted Zone

After falling from a great height, your only option is to shuffle down into the ruins of the city's canal and **maneuver slowly** through the wreckage as Cabal patrols lumber about above you. You're fortunate to **reunite with your Ghost** before leaving the city for the wilds of the countryside.

Severe Damage Inflicted!

Your current health and wellbeing are critical. Check your Character Menu to learn the exact nature of your damaged equipment; your armor can best be described as "scorched" and offers little protection. You have but a single Kinetic weapon (Sidearm) and a damaged Ghost. However, that fall didn't kill you.

② City Outskirts

Super: Not available **Grenades:** Not available
Warning: Restricted Zone

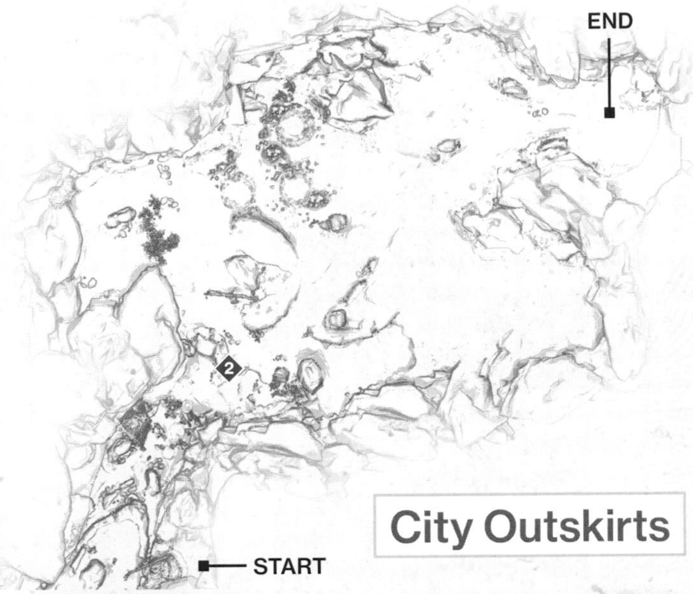

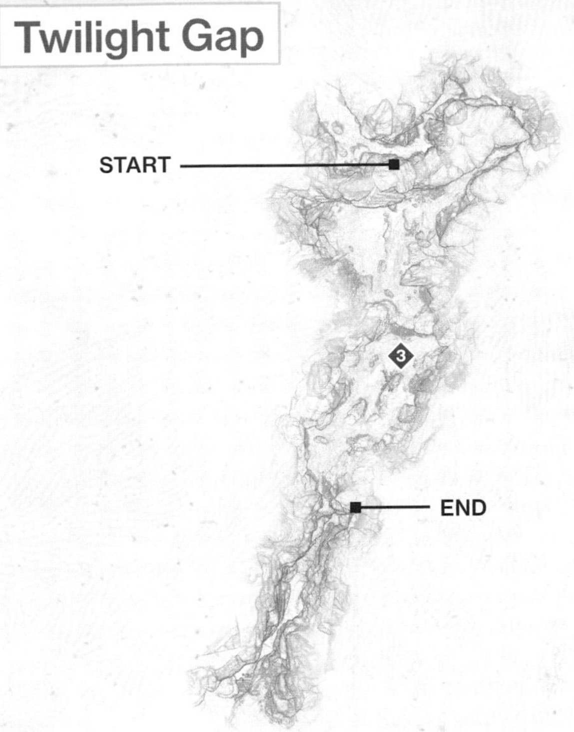

Stumbling into the sunlight, you continue your vision: a bird of prey flies from its perch into the snow-covered crags ahead. Drop down to a remote **Guardian outpost**, where you can reach down and grab an **SMG (Energy)** from the deserted area. Deserted, that is, until you witness **a pack of War Beasts** bounding to your location.

Restricted Zone! Your Light Fades Away

This is your first Restricted Zone, which requires caution (especially in your current fragile state). Your Ghost cannot resurrect you here, so ensure that you aren't mauled to death by War Beasts, or you'll have to retry this wandering.

The War Beasts attack in a large pack but charge you around three at a time. See if you can aim down your sights and pick off (or wound) as many beasts as you can at range (**shoot their heads for optimal damage; a critical hit aiming plan you should now be very familiar with**). Then, finish them with gunfire or a melee attack at closer quarters (as they only exist to charge and savage you). The first War Beast that you defeat spills out ammunition. You may want to switch to the SMG for this battle, if you're getting overwhelmed. Stay at the outpost for the battle, as you have a good view of the incoming foes. After the battle, your first Objective begins: follow your vision across the rocky ground and **up the snowy gully**, as the bird circles in the distant sky.

③ Twilight Gap

Super: Not available **Grenades:** Not available
Warning: Restricted Zone

Follow the falcon through the snowy gorge to a cliffside path, where you can witness the full horror of the Cabal attack. Continue around, heading up through a mountain pass and down into a rocky slope to a snow-lined clearing.

When you drop down, a **Legionary and around 15 War Beasts** appear (gradually; the beasts arrive in packs of 3-5 foes). If possible, move to the base of the central rock where the Legionary appears from, and headshot him before he can fire. That way, you aren't dodging his attacks while thwarting the War Beasts. Then, step back and tackle the four-legged fiends with your **SMG and melee swipes**; **keep moving**! You can flee the area by running directly ahead, but it's better to learn how to remove War Beasts as a threat and attack them with nimble maneuvers, then retreat to higher ground.

Bullet Spread and Precision Kills

By this point, you may have noticed that long-range shots with your SMG (both when manually aiming or aiming down the sights) result in much less accurate bullet strikes. This weapon suffers from bullet spread at longer ranges. The Range stat on each weapon implies a falloff point where optimal damage decreases the further you get from your target. Damage numbers can help you track the sweet spot where you're at maximum effective range before the value of the damage begins to go down. It's worth learning about this in the Field Manual chapter so you can figure out whether to employ weapons that enjoy more precise takedowns at longer range or greater damage at shorter ranges. The variety of weapons soon available also helps mitigate your current dilemma. It's also worth studying how to more effectively land Precision Kills (yellow damage indicators show a precision shot, and if one of these kills the target, this is recorded as a Precision Kill).

The rocky crag and gorge area you're descending to reach the perched falcon is a little more treacherous than you might be expecting. Ensure that you **cross the fallen log** via the middle of it, or you can slip and fall. It's also important to leap the gap from the lower of the two protruding rock ledges, or you won't make the jump. Remember that you don't currently have your Movement Mode! Once across, head to the sunlight, and make an attempt to leap another gap to **reach the falcon's perch**. This is always impossible, so you fall to the clearing at the base of the gorge.

You wake up at the end of your vision: **Hawthorne** and her pet falcon **Louis** (the bird you've been following) welcome you to their band of resistant refugees. You're given your first **Power weapon** (hold the swap button to equip it) and taken to the base of resistant operations in the European Dead Zone: **the Farm**.

Important Ally:

Suraya Hawthorne (and Louis)

"The name's Hawthorne. And this is Louis, the best pilot we've got!"

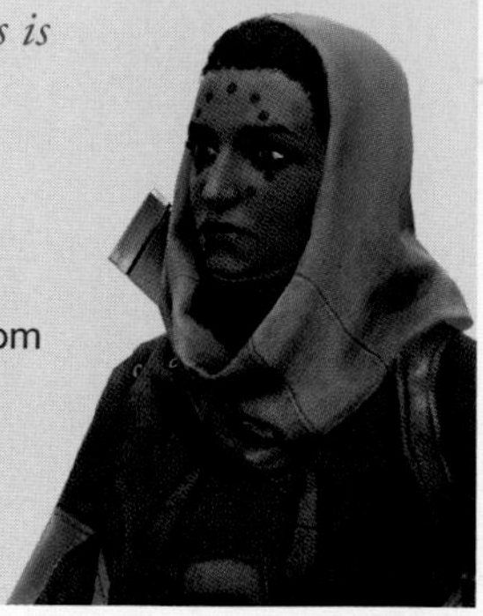

Hawthorne is an adept huntress and markswoman, with a keen sense of foraging and the land. She leads the resistance in the wilds of the EDZ from a ramshackle base of operations known as the Farm, where she is the Overseer. She dotes on her pet falcon named Louis.

The Farm

European Dead Zone

Welcome to the Farm! It's worth spending a while **exploring this base of operations** in the EDZ, as you'll return here time after time as you improve the level of your Guardian and complete more Campaign Missions. Before continuing your Campaign, it is recommended that you complete any or all of the following:

Darbi 55-30 (Postmaster): When shipments of goods arrive, they are sorted at this open-air post office. Darbi 55-30 will be happy to **provide you with items you acquire** during missions that are rare or important enough to be saved, if you didn't pick them up. (This can occur if your inventory is full, you ignore or do not see the item, or the item falls into an area you can't reach.) Darbi 55-30 currently has nothing for you.

Tyra Karn (Archivist): This wise woman offers the **decoding of engrams** that you may have found during your explorations. She mentions the dangers in the vicinity when you talk to her. Return here once you need an engram deciphered, after which it is turned into an item and placed in your Character Menu (or Postmaster if your menu is full of that item type).

Hawthorne (Overseer): The Farm Overseer and her bird friend explain the finer points of clans, **sell gear** that is more protective than your current rags, and offer other services.

Vault: Note that the sunken fountain area between the Postmaster and Archivist has two vault stations where you can store items that you want to save or share with your other two characters, or that can't face dismantling. It's worth checking this out to learn how the vault works.

Remember, you can save your favorite weapons from a veteran character (and armor if your subsequent character is of the same class) and let a new character use them, which really helps during subsequent replays!

New Item or Information

When entities of interest have something new for you, their icon changes color to green.

Other Activities: Make sure you take time to thoroughly explore the Farm. There's more than just a **soccer pitch** to slide around in. Have you jogged atop the **water wheel**, for example?

Character Menu: Inspect your Character Menu to **check the statistics** of the three weapons you have accrued (including the new Power weapon). Note that the armor you are wearing is among the worst imaginable. It's up to you to complete missions (and other tasks) to increase your **Glimmer** total and gain **Reputation** with certain Vendors (like Hawthorne) so you can afford better gear.

Also, take the time to learn how your **Armor, Agility, and Recovery** are affected depending on what you wear. Finally, note that your **Super ability** is currently compromised; beginning the next Campaign Mission is a priority.

New Mission Available: Open your Director and click on Earth to launch Spark, the next mission.

Down on the Farm

The Director (Atlas) chapter of this guide has a full list of activities, vendors, and other advice when visiting this location, including future visitors to this place as your Campaign continues. Consult that chapter for further information.

Spark – Pt. 1

Objectives: Go to the Shard.

Recommended Level: 1
Recommended Power: 10

All is not lost! Though your world is in shattered shards, this is the time to begin piecing them back together. Exploration of a ruined land begins by venturing deep into the forest near the Farm, drawn to a segment of the Traveler's might: a Shard of glowing power. Communing with it restores some of your previous Guardian prowess, enabling the most powerful of your attacks. Only then is it recommended that you explore further.

Make sure that you've explored the Farm, spoken to Hawthorne at her "perch" for the first time, checked out your rather ragged selection of armor, and studied the functional (but not fantastic) selection of weaponry you own. You are encouraged to complete this mission immediately. This is because you receive your Super ability at the end of this mission (as well as being able to use your Movement Mode).

A New Beginning

From this mission onward, and once your Super ability is acquired, your character starts to level up, can use ability points to purchase grenades, and can learn the finer points of different weaponry and armor as they collect or find interesting items. Complete this mission, and you have full control over your **destiny**!

Quarantine Sector 236

Restricted Zone

Enemies Encountered

FALLEN: Marauders

Objectives

Go to the Shard.

New Actions to Learn

Power Weapons
Listening for Enemies

1 Marauders' Grotto

Super: Not available **Grenades:** Not available

Head down to the road and **crouch** to maneuver through the rusting barricade and into a murky and overgrown forest area. **Leap the gap in the road**; if you don't make it, climb back up and practice until you can accurately land jumps. Press on into a pitch-black tunnel. As Ghost illuminates your path, switch to your **Power weapon** when prompted. Since this is usually a shotgun, you can make short work of the troublesome Fallen just ahead and below.

Drop into the **grotto** with your shotgun fully loaded. As the **Fallen Marauders** scamper at you with their functional cloaking devices, pick out the blue shimmers and blast them before they get close. They can easily kill you with their knife-wielding melee attacks, so standing firm and shooting them across the grotto is a good plan. Keep aiming and fire between reloads so the last of the Marauders doesn't get to melee range.

You can strafe and use an SMG if you want, but this isn't as effective in this particular location. After the fight, climb the opposite side of the grotto, and follow the tunnel.

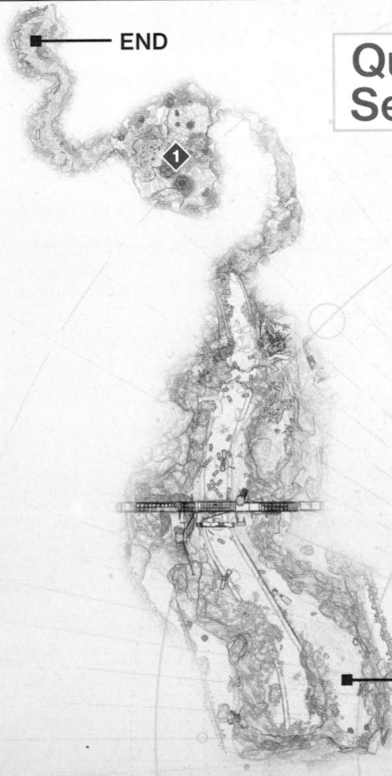

Quarantine Sector 236

Blackened Forest

Restricted Zone

Objectives

Go to the Shard (continued).
Traverse the Forest.
Defeat the Fallen.

Enemies Encountered

FALLEN: Dregs, Marauders, Wretches, Captain
SUB-BOSS: Rankkov the Survivor

New Actions to Learn

Loot Chests
Switching Equipped Weapons
Abilities: Grenades
Abilities: Jumping
Abilities: Super
Orbs of Light
Gaining Levels
Gathering Resource Materials

2 Abandoned Mine

Super: Not available **Grenades:** Not available

The tunnel opens up into a mine cavern and out into the remains of an old corrugated metal mine structure, now choked with brambles and undergrowth. Immediately ahead of you is a **Loot Chest**. It contains a new weapon and is one of the many different types of chests available if you know where to find them! You may receive a weapon from this chest that is the same type as one you are already carrying, so **weapon comparing** at this time is a good idea. Then, climb the steps to reach a rickety balcony overlooking **the Dark Forest**. In the distance is the **Shard of the Traveler** that you seek.

Comparing Weapons of the Same Type

At this point, it's wise to check your Character Menu and compare both weapons to determine which has better statistics. However, don't judge either weapon's effectiveness with a simple stat comparison – use both weapons in combat first! Remember that Energy weapons using Arc damage are more effective against (most) Fallen energy shields, so use those as a priority when facing Fallen Captains. Match the weapons damage type to the energy shields damage type for optimal damage. It causes the shields to explode, dealing bonus damage to the shielded unit and any other Combatants nearby. The shielded unit will also stagger, giving you an additional window to damage the combatant.

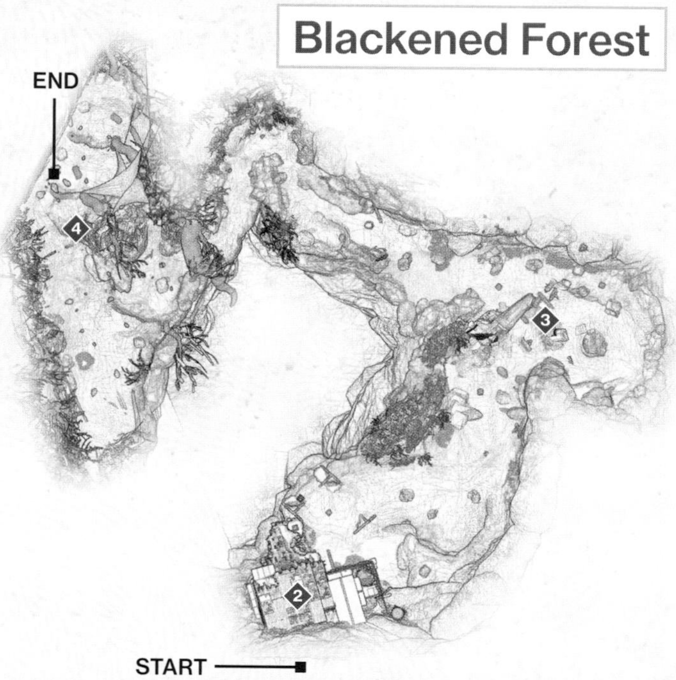

3 The Dark Forest: Crash Site

Super: Not available **Grenades:** Not available

Drop down the rickety mine building's broken balcony to the forest floor below and head slightly downhill, slowing as you reach a small fire. Ahead and left is a **Cabal Ship**, and a **cluster of Fallen Dregs** pours out of the ground like ants as you head toward it.

At this point, it's worth remembering you're outnumbered. Although the enemies are not really a threat on their own, in a group, they can be trouble for the overconfident. (Not to mention there's a **Marauder** lurking among the rocks and wreckage ahead.)

Therefore, remain at range and tag all the Dregs that you can with **headshots** as they disembark from the front of the ship. Note any that are scampering to the left; advance and remove them first, then turn right to the main path into the crash site and watch for incoming grenades. Use trees and boulders for cover, and aim and shoot the heads of all Dregs in the vicinity. **Take it slowly and methodically** so you're not overwhelmed. If a Dreg is close, turn and charge, then melee attack it to death with a single blow.

There's a Marauder lurking among the wreckage, too, so listen for his gurgling and back up so you aren't stabbed to death. Look for where Dreg grenades are being lobbed from and tackle the foes from range, or charge them and execute with melee attacks. There are **around 15 Dregs** to defeat in this general vicinity. Don't forget to use your radar to determine where the stragglers are.

Continue deeper into the forest, making steady but cautious progress up a ravine with boulders on either side and Dregs on and around these boulders. Tackle them proficiently; you don't want to be struck from behind. This is especially true farther along the ravine when you're attacked by a cluster of **Wretches**, Dreg-like Fallen with impressive close-combat staves. Stay back and let the eight Wretches come to you, **aiming for their heads** and dropping them way before they reach close-combat range. Then, continue around the corner, passing the glowing fungi, toward a massive tree root.

Watch out for a Fallen Marauder's close-combat knife attacks. Strafe to avoid being struck by that, and back up as a couple of Dregs and Wretches add to the fracas. Remove the foes closest to you first, retreating back around the boulder corner if necessary. Then, select your favored Marauder-killing weapon and remove the cloak of this semi-transparent foe, aiming at the head and removing this threat entirely. A charge and melee strike to finish is also optional and worthwhile if you're emptying a clip and don't want to be caught reloading or changing weapons.

4 The Dark Forest: Shard Site

Super: Thoroughly recommended (when available)
Grenades: Not available

Captains Battle: Head up the grassy gully, methodically dispatching the **Dregs**. Don't become transfixed by the massive glowing Shard wall as you reach the **Shard site** itself, as the place is teeming with Fallen, including a couple of **Captains**. Make quick work of them, matching your Energy weapon to their shield type, and mop up any stragglers. When Ghost indicates it is time to get your light back, the combat shifts to a final confrontation; with a Fallen Captain named **Rankkov the Survivor**. Let's try to make this his last battle, shall we?

Sub-Boss Rankkov the Survivor: Normal Combat (Optional): There are columns of Boundless Light dotted around the arena, so using normal combat means to dispose of Rankkov is not necessary. However, if you must, try the following tactics:

The Captain is much tougher than your previous foes, and he may carry a **Scorch Cannon** that can kill you in two or three direct hits, so remain in cover! Make a series of precision hits to the Captain's head until **the first third of his health is gone and he changes position.**

Move away from the raised mound of boulders where Rankkov teleports to. Drop into cover, and pepper away at his head with precision shots until he loses around **two-thirds of his health** and teleports to the central ground area. During this time, if you're struck from the flanks by lesser foes, quickly turn and remove the Dreg and Wretch threats before returning to concentrate on the Captain. Then finish him using similar tactics; stepping out from cover, hitting him with precision strikes in the head, and stepping in again.

Rankkov the Survivor: Boundless Light Combat (Recommended): Ghost indicates that this is time to get your light back, and a quick check of the **Character Menu** and your **Super Subclass Menu** reveals that one of your Guardian's **Supers is now active**! Not only that, but your Guardian's initial **grenade ability** and **jumping ability** are also unlocked. This means you have considerably more potency in your attacks from this point on. Time to show the Fallen how impressive you've become!

Check the area for the columns of light, and step into them to **instantly fill your Super and grenade**. The latter isn't really needed, as you have pretty much unlimited Super abilities, so launch it at once and start to demolish the hapless Dregs and Wretches in the vicinity. But make sure your main focus is repeated pounding into the hide of Rankkov! The type of Super depends on your Guardian class.

Titans unlock the **Sentinel Shield Super**, the **Magnetic Grenade**, and the **High Lift Jump** from the **Sentinel** Titan Subclass.

Hunters unlock the **Arc Staff Super**, the **Skip Grenade**, and the **High Jump** from the **Arcstrider** Hunter Subclass.

Warlocks unlock the **Daybreak Super**, the **Solar Grenade**, and the **Strafe Glide Jump** from the **Dawnblade** Warlock Subclass.

Combat now becomes a **maelstrom of Supers**, directed into the hides of at **least 40 Fallen** that appear in waves. **Dregs, Wretches, Marauders**, and finally the **Sub-Boss** Captain Rankkov should all feel your wrath. This is the ideal time to perfect your Super: learn how to react both on the ground and in the air. Learn whether your Super has combos and alternate strikes, and how easily it cuts through enemies. **Columns of Boundless Light** mean that as soon as one Super is finished, you simply need to jump into another light column and start the Super again. You can certainly waste ammunition strafing at Fallen, or lobbing a grenade if you're low on health and rushing to another Column of Light, but culling 90 percent or more of the foes with your Super is the only way to competently complete this mission!

Even the toughened shield and hide of the Rankkov the Survivor cannot withstand your Super attack! Complete the mission, usually **increasing your level to 2**, which unlocks stronger gear, new abilities, and access to harder missions. The mission ends, and you're transported back to Orbit.

Gathering Resource Materials

Now that you're able to freely roam throughout the EDZ, it is worth learning the indigenous resource that grows in each of the four planet-like zones you'll be traveling to. Check the Field Manual chapter for more information.

Additional Guardian Subclasses

Currently, you have only one of three possible Subclasses unlocked for your Titan, Hunter, or Warlock. Should you wish to unlock the other two Subclasses, the (optional) Campaign Mission Spark – Pt. 2 must be completed. Find information on this from Devrim Kay in Trostland.

Orbs of Light

During any battles you may have with other Guardians (including your mentors), your judicious use of your Super occasionally produced Orbs of Light. These are smaller, more common forms of the Traveler's Light (like the much rarer columns you were bathing in), and they partly refill your Super. Usually, these are by-products of a fellow Guardian when they use their Super. Orbs only spawn for other Guardians. The optimal strategy is for fireteams to take turns using their supers to feed each other orbs. You will only ever see and collect orbs from other players' Supers or orb-creating perks.

Activities to Attempt

At this point, you should head into the EDZ and find Devrim Kay at the church tower in Trostland. Start a more freeform exploration investigating the following:

- Lost Sectors (throughout each zone in the EDZ).
- Adventures (throughout each zone in the EDZ).
- Public Events (throughout each zone in the EDZ).
- Rosters and likeminded players (cooperative missions and Public Events).
- Joining clans (see Hawthorne at the Farm) (helping others or receiving advice).
- Gaining Reputation with Devrim (Trostland) and Hawthorne (at the Farm) (to unlock better gear).
- Purchasing items from Devrim and Hawthorne (at the Farm) (to improve your armor and weaponry).
- Using your vault to store items (at the Farm).
- Checking missed items at Darbi 55-30 the Postmaster (at the Farm).
- Visiting Tyra Karn the Archivist to decipher engrams to unlock better gear (at the Farm).
- Visiting Tess at the Eververse store for engrams and gear (at the Farm).
- Completing Mission: Spark – Pt. 2 (providing you've found the randomly-looted strange Artifact).
- Completing Mission: Combustion (at EDZ: Trostland).

Spark – Pt. 2

First Trip
Recommended Level: 4
Recommended Power: 40

Second Trip
Recommended Level: 15
Recommended Power: 150

The time has come to further improve your Guardian's exceptional and superior abilities. Once again, you are drawn to a Shard. But this segment of the Traveler's awesome power is hidden deep within the Dark Forest, amid reports of Fallen (or Taken) activity. Taking this trip requires a "key" of sorts: an Artifact that allows access into a previously unexplored zone. When you get to this zone, you'll understand why.

This unlocks **the other two Subclasses** of your Guardian (giving you access to two other Supers and associated Abilities). To access this mission, you must have **acquired a strange Artifact**: a randomly found item with the same name. After taking it, a black, diamond-shaped icon appears in your Abilities Menu, like the one indented at the start of this paragraph. You can undertake this mission now or in the future, depending on when you want to unlock the next Subclass of your Guardian.

Before you venture into the Salt Mines north of Trostland, it is also worth visiting **Devrim Kay**, one of the Haven Holdouts and a resistance fighter who guards the remains of the old church. You have both gear and Reputation to grant him.

The Dark Forest
European Dead Zone

Objectives
- Enter the Dark Forest.
- Continue exploring the Dark Forest.
- Clear out the enemy force.
- Enter the portal.
- Explore farther into the forest.
- Clear out hostiles around the Dark Shard.
- Commune with the Traveler's Shard.
- First Trip: Defend the Shard from the Fallen.
- First Trip: Leave the Dark Forest.
- Second Trip: Fight your way out of the Dark Forest.

New Actions to Learn
- First Trip: Titan Subclass: Striker
- Second Trip: Titan Subclass: Sunbreaker
- First Trip: Hunter Subclass: Gunslinger
- Second Trip: Hunter Subclass: Nightstalker
- First Trip: Warlock Subclass: Voidwalker
- Second Trip: Warlock Subclass: Stormcaller

Enemies Encountered

FIRST TRIP: FALLEN:	Dregs, Vandals, Captains, Shanks, Tracer Shanks, Shanks (Large), Servitors
FIRST TRIP: FALLEN: SUB-BOSS:	Servitor
SECOND TRIP: TAKEN:	Psions, Vandals, Captains, Wizards, Goblins, Phalanxes
SECOND TRIP: TAKEN: SUB-BOSS:	Haraal: Venom of Oryx (Wizard)

1 Entering The Dark Forest
Super: Optional **Grenades:** Optional

A strange power from the Artifact you've collected is drawing you toward the Dark Forest. Locate it by visiting **the Sludge** Sector of the EDZ and heading toward the northern side of this area, jumping up a **narrow waterfall**, through a narrow crevasse, and into a strange, grotto-like cavern with a glistening and shallow pond. A small island at the far end of this area has a **Taken Portal**. Step into it to transport yourself deeper into the forest.

The Dark Forest

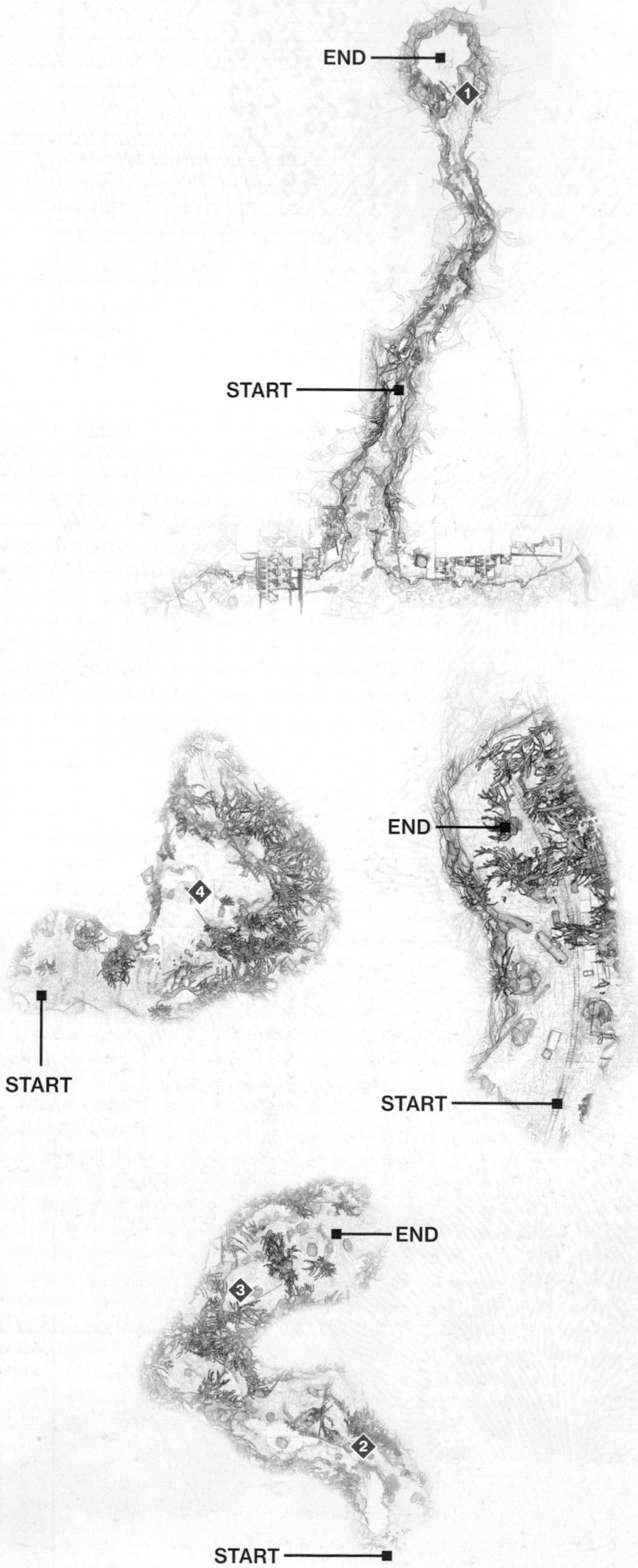

Exploring The Dark Forest

Super: Not recommended
Grenades: Not recommended

You appear in a strange and ominous glade. Wander along the riverbank. You encounter an **oddly ethereal statue** of your Guardian Mentor (Zavala, Cayde-6, or Ikora). It tells you more about what you want to know. A second statue of your mentor is waiting to be discovered farther along the forest glade. Find a third statue of Lord Shaxx, and then a fourth of a Centurion. They too reveal secrets: the revelations of the Artifact and the possibilities you could gain by unlocking your Guardian's remaining two Subclasses.

Statue of Limitations

Depending on the Guardian class you are using, the statues that you encounter are different. You're unlocking one of your Titan, Hunter, or Warlock Subclasses, and only those of your Guardian.

Combat at the Lake

Super: Recommended **Grenades:** Recommended

After finding the second Subclass statue, turn your attention to the arriving enemies.

First Trip: These are **Fallen**, a cluster of Dregs scurrying around in the shallow lake. Tackle them, along with a couple of Vandals (who can impede your progress with their nasty ranged rifle fire). Continue to fight more Dregs and two more Vandals, and expect Dregs with a Captain who employs an Arc Shield.

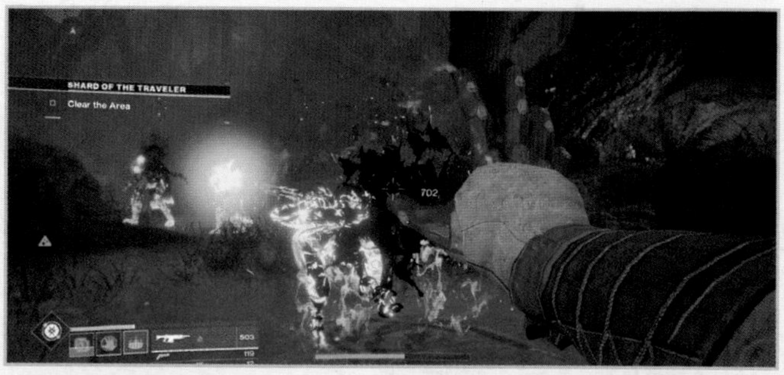

Second Trip: These are **Taken**; four Psions are blinking into existence in the shallow lake. Tackle them and a couple of Taken Vandals. The Vandals can conjure a dark dome of protection that you must run through to reach and attack them, as your ranged weaponry bounces off.

Tackle more Taken Psions, two more Taken Vandals, and then a cluster of Psions and a Taken Captain with a Solar Shield. Think of them as tougher versions of the Cabal and Fallen counterparts.

With the lake area cleared, **a portal opens**. Enter it.

Head out of an ancient railroad tunnel and along the forest floor, pausing to hear some words of wisdom from more statues on your way to another portal.

4 The Traveler's Shard

Super: Recommended **Grenades:** Recommended

This portal transports you to a glade of twisted trees where **the remains of a Dark Shard** are present; its power has beckoned foes to the vicinity. This is where the action begins to get consistently dangerous.

First Trip: Approach a Captain with an Arc Shield flanked by two Shanks, and defeat them. Then, scour the trees around the lake for Vandals and additional Shanks to dispatch. Another Captain (Arc Shield) and Shanks arrive.

Second Trip: Approach a Taken Trap (a ball of writhing blackness), and shoot it. If you step too close (which is especially problematic because you can stumble into them while in combat), it can damage you. Either way, it explodes, and a small contingent of Taken emerges.

Expect to face a couple of Taken Captains at a time, a half-dozen Taken Psions, a quartet of Taken Vandals, and other clusters of these foe types. For this reason, clear each area methodically, and don't rush or run into another Taken Trap.

Defeat foes until the objective updates, enabling you to commune with the Traveler's Shard. Approach and **interact with the Shard**. You immediately acquire a new Subclass!

You also immediately acquire an influx of foes that must be quelled before you can escape this place.

First Trip: Vandals and Shanks (and periodically, a Heavy Shank) appear, but these are soon superseded by Servitors. The Servitors have a small cluster of foes they are linking to, giving the entire cluster invincibility (aside from the Servitor).

Expect around a dozen Servitors to appear, around two at a time, from different parts of the forest perimeter. Shoot the Servitors first, then take out the rest of the foes. The last Servitor is a Sub-Boss with more enemies surrounding it, though the tactics to defeat it are the same. When all Fallen are defeated, **take the portal and escape this place**, concluding the mission.

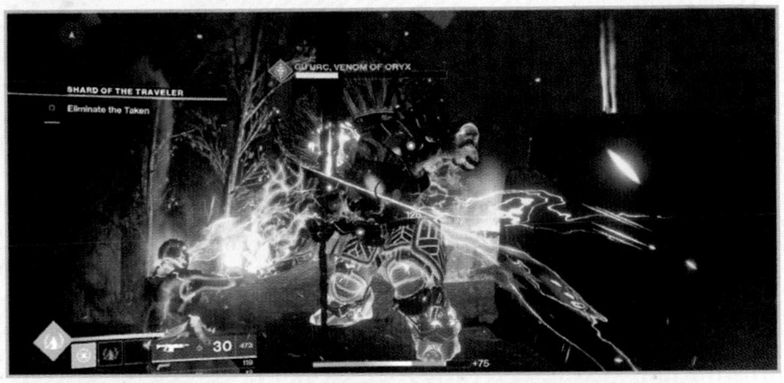

Second Trip: Taken Wizards (with Void shields) and Taken Goblins appear. These can be most dangerous because the Goblins tend to link to their Wizard masters. If you see them linked with green energy, shoot the Goblins, since the Wizards are more or less indestructible. Obviously, you should employ your new Super at every opportunity. Once you've culled around four or five groups of Wizards and Goblins, a portal opens up.

Second Trip: The action hasn't let up yet! There are around four groups of Taken (Goblins and Phalanxes) on the **railroad tracks back toward the tunnel**. All must be defeated; focus on the Goblins if they are linked to the Phalanxes, and sidestep the latter's shield blast or face serious damage. As ever, rush into the Columns of Boundless Light, replenish your Super and grenade, and use both immediately. When you've defeated all foes, enter another portal.

Second Trip: The initial **lake and forest glade** is now teeming with Goblins protecting their Wizard masters. Produce your Void weapon when removing Wizard shields, and drop the Goblins protecting Wizards before turning your weapons on the Wizard itself. Better yet, use continuous Supers and grenades as you wade through five clusters of these foes.

New (and Familiar) Super Attacks

Though you can face your enemies with conventional weaponry, it is better to step into a Column of Boundless Light. These are scattered around the vicinity and instantly charge your (new) Super and Abilities. Use this to practice your new Super, and find additional columns as combat continues. Wipe out all incursions in this glade, ideally perfecting your new Super in the process! Veteran Guardians may remember utilizing the two unlockable Subclasses during their earlier adventures.

The last cluster involves around eight Taken Goblins all adding to the power of a **Sub-Boss, a hardened Taken Wizard named Haraal, Venom of Oryx**. He tends to summon Taken Thralls and also has reappearing Taken Goblins. Stay on higher ground, use Supers and grenades, and then continuously bombard the foes with regular weaponry as you head to the next light column. Once you've slaughtered his Goblin minions, ensure that he dies like the rest! **When you've defeated all Taken, take the portal and escape this place**, concluding the mission.

Combustion

Recommended Level: 3
Recommended Power: 30

With at least one of your Super abilities available, you can begin the long journey of rebuilding your Guardian's prowess. The first stop is the ruins of an old town in the European Dead Zone. A derelict mine is teeming with Fallen, and Hawthorne needs a signal booster. Before you venture into the Salt Mines north of Trostland, it is worth visiting Devrim Kay, one of the Haven Holdouts and a resistance fighter who guards the remains of the old church. You have both gear and Reputation to grant him. He also orders you to that you attempt your first Adventure in the vicinity, if you've not done so already.

Salt Mines

European Dead Zone

Enemies Encountered

FALLEN: Dregs, Captains, Vandals, Wretches

Important Allies

Devrim Kay

Objectives

Enter the mine.
Rendezvous with Hawthorne.
Defeat the Fallen.
Call the elevator.
Find another elevator.

New Actions to Learn

Detonating Explosive Barrels

Trostland (EDZ)

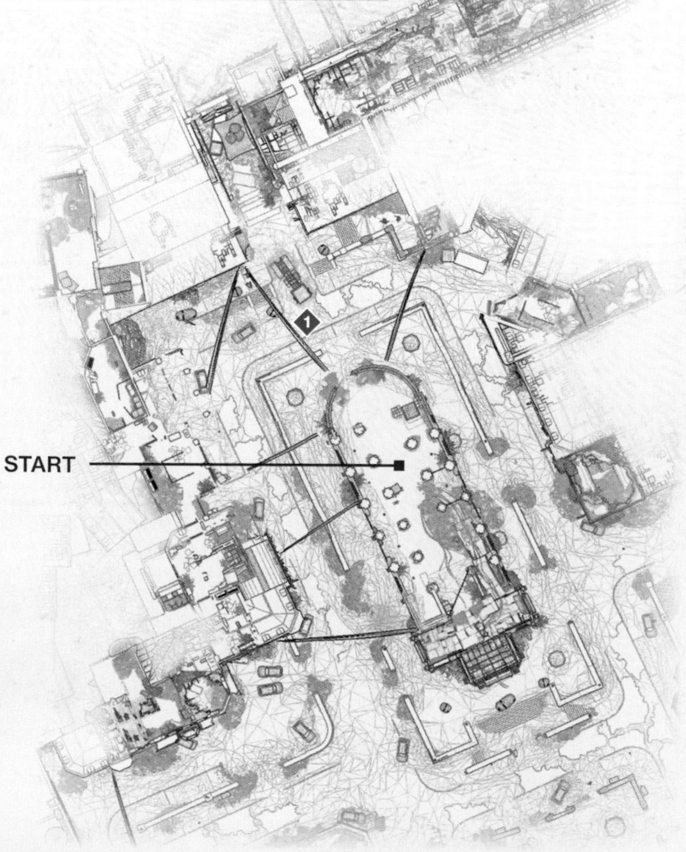

Salt Mines (EDZ)

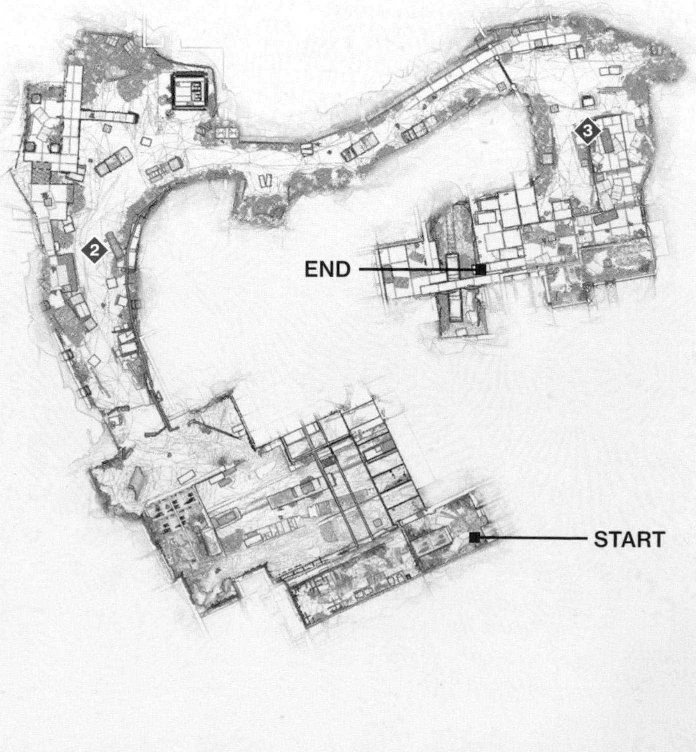

1 North Trostland Salt Mine Entrance

Super: Not recommended **Grenades:** Optional

You begin your assault into the Salt Mines **at the church** in Trostland, with a **group of Fallen guarding the entrance**. It's a straightforward matter of removing the cluster of Dregs, whittling down the Captain's Arc Shield and taking him down before the shield recharges, and then tackling the couple of Vandals and Dregs in the rubble of the structures to the right of the entrance. You are doing some close-quarters fighting, so have your melee attack ready to back up your weapon of choice.

Here come the **Vandals**. Treat them as slightly hardier Dregs: aim at their heads and dodge the incoming projectiles from their Shock Rifles. These rifles have a slower firing cadence than a Dreg's shock pistol and can be fired farther. Rushing forward with melee strikes works, as well.

2 Salzwerk Mine Outer Depot

Super: Not recommended **Grenades:** Optional

Wind your way **into the mine depot**, listening to Hawthorne as you go. This objective is quickly changed to a new one, as you must clear the area between the imposing **"Salzwerk" mine entrance** and the elevator shaft. Follow the Dregs in, looking up so you aren't surprised by a **Wretch ambushing you** from the ceiling. Melee or headshot him before entering the depot interior.

Enter the depot, which has **two main routes through to the elevator**. The first route is taking the dilapidated **metal stairs on your left**, leading to a rusty gantry and box-shaped structure ahead of you. Choose this if you enjoy removing foes from height and the advantage that gives you. The other path is walking the **main floor of the mine** itself; there are four initial Dregs darting from crates on both sides, and a Vandal sniper at the far end. Charge in, and expect to be overwhelmed. Instead, stay back and pick off the foes you can see before moving forward (using either route).

You could rush along the **right side of the floor**, leaping over a pipe and hiding behind the rusty truck cab, but three Vandals on the gantry to your left can easily locate you. You can perfect the technique of sprinting around the objects the Dregs are hiding behind and melee striking them into submission. Then, move onto the gantry to clear the Vandal snipers and any remaining stragglers.

Or, you can **stay on the left gantry** and systematically remove Vandals and Dregs from the gantry itself. Advance into the hut and around to lob a grenade down on the Dregs below before tagging them easily from the protruding gantry. You can also try moving in the air and firing down on Dregs as you land. There's also a **red barrel with a flashing diode on it**; this is **explosive** and can be detonated if you shoot it. This causes commotion, alerts foes, and may not catch Dregs if you don't hit it quickly enough. Still, these are worth shooting later into this mission. Just don't stand near one when it explodes, as it can hurt!

After **calling the elevator**, you surmise that it is definitely out of order. Open the large rusting tunnel grating, and continue deeper into the mine.

3 Salzwerk Mine: Inner Yard

Super: Optional **Grenades:** Recommended

Head down the tunnel, entering (via the opening on the left) a **large inner yard** with a lower roof than the previous chamber. It hosts a **cluster of Dregs with a Captain on the far platform**. Lob a grenade or shoot the explosive barrel by the Captain to wake everyone up before rushing along the left wall and onto the platform, finishing the Captain before his shields recharge. Swift executions are advisable.

Or, you can **creep along the left side**, executing the Dregs and Vandals as you go, backing up if the foes become too numerous, and leaving the Captain for last. **Watch for two Wretches** coming in from the chamber exit; they sneak in and around the darkened areas on the far side of the chamber. These hostiles can impede your progress if you're overrun while on the rusting platform.

Alternately, you can **use your weapon's sights** and tag each Dreg and Vandal from the entrance to the inner yard, slowly working your way around the left side and onto the rusting platform. Dispatch all foes from range, including the Captain, and tackle the two Wretches as they run in from the broken gantry bridge in the **Restricted Zone** ahead of you.

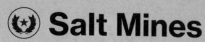

Salt Mines

Restricted Zone

Enemies Encountered

FALLEN: Shanks, Dregs, Vandals

Objectives

Find another elevator (continued).

New Actions to Learn

Investigating Objects (Scannable)
Long-range Power Weapons
Disarming Laser Traps

Inner Mines

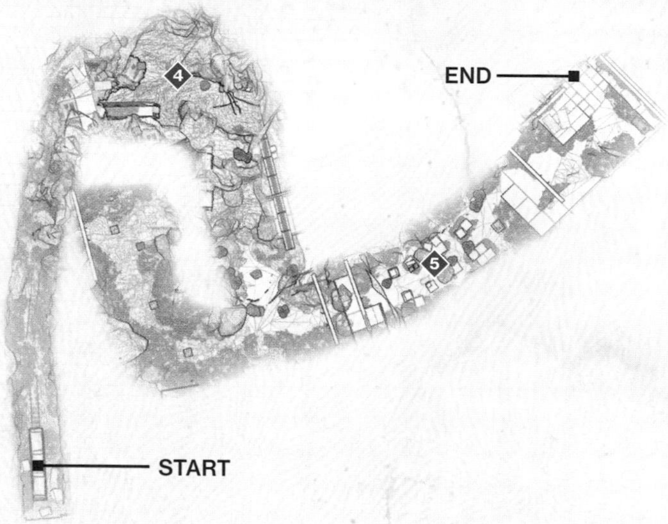

Scannable Objects

This is one of more than 100 scannable objects you can optionally investigate, which are dotted across all the four main worlds. Have you found them all? The Director chapter of this guide offers hints at where they are. Don't worry; you can go back and find all of them after a mission is finished.

4 Sinkhole

Super: Not recommended **Grenades:** Not recommended
Warning!: Restricted Zone

Head through the exit to a broken gantry over a lower mine tunnel. Before you drop down, leap across the gantry gap to an upper ledge where there's an **old computer terminal (scannable object)**. Investigate it to receive some information, and then drop down. Follow the open tunnel until the ceiling lowers enough for you to **crouch**, and slide into a tight connecting chamber. The remains of a resistance fighter lie at the exit into a huge sinkhole with light from above. Before you peer down the massive hole, **grab the Sniper Rifle**.

Step to the **edge of the massive hole** and peer over; deal with a trio of **Shanks** first. These Fallen robots shoot moderately damaging turrets and are more of a pest than a real threat. However, they are of priority concern now and should be defeated using sight-aimed gunfire.

Step back from the edge so you aren't peppered with small-arms fire from the couple of **Vandals and Dregs on the lower ledges** surrounding the hole deep below you. Only step to the edge once you've destroyed the first three Shanks. You have a couple of seconds to lob down a grenade, try **extreme-range takedowns** with your Kinetic or Energy weapons, or bring out the **Sniper Rifle** and tag these foes with headshots. Switch (and step) back a few seconds later as six more Shanks appear. Expect a couple more Dregs on the lower ledges, too.

You could also **drop down** and engage the foes with a shotgun at closer quarters, though the Shanks become more of a problem once you give them the height advantage.

Feel free to perfect the slowing of your fall with a **Movement Mode activation** before you reach the ground after dropping off the upper ledge. The timing of this depends on your Guardian class.

Head deeper into the sinkhole into a **pitch-black, steep tunnel** with five Shanks at the entrance and five assorted Fallen (Vandals and Dregs) at the far end. Once you've dealt with the Shanks, it's worth tagging the other hostiles from range if you can. Soften the lower foes up with a grenade (if available), and then descend and melee attack any that remain. With the area secured, enter the door marked with a "**Vorsicht**" sign ("Attention" in German).

5 Laser Trap Tunnel

Super: Not recommended
Grenades: Not recommended

Although the rusting metal doors are swung wide open, the tunnel ahead is less than welcoming, with more than a dozen laser traps for you to contend with. These are easily neutralized, but being caught in the explosion after you fire at the explosive end of the laser can kill you. Step back from the door, and **fire at the first laser** (lower-right side).

Step through into the main tunnel with a mesh of lasers. **Look up and left** and shoot one laser, then a second on the limestone ground ahead and left, detonating the first cluster of lasers (ideally, without you being nearby). Then, advance.

When you reach the area shown in the previous picture, you can't aim at the closest laser trap from your current angle. Stay back and **aim at the traps beyond the first one**; detonate the one on the ceiling, then two on the rubble, and then skirt to the left of the rusting storage shelving. **Look back,** and you can now spot the laser, either destroying or ignoring it. Head farther up the tunnel so you aren't caught by the explosion.

Salt Mines

Restricted Zone

Objectives

Call the elevator.
Restore power.

Enemies Encountered

FALLEN: Vandals, Dregs, Wretches, Servitors, Boss: Leech Servitor, Shanks

Mine Chamber

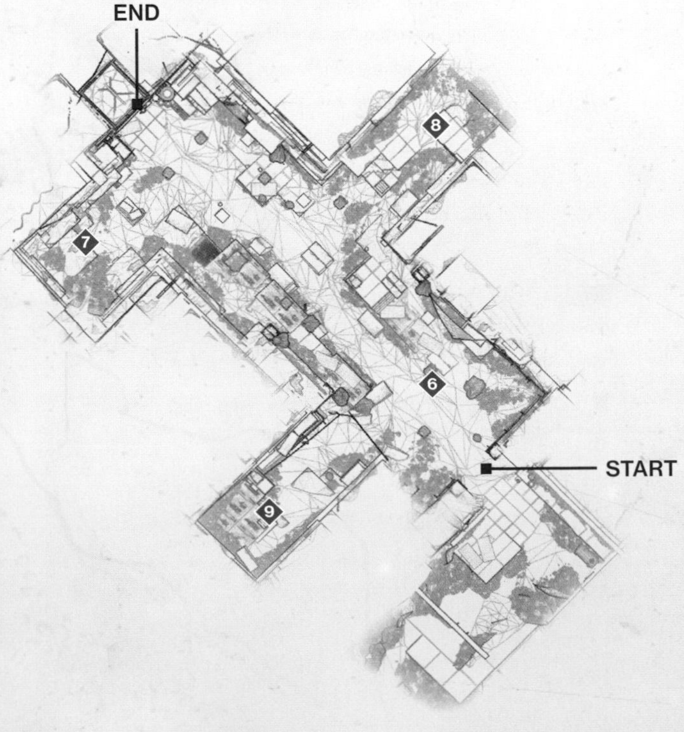

6 Main Quarry

Super: Recommended **Grenades:** Recommended
Warning!: Restricted Zone

The previous laser trap tunnel wasn't a Restricted Zone. However, as darkness clouds your vision, know that you're in for some trouble as you advance down a **high-ceiling main quarry**, splashing through some shallow water to reach and **call the elevator**. The power is out. But the Fallen are most definitely in!

This quarry has a **central lower ground** area and **three equidistant side slopes,** two on one side and one in the middle on the other. Though you can dash around, taking up cover and using jumps to reach enemies you want to slay before scurrying back to replenish your health and gather dropped ammo, there's a slightly safer and more methodical approach.

Forewarned and Forearmed

Be ready for a protracted battle. Before you call the elevator, you should check the entire chamber for hiding places, gantry platforms, explosive barrels (clustered near the elevator), and sniping positions. Also, check your Character Menu before tooling up with your favored weapons for tackling the Fallen and the giant globe-like Servitors that are the major problems you face.

7 Start by heading up the slope just to the side of the powered-down elevator. From here, you can spot a Vandal and Servitor appearing across the quarry chamber at Location 8, and drop them with accurate sniper rifle fire (if you're quick). But don't worry too much about them at the moment. Instead, **back up, using the blocks of stone and height as cover**, and shoot at the Dregs and Vandals below you in the waterlogged main area. Tag any of the strewn red explosive barrels to soften them up. If a grenade comes flying at you, sidestep it and shoot the Dreg responsible. Stay in and around this slope, and engage the first **Servitor** as soon as possible.

These giant floating globe-like drones aren't particularly adept at delivering killing blows, but they can provide immunity to Vandals and Dregs that are near them. **When your first Servitor floats in, make it a priority target.** Destroy it quickly, perhaps with a grenade (as you're close enough for it to be effective) before finishing the infantry it was protecting. Remain in the side slope vicinity, whittling down the enemy Dregs and Vandals. Soften up Vandals and then melee attack them if they're close. You may discover groups of Dregs and Vandals on the platform between here and Side Slope 6, but don't worry about them now (unless you can lob a grenade to wound multiple foes).

8 When there are little to no threats near the elevator, **sprint over** to the middle slope where the **Servitor** and possibly two or three Vandals are. Maneuver all the way to the platform at the top so you have the cover to hide from this enemy fire. You can now demolish the Vandals, the Servitor, and any foes on the platform diagonally across from you on the opposite side of the main thoroughfare. Stay in this **excellent cover** until little or no threats present themselves. Then, scoot over to the third side slope.

9 When half of the quarry area is more or less devoid of Fallen, move across to the entrance area where you entered. Make short work of the **eight or so Dregs** before turning your attention to the **Servitor** on the last side slope. **Ensure that this is your final foe.** If you charge up to the very top of the slope, the Servitor moves down, allowing you to shoot it in its "eye" easily and quickly. Use the blocks of stone and corner of the gantry area as cover.

Servitor Takedown Tactics

No matter what their size, Servitors are tackled as a priority because they can safeguard other Fallen forces with an electrical arc of protection. Combat this by aiming at their central eyes, dodging the bolts of energy they fire from this location.

End Combat Boss: The reason for defeating all of the Fallen infantry before both Servitors becomes clear. As soon as the last Servitor explodes (whether or not there are other enemies to face), a massive **Leech Servitor** appears, with even more damaging eye attacks and the usual ability to "nourish" the remaining enemies. These are **Shanks** and (later) the more dangerous **Resilient Shanks** (toughened variants), as well as any Vandals and Dregs you may have mistakenly left alive before destroying both Servitors.

Remain in and around Side Slope Location 9 as the Leech Servitor appears at the far end. Concentrate on **shooting its central eye** with your favored ranged weapon (a Sniper Rifle is ideal), switching quickly to remove Shank threats that get too close. **Be patient** and whittle down the Leech Servitor. It has a massive constitution, and the longer you leave it alive, the more Shanks there are to cause trouble. **Focus on the Leech Servitor**, damaging Shanks only if they encroach on you or you need more ammunition (which they drop). Continue the bombardment until the Leech Servitor finally yields. Then, mop up any remaining Shanks.

With the Fallen forces defeated, the power to the elevator is restored now the Servitors aren't disrupting the electrical circuits. Simply **enter the open elevator**, and ride it up. Along the way, expect additional Fallen to arrive. These optional targets are a good way to **hone your long-range headshots** as you pass by gantries and chambers with Dregs and Vandals. Any **Shanks at close quarters are a priority**, as they can harm you more easily. Don't ignore these enemies, either; they could drop an item you need, although you'd have to visit the Postmaster to obtain it.

The elevator arrives atop the mine, allowing access to an exterior area. Head down the **grassy cliff path** to finally **rendezvous with Hawthorne** and conclude this mission.

Hope

Recommended Level: 4
Recommended Power: 50

This mission is the first exploration of the moon Titan, with its methane seas and lurching rig structures. You are here to secure the main shipyard's command center and rendezvous with Sloane, the Fleet Tactician of the resistance. After some precise and vertigo-inducing jumps, you face a revolting new enemy menace: the swarm-like Hive that are not only active on this planetoid, but have left their revolting secretions everywhere.

Sinking Docks

Seas of Titan and Restricted Zone

Objectives
Secure shipyard command center.

Enemies Encountered
HIVE: Thrall, Acolyte, Knight

Falling Short

Your Guardian class makes the jumping a little more difficult or "precise," as does the jump type you might have chosen. If you're constantly (and literally) falling short, vary your timing between the first and second jumps while airborne. Titans have a slightly easier time of it, and Warlocks have the trickiest maneuvers; so if your Warlock is falling short, double-tap your jump button faster, for greater upwards boosting.

1 Initial Superstructure

Super: Not recommended
Grenades: Not recommended

The main order of business is to find and secure the shipyard's command center, located on one of the massive rig islands farther into this facility. You begin on the **outer (western) edge** and must accomplish some deft maneuvering first.

Begin by **jumping to clear any gantry gaps** you see, working from one large platform to the next. Watch as large containers slide into the stormy methane ocean en route to some narrow platforms on the gigantic pilings of the superstructure. **Careful landing and Movement Mode activation is required** so you don't fall into the frothing seas. Once inside the red vertical piling tower, **shoot the secretions** coating the entrance and exit as you ascend to an upper red pipe and more precarious gantry jumping. Finally, leap across to the interior entrance marked "Kemphaan" in giant lettering, and enter.

2 Kemphaan Rig (Restricted Zone)

Super: Not recommended **Grenades:** Optional
Warning!: Restricted Zone

The walls of this massive rig are coated in disgusting secretions, and it isn't long until you witness the revolting entities responsible. Your presence wakes around **eight Hive Thralls**. Back up, shooting them in the head before they maul you, and use melee attacks with quick maneuvers so you aren't swarmed. The next chamber has another eight or so Thralls.

Feel free to **back up** into the previous chamber to avoid getting mauled, and use melee attacks after emptying a clip of ammo to finish off these foes. Then, reload afterward. With the coast clear, turn right at the entrance right of the large pipes labeled "1, 2, 3." This leads to a farther **storage chamber with a final cluster of Thralls**. Deal with them in the same manner as before. Then, exit the rig onto another highly precarious (and partly broken) gantry platform.

3 Poelruiter Rig

Super: Optional **Grenades:** Optional
Warning!: Restricted Zone

Leap across the gaps in the gantry platform and into the side entrance of the "Poelruiter" rig. At the doorway near the sign for "Bay 3," you must begin a **sweep of Hive Acolytes**; around eight are lurking in the two-level chamber beyond. You can elect to slowly tackle foes from the doorway with well-aimed gunfire down your sights, or leap onto the upper area of turquoise metal flooring and use more aggressive tactics. A well-aimed grenade also works to clear the area out. Acolytes don't respond well to being **shot in the head**, so make that the target of choice for dispatching them.

Step into the **cylindrical vent chamber** with the large floor fan, and drop down.

Acolyte Learning and Burning

Hive Acolytes are the most numerous of enemies that fire weaponry (compared to the Thrall foes that just charge and claw at you). Acolytes have no real protection aside from their bony hides, so concentrate your fire at their craniums, and dodge or seek cover to avoid their gunfire. They go down after two melee attacks, so you may want to soften them up with gunfire first. However, be aware that some Acolytes have learned a highly damaging flame grenade ability that can set you ablaze if you're caught in the pool of fire they conjure (although this is rarely seen).

Drop down onto the **red-colored metal cargo platform**. Thralls are active in the vicinity, and more appear the longer you wait around here. Feel free to take your time if you want to accrue more kills.

Your main task is to defeat the trio of Acolytes on the lower platform, then drop another four or five on the **gantry steps ahead and left** of your initial landing position. Then, ascend a vertigo-inducing set of gantry steps that would definitely fail a safety inspection, and go up into a circular doorway.

4 Super: Recommended Grenades: Recommended

Enter a corridor, peering through a gap between walls to see a strange **green fire** in the mid-distance, an indication that a **Hive Knight** is present. You can rush up the small steps to the left, lob in a grenade, and wound the cluster of Thralls, the Knight, and Acolytes. You could also storm in using your Super, or shoot a sitting Thrall from the entrance and coax the Thralls to charge you, dispatching them all relatively easily before heading up and into the main chamber where the Knight resides.

The Knight should be your priority. After reading up on this foe's tactical strengths and weaknesses in this guide's Bestiary, you know to strike the head and wait for the shield to dissipate.

Then, you remove the small amount of health they gain and the rest of the foe's constitution until they are dispatched into the ether. **Seek cover for the Knight's Boomer weapon**, which has a wide-spreading number of projectiles, none of which is particularly pleasant to be hit by.

Head farther into the **upper cargo bay**, now illuminated by a sickly yellow glow from a nest-like secretion in the main bay itself. Deal with Acolytes on the raised platform, then turn your attention to the **Knight by the Hive "nest."** If he's heading your way, make him a priority. However, if he's staying on the far side of the "nest," tackle the Acolytes first. Use the large pillars (one in the raised area) for cover. There's little need to charge in unless your Super demands it.

With all foes vanquished, head to the right of the window onto a precarious covered **tube gantry** that links the Sinking Docks to Siren's Watch, and proceed to the main rig itself.

Siren's Watch

Seas of Titan

Enemies Encountered

HIVE:	Thralls, Acolytes, Knights
SUB-BOSS (KNIGHT):	Ubara, Hive Prince

Objectives

Secure shipyard command center (continued).
Destroy Hive spawn pods.
Secure shipyard command center (continued).
Rendezvous with Zavala.

Important Allies

Sloane

Siren's Watch

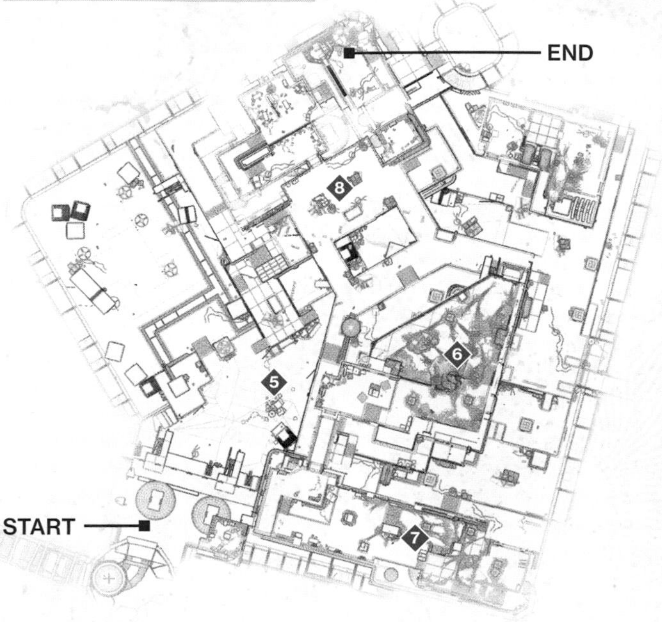

5 Main Cargo Bay (Exterior)

Super: Optional **Grenades:** Recommended

Surprisingly, your first action as you step onto the rig isn't mowing down Hive deviants. Instead, it's **acquiring a grenade launcher**. Open the door, and there's little time to be bewildered by the sheer size of the Base structure. A cluster of around **eight Thralls is streaming down the exterior gantry steps** ahead and left of you. A quick and single grenade strike can defeat them. But if you're not that fast, just back up into the chamber you came from and tag them as they charge, before they arrive at your door.

Grenade Launcher: Worth a Punt?

This Power weapon is obviously adept at badly wounding groups of foes if you can accurately aim it. Use the same technique you adopted when throwing grenades: aim the projectile at where you think an enemy will be when it lands and explodes, rather than where they are currently. Don't forget to try it out in the forthcoming battles. Grenade Launcher projectiles also inflict good impact damage.

After learning how to plant a grenade right at your enemy's feet, start to practice direct hits. The combination of a grenade impact and the ensuing explosion is the highest damage output for this weapon.

Keep in mind different Grenade Launchers have different projectile speeds and blast radii (as shown in the weapon stats), so your intuition may need to be adjusted as you try different GLs and settle on the one you like best.

Take a moment to check the vicinity. You see a large open platform to your left, stairs and gantries ahead and left, and the **main Hive forces directly ahead of you, between the two giant metal structures**. This is where you should head; you can investigate the side walkway, but the enemies on Siren's Watch still require you to defeat them. Your assault on the main thoroughfare may begin with more **Thralls**, followed by a battle against around **eight Acolytes and two Knights.** The Knights arrive one at a time unless you're charging the area in a foolhardy move begging for you to be overrun. When Ghost recommends scoping out the rest of the area, find the open door leading to an **interior "nest" chamber** filled with revolting Hive sacs. This is across from a small **Comm Tower** building with "02" on the side of it. Use that and the pallet of loose luggage at the foot of it as landmarks.

The Side Walkway Sidestep

The side walkway offers a more compact area of pipes and metal stairs that lead to a couple of Loot Chests. Check the Director chapter for detailed analysis of the many side thoroughfares and chambers of Siren's Watch. You can also reach the main spawn pod chamber via a second entrance from here, which offers less of an overall view into the chamber compared to the main route.

Loot Chests and Scannable Objects

You may want to spend some additional time searching gantries, smaller offices, bunker rooms, and other facility areas off the beaten path for Loot Chests and scannable objects. However, it's better to seek these out once you return here after the mission is complete, so you can hunt down these collectibles at your leisure.

6 Spawn Pod Chamber

Super: Recommended **Grenades:** Recommended

Regardless of which lower entrance you entered this chamber from, the plan is still the same: Sloane wants you to destroy the revolting, giant **yellow egg sacs dotted around the chamber**. There is also a large contingent of Hive to worry about, with **Thralls** on the lower level, around eight **Acolytes on the stairs,** and one or two **Knights on the upper platform** and exit. You have several options here:

Produce your **grenade launcher** and lay waste to most of the foes in this chamber from the entrance door. Follow up with precise ranged-fire bursts at the stragglers and sacs. Then, slowly and methodically clear the lower ground, climbing the interior steps when few threats remain, and clear the area competently.

Use a **different Power weapon**, such as the shotgun, to inflict large close-combat damage as quickly as possible. However, this weapon should be focused on enemies (not the sacs) due to its limited ammunition. The shotgun offers impressive damage, but this plan is a little more dangerous.

Standing outside and tagging the sacs, then delivering more gunfire and melee attacks to any foe heading to intercept you is another great idea. You can out-manuever enemy attacks by backing up or strafing in the exterior area rather than being constricted inside the nest pod chamber.

Grenades are also an option, but using them on clusters of foes makes more sense than wasting them on the sacs, which don't fight back! Your **Super is also a viable option**, though you may want to save it for the next chamber beyond this one because there are additional foes to face. Still, it's worth considering if you're having trouble clearing the room.

7 Computer Room

Super: Optional **Grenades:** Recommended

Ascend the spawn pod chamber, cross a short connecting tube tunnel, and turn left as you enter a **computer room** with a large window. Ignore the view and concentrate on demolishing the Hive forces here. Start with the nearby **Acolytes** before defeating the **Knight**. This is a good spot for a grenade if you want a quick clear-out. **The action continues outside** up a ramped cargo bay with a **Knight and around six Acolytes**, which leads around to the main spawn pod chamber doorway. You've completed a circuit and removed considerable Hive forces along the way.

8 Command Center Climb

Super: Recommended **Grenades:** Recommended

Now that you're back at the **Comm Tower 02 exterior**, head to the pallet of luggage and use it as cover, firing at Acolytes along the way. Look ahead with the spawn pod chamber door to your left. The **command center is above and right of you**, where additional Acolytes are appearing from. Make slow and steady progress up the metal steps to the low roof attached to the Comm Tower 02, and hide behind the AC units as you clear this metal flat roof of foes.

Leap the gap to the upper metal steps left of the two large light orange pipes. They lead up to an **open roof platform with a large square-shaped hole** leading down to the initial thoroughfare you traversed before you entered the spawn pod chamber. On this roof is the **last major battle** you'll face, with an **initial eight Acolytes and a Knight** to defeat. Use the cover opportunities and force yourself up to this roof platform; attacking from below limits your opportunities for takedowns. When this first wave of foes subsides, **another eight Acolytes and the Sub-Boss Ubara, Hive Prince (Knight)** arrive!

Sub-Boss: This battle is violent but relatively straightforward as long as you're spatially aware of how you can reach this upper roof platform. (You can also use the stairs on the opposite side near the entrance you first came from, where the Thralls charged down from.) The main fracas occurs in the area around the square-shaped platform hole. Just cover either side of it. As Ubara, Hive Prince arrives, **sprint to the raised section of roof** and clear it of a few Acolytes so you have a slight height advantage. **If you have a Super, use it.** If you have a grenade, throw it (ideally at the Sub-Boss). Otherwise, make nearby Acolytes your first target, then Ubara, who takes about three times as much damage compared to a regular Knight before he falls.

With the battle over, go to the **command center door**, open it using Ghost, and head through to a gantry way and a meeting with Zavala himself. The mission concludes, and you can now meet and greet **Sloane** in person.

Activities to Attempt

You now have permanent access to a Landing Zone, as well as Adventures and an additional Campaign Mission on Titan. Remember to gather tokens to raise your Reputation with Sloane so you can obtain her gear. She also sells some gear of interest, if you can afford it.

Important Ally:

Sloane

"Ah, it's a hell of a view, isn't it?"

Sloane is the Fleet Tactician and a key ally on the moon of Titan. She works with Zavala to plan counter-offensive attacks against the Red Legion. Visit her to gain insight into the current conditions on this moon.

Riptide

Recommended Level: 4
Recommended Power: 50

You may have pushed back the Hive threat somewhat, but the shipyard of Titan is still without power. Fortunately, there is a massive generator rig out in the southern reaches of this base, with a series of huge energy converters that can turn the raging methane seas into all the power Sloane will need. Naturally, the Hive's disgusting secretions have compromised the converters. You're here to attempt the clean-up operation.

The Rig

Seas of Titan

Enemies Encountered

FALLEN: Vandals, Dregs
HIVE: Acolytes, Shrieker, Knights

Objectives

Restore shipyard power.

1 Shrieker Bridge

Super: Optional **Grenades:** Optional

You begin your mission at **Siren's Watch**, and it's a simple drop and sprint down to the two **connecting towers (01 and 02)** that link Siren's Watch to **the Rig**.

Once you're exploring this new area on Titan, edge forward to witness a pitched battle between **Fallen and Hive forces**. Acolytes are engaged against Dregs and Vandals. You can watch this, but there are no sides to take; both enemy groups will turn on you. Remove the closer Acolytes first, use the crate to hide behind, and then drop the Fallen foes before moving along a ledge with a **view of a bridge ahead and left**.

This bridge is being assaulted by Fallen, but the large floating sentry known as a **Shrieker** with its incredible rate of void projectiles is laying waste to them. Add to the Fallen's troubles by tackling the Vandals and Dregs on the near side of the bridge, clearing the area so you can focus on the Shrieker yourself. You can choose from several tactics:

Patiently **sidestep out from the cover** afforded by the bridge pillar with a weapon aimed at the Shrieker's central "core" (its precision hit spot), then step quickly back again before the Shrieker's bombardment of orb-like bolts strikes and kills you. Repeat until one of you is dead.

Shoot the Shrieker from distance using a **sniper rifle**, prior to arriving at the bridge. The crate the Acolytes were fighting from when you first encountered enemies is a good cover spot. A **sticky grenade** (which only **certain** Guardians can spend ability points on to choose) is worth lobbing if you can get it to hit the Shrieker itself. Even if you miss, the grenade can damage the Acolytes and Knight you need to pummel next.

A **Super** is also an option, though Supers that mainly deal damage at ground level aren't as potent as attacks from the skies, for obvious reasons (the Shrieker is stationary but airborne). This makes short work of the Hive ground forces, however.

The Rig

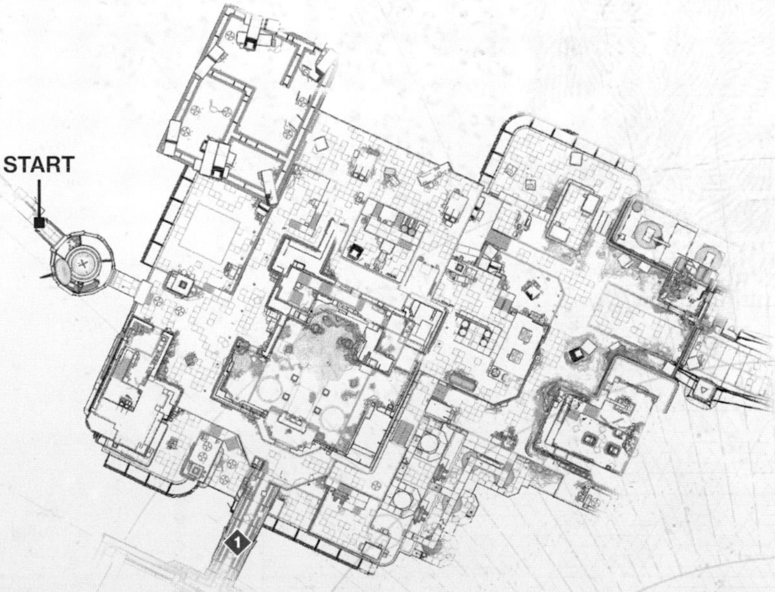

With the Shrieker neutralized, optionally turn 180 degrees around and explore the darkened room behind the bridge (for a scannable item or two) before **crossing the bridge**. The **six or so Acolytes and Knight** shouldn't be a problem, as you have good line of sight for ranged headshots and cover across the bridge if you want to tackle them at closer quarters. A **grenade** is a good way to soften them up. Then, enter the huge rig building with the **sunburst logo above the bridge**, go into the dark cargo ramp room, and take a left, heading up through the secretion-filled side gantry corridor.

Tidal Anchor

Restricted Zone

Objectives
Restore shipyard power (continued).
Fix the wave energy converters.
Flip the circuit breaker.

New Actions to Learn
Disarming Motion Traps

Enemies Encountered
HIVE: Acolytes, Knights, Acolytes, Cursed Thralls, Wizards
FALLEN: Dregs, Vandals, Exploder Shanks, Captains, Wretches, Tracer Shanks

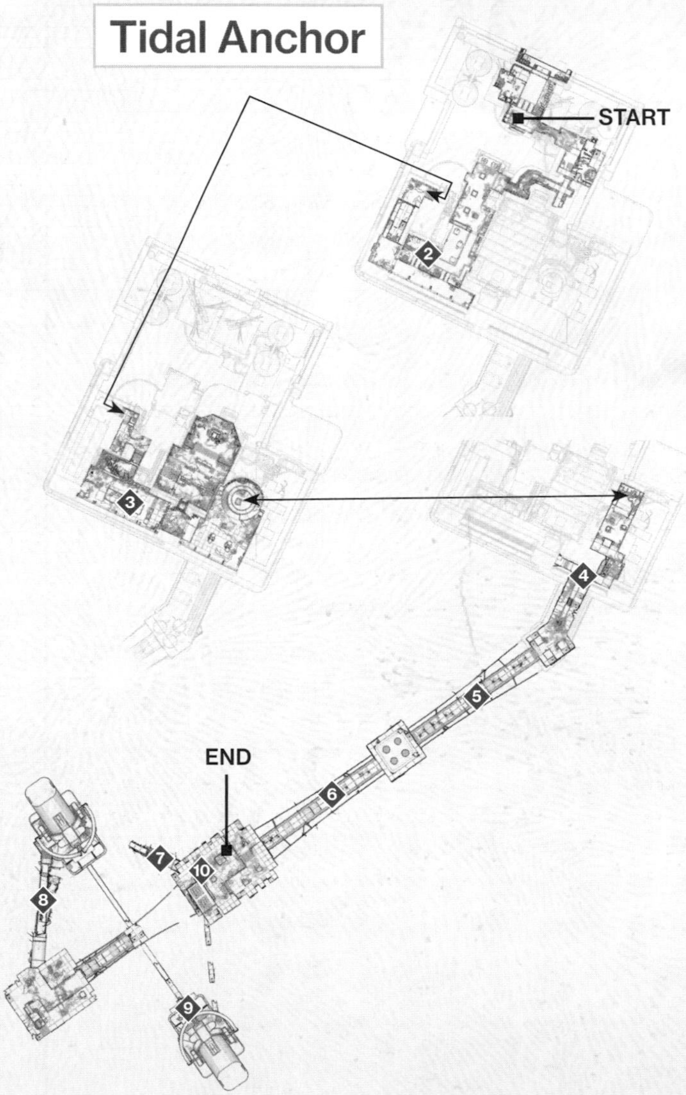

2 Sunburst Rig: Wave Converter Control Room

Super: Optional **Grenades:** Optional
Warning!: Restricted Zone

Enter the **Restricted Zone,** and help a group of **Fallen Vandals and Dregs** mow down a cluster of **Hive Acolytes** before turning your weapons on the Fallen. You can just catch a Fallen ship taking off from the exterior seas through the window of the control room you're assaulting. Sidestep left, and concentrate your fire (and melee) on any nearby Dregs. Then, quickly react to and shoot at the **Exploder Shanks**; these floating bombs need to detonate and wound the Fallen in the vicinity, rather than you. Make them **priority targets**.

Stay back from the circular doorway and "Bay 03" pillar until you've neutralized the immediate threats before heading forward and tackling a **Fallen Captain flanked by two Vandals**. With the closest threats gone, access the "golden age console" so the **wave energy converters** can start to restore power to the main base. Alas, two of the converters didn't start. Your objective now is to **manually bring them online**.

3 Sunburst Rig: Machine Corridor (Lower)

Super: Optional **Grenades:** Optional

Enter the door that opens, and carefully navigate the dark stairwell. There are two areas of concern, the first of which involves three **motion traps** that trigger when you move close to them. These can damage and slow your movements. Shoot them before they activate (they have a red diode and look like round mines) or just after they activate, before the small floating "ball" bomb expands. Alternately, rush through so they activate behind you. This latter plan isn't the best because the ground below the gantry is too toxic to stand on and will kill you.

Instead, make slow progress down to the stairwell door. When it slides open, **surprise a Dreg and a Wretch** attempting a manual door opening by quickly removing them as threats. Then, head down the stairs (the door they were prying open is inaccessible).

It seems the Hive have made themselves at home at the bottom of the stairwell, though you can still see out into the methane ocean as you enter the **lower windowed corridor**. Before stepping into the corridor, remove **Dreg** threats and shoot the **two Exploder Shanks** before they invade your personal space. Step out and look left: **two Vandals** and some milling **Dregs** are in this open corridor area. You can tackle them head-on, sneak between the windows and machine platforms in the middle of the corridor and outflank them, or land atop the platforms and use them for their height and cover advantage.

Step up to the connecting corridor **room filled with laser traps**. Then, step back and shoot at any of the small cylinders on the ceiling or ground. The entire mesh of lasers is activated, and the room detonates. Pass through, then **drop down the large circular hole**, boosting just before you land so you don't crash.

4 Sunburst Rig: Red Deck (Lower Exterior)

Super: Optional **Grenades:** Optional
Warning!: Restricted Zone

Dangerous Jumping Ahead!

From this point on, it's worth understanding that your class-specific jumping prowess will be put to the test. For the immediate area, watch your head, as you're easily able to hit the roof of the deck platform you're on and fall short. Later on, you have some adept maneuvers to land that involve very precarious and broken gantries. Take it slow and steady so you don't plummet into the methane ocean.

Immediately **destroy the two Shanks** floating between you and the farther section of red gantry platforms. In the distance are two new **Tracer Shanks,** as well, and the strength of their Wire Rifle is almost as damaging as a sniper bullet. It's important to dodge this fire and make them priority targets, and you can try sniping all airborne foes from the initial platform. The **half-dozen Dregs and a Vandal** are more of a nuisance.

Step through the open hatch to your left, ignoring the revolting worm but concentrating on the **motion trap**. Destroy it before it activates, or you'll be slowed and become much more of a Tracer Shank target. As the gantry splits into two parallel platforms, **take the right-side one** so you can work your way forward and then left to mop up the last Tracer Shank. Slow and steady takedowns are worth attempting here.

5 Bridge and Tower 01

Super: Optional **Grenades:** Recommended
Warning!: Restricted Zone

Head to a **precarious narrow bridge leading to a large tower** (marked "01") connected to a couple of the massive energy converter arms. This span has **four Shanks, a couple of Vandals and some Dregs** on the bridge, and a **Captain** at the far tower platform. Concentrate on taking down the four Shanks first. You don't want to be spinning around, looking up, and dodging Shank fire when you're on the bridge, as you can easily fall. Instead, tag them from range, then start your bridge assault.

Lob a grenade if you want, then drop the Fallen infantry (Dregs, then Vandals) from closest to farthest threats. **The wall-like bridge support clamps on either side make reasonable cover**, though grenades can easily land near you. Remaining stationary is not advised. As you head up the far side of the bridge, a force of **Hive foes led by a Knight** attacks the Captain (if you haven't slain him yet). Of greater concern is a **cluster of Cursed Thralls**; they are charging straight at you, and although they shamble at a slower rate than normal Thralls, they will explode on contact!

This is the prime opportunity to **lob in a grenade** from a launcher or your ability. The Cursed Thralls are just like their lesser brethren but more explosive. This is highly dangerous for you at close quarters (retreat!), but it's just as problematic for the enemy at range. Make use of this foe's explosive qualities and ensure that the grenade or accurate headshots **strike a Cursed Thrall so a group explodes, ideally wounding the Knight and Acolytes in the process**. One shot at a Cursed Thrall usually causes a chain reaction that destroys all of them. Then, rush the tower, running around the perimeter into and out of cover, and remove the Acolytes and Knight.

Aargh! I'm on Fire!

Do you see those fireball-shaped objects being lobbed by the Acolytes at the far end of the bridge? Those are incredibly problematic because they land and start a raging fire that can cause continuous damage even after you've moved away from it. Leap the fire, avoid getting struck by it, and keep an eye open for these attacks. As you have limited maneuverability on the bridge, elect to retreat and tackle these foes from range. Or, execute a Movement Mode and head in to slay them with extreme violence, hopefully without being overwhelmed. Mop up Acolytes before taking on the Knight for these reasons. For more information on Notifications, consult the Field Manual chapter.

Aargh! Come Face My Ire!

If you're having difficulty with this section, you may want to try the following plan. When there are only a couple of Vandals and the Captain left, move between the third and fourth set of bridge clamps. Focus your gunfire on the Acolytes and Knight, tagging them as they rush in so they have little time to establish themselves. Shrug off a bit of damage, then aim at a Cursed Thrall before the cluster of them manages to head down the steps. The Acolytes are too close to use their burn attacks, and the exploding Thralls kill off everyone.

6 Bridge and Tower 02

Super: Optional **Grenades:** Recommended
Warning!: Restricted Zone

A **second bridge** links Tower 01 to Tower 02. Initially (and suspiciously) devoid of foes, the enemy soon appears as you reach the middle of the bridge. **A host of Cursed Thralls** blinks into existence behind the support clamps, and more pour down from the steps to Tower 02. Normal and faster-moving **Thralls** are also part of this horde. Back up just a little, and shoot the closest Cursed Thralls you can see. The trick is to **burst open a Cursed Thrall so it detonates** and takes a group of others with it. Keep this up with quick and accurate headshots, and you can down both types of foe. If any Thralls get through, melee attack them and back up a little.

Force yourself forward, where **a group of Acolytes and a Knight** appear. If you're in the center of the bridge or farther from them, the Acolytes use their fireballs, which can cause no end of problems. If you're not sniping from long range, **take a chance and charge up the bridge and into Tower 02, lobbing a grenade at the Knight** as you reach the last bridge clamp. It's worth taking a couple of hits as you rush the tower instead of shrieking as you're coated in magical fire! When you reach the tower, **use the walls as cover**, and the fighting becomes much more straightforward.

7 Tower 02 to First Convertor Tower

Super: Not recommended
Grenades: Not recommended

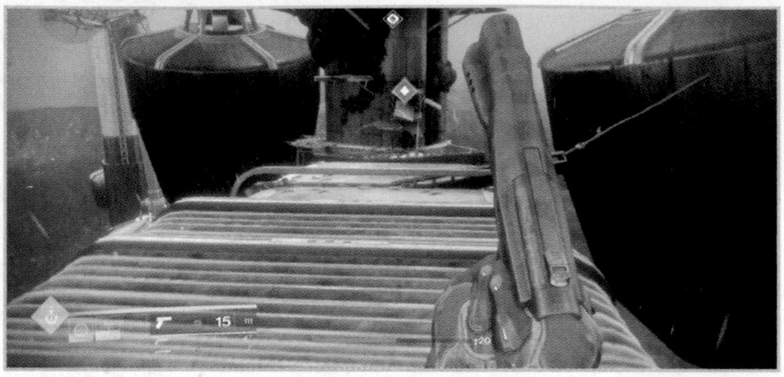

From Tower 02, you have the precarious route **across a partly destroyed covered bridge** (though you're moving along its roof) to the twisted gantry ledges of the convertor tower. Perform a quality jump, then leap up the gantries and into the secretion-coated doorway. **Head up the inside of the tube-shaped tower**, shooting (or melee striking) the revolting **Hive spittle coating on the central mechanism**. Then, continue up and out. That's the first converter good to go!

8 First Convertor Tower to Tower 03

Super: Not recommended **Grenades:** Recommended

Exit the top of the converter tower tube, and gaze to your right. You must now carefully traverse **the remains of a cable bridge** leading to Tower 03. Use the sections of the broken bridge as platforms to descend onto; you want to enter Tower 03 at the opening directly below the remains of the covered bridge above it. **As you arrive, repel a Knight and three or four Acolytes**. A quick grenade into the hide of the Knight can really help remove it as a threat.

9 Tower 03 to Second Converter Tower

Super: Optional **Grenades:** Recommended

Face toward Tower 02, **run along the section of cable bridge, and then leap up to the half-destroyed gantry above it**. You haven't reached Tower 02; instead, turn right, and face the second converter tower (with the two gigantic buoy-shaped generator arms on either side of it).

Leap the two gaps in the gantry bridge, and **prepare for another four Acolytes and a Knight** as you reach the platform attached to the tower. Lob in a grenade or use your Super to make short work of the Hive foes. Otherwise, **make use of the cover** afforded here, and keep running and gunning.

With the coast temporarily clear, **enter the converter tower, descend down the tube-like interior**, and remove the secretions from the **central piston mechanism, just like before**. That's the second converter fixed! Now to flip the circuit breaker and bring this entire base online.

10 Second Converter Tower to Tower 02 Roof

Super: Recommended. **Grenades:** Recommended.
Warning!: Restricted Zone

The circuit breaker is on the roof of Tower 02, so naturally, you'll need to nimbly leap a series of gaps as you maneuver across the remnants of a gantry bridge from the converter tower. **Jump left slightly as you reach the tower exterior**, landing on the gantry steps. Head up and around to a host of problems, not least the screaming, banshee-like wail of **two Hive Wizards**!

There's not one, but two Wizards on this roof platform, and that's not including a small horde of Thralls, and some Acolytes. This is a particularly tricky fight to win, so quick thinking and taking cover are the best overall plans.

As you round the corner from the gantry platform, start by **focusing your attention and firepower on the Wizard directly in front of you**. Shoot it with a **Solar Energy weapon,** and continuously batter it with gunfire until it dies before even worrying about anything else (you don't want it to recharge its shield). The foe is close enough for weapons like sidearms or shotguns to be most effective on it. **Then, sidestep right into the hiding area** behind the secretion-covered crates. As you step into cover, **lob a grenade at the Acolytes and Thralls** milling around in the middle of the roof.

Did That Wizard Come from the Moon?

No, it was mostly likely summoned from another dimension, but your greater concern is dispatching the two of them with extreme prejudice. Wizards are airborne foes, making weapons that strike the ground (like grenades) far less potent, unless they're sticking to the Wizard. Furthermore, the Wizard has a Solar Shield, meaning that a Solar Energy weapon is preferable when removing this protection. Try not to stop firing at the Wizard until it is defeated. Its shield recharges a few moments after the Wizard isn't hit anymore, just like a Fallen Captain. With this in mind, you must assess whether to clear out other foes first (who might stop you from fully committing to killing a Wizard), or shrug off all attacks and focus all your firepower on a Wizard.

As for the Wizard's attacks? The orbs must be sidestepped, and the poison cloud it unleashes when wounded stepped away from. (You don't want to be constantly impeded with poison damage in addition to everything else!) The lack of clarity of vision through the cloud doesn't prevent your weapons from damaging the Wizard, so keep on firing!

After you clear the remaining Acolytes from the roof, **a group of Thralls** appears, **along with more Acolytes.** Keep one of the previous Acolytes alive and **shoot the second Wizard from cover**, or charge its location on the raised area of the roof ahead of you. Demolish the Wizard before seeking cover atop the raised area or back behind the crates where you initially hid. Another option is to rush the second Wizard's location and tackle it from close quarters, which is good if you have more potent close-combat weaponry.

Stay mobile, and aim for any Thrall stragglers.Target the regular Thralls as a secondary concern, melee striking them if they finally reach you. With **only five or six remaining Acolytes** left to worry about, you can take a little time to recover behind some scenery. Then, remove Hive threats as you see them.

Other options include backing up around the initial gantry steps and taking on foes one at a time. You can also **launch grenades** (from a launcher) into the fray to soften up your targets. Aiming down the sights at the far Wizard is recommended, but staying motionless or just behind the initial cover is not. Scamper along the left side of the roof to where the circuit breaker is. This is also by far the best time to **use your Super**, concentrating on dispatching both Wizards while you use it; anything else is a bonus.

When the mayhem is over, **shoot the Hive secretions off the circuit breaker and flip it**, restoring power and completing the mission.

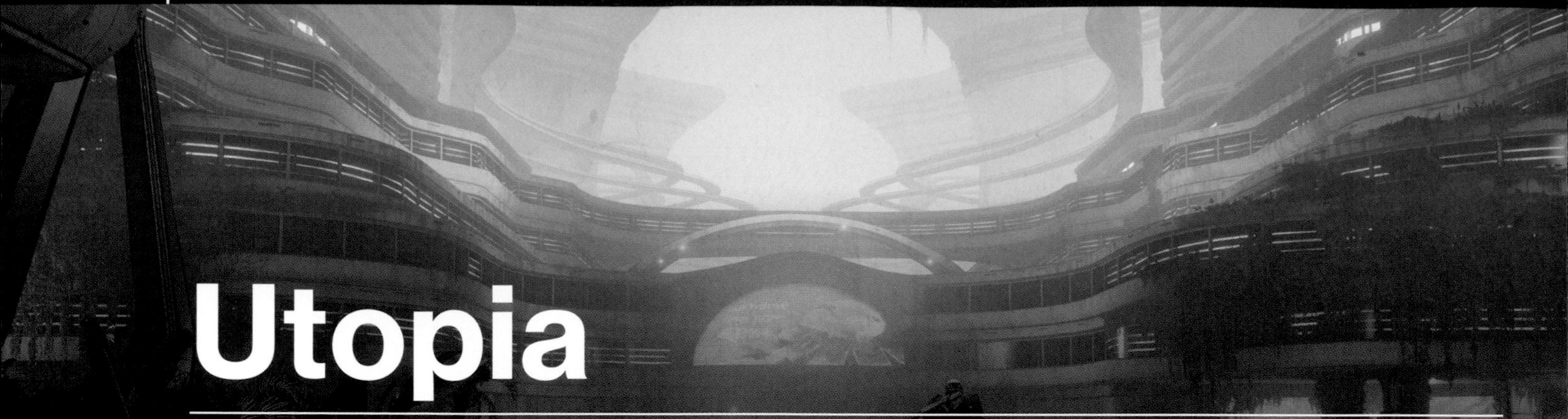

Utopia

Objectives: Enter the Festering Halls, Find an access terminal, Find a CPU, Escape!

Recommended Level: 6
Recommended Power: 60

Holliday needs an advanced CPU to decrypt Red Legion intel that the Resistance has gathered. This Golden Age Arcology must have one still working. Time to head to the Festering Halls. This Sector is particularly difficult to navigate, as the Hive have left their mark (and their minions) everywhere. Expect a number of dangerous battles until you reach a series of shafts and duct passages that requires fewer weapon rounds to expend and more precise jumps, falls, and scampering to get through. Once you've located and retrieved the CPU, you must escape, ideally using an APC and a series of ramming maneuvers. Before that happens, though, the Festering Halls await.

Access Terminal

Seas of Titan

Objectives

Enter the Festering Halls.

Find an access terminal.

Enemies Encountered

FALLEN: Dregs, Vandals, Servitors

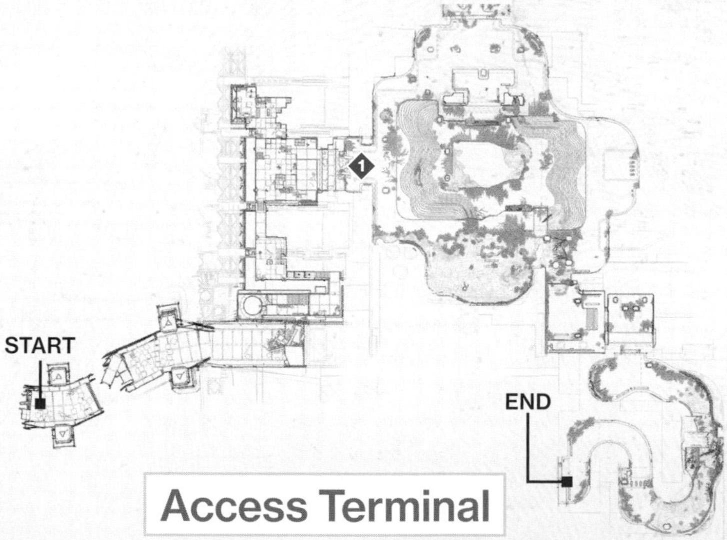

1 Festering Halls Entrance

Super: Optional **Grenades:** Optional

Head across the remains of a **large bridge** linking the Rig to Solarium, then up the steps to the **dark gantry platforms** enabling access into the Festering Halls. Along the way, battle back some **Dregs, Vandals, and a troublesome Servitor** (a priority target because it can keep Vandals immune from your attacks). Watch for two Dregs leaping from a lower platform just before you step to the right and demolish a Servitor close to a **malfunctioning LED wall**. Shoot through the LED panels to create a Guardian-sized hole, and then step into the main forecourt.

The plaza is expansive and overgrown, and the access terminal you are tasked with finding is **ahead and right** of your insertion point. A quick Ghost scan reveals the route: proceed through the empty and curved white corridors, passing through a turnstile and into the Festering Halls.

Festering Halls

Seas of Titan

Objectives

Find an access terminal (continued).

Find a CPU.

Escape!

New Actions to Learn

Gathering Cores

Driving: Construction APC

Enemies Encountered

HIVE: Thralls, Acolytes, Knights, Wizards, Shriekers, Cursed Thralls

HIVE: SUB-BOSS: Garmurg (Ogre)

2 Festering Halls Forecourts and Lobby

Super: Optional **Grenades:** Optional
Warning!: Restricted Zone

At the screened terminal by the oval-shaped door, plug in Ghost, and wait for the entrance to slide open. Drop down into the **dark and sunken inner forecourt**, with evidence of Hive nest-building in the vicinity. Don't venture up the wide set of steps that spans the entrance until you've dealt with around a **dozen Thralls** that charge you. Stay mobile, and back up while blasting their heads.

The **four Acolytes** that subsequently appear (and a **Knight**) are easily dealt with if you're not dodging Thralls trying to maul you. One of the Acolytes is a **toughened Revenant Acolyte** variant and should be a priority target, along with the Knight. It dies with a headshot or two just like its lesser brethren.

If you're concerned about giving the enemy the advantage of attacking from the top of the steps, **rush the far-left side** until you're at the same height. Use the pillar as cover before mowing down your foes. Strafing and accurate headshots easily deliver killing blows to the Hive, no matter where you are.

3 One of the Acolytes may have retreated into a darkened adjacent lobby. Don't follow it in until you've neutralized previous foes, as this lobby area has **two additional Acolytes and a Wizard**. Solar Energy weapon at the ready, concentrate your firepower on the Wizard first. Circle-strafe around the central pillar for cover, and remove the Wizard as a threat before the Acolytes fall to your hands (or guns).

4 The only way is down, **dropping through the floor** the Hive have eaten away at to a lower corridor with a **Knight** at the far end. Venture too far, and you reach a corridor lit with an orange glow. **A half-dozen Thralls** are charging your way and a **Shrieker** is ready to rake you with multiple void projectiles, along with **another four to six Thralls**. Step back, and tackle each foe type one at a time. Drop the Knight before reaching the start of the orange corridor. Then, step back and shoot the Thralls before they reach you. This only leaves the Shrieker.

Step out from left to right by the corridor entrance (where the wires are hanging down), deliver serious damage into the Shrieker, and retreat back if Thralls arrive. Strafe right, then left as you whittle down the Shrieker's energy.

5 Main Hall

Super: Recommended **Grenades:** Recommended
Warning!: Restricted Zone

Turn right at the location of the deceased Shrieker, and look down. Below is **a main hall**, now covered in grotesque Hive nesting materials. Before you descend down there, drop the **four Acolytes**. Then, watch for a couple of **Cursed Thralls**. When you reach the slight hump in the middle of the hall, look to the right and catch them before they explode at your feet.

Festering Halls

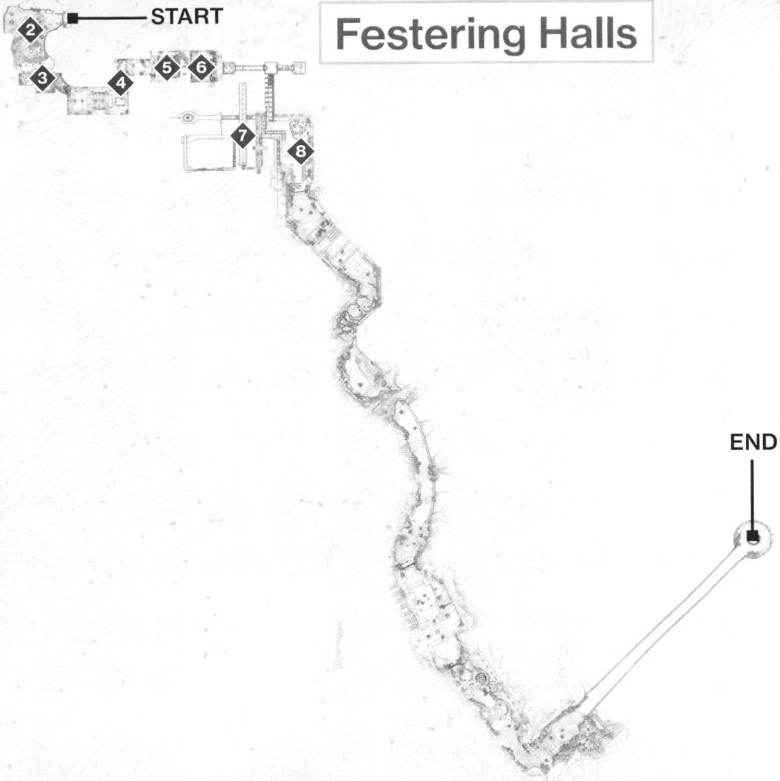

Around **four more Acolytes** are milling around their nests, with a ramp on the right leading to a **raised corridor where three Knights** reside.

You can use the revolting secretion scenery to hide behind, taking long-range headshot opportunities at the Acolytes and Knights as they present themselves. Check left and right to ensure no foes are incoming on your flanks. The biggest problem is the **barrage of projectiles** from the Knights' weaponry, which can badly wound you in seconds. It's a good idea to **charge up the right ramp** onto the raised corridor with a pillar for cover, and dart left and right while targeting headshots on the remaining foes from mid to closer ranges. **Or, lay waste to everyone using your Super**. You may want to keep your Super handy for the next fight, however!

6 Main Hall Sub-Boss

Super: Optional **Grenades:** Optional
Warning!: Restricted Zone

Sub-Boss: Take a moment before dropping down from the raised corridor where you fought the Knights. There's a particularly ferocious foe you may not have encountered before, a named **Sub-Boss Ogre, Garmurg!** Though its powerful close-combat ground slam can seriously damage you, the massive beam of energy from its **almost-continuous eye blast** can kill you in a couple of seconds. This foe is also joined by around **four to six Thralls**, making combat even trickier.

However, if you sidestep left around the main (gigantic) pillar and quickly deal with the Thralls, you can use this vertical cover, sidestepping out to shoot Garmurg in the "head" before seeking cover to replenish the damage you took. Try for some free hits as the Ogre climbs out of its hole. **Keep circling the pillar** and attempting direct and strong hits on the head until the Ogre falls, or just flee the chamber and drop into the shaft ahead. This is feasible without needing to use your Super, although that's also a good idea.

7 Festering Halls Descent (to Core Chamber)

Super: Not recommended
Grenades: Not recommended

After the Ogre, peer down the shaft it climbed up from, then leap to the far wall, **dropping down and use your Movement Mode** just before you land on the narrow platform at the door entrance below. Head down the connecting corridor to another shaft and **execute the same jump**, boosting just before you land on another tiny platform at a doorway. Traverse another short corridor to a third shaft. This one has a low railing and a blinking light illuminating a narrow ledge opposite the entrance. **Carefully step to the lit ledge**, turn around, look down, **and fall off**, using your Movement Mode to land carefully on the **orange-lit ledge** and lowest doorway.

Enter a maintenance corridor with evidence of Hive activity. **Shoot the secretion** preventing you from descending down, then drop into a **sloped maintenance corridor**. Shoot or melee **the grating** at the far end, then maneuver into **a long duct**. Ready yourself for **a couple of Thralls** when the lighting turns from orange to grayish-blue. Continue down the corridor, drop down again, and proceed a second time to **a dark and waterlogged canal-like corridor** with more **Thralls** and a Hive opening to your left.

Melee strike the secretions and follow the narrow Hive tunnel that opens to **another maintenance duct**, allowing you to drop down and shuffle toward a blue light. Drop down yet again (crouching and sliding is necessary) to a **pipe duct** leading to an open floor grating.

Drop through the floor grating, and land in the **Festering Halls core chamber**. A bottomless chasm surrounds you, so carefully **maneuver to the quantic core repository, then gather it up**. Hive forces are woken at this point, and because you need both hands to carry the core, you have little choice but to **depart through the circular doorway**. Time to escape!

8 Festering Halls Escape

Super: Not recommended
Grenades: Not recommended
Vehicle Available: Construction APC
Warning!: Restricted Zone

Dash up the stairs away from the Acolytes, and **access one of the parked APCs**. Your escape is now much less fraught but just as entertaining. The APC has no offensive capabilities in terms of weaponry, just good old-fashioned **ramming and crashing**! Keep an eye on the damage your vehicle is taking (at the top of your HUD), and accelerate hard. **Crash through the Hive columns** blocking your path, and drive into a massive cavern. This is one of many Hive tunnels that you must traverse, so simply run over the foes and keep your momentum going. You don't want to stop to try to kill everything, as that heightens the chance that your APC will take catastrophic damage.

Instead, **press forward, hitting Acolytes, Knights, Thralls, and Cursed Thralls with the front of your vehicle**, along with any nests you don't want to avoid. Of the foes attempting to slow you, the damage from the Cursed Thrall's explosion can be of moderate concern, so avoid it, swerving into as few Cursed Thralls as possible. Head through tunnels, across a bridge, and into a hallway, knocking down Cursed Thralls. The main hall also holds a Shrieker, which is only a concern if you're crazy enough to get out of your vehicle to mop up stragglers by hand. Then, it's back into a Hive tunnel before finally **exiting to an elevated roadway,** where Amanda Holliday arrives to extricate you just in time.

On Foot Antics

Can you escape on foot? No, you need the APC to break through the Hive column tunnel entrances and survive the dozens of foes in the vicinity. Can you get out of your vehicle in each area and start slaying everything on foot? Yes, but you're easily overwhelmed, although those seeking a real challenge could try this plan. Once your Super is spent, the sheer number of enemies becomes a problem, so take extra time when clearing each tunnel section. Or just use the APC!

Looped

Recommended Level: 7
Recommended Power: 80

You arrive on Nessus and you must complete a few tasks, courtesy of a failsafe device with possible knowledge of Cayde-6's whereabouts. Nessus is teeming with life, but unfortunately, these are robotic, fluid-loving killing machines known as the Vex. You must battle through the exotic and strange chambers heading deeper into the heart of Nessus. The constantly teleporting Cayde has some words of encouragement for you, just before a Hapax, the Convergent Mind hovers into view.

Artifact's Edge

Nessus, Unstable Centaur

Enemies Encountered
None

Objectives
Follow Cayde's signal.

Important Allies
Failsafe

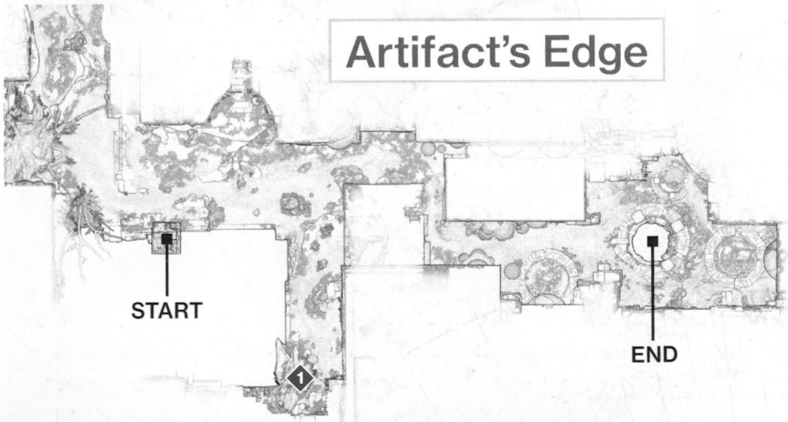

A Failsafe Plan

Super: Not recommended
Grenades: Not recommended

Drop down the energy chute, or take your life in your hands and leap off the top of the tower and boost jump just before you land. **Follow the signal to the rocks**, then right and up the ravine with the bottomless chasm to your right, making your way to the wrecked ship.

The Confusing Nodes of Nessus

The planetoid you're on is a maze of locations carved by the Vex, some with multiple vertical and horizontal exits. Hallows is a good example of this. You enter here from Artifact's Edge, dropping into the large circular hole before venturing into the depths below, with exits deeper and deeper—even down to the core! It is fortunate, then, that the Director chapter of this guide has maps to ensure that your navigation is as "fail safe" as possible.

Important Ally:

Failsafe

"May I help you with anything else? Like, I don't know, leaving?"

Failsafe is the Navigation AI of the Golden Age Colony Ship "Exodus Black".

Climb onto the hull of the craft and have Ghost interface with a terminal to access Failsafe, Cayde's "helpful" A.I. with a heart of gold and a screw loose. As the banter continues between her and Ghost, exit the area, **following the signal waypoints into Hallows**.

Hallows

Nessus, Unstable Centaur

Objectives
Follow Cayde's signal (continued).

Enemies Encountered
VEX: Goblins, Minotaurs

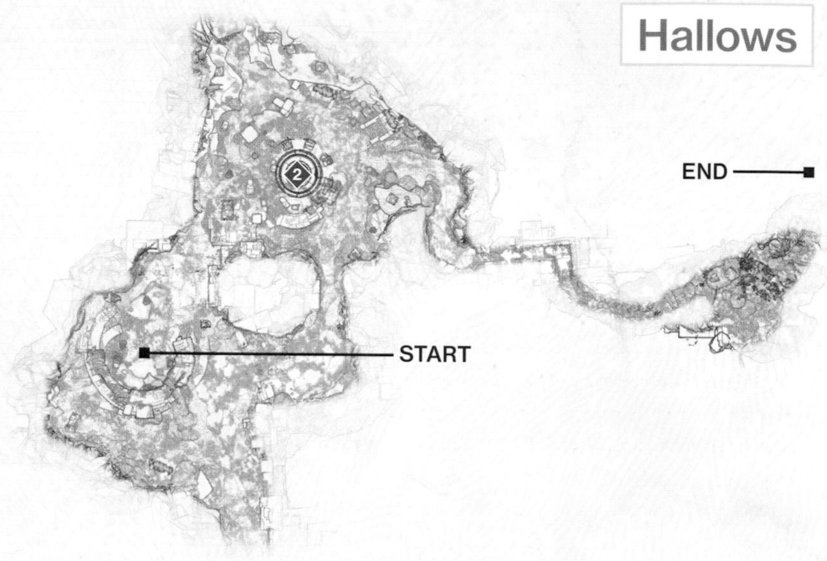

Drop down into the large hole at the surface of Hallows, as the stairs cut into the rim of the hole are for those who want to ascend. Follow the waypoints to a circular part of the subterranean area, where Vex architecture is embedded into this strange structure.

You find **Cayde hanging around here**, but he is forcefully blinked out of your existence and replaced by **a squad of six Vex Goblins** materializing from the columns surrounding the central plinth.

You risk death by standing in the middle of these columns, **so retreat** back up, and tag each Goblin in the lower torso where they glow white (their weak spot). Shooting their heads with a weapon that is less powerful than a sniper rifle usually results in the head being taken off, but the remaining body going "berserk." It charges at you and causes you damage as it arrives and (possibly) explodes. You can also destroy Goblins with a headshot if you've already shot at their "white point" and damaged them; this is an alternate way to remove them. Damaging and melee attacking them is also feasible.

Methodical torso shots to their precision hit location are needed here, especially as four or five additional Goblins arrive at two different portals, and then another six Goblins appear from the columns around the central circle.

The battle does not let up as **a larger Vex robot with a Void Shield, known as a Minotaur**, appears with six Goblins. Slay them, and expect two more Minotaurs and another dozen or so Goblins to come before the Vex trap you stumbled into subsides and no additional foes appear.

Minotaurs have nasty, damaging laser rifles, can teleport short distances (making your grenades tricky to land), and have a reasonably quick gait. Switch to a Void Energy weapon to make short work of those shields, then focus on the torso "white point" weak spot. Feel free to shoot off the head if you want to stop the Minotaur from teleporting or recharging its shields, but prepare to be bombarded with rifle fire as it goes berserk. Make these your priority targets.

With the appearance of the Minotaurs, this is a good opportunity to utilize your Super. **After the battle, follow the waypoints out of Hallows**, and head into the lower depths of this icy rock.

2 Vex Portal

Super: Recommended **Grenades:** Recommended
Warning!: Restricted Zone

Sunken Cavern

Nessus, Unstable Centaur

Objectives
Follow Cayde's signal (continued). Find Cayde-6.

Enemies Encountered
VEX: Goblins, Hobgoblins, Minotaurs

3 First Descent

Super: Not recommended
Grenades: Not recommended
Warning!: Restricted Zone

Weave your way through the connecting tunnel slowly to take a view of what appears to be the core of Nessus in **a gigantic void of darkness and glowing fire**. Look down at a dome-shaped (and inactive) energy catapult far below you.

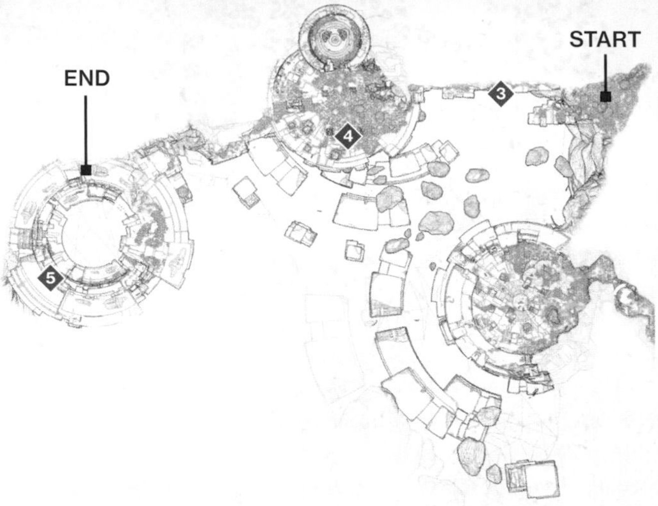

After being hit by your first shot, it creates a three-second invulnerable shield, similar to a Hive Knight. During this time, the shield replenishes, so make your first shot a single bullet from a burst-fire weapon to avoid wasting ammo. Lay waste to the Hobgoblin's "white point" lower torso weak spot before and afterward. Shoot this enemy's head, and it goes berserk like a Goblin. Note that a Hobgoblin cannot enter an invulnerable state while berserk, which is a potentially positive trade-off.

There are three Hobgoblins to worry about (one on the ground, and one on each column that warp in a few moments after you engage the ground foes). These should be your priority targets because they are longer-ranged threats than the group of Goblins and Minotaur that appears on the ground ahead of you. **Tag them at range from cover** before you're spotted, or while darting in and out of cover. Or, you can jump onto the cluster of columns in the center of the enemy group, land next to the Hobgoblin, and remove it with a shotgun or high-powered pistol. Then, drop a grenade and remove the rest of the foes from this vantage point.

Usually, simply sidestepping between the rocks without advancing too far forward and letting the first wave of six or so Goblins head into your low-recoil mid-range rifle (or hand cannon) fire is a good tactic. Then, when the Hobgoblins warp in, shoot them from their pedestal, and save a grenade for the Minotaur, severely damaging it without having to worry about removing its shield.

Sunken Cavern

Now, **make some precise, vertigo-inducing jumps**, landing on the huge floating block and sections of wall to reach the massive curved floor structure the catapult is attached to. If you haven't fallen into the inky blackness, you're doing well.

Energy Catapult Active

This energy catapult is now active and allows you to ascend back up to the entrance area (during future explorations of Nessus). However, this isn't necessary for the continuation of the mission.

4 Vex Plateau

Super: Recommended **Grenades:** Recommended
Warning!: Restricted Zone

Creep along the cover of this rocky plateau, visually checking the Vex entities in the vicinity. A new foe known as the Vex Hobgoblin is active in this area. It doesn't move quite as often as a Goblin but fires a sniper-like line rifle that is extremely damaging.

5 Second Descent

With this contingent of Vex defeated, you have **another couple of extremely vertical (and vertigo-inducing) drops**, avoiding a plummet into the void to an even lower floating plateau with massive crumbling walls. Head into the triangle-shaped hole entrance, and peer over the bottomless edge. Traverse a circular bottomless cavern of floating platforms **in a clockwise manner, proceeding to a Vex teleport gate.**

Scan if you Can

One of the most cunningly hidden scannable items is available if you can jump to the right wall from the top platform here. Consult the Director chapter for clues to its whereabouts.

Well of Giants

Nessus, Unstable Centaur

Objectives

Find Cayde-6 (continued). Defeat the Hydra.

Enemies Encountered

VEX: Goblins, Hobgoblins, Minotaurs, Hydra

6 Bottom of the Well: Hapax, the Convergent Mind

Super: Recommended **Grenades:** Recommended
Warning!: Restricted Zone

Enter a cavern with a bottomless chasm below, and jump across to a natural arch. Pass through it and around to the right, and leap to the triangular exit door. **Ride the huge energy well** down to the huge lower platform and its many columns and walls. It's worth **learning the layout** of this arena-like location **before you investigate Cayde-6**, who is floating above the central circle.

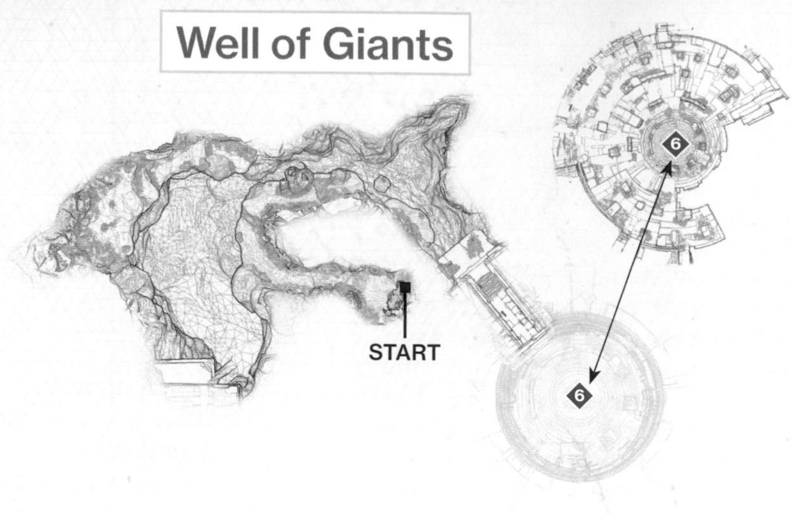

His chat is interrupted by **Hapax, the Convergent Mind**. This foe is armed with a devastating Aeon Maul cannon that can drop you in two or three hits. You must defeat it!

Boss: Hapax is your priority target. Though **the arena is soon swarming** with Goblins, a few Hobgoblins on the upper perimeter ledges, and Minotaurs that are more troublesome (as their weaponry is also highly damaging), the combat concludes quickly once you defeat the Hapax. However, it lengthens considerably if you leave it alone and wait for more and more enemies to teleport in. This is only a good idea if you want to gain XP and have the competence to run and gun, using the main walls to stand behind or on top of as you seek cover and become a moving target.

Aside from the Goblins that incessantly march on your location, distracting you from tackling the main beast, the **Boss's biggest defense** is its **impenetrable rotating shield**. Your shots need to **hit the Boss's central "eye" (its weak spot or precision spot) through the vertical gaps** in those shields, or you're simply wasting your ammunition.

The type of weapon that you use helps. A sniper rifle aimed from height and range is good in theory, but other foes usually see and bombard you before you can get an accurate shot. Shotguns and extremely close-range weapons are feasible, though the Hapax's Aeon Maul is more or less guaranteed to hit you, and three of them can kill you. It's better to **stay at mid-range, darting in and out (or up and down) from cover** and executing a well-lobbed grenade, followed by bursts of accurate gunfire at the Boss's eye.

Take note of Hapax's segmented health bar. Not only do you receive an encouraging yell from Cayde-6 each time a third of the Boss's health is removed, but **the beast teleports to a different location**. Keep an eye on that, and maneuver accordingly (closer to the new location). Also, keep a mental note of the three shield sections and how they are rotating. You can pop out of cover and shoot the Boss when it's just about to be exposed, and step back into cover just as the shield covers the Boss's eye again.

You want to deal **as much burst fire or hand cannon damage** as you can in between protective periods of defense. Alternately, execute your Super as soon as a gap appears in Hapax's shield.

When Hapax finally dies (which removes any other infantry Vex threats), resist the temptation to sprint to its remains to claim any items because **the head will explode**, which can kill you. Gather any items after this occurrence, after which Cayde-6 explains how you can finally free him. The mission then concludes.

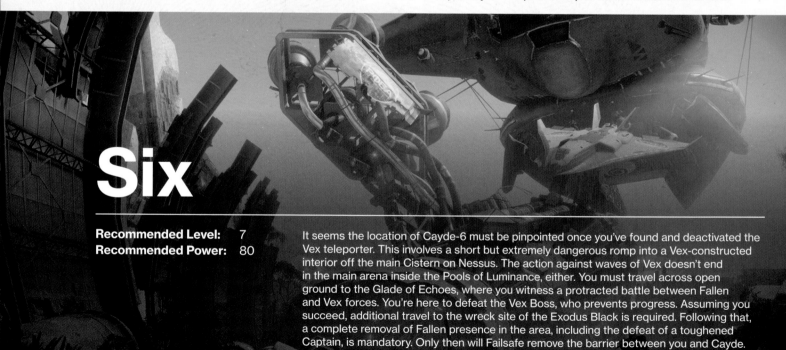

Six

Recommended Level: 7
Recommended Power: 80

It seems the location of Cayde-6 must be pinpointed once you've found and deactivated the Vex teleporter. This involves a short but extremely dangerous romp into a Vex-constructed interior off the main Cistern on Nessus. The action against waves of Vex doesn't end in the main arena inside the Pools of Luminance, either. You must travel across open ground to the Glade of Echoes, where you witness a protracted battle between Fallen and Vex forces. You're here to defeat the Vex Boss, who prevents progress. Assuming you succeed, additional travel to the wreck site of the Exodus Black is required. Following that, a complete removal of Fallen presence in the area, including the defeat of a toughened Captain, is mandatory. Only then will Failsafe remove the barrier between you and Cayde.

The Cistern and Pools of Luminance

Nessus, Unstable Centaur

Enemies Encountered

VEX: Harpies, Fanatics, Goblins, Hobgoblins, Minotaurs

Objectives

Deactivate the Vex teleporter.
Find Cayde-6.

Is an Exploration of Nessus Necessary?

Possibly: this mission takes place on the vast plateaus of Nessus. It is worth learning how each zone on this planetoid links to other areas. A thorough read of this guide's Director chapter can help you ascertain nearby threats, along with helpful areas to explore outside of the scope of this mission.

The Cistern

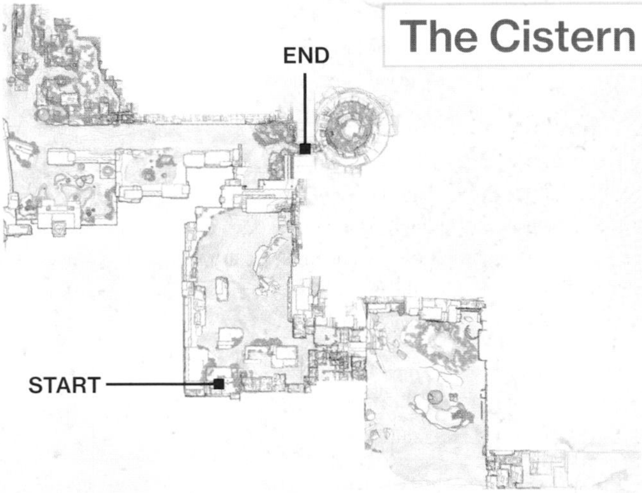

Pools of Luminance

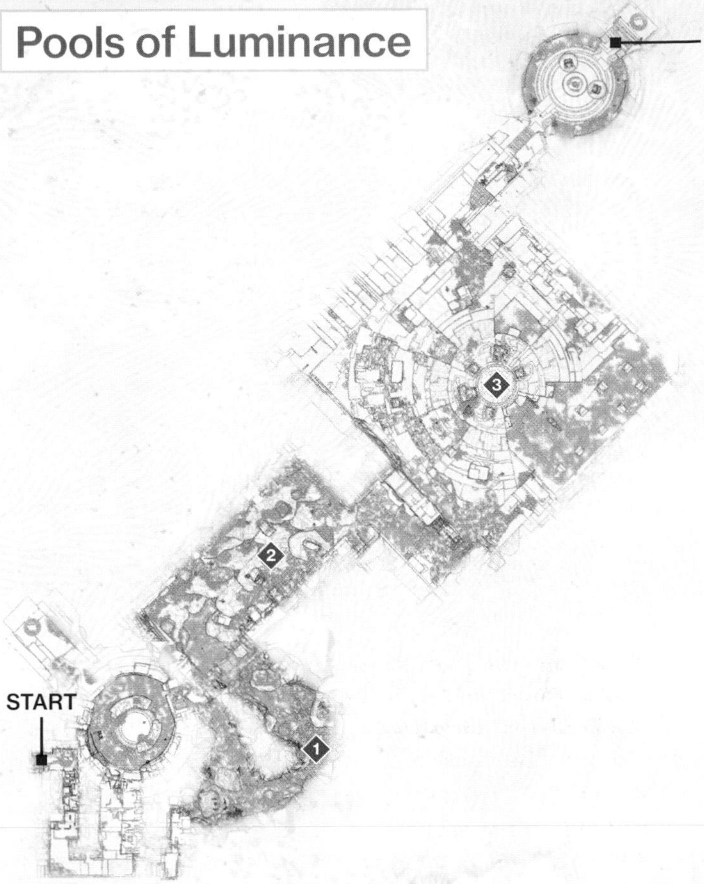

1 Radiolarian Stream and Cavern

Super: Not recommended
Grenades: Not recommended

You begin on a platform overlooking a giant Nessus plateau, but **Cayde's signal is coming from a nearby split in the wall**. Enter it, stepping into a tunnel-like warren known as **Pools of Luminance**, where you encounter a white liquid that's damaging to the touch: **Radiolarian (or "Vex mind") Fluid**.

Jump to the rocky outcrops and ledges as you navigate this fluid stream, then jump from the last ledge through a circular doorway and into an unstable-looking cavern.

2 Fortunately, the floor is firm, but the air is filled with the screeching of around a dozen **Vex Harpies** (which appear in flocks of about four or five at a time). Seek nearby cover, and methodically thin their number by firing at their central eye; the precision hit location. These foes are more of a nuisance than a threat, although their laser rifle-like beams are damaging. **When you've cleared the cavern**, seek the small connecting chamber with fluid on the floor, and head to the narrow golden wall.

3 Luminance Arena

Super: Recommended **Grenades:** Recommended
Warning!: Restricted Zone

Enter an **arena-like room** with a central circle on the ground raised from the entrance and a higher area at the far side of the chamber. There's a platform to your left and stepping stones to the right (the route to the left is more accessible). Note the block-like wall sections because these cover opportunities are crucial for the carnage to come. Prepare for **a protracted and extremely difficult battle** with waves of incoming Vex.

The first wave teleports in as you advance on the central circle. These are a new type of Vex, **the Fanatic**. Think of a Vex Fanatic as a headless Goblin, but not quite as furious. Fanatics use the same weaponry as a Goblin and will track and march directly toward you, exploding at close range and leaving an area of effect that damages others for a few seconds afterward. Aside from blasting them at range before they detonate and harm you, you can effectively defeat them by bringing them down in between the pillars. That way, other foes (particularly Goblins) are harmed and hopefully destroyed by a Fanatic's explosion and area of effect that stays active.

Blast the first wave (Fanatics) with accurate gunfire from your starting position cover. **The second wave (Fanatics and Goblins) then appears**; execute the same plan, dropping Fanatics as priority targets and ensuring that their ongoing explosions strike the Goblins. During the second wave, you will be outflanked and overrun by multiple Goblins. Start at the top of the ramp from the lower block wall, then retreat to it and melee attack any Goblins (but not Fanatics!) that get through. Your primary escape route is to your left, by which time, the third wave arrives.

By this point, you have **groups of Fanatics, Goblins, and a couple of Minotaurs all converging on your location**, with Harpies providing a long-range annoyance. Keep moving from the lower island with the two block sections of cover back and forth to the starting position, and drop Fanatics so they explode and take a couple of Goblins with them. When you're overwhelmed, sprint over to the other area you're comfortable holding, and block chokepoints with exploding Fanatics and headless Goblins (anything to cause a chain reaction).

Other options include **bringing out the big guns, AKA your preferred Power weapons** (grenade launchers for longer-ranged foes, and shotguns to quell any foes trying to overrun you, though you run the risk of being struck by their exploding damage). A thrown grenade is also useful to detonate at the feet of multiple foes. You can also leap atop one of the larger block defenses, crouch down, and tag foes quickly from this partial cover. Since you're atop a block but crouched, much of the Vex's ranged firepower hits the block instead of you. However, you're usually surrounded, so watch for flank attacks and jump away when it all gets too hectic.

Once you clear the incessant waves of Goblins and Fanatics, **the final wave** consists of the **Minotaurs, Harpies, and a few remaining Goblins** that remain on the upper platform and may have teleported in earlier. These are actually a little easier to destroy, as they aren't actively marching on your position. Long-range tagging of Harpies can be done at your leisure; shoot them first so you have fewer enemies firing at you from directions you can't control.

Then, move to mid-range, and tackle the remaining Harpies and the Goblins. Move to the central circle, but back up when the Minotaurs' weapon barrage starts to sting. Now is the perfect time to execute your Super, as it can cut through the usually troublesome Minotaurs without you worrying too much about being caught in any explosions. **Whittle down the enemies until the room is secure.** Then, gather any dropped ammo and items.

Not-so Super Attacks

Although using your Super is a great idea to thin the numbers, it's important to know how dangerous certain Supers are when employed against exploding foes, like the Fanatics. You can kill yourself easily with Supers that inflict damage at melee range, so ensure that your Super attacks are inflicted at longer distances, outside of the detonation range.

Finally, exit via the marked (slightly glowing) stepped tunnel into a Vex temple. **Gather the teleporter, which frees Cayde-6**, although you need to find him next. Step into the Vex gate behind the teleporter, sending you back to the entrance. From here, retrace your steps back to the expanse of **the Cistern**, scanning the area so you don't dash off in the wrong direction, heading left from the wall split entrance. You're on the right track if you pass by a Vex-like ball structure with a hole in it. **Continue your track until you enter the Glade of Echoes.**

Glade of Echoes

Nessus, Unstable Centaur

Objectives

Find Cayde-6 (continued).
Kill the Boss.

Enemies Encountered

FALLEN:	Dregs, Wretches, Marauders, Vandals, Captains, Servitors, Spider Tank (destroyed)
VEX:	Goblins, Minotaurs
VEX: BOSS:	Acanthos, Boss Minotaur

Glade of Echoes

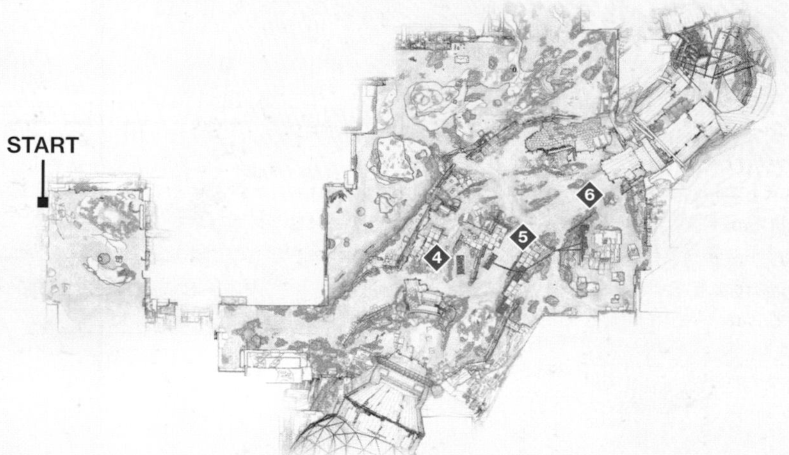

Slaying Acanthos the Boss Minotaur

Super: Recommended **Grenades:** Recommended

It seems **the Vex have a shield up**, preventing you from reaching the crash site of the Exodus Black (Cayde's ship and possible location). The shield is linked to **a gigantic, Minotaur Vex known as Acanthos**. This **Boss Minotaur** isn't the only entity standing between you and the crash site, though. A massive battle between Fallen and Vex is taking place, and you're caught in the midst of it!

Fighting Smarter, Not Harder

You may be initially overwhelmed by the battle going on throughout this zone, and it's easy to be caught up in protracted fights with Fallen and Vex. Instead, learn that the Boss Minotaur is the only entity you must defeat; all others are optional. Furthermore, there are three clusters of fighting occurring. The Boss Minotaur attacks at one, moves to the second at two-thirds health, and teleports to the final one at one-third health.

Finding a position to bring down the Boss Minotaur's health bar is more effective than leaping into the fray and hoping you can kill everything. You can, but it's going to take extreme dexterity, competence, and patience. Instead, think about employing longer-range Boss Minotaur takedowns from a hiding place at any enemy cluster. You can complete this entire battle without slaying anything other than this gigantic Vex!

The Boss Lowdown

The Boss Minotaur can crush you with a single foot stomp if you're foolish enough to think that close combat is the best way to defeat this towering adversary. Hang back and watch the highly damaging Torch Hammer bolts Acanthos fires from his main weapon (right arm). Aside from this and his two teleportation maneuvers as his health weakens, treat him as an insanely tough (and giant) Boss Minotaur. Aim for the white glowing lower torso to inflict proper damage, and stay mobile so you aren't pinned down and defeated by Acanthos' gunfire. Sticky grenades are more helpful, as he's so tall that explosions on the ground only inflict limited damage. Supers are an excellent idea, though ideally at the very start of the fight and once again at the very end (maximizing the use and recharge of your Super).

4 **Battle Cluster #1 (Waypoint #4):** The first of the three areas where you must reduce the health of Acanthos is where the Boss Minotaur and a small contingent of Goblins are battling against a Fallen Captain and his trio of Vandals (though other Fallen and Vex forces are in the vicinity). Try one of the following plans:

You can **sneak behind the action** via the massive skeleton of a spacecraft's fuselage onto the platforms on the other side where the Captain and Vandals are, and wipe them out. However, Acanthos can simply redirect all his offensive firepower at you. Stay away from the lip of the platform (so the Goblins can't hit you), and sidestep Acanthos' gunfire until he disappears. Then, look down and defeat any remaining Goblins now that Acanthos cannot protect them.

The other main plan is to **adopt a longer-range, indirect approach.** Ignore the main fighting, and circle around to the large stack of cargo containers beyond the Boss Minotaur on the far side of the main ravine road. Jump up to gain some height (and cover opportunities), and start some long-range sniping with a rifle that has low recoil. You can pepper the torso of Acanthos until he disappears without being struck at all, if you're far enough away. You'll use up a lot of ammo and can't hit his weak spot, but it's the safer option. Or, you can **snipe from the gigantic circular fuselage** section on the lower part of the zone to the right of where you first saw the Boss Minotaur, using the cover there if Acanthos turns to focus on you. Dart out, shoot his weak spot, then dive back into cover.

Also, be aware that a little farther down the "ravine" of crashed spacecraft parts (between waypoints #4 and #5) is **a smaller pitched battle** where a Captain and a group of Wretches fight a Minotaur and Goblins. Feel free to remove these on your way to waypoint #5, or leave them to finish each other off.

5 **Battle Cluster #2 (Waypoint #5):** The second area is **directly in the middle of the battlefield**, with multiple flashpoints of combat. Above the dirt road, there are Fallen foes on wreckage platforms, including a Captain with a shrapnel cannon, Vandals, and a Servitor providing protection to some Dregs. The Vex forces are some Goblins with a Minotaur on the dirt road and Acanthos himself near the smoking remains of a Fallen Walker. Your options are similar to before:

Head directly in from waypoint #4 **to the platform by the Servitor** on the "left" side of the road (if you're looking uphill), and use cover as you advance. Remove the Servitor as a threat first, then any Dregs. Target the Vandals and then the Captain before a protracted attack on Acanthos, using the same cover sidestepping plan as before. This is a long and drawn-out process, so save some time by lobbing in a grenade at any foe clusters or the Captain for quicker kills.

A variant of the previous plan is to jump on **the cluster of strewn cargo containers** on the right side of the dirt road, coming up behind the Captain with the shrapnel cannon and Vandals. Before dropping them at closer quarters, stay at range (the entrance through the open container), and shoot the Servitor from distance. Or, jump across the dirt road and land by the Servitor, dispatch it and the Dregs, then leap back. Remove the Vandals and Captain next, leaving only the Vex foes to worry about; concentrate your firepower on the Boss Minotaur, using the interior of the open container as partial cover. Then, use your height advantage to lay waste to the Goblins and Minotaur, or ignore them and press on.

A second variant of the previous plan is to **step into the open cargo container** near the Captain and two Vandals, removing the Vandals but remaining inside the container. Attack Acanthos next, and then worry about the Fallen Captain, the Servitor, Dregs, and finally showering hot death down on the Minotaur and Goblins on the road itself.

For those with only Acanthos on their minds, skirt the outer edge of the dirt road to the cargo containers, then **the gap behind the remains of the fuselage** on the opposite (right) side of the road. Find some excellent height and cover on the rocks or other scenery around here so you can easily pepper the Boss Minotaur with gunfire, ducking down or simply sidestepping to easily avoid his return fire. Though you may not be hitting his weak spot, he's still taking damage, and you can circumvent all other combat once he teleports for the last time.

6 **Battle Cluster #3 (Waypoint #6):** The Boss Minotaur's final stand takes place **farther up the dirt road hill**. The forces still battling at this point are Goblins on the road near Acanthos' feet (near the burning Fallen Walker) and two groups of Fallen: a Servitor and two or three Vandals in each group. You have two options:

Creep around the **left perimeter of the battle** and quickly tackle the Servitor and Vandals before facing down the Goblins they were attacking. Do this for both groups, moving continuously and being very aware that you could be overwhelmed. Lobbing a grenade and using your Super are both recommended at this point. Whether you focus your Super on the smaller foes or the Boss depends on the type of Super you're using. (It's more proficient to strike Acanthos at his weak spot, which makes airborne attacks much more potent.)

Or, you can **climb the rocks and scenery to the right** of the dirt road, firing down from above the fuselage section nearest the exit road. Shoot Acanthos in his weak spot until he yields, ensuring that you aren't struck by him during this frenzy of gunfire.

After that, you can leave the remaining enemies and escape through the dissipated energy wall, or you can mop up.

No matter how many enemies you've slain, once Acanthos falls, you should head uphill. Exit through the gigantic rib cage-like ruins of a massive rusting spacecraft, and head downhill (or through a large tube) into the crash site itself.

Exodus Black

Nessus, Unstable Centaur

Enemies Encountered

FALLEN: Dregs, Shanks
FALLEN: BOSS: Jaliks, Fallen Captain
FALLEN: Vandals, Marauders

Objectives

Rescue Cayde-6 and Failsafe.

New Actions to Learn

The Scorch Cannon

Exodus Black

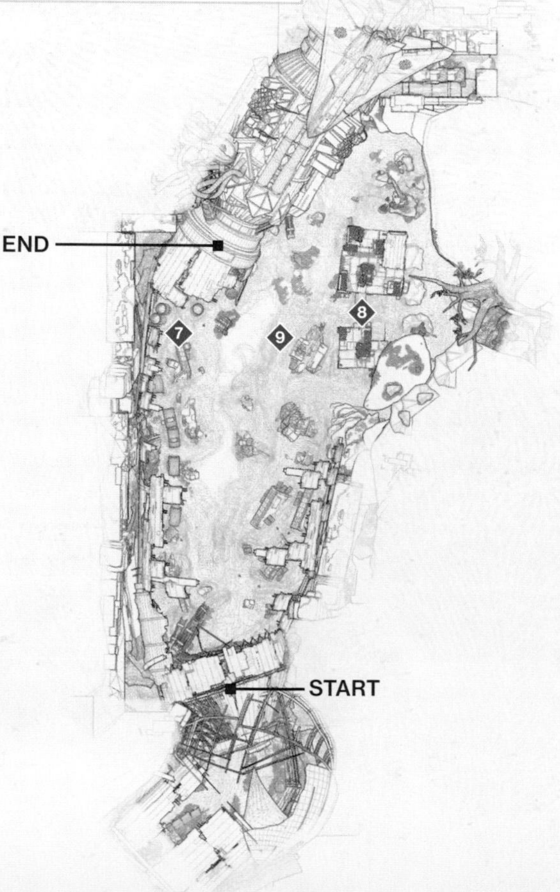

7 Fallen Captain Jaliks: Battle 1

Super: Optional **Grenades:** Recommended
Warning!: Restricted Zone

Boss: The Fallen are active in this shallow lake area where you find the remains of the Exodus Black. **Concentrate on the series of tubes** (one has a scannable object in it) leading to the large circular open hull with a blue energy wall preventing progress. You need to enter here, but only after you deal with all Fallen threats. A small group is already bombarding this entrance, led by an **impressively tough Captain named Jaliks**. Shoot Jaliks' shield with Void Energy weapons until he teleports away. Force your way to the Exodus Black's platform entrance to gain some height, and use the cover there as you fire down, dropping Jaliks' three Dreg friends. Watch for Shanks appearing from behind one of the upright cylinders along the perimeter fuselage wall. Around 10 more appear from Fallen dropships, so expect a protracted battle.

Even though you could be milling around the scattered tubes or lake, a more cunning position is **by the entrance to Exodus Black**, using cover as previously recommended and firing down at the dozen or so Shanks. Jaliks is your priority target, though, as his shrapnel launcher and impressive constitution make him a menace. Use the tactics you've employed for previous Captains, and remove the first third of his health. At this point, he disappears to a Fallen base on the rocky and slightly elevated ground farther into this Sector.

Initial Attack: Other Options

There are other ways to assault Jaliks and his flying robots. You can attack from across the lake using the assorted debris and rocks along the right side of the lake as cover. You can also employ long-range weaponry, mainly to focus your attacks on Jaliks until he teleports away.

It's worth clearing the immediate area around the Exodus Black entrance and the lake of Shanks and Dregs so you don't have to worry about them attacking as you assault the Fallen base itself.

8 Fallen Captain Jaliks: Battle 2

Super: Recommended **Grenades:** Recommended

Warning!: Restricted Zone

Boss: Jaliks has fled to the Fallen base, a compact set of platforms and crates bisected by a dirt road on the far-right area of this Sector. Watch for a cluster of Shanks en route to the base, along with some troublesome Jackals on the near side of the base itself. These are joined by four Dregs and four Shanks under the platform. On the far side of the road is the larger section of the base, with Dregs, Vandals, and Shanks (around four of each) to worry about.

Jaliks himself starts on the platform of the near base. As you attack, he shifts position, retreating down the ramp to the dirt road, up the ramp to the main base platform, and moving back and forth in this general area. With the threats now noted, it's worth executing one of the following cunning plans:

A frontal assault is fine to try, as long as you're not too enthusiastic and die trying to reach the first base. Take your time and remove the Shanks, Vandals, and Dregs first. Pay special attention to the Vandal snipers on the higher crates of the platform area. With few or no minor foes left on the initial base platform, rake fire into the Captain's shields.

You may need to do this three or four times because Jaliks is tough enough to make you retreat to find ammo, and he also retreats to the main base. Use the cover, sidestepping and pushing him back down the ramp to the road while **you stay on the initial base platform**. Remain here, and keep those headshots going for as long as possible (ignoring the other foes on the far base area). Finish him with a grenade and a Super.

A rear assault is also an option. Skulk around the perimeter of this Sector to the large rock stalagmites, using them as cover while you remove the threats under the platform (Dregs and Shanks). Then, leap atop the rocks and then across, landing on the platform itself. As you arrive, shoot the Vandals, then **use the curved "roof" section of the main part of the base to stand on** and as cover. Tag the Vandals on the initial base platform before turning your attention to Jaliks. Obviously, there are times when this roof section becomes compromised, so don't refuse to move from up here when necessary. However, bounding around here in between clearing lower areas and collecting ammo is a fine plan.

You can elect to **completely clear both bases of Fallen infantry first** before tackling the Captain. This isn't necessary, but it does allow you to focus completely on the main takedown.

There's also an **extremely high plateau** along the near side, right of the initial base area. Though it takes some deft jumping, you can reach this large ledge and then fire down on your foes. They can't really retaliate, especially if you back away from the edge to stop yourself being struck by incoming fire.

9 Conclusion: Scorch Cannon

Super: Not recommended

Grenades: Not recommended

Once Captain Jaliks falls, he drops a fabled **Scorch Cannon**, a highly dangerous rocket launcher that can lay waste to multiple foes while giving you a dangerous sense of invulnerability. A Fallen dropship deposits a group of Dregs, Vandals, Shanks, and a (regular) Captain in the lake area. Though you can use your regular weaponry, it's worth **tackling them with this new and impressively devastating cannon**. Blast from range, as pointing the cannon at a melee-range enemy (or your feet) is just as damaging to you. Strafe while tackling all Fallen threats; with this weapon, you can cut through the enemy easily. **After that, Failsafe opens the Exodus Black**, and you can finally meet this lunatic AI and Cayde-6.

Sacrilege

Recommended Level: 11
Recommended Power: 120

Ikora Rey has reappeared on this moon, where the secrets of the Traveler are yet to be uncovered. However, the Red Legion forces have certainly mined the area for both materials and information. As you arrive, a Cabal fleet is leaving in a hurry. It is only after a reconnoiter across the strange alien rock outcrops and into a series of caverns that once served the Cabal that the true terror of Io is discovered. The Taken are here! Battle your way back out of the interior, following the instructions of Asher Mir as you attempt to close the Taken portal, and you might just survive this!

Terrabase Charon

Io

Objectives

Determine what the Red Legion is doing on Io.

Enemies Encountered

CABAL: Phalanxes, War Beasts, Psions, Legionaries

Terrabase Charon

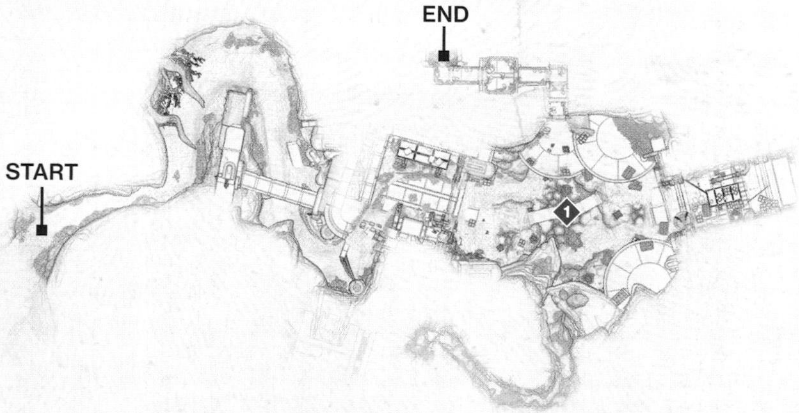

1 Cabal Depot Assault

Super: Optional **Grenades:** Optional

After the Cabal ships depart, **race to the Red Legion base**, through the **Lost Oasis** and into a Sector called **Terrabase Charon**. You're greeted by a small pack of War Beasts at the **exterior depot area**, guarded by a couple of shield-carrying Cabal Phalanxes. A couple of Psions are also present, so use the entrance cover and remove the threats, starting with the War Beasts, then the Phalanxes, and finally the Psions. The lower ground should be completely clear because the **upper ledge on your left** holds additional foes (a couple of Legionaries and a Psion to worry about). Feel free to leap to this ledge, or take the dirt road around and up to the right side of it.

Shields Up, Phalanx Down

If you haven't seen them before in the eastern Sectors of EDZ, you should be training your firepower on the center of their expanding shield until it retracts, knocking them back. After that, attempt a flurry of headshots to bring these foes down.

Checking the Ramps

Check under the two metal ramps for possible chests. These come in useful at the end of this mission, so it's wise to remember where they are for later.

The Wraith Mines

Io

Objectives

Determine what the Red Legion is doing on Io (continued).
Defend yourself against the Taken.
Rejoin Ikora.

Enemies Encountered

TAKEN: Psions, Phalanxes, Thralls

2 Bunker Busting

Super: Optional **Grenades:** Optional
Warning!: Restricted Zone

Venture down the connecting corridor into the Excavation Site II, and begin to explore the linked caverns. Strange rifts in the walls are a prequel to the problems you'll soon face; the Taken have arrived on this moon, which explains the Cabal's quick departure! **Avoid or shoot the Taken ball-like traps**, or run through them before they expand and slow you down.

Taken Aback

The Taken are extremely adept at combat and are very dangerous to your continued well-being. You are advised to take extra caution, recharging between chambers, making full use of your Energy and Power weapons, and learning how these enemies attack by consulting this guide's Bestiary.

Head into a cavern with a ledge ahead and above and an exit ahead of you. The ledges aren't your main concern; it's the multiple dimensional shifts announcing the rival of around a **dozen Taken Psions**, who have the ability to replicate themselves, and should therefore be priority targets. They fire rapidly and are more ferocious compared to the Cabal Psions they possessed. It's important to stay behind cover (or Movement Mode to the upper ledge), tackle closest threats, and gradually remove enemies from the cavern. If you want, you can back up and lob a grenade to catch the Taken just as they warp in.

3 **Exit the cavern at ground level**, moving up the steps of the linking chamber beyond. Go up to a second storage cavern, where multiple Taken Psions are stationed. Again, the cover affords you protection so you can drop foes at both close and far ranges. There's also a platform above and to the left. Use your Movement Mode to get up here (stay away from the edge of the platform), and you can whittle down the Psions before peeking over the lip of the platform to deliver more carnage down below. This is easier than charging across the ground.

The **upper storage chamber** wraps around and down to the initial cavern (waypoint #2), though the enemies you encounter on your return are yet more vicious: **Taken Phalanxes**! Remove them before attempting to escape, as a group of **Taken Thralls** soon overwhelms you. These slightly mindless foes act

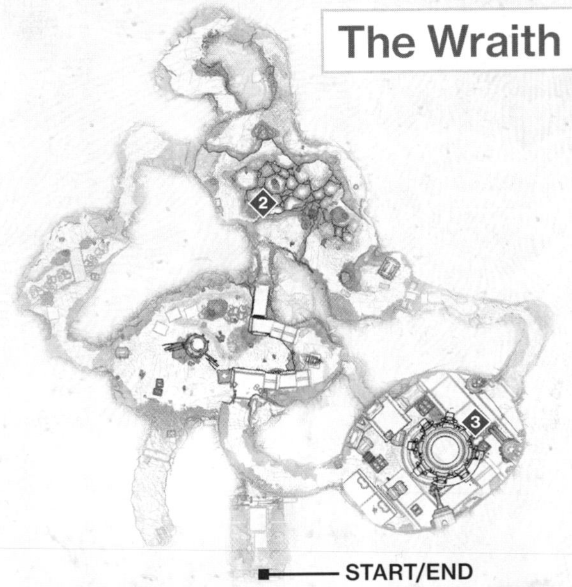

like their Fallen variants but have a quick and short warping teleport (meaning grenades are tricky to land), and they can very easily crush you. Jumping out of their grasp, backing up, and performing headshots is the plan here.

Shields Up, Taken Phalanx Up

You must learn (quickly) that unlike their Cabal counterparts, you should not shoot a Phalanx's shield, which blasts a massive jet of highly damaging matter at you. Strafe, dodge, or jump to avoid that (do this early, as it's difficult to avoid). Concentrate your firepower on the body parts you can see behind the shield, which is usually the Taken Phalanx's right foot. When you shoot and knock them back, the shield lowers, allowing you headshot opportunities.

Continue down to the passage with the Taken traps and the **strange glowing blue floor**. Slow your progress so you can drop the Taken Thralls milling around here, as you don't want to face them near any unexploded traps. When the coast is clear, pass through into the initial orange-hued rock cavern where you can face or flee from Taken Psions and a Phalanx. As the Taken are about to open a portal, it's time to **retrace your steps, out of the area and onto the surface again**.

Terrabase Charon

Io

Objectives

Seal the Taken portal.

Important Allies

Asher Mir

Enemies Encountered

TAKEN:	Psions, Thralls, Phalanxes
TAKEN: SUB-BOSS:	Wizard Elite x3
TAKEN: BOSS:	Centurion Boss

Terrabase Charon

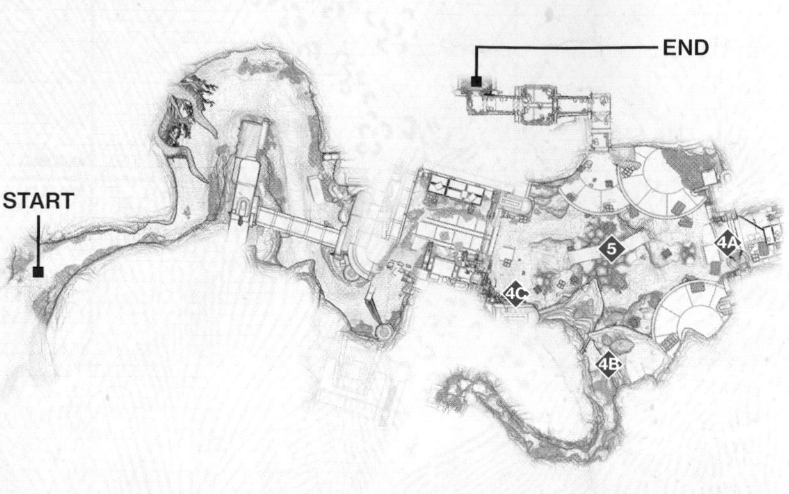

4 Cabal Depot: Portal Assault (Taken Wizards)

Super: Recommended **Grenades:** Recommended

As you arrive back outside, you're warned that the Taken are attempting to summon a portal, and **the ritual has already started!** This arena-like junction consists of three pathways: the platform you're on, the main route back to Lost Oasis, and a large hangar area to your right. Make short work of the Taken Psions on the platform, and then remember the location of this ledge. Once you defeat the three Taken Wizards, it becomes very important to use the height and cover afforded by this location.

Sub-Bosses: But for now, you must concentrate on the masses of Taken in the vicinity. Equidistant around this depot area are **three Taken Wizards**. Swiftly defeating each one is paramount to continuing your progress, and this isn't easy. Two Taken Phalanxes and around four Taken Psions guard each Taken Wizard. Additionally, the Taken Wizards can summon Taken Thralls to waylay you. It's worth starting with the **Taken Wizard immediately left of the platform**, as it is nearest and you have the stack of large pipes and other crate-like scenery to use as cover. Remove the foe's shield, and concentrate your firepower on its head.

Tackling Taken Wizards

Aside from summoning Taken Thralls, Taken Wizards can conjure a ball and launch a multitude of orb-like bolts that are highly damaging (their Necromantic Gaze attack). They also have a Darkness Blast of energy that can stop you dead in your tracks. They use Void Shields, so switch to an Energy weapon of the same type, and finish them with sticky grenades or your favored weapon and shots to the head.

You should take a few shots from other nearby foes in order to end the Taken Wizard's life. Breaking off from combat causes the Taken Wizard's shield to recharge, lengthening this dangerous combat considerably. **After you've dispatched the Taken Wizard, remove the Phalanxes, Psions, and any other Taken foes in the immediate vicinity** (in the first "third" of this arena). Another option is to battle the Taken Wizard's minions first. There's some tactical advantage of removing the Phalanxes before they can damage you with their shield attack.

You should be focusing your firepower on each subsequent Taken Wizard as often as possible. Don't land near to the foe, and then start firing. Take aim at this foe from extreme range, causing damage as you close to remove it as quickly as possible.

A clockwise maneuver to the next Taken Wizard (who is floating among the rocky outcrops) is wise because it is closer than the final foe near the main road entrance. You can stand atop the rugged ledges and face few other hostiles, so with some nimble leaping, you can remove this threat with relative ease.

The last Taken Wizard in the large flat expanse near the road entrance is the most troublesome. Its contingent of Taken infantry can easily deplete your defenses, especially if you ignore cover and leap down from the platform. You may want to approach from the rock formation after slaying the previous Taken Wizard, since there are more cover opportunities and places to retreat to. The only reason to attack via the open road entrance is if you favor a Super or can quickly reach the cargo crates cover near the Taken Wizard.

It's worth **expending your Super to demolish the first Taken Wizard** you encounter. Focus on hammering it with your attack. If you're fast enough and your Super lasts long enough, continue it by quickly heading to the second Taken Wizard. Using your Super on the Taken infantry is wasting your powers. Remember, the **crackling and gradually expanding portal** in the sunken central part of the arena is perhaps **the worst place to stand.** The enemy has the height advantage, and even the available protection under the ramps is soon negated as you're overrun by Taken Psions or Taken Thralls. Only head here to open the chests; otherwise, stay to the perimeter.

5 Cabal Depot: Portal Assault Vortex Mind

Super: Recommended **Grenades:** Recommended

The portal continues to open. It expands and the entire arena is encased in a black dome, effectively trapping you just within the perimeter and severely impeding your ability to stay around the edges of this location. Rifts appear, depositing Taken Psions. Stand atop the ramp near the three stacked cylinders and initial platform, and drop them as they head your way. Back up onto the platform, using the crates as cover until you've dealt with most of these foes and the final Taken entity appears.

Boss: This **highly dangerous Taken Centurion** is perhaps the most difficult foe you've faced. It can **bombard you with a Projection Rifle** that can kill you in three or four shots. It fires **homing orbs of energy** that find and explode, usually killing or badly damaging you. **Additional Fallen Thralls and Psions** appear throughout the fight. If you aren't properly prepared, expect to die a good number of times when facing him!

First, the **Vortex Mind seems to stay mainly in the sunken central part of the arena**, which means you should remain as far away from the barrage of attacks he generates as possible. **Stay around the upper perimeter**, ideally on the platform. Use your Movement Mode to go across to the rock outcrop for a different view or if one of these two vantage points becomes choked with lesser foes.

Any lower location means you're likely to be overwhelmed, first by the **Vortex Mind** firepower, and then by Taken Psions and Taken Thralls swarming your location. The only time you should think about heading into closer range is if you're using a shotgun, a maneuver both dangerous and effective. Second, make a more vertical leap or step to the edge, and **bombard the Boss with your favored weaponry**. A low-recoil rifle is good. You need eyes in the side of your head to watch for foes outflanking you. Stand on the platform, and it's slightly easier because lesser enemies can only reach you via the ramp and path to your left. **Intersperse your gradual Boss wounding with quick rakes of attacks against Taken Psions and Taken Thralls** checking the ramp to see any heading your way.

Third, **deal with the Vortex Mind's homing orbs by shooting them** yourself, or stepping into cover so the orb hits that and not you. Shooting is the better tactical plan, as you can quickly switch back to blasting the Boss's head. Don't be overly impatient in this fight, which usually gets you killed. If this Taken deity decides to launch multiple homing orbs, shoot them from as far away as possible, then focus on his head.

When you remove a third and then two-thirds of the Boss's health, additional lesser foes are summoned, though the attack pattern remains similar. Feel free to **launch a grenade or Super as soon as they have recharged from your Taken Wizard battle.**

As you must continuously move to avoid death, weave around the perimeter, using the rocks and crates for cover and resisting the temptation to head into the middle of the arena. Stay away from the edges of ledges, or you may be easily demolished by this enemy's gunfire. And **remain calm; this behemoth takes a while to drop!**

Once you've defeated the **Vortex Mind**, the mission concludes.

Important Ally:

Asher Mir

"As for you, meddling Guardian? I've a few choice things to say to you!"

While many Guardians have encountered the Vex, Asher Mir is one of the few Light-bearers who could be said to fully understand them. A member of an obscure sect of Warlocks, the Gensym Scribes, Asher has spent his entire Guardian life attempting to understand these cybernetic beings. He's a (somewhat) friendly face on the edge of the solar system.

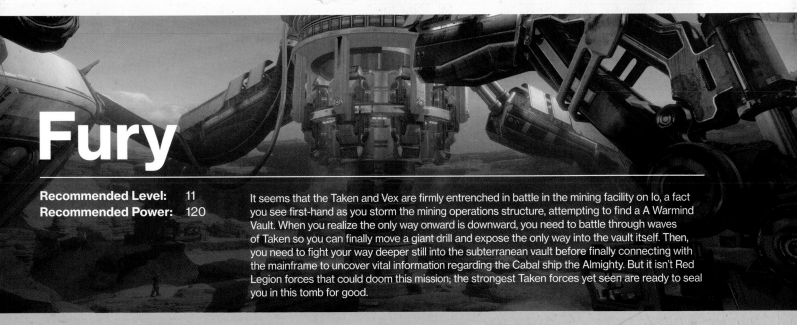

Fury

Recommended Level: 11
Recommended Power: 120

It seems that the Taken and Vex are firmly entrenched in battle in the mining facility on Io, a fact you see first-hand as you storm the mining operations structure, attempting to find a A Warmind Vault. When you realize the only way onward is downward, you need to battle through waves of Taken so you can finally move a giant drill and expose the only way into the vault itself. Then, you need to fight your way deeper still into the subterranean vault before finally connecting with the mainframe to uncover vital information regarding the Cabal ship the Almighty. But it isn't Red Legion forces that could doom this mission; the strongest Taken forces yet seen are ready to seal you in this tomb for good.

Giant's Scar

Restricted Zone

Enemies Encountered

TAKEN: Centurions, Psions
VEX: Goblins, Hobgoblins, Minotaurs

Objectives

Locate the Warmind Vault.

1 Mining Base

Super: Optional **Grenades:** Recommended

Make your way to the Sector known as Giant's Scar, where a small contingent of **Taken is battling Vex** guarding the base entrance. You can sit back and enjoy the carnage, or fight headlong into the warring Combatants. If you choose the latter, it's wise to stay along the bottom of the left perimeter rock cliff so you aren't overrun and can tactically choose the foes closest to you. Note that the Taken features a group of Psions led by a Taken Centurion. The Centurion has many of the attack patterns its Cabal counterpart uses.

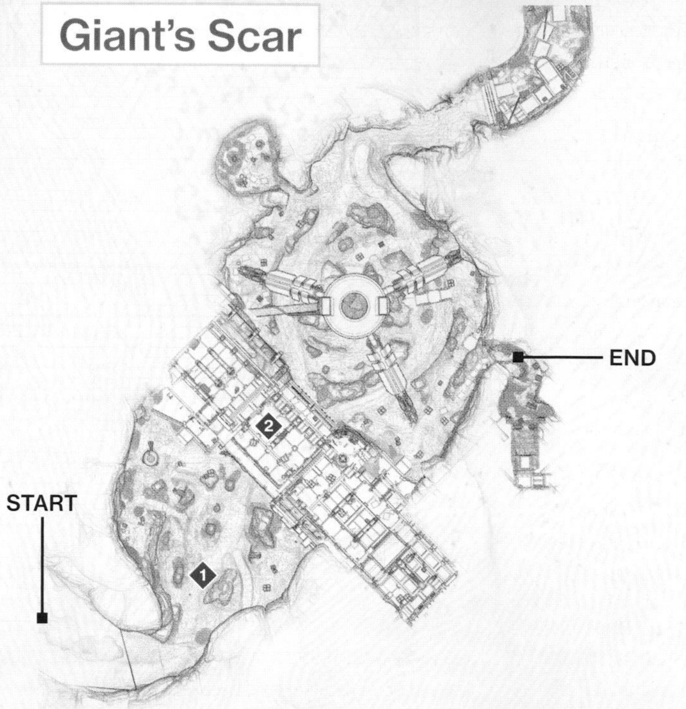

However, it uses an **Energy Shield** (usually Void), can teleport small distances, and prefers firing its homing orb, which you should shoot before it badly damages you. Or, find nearby cover and dart behind it so the orb hits the rocks and not your armor.

The Taken Psions are easier kills, after which you must be aware of two Vex foe clusters. There are Goblins and a Minotaur around the large cylindrical tower, and Goblins, a Minotaur, and a Hobgoblin on the entrance platform. Cover, a possible grenade lob, and lower torso shots are needed here. With the area devoid of foes, **head up the ramp and enter the base entrance**. Turn right once you're inside, head up an interior ramp, and go to a window overlooking a rather impressive mining drill.

2 Drill Site

Super: Recommended **Grenades:** Recommended
Warning!: Restricted Zone

Vex are teleporting to your location. Face two Minotaurs and a group of Goblins, lob in a grenade to start the fight, and switch to Void Energy weapons to remove Minotaur shields. Focus on the Minotaurs unless a Goblin is in your face (in which case, punch it twice). Feel free to back up or **use the upper windowed ramp area** to your left to gain the height advantage.

Push through the next large doorway into a storage chamber, where a Hobgoblin has taken up a camping spot ahead and left of you (above the sunken exit area). Kill him as the other Vex warp into view.

Then, **use the entrance doorway as cover**, and remove the advancing Goblins with ease. There are around 10 Goblins and two Minotaurs, and their close proximity to one another makes grenades, a grenade launcher, or your shotgun a good choice, along with normal Kinetic or Energy weapon fire.

With the Vex temporarily neutralized, check the upper ledges for a scannable object, then **inspect the orange-colored computer terminal**, powering it on. This unfortunately doesn't raise the drill, forcing you farther into the mining base. Head out of the exit (right and down of the terminal) and across the edge of the large exterior drill site, up to an arched entrance. Then, **head down into Excavation Site II**.

Scannable Globes of Darkness

Have you been checking the high storage ledges and other areas throughout this mining base for strange scannable objects? The place has a few black globes to check out. Don't worry, though; they're still here after you finish this mission, and it's easier to return here after the mission to complete your search for them (when you're not under fire).

Excavation Site II

Restricted Zone

Enemies Encountered

TAKEN: Centurions, Goblins, Phalanxes, Minotaurs, Wizards, Psions
VEX: Harpies, Hydra

Objectives

Locate the Warmind Vault (continued).

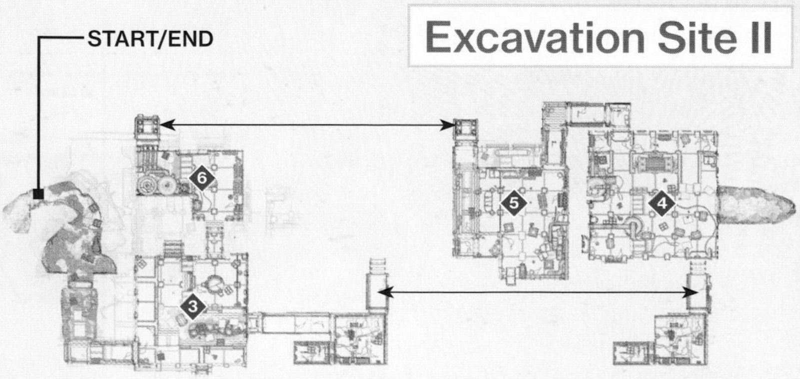

3 Storage Rooms

Super: Optional **Grenades:** Optional

Head down the rocky tunnel into the bunker, making your way **into a storage room** with a large black cylindrical tower in the far-left corner. Of greater interest is a small band of Taken—a Centurion and three Taken Goblins. These Goblins are much like their Vex counterparts but can warp small distances, meaning that constant readjusting in your aim is necessary. Also, you strike them in the head rather than the lower torso. **Use the metal fence sections as cover**, and drop them with regular gunfire. Save your best weaponry for future combat.

With the room secure, check it for a scannable object, then **depart via the orange ramped corridor** up to a warping Taken Phalanx. Drop it before it can bring out its shield. Then, head into the subsequent chamber.

Goblin up All the Energy

Taken Goblins have another trick: they can sometimes link to other Taken and provide them with enough sustenance to make their target invincible. If you see a greenish-turquoise glowing umbilical cord start to form from a Taken Goblin to another Taken target, remove the Goblin immediately. This becomes more and more important as this mission continues.

4 The **next storage chamber** has a few more Taken threats; a Centurion, two Phalanxes attacking from your left flank, and two Goblins on the slightly raised area across from an L-shaped thoroughfare. Drop the Goblins first if possible so they don't link to the other foes and give them energy. Then, use the copious cover to bring down the larger enemies one at a time. Put some distance or cover between you and the Phalanxes so their shield blast doesn't impede you. Note that **you return to this chamber** later into the mission.

5 Override Terminal Room

Super: Recommended **Grenades:** Recommended
Warning!: Restricted Zone

Wind your way up another orange tunnel and **into the terminal room**. Here, you must defeat any Taken hostiles before accessing the override terminal for the drill. **It's quite easy to die here.** The action begins when you spot something shimmering, the telltale sign of a **Taken Minotaur** in the vicinity. Deal with it quickly, then resist the temptation to panic as a couple of Phalanxes, then Taken Goblins and up to three more Taken Minotaurs, and four or five additional Phalanxes all arrive in two or three more waves. Now that you know the anticipated foes you'll face, it's time to do something about them.

Taken Minotaurs are slightly easier to tackle, assuming you can spot their shimmering invisible forms and blast them (in the central "eye head") while nimbly sidestepping their ferocious flame bolt projectile. Finish them with a melee strike if necessary.

Your close proximity to all foes in this chamber means shotguns are a good choice. Taken Minotaurs also like to teleport short distances, so quick reactions are key when pursuing and dropping them.

Taken Phalanxes are a bigger problem, as their shield is impenetrable when it's raised, and it only takes a second for them to fire a devastating energy bolt from it. It's a good idea to **keep moving, using the cover and making a "circle" maneuver around the perimeter of the room**. Leap up to the terminal console platform ahead and slightly left (as you enter this room) to gain a breather and fire down on the foes. Use the previous Taken Phalanx killing techniques (shooting the exposed areas their shield doesn't cover, or waiting until the shield has fired, stepping out of cover, and aiming at the head), and exercise patience. Rushing in usually gets you killed, unless you're launching your Super, which is also recommended when combat gets too crazy.

Taken Goblins are a real menace, **as they heal and make both Phalanxes and Minotaurs almost invulnerable**. Trace any "green glowing" enemies back to this foe, and blast them. Tackle Taken Goblins as soon as they warp in so they don't have chance to link to their tougher brethren.

Keep this plan up until the last of the Taken (usually a Minotaur) yields. You can then **leap to the ledge and access the wall terminal** to override the drill controls. Turn right, run along the narrow orange corridor, and drop down (with a second jump to slow your descent).

6 The Exit

Super: Optional **Grenades:** Recommended
Warning!: Restricted Zone

Enter a new storage area with a rock floor. Amid the orange light and blue energy windows of the scenery, there's **a Taken Wizard**.

It seems preoccupied with combat occurring in the next chamber, so seize this opportunity to rake it with **Void** energy bullets, and quickly drop it. A Phalanx just inside the next chamber can also be quickly removed. You soon discover the reason for these reasonably easy kills.

Enter the storage room with the L-shaped thoroughfare, and stumble into a **Taken Wizard and a group of Taken Psions battling a small flock of Vex Harpies and a Hydra**. Stay around the large black cylinder tower and watch the chaos, if you want. A better plan would be to quickly rid the room of the Taken Wizard, then move to the far raised perimeter area (where the room exit is). Use the metal fence as cover, shooting the Harpies and Taken Psions as these threats present themselves. Keep one or two enemies from each side alive as long as possible so the Hydra concentrates on killing them instead of you.

Remove threats until only one Taken Psion and the Hydra remain, then tackle the Hydra, **using the metal fencing as cover.** Expect another four Taken Psions to arrive shortly before or after you kill the Hydra; these shouldn't present a problem, given the cover available in this room. With threats dealt with, head **back up to the drill site on the surface**.

Giant's Scar

Io

Objectives
Locate the Warmind Vault (continued).
Use the Warmind network to scan the Almighty.

Enemies Encountered
VEX: Goblins, Hobgoblins, Minotaurs
TAKEN: Wizards, Psions, Phalanxes, Centurions

Giant's Scar

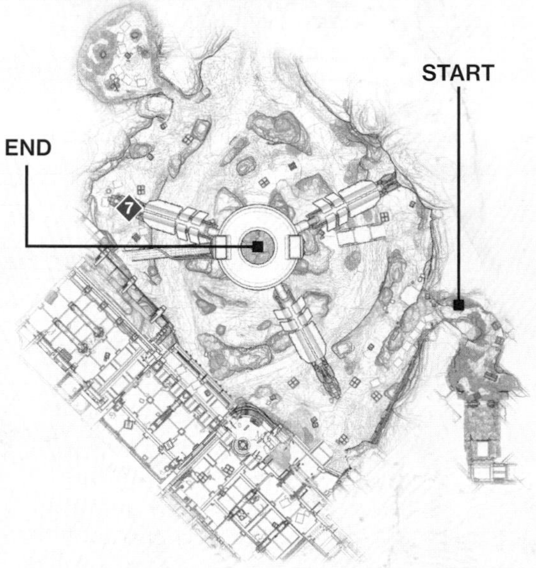

7 Return to the Drill Site

Super: Optional **Grenades:** Optional

The drill is now active! Unfortunately, so are the Vex, and incoming groups of Goblins and Minotaurs are teleporting onto the surface of the drill site. If you want to waylay your progress considerably, feel free to engage them. A better plan is to **locate the drill control cabin**, which is on the opposite side of the drill site arena as you emerge from the bunker, and jump across to it. Here, you're greeted by a couple of Vex Hobgoblins and a Minotaur; nothing you can't handle. Remove these immediate threats, then **access the drill control terminal and lift the drill**.

By now, expect around 12 or more Vex Goblins and a Minotaur or two to congregate on the dirt road below the cabin. You can remove or ignore them, but it's better to run. Taken hordes are also starting to arrive, and **the battle becomes prolonged and unnecessary if you stay here**. Avoid the Taken Wizards, Taken Psions, Taken Phalanxes, and Taken Centurions, and head to the central hole where the massive drill was raised from. **Stop at the edge, and jump to the upper side tunnel with the metal surrounding it.** Dropping straight down or to a lower tunnel results in death.

Warmind Vault JYS-2

Io

Objectives
Use the Warmind network to scan the Almighty (continued).

Enemies Encountered
TAKEN: Hobgoblins, Goblins, Minotaurs, Psions, Phalanxes
TAKEN SUB-BOSS: Modular Sigma
TAKEN BOSS: Modular Upsilon

8 Vault Infiltration

Super: Optional **Grenades:** Optional

Maneuver up the narrow tunnel and **into the initial vault chamber**. As expected, the area is teeming with Taken. Expect three Taken Hobgoblins and a Taken Goblin to attack as you enter. The former foes have some nasty beam weaponry to dodge, and the latter can link to the Hobgoblins, giving them near-invulnerability.

Also, note the slight red glow to the Hobgoblins when shooting them. They have a minor shields, so adjust your offensive ordnance accordingly. Taken Hobgoblins can teleport short distances but aren't the hardiest of foes. Use headshots and melee strikes to finish them if you're close enough.

Head up the steps, and drop a Taken Goblin and Minotaur halfway up. Then, remove the Taken Goblin linking to two final Hobgoblins as you **reach the mainframe core chamber**. With no further Taken activity, **head down to the sunken center of the chamber, access the mainframe**, and then prepare for the fight of your life!

Warmind Vault JYS-2

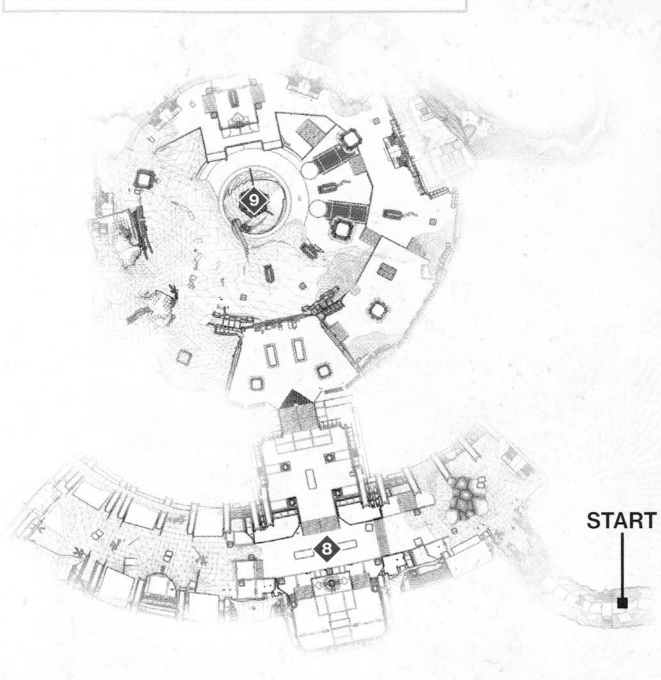

Preplan of Attack

It's worth making a thorough sweep of the mainframe chamber before you access the computer itself, prior to the forthcoming Taken battle. Learn where the small sunken tunnel is, the cover opportunities around the perimeter, the dead end of the sand pile and the lack of cover near it, and other minor cover opportunities like pillars.

9 Mainframe: Modular Upsilon Battle

Super: Recommended **Grenades:** Recommended
Warning!: Restricted Zone

Boss: A giant Taken, seemingly a giant Vex Minotaur now possessed by this parasitic foe, steps out of a rift. This is the **Modular Upsilon, and it is extremely dangerous**. It fires **highly damaging flaming bolts** in rapid succession, and three of these hitting you directly will likely kill you. If you're not behind cover, sidestep or leap away from them. Close the gap, and expect **a foot stomp** that's not only damaging but launches you backward, sometimes across the entire arena. Melee combat is tricky because of the firepower that Modular Upsilon wields, as well as its foot stomping. **It can also turn more-or-less invisible (like a Taken Minotaur)**, so track the slight glow of its "eye" and focus your firepower on that. Target its general body if you can't track its eye because of other foes or your position. Finally, **it receives invincibility from a Sub-Boss, the Modular Sigma**, so refrain from wasting your ammunition any time this behemoth glows a greenish-turquoise.

Sub-Boss: Modular Sigma is a Taken Goblin with more health and a determination to keep its huge brethren invincible for as long as possible. **This is your priority target.**

Although it fires a Projection Rifle, that's the least of your worries, since it spends most of its time moving to within 20 feet of Modular Upsilon and sending out snakes of energy.

Hit Modular Sigma in the head so it is temporarily destroyed, then make the most of the time it's gone by hitting Modular Upsilon in the "eye." **When Modular Sigma returns** (and it will; it only dies when Modular Upsilon is defeated), **destroy it as soon as possible.**

Then there's the small matter of the Taken Phalanxes, Centurions, and Hobgoblins that arrive to help protect Modular Sigma. These are infuriating to deal with, so **exercise extreme patience and care**, especially when facing the Phalanxes and their shield attack or the Centurion's homing orb. These foes appear consistently throughout the battle. Leave them, and you'll end up trying to force your way through four or five Phalanxes to reach Modular Sigma, with little or no cover. **Don't ignore the regular Taken infantry**, if only because they're your only source of ammo.

There are ways to minimize the hardship of this battle. Firstly (and most importantly), **know that Modular Sigma only gives Modular Upsilon immunity**; it isn't healed by this green energy link. This means that **any damage you inflict on Modular Upsilon is permanent**. With this knowledge, prepare a war of attrition. As each wave of foes appears to aid Modular Upsilon, attempt the following: **Remove all Taken Phalanxes, Centurions, and Hobgoblins in the vicinity**. **Defeat Modular Sigma. Then, remove as much of Modular Upsilon's health as your weaponry allows**; shoot its eye or its body, if you can't aim at the eye.

Use the upper perimeter, lower tunnel, and central mainframe pillar as cover. However, the location of Modular Sigma's appearance may cause you to venture into the sand slope. Try to find the dark alocve on the sandy hill to the left of where you entered this chamber. Few enemies can threaten you there, and you can more easily inflict damage on both bosses.

Grenade launcher, sniper rifle, and shotgun attacks are all advisable if you need to inflict damage quickly. Sniper fire is good if you can get a target at long range on both Bosses. Check your bullet count, and switch if you're dangerously low on bullets for one of your main weapons (Kinetic or Energy). **As the battle progresses, each time Modular Upsilon loses a third of its health, the link it establishes with Modular Sigma becomes longer**. This is actually helpful because you can more easily tackle Modular Sigma without incurring the wrath and firepower of Modular Upsilon.

Grenades are best used just as Modular Sigma and his Phalanx friends appear from a rift; damage as many as you can. Use your Super just after removing Modular Sigma so all your damage is inflicted on Modular Upsilon without it becoming immune. If this happens during a Super, immediately find and destroy Modular Sigma and other Taken infantry.

This is a ferocious and long-lasting battle. Patience is almost as vital as good weapon choices and deft maneuvering. When Modular Upsilon finally falls, the mission concludes.

Payback

Recommended Level: 15
Recommended Power: 160

You need to hitch a ride to the Almighty, and the start of this impressively foolhardy plan begins in the Tunnels of the EDZ. You must reach the Cabal's shipyards, where its main carrier is moored. You accomplish this by driving a Drake tank through the giant tunnel complex the Cabal have dug, delivering payloads of pain to a variety of Cabal infantry and vehicles before appearing outside at the base of a gigantic carrier craft. This must be crippled to lessen the possibility of a large Cabal presence following you in future missions, so perfect your tank driving skills. Complete these tasks with skillful precision rather than the chaotic manhandling of the Vanguard vehicle.

The Tunnels

European Dead Zone

Enemies Encountered

CABAL: Psions, Phalanxes, Legionaries, Centurions, Interceptors, Interceptor Pilots, Thresher, Incendiors, Goliath Tank, War Beasts

Objectives

Enter the Cabal base and hunt down the Viper.
Advance to the Cabal carrier located in their shipyards.

New Actions to Learn

Drake Tank Driving: General Maneuvers
Drake Tank Driving: Offensive Capabilities
Drake Tank Driving: Locking on to Targets
Drake Tank Driving: Locking on to Missiles
Drake Tank Driving: Zooming in on Targets

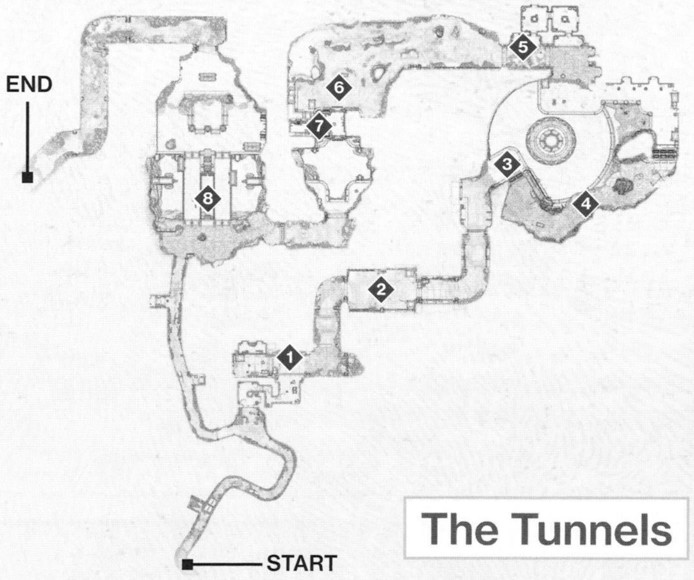

1 Cabal Tunnels to Tank Acquisition

Super: Optional **Grenades:** Optional

You begin in the Gulch (EDZ), entering a large tunnel structure carved out of the hillside by the Red Legion forces. Continue down the tunnel until you see an opening to your right; it's **a rocky cavern** with a small Cabal chamber, guarded by two Psions and a Phalanx.

Two Legionaries also appear. Make short work of this infantry, throwing your Super or grenade into the combat if you want (since you're about to drive a tank, you can afford to use up these powers). Otherwise, use the rocks as cover.

Watch for another Phalanx in the **connecting chamber to a massive tunnel structure**. It's so massive, in fact, that Amanda Holliday's ship arrives and deposits **a Drake tank**. You are firmly encouraged to enter and drive this vehicle for the remainder of this mission.

Tanks a Lot!

The Drake tank is a formidable piece of battle hardware, and it's well-suited to rampaging through this huge Cabal base. However, it isn't invincible. It's worth reading the Field Manual chapter to perfect your maneuvers, missile and cannon firing, and ramming techniques, and to learn about the shortfalls of this vehicle.

No Tank You: on Foot

Can you ignore the Drake tank and attempt the Cabal underground base assault on foot? Sure. Is it possible? Eventually. Is it advisable? Definitely not.

No Tank You: Interceptor

Can you utilize a Cabal Interceptor and maneuver through the base using this vehicle instead? Sure. Is it better than the tank? Nope. It has far less firepower, meaning you'll be leaping from its burning carcass and fighting off foes on foot before you know it.

2 Tunnels of Terror

Super: Not recommended

Grenades: Not recommended

Start up the tank, learning the basic maneuvers (the independent turret, the missile launcher and main turret cannons, locking on to enemies, and zooming in on targets) before trundling into the tunnel. As you go, make sure you observe and react to the following:

Main cannon: This fires a single shell that explodes with a wide area of effect. **Use this on clusters of foes, hardened targets like vehicles or more impressive enemies (like Centurions), scenery you want to destroy, and enemy vehicles you encounter**. The damage is impressive, but the firing is slow. For accurate attacks, fire when the target reticle turns red.

Missile launcher: You can fire a cluster of up to seven missiles. These have the advantage of swerving around cover to strike foes and are also **great for removing clusters of infantry**. The main reason to use missiles is to hold down the firing button so your **missiles lock on to a target**, usually guaranteeing a strike.

This is especially useful if your target moves quickly, like an enemy Interceptor or Thresher vehicle. **The missiles can also lock on to incoming missiles (usually from Threshers)**, negating the enemy's most devastating attack. Use this lock-on feature, or face a fiery tank that you must extricate yourself from. Finally, note that the blue circles under the tank icon (in the bottom-left part of your HUD) indicate the number of missiles that are ready to fire.

Cabal infantry: They prove no match for your vehicle; shoot them, run them over, or ignore them and continue along the tunnel structure.

Cabal barricades: You can run over these shield-like barricades without damaging your tank. Sometimes, enemies hide behind them; shoot at the barricades or ignore them as you continue forward.

Explosive barrels: Dotted about some corridors are yellow explosive barrels, which very lightly damage your tank if you run them over. This isn't something to worry about unnecessarily, and you can shoot these barrels from a distance; any foes caught by the blast are damaged.

However, your tank weaponry is much more potent than barrel explosions!

Roof artillery shells: You can aim your cannon or missiles at the trios of Cabal shells stacked on the roof, dropping them on foes underneath, if you want.

Begin your progress through the tunnels, continuously blasting anything vaguely related to the Cabal. Lay waste as the tunnel widens then narrows as you encounter your first Cabal Interceptor. Aim for the Interceptor Pilot to quickly stop the vehicle; the Psion driving the vehicle is a lot less tough than the Interceptor itself.

3 Cabal Cavern Climb

Super: Not recommended

Grenades: Not recommended

When you reach the first **tank summoning point**, before the tunnel opens up into a gigantic cavern, get out of the vehicle (without blocking the road) and summon a new Drake tank if the first one has taken any damage. There's no need to continue on with a damaged tank! Then, slow down as a Cabal Thresher hovers into view. It begins launching missiles, which you need to lock on to before releasing your own missile barrage to negate this attack. At the same time, use your main cannon to blast the Thresher into fiery pieces. You can also target the Psions on the far platform, blasting them with missiles so they don't snipe you, though the damage inflicted is minimal.

Time for a New Tank

Is your tank on fire? Then back up, get out before it explodes with you in it, and retreat to the previous tank-summoning circle, starting your assault of this area again. This is better than the suicidal plan of pressing forward on foot or in an Interceptor.

4 Swing right, mowing down a squad of Phalanxes with ease, rounding the corner, then backing up as a Thresher and Interceptor attack simultaneously. Lock on to the Thresher's missiles and neutralize them while you aim at the Interceptor Pilot, blasting that Psion and stopping the ground vehicle. Then, aim all your firepower at the Thresher.

Head around the gigantic natural rock pillar, firing at Centurions, Phalanxes, and another Interceptor as you go, and any Psions you see on the platforms away from the road you're on. **Pass (or use) another tank summoning point**. Head up the slope, training all weapons on the infantry cluster to the left. Turn left, staying at the far end of the road ledge as it narrows so you can easily and methodically destroy the Thresher, a couple of Centurions, and other ground forces. Then, head around, sharply turning right and delivering overwhelming firepower at an Interceptor and a few more Cabal infantry. **Park at the next tank summoning point**, but not before you remove the Cabal Centurion standing just inside the horizontal opening that leads to the door override.

5 Door Override

Super: Recommended **Grenades:** Recommended

Get out of your tank only after you've waited until no additional enemies are in the connecting chamber between you and the door override. **Remember that you can always return to the tank** and lay waste to other enemies you find inside, though it's easier to tackle the couple of Legionaries in the usual manner. **Head into the roughly cube-shaped chamber**, and turn left. The door lights turn to green, and it opens. Expect two Phalanxes to face inside a second identically sized chamber, along with two Psions and an Incendior you can explode easily.

Once in the second room, turn left and walk to the open door of a third room that a Centurion guards. Drop a grenade, rake his Solar Shield, and drop him. Using your Super just as you attack the Phalanxes (so it runs out after the Centurion is defeated) is a good idea. **Then, dash out to the giant blast door and the hologram unlock area**, using Ghost to open the tunnel door. Head back to your tank or the nearest tank summoning point, and proceed through this door.

6 An Enemy Tank

Super: Not recommended
Grenades: Not recommended
Warning!: Restricted Zone

You're entering a Restricted Zone, and there's an enemy tank at the end of the rocky tunnel you're trundling through. **Exercise more caution** than you may have attempted up to this point. Slow down, and drop roof shells on the two Psions standing on the low ridge ahead and left of you (or just blast them). Back up and tackle the two Interceptors before you reach the corner of the tunnel. Trundle forward, aiming at the two Centurions along the outer (right side) corner, staying to the right as you spot an enemy Goliath tank. Two more Interceptors flank it!

Sub-Boss: The odds are no longer in your favor; **you cannot stand and go toe-to-toe with the Goliath**, exchanging missile and cannon barrages, as it is tougher than your Drake tank. You can't stop and start or head across the uneven ground because getting stuck means you're a sitting target.

If your tank catches fire, retreat, optionally getting into one of the Interceptors you're previous fought, and head back to the tank summoning point to start again. Do not attempt to head forward on foot because you're easily overwhelmed, and the enemy tank must be defeated, too.

Instead, **retreat back along the tunnel** before the two natural pillars, and clear the area of Interceptors if they are close by. Trundle forward and inflict a massive barrage of well-aimed tank fire into the enemy tank. **Stop so its return fire hits one of the pillars** (hide behind one of them), then reverse back out of the enemy tank's range. Do this two or three more times, and you'll destroy it. Then, head back to the blast door, summon a brand-new tank, and **drive it toward a retracted bridge**, destroying the Cabal infantry guarding the entrance to the control room on the right side of it.

7 Bridge Control Room

Super: Recommended **Grenades:** Recommended

Use your Drake tank or an Interceptor to clear the dirt ground to the right of the retracted bridge of Cabal Phalanxes and other infantry. **Bound up the control room ramp on foot**, and make short work of the three Legionaries and a Psion behind you. Clear this room first before venturing into the subsequent room via the green-lit door; **inside the second upper chamber is a pack of War Beasts and a meaty-looking Cabal Centurion.**

The Centurion fires its weapon with alarming regularity, and two hits from this can kill you. It also has backpack rockets but usually doesn't employ them in these close quarters. Stay at the entrance door or the central cover block, and lob in a grenade before following up with precision headshots. A grenade launcher is also an option. Better yet, save your Super and easily drop this behemoth! Otherwise, tag the Centurion with sidestepping and accurate headshots without being struck. This foe guards the bridge controls; **activate the bridge,** and quickly return to the tank.

8 Battle of Bridge Cavern

Super: Not recommended
Grenades: Not recommended
Warning!: Restricted Zone

Drive across the bridge; you may want to lock on to the Psions behind cover on the opposite side, and train your main cannon on an incoming Interceptor. Run over the War Beasts, and don't spend time making precision maneuvers on the bridge because you can easily drive off to your doom. Instead, cross to the tunnel entrance, up through a connecting tunnel with a tank summoning point, and **into a huge cavern with two parallel bridges**, one of which you must cross to the other side.

Start by mauling the Cabal Infantry (an Interceptor, Phalanxes, Centurions, and a Centurion) on the near side of the bridge, as well as Psions and Centurions on the far yellow platforms. This keeps you from getting annoyed by other enemies as you attack the real menace guarding this cavern: two enemy tanks.

Sub-Bosses: Two Goliath tanks are parked on the opposite side of the bridge to you. Trundling over the bridge to meet them is exceedingly unwise, as they can easily overwhelm your tank with their fire. Instead, **slow down and hide behind the initial large rock and the rock pillar on the entrance side of the cavern**. Use this scenery to protect you. Then, edge out, zoom in on either of the tanks, lock on to any incoming missiles (from either tank), and let rip with your main cannon. Trundle to one of the two cover points previously mentioned. **Move between these points, concentrating on one tank at a time**, until you neutralize the first and then the second enemy tank. The rock pillar between the entrances of both bridges is particularly good to hide behind (letting the enemy's attacks hit it), but you must keep moving.Another option is to **slowly creep out from the entrance** until you can target the tank on the right side of the far part of the cavern, and concentrate your firepower solely on it. As long as you don't drive past the rocks you're using as cover, you can peep in and out of the entrance, avoiding the first tank's barrage. Then, move to the pillar and assault the other tank on the far-left side of the cavern.

You may need to **remove an Interceptor or two on the opposite side of the bridge**; do this by zooming in before firing to ensure accuracy.

With both tanks defeated, make short work of a Thresher that flies in before crossing either of the bridges. One of the tanks may have retreated to the exit area, but that's no matter. You can use either of the exit ramps as cover (so the Goliath's main cannon hits the top of the ramp, and not you) and lay waste to the second tank. Mop up a few infantry stragglers, then **head out of the tunnels** and into the EDZ Sector known as the Sunken Isles.

Ramming Speed

Another option is to forgo all this "combat" and "tactics" and simply speed into the cavern, over one of the bridges, up an exit ramp, and leave. Sure, you'll be bombarded with enemy fire from the Cabal infantry and tanks, but with some fast driving and a total disregard for your own safety, you can swerve past either tank and out of the tunnel. However, you may need to leave your burning tank and flee to the exit on foot. Enemies won't chase you into the main carrier landing bay.

Sunken Isles

European Dead Zone

Objectives

Disable the carrier's shield.
Destroy Cabal defenses.

Enemies Encountered

CABAL: Psions, Phalanxes, Legionaries, Centurions, Interceptors, Interceptor Pilots, Thresher, Incendiors, Goliath Tank

9 Generator Destruction: First Location

Super: Not recommended
Grenades: Not recommended

Although you can tackle them in either order, it's easier and safer to approach the one to the right of the giant Cabal carrier ship if you're looking at its exhaust pipes, **close to the lake**. Head down the side road slowly so you can destroy two Interceptors with long-range cannon shots without alerting the entire base.

Sunken Isles

Drive over the sharp "lip" of earth to the exposed core of the generator, which is being guarded by Cabal infantry and a Centurion. Destroy the Centurion, then simply **fire your cannon two or three times into the spinning core on the exposed side** until it explodes, and your objective updates. Engaging the enemy is optional; you're here to cleanly sweep through the main defenses, not get bogged down shooting every single Legionary (though that's also possible).

10 Generator Destruction: Second Location

Super: Not recommended
Grenades: Not recommended

Retrace your tracks to the main perimeter road, turn right, and work your way around to the high ground slightly above the second generator, and deliver punishment to an Interceptor. This route is preferred over the shorter, rough terrain or the tunnel below the carrier bay, as you're not as easily surrounded and you have a height advantage. Carry on past the main base doors (on your left), and launch missiles and cannon fire at the infantry ahead of you (Psions, Legionaries, and Centurions are likely targets).

Swing around and into the flat ground area by the generator, staying on the move as you tackle a Centurion and stop a Thresher from firing its missiles into your tank (use your locked-on missiles). Make short work of a second Interceptor, then aim two cannon blasts into the spinning core.

Boss: Your final act is to remove the Cabal defenses. This takes the form of **another three or four Interceptors and a Goliath tank**. Blast the closest enemies first, and then use the tunnel below the carrier bay as cover. This is a good place to hide and fire long-range shots at the Goliath as you move into cover, and you can easily access a new tank from the summoning point. Or, you can make a clockwise loop through the tunnel and out and around to the perimeter. Encroach on the tank's location (the road just above the second generator) using the same path as before and the large rock outcrops to retreat to. Just be sure you drive to a tank summoning point if your tank starts to catch fire!

Another trick is to drive up to the Goliath tank's location, and **circle the large boulder while bombarding the enemy tank** with missiles and cannon fire. It usually can't turn and strike you as quickly, leading to a quick dispatch.

Time to ground the carrier. Move to the perimeter road, and **look up at the carrier's gigantic exhaust ports**. Aim all you've got at the lower center of the ports until the craft is crippled. Remove any remaining vehicular threats to conclude the mission.

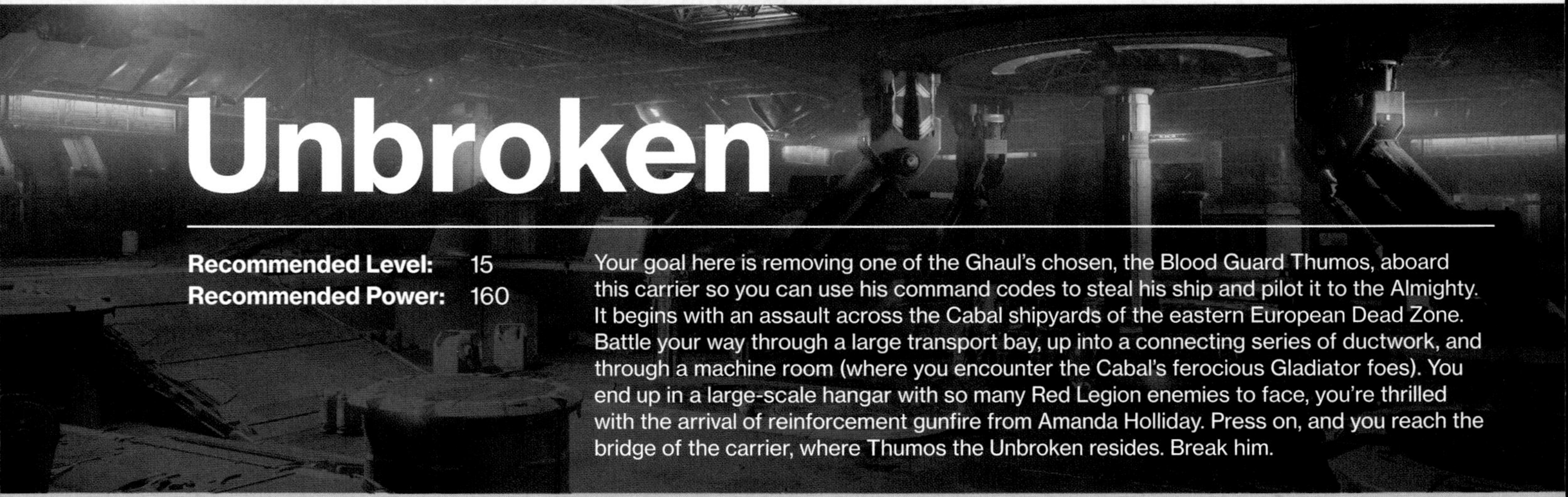

Unbroken

Recommended Level: 15
Recommended Power: 160

Your goal here is removing one of the Ghaul's chosen, the Blood Guard Thumos, aboard this carrier so you can use his command codes to steal his ship and pilot it to the Almighty. It begins with an assault across the Cabal shipyards of the eastern European Dead Zone. Battle your way through a large transport bay, up into a connecting series of ductwork, and through a machine room (where you encounter the Cabal's ferocious Gladiator foes). You end up in a large-scale hangar with so many Red Legion enemies to face, you're thrilled with the arrival of reinforcement gunfire from Amanda Holliday. Press on, and you reach the bridge of the carrier, where Thumos the Unbroken resides. Break him.

Legion's Hold

European Dead Zone

Objectives

Board the carrier.
Find a console.
Head into Legion's Watch

Enemies Encountered

CABAL: Psions, Phalanxes, Legionaries, Beasts, Centurion

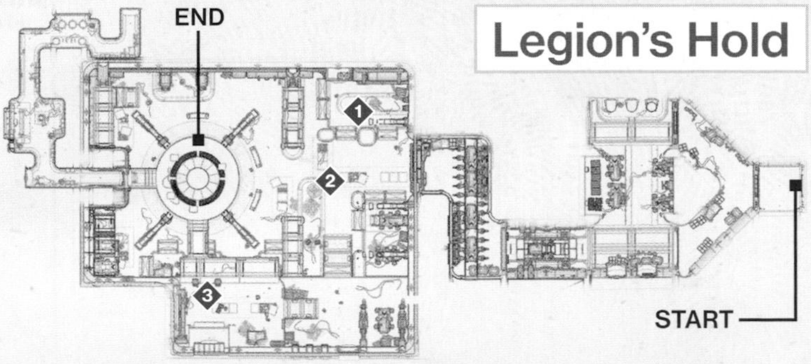

1 Hangar Assault

Super: Optional **Grenades:** Optional

Enter the giant hangar, where you're immediately on the defensive due to the large number of Cabal forces to face. Instead of rushing in and dying, **remain at the huge entrance** to the hangar, and drop the Psions and Phalanxes from range. Or, if you have closer-range assault weaponry, use the scenery along the right side of the main hangar road or the low cylindrical storage vat on the inner corner where the Psions first congregate as cover. Legionaries soon join these foes milling around near the storage vat.

Take Cover or Die

A squad of Phalanxes is on the upper ramp, and Psions with their beam rifles are at the ready on the gantry platform to the right of the ramp. Coupled with the enemies closest to you by the cylindrical storage vat, these foes can kill you in seconds if you're foolish enough to remain in the open. Take cover and focus on the closest foes first.

Make the Phalanxes your first targets because their shields can allow other enemies to use them as cover. **Then, drop the Psions, and finally, the Legionaries.** Remain in cover as the Cabal release a pack of War Beasts that bound down the ramp. Assuming you're hidden behind cover at the opposite end of the hangar, you can step back a little, and drop these foes at distance. If any reach you, attack them while shielding yourself from the Psions and Phalanxes on the upper ground by using cover.

2 There's no rush to push forward, so stay behind cover until you've neutralized all nearby ground-level foes (including all War Beasts).

You can then choose whether to attack the Phalanxes atop the ramp, or the Psions atop the gantry platform.

The latter is the best pick; the **Psions have long-range weaponry, so neutralizing them is safer**. Sidestep to the cylinder with the blue metal mechanism surrounding it (ground level), using it as cover and sniping at the Psions. Or, jump onto the gantry and assault the Psions at close range. (Warlocks may need to land on some higher scenery to complete the maneuver.)

If you're landing on the gantry, use the metal barricade fencing on your left as cover, lobbing in a grenade to soften up the Psions and Phalanxes. Then, lay waste to both sets of foes as you advance onto the top of the ramped area. Alternately, you can skulk up the left side of the hangar (along the same side wall as the entrance), **taking up cover on and around a parked tank** (unfortunately inaccessible) **in the corner**. Then, you can remove the Phalanxes and Psions from this direction. You have more cover opportunities from this angle, though you must cross the open platform atop the ramp, leaving you more exposed.

3 **Head up the shorter ramp to the upper platform,** where a few Legionaries, Psions, another pack of War Beasts, and a Centurion all must perish. This is a good time for a grenade or a Super (preferably the latter), focusing your rage on the Centurion. Or, shoot as many foes as you can before the War Beasts reach you, then back up and tag these four-legged fiends. Push up, use the good cover opportunities, and bring the remaining Cabal forces to their knees.

After that, **approach the right console** so Ghost can access the schematics, and the objective updates. **A large circular platform descends** across a short bridge. Jump across the platform and up into a high door leading to a connecting passage.

Legion's Watch

European Dead Zone

Objectives

Head into Legion's Watch

Take Thumos' command codes.

Kill Thumos.

Enemies Encountered

CABAL:	Legionaries, War Beasts, Gladiators, Psions
CABAL SUB-BOSS:	Blood Guard (Incendior), Blood Guard (Legionary), Blood Guard (Centurion)
CABAL BOSS:	Thumos the Unbroken
CABAL SUB-BOSS:	Blood Guard (Legionary Commander)

4 Machine Room Assault

Super: Optional **Grenades:** Optional

Follow the winding docking passageway up to an open door, behind which is a Legionary and three War Beasts. Quickly react to deal with this threat (backing up and firing).

Legion's Watch

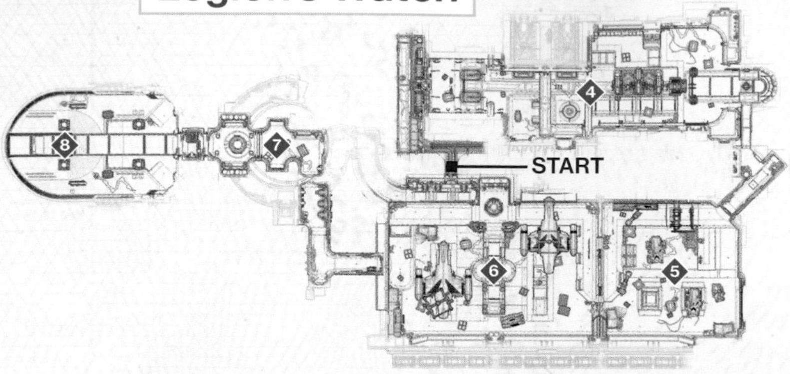

Then, look up and left, shooting out a ventilation grating before jumping up into a conduit.

Head up and left, landing on a large pipe and continuing through the conduit until you can shoot (or punch) out another grating, this time on your right side. Drop down to a Cabal bay teeming with foes, including a couple of deadly **Gladiators**.

Beware of Gladiatorial Combat

Gladiators are a ferocious, close-combat menace armed with a pair of Severus cleavers. They can use jump-jets like Legionaries, have a charge and doggedly track and leap at you, and have dense armor plates to help shrug off enemy fire. They are as fast as they are dangerous. Tackle them at range, as your close-combat capabilities are no match for them. A shotgun to the face is a good way to drop a Gladiator at melee range, but little else works. Your own melee attacks aren't that damaging, and you can be easily cut down while trying this out. You can find higher ground, sprint and weave behind cover, and backpedal while executing headshots, but a Gladiator is always a priority target, and an extremely deadly one.

Shoot the two Gladiators in the head immediately. Drop one before either reaches you, then flee the vicinity. Either go around the machinery to either of the perimeter edges of the room, or jump and land atop the smaller machinery scenery below the open grating you dropped through. You could jump back through the grating and attack from above, too. **Standing and fighting gets you killed.** A Super can save you here.

With the Gladiators defeated, head between the machinery, ideally along the right side so you can stay in partial cover and tag the Psions on the floor and gantry platform ahead of you. **Expect around six Psions and four Legionaries**; if the Psions retreat, shoot them in their jetpacks.

Edge farther into the bay, looking for the Phalanxes and Legionaries to the right of the pistons on the ground floor. Drop the two Phalanxes from range, then the two Legionaries. Don't venture too far forward too quickly: the far end of the room has a Sub-Boss, and two corner alcoves above you may be hiding a Psion that can snipe you easily.

Clear the alcoves by jumping and demolishing the Psions there, or lob up a grenade (or fire a grenade launcher, or use long-range weaponry). Then, land in the dead-end far area, dealing with additional Psions, a few Legionaries, and a named Sub-Boss—one of the fabled Blood Guards!

Sub-Boss: This foe is a large **Incendior with a tough Void Shield**. In all other respects, treat him the same as the Sub-Boss you faced back when you were infiltrating the command ship back on Earth (Mission 1; Pashk the Searing Will). Make the Sub-Boss a **priority target**. With the shield removed, shoot his head or fuel tanks. You can face him at close range, sidestepping his flamethrower and using the central pillar at the back of the chamber as cover. Alternately, you can fire on his minions from either of the upper side alcoves. Or, you can retreat back to the pistons, deal with Legionaries and Psions one or two at a time, then jump back and engage the Sub-Boss.

5 Docking Bay Assault: Hangar 1

Super: Recommended **Grenades:** Recommended

After the Sub-Boss falls, **leap to the small ledge** above where you fought him, head up the narrow corridor ramp. Break open a grating, and maneuver through a door and into the main cargo bay for the Cabal in the EDZ. You have incoming heavy firepower in the shape of **Amanda Holliday's ship**, which provides additional takedowns, as there's a small army of foes to face. **You must head through two docking bay hangars**. Begin by dropping the Psion and two Legionaries at the platform console, then look left and down, blasting Cabal Psions and Legionaries on the bay floor below. The three Psions are particularly important to dispatch. Stay on the near side of the bay and drop them, firing at any that try to flee with their jetpacks active. Fail to stop the Psions, and they hide and whittle away at your energy as you progress to tackle tougher enemies.

Sub-Bosses: Remain on the near ramp, and remove additional Psion and Legionary threats (around three Psions and a couple of Legionaries). The reason not to rush through this hangar becomes apparent as you reach the bay **door with the hologram lock**. Before using Ghost to hack it, you need to face down **two Sub-Boss Legionaries**. These Blood Guard foes act similarly to Kreth the Living Skyfire (back in Mission 1); they usually have **Arc Shields** and tougher armor than regular Legionaries. Concentrate on one Sub-Boss at a time. Use your Super, if you must.

Taking a Breather

Before continuing to the second hangar, you may want to wait for your Super and other abilities to recharge before accessing the door hologram. Switch to an appropriate Energy weapon, too; there's another Sub-Boss and more mayhem to come.

6 Docking Bay Assault: Hangar 2

Super: Recommended **Grenades:** Recommended

Sub-Boss: As soon as you open the door, there's a **Sub-Boss Centurion to worry about**. He has a Solar Shield, so concentrate on him while Holliday drops by to soften up the majority of the targets in the second hangar. You can remain low down on the ramp back in the first hangar so enemy fire can't strike you, then head up and defeat four Psions on the initial platform area. **Progress into the second hangar**, and use the platform barriers as cover, raining death down on various Cabal infantry (Psions, Legionaries, and Phalanxes) as Holliday helps with some barrages of her own. Stay on the initial platform so you can methodically deal with foes as you see them, from closest to farthest. If you rush into the hangar, the Sub-Boss at the far end will waylay you. Having to deal with him and the other infantry you've ignored makes the fight more difficult.

Slowly work your way right along the raised platform to the upper gantry that spans the middle of the hangar. The foes congregate under and around the gantry. Once you've dispatched the Psions guarding it, firing out and down from the alcove along the right wall (with the circular metal center and consoles along the perimeter) is helpful. Always remember to defeat Phalanxes, the Psions, then Legionaries whenever possible, due to the deescalating threats they pose.

Sub-Boss: A named **Blood Guard Legionary** (usually with Arc Shields), just like the two jokers you encountered previously, guards the far end of the second hangar. With Holliday's barrages dropping his lesser Legionary brethren, you can cut down his shield. Then, shoot his head or jetpack, using the ramp, the top of the parked Thresher, and crates as cover.

7 Bridging Corridors

Super: Not recommended

Grenades: Not recommended

Sub-Boss: Head up the interior ramp from the hangar exit, turning right and melee striking, then firing at around four Psions and a Legionary in the corridor ahead. Step through a narrower door, turning left into an insulated corridor, but don't sprint in here. Stay behind cover at the corner and remove the Psions and Legionary threats. The reason is yet another Sub-Boss, a **Blood Guard Centurion** with a Solar Shield. Fortunately, you have a circular central section of this corridor to maneuver around and use as cover as you avoid the Centurion's projectiles and remove his energy. The compact corridor means rushing in with a shotgun is hugely helpful, though your usual takedown tactics apply, too.

8 Thumos the Unbroken

Super: Recommended **Grenades:** Recommended

Boss: Advance into the large bridge room of the carrier, and back away from the console as **Thumos and two Sub-Boss Legionaries) appear**. Your plan is to defeat Thumos, but this takes a lot longer than previous Cabal Boss takedowns because of the reinforcements that arrive throughout the fight. Here's what to look out for.

Sub-Bosses: Thumos arrives with **two Commander Legionaries**. These Sub-Bosses have Arc Shields and should be prioritized so you aren't dodging all three foes' weaponry.

Use the giant ramp pillars, console stacks, and raised platforms on either side of the central ramp as cover, and tackle each Commander Legionary one at a time. This is a good point to use both your grenade and Super, so it recharges and you can use it again toward the end of the entire battle. **Use the entire perimeter** of the room, and jump away from the Commander Legionaries if they charge after you reduce their energy to under a third. With both Sub-Bosses neutralized, pick some cover to sidestep back and forth from, and fire rapid headshots into Thumos until a third of his energy is gone.

Thumos: With no other foes getting in your way, start to battle Thumos, **treating him as a battle-hardened Centurion**. Though he has no Energy Shield, he makes up for it with **a nasty vibro-sword, jetpack, and rifle** (although he isn't vicious with the rifle at range). When he unsheathes his sword, **back away, as melee combat with him usually results in your death**. Instead, move back, keeping him at distance while peppering his head with your favored weapon. Keep this up until the next wave of foes arrives, usually when Thumos is at around two-thirds energy.

Cabal infantry: Thumos summons **three to four Psions and a couple of Legionaries**. He tends to hover above the platform he ascended from, shooting at you. Remain behind either large ramp pillar, and drop the Cabal infantry with methodical precision. Then, tackle Thumos again, using the same tactics. You can run onto the main central ramp to gain unobstructed views of this foe, leaping over his head as he charges you. Perfect your "flying and firing" at his head so you're damaging him all the time, no matter what maneuver you're trying. Thumos sometimes switches to a void beam rifle during this battle, but that's reasonably easy to shrug off or avoid.

More Cabal infantry: With around a third energy left, Thumos summons a small pack of around **six War Beasts, a trio of Psions**, and (once the War Beasts are defeated) **a Gladiator** to really cause you problems. Shoot all but a couple of the War Beasts, using your Movement Mode to avoid being mauled and staying behind either ramp column so Thumos can't hit you. Tackle the Psions so there are as few foes as possible when the Gladiator appears. Then, make the Gladiator a priority target, staying active and using the stacked consoles and entire perimeter to backpedal around. Drop the Gladiator with headshots before he can kill you at melee range. If the Gladiator is getting too close, move across the chamber.

Final fight: With only Thumos left, the battle becomes a bit easier. This Boss isn't as vicious or maneuverable as his underlings. **He's tough, though, so continue to strike him in the head with ranged shots.** Watch for his jumping, which is more pronounced than in previous bouts (he lands on the side console and moves to different parts of the chamber). However, with continuous firing and perhaps a second Super, Thumos soon becomes "broken." The keys are acquired, and the mission concludes.

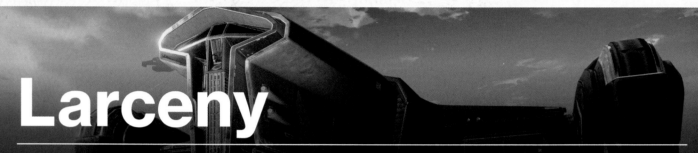

Larceny

Recommended Level: 16
Recommended Power: 160

You've taken out the previously unbroken Thumos and stolen his ship data. Before setting off for a journey into the sun, you need to appropriate the ship itself. This is easier said than done, as the expansive landing bay along the eastern side of the EDZ has even more Cabal to battle through. However, they're hindered somewhat by some upstart Fallen who are here to savage both you and the Red Legion. After a fierce battle, you end up at the ship, but it's going to take Ghost a while to hack it. Meanwhile, you must hold off multiple waves of Cabal ground forces intent on stopping your little game.

Legion's Anchor

European Dead Zone

Objectives

Steal Thumos' ship.
Board Thumos' ship.

Enemies Encountered

CABAL:	Legionaries, Incendiors, Phalanxes, Scorpius, Gladiators, War Beasts, Centurions
FALLEN:	Dregs, Vandals, Shanks
FALLEN: SUB-BOSS:	Servitor
CABAL: BOSS:	Centurion

1 Legion's Anchor Corridors

Super: Optional **Grenades:** Recommended

From the Sunken Isles, **head down the L-shaped corridor into Legion's Anchor**, where a Fallen incursion is currently underway. Remain at the entrance, using the partial cover and dropping the cluster of Legionaries, then the Fallen Dregs and Vandals firing upward and left of you. **Step into the loading bay**, jump onto the platform bridge and ramp, and follow it to the upper ledge, slowly removing the nearest foes as you go. **Note the yellow explosive barrel** you can shoot to clear the central bridge area of foes. Shoot the four Shanks before dealing with the remaining Cabal atop the ramp and ledge. Then, focus on exploding an Incendior and removing Phalanx shields before heading down the exit corridor to a windowed thoroughfare.

Turn left slowly at the next left corner, as **two rapid-fire sentry guns (Scorpius class)** have been stationed to waylay Fallen intruders. These can seriously deplete your energy, so use the corner wall as cover and rapidly shoot each one, aiming at the brightly lit weapon that activates. You have a second as the gun raises up and cocks into position; use this to lay waste to it. **Scorpius sentry guns are always priority targets** because they are stationary and can kill you in seconds.

Legion's Anchor

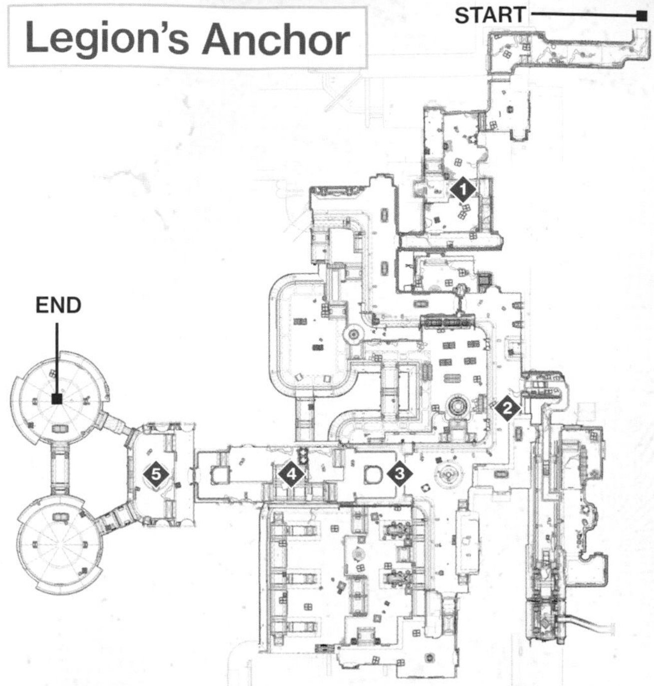

2 Viewing Corridors

Super: Recommended **Grenades:** Recommended
Warning!: Restricted Zone

The frequency and number of enemies from this point on becomes greater, so it's worth taking your time, **slowing down and clearing the following corridors with care**. Remove the Legionary, then step to the corner of the corridor to aim at a Dreg, Vandals, and Shanks as they close in on you. Deal with the Shanks first. Move to the ramp on the left side of the corridor, leading to a raised ledge where Dregs appear from. Tag them as they appear, along with two Vandals farther along the L-shaped raised ledge. Use the generators or lower barricade as cover. **Stay on the raised ledge and move around slowly** until you reach a central door console surrounded by Fallen.

Sub-Bosses: Aside from Vandals and Dregs, there is a named Servitor with a larger health capacity than normal. It doesn't need to be a priority target; with their highly damaging long-range rifle shots, Vandals should be the first foes you kill. **Also, explode the yellow canister just behind and right of the console island.** If the Servitor starts to link to Dregs or Vandals, focus on the Servitor instead. A well-timed Super can rid the entire area of foes here, but it's worth hanging on to your Super for a subsequent (and imminent) battle.

When the Servitor loses around half its health, around six Shanks join in. Back up to the corner of the raised L-shaped platform and use the cover, dropping all airborne foes in quick succession. Then, venture past the console island to a door that opens, **revealing a nasty surprise**!

3 **This is the time to lob in a grenade or use your Super.** Cabal hostiles comprised of a Gladiator, two Phalanxes, and two Incendiors are waiting behind this door.

If you can land a grenade and damage the Gladiator, finishing it with a headshot before it even has a chance to move, you can easily deal with the other four foes without needing to use your Super. Retreat to the L-shaped platform again if you must, but don't stand toe-to-toe with the Gladiator, or you'll be cleaved to death. Aiming at either of the Incendiors so their fuel packs explode is another way to soften up the Gladiator.

4 The cluster of Cabal was guarding **a long cargo bay** with two short and parallel corridors. Those open into a bay area with Psions (four on the upper platform, and four on the sunken central bay) and a Scorpius (right side of the upper platform). **Stay at range**, explode the Scorpius, then take aim and clear the central area of Psions. Don't head farther into the cargo bay until you've secured the initial area, as you find another Scorpius (right side of the right corridor) and a pack of eight War Beasts.

As you rattle off bullets into the exploding collars of the War Beasts, retreat a little, then deal with the Scorpius from range. There's another Scorpius guarding the left exit corridor and a couple of Psions to further waylay you; explode the sentry gun first. **Take your time, as the door these foes are guarding automatically opens,** revealing a Cabal Landing Zone with more automatic sentry guns. Stay out of their range of fire as you prepare for the following assault.

5 Cabal Landing Zone Assault

Super: Recommended **Grenades:** Recommended
Warning!: Restricted Zone

A protracted battle commences at this point, lasting until the end of the mission. Before you step into the fray, it's worth **learning the three areas of combat** you'll be accessing.

Covered ramps: There's the initial bay area that overlooks the two LZ platforms. Currently, a Scorpius is firing ahead and right of you. Destroy it, then watch for Legionaries on the lower ramped area.

Empty LZ: Ahead and left of you down an open-air ramp is a large Landing Zone with some yellow explosive canisters (save them for later) and a small group of Legionaries. These are easy pickings.

Ship LZ: Ahead and right of you, linked by a bridge between both LZs, is a gap you can leap across, leading to an LZ with the ship you need to hijack. Currently, a Scorpius is positioned on the edge of the LZ, pointed at the entrance you came in from. Behind it is a quartet of Legionaries. Shoot the Scorpius from cover at the covered ramps, or after crossing the bridge from the empty LZ. Remember you can move back and forth from the covered ramps to this location; use this route if the bridge and empty LZ become too crowded when Cabal reinforcements arrive.

Clear the entire area of the two Scorpius guns and the dozen or so Legionaries. Then, venture behind the ship (ship LZ), and **use Ghost to hack into it** (hijack the ship). This is going to take some time to complete, so you'll need to repel incoming enemies when this is going on.

As soon as the hijack begins, **a wave of Cabal start dropping into the covered bay**. Expect four Legionaries, a Gladiator, a couple of Psions, and up to four War Beasts. **Long-range sniping** with immediate and quick takedowns from the ship LZ is a good idea. Leaping to the covered bay is also an option, but you can be quickly overwhelmed. You may want to face the Gladiator at the empty LZ. It's a good idea to clear the Legionaries and War Beasts from range and from either of the LZ platforms before leaping onto the covered bay to deal with any Psion stragglers.

As you're mopping up Cabal from Wave 2, **a dropship deposits** a squad of Phalanxes, Legionaries, and a Centurion (with a Solar Shield). If you're at the covered bay, you have a slight height advantage and can face the Cabal on the connecting bridge, using area-of-effect weapons to detonate and send foes flying off to their doom. A similar plan is available if you're on the ship LZ. **It's worth removing most of the foes from range first**, then heading in to deal with the Centurion and firing at the yellow explosive canisters to soften up foes as the situation allows.

The action isn't letting up! As you defeat the final foes of the previous wave, expect around eight Psions, four Incendiors, and a couple of Legionaries to appear **in and around the covered bay**. **Shoot the Incendiors first** because they are easy to tag, and their explosions can damage the Psions. Then, hunt the Psions, coaxing them onto the empty LZ where there's cover for you but enough space to fire on Psions without obstruction. As the Psion menace is abated, **check the ship LZ; there's a Centurion** ready to battle!

Boss: At the end of this battle, try to stay on the empty LZ, especially as the Centurion arrives. He uses the weaponry associated with this enemy type, so seek cover, and **coax the Centurion onto the bridge between the empty LZ and the ship LZ** (where he appeared). At this point, produce a grenade launcher, and punt projectiles at the foe until he's staggered and finally sent falling off the side of the bridge. Use your Super and grenade, too. If you don't have area-of-effect weapons to push him off the bridge, face the Centurion with some sniper fire at range or continuous headshots as you move to the different cover options around the empty LZ. Staying at range and in cover and whittling down the foe's health as he plods toward you is a slower (but no less competent) way to finish this fight.

With the Centurion defeated, simply **board the ship** and conclude this mission.

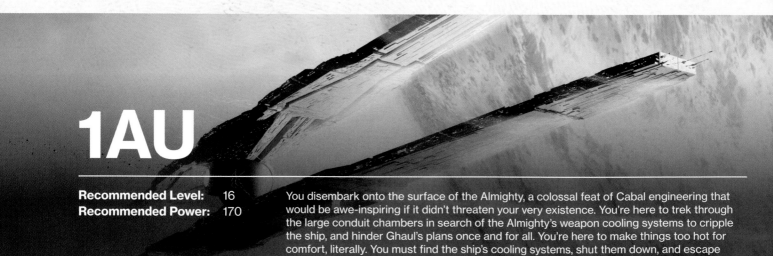

1AU

Recommended Level: 16
Recommended Power: 170

You disembark onto the surface of the Almighty, a colossal feat of Cabal engineering that would be awe-inspiring if it didn't threaten your very existence. You're here to trek through the large conduit chambers in search of the Almighty's weapon cooling systems to cripple the ship, and hinder Ghaul's plans once and for all. You're here to make things too hot for comfort, literally. You must find the ship's cooling systems, shut them down, and escape before the entire ship overheats into a planet-sized ball of molten death.

Starboard Landing

The Almighty

Objectives

Follow the fuel streams to the Almighty's weapons systems.

Enemies Encountered

CABAL: Legionaries, Psions, Scorpius, Gladiators, War Beasts, Incendiors, Phalanxes

Starboard Landing

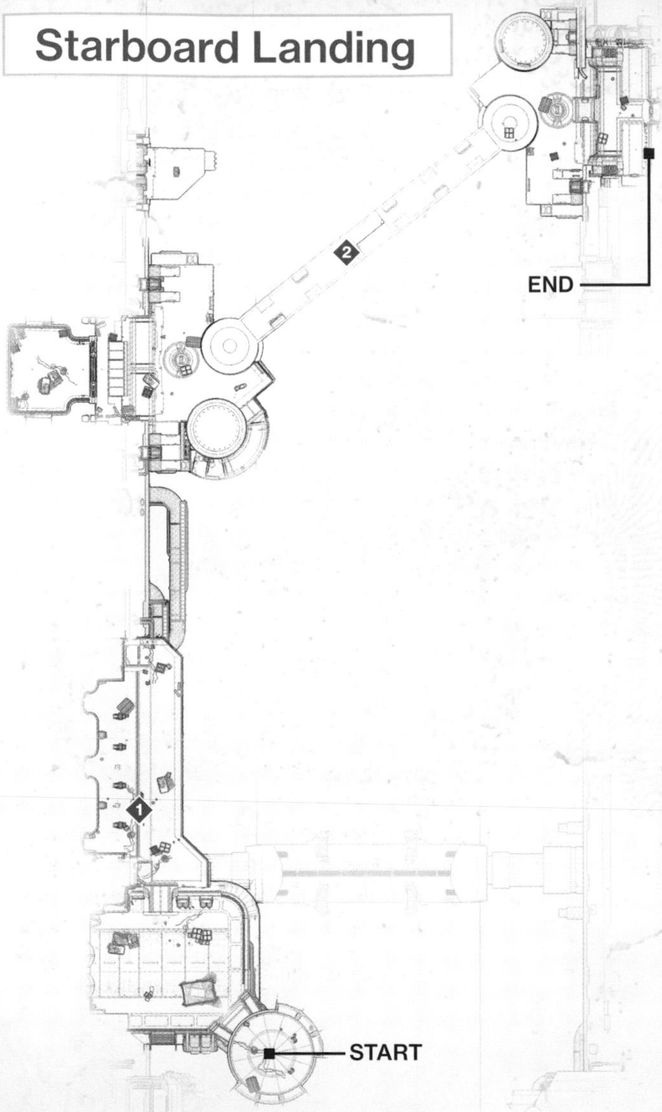

❶ Fuel Stream Corridors (Exterior)

Super: Optional **Grenades:** Optional

Drop down to the platform and deal damage to a few Legionaries, using the crates as cover (or land on and fire down from them). **Head down the ramp**, engaging Psions behind cover on both sides of this **long exterior corridor**. Expect no more than a dozen Psions and four Legionaries stepping out from the left. Methodically check behind cover, and bring down foes closest to you. **Shoot the yellow explosive canisters** to wound hostiles hiding near them.

Jump and land on the exposed pipe with the narrow gantry atop it. You're close to the fuel stream and a bottomless drop into space, so keep yourself properly anchored by landing firmly on the gantry.

Shoot the Legionaries on the curved grating ahead, and follow it around to the right to a second expansive platform. **Your first adversary is a Scorpius**; destroy that before it does the same to you. Then, move onto the platform, tackling four Psions and a Gladiator. The space allows you to easily back up and headshot the Gladiator, optionally detonating explosive canisters to wound him as you maneuver.

Standing atop some crates and firing down also works, though the Gladiator can use a jetpack to reach you. With the area devoid of Cabal, **use Ghost to access the bridge controls**, and extend the bridge across to the opposite side of the super-structure.

❷ Fuel Stream Bridge

Super: Optional **Grenades:** Recommended
Warning!: Restricted Zone

Just as you produce Ghost to access the bridge controls, you have two main assault options as three Cabal dropships swoop in, releasing a small horde of foes onto the bridge and the main entrance on the opposite side. You can:

Remain by the console, using ranged weaponry to easily tag around six War Beasts as they bound in your direction. **Stay where you are**, and drop a couple of Incendiors and Phalanxes as the opportunity arises, along with two Legionaries slowly advancing across the bridge. **Use the raised barriers on the edge of the bridge as cover**, if necessary. Lob a grenade if you must; it is more effective because the enemy can't really dodge it in the confined space. Then, rush to the far side of the bridge, where additional combat begins.

Or, you can **rush across the bridge** just as it starts to pivot. When both sections link up, you can execute a Super and rampage through the aforementioned foes. You can also flee to the far side of the bridge, optionally using your Movement Mode to get up to the large cylindrical platform on your left and attacking everyone from up there. This isn't as safe, but it's an option.

Assuming you attempted the first bridge-crossing option, drop foes closest to you first, then Phalanxes. Because they shield other enemies, they cause you the most trouble. There are around four more Legionaries on the raised area by the main door, along with an explosive canister; hit that to soften up multiple foes.

Mineral Processing

The Almighty

Objectives

Follow the fuel streams to the Almighty's weapons systems (continued).

Find a way to turn on the grinder.

New Actions to Learn

Gathering Fusion Cores

Enemies Encountered

CABAL: Legionaries, War Beasts, Phalanxes, Gladiators, Incendiors

CABAL: SUB-BOSS: Centurion

Mineral Processing

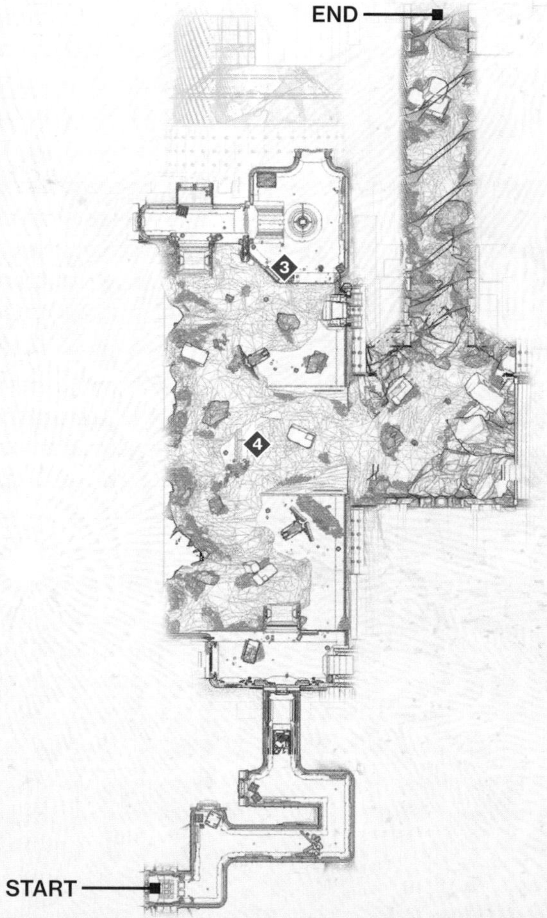

3 Ore Grinders Chamber

Super: Recommended **Grenades:** Recommended

Warning!: Restricted Zone

Head through the linking corridors into a large chamber. You see a series of circular chute doors to your left, masses of ground-up rock on the floor ahead of you, and a massive grinder along the right side of the chamber, where you can easily defeat two Legionaries. Ghost recommends that you get this grinder started, so **head over to the control room on the opposite side**, dropping two more Legionaries. Save the exploding canisters for the main fight to come. It seems the Red Legion is using the remains of the planet Mercury as fuel.

Search the grinder control area for a selection of **fusion cores** (ball-shaped objects you can grab), and carry one to the console with the circular open door.

Insert the core, and the massive grinder closes up and starts removing the huge rock wall that's preventing your progress. While it eats away at your exit option, Red Legion are inbound. **Prepare for a protracted battle.**

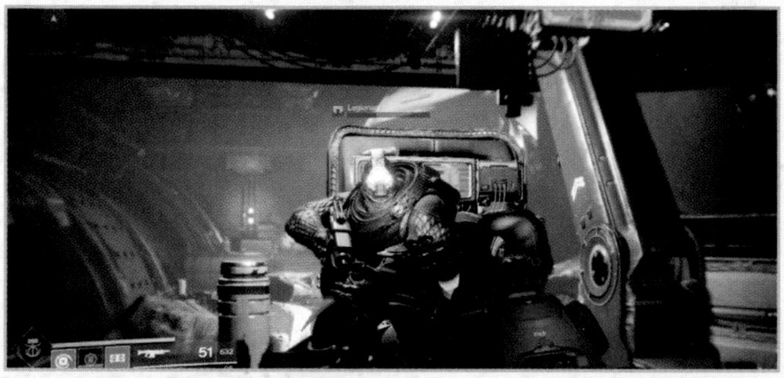

4 **Remain on the control room side** of the chamber, and snipe at the Legionaries and Phalanxes dropping in close to where you entered, along with a pack of War Beasts on the right side. These foes are immediately joined by two Gladiators, and they are your priority targets. Shoot them in the head as they bound and jet-pack their way across the chamber. Because **you're on raised ground** by the grinder controls, they can't quickly charge you, affording enough time for you to drop both of them without a lot of tricky dodging.

Then, concentrate on nearest foes, with War Beasts and Phalanxes top of your list. When the control room starts to get overrun, jump out in the chamber, and fight the Cabal among the rocks. Incendiors have joined the throng, and other foes (usually Legionaries and Incendiors) are dropping in from the large circular chute doors opposite the grinder. **Know where your reinforcements are coming from**, and drop a grenade (from a launcher, as well as your ability) if you can. **Jumping in and shotgunning foes in the face** is amusing and works well, as does landing on scenic objects for a few seconds so you aren't swarmed on the ground.

Bound to the raised entrance platform where you came from, too; the height helps you waylay foes so they have to use their jetpacks or the ramp. **Detonating Incendiors and blasting all explosive canisters** is another excellent plan, as is using your Super.

Sub-Boss: After the first wave of enemies, **expect a named Centurion** with a Solar Shield to appear. Treat him just like any other Centurion: blast his shield with an appropriate Energy weapon and aim at the head, shrugging off other attackers so this Centurion dies before his shield recharges.

With the enemy defeated in this area, the grinder finishes burrowing, allowing you **access deeper into the Almighty**.

Sunside

The Almighty

Objectives

Follow the fuel streams to the Almighty's weapons systems (continued).

Enemies Encountered

CABAL: Legionaries, War Beasts, Incendiors, Gladiators, Psions

CABAL: SUB-BOSS: Centurion

5 Cargo Corridor 1

Super: Optional **Grenades:** Optional

Venture into a darkened rubble-filled chamber with a door up and right of you. Step to it, and it opens, revealing a Legionary and War Beast ambush. Step back and down so you have enough time to rake the War Beasts, then finish the Legionary before **proceeding into the cargo corridor**. Note the small platform ledges on each side of this relatively narrow corridor; tackle a couple of Legionaries and a Incendior, but don't rush forward because there's a Gladiator to deal with. Shoot him from range, ideally dropping him before he can cleave you.

Only then should you head down the shallow ramp, using the two central generators as cover and removing the remaining Incendior and a couple of Legionaries. Yellow explosive canisters are also helpful to shoot here.

Continue down the corridor to the window at the far end, showing the monumental power of the Red Legion's ship. You're now expected to head outside, with the full rays of the sun burning through your armor, and maneuver across the ship's superstructure.

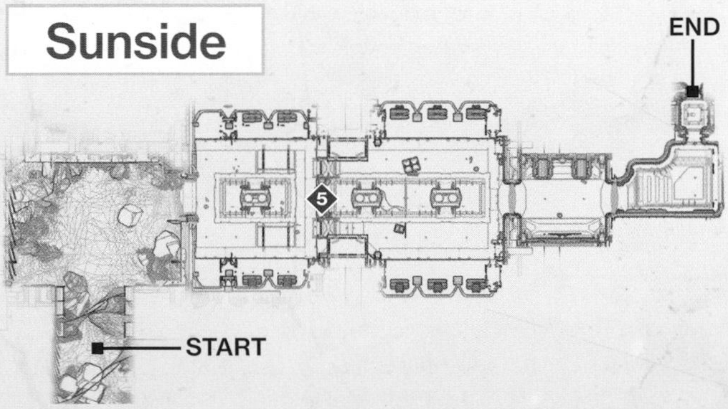

6 Exterior Superstructure

Super: Optional **Grenades:** Recommended

Warning!: Restricted Zone

Sprint down the shallow and searing slope of the super-structure, **stepping into the shadow of the scenery and heat shields** to avoid being fried. Rush to the two larger shields, where you must engage (or ignore) a couple of Legionaries. Once you're in shadow, start the fight.

To your right are two parallel bridge spans. From your elevated cover, shoot the Legionary duos on either span (or both), using grenades if necessary, **then sprint across to the shadow of a large shield** on the opposite side. Venture back up the slope, stepping into cover as you engage Legionaries streaming down from the exit door. Stay cool, and aim at their heads as you push forward. Stop at cover, **ideally at the area in the middle** where the heat shield and dome-shaped section of the ship are located.

Let the enemy come to you, using the dome to run around for additional cover (from both enemy fire and the heat). Then, sprint and jump onto the small platform with the exit door, running inside and out of immediate danger.

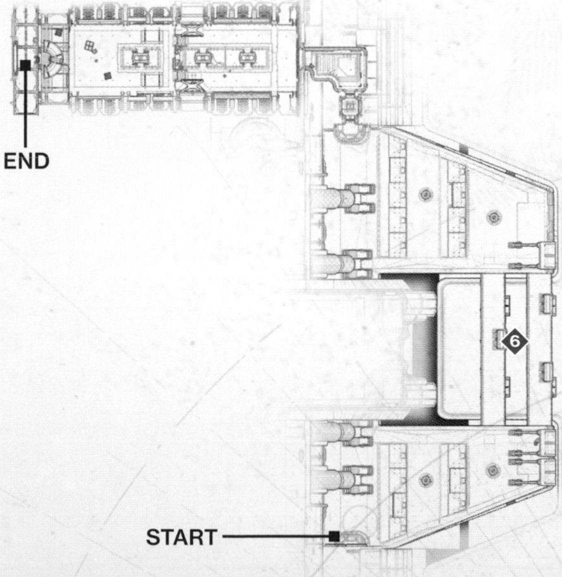

The Action is Heating Up

During your time moving across the exterior of the Almighty, you're constantly taking burning damage until you find respite behind the ship's heat shields or structures, anything that casts a shadow. Remain in shadow whenever you need to replenish your energy, and try to attack from these points. Minimize your combat with the Cabal outside of this cover, as you're easily defeated due to constantly losing health.

7 Cargo Corridor 2

Super: Recommended **Grenades:** Recommended
Warning!: Restricted Zone

Enter a similar cargo corridor to the one previously accessed, though you're approaching from the lower ground end. **Leap to the raised area** halfway along the corridor, and watch three Gladiators drop into view, along with a trio of War Beasts, two Incendiors, and a couple of Psions along the back platform. **The Gladiators are a real concern**; blast any explosive canisters to weaken them, then train your weapons on the closest Gladiator, backing up where necessary. You can jump to a small high platform on either wall, but these foes can follow you there. **It's better to leap atop the generators in the middle of the corridor**, and dodge while you drop the Gladiators. Or, use your Super and kill all three easily. Stay at the lower end of the corridor where the Psions can't snipe you.

Deal with the Psions last. Shoot the canister on their platform as you boost up and tackle them at close quarters so you're not sniping them from range (which takes too long). **Then, climb the curved platforms around the massive chain to exit the chamber.**

Another option is to charge immediately to the far end of the corridor, removing both Psions and then firing down on the Gladiators, War Beasts, and Incendiors from there or the chain platforms. Or, simply escape without clearing the room, but that's more dangerous.

8 Cargo Corridor 3

Super: Optional **Grenades:** Recommended
Warning!: Restricted Zone

At the top of the curved gantry platforms is **access to a red-hued corridor entrance**. Meet two Legionaries, a Phalanx, and a Gladiator here, using the scattered cover opportunities at the corridor entrance. Grenades or shotguns to drop the Gladiator are good ideas.

Then, step to the corridor entrance, aiming at the Phalanx's shield, and back up as another Gladiator comes charging down. Deal with him, then Legionaries and another Phalanx and two Legionaries, making sure you **don't push down the corridor too quickly**.

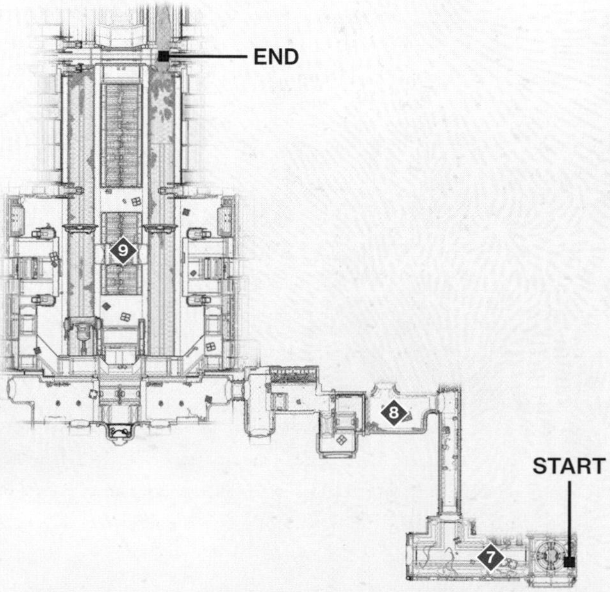

9 Main Grinder Chamber

Super: Recommended **Grenades:** Recommended
Warning!: Restricted Zone

After some corridor and ramp maneuvering, you arrive at the huge **main grinding chamber**, with ore tubes linking this location to the weapons systems of the ship itself. From here, you can easily ignore all enemies and jump to the central part of the chamber (avoiding the grinder). **Sprint along to the exit gravity tube ahead and to your right.**

Sub-Boss: A more proficient use of your time is to clear the area first. Cabal forces are on the lower sections of metal flooring on either side of the grinder, **so approach via the ramps**. The recommended route is **down the left gantry ramp, dropping through the hole in the lower gantry platform to floor level**. Remove immediate Legionary threats, then destroy a couple more Legionaries, an Incendior, and a named Centurion emerging from a doorway in the far-left corner of this area. Remain steadfast, and drop the Centurion so you can turn and dedicate your subsequent ammunition to shooting incoming Legionaries and Psions using their jetpacks. **Use the console wall and support pillars as cover.** Then, you can tag Psions across the chamber from this cover, hitting them in the head before jumping over to finish any stragglers. Expect around a dozen Psions in and around the curved sunken gravity tube entrance, and then exit.

A Huge Mistake

If you head down the right gantry ramp from this chamber's entrance, the Centurion that appears from the far-left area has time to boost across and start launching his cluster missiles, making him a little trickier to take down. It's wiser to remove him by rushing his location using the previous recommended plan.

Sunside

The Almighty

Enemies Encountered

CABAL: Legionaries, Psions, Incendiors

Objectives

Follow the fuel streams to the Almighty's weapons systems (continued).
Destroy the Almighty's weapon cooling system.
Escape the Almighty!

New Actions to Learn

Interceptor Driving: General Maneuvers

10 Cooling System Takedown

Super: Recommended **Grenades:** Recommended

Ride the gravity tube, drop down a massive pipe, and land at an Interceptor depot. **When the door opens, shoot the canister** to your left so it explodes, killing both Legionaries. If available, use your Super and grenade to clear the depot, as you **spend most of the remainder of this mission on an Interceptor**. Or, just drop down, climb into the Interceptor, and destroy every Psion and Legionary in the vicinity.

Vehicular Cabal Slaughter

Use this Cabal vehicle against the Red Legion similar to how you drove the Drake tank earlier in the Campaign. The craft is reasonably maneuverable, can boost and strafe easily, and has solar rockets to strike foes and the cooling systems. Pay attention to the damage you're taking, and find additional Interceptor summoning points throughout the super-structure of the Almighty.

Your Worst Foot Forward

Can you ignore the Interceptor and attempt an assault on the Almighty on foot? Sure. Is it possible? Definitely not. Prove us wrong!

Boost into a curved hall with barriers, explosive canisters, and around a dozen Incendiors and Legionaries. Shoot them using your Interceptor's solar rockets or blast the canisters for area-of-effect damage, hitting more foes at once (then finishing with the Interceptor's firepower). **Head to and then wait at the green-lit door**, which opens and allows access onto the exterior of the weapons systems area.

11 **Once you're outside, firing at foes becomes a secondary action**, compared to locating and destroying a series of cooling fans (waypoints 10, 11, and 12). These appear on your HUD after scanning with Ghost, and they are easy to spot. Clear the immediate area of Cabal infantry, **staying mobile** so foes don't concentrate their firepower on you.

Locate the large flat-domed cooling vent, and position your craft by the door gratings. When those open, **fire at the interior fan** with the Interceptor's rockets. Don't let up, and ignore enemy firepower hitting your craft. **It takes four or five rocket barrages for the cooling system to explode.** Then, boost away to the next location.

The second cooling dome is identically designed, so circle around it until you find the door gratings, dropping Cabal infantry as you wait. With the grating open, fire four rocket barrages, then boost across a bridge, through a doorway, and around to the main cooling system.

Sunside

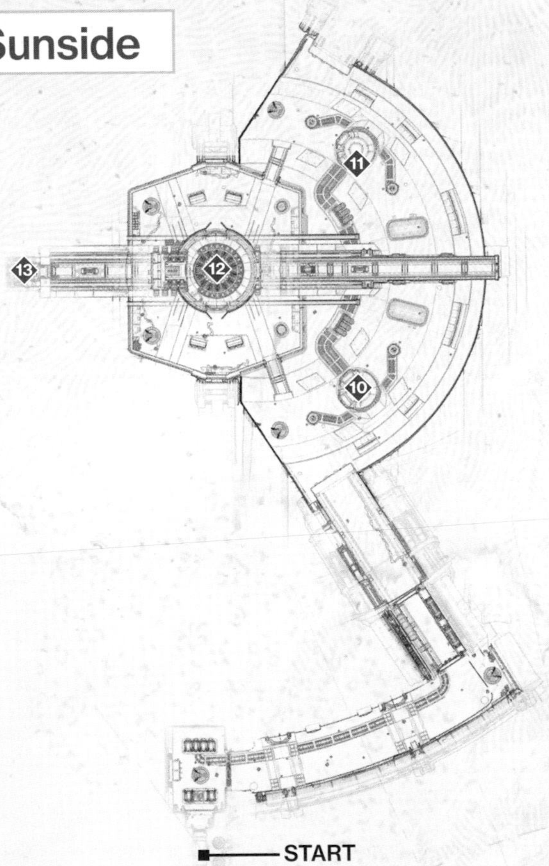

12 This system is set up a little differently. When you're at the large curved platform with a couple of barricades, clear the area of Psions and other pesky foes. Then, **wait for the main cooling vent doors to open** in the much larger domed structure. **Blast the final fans, then drive your Interceptor to the entrance doors** and rake the incoming Legionaries rushing in from the left. Hop out of your vehicle, as the final part of this mission is on foot.

13 The enemy presence is light, and **you have an electron reservoir to cripple**. Accomplish this by entering the corridor left of the destroyed cooling system, **grabbing a fusion core**, and jumping up and through the connecting corridor with an overheating floor. Your armor takes some damage, but this is necessary to **reach the circular conduit to the Almighty's core**. Drop the fusion core into this receptacle, and then flee.

The Almighty is disabled. Time to get to the escape dropship in under a minute. As the timer counts down, turn 180 degrees and jump onto the top of the super-structure (above the corridor you just ascended from). **Sprint across (and jump over) the rapidly exploding and overheating floor.** Bound to the waiting ship (competent Guardians should have around 30 seconds left on the clock), and conclude the mission.

Chosen

Recommended Level: 19
Recommended Power: 190

Though the Last City is in ruins, the tide is turning in your favor, and the liberation into a new era of light is about to begin. Just ensure that it isn't Ghaul himself who controls the Traveler! To stop the Cabal leader, you must first gain entry to his ship by reaching a rally point where your Guardian Mentors are holed up. You achieve this by battling Cabal forces across the city, then taking careful jumps across the rooftops to the rally point itself. As you'd expect, you're selected to face the great Ghaul himself. It seems he's learned his own abilities, so prepare to fight Ghaul with light in this final confrontation.

Peregrine District

Last City Liberation

Objectives

Rendezvous with the Vanguard.

Enemies Encountered

CABAL: Legionaries, Phalanxes, Incendiors, Centurions, Psions, Gladiators, Centurion, Scorpius Sentry Gun

CABAL: SUB-BOSS: Incendior

Peregrine District

1 Assault on Cabal Barrier 1

Super: Recommended **Grenades:** Recommended

The liberation of the Last City begins. Start by **executing some careful jump drops to the ground** (let's not start this mission by cratering, okay?). You can maneuver your drops to land on a low roof of a building to the right, if you want. This gives you some height to lay waste to Legionaries as you **head up a rubble-filled street**. Tackle four Legionaries by the small kiosk, then head farther up the street **to a courtyard** where a main force of Cabal is **guarding a barricade** (the orange energy wall to your left).

Open up and Let Me In

The Cabal barriers here, and throughout this mission, they're on a timer. You need to keep an eye on the orange energy walls, and pass through them when they disappear. These walls usually open after you've neutralized all immediate Cabal threats. However, they close quickly, leaving you to face the same threats again. This can continue for a while, so always head through the open barricades as quickly as possible, even if there are foes left in the previous area.

Prepare to fight a few Legionaries, two or three Phalanxes, and a Centurion with a Solar Shield. A Super and grenades early on are great, as you have time to recharge these Abilities for the assault on the second barrier. Use the cover of the crates and the Cabal dome on your right, and stay close to the left side of the rubble-filled courtyard, where the barrier wall is.

An Incendior and Phalanx reinforcements arrive; after that, expect the same initial forces (Legionaries, Phalanxes, and a Centurion) to head through the barrier wall, so break off the engagement and head through the doorway. If you don't, you'll simply have to finish the foes again, and watch for the next time the doorway opens. Should you see other Guardians in this space, it is recommended you team up with them for maximum firepower. Help them return to the action by resurrecting them!

2 Assault on Cabal Barrier 2

Super: Recommended **Grenades:** Recommended

Once you're through the first barricade, **head along the remains of an ornate concrete walkway by a canal**, cross a bridge, and proceed up a rubble-strewn street while quickly dropping around eight Psions along the way. There are Phalanxes on the opposite (right) side of the canal and Legionaries around the bridge. You can ignore them, if you're in a rush.

Slow down at the next courtyard, though. There's a ruined building to your left (good to jump onto and use to strafe foes below you), a Cabal dome on your right (good for cover), and Legionaries to strafe. Expect 4-6 of them, a couple of Phalanxes, an Incendior, and a Centurion (with a Solar Shield).

Defeat all of them, and six more Legionaries appear from a side entrance and behind the dome and ruins, followed by a Centurion (Solar Shield), Phalanxes, and an Incendior. The reinforcements are the same as before. **At this point, look for a break in the barrier and flee**; it's usually after the second wave of foes are vanquished.

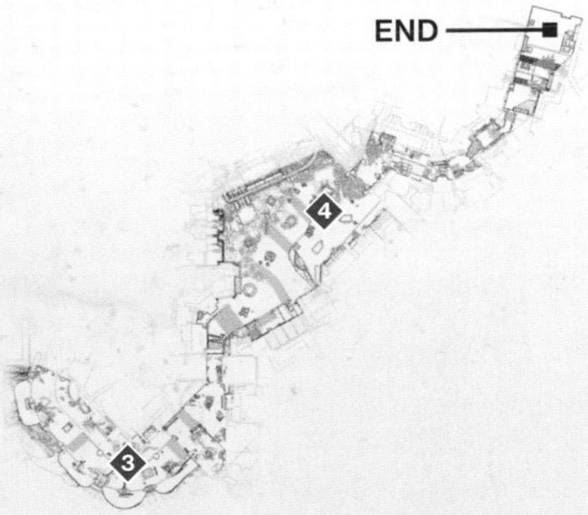

3 Bazaar Thoroughfare

Super: Recommended **Grenades:** Recommended

Leap onto a balcony, and **head into a market bazaar corridor** with two levels; stay on the upper-left level to gain a height advantage. Shoot a Psion from range before backing up and concentrating your firepower on a charging Gladiator. Expect around eight Psions and a second Gladiator as you turn the left corner slightly and **reach a stepped courtyard area**. You can rush through, stand and fight, or back up and wait for foes to reach you so you're not overwhelmed. Exit via the open iron doors ahead and left.

4 Market Courtyard

Super: Recommended **Grenades:** Recommended

Head up a number of stone steps leading to a market with a large archway on the upper **far side of a courtyard teeming with heavily armored Cabal foes**. The easiest way through here is to simply **ignore all enemies** and jump, then sprint through the archways, as this area has no barrier you need to wait for.

If you elect to stand and fight, you may want to slow down. Drop the Legionary halfway up the steps, then slink around to the left, ascending over the rubble and using the various columns in the courtyard as cover. Dispatch two Phalanxes and strafe in and out of cover while bombarding the head of a Centurion, your priority target. When he falls, resume attacks on the Phalanxes and a couple of Incendiors (depending on which is threatening), and mop up a couple of Legionaries to clear the area.

Sprint along and **up a series of corridors and rooftops** until you can see the Traveler and the draining of the light. A set of rooftop maneuvers to the rally point is now called for.

Cabal Confrontations

From this point, attacking the Cabal, especially those on rooftops you don't need to reach, is purely optional. Since you have a series of death-defying airborne platform maneuvers to complete, remain focused on the route to take instead of combat antics.

5 Rooftop Maneuvers

Super: Optional **Grenades:** Recommended

Take your time, looking to the right from the initial rooftop, and **jump to the yellow metal stairs on the subsequent roof**. Land on the ivy-covered cabin roof, watching for a Legionary and other Cabal diagonally ahead and left of you, on a rooftop you can optionally jump to and secure.

If you head across, leap to the curved platform where the first Legionary was, then jump so you don't fall short. There are Legionaries, Phalanxes, and a Sub-Boss Incendior to deal with.

A better plan is to simply stay on the right side and **jump across to three tiny square-shaped grate platforms attached to vertical poles.** Prevent yourself from overshooting these targets by steering in the air so you hit the vertical poles and drop down, or hit the jump button again to descend if your Guardian power allows it.At the third tiny platform, look ahead and right, then jump to a building balcony (attached to a green tenement block). Then stop!

6 **Just around this corner is a Scorpius sentry gun.** Step out of cover, shoot it or lob a grenade, then step back. Simply running at it gets you mowed down. Move to where the Scorpius was, and **take one of the diagonal gantry girders to the yellow building**, swing right, leap up where the ladder is, then look left. **Ahead is an outdoor covered rooftop.** Jump to it, slaughtering a Phalanx and Incendior as you arrive. There are a second Phalanx and a Legionary on the upper level.

Work your way around to the edge of the rooftop and **jump to the balcony** on the rally point building (with the salmon-colored semi-circular neon lighting). Drop an Incendior and a couple of Legionaries as you move up and right to a final set of steps **and finally rendezvous with your team.** With your Guardians badly wounded, it's up to you to finish the leader of the Red Legion yourself! Cayde opens up a teleport; enter at your own risk.

Systems Deck

Last City Liberation

Objectives
Defeat Ghaul.

Enemies Encountered
CABAL: War Beasts

Systems Deck

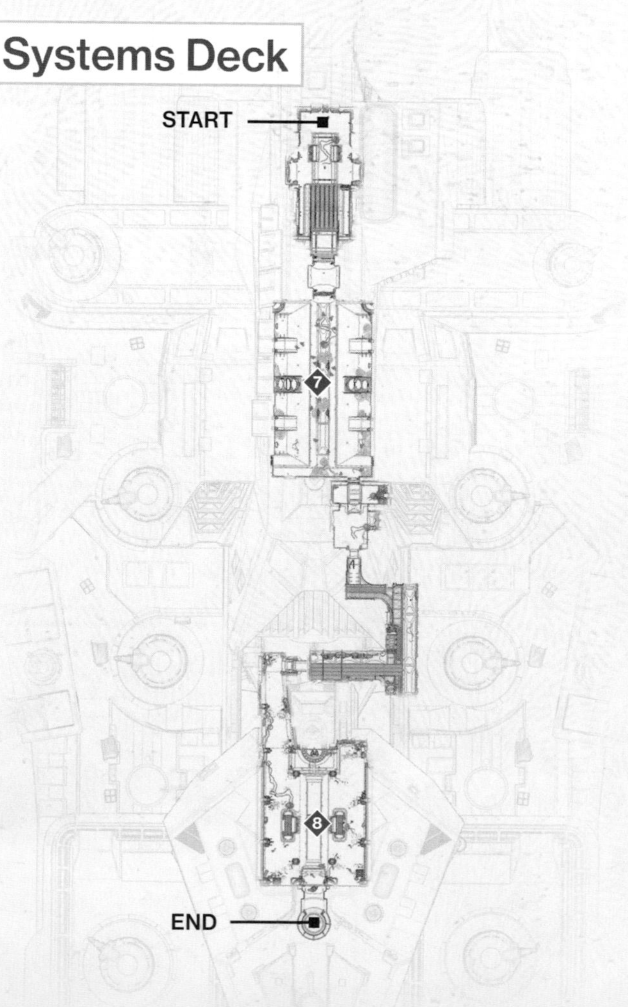

7 War Beast Chamber

Super: Recommended **Grenades:** Recommended
Warning!: Restricted Zone

You appear inside Ghaul's command ship. Head forward, and when the door opens, reduce your speed and noise to a minimum, as you reach **a cluster of sleeping War Beasts**. You can move slowly around them (head left of the pillar) toward an exit doorway, going to a subsequent maintenance doorway and up a maintenance shaft area. You can do this without waking up any foes. If you stand on any War Beasts or move too close to them, they wake up!

Or, you can **shoot at the War Beasts while backing up**, dropping a barricade or grenade so they can't easily get through the entrance door. Retreat back up the entrance corridor as the War Beasts charge you. This can result in your death, but it's worth a try if you're adamant about killing everything.

Alternately, you can **sneak through the room before sprinting to the exit** into the maintenance shaft area. Turn around and shoot at War Beasts from this vantage point, dropping down to tackle foes before retreating back here if anything gets too close for comfort. Then, you can gradually reduce the number of foes from here. Grenades are worth dropping in this confined area. Boost up past the yellow pipework to a higher gantry, then around to the red-lit pipes, running by them up a ramp and into the upper cargo bay of the ship.

Quarterdeck

Last City Liberation

Objectives

Defeat Ghaul (continued).

Enemies Encountered

CABAL:	Psions, Phalanxes, Legionaries, Incendiors
CABAL: SUB-BOSS:	Incendior
CABAL: BOSS:	Dominus Ghaul

8 Command Ship Cargo Bay

Super: Recommended **Grenades:** Recommended

Warning!: Restricted Zone

Head up the ramp to a **relatively compact cargo bay area**. Streaming out of the far door are six Psions (three moving to each side of the bay) and a couple of Phalanxes, Legionaries, and an Incendior Sub-Boss (Void Shield). **Head around the left side of the room's perimeter** so you can quickly neutralize half the Psions, then attack the closest targets, with Phalanxes being the main concern because they can shield others.

Remain at range, and tackle the Sub-Boss Incendior last unless you're confident you can defeat him without breaking off the attack and letting his shields recharge. Then, move through **to the circular elevator**, allowing access to the command ship's exterior.

Another option is simply to charge forward, passing by all enemies to the elevator and riding it up, ignoring all combat.

9 Final Confrontation: Dominus Ghaul

Super: Recommended **Grenades:** Recommended

Warning!: Restricted Zone

Defeating Ghaul: Reconnoiter: After heading along the outer spine of the craft, you face down Ghaul, and combat begins. Just **aim at his head** until he moves out of range and the complexities of combat increase. At this point, you should explore the structure of the battlefield (in this case, the command ship you're fighting on).

Traveler's Light: Ghaul flies around this craft, returning to bathe in a column of unnatural light from time to time. This column is directly ahead of you (as you enter the fight), and **it's not worth moving any farther** toward the front of the ship than this point.

Linked tunnels: There is a lower section on either side of the upper "spine" of the craft, each with a tunnel that links to a central tunnel and then to the opposite side.

Quarterdeck

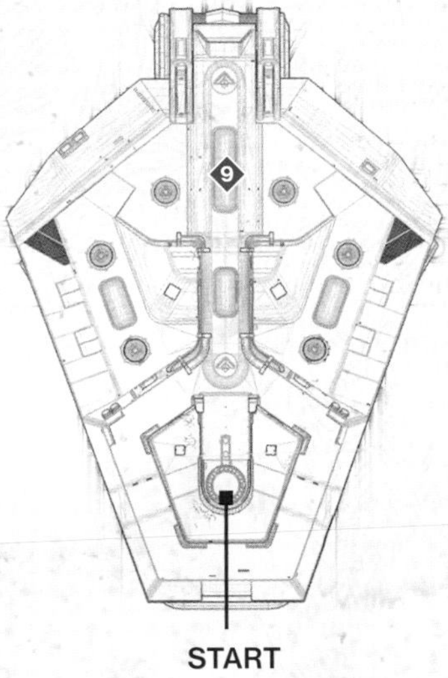

Here, **you can rush to replenish your energy if you've been struck or if you need to reload, change weapons, or hide**. Note the tall metal cylinders on the craft at each entrance; look for them during combat so you know where to head. Also, note a second central tunnel farther back under the main spine of the craft, which is useful for moving back and forth between the lower exterior sides.

Cover opportunities: The metal cylinders and various metal barriers along the sides of the craft can **act as cover**. In general, though, there aren't many areas to hide behind, aside from the tunnels.

Columns of Boundless Light: During the second and third parts of the battle, the rear part of the craft on each side has a Column of Boundless Light, which **automatically recharges your Super and Abilities.** This is critical to reach during an otherwise lengthy battle.

Cabal infantry: Expect **Psions and Legionaries** to help their master all the way through combat. During parts two and three, **Incendiors and Phalanxes** also appear, arriving on the super-structure to annoy and impede you. Periodically clear these foes, usually by rushing them with headshots and a melee attack to finish. These actually become **useful because the ammo they drop replenishes your supplies**, especially helpful for your Power weapons.

Begin by focusing on the removal of Ghaul's first third of his health. **Ghaul spends most of his time in the air** and has three main attacks.

His **foot-stomp** (executed after landing) is highly damaging at close range, so stay away from him unless you're waving a shotgun in his face as you charge forward and back. He has **a grenade launcher** that punts out a grenade one at a time; strafe or jump away from that. He also has a **variation on a Guardian Super attack**: a flaming sword he lobs down while flying. This can damage you severely, so quickly jump away from it before it strikes you.

React by **aiming all your firepower at Ghaul's head**. Fast-firing rifles or hand cannons are great. Shotguns are dangerous but effective. Sniper rifles are tricky because he keeps moving. Grenades and launchers are tricky because he can easily avoid those projectiles in the air. **Be sure to launch your Super**; connect with Ghaul's head, and don't worry about "wasting" it, as there's more light available soon. Continue to punish Ghaul's head until he loses his first third of health and **retreats to his column, the Traveler's Light**.

As Ghaul retreats into his maelstrom of purple light, **remove all Cabal infantry threats**, as many as possible once a new dropship arrives to deposit more Psions and Legionaries on the super-structure. While you're fending off the lesser foes, **step into either Column of Boundless Light** on the ship, recharging your Super and Abilities. When the purple column disappears, you can focus on removing the second third of Ghaul's health.

Ghaul attacks with his grenade launcher (two grenades at a time now), still has his foot-stomp, and has learned **a variation on a new Super**: a crackling maelstrom and some deadly melee strikes. However, a quick-thinking backpedal usually results in this attack missing. **Return the favor with a Super** just after Ghaul finishes his, when he's most exposed. Couple this with **any Abilities you favor** before returning to a Column of Boundless Light and recharging. Repeat the Super attack until Ghaul's health ebbs away to a third. Alternately, **headshots from your favored weapons** eventually do the trick, though you need to keep moving (and hiding) to avoid his wrath.

The light is affecting Ghaul, and the tide may be turning. While he's writhing in his purple maelstrom, **make short work of the Cabal infantry on deck**, using your grenades (and grenade launcher) to clear the area and perhaps pick up ammunition. **Bathe in either Column of Boundless Light** so your Super is ready to go. Note that the columns move to the lower part of the craft, near the tunnels.

Ghaul himself uses **both the previous Supers** he has acquired from the Traveler's Light, after attempting to strike with his final super, a giant void shield which he can hurl at you. This is easily dodged if you watch Ghaul conjure the ball and leap before it arrives. Though he's more vicious, and **you'll usually need to use the tunnels to protect you**, he eventually yields to several Super attacks directed at his head, or countless bullets aimed at the same place. **Keep on the offense**, returning to bathe in more light for a recharged Super until Ghaul takes a tumble he doesn't get up from. The mission is over. **The Red Legion has been defeated!**

We've Only Just Begun!

Get yourself back to the Tower; there's little time for celebrations, but a whole lot more to unlock, including missions, weapons, and masses of loot. The battle is over, but the war has just begun.

Overview

Guardians may elect to complete one of the available Strikes, accessed from the Director once they are unlocked. This is a co-operative mission for three fireteam members that requires the assault on a particular enemy, the removal of consecutive enemy clusters, and possible Sub-Boss takedowns before a final confrontation with a tougher foe. Rewards include quality and Strike-specific loot.

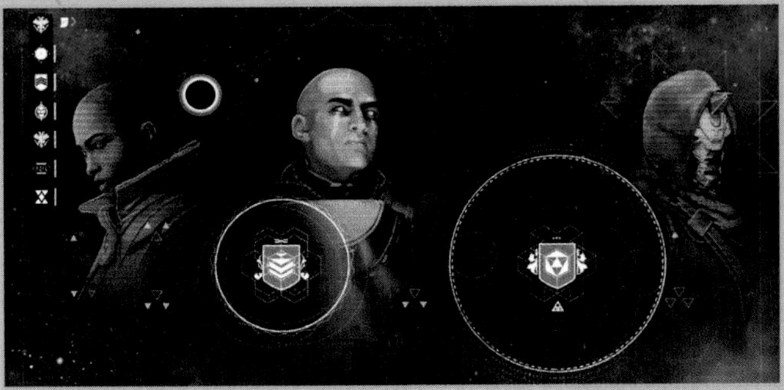

Available Strikes

At launch, there are **five available Strikes** across all gaming platforms, located across four different Worlds. They unlock once the Vanguard mentors return to the Farm:

Name of Strike	Strike Recommended Power	Nightfall Strike Required/Recommended Power*	Location
The Pyramidion	140	230/240	Io
The Inverted Spire	140	230/240	Nessus
Exodus Crash	140	230/240	Nessus
The Arms Dealer	140	230/240	European Dead Zone
Savathûn's Song	140	230/240	Titan

(* Recommended level for Strikes/Nightfall Strikes)

Nightfall Strikes

As you might expect, there are **higher-difficulty variations** of each available Strike, which are **usually selected for availability (after game launch) by Bungie** and may not be available to play on a consistent basis. Look for these missions, which may **reward you with Exotic loot**.

Enemies are usually tougher, and differing enemies may appear in clusters as you encounter them throughout the Nightfall Strike, compared to a usual Strike.

Expect a number of modifiers that vary your game. Since Strike enemy groups are variable, you may witness completely different squads of enemies.

Nightfall Strikes have (usually) two **modifiers** that add an additional element of difficulty. Different tactics may be required in order to complete the Strike. Modifiers are chosen by Bungie each time a Nightfall Strike becomes active.

Strike Information: General Overview Access

The remainder of this chapter is devoted to the five Strikes and more precise knowledge of each set of encounters, along with tactics on completing each one. As the limitless variation of Nightfall modifiers may change the tactics significantly, utilize the following information based on the original Strikes. The information is here so you have a good overall understanding of when the most problematic foes are encountered, what general variations there might be, and "best-case" strategies.

Note that each section gives you general advice on whether to use your Super or your grenade Ability, the general differences between a Strike and its Nightfall version, and any weak point for the end-of-mission entity you face. As always, you may want to employ differing tactics depending on the specific situations presented to you.

The Pyramidion

Strike: Recommended Power 140
Nightfall: Required Power 230
Recommended Power 240

Asher Mir requests your presence investigating the main Vex pyramid structure on Io. It soon becomes clear that this is the main conduit for Vex activity throughout the solar system and a base of power for this enemy. You must negotiate the vast floating platform interior of this void structure, navigating past laser defenses and hordes of Vex foes, including enemies very rarely encountered. After locating the main conduit, you must drop down and engage the genesis mind of this seat of power.

The Rupture

Restricted Zone

Enemies Encountered

VEX: Goblins, Harpies, Hobgoblins

Objectives

Approach the Pyramidion entrance.
Activate the Vex altars (2).
Defeat the Vex.
Enter the Pyramidion.

1 Pyramidion Entrance Altars

Super: Optional (one player)
Grenades: Recommended (one player)
Variations: Additional Hobgoblins, Storm Minotaurs.

A more cunning method of entering the Pyramidion structure than "attack everything" is required, especially as the surrounding sides of the central sunken area are great for long-range sniping. Send your meatiest teammate down there to inflict close-quarters hurting on the assembled Vex forces, which are usually toughened Goblins and Harpies. Have your other teammates **snipe from the side and offer covering fire** (dropping any Hobgoblins that have appeared atop the pillars). When fewer foes are presenting themselves, be sure to **stand in the circular altars of light** (there are two within the sunken entrance area); have one teammate at each altar to quicken the unlocking process. With remaining stragglers dealt with (including a couple of toughened Harpies), simply descend into the now-open structure.

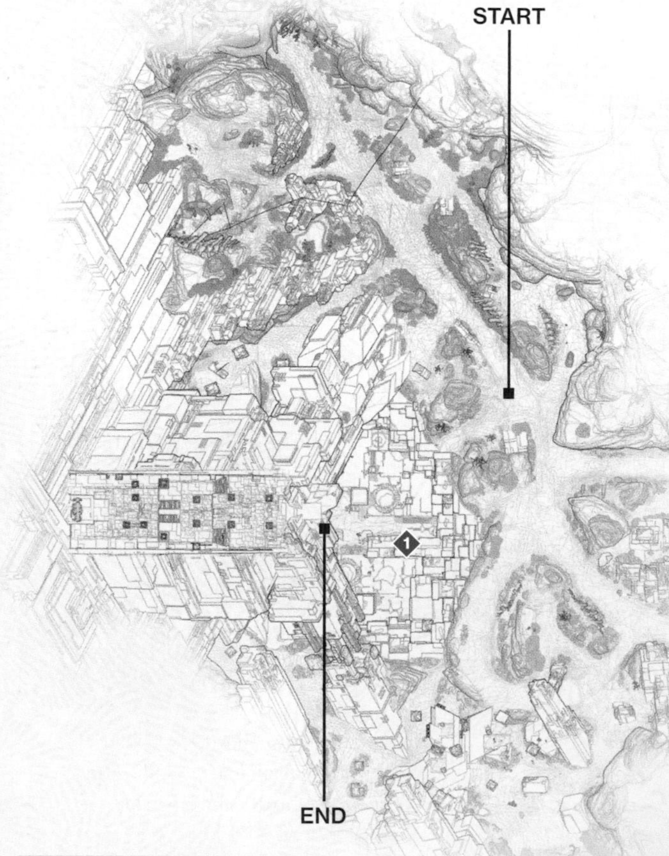

The Rupture

The Rupture

Restricted Zone

Objectives

Find the first warpgate.
Defeat the Vex.
Find the next warpgate.
Activate the Vex altars (3).
Locate the last warpgate.
Hack the network towers (4).
Reach the final warpgate.
Enter the conduit.
Defeat the Boss Hobgoblin.

Enemies Encountered

VEX: Goblins, Minotaurs, Hobgoblins, Harpies, Hydras, Cyclopses
BOSS: Brakion, Genesis Mind (Hobgoblin), Fanatics

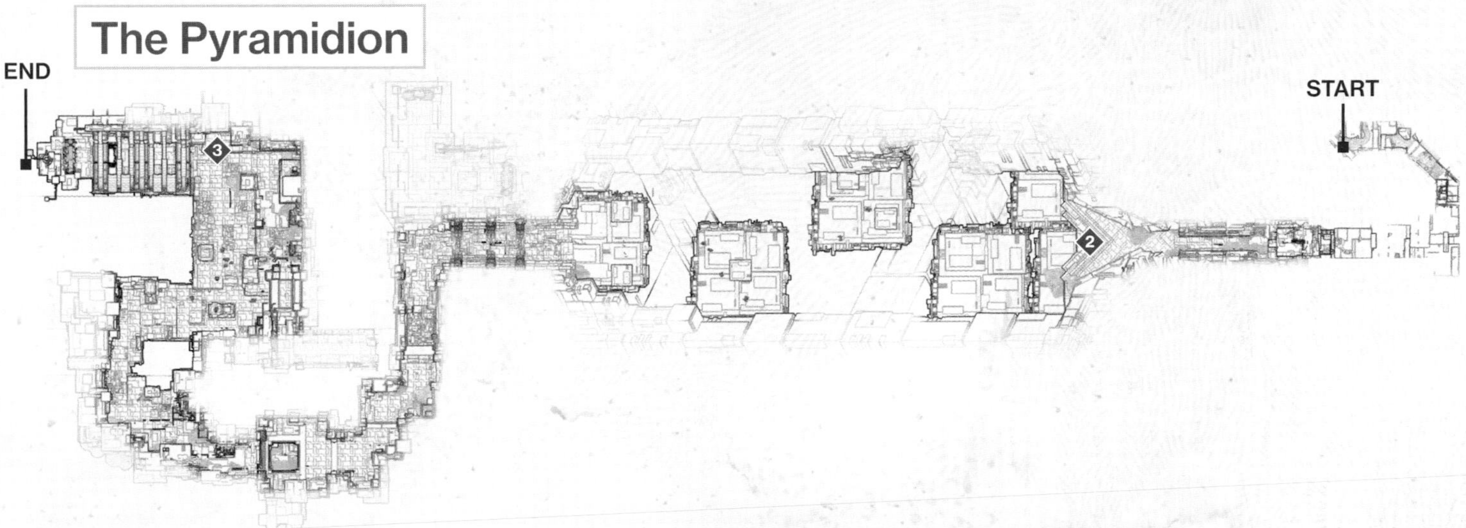

2 Colossal Steps

Super: Optional (one player)
Grenades: Optional (one player)

Resist the temptation to gawk at the incredible Vex architecture, and instead, make short work of the Goblins guarding **the gigantic stepped chamber**. Drop onto each step, watching for the telltale signs of Vex teleports warping **Goblins and a Minotaur onto three of the steps**.

Have one teammate attack at close quarters with two others on higher steps, providing sniping fire. Continue a measured descent, with one teammate tagging each Hobgoblin on either side of the circular exit. Then, demolish the Goblins and Minotaur on the final step and land on it.

Pass between the first **three white laser traps**. Cut down the Goblins in the connecting passage, then jump over the laser floor. Jump over the next laser wall, and slide under the next. Then, steer yourself during the drop so you miss all of the lasers during the descent.

3 First Warpgate

Super: Recommended (one player)
Grenades: Recommended

Out from the laser traps, remain on the higher platform as you look across to the first warpgate through an archway opening that looks a little like a ribcage. **Dispatch Harpies, then the Goblins** in your immediate view before heading across this exterior chamber. At this point, have one of your teammates execute a Super; there are **more than a dozen Goblins, a couple of Minotaurs, and some toughened Harpies** on this platform. **Don't overcommit** and push too far forward because you'll be swamped. Instead, lob in grenades, and make steady progress around to the warpgate arches. Here, there is **a flock of Harpies** to neutralize; expect about 10. You'll know if you've defeated all the Vex because this triggers the warpgate to open.

4 Altar Room

Super: Recommended (two players)
Grenades: Recommended

Once you're through the warpgate, **time your movements through the next set of laser traps**. They disappear and reappear, so move just as the lasers shut off. Watch the rhythm of the lasers before predicting when they shut off, and step through (or fall down) to the altar room.

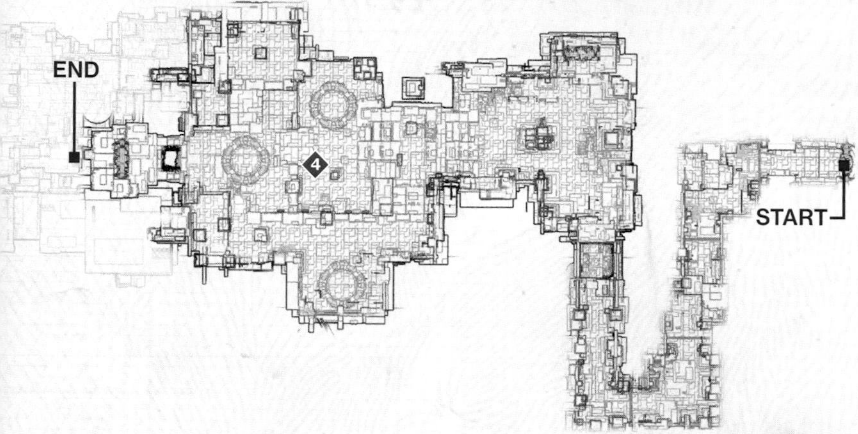

This chamber requires you to **activate three Vex altars**, just like you did before entering the Pyramidion. The altar chamber is large and **packed with Vex**; Harpies are in the center, with a Minotaur, Goblins, and Hobgoblins on the far side toward the (currently inactive) warpgate. Thin out the Vex first, and **make the sniping Hobgoblins a priority**. When very few foes are left, have two players head to the first altar to activate it. **Reinforcements arrive each time an altar is activated** (usually Minotaurs and Goblins), and a Hydra appears when all three altars are active. Employ a Super if needed when clearing this area. Otherwise, remain on the perimeter of the room so you're not overwhelmed. **Save a Super for the Hydra**, unless you want a protracted fight. With the warpgate functional, leap through it.

5 Conduit

Super: Optional (one player) **Grenades:** Recommended

A long conduit chamber is visible, with a number of laser traps and Vex Hobgoblins, Goblins, and Harpies in between them. Time your sprint through the first couple of walls, then take down the Hobgoblins and then the other foes before heading into the tube-like conduit. Time the dash through the rotating lasers so you sprint at either side in one continuous run; just time it based on the initial rotating laser, and you should be fine. Then, drop into the teleport.

6 Tower Platform

Super: Recommended **Grenades:** Recommended
Variations: Additional Hobgoblins.

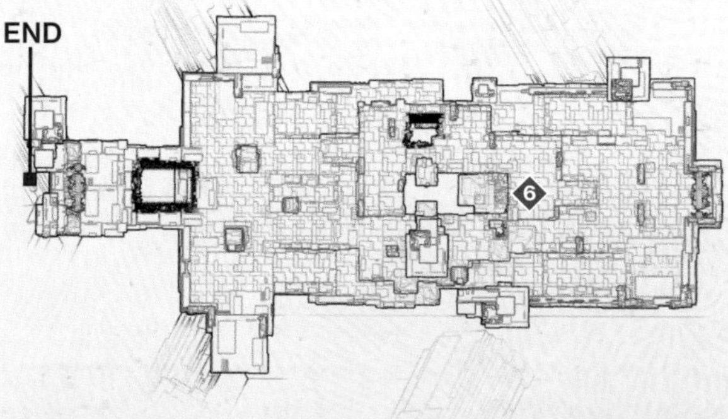

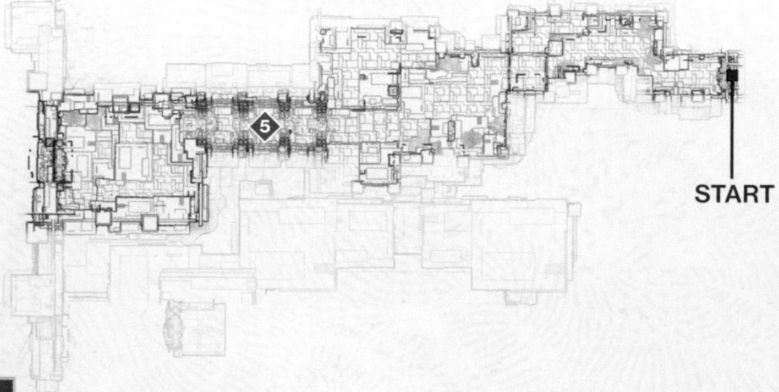

Step onto a long platform with a central sunken area and a teleport at the far end. Ahead and on either side of the platform on two small plinths are some **stationary Cyclopses**, a rarely encountered Vex.

This foe fires a nasty laser, then a barrage of lasers when it's been damaged. Before you remove these threats, **tackle the enemies atop the pillars**, and make slow (but steady) progress through this chamber. If you're dying, you're being swarmed by multiple clusters of Vex; a Minotaur and Goblins appear around each of **the network towers you must hack**. It's usually a good idea to tackle these tower hacks methodically, with your entire team focused on one location at a time.

Approach each of the white glowing small towers, and completely remove any threats in the immediate vicinity. As the last Vex hostiles fall, have one teammate do the hacking while the other mops up and the third ascertains the next nearest tower. Repeat this plan two more times. If you're skilled enough or don't have the time, you can try the slightly more dangerous plan of having two teammates tackle a tower separately, with the third providing covering fire. Minotaurs are especially deadly here, so make them priority targets after you've aimed at the Cyclopses' eyes.

7 Conduit and Final Altar

Super: Recommended **Grenades:** Recommended
Boss Weak Spot: Red head slit, then torso opening.

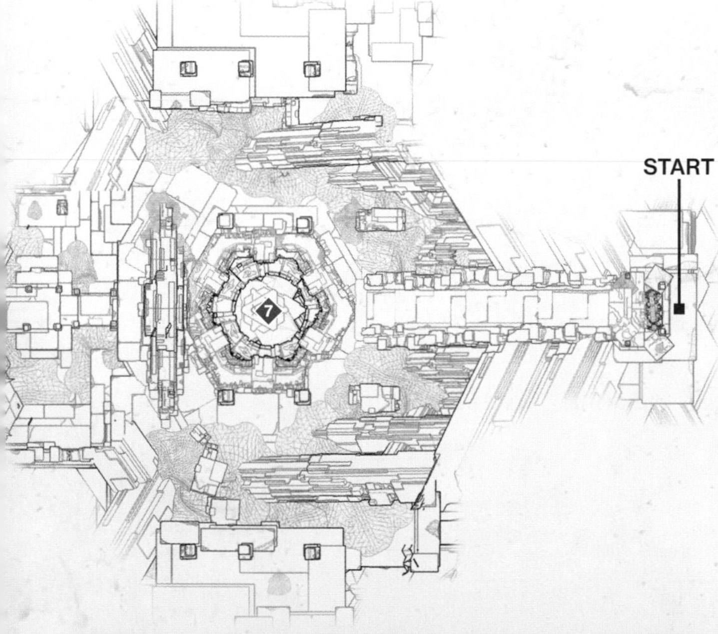

Once you're through the last warpgate, drop down the colossal conduit to a roughly triangular altar chamber with numerous gaps in the floor (leading to bottomless death drops) and a final altar to step into. This summons a truly frightening (and massive) **Boss Hobgoblin**, the genesis mind of the Pyramidion itself!

From the start of the battle, it is important to know where the Boss Hobgoblin appears from (the edge of the arena closest to the altar you stand on).

Situate your team so that the available **low block cover opportunities are known and utilized.** Then, train all your **firepower on the Boss' head** as soon as it appears. Wreck him with your fire and sticky grenades until he retreats to a raised perimeter of the battlefield and puts up an **impenetrable white shield.** A host of Goblins is then summoned.

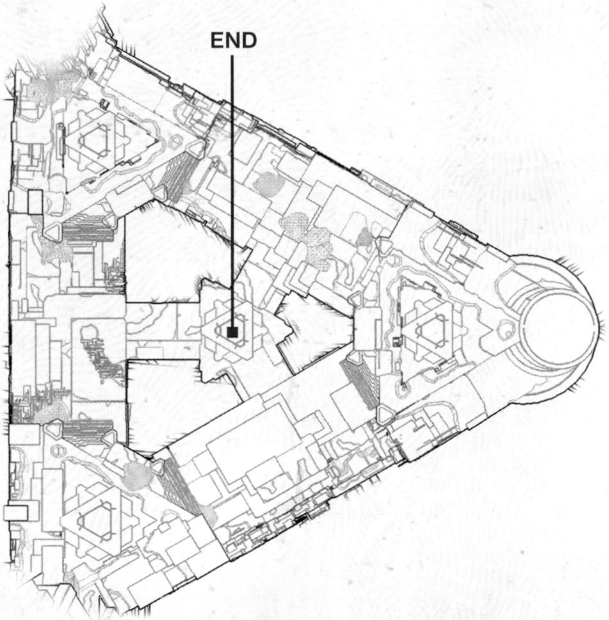

Stay active, concentrate on removing the multiple Goblins (area-of-effect attacks work before the Goblins spread out), and then **stand on an appearing altar circle** to weaken the Boss Hobgoblin's white shield wall. A second wave of Goblins then appears on the opposite side of the front of the wall, with a second altar circle to stand in. **Remove the foes, and activate this second altar.** The white wall shield collapses, enabling you to damage the Boss Hobgoblin again. During this time, the Boss Hobgoblin may raise or drop the low block wall sections, so **hiding places are not guaranteed.** Instead, back up and use your favored ranged weapon, or close in and remove Goblins with a shotgun (depending on your play style).

When the Boss Hobgoblin is prone, waste no time in bombarding him in the central red head slit, avoiding his vicious and powerful red laser sniper rifle. This is the time to launch grenades and Supers into the foe; do it **as soon as the shield wall drops so you can inflict the maximum amount of damage possible** before another wall goes up. Note the red glow before the Boss Hobgoblin fires his rifle. When you see it, strafe quickly into cover so it doesn't badly damage you.

Expect to deal with two or three shield walls before the Boss Hobgoblin loses a third of his health. **On subsequent wall shield removal plans, watch for additional foes to appear**, like Minotaurs and the Goblin hordes.

More expert players tend to wait for Vex to "fall in" and land on the ground, and they dispatch enemies near where they first appear while remaining in cover. Then, they target the foes at the second altar area from distance. It's also a **great idea to split up** (it only takes one of you to stand at an altar); make your team more difficult to fire at by attacking in all directions.

With around a third of his health lost, the **Boss Hobgoblin attempts a rampage** across the arena. Find cover, split up, and bombard him with your favored weaponry. Supers are reasonable at this point, but the Boss Hobgoblin usually teleports when he's hit by enough damage, meaning that you can waste some of your Super sprinting to reach him again.

At this point, the **Boss Hobgoblin throws out a nasty belch of purple flames** that coats the surrounding area where you're standing. Leap quickly out of the way, and don't spend time thinking the cover is going to help you. The burning damage spreads out around the blocks you're hiding behind. Goblins are summoned as the Boss Hobgoblin continues this rampage.

To further annoy you, **he removes and summons block sections in separate areas of the arena**, so split your team up and attack from three different directions. Watch for the purple fire gouts, too.

With around one-third of his health left, the **Boss Hobgoblin starts a more manic assault**, summoning Harpies and Goblins (and sometimes Fanatics) to aid him. Deal with them in your immediate area, then spread your team out to the three different corners of the map. Use block cover, and train your weapons and Supers on the giant foe until you **blow his head off**. Then, switch to the torso opening glowing white, circle-strafing around the now-crippled foe until he finally goes down.

The Inverted Spire

Strike: Recommended Power 140
Nightfall: Required Power 230
Recommended Power 240

Cabal mining activity on Nessus has unexpectedly woken a powerful Vex presence, and the ensuing conflict across multiple Sectors requires Guardian investigation. Your team must access the Cabal drilling operation away from the main Sectors of this planetoid and wade through any defenses as you search diligently (and violently) for evidence of Modular Mind activity. The final showdown occurs all the way down a multiple-tiered inverted spire, where a Boss proves that the Vex are a real force to be reckoned with.

The Cistern

Nessus, Unstable Centaur

Objectives

Investigate the Cabal.
Defeat all hostiles.
Access the conflux.
Press forward.

Enemies Encountered

CABAL: Legionaries, Phalanxes, Psions, Centurion
VEX: Goblins, Minotaurs, Cyclops

1 Pedestal Platforms

Super: Optional (one player) **Grenades:** Optional
Variations: Vex enemies (Goblins, Minotaur, Cyclops) on the exit promontory.

Assault the Landing Zone in the southeastern area of the Cistern, where a group of Cabal (Legionaries and Phalanxes) is engaged in battle with the Vex (Goblins and a slightly toughened Minotaur). The fight is relatively straightforward, as you have the height advantage and can also attack from the block walls surrounding the LZ.

Access the pulsing conflux, hacking it so a series of floating blocks appears over the bottomless chasm ahead and along the southern perimeter of this Sector.

Carefully jump across the blocks (or take the slightly shorter route across the even smaller blocks to the right of the main route) to a block promontory with a Vex cannon above it. **Jump into the cannon** to propel yourself across to a second larger promontory with a small contingent of Cabal (or Vex, depending on the variations). Expect Legionaries, Psions, and a Centurion to waylay you. Use the tube-like structure as cover as you easily bring down these forces and then leap through another Vex cannon, traversing deeper into these vast floating block structures.

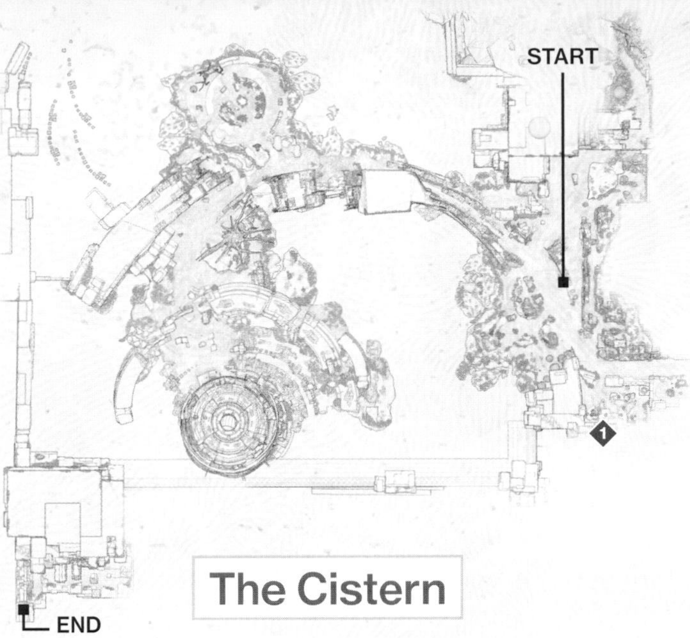

The Anchor

Restricted Zone

Objectives

Traverse deeper.

Press forward.

Enemies Encountered

VEX: Goblins, Hobgoblins, Fanatics, Hydras

2 Anchor Chasm

Super: Recommended (one player) **Grenades:** Optional

Variations: Hobgoblins on the upper ledges, Cabal forces (Sub-Boss Centurion) in the main L-shaped ledge.

Enter the gaping chasm and look to the right from the entrance perch. **Snipe the Goblins** on the lower block "bridge," and then jump to it. Watch your step: aside from the ledges to leap to, this is a bottomless crevasse. **Look out for Hobgoblins sniping from the far blocks** on the upper and lower areas. Have one of your team **jump to the higher plinth** attached to the right wall, as there's a good view (and you can step back into cover). Here, you can spot the Goblins, Fanatics, and two Hydras roaming the L-shaped main ledge to the exit, and lob grenades at them with impunity. You must defeat all these foes, and wading in is a little more dangerous due to the possible death drops along the inner side of the ledge.

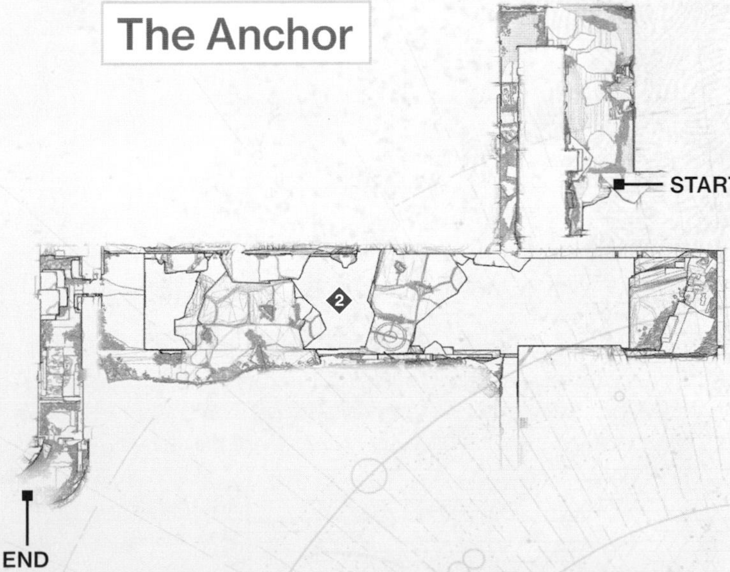

However, at least one of your team should try this to cause a distraction. **The ledge is wide enough for you to dodge incoming fire**. Once you've defeated one or both Hydras, press forward.

There is **a sunken area with a Vex catapult** slightly off the side of the ledge, but milling around here just gets you shot at. You can use it to outflank the foes by landing down here, jumping up to the exit passage, and then turning to face down remaining foes. However, this isn't as cunning of a plan, as you can easily miss the catapult or get confused in the sunken darkness of this lower platform.

Legion Drill Site

Restricted Zone

Objectives

Press forward (continued).
Approach the drilling site.
Eliminate drill site security (2).
Board the Cabal drill.
Reorient the transit system.
Repel all attackers.
Cross to the dig site.
Get clear of the drill.
Investigate the dig site.

Enemies Encountered

CABAL: Psions, Gladiators, Legionaries, War Beasts, Phalanxes
SUB-BOSS: Blood Guard (Centurion), Centurions, Incendiors, Blood Guard (Incendior)
VEX: Goblins

Legion Drill Site

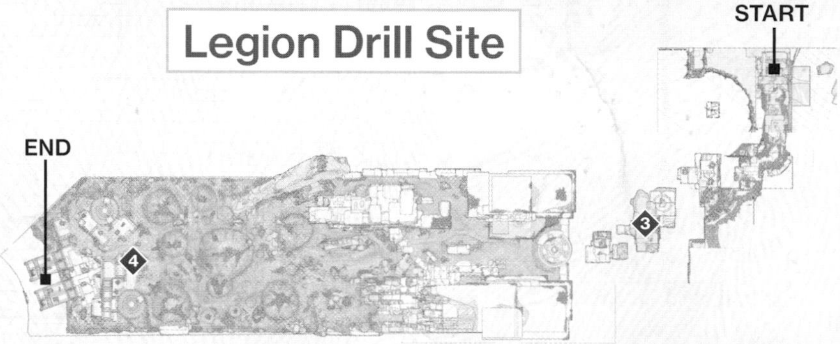

3 Stepping Stones

Super: Recommended **Grenades:** Optional

You appear high above a huge expanse of block architecture, with the strip mining of the Cabal visible in the far distance. Getting there is the first challenge. Stop at the edge of the large red moss-covered block towers, and **snipe the Cabal Psions** atop the nearest one before jumping onto it. To the right of the moss-covered block is an attached gray promontory with a small block section and a scarred circle carved into the stone. **Land here, and expect to face at least two Cabal Gladiators.** If you can land on the block section, you can use the slight height and cover to dodge the Gladiators as you slaughter them. Then, simply **snipe a couple of Legionaries on your way down** to the last stepping stone, then head to the **Vex altar circle, where a group of Goblins** must be quickly defeated. Immediately wind your way across any of the short Vex paths, and go into the crater zone.

4 Cabal Mining Base

Super: Recommended **Grenades:** Recommended
Variations: Vex forces between Sub-Bosses in the mining base.

Rush (or drive) across the crater zone, ignoring any small skirmishes between Vex and Cabal forces (there's no need to get involved); expect Goblins and War Beasts in this area. **Slow down as you reach the edge of the mining base. You have two "drill officers" (Sub-Boss Legionaries) to tackle**, as well as a host of Legionaries who have jet-packed into your view. Each Sub-Boss is situated (to begin with) inside one of the two low circular structures, which usually has a Psion sniper on the roof. Between these two structures is a mass of Cabal infantry: Phalanxes, Psions, and Legionaries, usually led by a Centurion with a rapid-fire cannon.

Sub-Bosses: There's a lot to recommend if you first focus your firepower on this central cluster of forces from the crater zone. **Start with any Psions** atop either base building; drop them as your team arrives in the general area. Annihilate the Cabal between the two circular buildings (or Vex, if this is a Strike variation). Then, **take each Legionary Sub-Boss one at a time**. Since they tend to hide inside the circular building, you can have one player rake the entrance, removing Phalanxes and other infantry as well as hitting the Sub-Boss drill officer. Another teammate can fire through the open windows and lob in grenades. This can topple the foe in seconds. Repeat the process with the remaining Sub-Boss in the other building.

Your next task is to board the Cabal drill. At this point, venture down to the two ledges with the Cabal energy catapult (AKA "transit system") on each of them. On the way, expect to **deal with a couple of Centurions**. With your team, predetermine which of the two catapults you want to activate. Have one member access the nearby switch to power it up while the other two tackle a Centurion each and any remaining Cabal stragglers. Remember that **the energy catapult must be glowing orange** before you jump into it, or you'll simply fall to your death in a most embarrassing manner.

5 Drill Rig

Super: Recommended

Grenades: Recommended

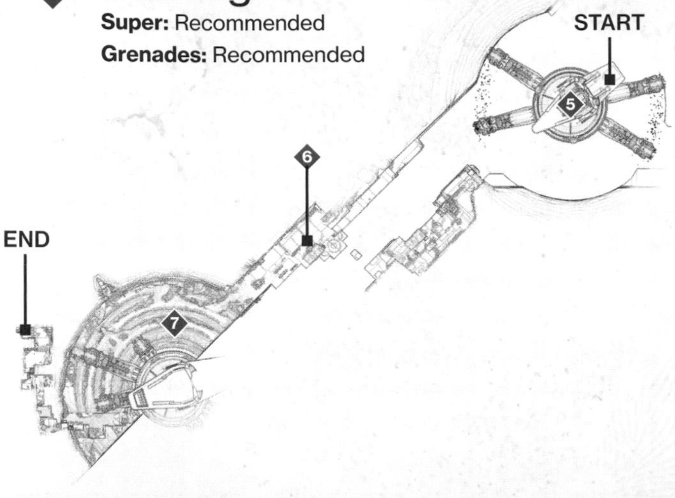

Ensure that the three of you are **catapulted onto the Cabal drill rig in unison**, as the battle to come is the most difficult you've encountered so far. As the first teammate lands on the platform above the drill rig's circular control room, a door opens, and Cabal forces appear (Phalanxes and Legionaries). **A quick, well-placed grenade damages all of them**, after which you can mop up stragglers. Predetermine who's going to throw the grenade, and ensure that all your teammates have Supers at the ready before you drop down into the rig's control chamber.

The action commences immediately with **a group of Gladiators to defeat**. Have one teammate **complete the objective** as soon as possible. The "transit system" (a slowly rotating Cabal catapult) must be moved into position, and wasting time ignoring this objective simply means more time fighting a crazy number of foes. Pull the lever on the raised perimeter terminal, and watch the system reset count up. However, your main focus is on further Cabal incursions.

Expect a group of **Legionaries and a couple of Gladiators to drop in**. Priority targets are the Gladiators; keep moving around this compact circular chamber so they don't strike and kill you. Launch a Super at this point. Then, have a teammate continue with their Super as **a pack of War Beasts and a second wave of Legionaries and Gladiators appear**. Lob grenades and basically expend all your weaponry to ensure that you survive this onslaught. But keep an eye on the objective; when the transit system has reoriented itself, you can leave, even if there are still Cabal in this control room.

6 Vex Gorge and Cabal Quarry

Super: Recommended **Grenades:** Optional

Variations: Vex forces on the tiered quarry area (Goblins and Hobgoblins).

Enter the Cabal catapult that's glowing orange (not the one that isn't in use), and fly across to a long gorge of probable Vex construction. Edge forward, and **while one teammate tackles the Incendiors** on the covered ledge you're moving through, **have two teammates snipe the Psions** on the (inaccessible) lip of the gorge to your right, across the bottomless chasm.

Otherwise, you're picked off as you leap across the pillars to a lower section on the opposite side. Between you and the drill site is a group of **Phalanxes, Incendiors, and a Sub-Boss Incendior**. You have plenty of range and cover, along with an optimal opportunity to launch a Super or lob grenades to remove these threats.

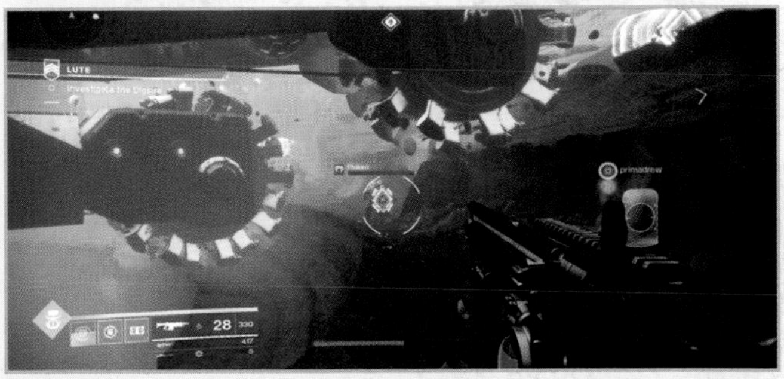

7 Approach the quarry, with its massive and deadly rotating quarrying arm machines. There are multiple arms, and being struck by any of them kills you. The trick here is to **drop down onto one of the tiered grooves** and simply make a counterclockwise run around to the entrance into the Inverted Spire Sector. As long as you aren't jumping, all of the quarry arms pass you by **if you're positioned on this tier**. The "tier" in question is shown in the previous picture. There are actually three safe paths, the lowest two are equally safe. These walkable paths feature dark brown dirt, whereas the paths that the arms travel in are light, bare rocks.

Teammates can be struck by an arm, so bunch up and follow each other closely, without being hit. If this isn't possible, **look for alcoves** along the route (always on the right-side), and step in to avoid the arms. The Phalanxes, Psions, and War Beasts are a secondary distraction. Soak up a bit of damage by remaining in the relative safety of the recommended tier, and remove these Cabal threats as you encounter them. **Psions should be the priority targets**.

With the quarry navigated, drop down into the initial safety of the drill site, but don't investigate further until all three of you are in the entrance corridor to the Inverted Spire. This is where combat gets even crazier!

The Inverted Spire

Restricted Zone

Objectives

Investigate the dig site (continued).
Defeat the Modular Mind.

Enemies Encountered

VEX: Harpies
BOSS: Protheon, Modular Mind (Minotaur), Goblins, Fanatics

The Inverted Spire

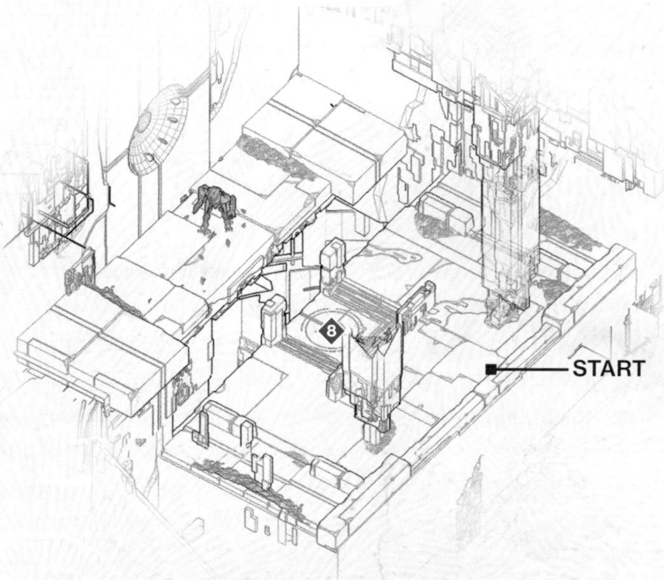

8 Guardian Platform

Super: Recommended **Grenades:** Recommended
Boss Weak Spot: Head, then torso opening.
Variations: Additional troops (usually Hobgoblins).

Carefully drop down the massive vertical conduit you enter, and start tackling a group of Harpies. **Take defensive positions** around the different parts of the perimeter before the last Harpy is shot, as removing the initial foes causes **the Vex Boss Protheon** to be stirred. He warps in under the large circular white portal light. Note the gap in this battle chamber along the middle of the floor, meaning you must be careful how you step and land during jumps.

Boss: The battle with Protheon starts now. Rattle off as many aimed shots into the white light **in the center of Protheon's head**, directly striking him as often as possible while avoiding the purple energy bolts from his massive weapon. If you've split up and you're **using the two low stone block sections as cover**, as well as the two pillars on the opposite perimeter of the arena, you can remove his health relatively quickly.

It's worth predetermining **one member of your team to immediately jump in and tackle Harpies** that appear as the battle continues. The **other two teammates should be leveling all firepower at the Boss**, including Super attacks and the stickier of any available grenades. **Keep moving**, or die under a hail of Protheon's gunfire. When you've removed around a third of his health, Protheon disappears. And moments later, so does the floor!

9 Radiolarian Circle

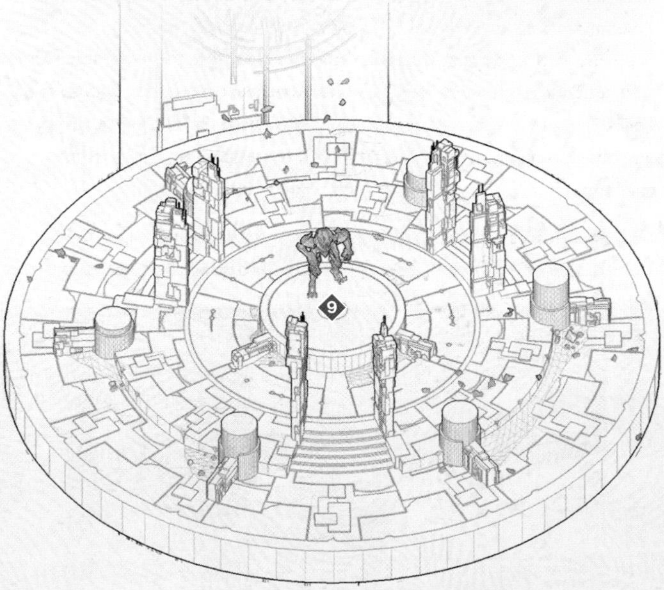

Your team plummets to a large circular island (and should jump to prevent damage upon landing). Try to **land on the short cylindrical pillars** around the edge of the circle, and split up. Moments later, Protheon appears again, and combat continues. The plan is to inflict as much damage to the Boss's head as it is safe to do. **When Protheon punches the ground, it subsequently becomes distinctly molten**, and it can kill you in seconds. T his is the reason for standing atop the low circular pillars, which aren't affected. The ground heats up and explodes. The burning ground does a small amount of damage; the blast is stronger, and will knock you up and out of the arena if you are not careful.

After the punch, the innermost ring glows and bursts, and just after outermost ring does the same. Stand on those pillars, run between the two rings, or just jump in the air to escape each blast.

Combat continues. If Protheon is aiming directly at you, **attempt to perfect a sideways jump** to a nearby circular pillar so you can keep aiming at his head at all times (or Hobgoblins, if this is a Strike variation). Any other teammates should be pounding Protheon in the cranium as much as possible. At this point, more than a dozen Goblins enter, and more molten ground transformations occur. The **Goblins are more of a distraction**; only defeat them if they are too close, though you're more likely to be constantly circling the perimeter of this arena so you're not burned alive. **Time for a second teammate's Super!** As Protheon is damaged to around one-third health, he disappears again. Look down, and look out!

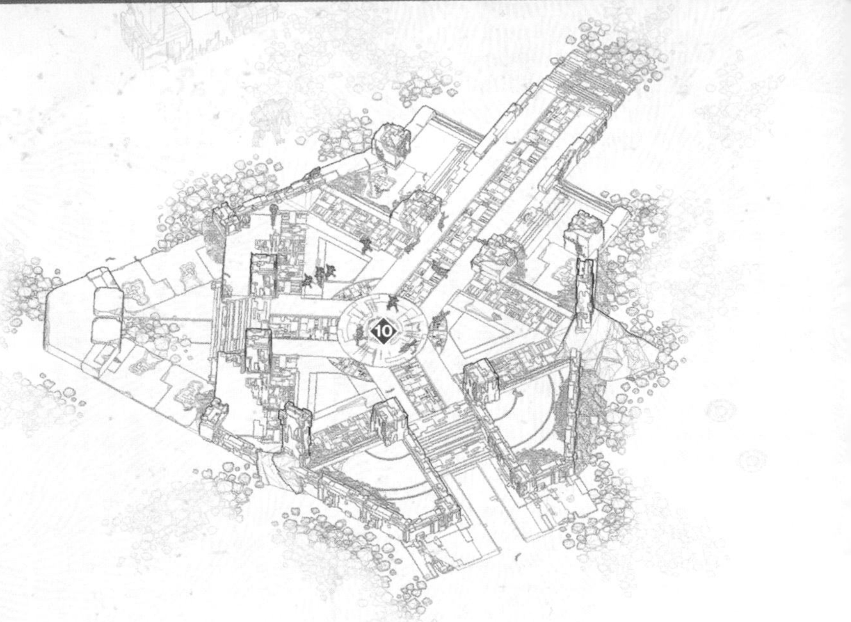

10 Tower Base (Final Conflict)

Your team falls (and hopefully jumps to avoid the impact just before reaching the ground), landing on a roughly circular base of this inverted spire, where Goblins are present. Remove them, as they are more of a problem this time. Moments later, **Protheon makes his presence felt, shooting out larger blue bolts of energy**. He stands on the Radiolarian lake that surrounds this island, which is deadly if you step on it. With limited maneuverability, **take every advantage you can in regard to the block scenery**; use it to hide behind or stand on top of so you can avoid further Vex infantry incursions.

Shoot the Boss's head, continuing to aim as he tracks around the perimeter of the island. When another wave of Goblins and Harpies appears, lob in a grenade as they rise out of the lake, and take down multiples at a time. **Protheon has attacks from a weapon fused to each arm** (a rapid-fire rifle on his right arm, and a larger slower-firing cannon on his left, with missile impact that can temporarily blind you). Avoid these, and keep pressing the attack.

When Protheon loses around five-sixths of his health (halfway between the last third and his ultimate defeat), **he loses his head—literally**. A torso slit opens, and this is where you must aim for the remaining moments of the battle. **It's at this point that Protheon becomes even more dangerous**. He rampages onto the island **and summons a horde of Fanatics** (as well as Goblins and Harpies) to thwart you. **Fanatics will home in and explode at your location**, which can kill all three teammates in seconds if you're not paying attention. Break off from striking Protheon for a second, use the scenery (especially the tops of the low pillars), and **shoot all Fanatics as priority targets**, provided a teammate isn't caught in the explosion. Request that your team flees to the edge of the island, and detonate the Fanatics in the middle. Then, return to fighting the Boss until he finally crumples. Don't forget to use your Supers to finish the job.

Exodus Crash

Strike: Recommended Power 140
Nightfall: Required Power 230
Recommended Power 240

It appears that Failsafe has been compromised after a contingent of Fallen touched down on Nessus and raided a secondary crash site near the Exodus Black. Your team is tasked with tracking a series of arc pulses left by the Fallen's weapons in preparation for finding and defeating this raiding party and their leader.

Prodromus Down

Restricted Zone

Enemies Encountered

VEX: Minotaurs, Goblins, Fanatics, Hobgoblins, Hydras
FALLEN: Vandals, Shanks, Captains, Dregs
SUB-BOSS: Servitor (2), Overcharge Shanks

Objectives

Pass through the electrical fields (100%).
Fight into the base.
Infiltrate the hideout.
Gather Fallen data.
Defend Ghost (100%).
Kill the Servitors (2).
Press onward.

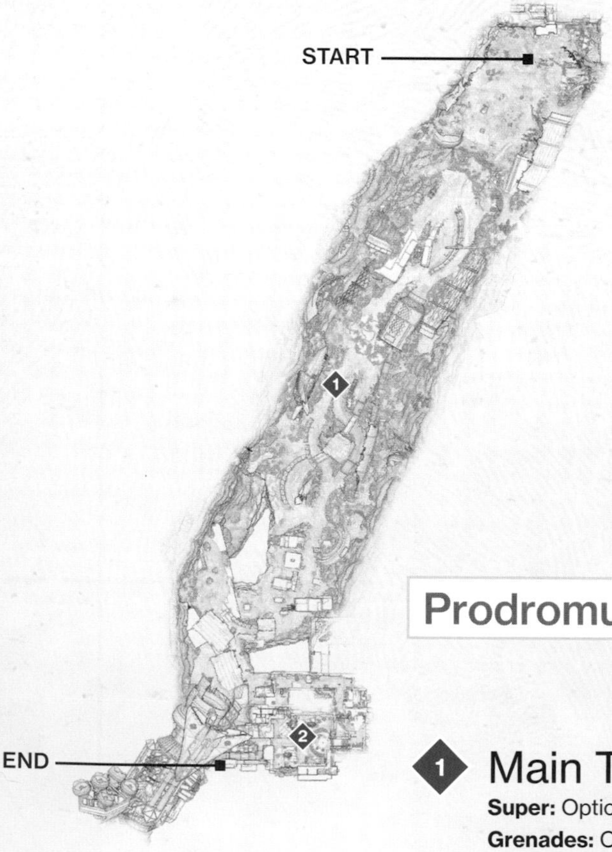

Prodromus Down

1 Main Trench

Super: Optional (one player)
Grenades: Optional
Variations: Fallen foes instead of Vex enemies.

You begin in a rarely visited Sector of Nessus, Prodromus Down. **This massive trench has a number of Vex guards**. Minotaurs and Goblins (or Fallen Captains and Vandals, if this is a variation) are stationed around the roadways that twist through the scattered ship wreckage all along this massive shallow scar. Though you can race forward, **optionally using Sparrows**, it's worth hanging back and methodically tackling the foes one cluster at a time, especially **the group of Fanatics** (who swarm and explode at close range). Tagging them from distance with long-range fire removes multiple threats at once.

As you progress forward, **split up and have each teammate head for a shaft of light**. These cylindrical electrical fields are instantly analyzed once you reach one, and there are only a few to find (usually six). You may find it easier to utilize a Sparrow, or better yet, a Pike that is parked in the vicinity with offensive weaponry. Blast another cluster of Fanatics, and watch for more of them if you take the main road (or Vandals, if this is a variation). As you start heading uphill **toward a ruined fuselage**, remove Minotaurs and Goblins as a threat before starting an assault on some sniping Fallen Vandals. If you can **make it all the way to the low ceilings of the cargo storage exit** from this trench, so much the better. Battle more Fallen at this entrance; Shanks, Vandals, and a Captain await you before you can head into the interior.

2 Cargo Storage and Transmitter Chamber

Super: Recommended (one player)
Grenades: Recommended
Variations: Laser traps throughout the cargo storage, more Wretches, toughened enemies, two giant Shanks after Servitors battle.

Quickly push through the narrow low-ceilinged storage area once the barrier fades at the entrance (after you've neutralized all foes outside). **Push your way up into the transmitter chamber**, fighting Goblins and Dregs as you go. You can actually ram your Pikes up into this area and finish these foes with this vehicle's weaponry while staying protected by its structure.

Once you've killed the Fanatics and Hobgoblins already in the room, park near the yellow transmitter beacon.

You must now secure the room from an onslaught of both Vex and Fallen foes as **Ghost gathers data** on the Fallen from the transmitter. Remain close to the raised circular platform at the entrance, and **note the dark wall areas around the room that foes can spread out from**. Lob in a grenade before the clusters of Dregs and Overcharge Shanks head out of the first one. Overcharge shanks will electrocute some floors in this room: the two spots where the servitors fight from, and the platform you must stand in to progress. You can still use Pikes here to make short work of the foes before they venture too far into the room. Expect waves of teleporting Goblins, Overcharge Shanks from a wall hole, and then two annoying Servitors.

Sub-Bosses: Two toughened Servitors drop in to thwart you. As they are protecting the Overcharge Shanks that also make an appearance, **make the Servitors priority targets**. A Super and grenades are fine to use at this point. Goblins and Vandals also soon turn up after the Servitors. To prevent this from becoming a bloodbath, remain near the transmitter, using the surrounding cover and hammering the Servitors, then the Overcharge Shanks, and finally, anyone else left standing.

Here comes a Hydra! It teleports in with a couple of Minotaurs, but if all three of you are focusing your firepower on it, defeating it is straightforward. **Do this quickly, as a cluster of Fanatics then appears** and should be a priority due to their explosive tendencies (just like the Overcharge Shanks). With these foes defeated, the analysis is complete and the barrier retracts, allowing you access into Exodus Black Sector.

Exodus Black

Nessus, Unstable Centaur

Objectives

Pass through the electrical fields (100%).
Hunt the Fallen.

Enemies Encountered

FALLEN: Dregs, Vandals, Captain

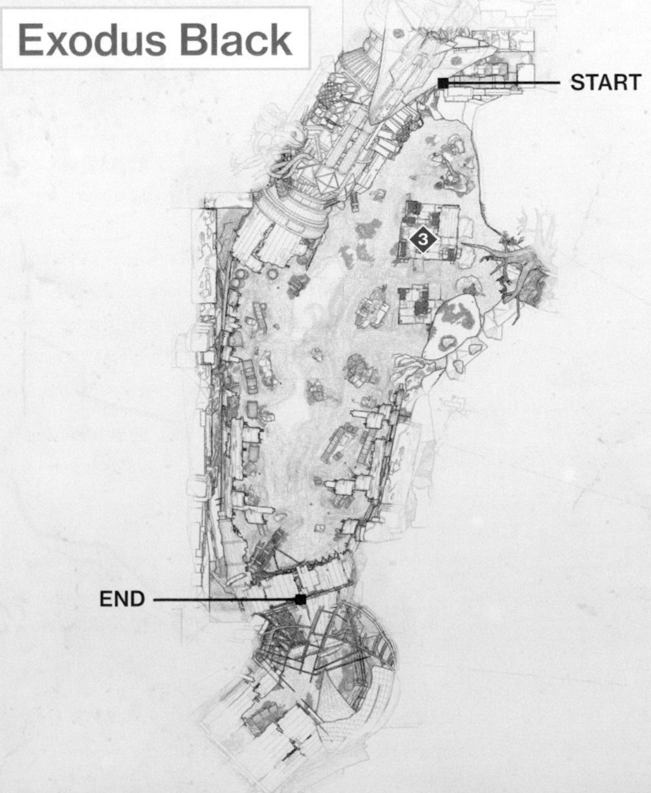

3 Fallen Base

Super: Optional **Grenades:** Optional
Variations: Hydra and possible Cyclops incursions in the lake area.

A **second series of electrical field columns** must be analyzed. Before you assault the ramshackle Fallen base in this Sector, check for a visual on the electrical fields, and have each teammate rush to two of them. Or, cluster up and advance in a pack, if you want. **Remember that you don't have to kill absolutely everything.** If time is a factor, just step into each electrical field and then flee, heading to Glade of Echoes with some immediacy.

There are three fields in and around the base: one atop the high plateau, and the other two in the lake and jumble of rocket parts close to the Exodus Black crash site itself. There aren't many enemies at this location (only the Fallen you usually encounter here), so **there's little reason to stick around**. However, it's worth finding and removing a Dreg from its Pike vehicle and using that to speed into Glade of Echoes.

Glade of Echoes

Nessus, Unstable Centaur

Objectives

Hunt the Fallen (continued).
Defeat the Assault Walker.

Enemies Encountered

FALLEN: Dregs, Vandals, Captain, Assault Walker, Giant Shank, Shanks

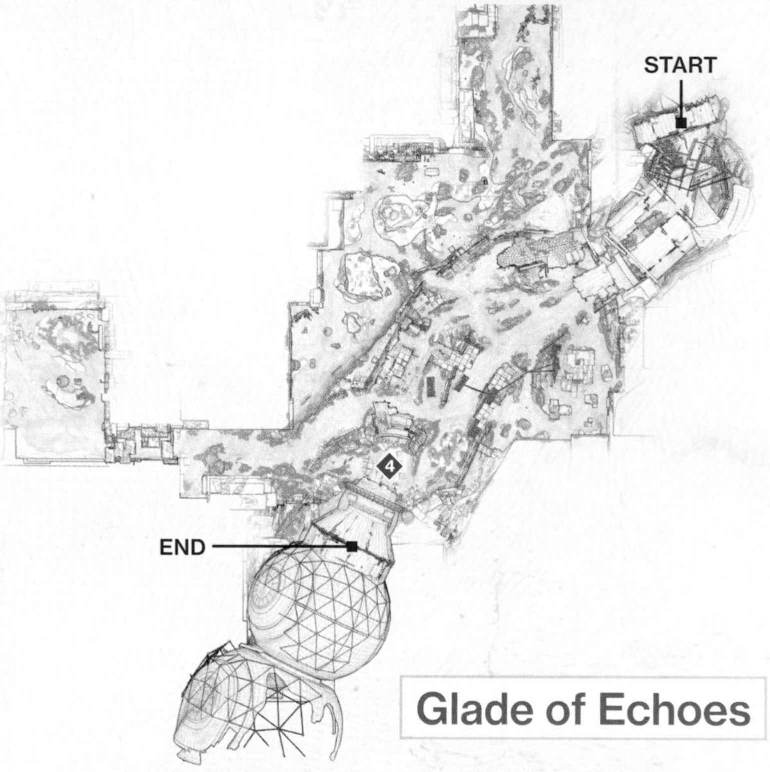

Attack the Walker by shooting its cockpit head or any of its **legs until it slumps forward and exposes its orange glowing "neck" engine interior**. Blast that to inflict heavy damage. Repeat this plan until one of you explodes. During this time, expect Shanks to be summoned, but these aren't particularly troublesome.

If you aren't using Pikes, split your team so everyone **attacks from three disparate angles**. You have enough cover and jumping room to ensure that this Walker is taken down easily, and one of you can try a Super if the battle is lasting too long.

Enter the circular fuselage structure the Walker was guarding. There's no need to waste time clearing the area of other foes; you must now fight to the source of the new Fallen tech.

4 Entrance to EX-077 Command: Tank Battle

Super: Recommended **Grenades:** Recommended
Variations: Additional Heavy Shanks.

Hopefully, you've apprehended enough Pikes for each team member (some empty Pikes sometimes appear nearby, so look for them), and you're boosting downhill toward the giant fuselage wreckage to engage in combat with a **Fallen Walker**, flanked by a giant Shank. While there are pockets of Fallen resistance (usually infantry) throughout this Sector, it isn't imperative to cull every single one of them. Concentrate on removing the Shanks, then peppering the Walker with Pike fire. Though the damage isn't that impressive, the rapid fire and extra protection this vehicle gives you is advantageous, especially because you can save your ammo and Supers for the Boss battle to come.

EX-077 Command

Restricted Zone

Objectives

Fight to the source.
Destroy the Shanks.
Kill Thaviks the Depraved.

Enemies Encountered

FALLEN: Dregs, Wretches, Vandals, Overcharge Shanks
BOSS: Thaviks the Depraved (Marauder), Servitors, Marauders, Captains

5 Dark Platforms

Super: Recommended (one player)
Grenades: Recommended
Variations: Vex Harpies and Goblins appearing

Prepare for the violence and intensity to be ratcheted up a couple of notches as you enter the **near-complete darkness of a dome-shaped interior chamber** after navigating a narrow and fiery entrance.

EX-077 Command

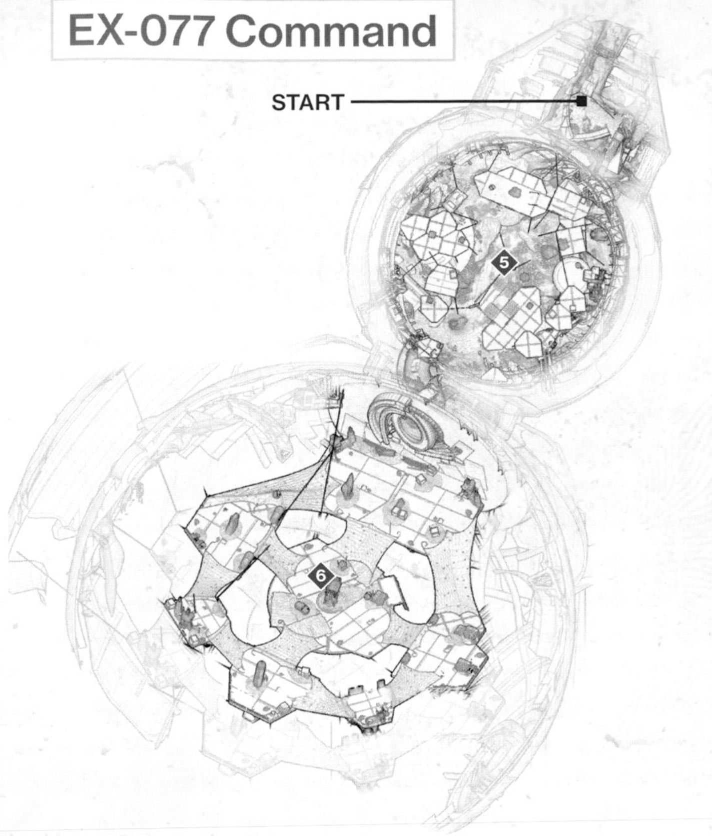

Ditch the Pikes if you still have them, and battle Fallen ahead and above you. This chamber has **several hanging platforms you must jump across** in order to exit. Fortunately, there are only Dregs, Wretches, and Vandals to worry about in here. Climb the gantry steps, then **look for the narrow orange lights indicating a platform above you** in the dark. Leap these stepping stones, defeating any foes on each subsequent platform, ideally using a close-range assault weapon **like a shotgun**. A teammate can remain at ground level to snipe from distance to cover you, if you're having trouble. When you reach the connecting tube passage that exits, wait so all three of you can head into the Boss chamber together.

6 Dark Platforms (Boss Battle)

Super: Recommended **Grenades:** Recommended
Variations: Toughened enemies and Boss, increased number of enemies.
Boss Weak Spot: Head

Stand atop the chasm chamber, and snipe the **Overcharge Shanks** down below. Notice how they are **electrifying the platforms**? This is a key problem to overcome during the ensuing battle with the Fallen leader, as you are damaged and slowed if you wade through this electricity. For the moment, blast all Shanks before dropping down, remembering that there's a bottomless chasm below you.

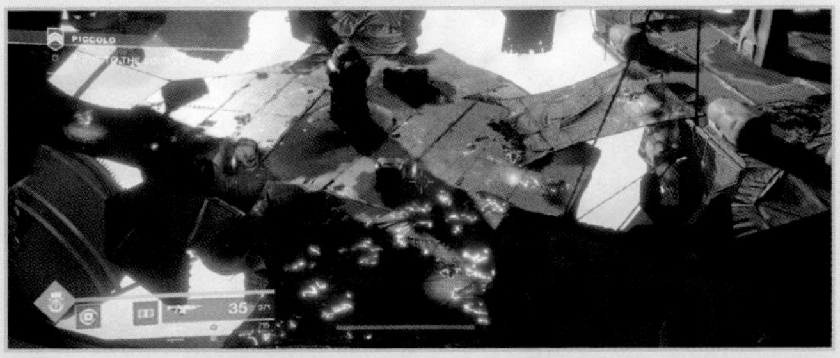

Boss: The source to be fought is a larger **Captain-sized Marauder Boss named Thaviks** (and his Overcharge Shank minions), and he's particularly troublesome. **He's fast and can scurry away or charge you in seconds. He has a highly damaging shrapnel launcher**, so make sure your dexterity and jumping are on point, especially during closer altercations. **He also has a cloaking device**. Look for the shimmering blue of his form and attack accordingly; there's no reason to let him remain untouched because this simply elongates an already fraught combat. Finally, **he attacks with melee strikes if you're close enough** and during the latter part of the battle, so expect a quick death if you don't back up.

As you might expect, your initial task is to remove the first third of the Boss' health. Concentrate all your team's firepower and launch one Super to effectively **remove this health as quickly as possible**. Unless Shanks and Vandals invade the entire platform area, **have at least two of your teammates make this a priority action**. The third player should check the various pods and other entrances around the perimeter of this arena for incursions of Overcharge Shanks and electrified floors. The floors can really stop you in your tracks (literally, they slow you down). Using your Movement Mode to go over them, landing on precarious scenery so you aren't struck by the electrified floor, and staying away from those areas while removing Shanks as quickly as possible are all good ideas.

For the first third of his health, Thaviks fights from the far end of the room. He teleports out of the arena every 10 percent of health he loses, and comes in by the shank spawners with refreshed camo (it does not regenerate like normal).

At 30 percent of his health gone, Thaviks retreats and waits for the minor combatants to be killed. Thaviks then switches to the entrance side of the room, spawning enemies, shanks, and teleporting from there.

At 40 percent, Thaviks retreats again and waits for all enemies to be killed. Then, he enables all 4 shank spawners, and will teleport in by any of the 4 - this time, with blades instead of a shrapnel launcher.

The last part of the battle involves **Thaviks being even more aggressive in his melee capabilities** and Overcharge Shanks electrifying more of the arena. Your plan here remains unchanged from earlier, though it helps to attack from multiple angles. **Have teammates with one or two Supers ready** to inflict a deadly amount of damage until the Fallen foe finally drops.

The Arms Dealer

Strike: Recommended Power 140
Nightfall: Required Power 230
Recommended Power 240

The Cabal warrior-leader known as Primus Zahn is active in the Cabal-controlled stronghold on the eastern side of the EDZ. Your team is tasked with breaching the Sectors under Cabal command while also dealing with intermittent Fallen incursions and working your way to the main cargo deck where Primus Zahn is said to be located. Along the way, you must neutralize a number of Zahn's trusted brethren and lieutenants. Expect almost every type of Cabal force to be active, including Thresher ships.

Legion's Anchor

Restricted Zone

Objectives

Overload Primus Zahn's systems.
Secure the area.
Force an explosion.
Kill Zahn's Lieutenant.
Find Zahn (continued).

Enemies Encountered

FALLEN: Captain, Vandals, Wretches, Servitors, Shanks
CABAL: Legionaries, Phalanxes, Psions, Centurions, War Beasts, Threshers
SUB-BOSS: Bracus Nor (Legionary), Bracus Vox (Legionary), Zahn's Lieutenant (Legionary)

1 South Cargo Docks

Super: Recommended (one player)
Grenades: Recommended

Alternate Version

There are two versions of this Strike; one with Cabal forces to fight and another with Cabal and Fallen forces. Adjust your tactics accordingly.

Begin to work your way along the windowed interior corridor. Use the yellow canisters to detonate close to any Fallen nearby (including a Captain). **Access the computer monitor**, which opens the door to the south cargo docks.

Sub-Boss: Dropships are depositing Cabal Legionaries and Phalanxes into a Fallen contingent of Vandals and a Captain. **A Sub-Boss Legionary (Bracus Nor) is leading this Cabal assault** and should be shot in the head until he yields.

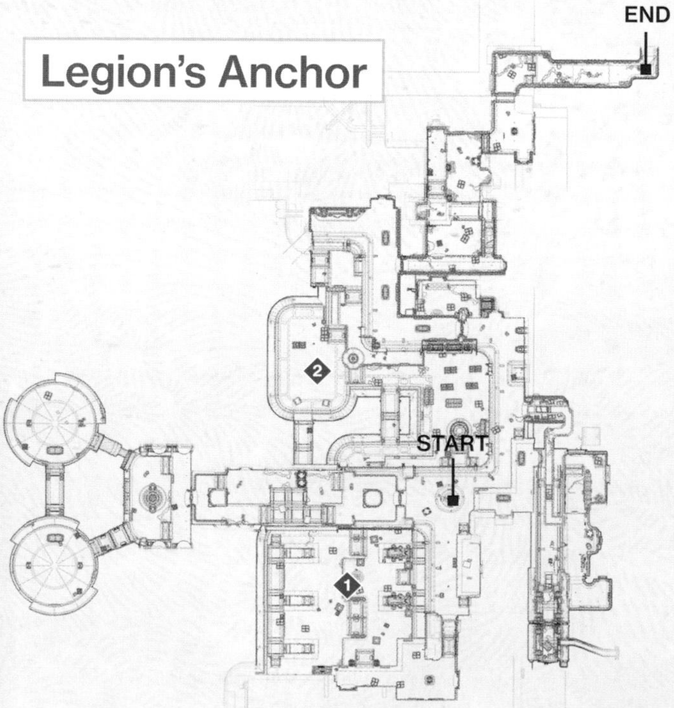

Stay on the perimeter of the bay while one or two teammates engage the foes at closer quarters. Scenery is easily available to hide behind. Have one teammate hover over the fusion ball dispenser as the enemy presence is whittled down. **Then, grab the ball as soon as the objective requests that you force an explosion.**

2 North Cargo Docks

Super: Recommended (one player)
Grenades: Recommended

Sub-Boss: A second Legionary (Bracus Vox) is waiting to engage with a melee weapon as you run under the connecting super-structure platform to the north cargo docks. **Cover the ball carrier,** and then spread out with one player leaping up onto the left perimeter edge and the other leaping right. Protect the ball carrier as he or she **inserts the fusion ball into the circular receptacle that a Centurion guards**. Focus your firepower on enemies attacking the ball carrier until the fusion ball is released. Take down Psions, War Beasts, and then the Centurion as you sweep the main docks.

By this time, **focus on blasting a Thresher out of the sky (a Super is helpful here), and watch the north ramp for Zahn's Lieutenant** (a toughened Legionary you can quickly drop with a Super), as well as some Fallen Servitors. Focus your firepower here after you clear the main cargo docks. Then, mop up any Fallen Vandals and other stragglers.

Access the windowed corridor, and head **into the tiered loading bay**. You have the height advantage, so use it, and blast yellow canisters for extra explosive damage. There are only a few enemies here, mostly Fallen Shanks and Vandals. Then, head through the connecting corridor into Sunken Isles.

Sunken Isles

Restricted Zone

Objectives

Find Zahn (continued).

Enemies Encountered

CABAL: Legionaries, Phalanxes, Threshers, Centurion
SUB-BOSS: Bracus Crull (Legionary)

Sunken Isles

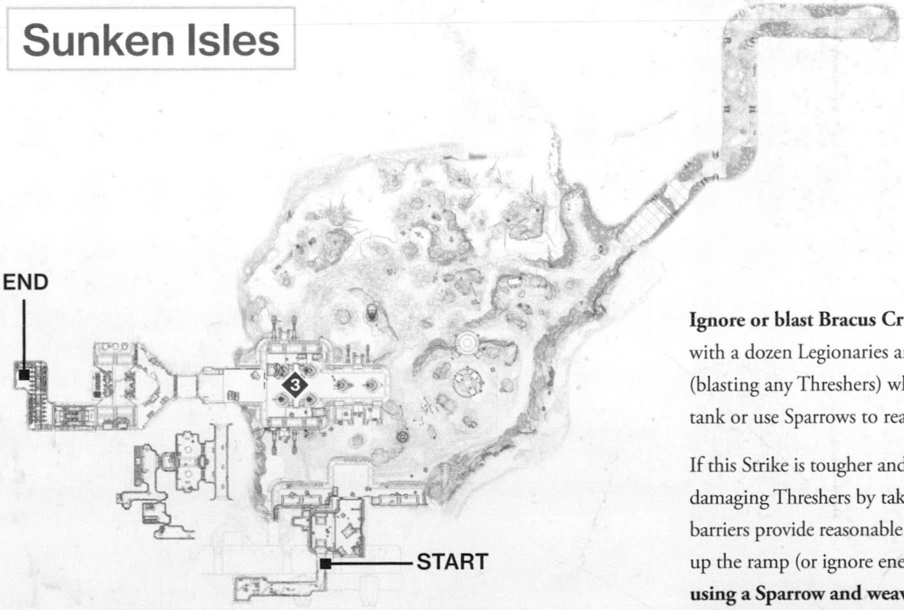

3 Antics on the Carrier On-Ramp

Super: Recommended (one player)
Grenades: Recommended
Variations: Drake tank unavailable

The plan is to **head out of the cargo bay and up into the carrier ramp**. This is easier said than done, as there's a sizable Cabal presence in the vicinity, with a large number of troops on the ramp itself. As you exit, clear all nearby enemies in the rough ground just outside (Legionaries and Phalanxes are milling around here). **If Hawthorne has dropped a Drake tank (to your right as you exit), quickly use it.** Drive it up onto the ramp deck and into the gigantic carrier craft to the next combat zone.

Ignore or blast Bracus Crull, another Sub-Boss who is on the ramp along with a dozen Legionaries and Phalanxes, and a Centurion. Provide covering fire (blasting any Threshers) while your teammates either ride on the side of the tank or use Sparrows to reach you. Enter the Legion's Hold hangar in unison.

If this Strike is tougher and there's no tank to take, you'll have to waste time damaging Threshers by taking cover in and around the cargo bay (the outside barriers provide reasonable cover, but remaining inside is safer). Then, wade up the ramp (or ignore enemies if time is a factor), and boost through them **using a Sparrow and weaving maneuvers**. Or, take a shortcut by activating your Movement Mode up from near the carrier ramp tunnel so you avoid the majority of the foes on the ramp. Having one of your teammates executing a Super against these enemies and Bracus Crull is a good way to remove them as a threat, but **don't split up**!

Legion's Hold

Restricted Zone

Objectives

Access elevator controls.
Clear a path.

Enemies Encountered

CABAL: Goliath Tanks, Legionaries, Incendiors, Centurions, Bracus Vox (Legionary), War Hounds
FALLEN: Captains, Shanks

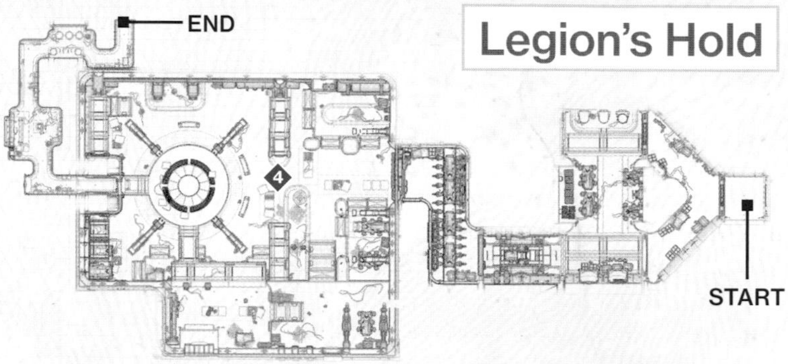

4 Trouble in the Hangar

Super: Recommended (one player)
Grenades: Recommended
Variations: Drake tank unavailable, mines on the ramps, additional enemies, elevator control locations may change

Let's hope you still have use of a Drake tank, as there's likely to be an enemy **Goliath tank** waiting as you enter the Legion's Hold hangar.

If you've used a Drake tank before (and employ cover as well as both of its weapons), you can destroy it almost immediately, then rake the remaining infantry as you wind your way up the ramps. Better yet, **have your teammates concentrate on removing the foot soldier foes en route to the bridge controls**. When a **second Goliath tank appears on the circular platform**, with a Bracus Sub-Boss shortly afterward, vary your attack direction.

Have your Drake tank batter the priority foes from the ground (where the first tank was destroyed) while one of your teammates executes a Super. With good timing, you can inflict massive damage in seconds.
Then, stay back as you kill the Bracus brother; sometimes, a pack of War Beasts bounds out of the door behind him.

If you're approaching on foot, scenery and hard-hitting weaponry are much more important when attacking the tank. **Split up on the ground area, and focus all firepower on the tank, then on any foes at ground level**. Then, it's best to ascend to the bridge controls as a group. Watch for mines as you head up the ramp, as well as a possible influx of Fallen. Note that **the location console with the bridge controls sometimes varies**, so look for the waypoint diamond to confirm where you're going. The second Goliath is relatively easy to tackle because it can't drive anywhere (assuming more than one of you is attacking it). Have one player time their Super to both defeat the tank and inflict serious damage on the Sub-Boss.

Flanking

There's a cunning flanking manuever to try as well; cross the floor of the hangar, under the circular platform, and leap up the left side where the machinery is, to the area behind most of the foes!

Echion Vae

Restricted Zone

Objectives

Hack the door.
Break through.
Defeat Primus Zahn.

Enemies Encountered

CABAL: Basilisk Flamethrowers, Legionaries, Centurions, Phalanxes, Incendiors, Psions, War Beasts
FALLEN: Vandals, Servitors
BOSS: Primus Zahn (Legionary)

5 Echion Vae

Super: Optional (one player) **Grenades:** Optional
Variations: Tougher foes, elevator control locations may change

Navigate the hangar bay and two platform bridges ahead of you. **Priority targets are the flamethrowers atop these bridges**, and then the closest foes to you. Mop up and slowly advance (as the Fallen are dropping in Vandals and Servitors), **using the scenery to your advantage**. There's an alcove on the upper-right area and suspended tanks on the left side of the hangar; both are good places to provide covering fire.

Echion Vae

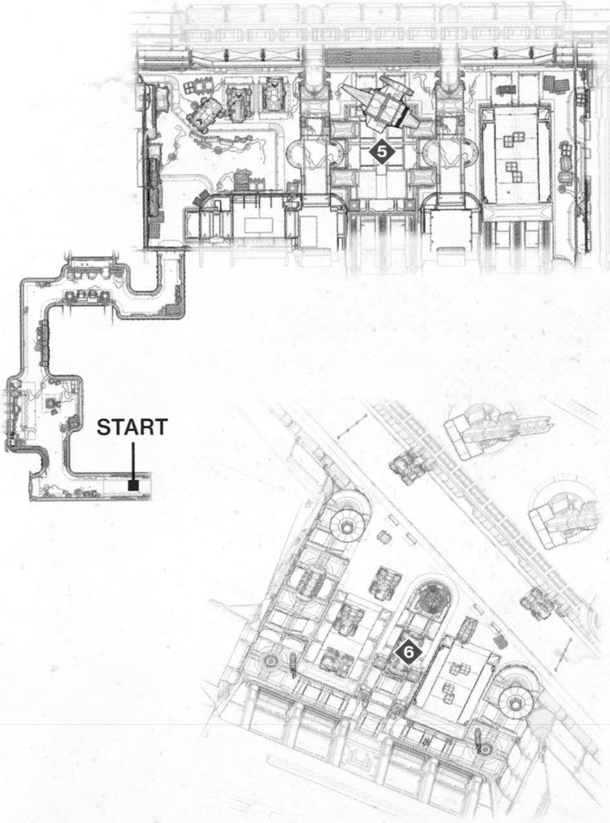

Your main plan is **defeating a couple of Centurion henchmen next to Primus Zahn**, who makes his first appearance. If the three of you can focus on each target at the same time, they fall in seconds and Zahn retreats quickly, prompting you to head onto a giant cargo elevator and mop up both Cabal and Fallen infantry. The crates and other scenery makes this relatively straightforward. Save your Supers for the final battle to come.

If your foes are giving you grief, it's worth **prioritizing your targets and demolishing them together, but from different locations within the hangar**. One teammate could be atop a hanging tank. Another could be on the ground, soaking up enemy fire, with the third atop one of the platform bridges or in the alcove.

6 Primus Zahn's Last Stand

Super: Recommended **Grenades:** Recommended
Variations: Toughened foes, Psion headhunters (snipers), solar charge location may change
Boss Weak Spot: Head

Primus Zahn peers down from atop the elevator on the cargo deck and hits hard with his sniper rifle. You'll be cursing this weapon frequently during the remainder of this Strike, so hide behind the crates, and when you're at the open deck, split up. **Take care of the flamethrower sentry guns immediately** while a second player **executes a Super at Zahn** and the third follows up with hard-hitting strikes and a grenade (also at Zahn). The trick is to **remove the first third of Zahn's health as soon as you can** so the battle doesn't get too protracted. As you'd expect, you're focusing all your regular firepower at Zahn's head. When a third of his health is removed, Zahn jets up to a high platform you can't reach, protecting himself with a solar dome of energy.

Between stages, a host of Cabal arrives from doors and dropships. **Expect dozens of Legionaries, Phalanxes, Incendiors, and a couple of Centurions to cramp your style**. You must defeat them, though staying on the perimeter edge where the flamethrowers are helps you from being swamped. As soon as it becomes available, **rush to grab the solar charge. Run it across the deck to the circular depositing conduit**, removing Zahn's platform protection and starting the second stage of battle.

Zahn flies down, and more flamethrowers and a pack of War Beasts are summoned at the ramped gantry on the perimeter of the deck. If you stay at the edges, you can use the nearby cover and the height of the ramp to avoid some of the incoming fire. **Zahn will train his sniper rifle on one of you, so it's wise to launch a Super** at this point. Have two or all teammates focus on Zahn (one could be coaxing the Cabal infantry away from this fight). You want the toughest Guardian taking the brunt of the sniping while the other rakes Zahn's head. Keep up the pressure until the second third of Zahn's health is lost (or thereabouts), and he boosts up to a different platform.

While Zahn is up on his protected platform, retreat to a far part of the deck so he finds it harder to snipe you. The last part of the battle involves **Zahn dropping down from his upper platform and engaging you at closer quarters** with what appears to be the world's most dangerous shotgun (which bounce-shoots you if you're close to the ground). You should have perfected your Movement Mode to the side or backward, landing on any of the low mechanical structures through the deck without seeing them to step on. Use the height and partial protection of this scenery while whittling down Zahn's health. If two or three of you can do this from different angles, there's hope to finish this fight. **Got a Super, a shotgun, or another close-quarters weapon you favor?** Then it's time to use every last offensive technique at your disposal.

Savathûn's Song

Strike: Recommended Power 140
Nightfall: Required Power 230
Recommended Power 240

It seems there's a mastermind at work inside the depths of the base on Titan, a dark heart that must be skewered so the hated Hive can be removed from this place once and for all. Head deep into the Arboretum Sector, battling through revolting secretion-filled chambers, shattering strange crystals, and locating a hidden tunnel into the deepest parts of the planet. This is where an immense Shrieker is said to reside. Head to the source, and defeat it.

Solarium

Titan: New Pacific Arcology

Enemies Encountered

HIVE: Acolytes, Wizards, Thralls, Cursed Thralls, Knights
SUB-BOSS: Ogre

Objectives

Gain access to the Arboretum.
Hack the door (2 protocols).
Defeat hostiles.
Clear out the Hive.
Find the source.

Solarium

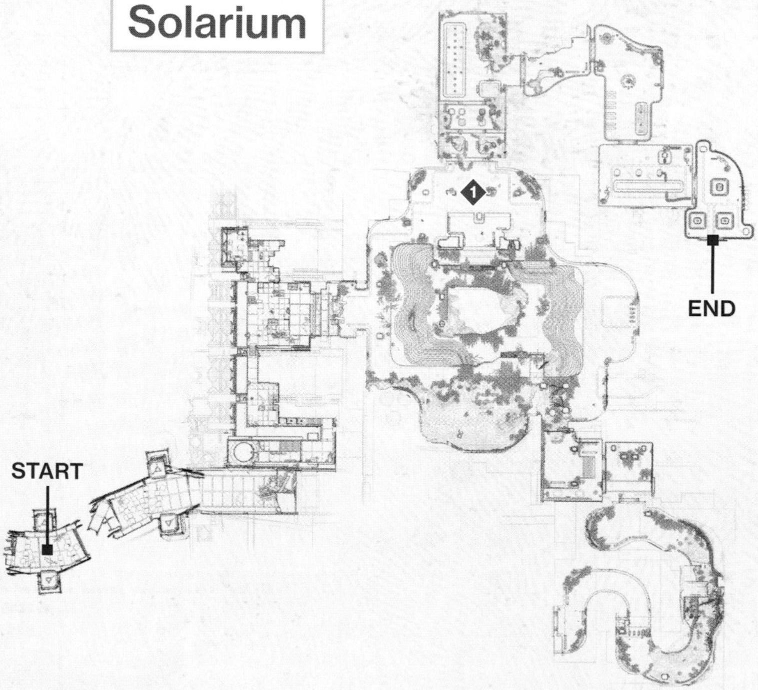

1 Lobby and Arboretum Entrance

Super: Recommended (one player)
Grenades: Recommended
Variations: Toughened enemies, different enemies

Cross the bridge, head up **into the platform chamber with the broken LED wall**, and engage the cluster of Acolytes in quick and violent combat. **Squeeze through the gap into the large open lobby**, and head left (north) toward the additional Hive foes. The initial hostiles include a few Acolytes and a Wizard. Destroy them, and avoid the Hive traps (the glowing anchor-like devices on the ground), which can damage and immobilize you. **While Ghost hacks the door, spin around and repel a group of charging Thralls led by a Wizard.** Execute the closer enemies first. Next, expect Acolytes and Cursed Thralls to drop in; remove the explosive Cursed Thralls as a matter of urgency. Use a grenade to soften up one of the two Knights that also appear, but save them for last.

Sub-Boss: When the door opens, you may want to punt or lob in a grenade to remove the cluster of Thralls before they charge and separate. Instead, just back up and remove them first. The reason is simple: **when you step to the second inner door, there are an Ogre, Knights, and Acolytes in the green chamber beyond.** Back up so there's room to find cover, or the Ogre's facial maw beam can cut you down in seconds. Step to the side of the door opening, have all three of you focus on the Ogre first, and then mop up the Knights and Acolyte stragglers. **A Super used on the Ogre is not a wasted opportunity.** Then, head farther down the corridors into the Arboretum itself.

Arboretum

Restricted Zone

Objectives

Find the source (continued).
Disrupt the void ritual.
Find the source (continued).
Scan the object.
Locate the crystal cave.
Destroy the crystals (6).
Kill the first Ogre.
Kill the second Ogre.
Destroy the crystals (6).
Disrupt the void ritual.
Make your way back to the plug.

Enemies Encountered

HIVE: Acolytes, Wizards, Shriekers, Knights
SUB-BOSSES: Ogres, Shriekers

Arboretum

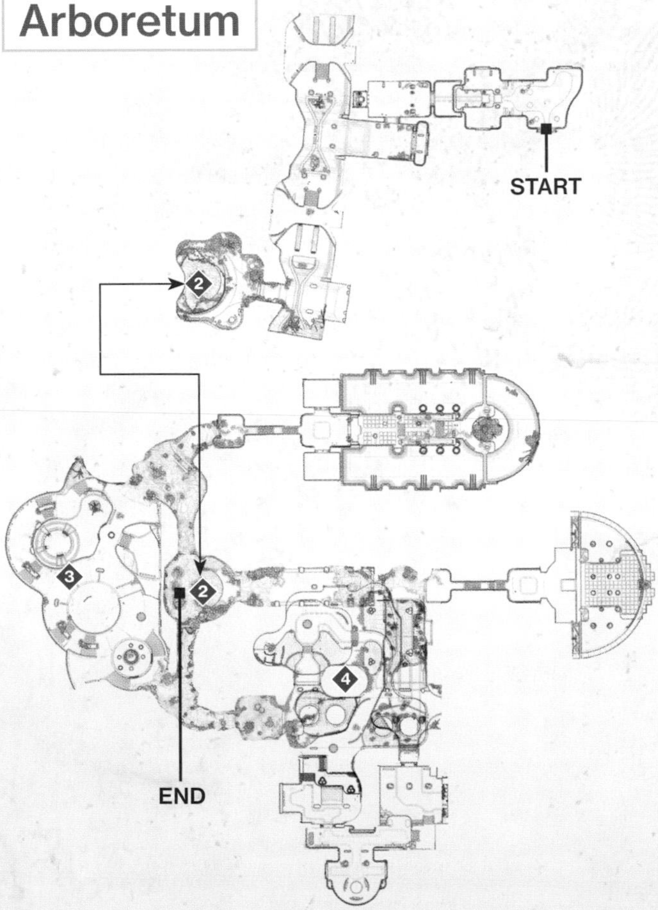

Make short work of the minimal Acolyte threats, avoid the Hive trap, and **head through the pinkish entrance corridor into the main hall.** Once inside the hall, make a left turn. Have two teammates remove the additional Acolyte threats and engage a Void Wizard. The toughest of your team must immediately vault up the steps to **grab a void charge (a ball of void energy) and run it forward to an area just below a floating Hive Shrieker.**

As you're cut down in seconds from Shrieker fire, you may want to delay grabbing this and focus on defeating the Shrieker using the weaponry all three of you have. A better plan is to quicken this by having two teammates hit the Shrieker while one of you deposits the void charge into the receptacle, opening the path deeper into the Arboretum (this usually dismisses the Shrieker, too). Launching a Super is a reasonable plan, but if you can finish off foes in the main hall without using it, it's helpful for the next major confrontation.

Drop down into the Pit, and scan the strange chained object in the middle of the Hive nest. You're tasked with finding more of these crystals, though this area is sometimes referred to as a "plug" (as it is sealing a lower area you must eventually break into). You can attack the remaining chambers of the Arboretum once you find and destroy the crystals in an adjacent cave (though variations exist where you enter different parts of the Arboretum first).

2 Main Hall and The Pit

Super: Recommended (one player)
Grenades: Recommended

3 Bio-Dome Mezzanine

Super: Recommended
Grenades: Recommended
Variations: Entering a Sector in a different order, entering this area and disrupting a Hive ritual instead of taking down two Ogres

Sub-Bosses: Head into one of the side chambers off The Pit. Engage Acolytes and a toughened Knight in combat before blasting (or punching) the **six glowing crystals embedded in the Hive cave** until the blocked doorway becomes accessible. Enter the mezzanine.

There's little time to look at the view of the massive bio-dome you're in; **focus your attention instead on the vicious Ogre. Beware of Knights, Acolytes, Hive anchor traps, and a second Ogre in the upper mezzanine** you must pass through. Acolytes and two or three Hive Wizards back up the Ogre. As you'd expect, killing all of them isn't easy if you rush the area, so hang back and remove foes at range if possible. Alternately, execute a Super. After you clear this mezzanine, head into a second crystal cave.

4 Upper and Lower Mezzanines

Super: Recommended **Grenades:** Recommended

Variations: Entering a Sector in a different order, entering this area and taking down two Ogres instead of disrupting a Hive ritual.

Reach another crystal cave from the bio-dome mezzanine (which is linked to the Pit), and after dropping the enemy Acolytes, destroy the six crystals. You're able to access the **upper mezzanine area, where you must halt a void ritual.** This is achieved using the same technique as earlier, but there are far more problematic threats at this point. Take defensive positions behind and around the low walls, and tackle the nearer Acolytes and Knights first. **Dodge the anchor traps and press forward into the mezzanine area, where two Void Wizards are being summoned.** Make them priority targets for one of your teammates while the other two take on the nearest Knights and Acolytes.

Sub-Bosses: The action now borders on the ludicrous. You're expected to head into the lower mezzanine, battle against multiple Acolyte and Knight threats, take down an Ogre, and then **slot in a void charge that two Shriekers are guarding.** You can grab the charge (which one of you gathered from the area above where the Wizards were), sprint down over low walls, and die. Or, you can work as a team, grabbing the void charge when your teammates are ready to cover you, and then using the lower mezzanine scenery as cover. This is especially important as you reach the Shriekers due to their rapid-fire offense. **Jump to the white columns and planters so you're not struck by too many attacks.** Have the two teammates without the charge launch their Supers: one to kill the Ogre before the Shriekers, and the other to take on the Shriekers while the charge is slotted.

When the madness temporarily ends, head down the L-shaped main hallway and back to the Pit, **where two Wizards are waiting**. Remove them as threats, and the plug is removed; the anchor crystal dissolves, and you drop down into the Chasm of Screams.

Chasm of Screams

Restricted Zone

Enemies Encountered

HIVE: Cursed Thralls

BOSS: Dark Heart (Shrieker), Acolytes, Knights, Thralls, Ogres

Objectives

Find the source.

Destroy the Dark Heart.

5 Hive Burrows

Super: Optional (one player)

Grenades: Optional (one player)

Tear through the Hive tunnels, **backing up as you spot Cursed Thralls running your way**. There is a horde of them, so don't race too quickly into their explosive ranks. Instead, back up a little, and tackle the ones closest to you. Take your time; you want all three of your team's Super attacks and grenades to be functional for the final confrontation.

6 Chamber of the Dark Heart

Super: Recommended **Grenades:** Recommended

Variations: Three appearing Ogres, toughened foes and Boss.

Boss Weak Spot: Central "eye."

Enter the final chamber, and make a quick sweep if you're unfamiliar with the area. There's a sheer and deadly drop with floating platforms along the eastern (far) side, a large multi-tiered balcony platform with a huge crystal, and numerous Hive entrances in the western perimeter wall.

Chasm of Screams

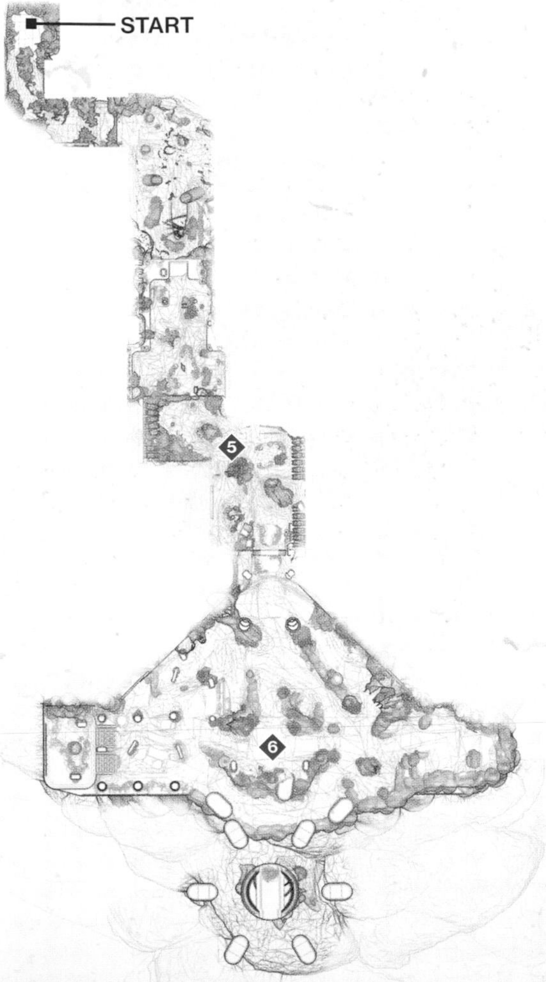

When you're ready and your team has spread out into position with a good view of **the large crystal, have one teammate smash it open** to reveal **a giant Shrieker known as the Dark Heart**. You're here to destroy it.

Not dying usually occurs if your teammates know exactly what job they have to do (in addition to killing the Dark Heart). **First, split up so the Boss and any incoming Hive foes have to work harder to take you down**. Have one teammate whose sole responsibility is destroying the Dark Heart, breaking off from combat only when Hive infantry are on them or the Dark Heart becomes invulnerable. A second teammate should focus on the Dark Heart but actively remove enemy threats as they arise. The third teammate should be shooting at the Dark Heart but focusing mainly on the Hive enemies, letting others know where there are too many to deal with.

This is the player who should be familiar with when and where foes appear. He or she can lob in a grenade to damage multiple foes as they arrive, before they spread out.

First, though, you should be trying to **whittle down the first third of the Dark Heart's energy. Strike the eye** (in particular, the jagged groove across the eye). Keep this up for as long as you can, even if you're being struck by Hive infantry, until the eye closes up and the Dark Heart floats to one edge of the battle area. Then, deal with a sudden influx of Acolytes and Knights.

When the Dark Heart opens up again, it floats to the opposite (higher) end of the balcony, and an almost constant stream of Acolytes becomes a problem. **With one teammate trained on that eye and two others switching from eye destruction to Hive infantry takedowns, make slow but steady progress removing more Boss health**. Keep moving and keep jumping in and out of cover to avoid the Shrieker energy bolts and (later) some void energy balls that the Dark Heart spits out in all directions. **Save your Super until the arrival of two or three Ogres**. These beasts can really cause you problems, but tackling them in record time and with perfect Super takedowns allows you to quickly focus your attention back on the Boss. Or, shoot them from two or three different directions so they can't blast you all.

By now, you should be familiar with **stepping out of cover, blasting that Dark Heart's eye, and stepping back into cover before you're battered by its homing energy bolts**. But once two-thirds of its health is lost, it teleports to the top of the floating platform with revolving ramps around it. Two or three Void Wizards also make an appearance. This is another ritual, and it's stopped in the same manner. With two teammates each tackling the Wizards, one of you must **grab the void charge on the main balcony** before leaping up onto the suspended and rotating ramps and central floating platform. **Slot the charge in, enabling the Dark Heart to be hurt**. Shrug off fire and focus on stopping the ritual, even if it means you die.

The final minutes of the battle **involve you removing any remaining Wizards, then battling the Dark Heart in a real war of attrition**, staying in cover and blasting the Shrieker before diving back into cover. Watch for Cursed Thralls during this time; back up so you're not struck as they explode. Launch any remaining Supers you can before this fearsome eyeball blinks its last.

Crucible

Overview

The Crucible is a series of fast-paced contests that pit Guardians against one another in open combat. Some come to find honor and renown; some come for more tangible rewards. No matter your reasons, you'll find the Crucible a suitable setting to hone your skills.

Quickplay contains a rotation of exciting match types with relatively straightforward rulesets. It's intended to provide a more casual experience, suitable for Guardians interested in a bit of spirited competition. You can access this playlist via the Director as soon as the Crucible is unlocked.

The **Competitive** playlist features two challenging objective-based match types. With a strong emphasis on combat proficiency and team tactics, this playlist is intended for skilled Guardians determined to compete at the highest level. The Competitive playlist becomes available once you've completed two Quickplay matches.

Each playlist contains a specific selection of map/mode combinations. Upon joining a playlist, you're automatically teamed up with (and pitted against) other willing competitors.

While participating in the Crucible, actions like defeating enemy Guardians and completing match-specific objectives grant Experience. Upon completing a match, each participant receives a large amount of Experience, a Crucible Token, and at least one randomly selected piece of equipment. You also have the chance to complete daily Challenges and weekly Milestones for additional rewards.

Unlocking the Crucible

You gain access to the Crucible upon completing the Campaign Mission: Spark, though higher levels of competition become available only as your Guardian grows more powerful.

Level Advantages

Whether you're in Quickplay or the Competitive playlist, you'll find that Level Advantages are disabled. This means that weapon Attack values, Defense values, and Power levels are all standardized. Weapons deal damage based on their archetype; armor offers no additional mitigation.

A Matter of Luck

While the Competitive playlist features a higher reward rate due to longer matches, the Quickplay and Competitive playlists draw from the same pool of potential items. Furthermore, your performance has no effect on the number or quality of rewards you receive.

Teams

Regardless of the game mode, every Crucible match features a 4v4 team format. Both playlists accommodate fireteams of up to four players, so you're free to play with a premade team of trusted allies. Otherwise, you'll be grouped with one or more randomly selected Guardians.

Team Assignments

Returning players should note that Crucible teams no longer have official designations—they're simply displayed on your screen as "Your Team" and "Opponents." This streamlined system means that when it comes to the color-coded display and objectives, you're always a member of the blue team.

Team Starting Areas

Each team begins a match in one of two predetermined locations. These areas are always located across the map from each other, allowing Guardians to scramble for strategically important locations once the match begins.

A map's team starting areas can vary between match types, but they're always consistent within a specific map/match combo, and any mode-specific variations tend to be minor.

Teamwork

Whether you're running with friends or teamed up with strangers, working with your allies is an important part of the Crucible. If you're looking for a crash course in teamwork, consider the following advice:

Communicate with your teammates. Use of the team voice channel isn't required, but it's one of the best ways to ensure effective teamwork. Your team's performance is bound to improve when everyone is kept apprised of high-priority targets and objectives.

Understand the User Interface (UI). It can be easy to develop tunnel vision in the heat of battle, but the UI provides a number of ways to keep tabs on your allies. When open communication isn't an option, knowing where your teammates are heading is the best way to predict what they're hoping to accomplish.

Of course, knowing how your teammates are faring always makes it much easier to determine your best course of action.

Team-firing is key. Experienced Guardians tend to know exactly how much damage they can safely absorb, and most will decide whether to engage or retreat within the opening seconds of a firefight. Team-firing helps take the option to retreat off the table. If you're communicating with your team, coordinate your attacks for maximum impact. Otherwise, just make an effort to join in on any firefights that break out. In a close battle, a little extra firepower can make all the difference.

Find strength in numbers. Try to stay near at least one teammate at all times. It allows for consistent team-firing, maximizes the effectiveness of support-related Class Abilities, and helps ensure that an approaching enemy never goes unnoticed. Just make sure you leave enough space to minimize the effects of incoming splash damage.

PvP Display

Crucible Heads Up Display (HUD)

Located at the top of the screen, the Crucible HUD displays useful information about your teammates, your opponents, and the overall state of the match:

- The remaining time is displayed at the top of the HUD.
- Team scores are related via the color-coded progress bars and tally boxes near the center of the HUD.
- The icons grouped on either side of the HUD represent the members of each team.
- The bottom of the HUD is reserved for match-specific objectives and features like allotted lives, available Revive Tokens, and controlled zones.

While all of this information will prove useful during a match, the Guardian icons warrant special attention. Initially, these icons display each Guardian's currently equipped Subclass. However, these icons can change to reflect important developments as they occur:

- A skull indicates a defeated Guardian.
- A gold icon means that the corresponding Guardian has a fully charged Super Ability.
- A pulsing gold icon means that the corresponding Guardian has activated their Super Ability.

Motion Tracker

The motion tracker is useful in PvE, but it's an essential tool in PvP—and one that new players tend to underuse. Before you step foot in the Crucible, remember that the motion tracker's radial grid shows:

- Approximate locations of nearby enemies (direction and range)
- Locations of nearby allies
- Elevation of nearby allies
- Status of nearby allies (active/defeated)
- Locations of nearby objectives
- Locations of nearby Power Ammo

Just outside of the radial grid, markers are used to indicate detected allies, objectives, and Power Ammo that are otherwise out of range.

Motion Tracker Ranges

Segment Location	Indicated Range
Outer Ring	24-48 meters
Main Ring	6-24 meters
Center	0-6 meters

Proper use of the motion tracker can take a bit of practice, but it's a skill that's well worth developing. As you become familiar with each battleground, combining your knowledge of the terrain with the information contained on the motion tracker will lead to greatly improved situational awareness.

Crouching and Cloaking

The motion tracker has a difficult time detecting crouched enemies. Instead of registering as a steady glow, a nearby crouched target is detected once every three seconds. Of course, cloaking Abilities (such as Vanish in Smoke) make enemy targets even tougher to detect.

Notifications

During PvP combat, you'll find a variety of notifications appearing on your screen:

Alerts: Urgent messages are typically displayed just below the Crucible HUD. The most common alert is "Last Guardian Standing," indicating that you're the last surviving member of your team.

Map Location: The area just below the motion tracker indicates your current map location.

Medals: Appearing just above the center of the screen, medals are typically used to acknowledge skillful play during PvP. While an earned medal offers no benefits, it serves as a useful indication of your performance.

Combat Feed: Located in the lower-left corner of the screen, the combat feed (sometimes called the "kill feed") offers a variety of notifications. The bulk of these have to do with Guardian deaths, listing the victim, the victor, and the weapon type that struck the killing blow. However, you'll also find updates about active Super Abilities, collected Power Ammo, and more.

Loadouts

You can use all weapons, armor pieces, and Abilities at your disposal in the Crucible. However, most players find that some loadouts are better suited to competitive play than others. After all, your fellow Guardians are sure to be more formidable and far less predictable than the enemies you face out in the wild.

It can take significant experimentation to find the best mix of items and Abilities, especially because arsenals and playstyles both tend to change over time.

Subclasses and Abilities

Every Subclass has a place in the Crucible, and you're under no obligation to select one over another. However, if you find that your PvE playstyle is at odds with your PvP goals, it might be time for a change.

Experimenting with different Subclasses, Grenades, Movement Modes, and Melee Abilities can be an enjoyable and illuminating experience, and it's worth trying every available combination at one point or another. Still, if you're looking for a place to start, take a step back and consider the basics:

- **Solar Subclasses** tend to focus on powerful, direct-damage attacks.
- **Arc Subclasses** tend to focus on short-range, multi-target attacks.
- **Void Subclasses** tend to focus on survivability.

Once you've chosen a Subclass, take a closer look at the abilities it offers.

Movement Modes

In PvP, hang time is more of a liability than a benefit—an airborne Guardian makes for an easy target. Start with a Movement Mode that favors directional control. If it doesn't suit you, swap it out for something else.

Blink

When it comes to Movement Modes, the Voidwalker's Blink deserves special mention. This short-range teleport is particularly well-suited to PvP. It takes a great deal of practice to master, but it's a remarkable evasive tool.

Grenades

While specifics vary, grenades generally fall into at least one of five basic categories:

- **Seeker grenades** produce one or more projectiles that home in on nearby foes. They're great for blind (or panicked) tosses near a suspected enemy location.
- **Persistent grenades** produce damaging fields or other lasting effects. They're useful map control tools, perfect for blocking off chokepoints or chasing opponents from strategically important locations.
- **Blast grenades** produce a straightforward explosion. They tend to deal fairly high damage.
- **Sticky grenades** can attach to targets. They take a bit of skill to use, but a well-thrown sticky grenade usually deals considerable damage.
- **Status grenades** afflict enemies with temporary effects. The clearest examples are both found in Titan Subclasses: the Striker's Flashbang Grenade disorients enemies, and the Sentinel's Suppressor Grenade prevents enemies from using Abilities.

Once you've identified your available grenade options, consider how it meshes with your playstyle and how useful it might be in a specific match type.

Class Abilities

Your choice of Subclass has no effect on your available Class Ability (assuming you've unlocked them, at least). All Class Abilities can be useful in PvP. Selecting one is usually just a matter of supporting your intended playstyle.

Titans will find that Towering Barricade is the better choice for defensive applications. The extra height makes it a much better option for providing cover at strategically important locations like Capture Points and Power Ammo spawns. It's also a better option for blocking chokepoints and flanking routes. However, Rally Barricade's ability to instantly reload your weapon makes it the better offensive option.

A Hunter who favors close combat should take a hard look at Gambler's Dodge. Using this Class Ability near an enemy automatically recharges your Melee Ability. If you prefer to keep a bit of distance between yourself and your enemy, Marksman's Dodge is the better option. A well-timed Dodge will reload your weapon, minimizing your downtime during heated encounters.

An Endless Cycle

While all Subclasses feature intriguing Ability combinations, it's worth noting that Gambler's Dodge is a particularly useful option for Arcstriders who opt for to follow the Way of the Warrior. The combination of Gambler's Dodge and Combat Flow creates a potent loop. Dodging near enemies recharges your Melee Ability, and your melee kills recharge your Dodge.

If you're playing as a Warlock, simply weigh the benefits of Healing Rift's group healing against the Empowering Rift's damage boost. They're both excellent support skills, so the choice often comes down to which effect your teammates are likely to prefer—especially because your allies must stay within your Rift to enjoy its primary effect.

Melee Abilities

Melee Abilities come bundled with unique and powerful effects. When you select a Melee Ability, consider the impact the related enhancements might have on your Super Ability, Class Ability, and more. It can be a difficult choice (of course, it's easily reversed). It's usually best to simply choose the option you find most appealing and give it a whirl.

For details about Melee Abilities and their bundled effects, please refer to this guide's Field Manual.

Weapons

Finding the right combination of Kinetic and Energy weapons can be a complicated task. Obviously, you must select from the weapons available to you, but that's just the beginning. The right choice depends on everything from the specific map/match combo to your skill level with a particular weapon archetype. Again, experimentation is your best option, but there are a few factors worth focusing on.

First, consider range. Does the map support long-range weapon use, or are you more likely to spend your time running through a maze of tight corridors? Never bring a scout rifle to a submachine gun fight.

Next, consider flexibility. While you're free to equip a Kinetic weapon and Energy weapon of the same archetype, it's rarely wise to do so. Crucible maps generally feature varied terrain, and the ability to adapt as the battle moves from one location to the next is an important part of effective play.

Then, consider your default playstyle. Habits can and do change over time, but you've probably got a good idea of how you'll react when things get hairy. If you tend to go charging in for a melee attack, even when you're exposed and outnumbered, own it. Drop a short-range weapon into one of your slots. If you head for cover the moment your target spots you, be honest with yourself and grab something suitable for long-range combat. Use your remaining weapon slot for something more map/match appropriate, and work on breaking any bad habits you might have.

Finally, consider your Power weapon. Once you've got your Kinetic/Energy weapons sorted, use the same process to narrow your search for a Power weapon. Consider the likely range of combat (make sure you factor in potential splash damage), the flexibility it might add to your loadout, and any persistent habits that might undermine your use of a particular weapon.

Armor

In the Crucible, assembling the best mix of armor usually boils down to three factors:

1. The supported attributes
2. The attached mods
3. How cool it looks

You may be able to overlook aesthetic concerns, but you should always consider the two remaining factors.

As for attributes, your goal is to strike the proper balance between Resilience, Mobility, and Recovery. As always, the most effective combination depends on your playstyle and skill level. One word of warning: there's no benefit to boosting an attribute above 10. Go any higher than that, and you're wasting points.

When it comes to mods, the benefits you choose are entirely up to you. Determine the mods that support your playstyle, then work toward assembling a proper collection.

Combat

Most of the skills you develop outside of the Crucible will prove useful within it, but competing against your fellow Guardians can be a jarring experience. Luckily, you can do several things to ease the transition from PvE to PvP.

Keep moving. Seriously—this is one of the most important habits you can develop, and the sooner you do so, the better off you'll be. In the Crucible, taking cover is more a matter of breaking line of sight. Your opponents won't hang back and wait as you hunker down to regenerate health. Unless you're collecting Power Ammo, dealing with a charge, or reviving an ally, you should be moving.

Understand ammo. You begin the match with a set amount of ammo for your Kinetic and Energy weapons. You can restock this ammo by collecting drops from defeated Guardians. You also receive a fresh supply of ammo after return to battle following a death (a less desirable option, to be sure.) You can only collect Power Ammo from designated spawn points. It only appears at certain times, and each crate can only be collected by a single Guardian.

Understand range. This has already been covered, but it's worth repeating. Each weapon has a specific range of efficacy, and it's important to keep that in mind whenever you engage in a firefight.

Understand sniping lanes. Essentially, any high-traffic area that features a decent line of sight can be considered a sniping lane. This means that each map's most effective sniping lanes tend to change as players learn to avoid certain areas.

Aim for the head. When two Guardians square off, every bullet counts. Remember that Level Advantages are disabled during all Crucible matches. If two Guardians are firing similar weapons under similar conditions, Precision Damage is usually the deciding factor.

Pre-aim for the head. Well, with rapid-fire weapons, it's usually best to pre-aim for the neck. At any rate, "pre-aiming" simply involves predicting where an approaching opponent will appear, and making sure that your sights are in place. As you become familiar with each map, you can use the terrain to help determine exactly where to aim.

Crouch wisely. Crouching renders you invisible to motion trackers, but only for a few seconds at a time. It makes you a smaller target, but it also slows down your movement. Crouching can be very effective, no doubt, but timing is everything.

Slide freely. Sliding is a great way to execute a level change as you're sprinting through a vulnerable area. There's more than a little luck involved, but a well-timed slide can drop your head directly under an incoming shot. It's also a stylish way to initiate a crouch, meaning that sliding allows you to pulse on the motion trackers of nearby opponents.

Sprint often. The faster you move, the harder you are to hit. It's important to note that you can't sprint and reload a weapon at the same time. Reloading will drop you out of a sprint, and sprinting will cancel a reload.

Cancel your jumps. Again, an airborne Guardian tends to make an easy target; avoid lingering in the air. Press Jump while your Movement Mode is active to drop to the ground (for some classes), or better yet, aim down sights for a split second to hit the ground even faster.

Put it all together. Moving is good; moving in unpredictable ways is better. Sprint, slide, jump, zig, and zag your way through dangerous areas. Mix it up as much as possible. When you're in the line of fire, it's best to keep your enemies guessing.

Mind your Supers. How and when you use your Super Ability is entirely up to you, but keep in mind that your allies are bound to be grateful for any Orbs of Light you might create in the process.

Be a team player. You won't always agree with your team's basic strategy, but when you can't get convince your allies to follow your lead, it's generally best to follow theirs. The same applies for commonly debated issues like the use of Super Abilities and Power Ammo. If victory is your priority, do whatever you can to make sure everyone's on the same page.

Expect to lose. Losses are inevitable, and if you're playing with a team of randomly selected Guardians, you can't realistically expect to win more than half the time. It's fine. Don't worry about it. You'll still get your Crucible rewards, and you'll have a new story to tell.

To move forward, look back. Try to learn something from every death, and don't wait until the match ends. When you come up short in a firefight, you'll always have at least a few seconds before you're returned to the battlefield. Use this time to ponder what went wrong and formulate a plan to avoid making the same mistake.

If you want to improve, practice. Practice with your favorite loadout, practice with new loadouts, and practice new playstyles and match-specific strategies. The more time you spend in each map, the more developed your situational awareness will become. And situational awareness is what separates top-level competitors from the rest of the pack.

Match Types

Quickplay Playlist

"Take risks and learn the art of war. But you have one focus: the enemy must fall."

—Lord Shaxx

Common Rules

All Quickplay match types feature eight-minute time limits.

Slain Guardians automatically respawn five seconds after defeat.

Clash

Objective

Clash follows a classic team deathmatch format. Put simply, the first team to score 75 kills wins the match.

Scoring

Clash is a straightforward eight-minute contest of combat proficiency. A team's score increases each time one or more of its members has a hand in defeating an enemy Guardian.

The match is awarded to the first team that scores 75 kills or to the team with the highest score when the eight-minute time limit expires.

Power Ammo

In Clash, the map contains three Power Ammo spawn points: one on each side of the map, and one in a neutral location.

- The neutral crate becomes available 20 seconds into the match. Once collected, this Power Ammo does not respawn.
- The two remaining crates appear 90 seconds into the match. At these locations, it takes 90 seconds for a Power Ammo crate to respawn between uses.

Basic Tips: Clash

Clash is about as straightforward as PvP gets, making it a great entry point for the uninitiated. Even so, there a few pieces of advice new players might consider.

Keep track of Power Ammo spawns. A game of Clash typically opens with a mad dash to the first available Power Ammo crate. Apart from that, Power Ammo strategies can vary from match to match. Is the opposition pushing into your side of the map? Is a teammate spending the entire match camping near a Power Ammo spawn point? Has a Power Ammo crate gone uncollected for a suspiciously long time? The way Power Ammo is treated can tell you a lot about the strategies in play, so adjust your tactics accordingly.

Efficiency is paramount. Clash's simple ruleset doesn't allow for much wiggle room. If you're losing more gunfights than you're winning, you're almost certainly hurting your team. Don't hesitate to retreat when things go south. Standing firm in the face of overwhelming odds may bring you a sense of personal satisfaction, but it's unlikely to yield any tangible benefits.

Stay loose. Clash is most definitely a team game, but not everyone treats it as such. Teammates can have wildly different playstyles and skill levels, and adjusting your tactics to fit them is one of the best things you can do to maximize your performance.

Control

Objective

Control uses a modified team deathmatch ruleset that awards bonus points based on location-based objectives. Teams fight to claim and hold up to three strategic battle zones. The number of points rewarded for defeating an enemy Guardian varies based on the number of zones held by each team.

Scoring

In Control, a team can increase its score by claiming Capture Points and defeating enemy Guardians. However, bonus points are awarded based on the number of zones held by each team. Essentially:

- Defeating an enemy Guardian grants a base score of +1.
- Claiming a zone's Capture Point grants +1.
- The **Zone Advantage** bonus grants an extra +1 per kill when a team holds the majority of zones.
- The **Power Play** bonus grants an extra +2 per kill when a team holds all three zones.

This means that, depending on the number of zones your team holds, defeating one Guardian can add anywhere from +1 to +3 to your score.

The match goes to the first team to score 100 points, or to the team with the highest score when the eight-minute time limit expires.

Power Ammo

In Control, the stage contains two Power Ammo spawn points: one on each side of the map. Both Power Ammo crates become available 90 seconds into the match. Once collected, it takes Power Ammo 90 seconds to respawn.

Control Zones

The map features three Control zones: A, B, and C. Each team begins the match with one zone under its control (A or C, depending on a team's starting location). Zone B starts off as neutral territory.

To capture a zone, simply stay within the borders of its Capture Point until it's awarded to your team. This process takes about 10 seconds, regardless of how many allied Guardians are present. A Capture Point cannot change hands while two rival Guardians are present.

> **A Quick Turnaround**
> Returning players should note that Control no longer features a de-capture phase. It takes exactly as long to claim an enemy-held zone as it does to claim a neutral zone.

Basic Tips: Control

Because it blends two very different objectives, Control supports a wide variety of tactics. The most effective strategies will vary from match to match, but there a few basic tips new players might fight useful.

Make every capture a solo capture. Capture Points tend to be in exposed areas, and claiming one is meant to be a risky endeavor. There's no benefit to doubling up with a teammate—the process won't go any faster, nor will additional points be awarded. Now, this isn't to say that teammates shouldn't support each other. It's just that a second Guardian would be far more useful covering the area from a nearby vantage point.

Do the math. The scoring system is fairly streamlined, so make sure you weigh the risks and rewards of claiming a Capture Point. A quick zone grab might put +1 on the scoreboard, but your gain becomes a net loss if your opponents are able to defeat you **and** retake the Capture Point. On the other hand, simply trading kills with an enemy Guardian can lead to big gains when your team has a Zone Advantage.

Choose the right grenade for the job. Seeker grenades and grenades that feature persistent/pulsing effects are particularly effective in Control. Hindering an opponent's attempt to capture a zone (if only for a few seconds) can give you an edge in zone defense.

Keep tabs on your teammates. Teamwork is always recommended, but Control is arguably the most strategically complex game mode in Quickplay. Take note of the Capture Points your allies prioritize, and adjust your tactics accordingly. No matter how skilled you are, you're bound to benefit from working alongside your teammates.

Supremacy

Objective

In Supremacy, a Crest is produced each time a Guardian falls in battle. The goal is to ensure that your team collects more enemy Crests than the opposing team.

Scoring

In Supremacy, scoring is a two-part process. First, your team must defeat an enemy Guardian. Then, a member of your team must collect the resulting Crest. Put simply:

- Collecting an enemy (red) Crest adds +1 to your team score.
- Collecting an ally (blue) Crest yields no points, but it does prevent the opposing team from scoring.

The match goes to the first team to collect 50 enemy Crests, or to the team with the highest score when the eight-minute time limit expires.

Power Ammo

In Supremacy, the map contains three Power Ammo spawn points. Locations and spawn rates are identical to those featured in Clash (assuming the map supports both match types).

- The neutral crate becomes available 20 seconds into the match. Once collected, this Power Ammo does not respawn.
- The two remaining crates appear 90 seconds into the match. At these locations, it takes 90 seconds for a Power Ammo crate to respawn between uses.

Competitive Playlist

"Stakes are high, and coordination with your teammates is vital. Leave personal glory behind, and together you'll crush the enemy."

—Lord Shaxx

Countdown

Objective

In Countdown, the map contains two charges. One team is tasked with detonating a charges of their choice, and the other team must prevent this from happening.

Countdown is a round-based match type. When a team fulfills (or fails to fulfill) its objective, the round ends. The teams then switch roles, and a new round begins. The first team to win six rounds of Countdown is declared the winner of the match.

Scoring

In Countdown, the only way to increase your team's score is to win a round. Although each team is assigned a primary objective when a round begins, you'll always have at least two paths to victory.

The attacking team ("Set the Charge") can:

- Arm a charge within the two-minute time limit **and** prevent the opposing team from defusing it.
- Eliminate all members of the opposing team.

The defending team ("Defend the Charges") can:

- Prevent the opposing team from setting a charge within the two-minute time limit.
- Defuse a set charge.

When one of these conditions has been met, the round is rewarded to the appropriate team.

Power Ammo

In Countdown, a stage always contains two Power Ammo spawn points: one on each side of the map. Power Ammo becomes available at both of the designated locations 30 seconds into the match. Once collected, it takes 30 seconds for a crate of Power Ammo to respawn.

Setting and Defusing Charges

Setting and defusing a charge is just a matter of moving within range and interacting with the object; the process is as simple as following an onscreen prompt. Of course, "simple" does not equate to "easy." When it comes to handling charges, new players should note the following:

- Once a round starts, the attacking team has 2 minutes to set a charge (or eliminate the opposition).
- It takes about 3 seconds to set a bomb.

- It takes more than 5 seconds to defuse a charge.
- When a charge is set, the clock stops and the map's remaining charge is taken out of play.
- Once set, it takes around 40 seconds for a charge to detonate. During this time, the opposing team can attempt to defuse it.

Lives and Revives

Countdown doesn't feature the unlimited (and automatic) respawns found in Quickplay match types. Instead, each combatant begins a round with one life and one Revive Token that can be used to resurrect a slain teammate. Note that while the Crucible HUD displays available "Revives" as a team resource, each Guardian is responsible for his or her own Token.

Revive Token

A gold icon in the bottom-right corner of the screen indicates an available Revive Token. When a Token is used or lost, the icon loses its color.

A Revive Token is consumed upon use, but it's also lost if the Guardian holding it is killed. This means that a given team can use a maximum of three Revive Tokens over the course of a round—the first death a team suffers always results in the loss of an unused Token.

A slain Guardian cannot be revived until 20 seconds after the time of death. It takes roughly 1.5 seconds to revive a valid target (although taking fire will prolong the process).

Basic Tips: Countdown

Countdown is a fast-paced game mode, and effective strategies tend to change with the ebb and flow of each round. However, there are a few basic tips that should help new players get off on the right foot.

Equip a scout rifle. Team-firing is always a worthy focus, but it's rarely more important than in Countdown. The combination of time constraints, limited lives, and location-based objectives turns every encounter into a high-stakes affair. A good long-range weapon makes it much easier to support your allies.

Agree on an objective. When your team is attacking make sure everyone knows which charge is the preferred target. If the target changes, ensure that everyone is kept up to date. Remember that setting one charge takes the other out of play.

Don't leave a job half-done. When your team is on defense, eliminating the opposition only ends the round if a charge hasn't yet been set. A detonation will cost you the round, whether or not your opponents are alive to celebrate. Keep your mind on the task at hand.

Use it or lose it. A well-spent Revive Token can change the course of a battle; an unspent Token offers no benefit. While there's nothing wrong with prioritizing skillful allies, enemy positions should be your chief concern. If you find yourself in a position to safely resurrect a fallen teammate, it's generally best to do so.

Survival

Objective

In Survival, each team has a shared pool of eight lives. Each death a team suffers removes one life from the pool. Outlast and/or outperform the opposing team to win a round; the first team to win four rounds is declared the winner of the match.

Scoring

In Survival, the only way to increase your team's score is to win a round. You can accomplish this in one of three ways:

- Defeat enemy Guardians until the opposing team is eliminated. To do this, your team must defeat a total of 12 opponents (four starting lives and eight more in the shared pool).
- End the round with more lives than the opposing team. Each round has a base time limit of three minutes. If time runs out while the teams are tied, the round enters a one-minute overtime phase.
- Claim the tie-breaker Capture Point. This can only be done when a round moves into overtime.

If an overtime phase ends in a tie, both teams forfeit the round. Scores remain unchanged, and the match proceeds to the next round.

Power Ammo

In Survival, the stage contains a single Power Ammo spawn point located in a relatively neutral area. Once collected, it takes the Power Ammo crate 75 seconds to respawn.

Overtime

A Survival round has three minutes of regulation play. If both teams have the same number of remaining lives when the clock runs out, the round moves into overtime. An additional minute is added to the clock, all remaining lives are removed from team pools, and a special tie-breaker Capture Point appears somewhere on the stage (typically in a neutral location near the center of the map).

To win in overtime, you must eliminate the opposing team or claim the tie-breaker Capture Point.

Claiming the Tie-Breaker

To claim the tie-breaker Capture Point, a Guardian must spend approximately 15 consecutive seconds within the indicated area.

Lives and Respawns

The nature of a shared life pool means that team respawns are handled on a **first-come, first-served** basis. When a Guardian is defeated, one life is immediately removed from his or her team pool. After 10 seconds, the fallen Guardian automatically respawns somewhere on the map.

If a life pool is empty at the time of a Guardian's defeat, the combatant is "knocked out" and unable to return for the duration of the round.

Basic Tips: Survival

Survival may lack a bit of Countdown's urgency, but things tend to happen very quickly. Experienced players are sure to develop their own preferences over time, but there are a few things that new combatants can do to improve their chances of victory.

Equip an auto rifle. Survival tends to take place on more compact maps, and the flexibility of a mid-range rifle is bound to prove useful. Unless your build relies on a specific Kinetic/Energy weapon combo, consider pairing a good auto rifle with whatever's most appropriate for the specific map.

Save your Super. This may go without saying, but a fully charged Super Ability is a valuable commodity. Use it only when it's likely to affect the outcome of a round.

Secure the Power Ammo. The map contains only one Power Ammo spawn point, so this location tends to be heavily monitored and hotly contested. Whether you intend to collect Power Ammo or use it as bait, coordinate with your team to minimize the chances of the ammo falling into enemy hands.

The Dead Cliffs

Quick Play

Competitive

European Dead Zone, Earth

The Dead Cliffs

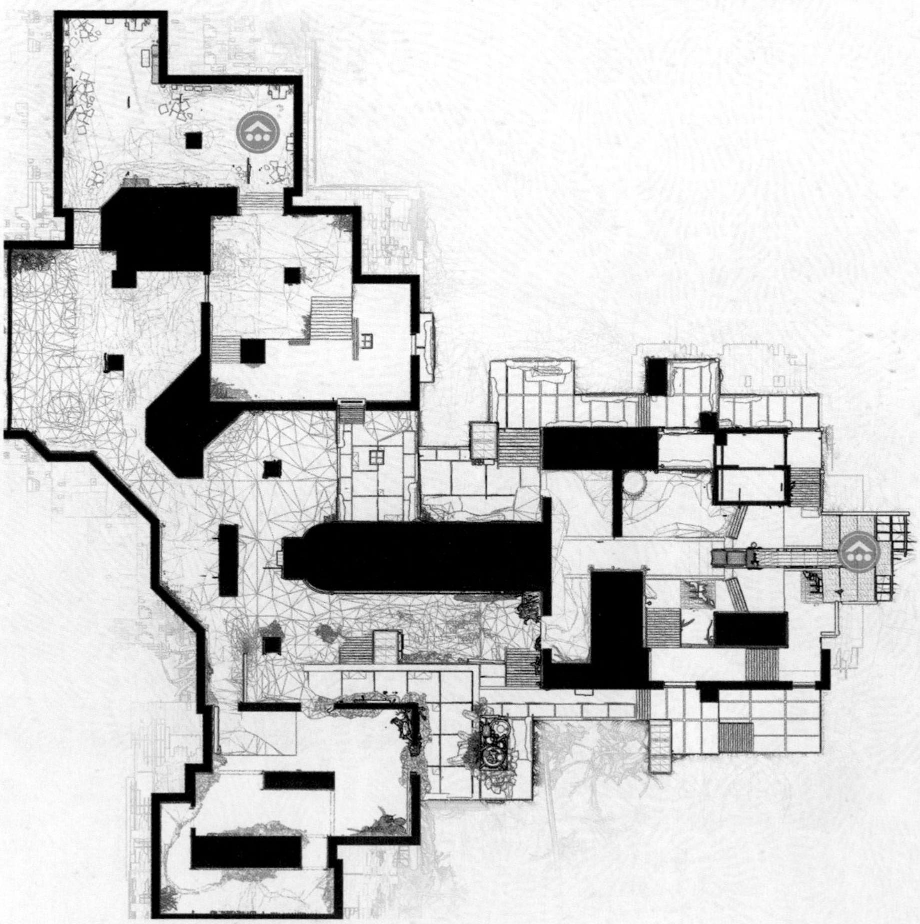

Crucible Map Icons

Before you dive into the Crucible maps, take a moment to review the significance of each icon.

Team Starting Area
A map's team starting areas can vary between modes, but these icons indicate the most common starting areas.

Power Ammo
Power Ammo only spawns in specific locations, and only at certain times. Locations and restock times vary based on match type.

Capture Point A
These location-based objectives only appear in games of Control.

Capture Point B
These location-based objectives only appear in games of Control.

Capture Point C
These location-based objectives only appear in games of Control.

Tie-Breaker Capture Point
Tie-breaker Capture Points only appear when a round of Survival goes into overtime.

Charge
Charges only appear in games of Countdown, typically on opposite sides of the map.

Overview

As a whole, the Dead Cliffs is a fairly small map, and its layout and landscape generally support short- to mid-range combat. Guardians who favor long-range weapons will find a few serviceable sniping lanes, but it's recommended that you equip at least one mid-range weapon during any visit to this map.

As the name suggests, the Dead Cliffs features a good number of sheer drops. Whether you're traversing gaps or engaging in cliffside firefights, be mindful of the map's boundaries. Even an experienced Guardian can suffer a fatal fall in the heat of battle.

The inaccessible structure at the center of the map houses a large piece of exposed machinery. The gaps in the grate aren't large enough for a Guardian to pass through, but you can lob grenades between the bars. While it's unlikely that a blind toss will hit an enemy, it can be a useful distraction tactic when your team is making a coordinated push across the map.

The Dead Cliffs Map Locations

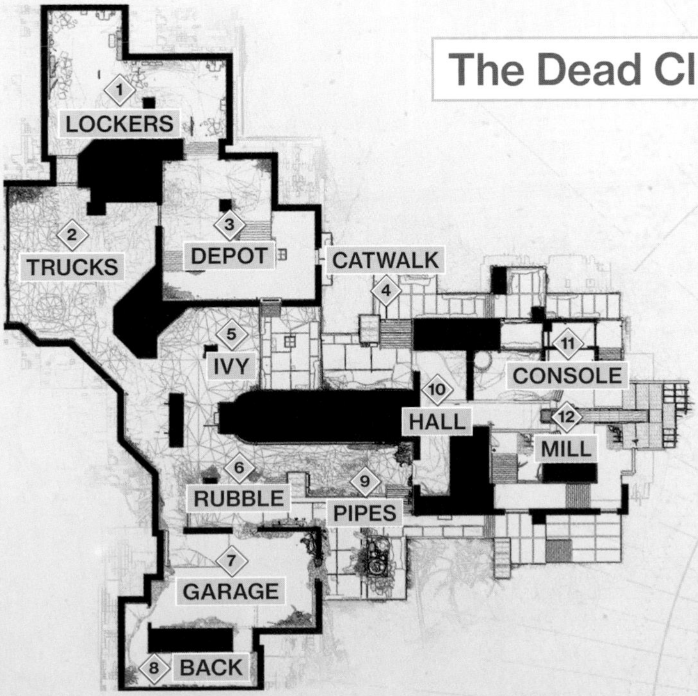

Survival

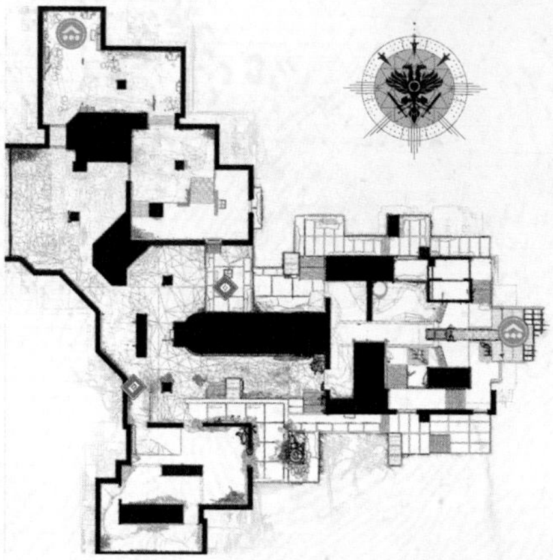

Clash

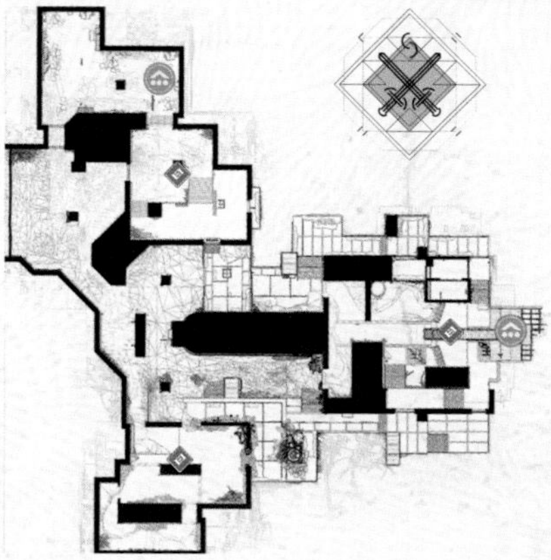

Control

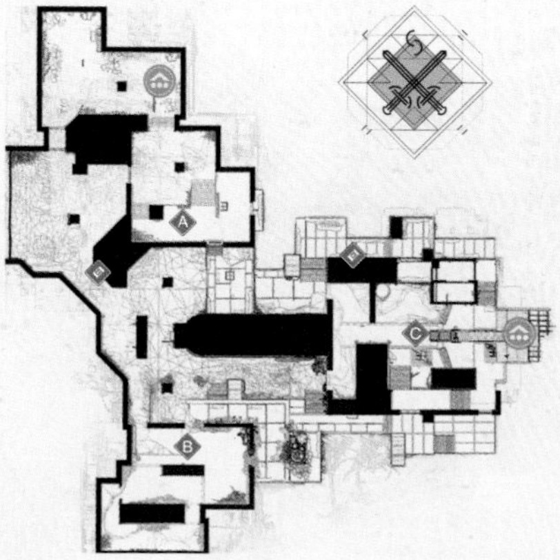

1 Lockers

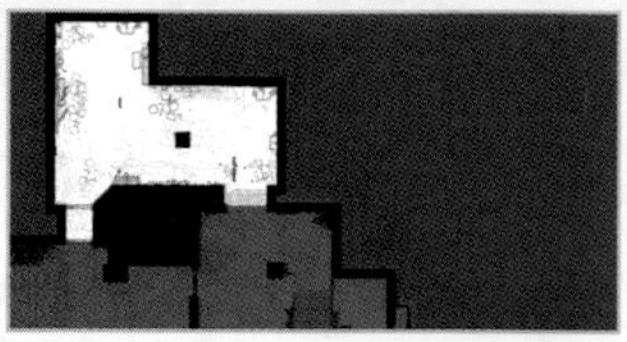

In most match types, **Lockers** serves as one of the map's starting areas. With two points of entry, a level floor, and relatively little cover, this large, dimly lit interior space supports more aggressive tactics. Firefights that break out in this location tend to end quickly and decisively.

It's often used as a flanking route between **Trucks** and **Depot**, but **Lockers** also offers excellent lines of sight into these areas. Those relying on long-range weapons would be hard-pressed to find a more suitable vantage point on this map.

2 Trucks

Key Location: Trucks

During Control matches, **Trucks** contains one of the map's three Power Ammo spawn points

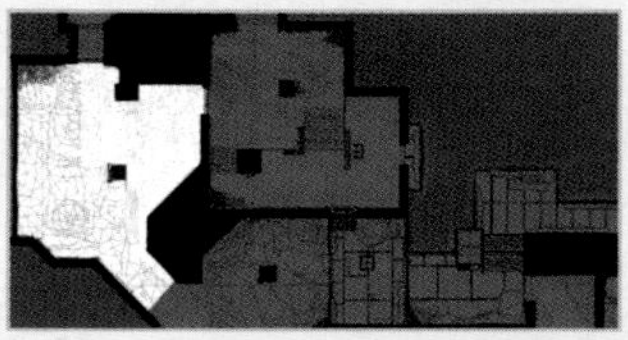

For the most part, **Trucks** acts as a junction between **Lockers**, **Depot**, and **Ivy**. However, this popular movement lane also serves as a Power Ammo spawn point during Control matches.

3 Depot

Key Location: Depot

During Clash matches, **Depot** contains one of the map's three Power Ammo spawn points. During Control matches, this location contains Capture Point A.

This interior space features a multi-leveled floor, a raised ceiling, and multiple cover options. It also boasts four points of entry, making **Depot** a difficult location for any team to hold.

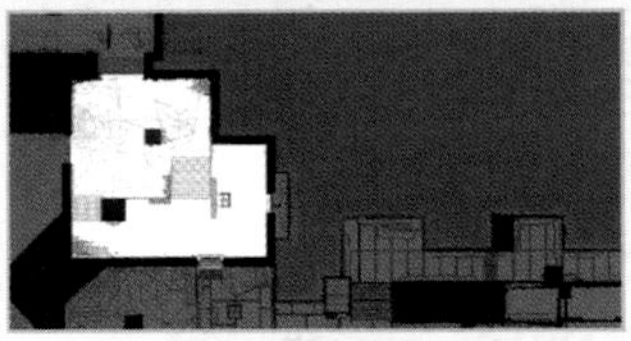

Strategically speaking, **Depot** is a key location during all Quickplay matches. In Clash, Power Ammo spawns on the room's central pillar. During Control, it houses one of the map's three Capture Points and provides an excellent line of sight to the **Catwalk** Power Ammo spawn. In either case, **Depot** is generally a hotly contested location.

4 Catwalk

Key Location: Catwalk

During Control matches, **Catwalk** contains one of the map's two Power Ammo spawn points.

With its varied terrain and multiple points of entry, **Catwalk** tends to be a very popular movement lane.

The combination of height changes and sharp turns makes it fairly easy to break line of sight in this area. However, be mindful of the low railings—a poorly timed jump can easily end in a fatal fall.

During Control matches, **Catwalk** also contains one of the map's two Power Ammo spawn points. Whenever you attempt to claim one of these spawns, be particularly mindful of enemies that might be lurking within the confines of **Depot**.

5 Ivy

Key Location: Ivy

During Survival matches, any tie-breaking Capture Points that appear will do so in **Ivy**.

Due to its position near the center of the map—along with the fact that it connects to **Depot**, **Trucks**, **Catwalk**, and **Rubble**—**Ivy** tends to get a significant amount of traffic during all match types.

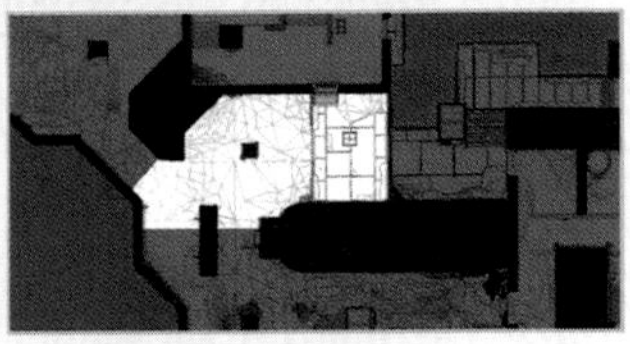

Ivy is a particularly important location during Competitive matches. Whenever a Survival round ends in a tie, the overtime Capture Point appears in this area.

6 Rubble

Key Location: Rubble

During Survival matches, **Rubble** contains the map's only Power Ammo spawn point.

With a simple layout and limited cover options, **Rubble** is a fairly exposed location at one end of a major sniping lane. During Survival matches, **Rubble** serves as the map's only source of Power Ammo, making it both a priority destination and favored target zone for dedicated snipers.

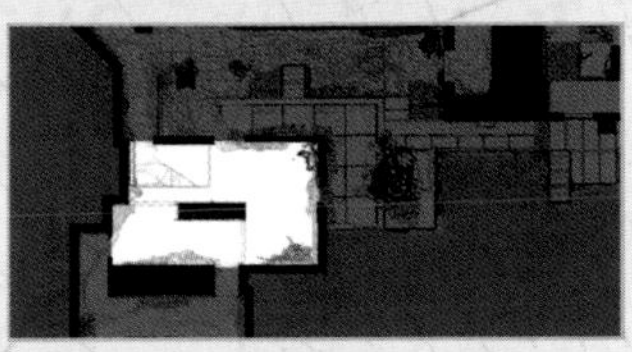

7 Garage

Key Location: Garage

During Clash matches, **Garage** contains one of the map's three Power Ammo spawn points. During Control matches, this location contains Capture Point B.

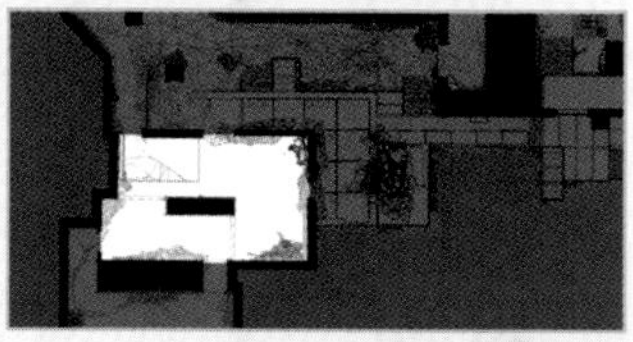

Garage is one of the map's smaller interior spaces, but you'll find this enclosure to be a strategically important location during any Quickplay match. During Clash, **Garage** contains the first available Power Ammo spawn; during Control, this location holds one of the map's Capture Points.

As key locations go, **Garage** is a relatively defensible structure. Because **Back** is only accessible from within the enclosure, securing **Garage** essentially eliminates two of the location's four points of entry.

8 Back

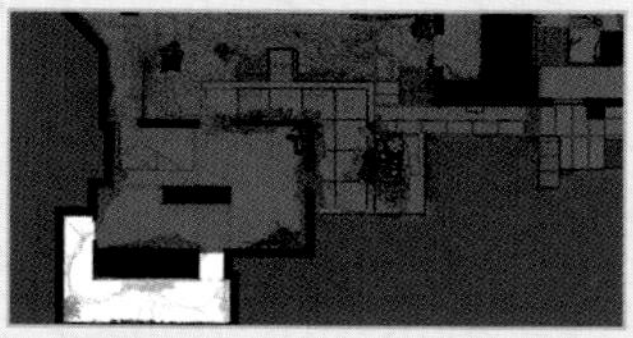

Because **Back** is only accessible via **Garage**, this narrow passage is more of a fallback position than a movement lane. Like any tight space, it's also a great spot to trap an elusive target or stage an ambush for an overeager attacker.

9 Pipes

Pipes features varied terrain, a sheer drop, and the tangle of hardware for which the location is named. It's also located in the middle of a major sniping lane, making the cover it offers particularly valuable.

10 Hall

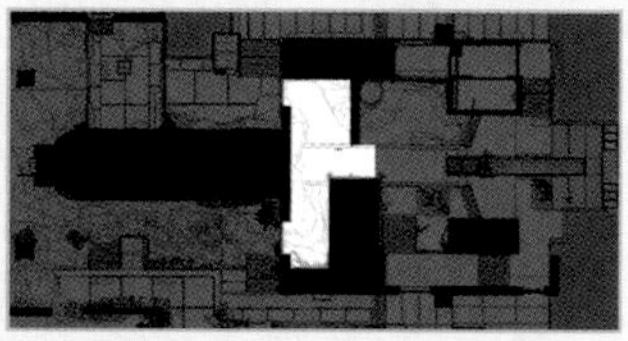

This interior location is essentially a three-way junction connecting **Catwalk**, **Mill**, and **Pipes**. A low ceiling restricts vertical movement, making it one of the map's better spots for Guardians who favor splash damage.

11 Console

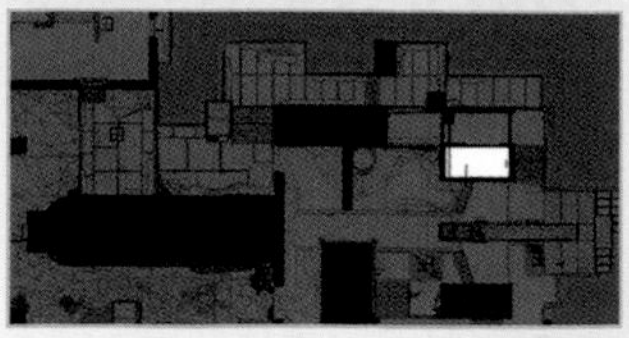

Located within **Mill**, this small enclosure serves as a nice piece of cover within what's typically a strategically important area. It's a great spot for stop-and-pop tactics, but it's easily flanked. Avoid lingering here for more than a few seconds at a time.

12 Mill

Key Location: Mill

During Clash matches, **Mill** contains one of the map's three Power Ammo spawn points. During Control matches, this location contains Capture Point C.

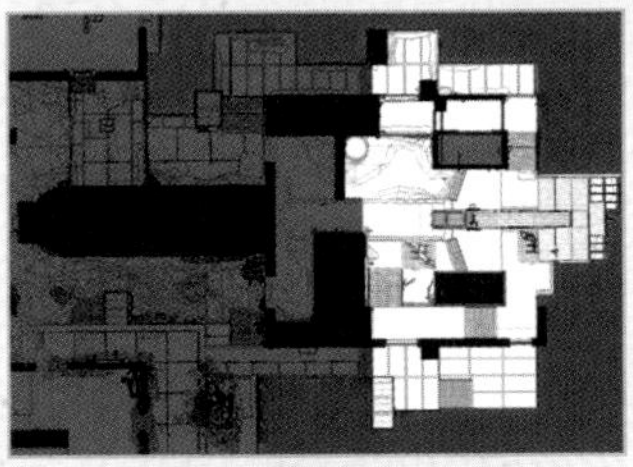

Consisting of both interior and exterior spaces, **Mill** is easily the map's largest location. Inside, you'll find varied terrain, a high ceiling, multiple cover options, and a variety of entry points. Outside, you'll see narrow walkways and some of the map's best sniping positions. In any case, **Mill**'s position at the edge of the cliff makes fatal falls a legitimate concern.

In Clash, **Mill** contains one of the map's three Power Ammo spawn points. During a Control match, it holds one of three Capture Points. In most game modes, **Mill** also serves as a team starting area.

Endless Vale

Quick Play

Arcadian Valley, Nessus

Endless Vale

Overview

Endless Vale is compact and roughly symmetrical, featuring similar movement lanes and cover options near each of the team starting areas. Firefights can break out anywhere, of course, but the bulk of the action tends to take place near the center of the map.

The map includes some passable sniping lanes, but nothing that will test the limits of a long-range weapon. Line of sight tends to be limited, and the center of the map can be downright claustrophobic. In most cases, you're likely to find that short- and mid-range weapons yield the best results.

Sheer drops and high walls are easy enough to identify, but the map also features some less obvious boundaries. The bodies of water along the edge of the map are considered off-limits. Step into one of these, and you only have a few seconds to return to the designated battleground.

Endless Vale Map Locations

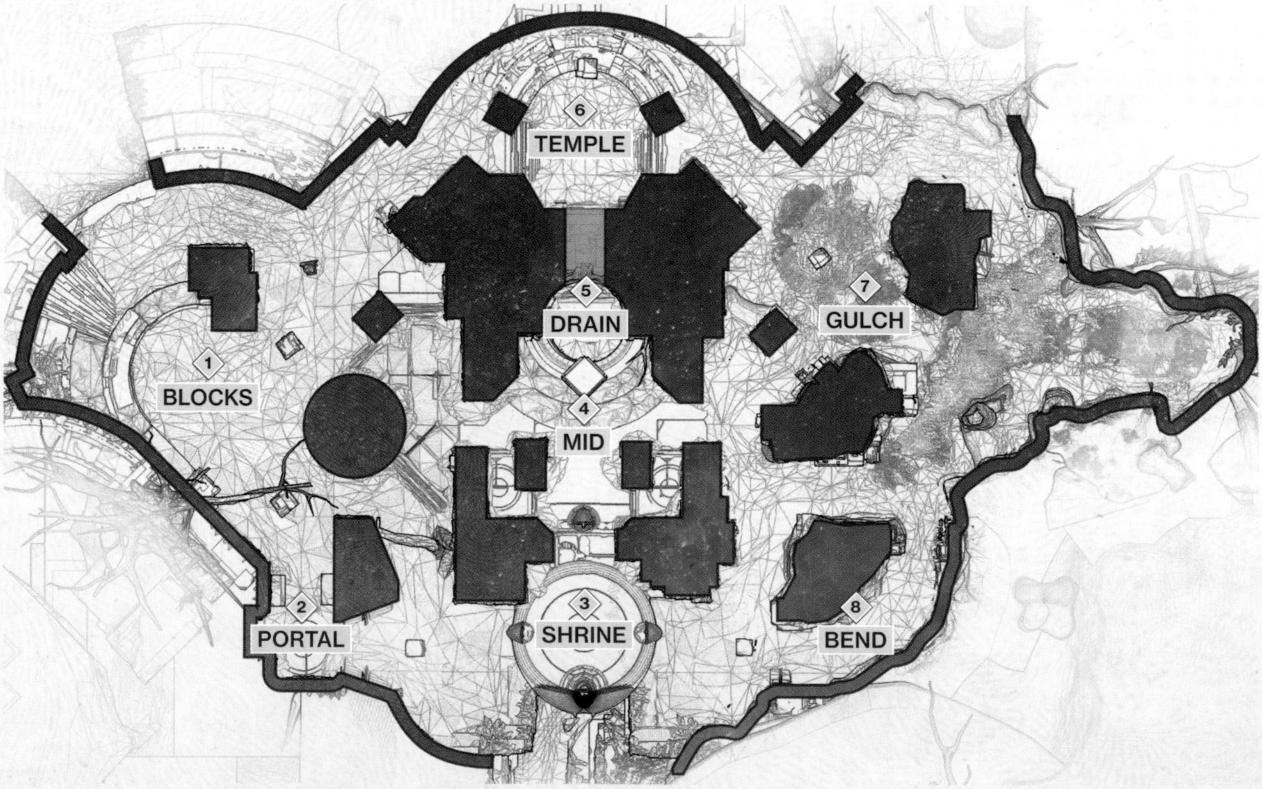

Clash, Supremacy

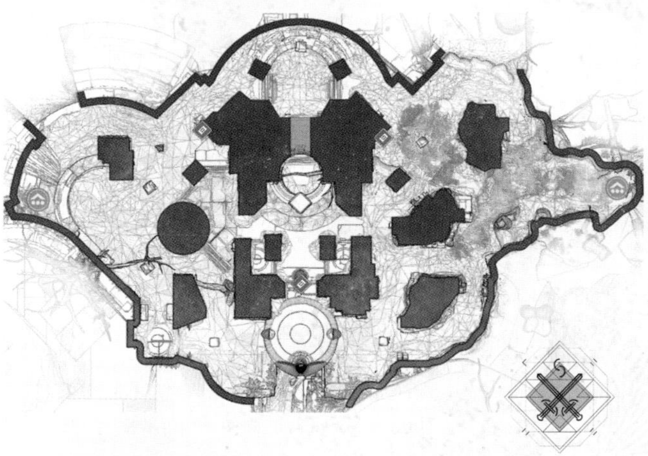

Endless Vale: Control

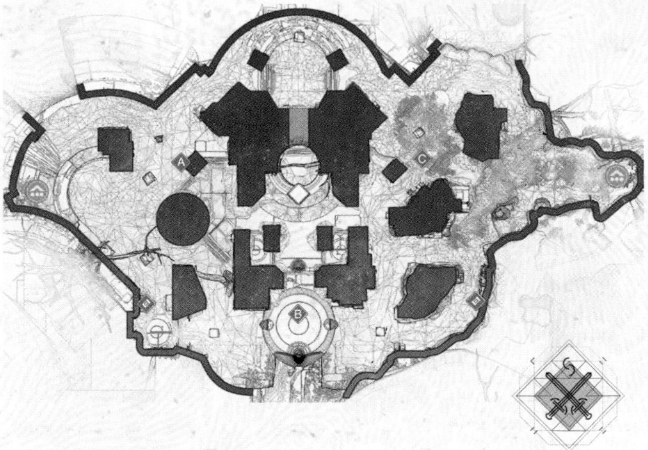

1 Blocks

Key Location: Blocks

During matches of Clash or Supremacy, **Blocks** contains one of the map's three Power Ammo spawn points. In Control, this location contains Capture Point A.

Blocks typically serves as one of the map's team starting areas. It's a relatively large space with some decent cover options, making it one of the better settings for mid-range gun battles.

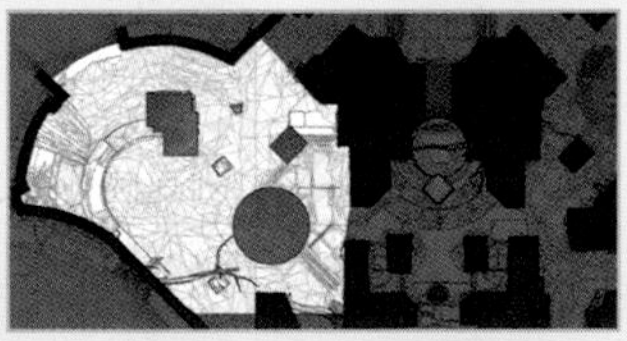

This location plays an important role in all Quickplay matches. In Clash or Supremacy, **Blocks** contains a Power Ammo spawn point. During games of Control, it holds Capture Point A.

2 Portal

Key Location: Portal

During games of Control, **Portal** serves as one of the map's two Power Ammo spawn points.

Due to its size and placement, **Portal** is typically used more as cover than as a flanking route. It offers a nice line of sight into Shrine, but the surrounding walls make it difficult to avoid incoming splash damage.

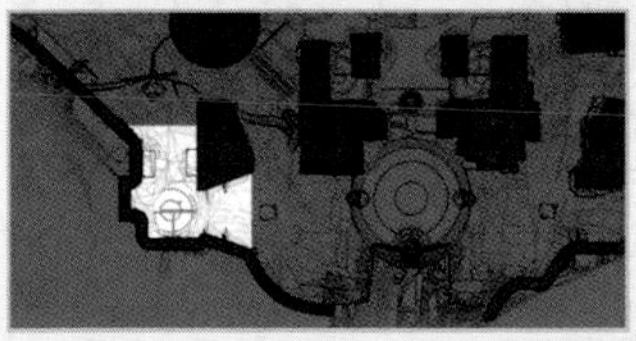

During Control matches, this location contains one of the map's Power Ammo spawns.

3 Shrine

Key Location: Shrine

In games of Clash or Supremacy, Shrine serves as one of the map's three Power Ammo spawn points. In Control, this location holds Capture Point B.

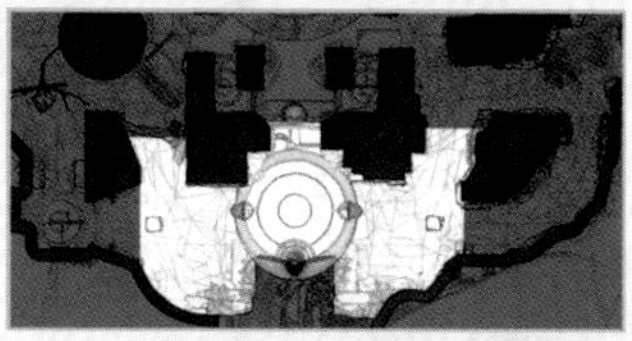

While the location includes some flat ground, **Shrine**'s defining feature is its central platform. Due to its height, this circular altar obstructs what would otherwise be one of the map's best sniping lanes. Of course, this makes the platform itself a dangerous place to linger. The surrounding objects offer minimal cover, and the extra height serves to put posted Guardians on full display.

Shrine plays a key role in all Quickplay match types, making it a hotly contested location in virtually any game.

4 Mid

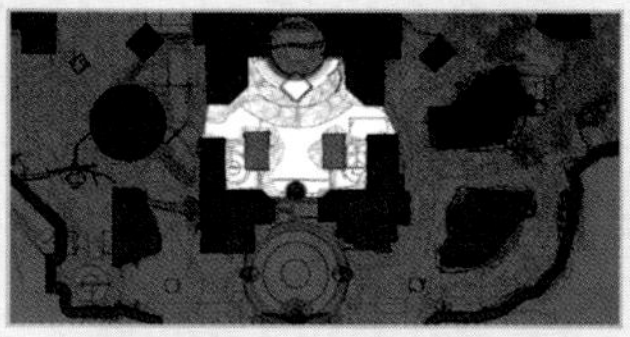

Placed at the center of Endless Vale, **Mid** is a widely used intersection and the closest thing the map has to a chokepoint. While it offers a clear path between **Blocks** and **Gulch**, cover is rarely more than a step or two away. It's a good spot for short-range combat, and the tightly clustered cover options make a quick run through **Mid** one of the better ways to disrupt incoming team-fire.

5 Drain

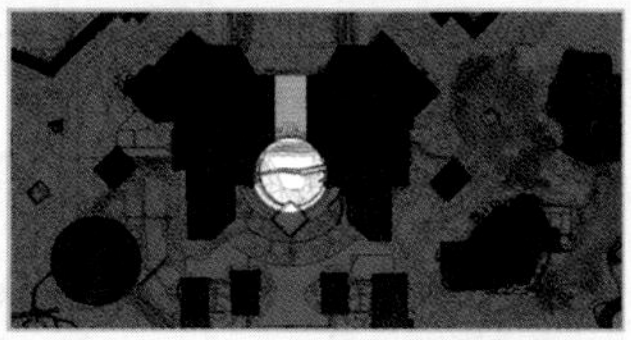

Connecting **Mid** to **Temple**, **Drain** adds a level change to what would otherwise be a simple hallway. This quick transition is a great way to break line of sight, but using it can leave you vulnerable to whatever's waiting on the other side.

6 Temple

Temple is a fairly large interior space with some nice cover options around its perimeter. The raised ceiling allows for a fair amount of vertical movement, and multiple points of entry support flanking maneuvers or quick escapes. This location also offers excellent lines of sight into **Blocks** and **Gulch**.

7 Gulch

Key Location: Gulch

During games of Clash or Supremacy, **Gulch** contains one of the map's three Power Ammo spawn points. In Control, it holds Capture Point C.

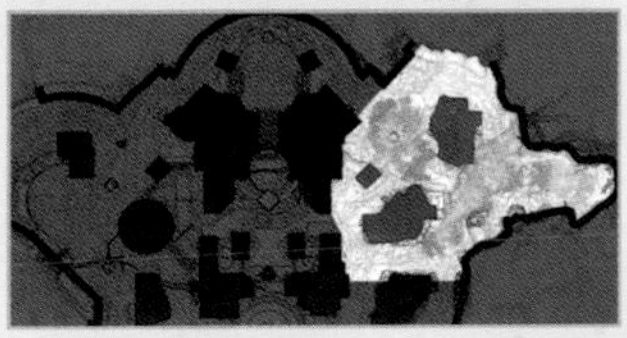

Despite some minor variations and a wildly different aesthetic, **Gulch** is essentially a mirror image of **Blocks**. It's roughly the same size as its counterpart, it shares a similar layout, and it generally serves as a team starting area. Here, a good mid-range weapon is likely to be your best bet; however, those who favor long-range rifles should find some potentially useful vantage points.

Like **Blocks**, **Gulch** plays an important role in all Quickplay matches. In Clash or Supremacy, **Gulch** features a Power Ammo spawn point. During games of Control, it contains Capture Point C.

8 Bend

Key Location: Bend

During games of Control, **Bend** serves as one of the map's two Power Ammo spawn points.

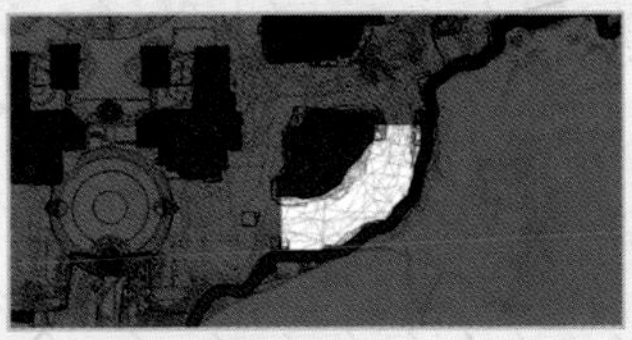

In contrast to the sharp angles of **Portal**, **Bend** features a gentle curving path. It's a decent place to break line of sight during hectic firefights, and it offers a semi-protected view into **Shrine**. Like its counterpart across the map, **Bend** also serves as a Power Ammo spawn point during Control matches.

The Fortress

Quick Play

Competitive

European Dead Zone, Earth

The Fortress

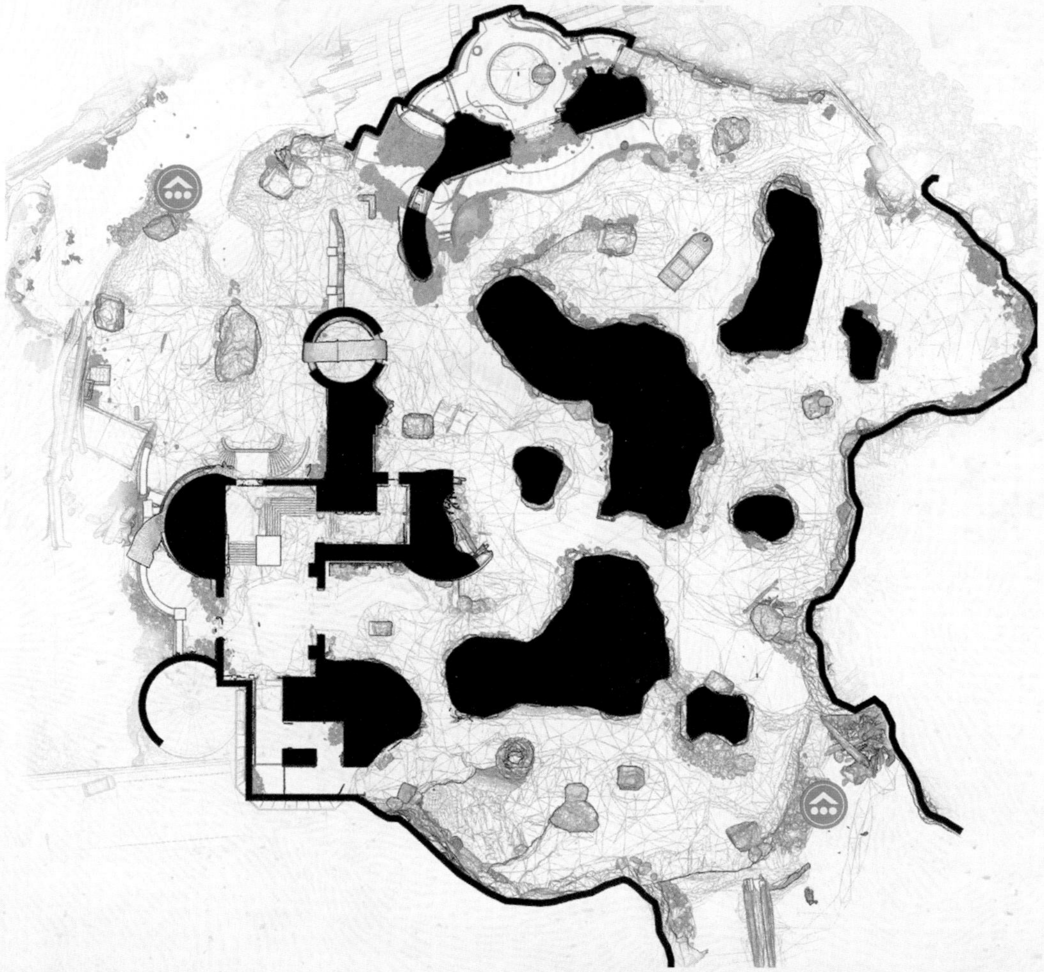

Overview

The Fortress is a large and varied stage, with some excellent sniping lanes. Regardless of your Power weapon preferences, consider equipping a good scout rifle whenever you visit this map.

Of course, not every location supports long-range combat. The Fortress includes some tight spaces, and many locations feature uneven terrain and plenty of cover options. In most cases, pairing a scout rifle with a short- or mid-range weapon is your best bet.

Much of the map's border is defined by a large body of water. While you can safely venture into the shallows of **Shore** and **Grotto**, open water is most definitely out of bounds.

The Fortress Map Locations

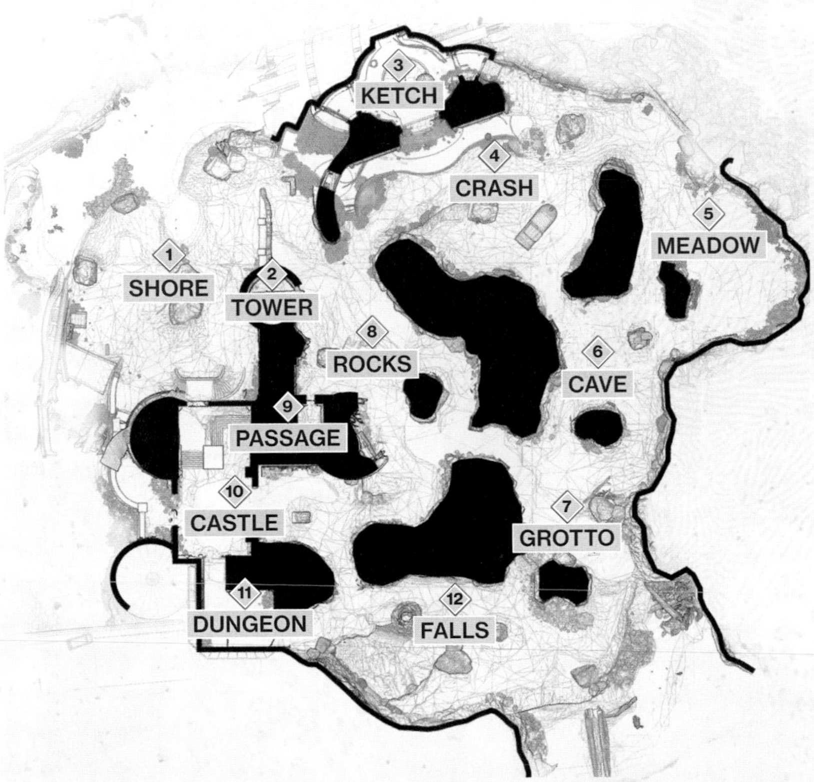

Supremacy

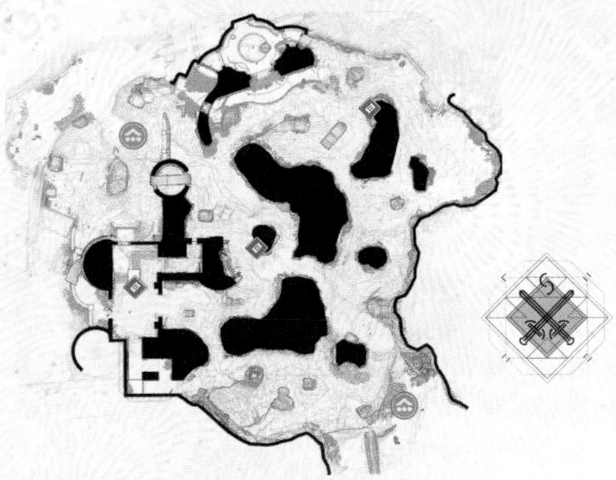

Countdown

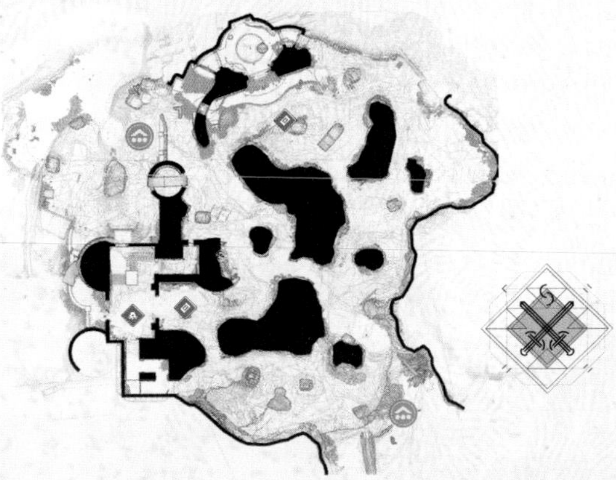

Control

1 Shore

Shore is a large exterior location that typically serves as a team starting area. The terrain offers some natural cover, but this location features an open layout suitable for large-scale skirmishes.

2 Tower

Key Location: Tower

During Control matches, Tower contains one of the map's two Power Ammo spawn points.

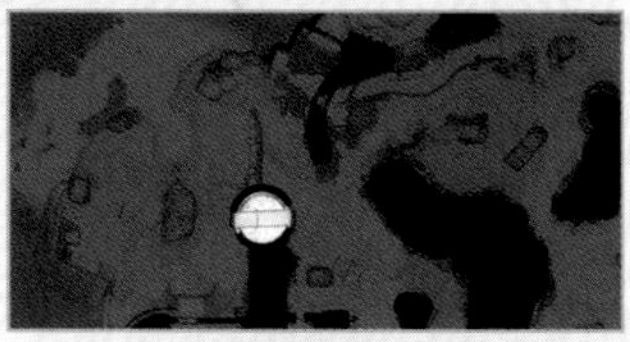

Nestled between two sizable battlegrounds, **Tower** is a small but significant part of a major movement lane. A nearby rock formation obstructs the view into **Shore**, but this open structure features an excellent line of sight through **Rocks** and **Crash**, particularly if you jump up to the ledge above the main passage.

During games of Control, **Tower** also serves as a Power Ammo spawn point.

3 Ketch

Key Location: Ketch

During Control matches, **Ketch** contains Capture Point A. In Countdown, it holds one of the map's two charges.

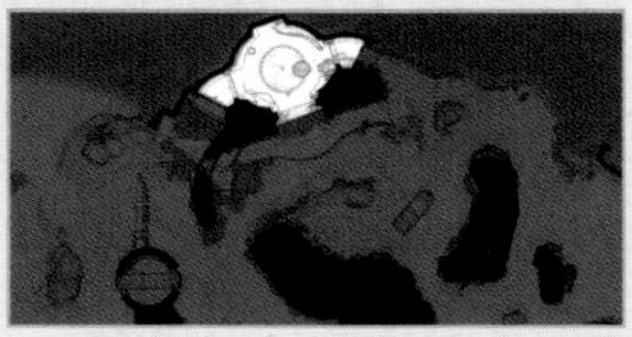

While **Ketch** is contained within a large piece of wreckage, the interior space is relatively compact. This makeshift structure features three points of entry, one of which is fitted with an automated door. This location provides some nice cover options and a decent view of the surrounding areas.

In most cases, you'll find that **Ketch** is a strategically important location. During games of Control, it contains Capture Point A; in Countdown, one of the map's charges appears within this enclosure.

4 Crash

Key Location: Crash

During games of Supremacy, Crash serves as one of the map's three Power Ammo spawn points. In Countdown, this location is one of only two sources of Power Ammo.

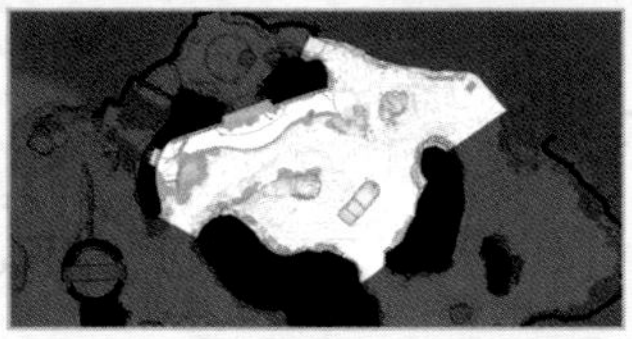

Crash is a fairly large exterior area. Much of this location is tucked between sizable rock formations, but a good portion of **Crash** stands as one of the map's most lethal sniping lanes. This heavily traveled area also serves as a source of Power Ammo during games of Supremacy or Countdown.

5 Meadow

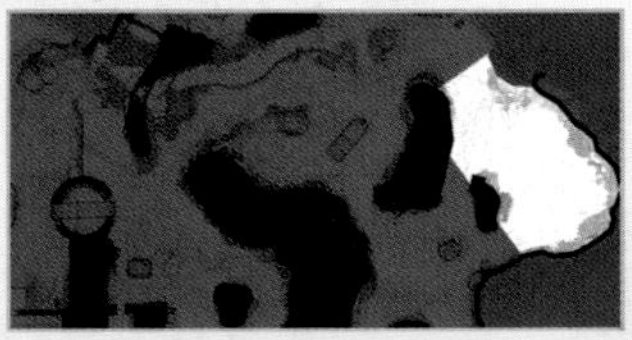

Placed along the perimeter of the map, **Meadow** is most often used as a flanking route between **Cave** and **Crash**. It's one of the map's smaller exterior spaces and offers very little cover, but it does make for a useful vantage point.

6 Cave

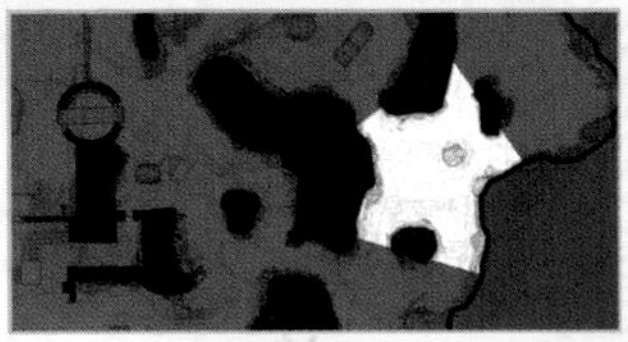

Cave consists of a few cover options within an otherwise empty enclosure. It has five points of entry, divided among three adjacent areas. It tends to see a lot of foot traffic over the course of a match, making **Cave** a fairly good spot to go looking for trouble.

7 Grotto

Key Location: Grotto

During Control matches, **Grotto** contains Capture Point C.

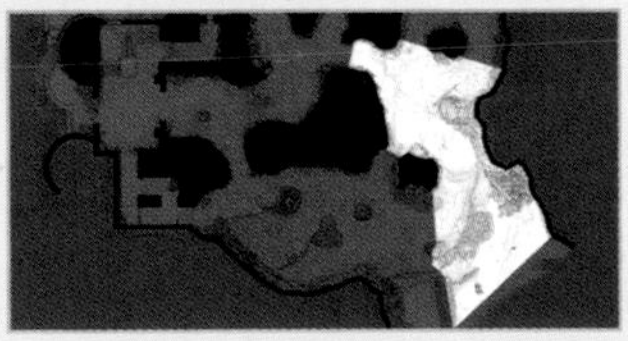

Grotto is a large but relatively narrow location that stretches from the border of **Rocks** clear to the edge of the map. It features some nice bits of natural cover, but multiple points of entry make it a difficult area to hold.

In most match types, **Grotto** serves as a team starting area. During games of Control, it also contains one of the map's three Capture Points.

8 Rocks

Key Location: Rocks

During Supremacy matches, **Rocks** serves as one of the map's three sources of Power Ammo.

Located at the center of the map, **Rocks** tends to be a heavily used intersection. It's too large to be considered a chokepoint, but this location is part of a fairly effective sniping lane. During games of Supremacy, **Rocks** also contains a Power Ammo spawn point.

9 Passage

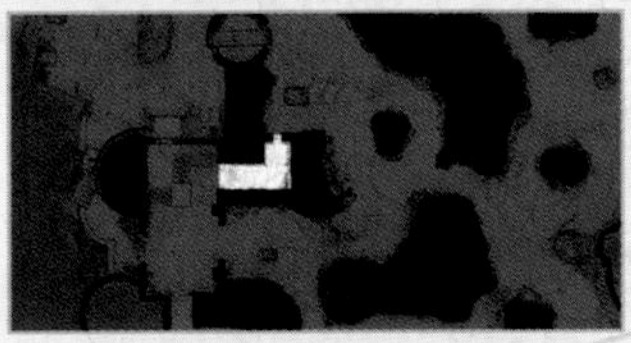

The appropriately named **Passage** is a narrow path connecting **Castle**'s interior space to **Rocks**. It's a useful flanking route and—thanks to a right angle that limits line of sight—a handy place to fall back and recover during hectic firefights. Like any tight space, **Passage** is a great place to ambush overeager pursuers.

10 Castle

Key Location: Castle

In games of Supremacy, **Castle** contains one of the map's three Power Ammo spawn points. In Control, it holds Capture Point B. During Countdown, it contains both a charge and a Power Ammo spawn point.

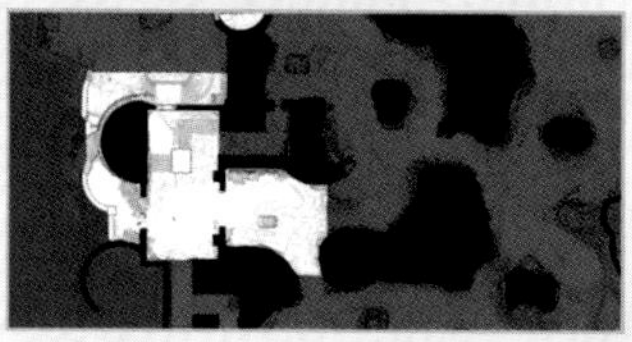

Castle is a strategically important location in all match types, so it tends to be a hotly contested area. The main structure's walls provide decent cover, but points of entry are arranged in such a way that coordinated assaults can be difficult to repel.

When it's not hosting heated firefights, **Castle** serves as a useful vantage point. It offers a particularly good view of **Shore**, but a well-positioned sniper can pick off targets approaching from **Rocks** or **Falls**.

11 Dungeon

Located between **Castle** and **Falls**, **Dungeon** is a small distinct area unlike anything else on the map. It's a useful flanking route and one of the map's best settings for short-range combat.

12 Falls

Key Location: Falls

During games of Control, **Falls** features one of the map's two Power Ammo spawn points.

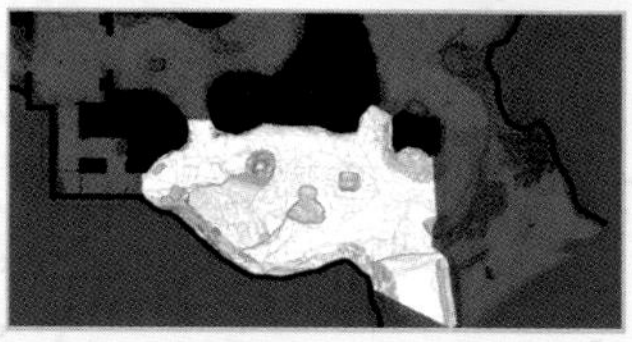

Falls is a fairly large location. While it does feature a very effective sniping lane, the combination of uneven terrain and natural cover makes it somewhat easy to break line of sight during long-range gun battles. Still, it tends to see a lot of foot traffic, and it serves as a source of Power Ammo during games of Control.

Legion's Gulch

Quick Play

European Dead Zone, Earth

Legion's Gulch

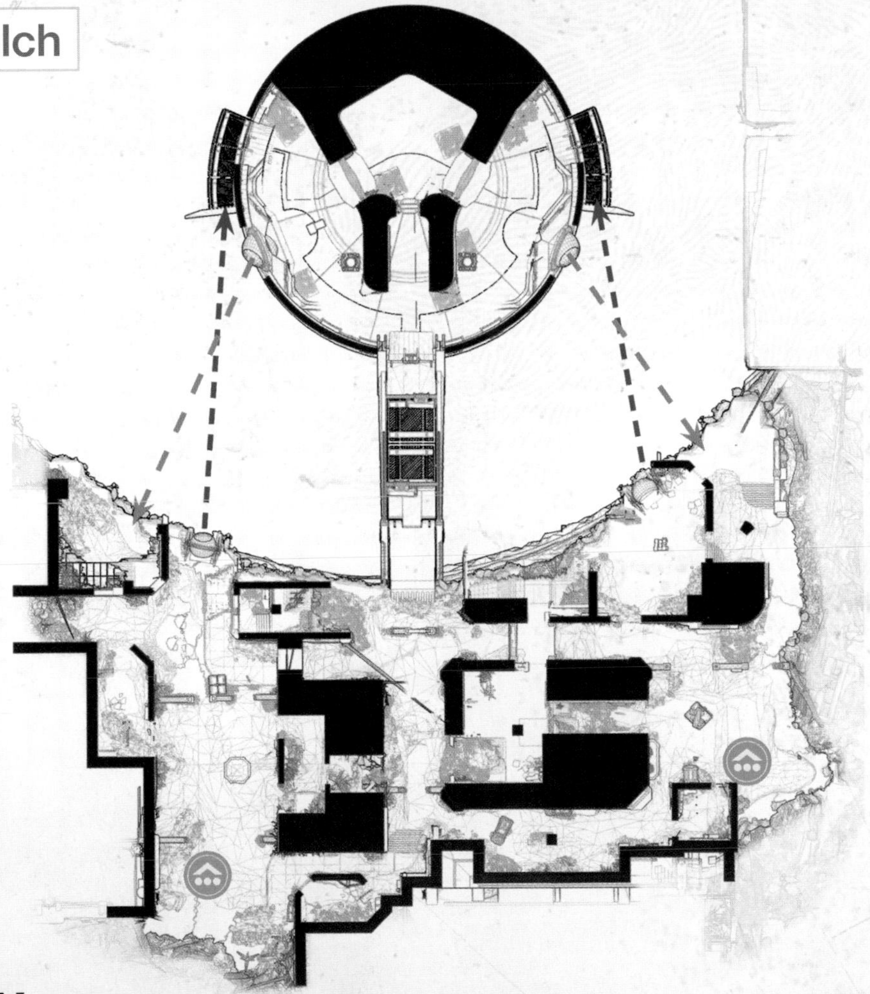

Overview

Legion's Gulch is a fairly large map, but thanks to a massive Cabal drilling platform, much of it has been rendered unusable. The result is a stage that features two very different settings separated by a sizable canyon. The damaged terrain means that sheer drops are commonplace, but the map's border also boasts some less obvious off-limits areas.

A once-bustling city accounts for most of the playable area. Short-range weapons can be very effective in this maze of crumbling buildings and narrow footpaths, but the cityscape does feature a few clearings and some surprisingly effective sniping lanes.

While there's a bridge running between the city ruins and the drilling platform, you'll also find four launchers scattered around the canyon's edge. These devices allow for quick and easy gap traversal, but using them leaves you fairly vulnerable to incoming fire. Before you step into a launcher, try to weigh the convenience against the potential risk. Airborne Guardians make tempting targets, and designated Landing Zones can be very effective ambush sites.

Legion's Gulch Map Locations

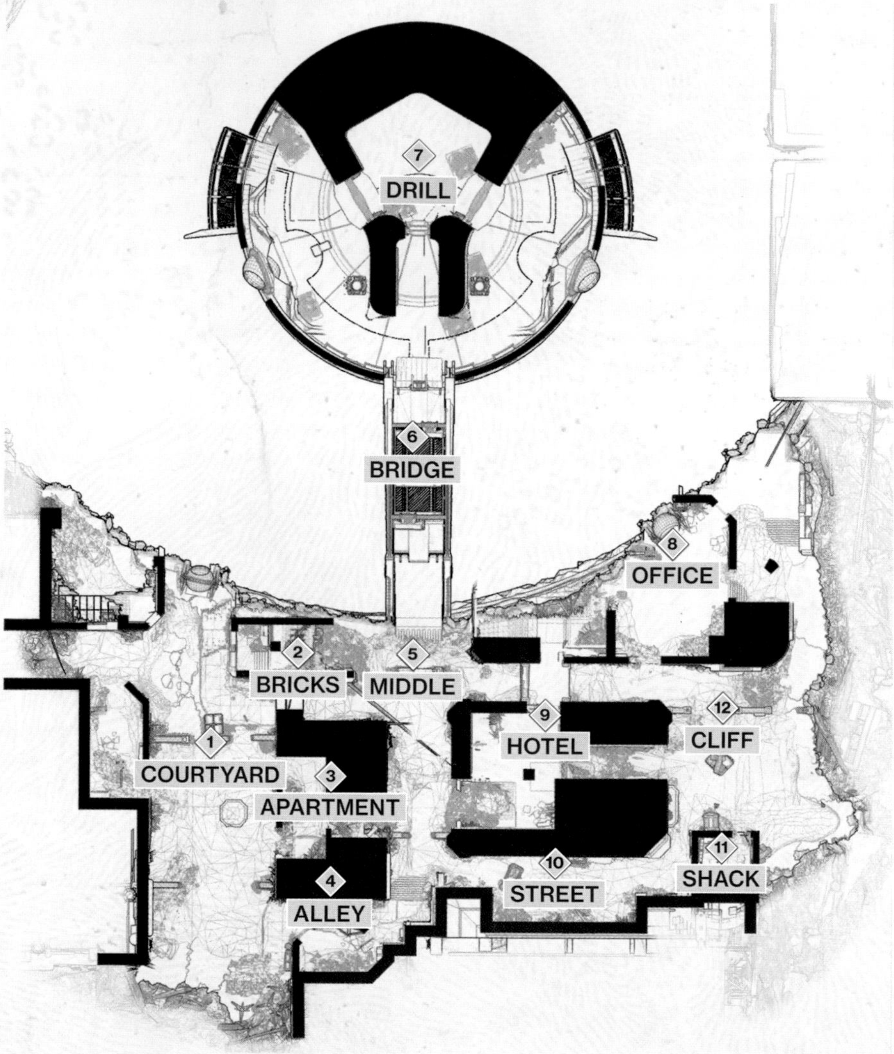

Clash, Supremacy

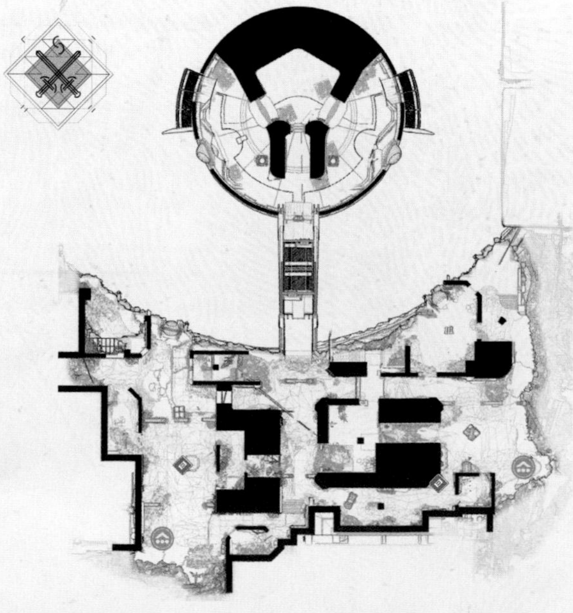

Control

1 Courtyard

Key Location: Courtyard

During games of Clash and Supremacy, **Courtyard** serves as one of the map's three sources of Power Ammo. During Control, it contains both a Power Ammo spawn point and Capture Point A.

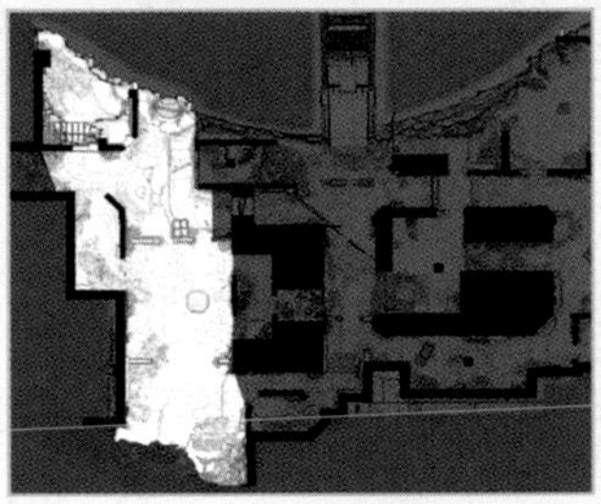

One of the map's largest locations, **Courtyard** features a wide variety of cover options. However, it also has a Cabal launcher and multiple points of entry, making this long strip of land something of a sniping lane.

Courtyard serves as a team starting area, a major movement lane, and a source of Power Ammo in all Quickplay matches. During Control, this location also holds one of the map's Capture Points.

2 Bricks

Bricks is a fairly small location, but it features three distinct paths connecting **Courtyard** to **Middle**. One of these paths offers a good amount of cover; another is part of a decent sniping lane. The third path is a very narrow strip of land running along the gap's edge.

3 Apartment

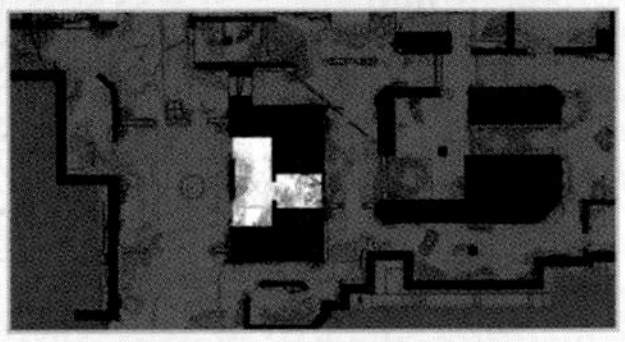

While this badly damaged building hardly qualifies as a structure, it does offer a good amount of cover for Guardians moving between **Courtyard** and **Middle**. It makes for a decent vantage point, and it can be something of a bottleneck during heated skirmishes

4 Alley

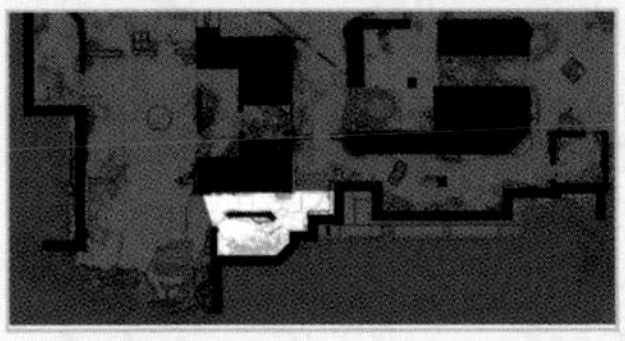

Alley features a narrow passage wedged between an inaccessible building and a small empty structure. It's a useful flanking route, but it also serves as a popular vantage point for Guardians monitoring **Courtyard** or **Middle**.

5 Middle

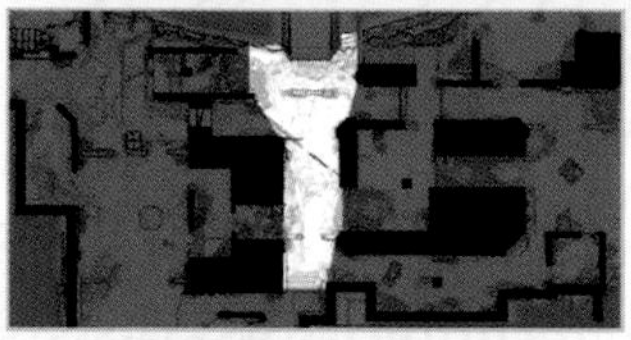

Located at the center of the cityscape, the aptly named **Middle** tends to see a lot of foot traffic over the course of any match. It features some useful cover options, multiple flanking routes, and a short but serviceable sniping lane.

6 Bridge

Key Location: Bridge

During games of Clash or Supremacy, **Bridge** features one of the map's three Power Ammo spawn points.

Bridge serves as a straightforward path between **Drill** and **Middle** that features some welcome cover options. During games of Clash or Supremacy, it contains a Power Ammo spawn point.

7 Drill

Key Location: Drill

During games of Control, Drill contains Capture Point B.

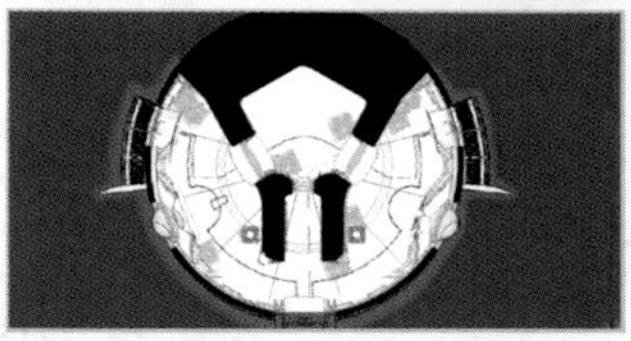

In contrast to the crumbling cityscape across the map, **Drill** features the industrial aesthetic found in all Cabal facilities. Despite some interior walls and an automated door, this circular platform stands as one of the map's largest battlegrounds. In games of Control, it also hosts a Capture Point.

Drill is a suitable spot for decisive firefights, but the available launchers support quick transitions in and out of the area. When you need a moment to recover from heavy damage, a quick jaunt into **Drill** is often your best option.

8 Office

Key Location: Office

During games of Control, Office serves as one of the map's two Power Ammo spawn points.

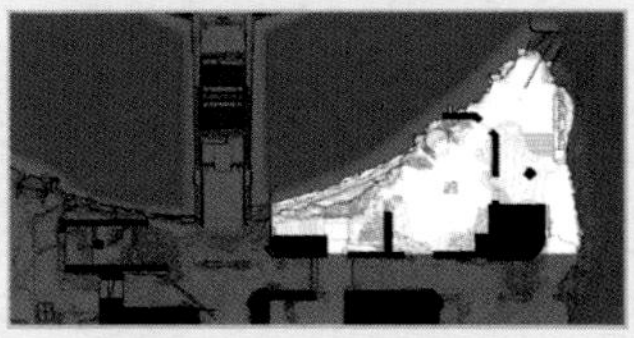

While **Office** includes a sizable exterior area, it also contains the cityscape's largest accessible structure. The interior space offers a few bits of cover, multiple points of entry, and a Cabal launcher for quick access to **Drill**. A low ceiling limits the potential for vertical movement, but **Office** tends to be a frequently visited area.

During games of Control, **Office**'s exterior space features one of the map's Power Ammo spawn points.

9 Hotel

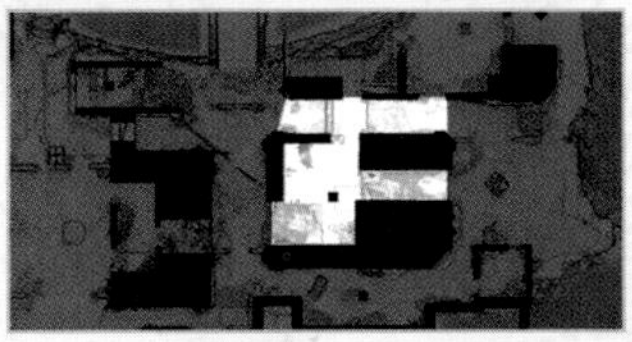

For what tends to be a heavy-traffic intersection, **Hotel** is a decent place to recover between firefights. It features a central piece of cover and three points of entry, making it possible to escape from all but the most coordinated of attacks.

10 Street

Key Location: Street

During games of Clash or Supremacy, **Street** contains one of the map's three Power Ammo spawn points.

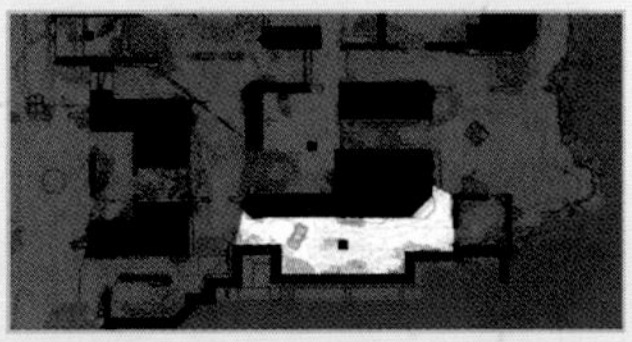

As a narrow throughway with some nice cover options, **Street** tends to be a popular flanking route and serviceable sniping lane. During Clash and Supremacy, it's also a source of Power Ammo.

11 Shack

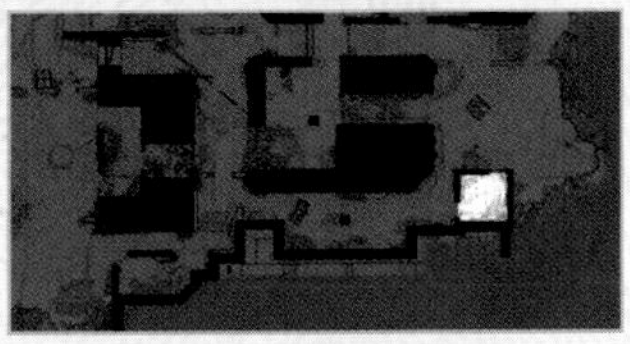

As a small structure tucked away in the corner of the map, **Shack** provides welcome cover from nearby firefights and great lines of sight into adjacent areas.

12 Cliff

Key Location: Cliff

During games of Control, Cliff contains Capture Point C.

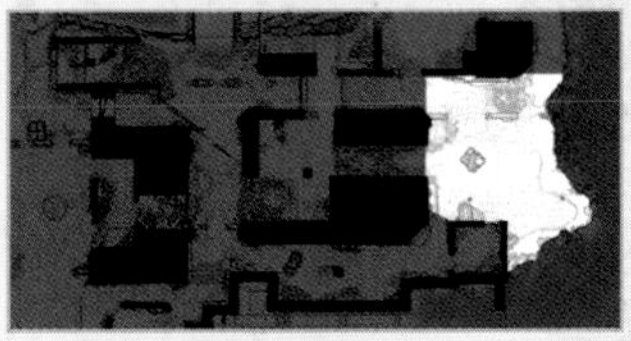

Apart from a few pieces of cover, **Cliff** is a fairly open exterior space. It typically serves as a team starting area, but during games of Control, it also contains one of the map's Capture Points.

Altar of Flame

Quick Play

Competitive

Caloris Basin, Mercury

Altar of Flame

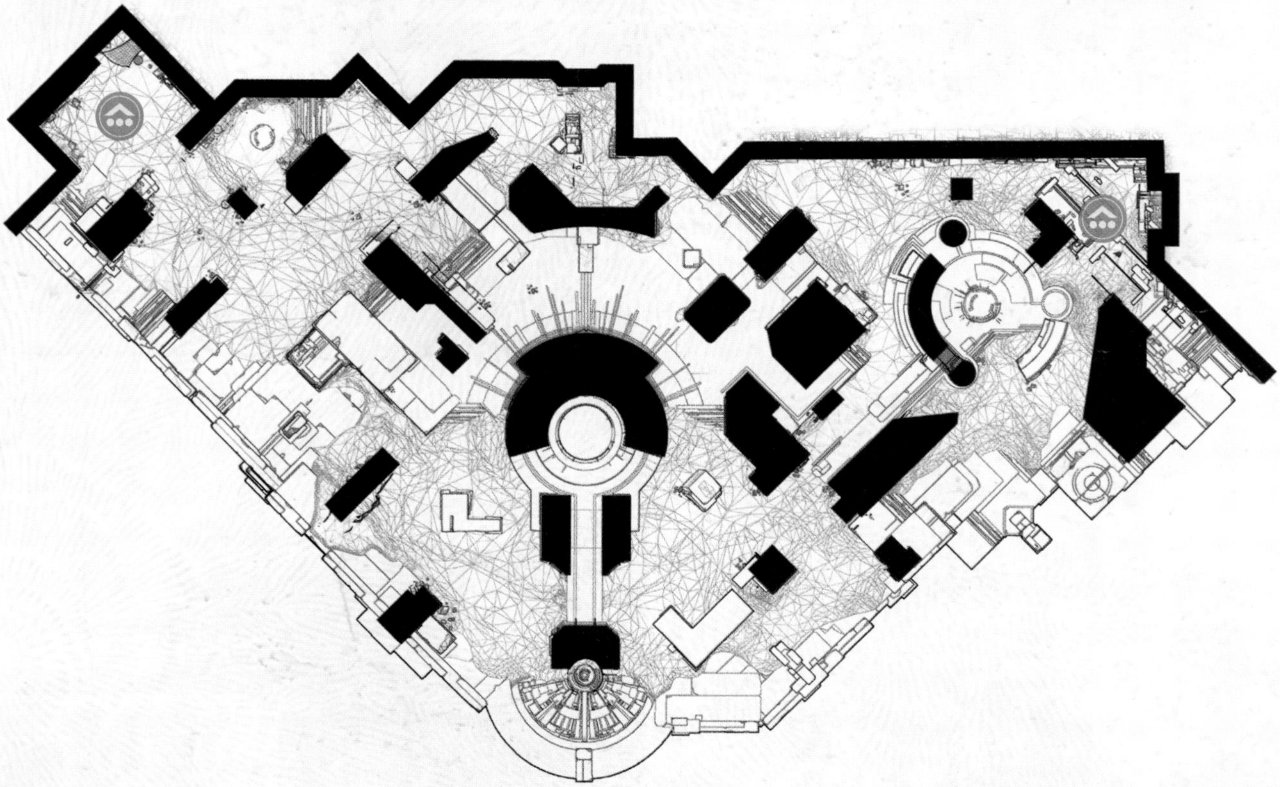

Overview

Altar of Flame is a fairly compact map, and the nature of Vex architecture can give even its largest areas a somewhat claustrophobic feel. Short- and mid-range weapons can be very effective, but long-range weapons still have their uses on this map.

Altar of Flame is largely an outdoor space, but it does have its share of overhangs and low ceilings. You'll also notice that this stage features a variety of lighting conditions. As you move from place to place, consider how your surroundings affect your mobility and target acquisition.

More than half of the map's border allows for fatal falls, but a few of the irregular ledges that mark these areas make for effective vantage points. Don't shy away from using them—just be mindful of your footing.

Altar of Flame Map Locations

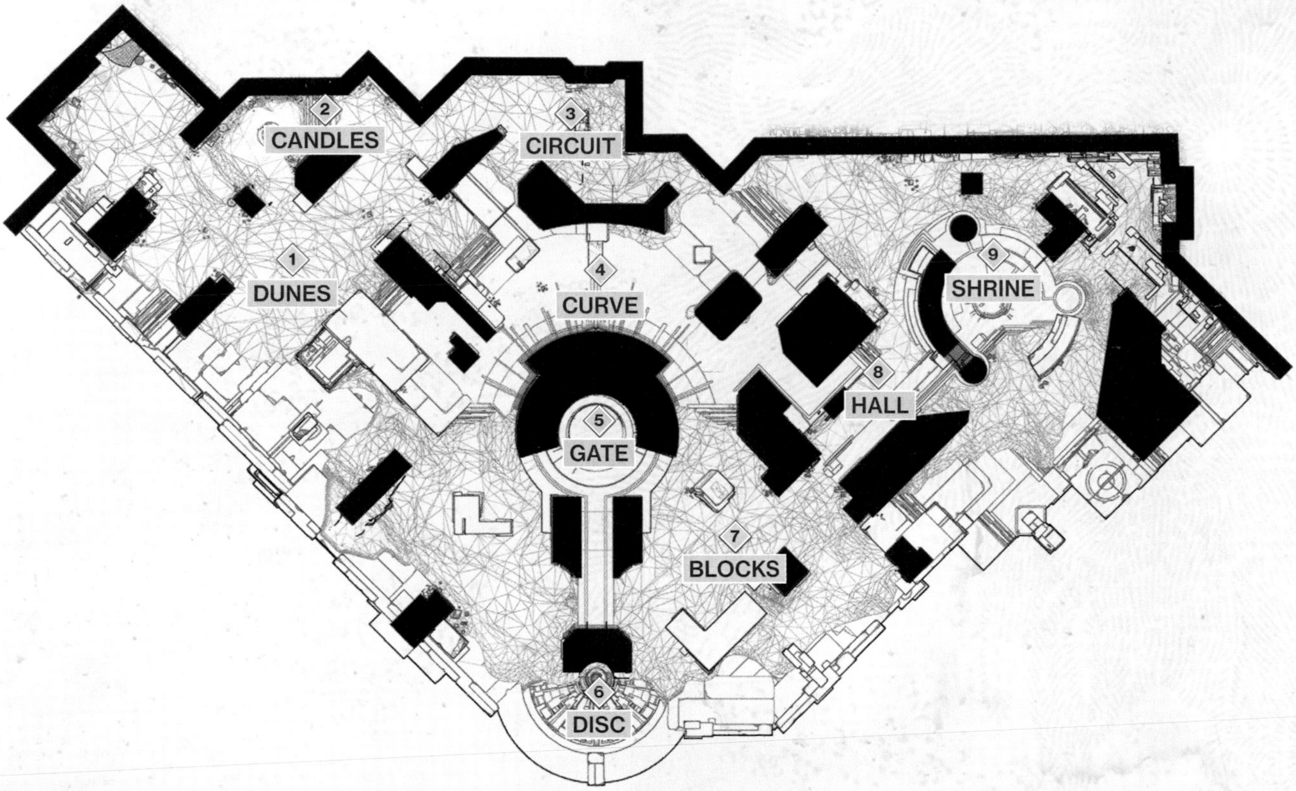

Survival

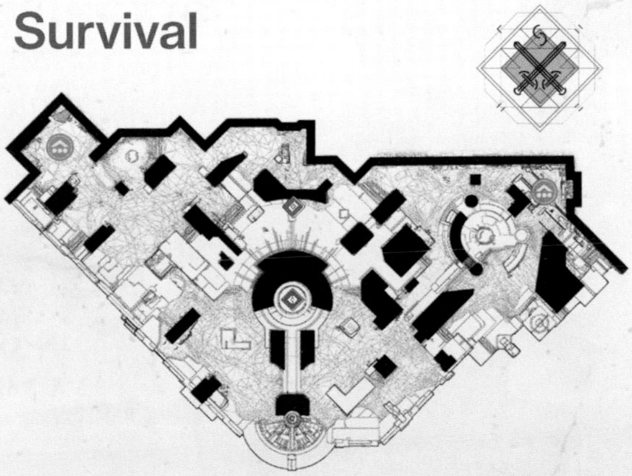

Clash

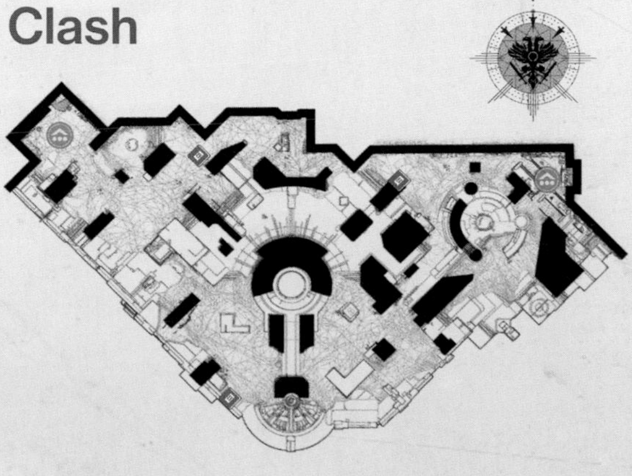

Control

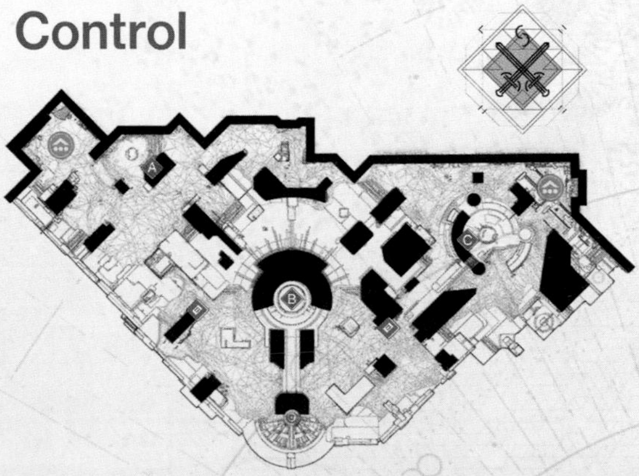

1 Dunes

Key Location: Dunes

During games of Control, **Dunes** contains one of the map's two Power Ammo spawn points.

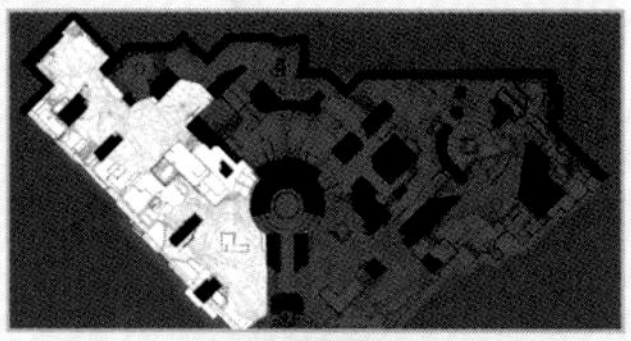

Dunes is a very large area featuring uneven terrain, multiple movement lanes, and extensive cover options. This location also includes the map's only true interior space, a sparsely decorated room that typically serves as a team starting area. During games of Control, this location is also a source of Power Ammo.

Due to its size, **Dunes** tends to be a high-traffic location. While it does contain some relatively open spots, Guardians in this area are rarely more than a few steps away from cover.

2 Candles

Key Location: Candles

During games of Control, **Candles** contains Capture Point A.

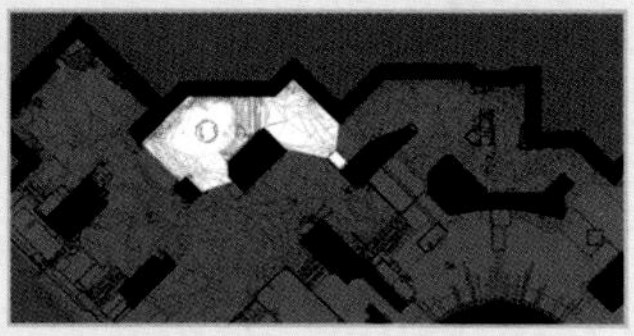

Candles is a fairly small area, but it tends to see a lot of visitors over the course of a match. Although it features four points of entry, some well-placed obstacles limit line of sight from adjacent areas. In most cases, this location serves as a popular flanking route. During Control, it contains one of the map's Capture Points.

3 Circuit

Key Location: Circuit

During games of Clash, **Circuit** contains one of the map's three Power Ammo spawn points.

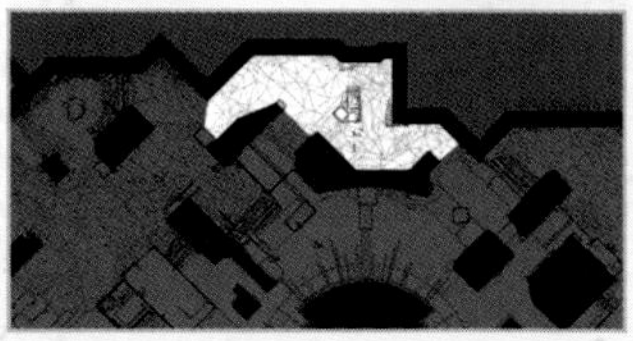

A metal corridor with three points of entry and a low ceiling, **Circuit** is a useful movement lane and a good spot for aggressive tactics. It's wide enough to allow for lateral movement, but a very low ceiling covers much of it. During Clash matches, this location also serves as a source of Power Ammo.

4 Curve

Key Location: Curve

During Survival matches, **Curve** contains the map's only Power Ammo spawn point.

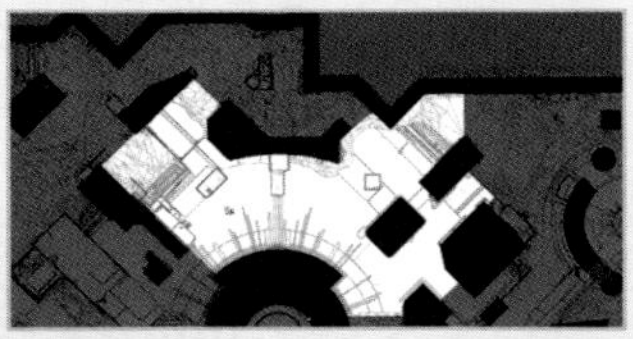

Wrapping around the center of the map, **Curve** tends to be a frequently visited and fairly dangerous area. Despite some solid cover options, it's a wide movement lane that can leave occupants open to fire from adjacent areas. It's a particularly important location during games of Survival, when it serves as the map's only source of Power Ammo.

5 Gate

Key Location: Gate

During games of Control, **Gate** contains Capture Point B. In Survival, it hosts the Capture Point that appears whenever a round ends in a tie.

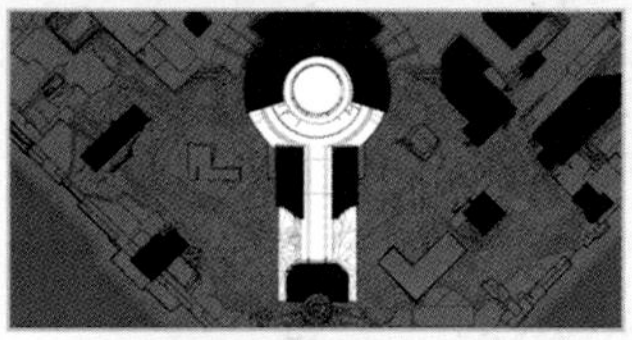

Located in the center of the map, **Gate** consists of a round platform connected to a narrow sloping path. The surrounding walls make **Gate** something of an open structure. In most cases, this location is a useful (if somewhat conspicuous) vantage point.

Gate is a relatively small location, but it tends to be an important one. It contains a Capture Point during Control, or whenever a round of Survival goes into overtime.

6 Disc

Key Location: Disc

During games of Clash, **Disc** serves as one of the map's three Power Ammo spawn points.

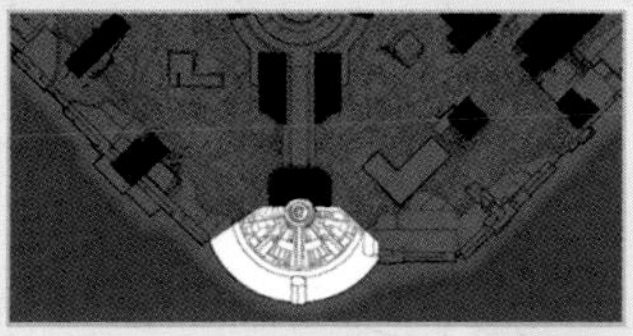

Disc is a small exposed area located between two fairly effective sniping lanes. It's most commonly used as a flanking route, but it does serve as a source of Power Ammo during Clash matches.

7 Blocks

Key Location: Blocks

During games of Control, **Blocks** contains one of the map's two Power Ammo spawn points.

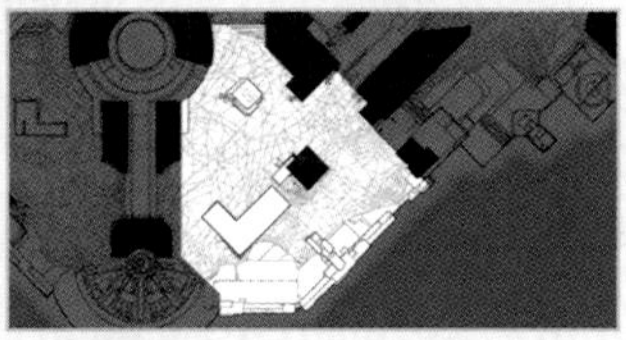

Blocks is a sizable area with some nice cover options, but it's located alongside multiple sniping lanes. The adjacent areas feature some very effective (and dimly lit) vantage points, so make good use of the available terrain, especially if you intend to grab the Power Ammo that appears here during Control matches.

8 Hall

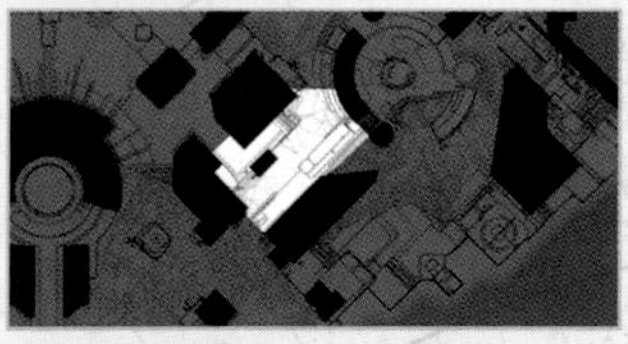

Hall is a useful flanking route and one of the map's most popular sniping points. It features a great line of sight through **Blocks** and plenty of handy escape routes in case things turn sour.

Shrine

9

Key Location: Shrine

During games of Clash, **Shrine** contains one of the map's three Power Ammo spawn points. During Control, it holds Capture Point C.

While **Shrine**'s most notable feature is the circular platform for which it's named, this sizable location also includes some nice flanking routes along the map's border. **Shrine** is typically a team starting area, but it's also a key location in Clash and Control.

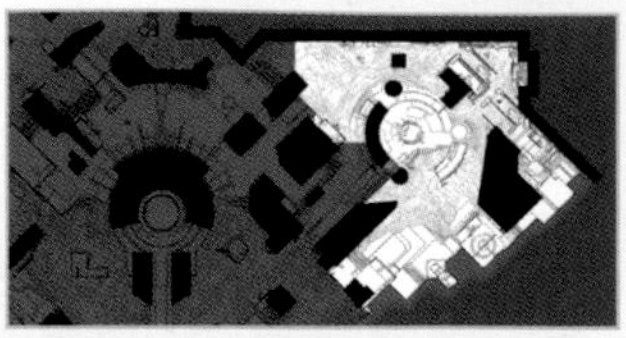

Much of this location is dimly lit, and the available cover makes it a fairly good fallback point. It's a great area to shake determined pursuers and a popular spot for designated snipers.

Vostok

Felwinter Peak, Earth

Quick Play

Competitive

Vostok

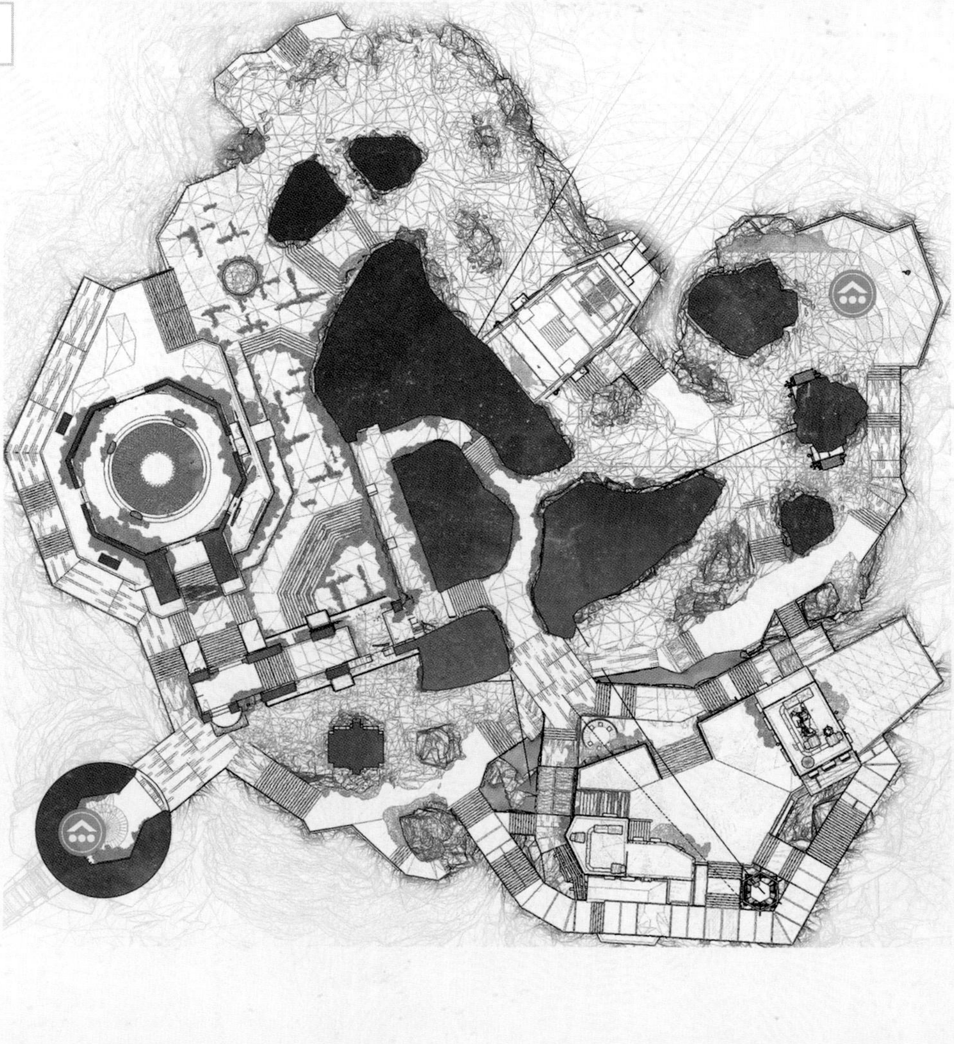

Overview

Vostok is a large map with some excellent sniping lanes, making it one of the Crucible's best stages for long-range firefights. A scout rifle is strongly recommended, and those who favor sniper rifles would be hard-pressed to find a better setting.

Most locations offer adequate cover in the form of rock formations and/or manmade structures—but thanks to some outstanding vantage points, few locations can be considered safe from sniper fire.

Vostok also includes some multi-level structures. Remember to utilize *all* of the information your motion tracker provides. Whether you're pre-aiming or using a grenade to flush an opponent out of cover, misreading your target's elevation can be a costly mistake.

Considering its location on Felwinter Peak, it should come as no surprise that Vostok contains a large number of sheer drops. It's also worth noting that some of these drops are located along important flanking routes. Airborne Guardians generally make for vulnerable targets, so before you leap across a gap, consider the likelihood of incoming fire.

Vostok Map Locations

Survival

Clash, Supremacy

Control

1 Wall

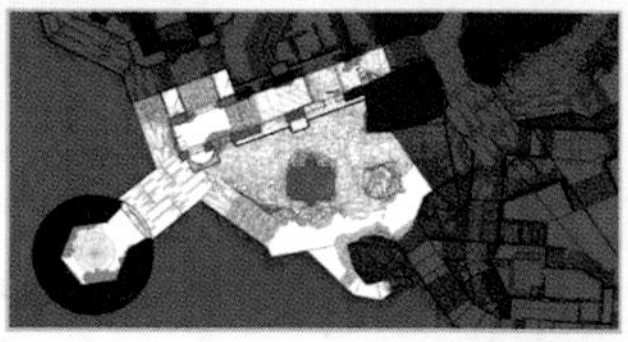

In most game modes, **Wall** serves as a team starting area, and it also serves as an excellent vantage point into adjacent locations. The structure that this area is named for combines a raised platform with solid cover options, making **Wall** a popular sniping point.

2 Dome

Key Location: Dome

During games of Clash and Supremacy, **Dome** houses one of the map's three Power Ammo spawns. In Control, this structure contains Capture Point A.

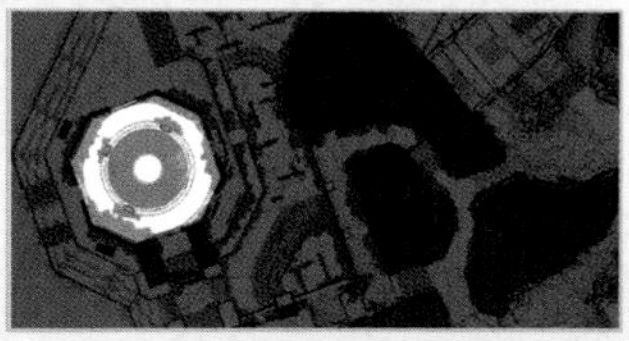

Located within the borders of **Temple**, **Dome** brings some much-needed cover to what would otherwise be a fairly open battlefield. It also serves as a key location in all Quickplay matches. Power Ammo spawns in this structure during games of Clash and Supremacy; during Control, **Dome** houses Capture Point A.

Dome features sturdy walls and some freestanding cover options, but it also has four points of entry. Coordination is essential for any team hoping to hold this location.

3 Temple

Key Location: Temple

During Survival matches, **Temple** contains the map's only source of Power Ammo.

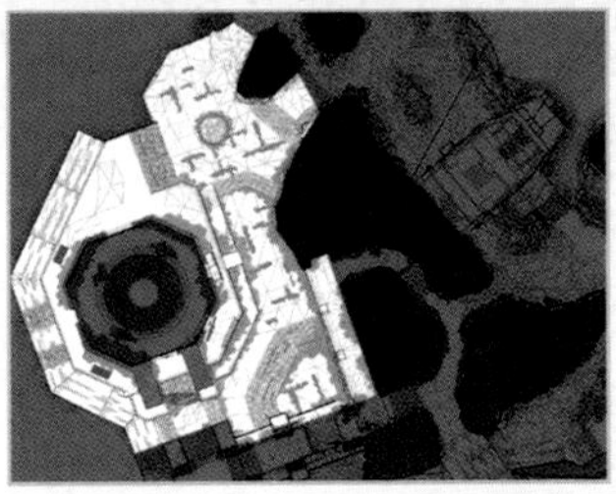

Temple is one of the map's larger locations. It features some varied terrain and nice cover options, but the layout makes this area a popular sniping lane. Avoid lingering out in the open.

In most game types, the fact that it surrounds **Dome** accounts for the bulk of **Temple**'s strategic importance. However, during Survival matches, **Temple** serves as the map's only source of Power Ammo.

4 Tram

Key Location: Tram

In games of Clash or Supremacy, **Tram** serves as one of the map's three Power Ammo spawn points. In Control, it contains Capture Point C and one of the map's two Power Ammo spawn points.

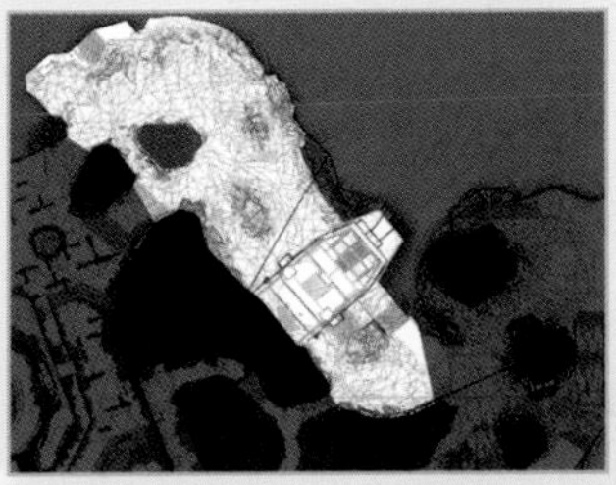

This is a relatively large area with some nice cover options, but the path that runs through it tends to be a popular sniping lane. **Tram**'s most notable feature is easily its gondola station. This open structure plays a key role in every Quickplay match type, and it serves as a useful vantage point for long-range experts.

5 Cave

Located at the center of the map, this narrow passage features four points of entry. This makes **Cave** a useful flanking route and the closest thing this map has to a chokepoint. It's also an excellent spot for close-quarters combat. Short-range weapons, short-range melee attacks, and splash damage all shine in the confines of this corridor.

6 Bridge

Bridge is a relatively small area that serves as something of a four-way intersection. A raised walkway (which the area is named for) runs between Deck and Cave.

The low road runs between the borders of Wall and Rock. It's located near the center of a major sniping lane, so be mindful of the surrounding vantage points.

7 Deck

Key Location: Deck

During games of Clash or Supremacy, **Deck** contains one of the map's three Power Ammo spawn points. During Control matches, Capture Point B appears at this location.

Deck features a level surface surrounded by a series of steps and walkways. The central platform is a key location in all Quickplay modes, and while a low wall helps mitigate the threat of long-range attacks, this frequently contested area is far from safe. Luckily, the surrounding walkways provide plenty of escape options.

8 Turret

Turret stands as one of the map's most useful vantage points. This small structure features multiple points of entry, great cover, and an unbeatable line of sight into **Wall**.

9 Tower

Key Location: Tower

During Control matches, **Tower** features one of the map's two Power Ammo spawn points.

Tower features a sizable platform connected to a tall, accessible structure. The interior space provides an outstanding line of sight into Rocks, making it one of the map's most effective sniping spots. Of course, this makes also makes the building's upper window a frequent target for counter-snipers.

10 Rocks

Key Location: Rocks

During Survival matches, any Capture Points that appear will do so in **Rocks**.

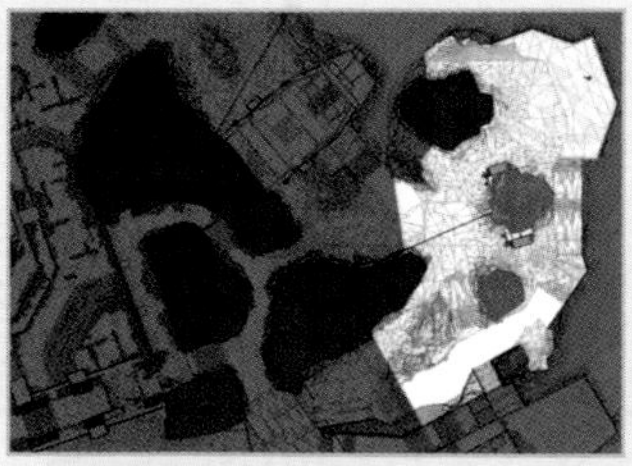

This area may be defined by its large, craggy formations, but **Rocks** features a fair amount of open ground. However, considering that it's part of two major sniping lanes, it's generally best to stick near cover.

In most match types, **Rocks** serves as one of the map's team starting areas. During Survival matches, this location hosts the tie-breaking Capture Point that appears whenever a round reaches overtime.

Midtown

The Last City, Earth

Quick Play

Competitive

Midtown

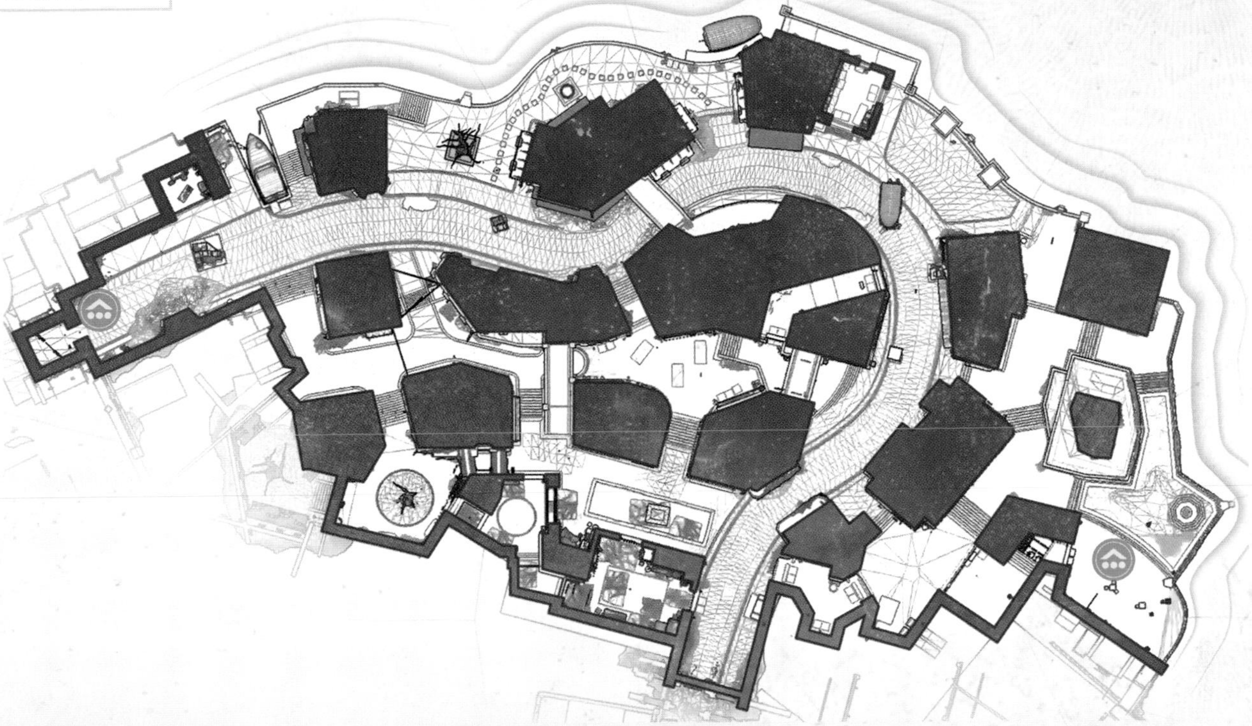

Overview

While it may be a stretch to call Midtown a symmetrical map, it does have a fairly balanced distribution of movement lanes. It consists of some relatively open areas connected by narrow paths, so you can virtually use any weapon effectively in at least a few areas.

Of course, there's no guarantee that your enemies will frequent your preferred locations. It's recommended that you equip at least one long-range weapon, but a short- to mid-range weapon is sure to come in handy.

This map also features several interior spaces. Some of these are significant structures with multiple points of entry; others are little more than alcoves. Whether you're looking for an alternate route or a bit of emergency cover, remember that heading indoors tends to limit your vertical mobility.

Much of the map's border is defined by the adjacent body of water, which serves as something of an environmental hazard. Fatal falls may not be common, but they're entirely possible.

It's also worth noting that the terrain tends to slope upward as you move away from the waterfront. Most of the available paths include steps or ramps that can enhance or hinder evasive maneuvers.

Midtown Map Locations

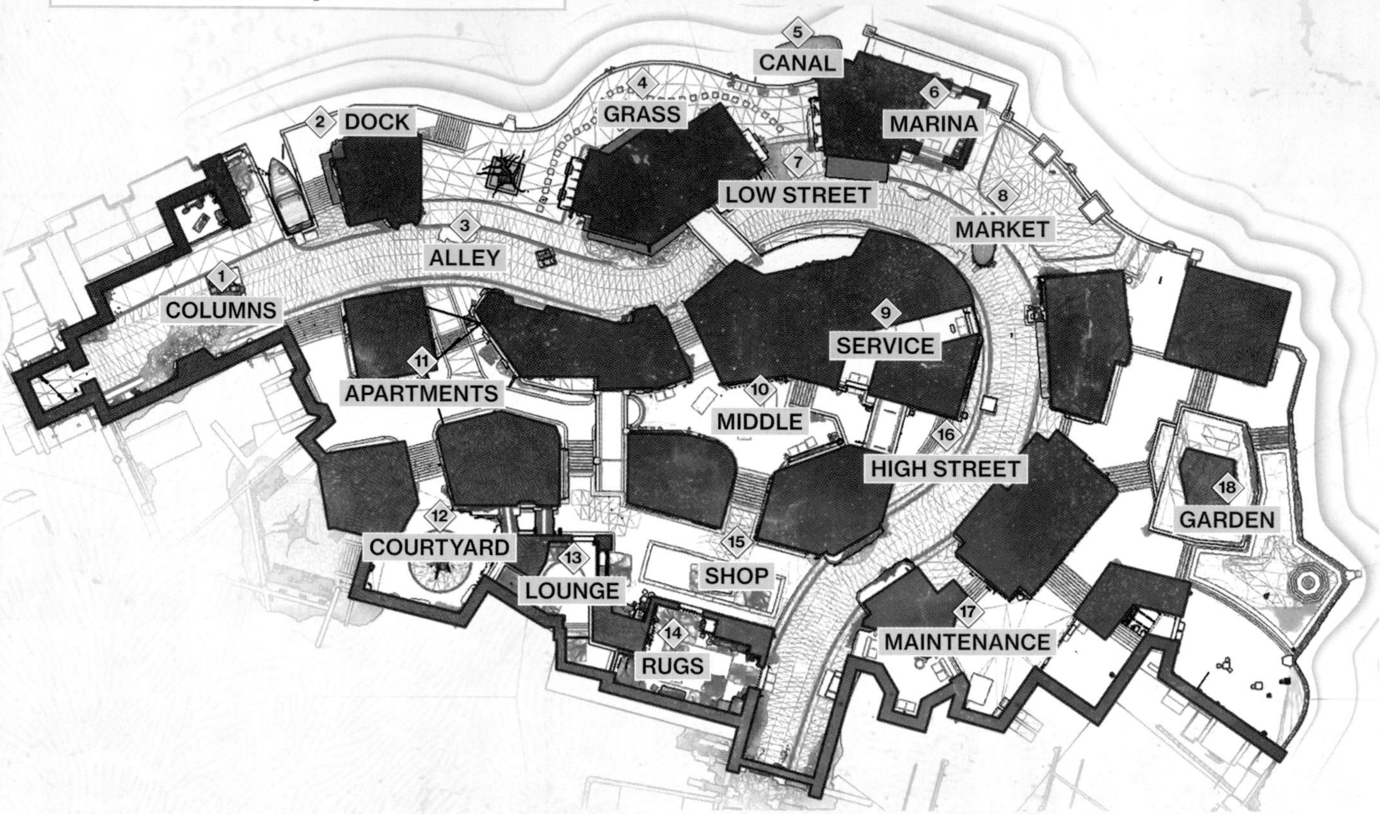

Clash, Supremacy

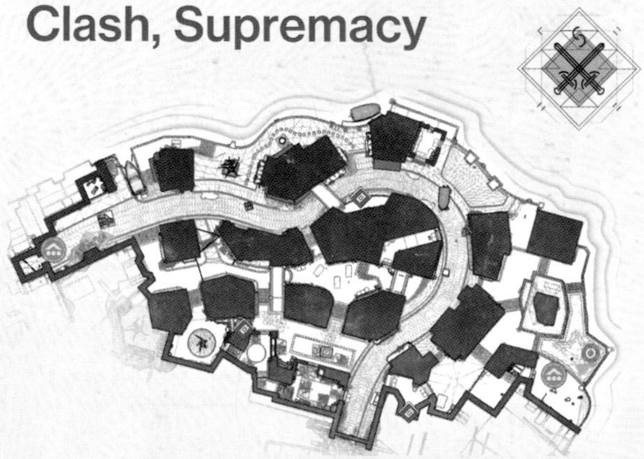

Control

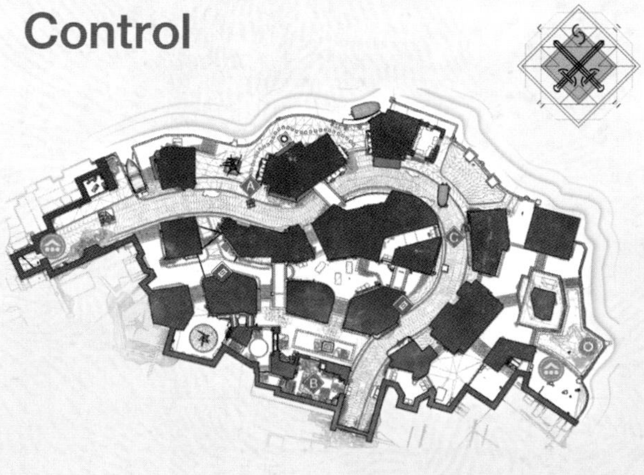

Countdown

1 Columns

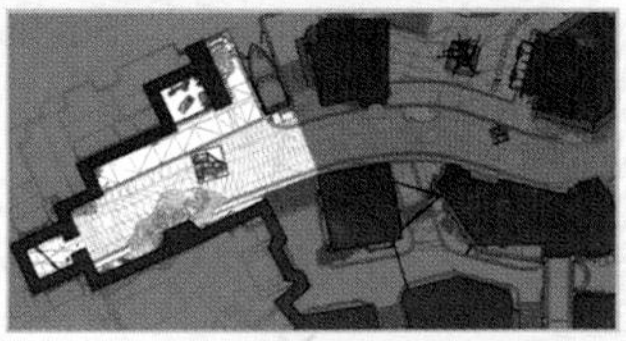

Columns typically serves as one of the map's two starting areas. It features some solid cover and a nice line of sight down a major movement lane. However, it also has what amounts to one large point of entry. This makes the area something of a mixed bag during a firefight, but it's still a popular spot for designated snipers.

2 Dock

Its limited points of entry, combined with the cover the adjacent building offers, make this narrow path a good spot to recover in during hectic firefights.

3 Alley

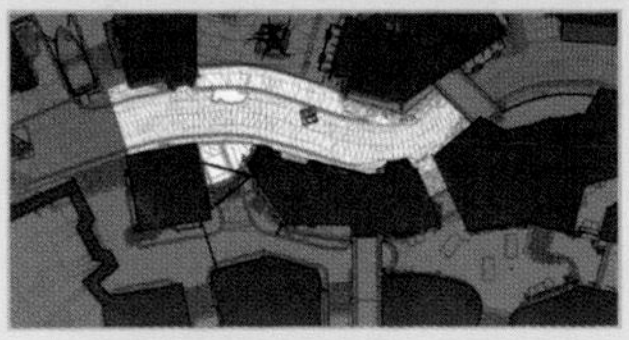

Alley is part of a major movement lane—which means it's also part of a popular sniping lane. It's one of the map's prime spots for long-range gun battles, but you'll find relatively little cover within its borders.

4 Grass

Key Location: Grass Control

During Control matches, **Grass** contains Capture Point A.

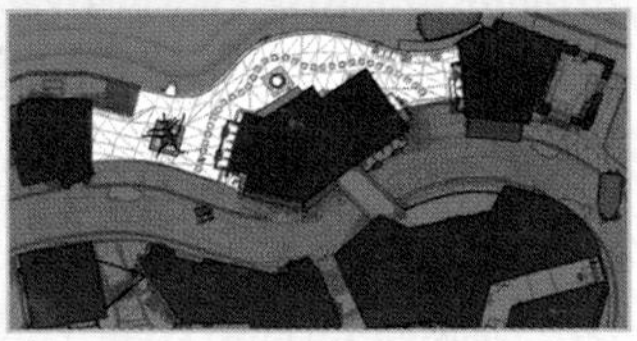

Located between the water's edge and an inaccessible building, **Grass** serves as one of the better flanking/escape routes on this side of the map. During Countdown matches, this location also holds one of the map's two charges.

5 Canal

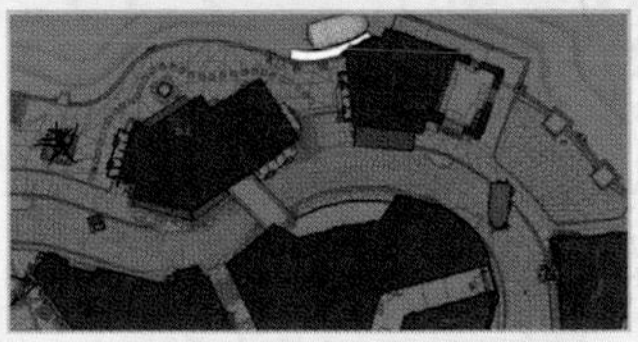

This tiny location is essentially a stepping stone between **Grass** and **Marina**. It's also a handy spot to break line of sight when you need to draw an opponent into a close-quarters fight.

6 Marina

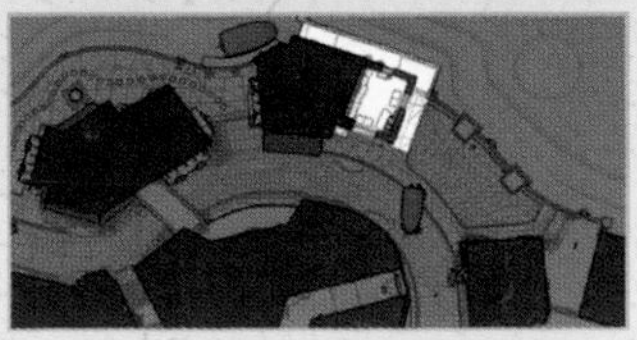

Marina features a narrow ramp wrapped behind one of the few accessible structures on this side of the map. The interior space is relatively small, but it offers some useful cover and plenty of escape routes.

7 Low Street

Key Location: Low Street

During Clash and Supremacy matches, **Low Street** contains one of the map's three Power Ammo spawn points. It also serves as a source of Power Ammo during Countdown.

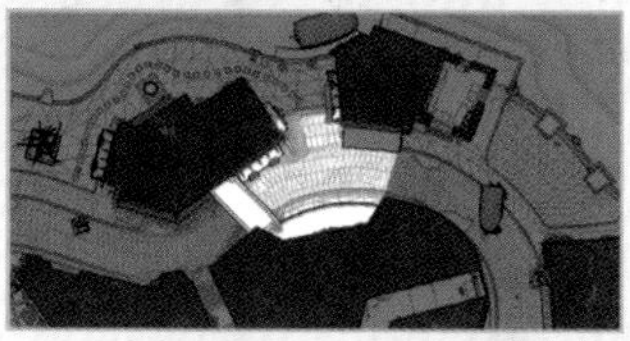

During games of Clash and Supremacy, **Low Street** acts as the map's central Power Ammo spawn point—making it a hotly contested location in most Quickplay matches. Placed near the center of a major movement lane, it's a difficult position to defend. However, it does feature a raised ledge that serves as an excellent sniping point.

8 Market

Key Location: Market

During Control matches, **Market** contains Capture Point C. In Countdown, this location holds one of the map's two charges.

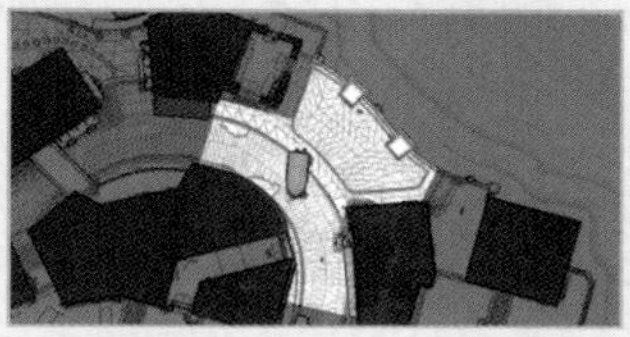

Market is one of the map's larger and more open locations, but its most notable feature is the makeshift kiosk at its center. This repurposed boat is a limited but useful option for cover during mid- to long-range firefights, and the connected paths offer multiple escape routes in case things get too hot. It also serves as a key location in Control.

9 Service

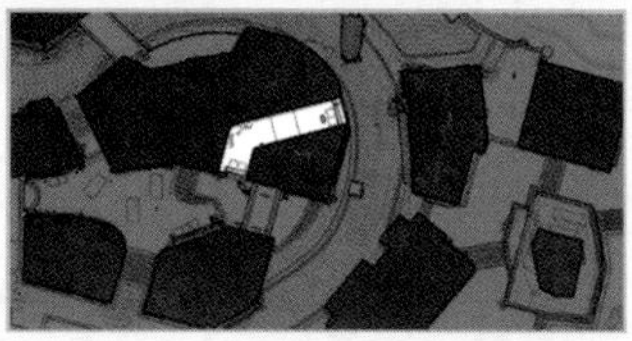

This narrow passage is typically used to avoid or flank enemies, but like any tight space, it's also a great place to stage an ambush for an overeager opponent.

10 Middle

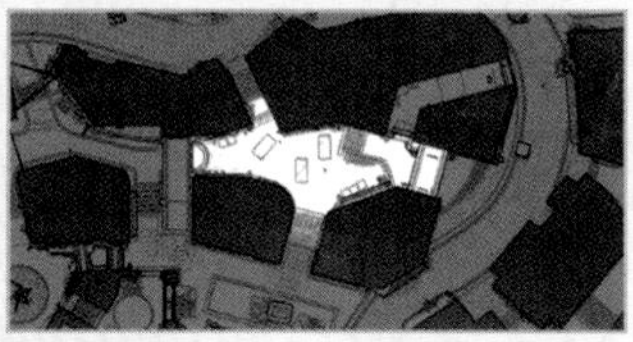

This appropriately named location is the map's central intersection. If you're having trouble finding a target, making a beeline to **Middle** is usually the quickest way to stir up some action.

11 Apartments

Key Location: Apartments

During Control matches, **Apartments** contains one of the map's two Power Ammo spawn points. It also serves as a source of Power Ammo during Countdown.

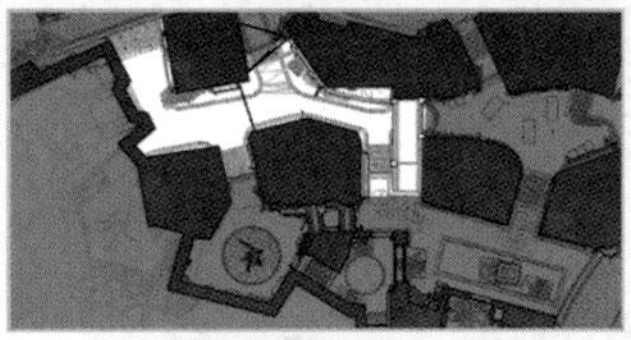

Apartments is a popular movement lane with multiple points of entry, making it a particularly good spot for hit-and-run tactics. It also serves as a Power Ammo spawn point during games of Control.

12 Courtyard

Key Location: Courtyard

During Clash and Supremacy matches, **Courtyard** contains one of the map's three Power Ammo spawn points.

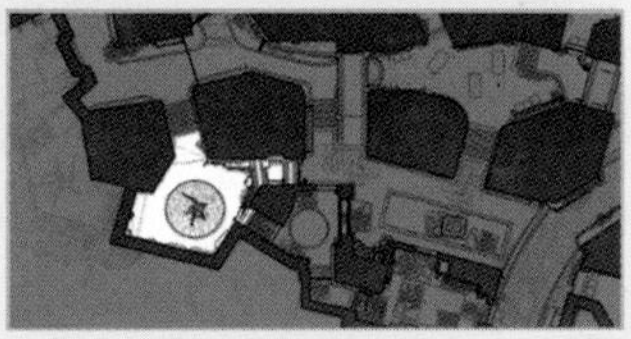

Tucked away at the corner of the map, **Courtyard** is a good place to regroup and assess between skirmishes. It offers impressive lines of sight into multiple areas, and its narrow points of entry make it one of the map's more defensible locations. It also connects to multiple movement lanes, so a quick retreat is usually an option.

13 Lounge

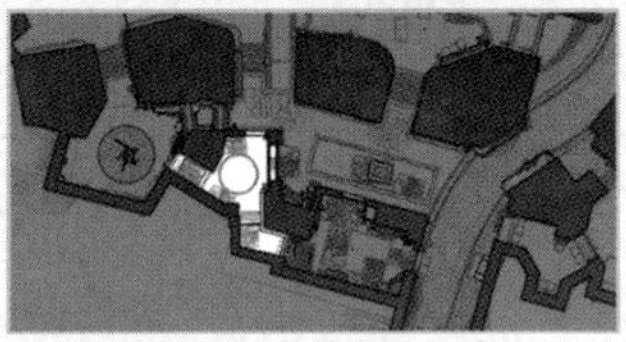

This open structure offers a bit of cover with a good line of sight into **Shop**, but it also features some narrow hallways and a very low ceiling. Essentially, it's a movement lane with very little room to move, a perfect spot for those who favor close combat.

14 Rugs

Key Location: Rugs

During Control matches, Rugs contains Capture Point B. In Countdown, it houses one of the map's two charges.

Rugs is a dimly lit structure located along the edge of the map. It's large enough to accommodate evasive maneuvering, but its ceiling does limit vertical movement. Its walls offer solid cover from nearby firefights, but the placement of its entry points makes it a difficult location to hold.

Rugs is a strategically important location in games of Control and Countdown. It also serves as one of the map's best sniping points. Using the doorway for cover, a long-range expert can fire clear through **High Street** and into **Market**.

15 Shop

Shop is one of the larger exterior spaces on this side of the map, making it part of a popular sniping lane. It also connects to all six of the adjacent locations, presenting a staggering number of flanking options. A small kiosk provides limited cover, but defensive players would do well to stake their claims elsewhere.

16 High Street

Key Location: High Street

During Control matches, **High Street** contains one of the map's two Power Ammo spawn points.

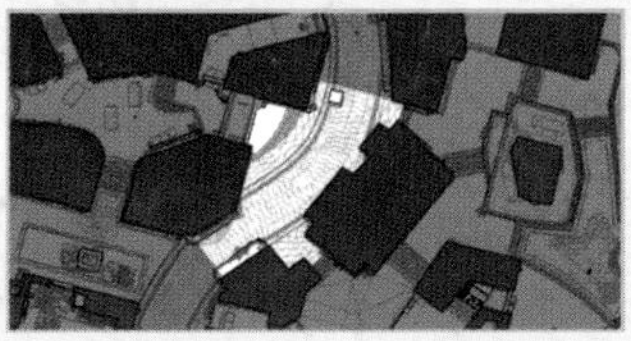

A wide path with a slight curve and limited cover, **High Street** is a precarious location. Moving out in the open leaves you vulnerable to long-range fire from at least two directions, meaning it's better used as an intersection than a throughway. However, it does serve as a Power Ammo spawn point during games of Control.

17 Maintenance

Key Location: Maintenance

During Clash and Supremacy matches, **Maintenance** contains one of the map's three Power Ammo spawn points.

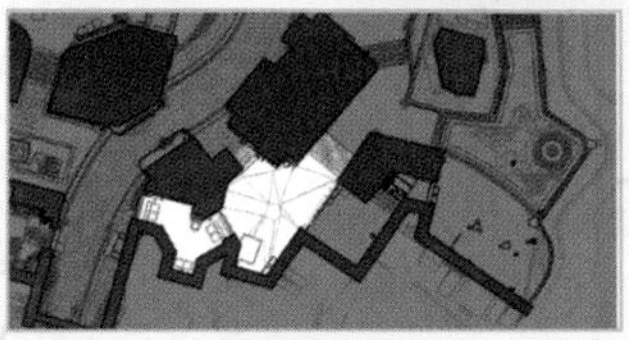

While **Maintenance** does include a significant exterior space, this location is truly defined by the raised passage that connects to **Shop**. Using this passage requires a well-timed jump, making it both a popular escape route and a useful vantage point. During games of Clash and Supremacy, this space also contains a Power Ammo spawn point.

18 Garden

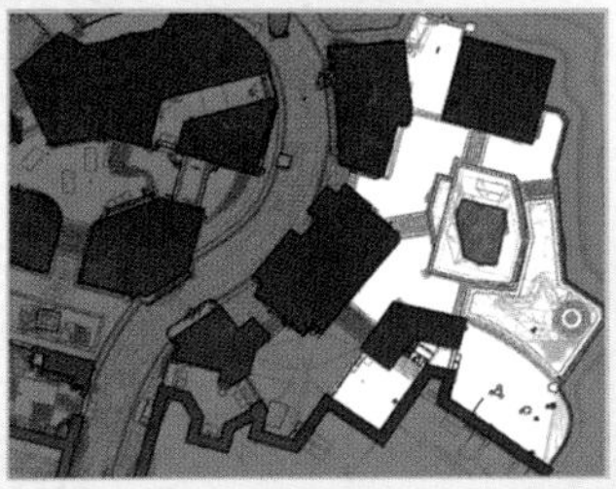

A large location with some varied terrain, **Garden** is a relatively open area with multiple points of entry. The central planter offers considerable cover, but the surrounding buildings limit lines of sight into adjacent areas.

In most match types, this location serves as one of the map's team starting areas.

Javelin-4

Warsat Launch Facility, Io

Quick Play

Competitive

Javelin-4

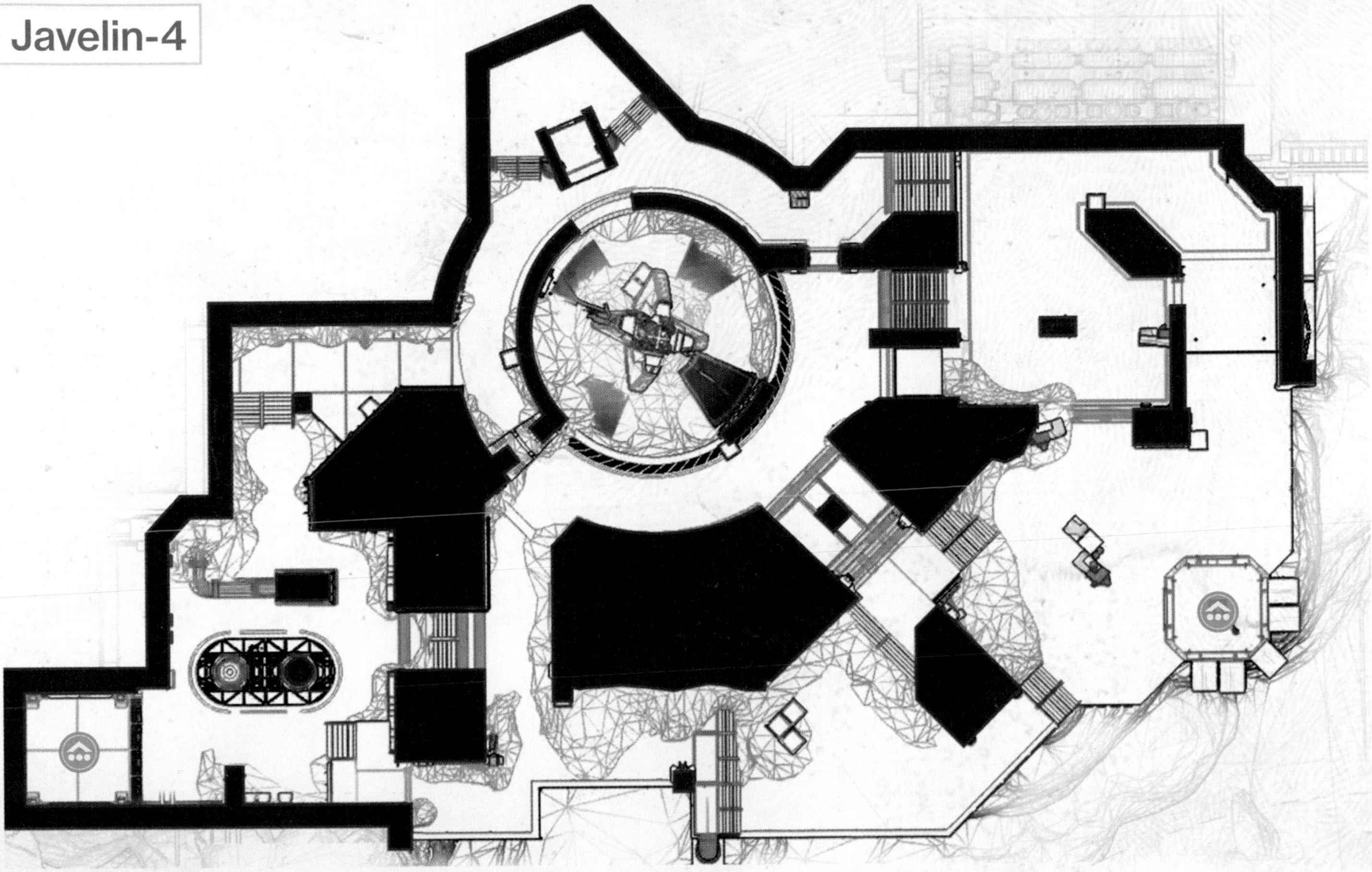

Overview

Javelin-4 includes some sizable interior spaces, but the facility's exterior locations combine to form one very large, fairly open area. A sheer drop ensures that fatal falls are possible, but the limited cover is what makes these outdoor locations so dangerous. Even the most protected spots are easily flanked.

While nature is in the process of reclaiming a few bits and pieces, most of the map features the clean lines and sharp corners one might expect to find in such a facility. This allows for an abundance of useful vantage points and some very effective sniping lanes. Consider equipping at least one mid- to long-range weapon whenever you visit this stage.

Of course, the facility does contain a few smaller areas. Many locations have curves or sharp corners that severely limit line of sight; those who favor short-range weapons will find some suitably tight spots. When in doubt, select weapon combinations that allow you to adjust your tactics as the action moves from location to location.

Javelin-4 Map Locations

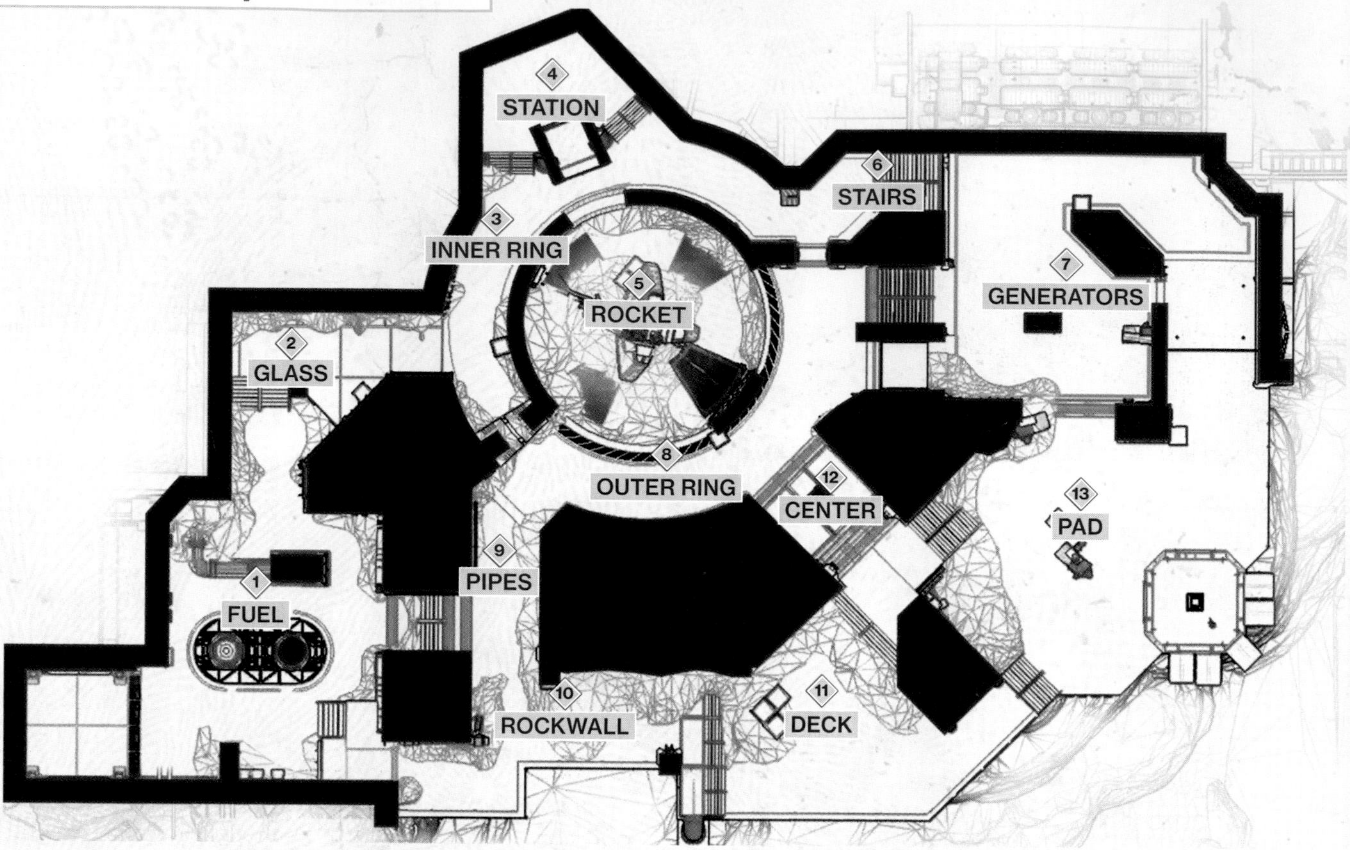

Survival

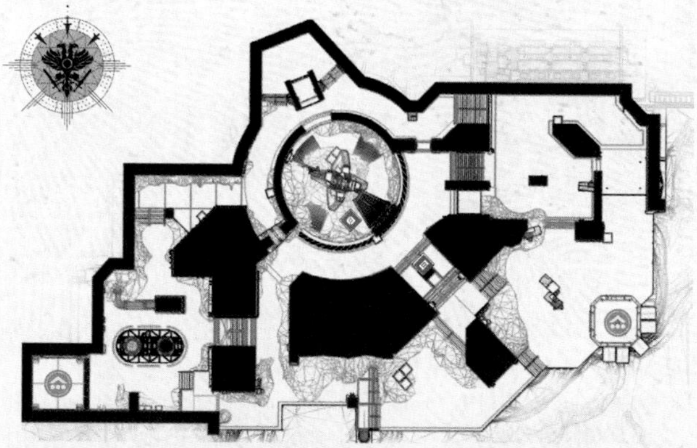

Control

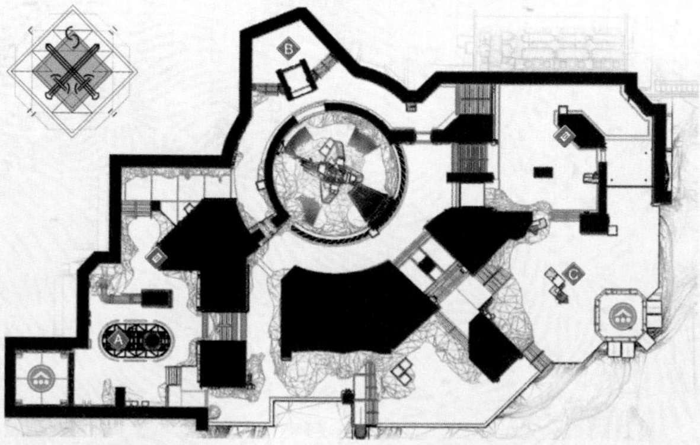

Clash, Supremacy

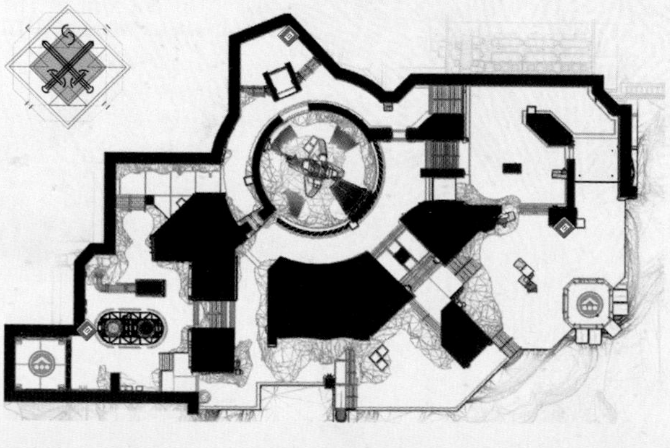

1 Fuel

Key Location: Fuel

During games of Clash or Supremacy, **Fuel** contains one of the map's three Power Ammo spawn points. In Control, this location holds both a Power Ammo spawn point and Capture Point A.

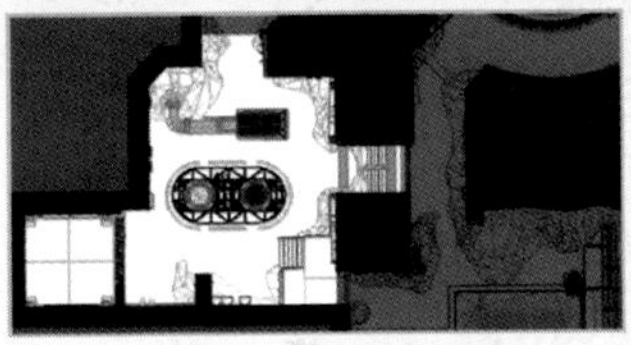

Fuel is a large interior space with three points of entry and some excellent cover options. It typically serves as a team starting area, but **Fuel** also tends to be a strategically important location during Quickplay matches. It's a source of Power Ammo during Clash and Supremacy. In games of Control, it holds Power Ammo and one of the map's Capture Points.

2 Glass

Glass is a relatively small area, but it stands as a popular flanking route and sniping point. The central pillar is a nice bit of cover, giving a well-positioned Guardian an excellent line of sight into **Fuel**.

3 Inner Ring

Key Location: Inner Ring

During games of Clash or Supremacy, **Inner Ring** contains one of the map's three Power Ammo spawn points.

Connecting to five adjacent areas, **Inner Ring** tends to be a heavily used movement lane, especially in Quickplay matches. During games of Clash and Supremacy, **Inner Ring** serves as a source of Power Ammo. In Control, this corridor is the only route to and from the map's neutral Capture Point.

4 Station

Key Location: Station

During games of Control, **Station** contains Capture Point B.

Station is a fairly small location, but it's a useful vantage point with a good amount of cover. During games of Control, this raised platform contains Capture Point B. **Station**'s size and shape make it particularly vulnerable to splash damage, and a coordinated attack can limit potential escape routes.

5 Rocket

Key Location: Rocket

Whenever a round of Survival enters overtime, a tie-breaking Capture Point appears in **Rocket**.

Located in the heart of the facility, **Rocket** tends to be a frequent setting for large-scale firefights. The central components serve as one massive piece of cover, there's no ceiling to worry about, and the adjacent areas allow Guardians to advance and retreat as needed.

Rocket is a particularly important location during Survival matches. Whenever a round enters overtime, a Capture Point appears just inside of this area.

6 Stairs

Running between **Generators** and **Outer Ring**, **Stairs** is a fairly straightforward flanking route. Like any confined space, it's also a good spot for ambushing overly aggressive opponents.

7 Generators

Key Location: Generators

During games of Control, **Generators** contains one of the map's two Power Ammo spawns.

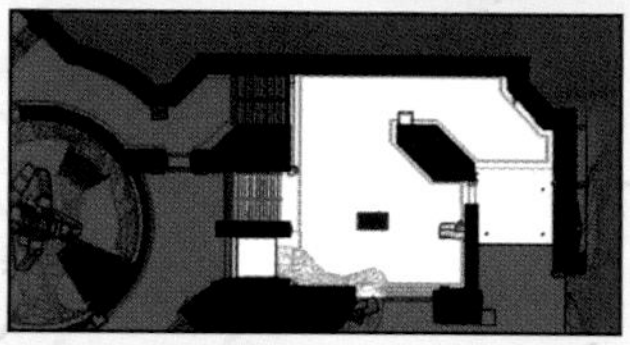

Generators is a large interior space divided by some sizable pieces of cover. It contains multiple flanking routes and some useful vantage points, making it a popular location for Guardians monitoring **Rocket** and **Outer Ring**. During Control, **Generators** also serves as a source of Power Ammo.

8 Outer Ring

Outer Ring is a major movement lane, but due to its open layout, it's also a popular battleground. Any skirmish that breaks out in or around **Rocket** is bound to make its way into **Outer Ring** at one point or another.

9 Pipes

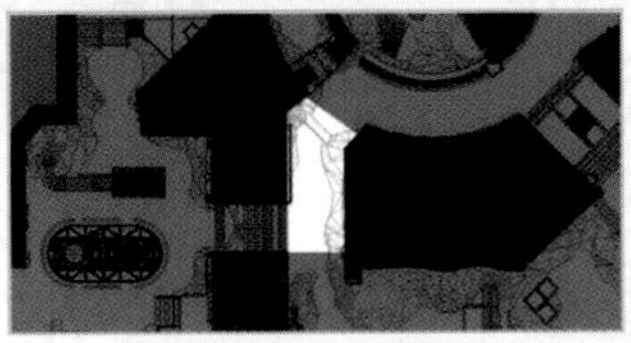

Pipes is a small but important hallway that connects **Fuel** and **Rockwall** to **Outer Ring**. It's a nice spot for short-range combat, and it serves as an excellent vantage point for Guardians monitoring adjoining locations.

10 Rockwall

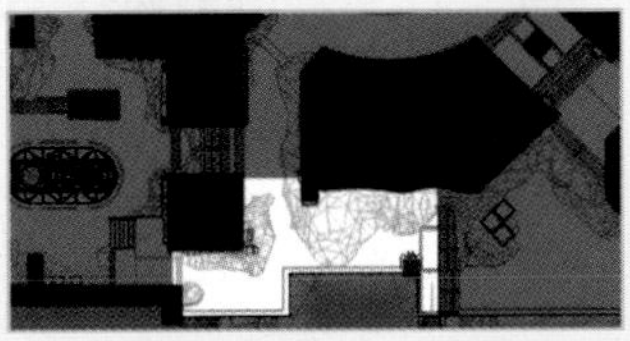

As the map's smallest exterior area, **Rockwall** is more frequently used as a movement lane than a battleground. It's wide enough to allow for evasive maneuvers, and it's a useful vantage point, but it doesn't offer much in the way of cover.

11 Deck

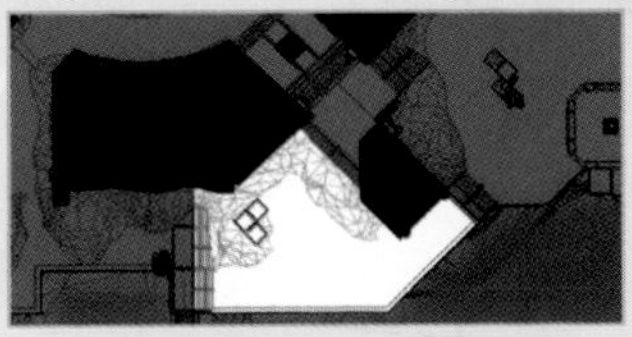

Deck is sizable exterior space with a fair amount of open ground and great lines of sight into adjoining areas. Of course, this also makes the location susceptible to long-range fire from multiple directions. It's a useful vantage point, but positioning is important. Take advantage of the limited cover, and favor brief visits to avoid being flanked.

12 Center

Key Location: Center

During games of Survival, **Center** contains the map's only Power Ammo spawn point.

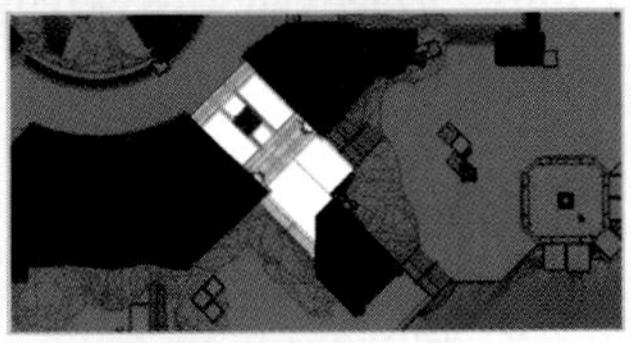

Center consists of an outdoor platform connected to an interior corridor. It's something of a chokepoint, but it does offer a decent amount of cover for a location its size. During Survival, **Center** also serves as the map's only source of Power Ammo.

13 Pad

Key Location: Pad

During games of Clash or Supremacy, **Pad** contains one of the map's three Power Ammo Spawn points. In Control, this location contains Capture Point C.

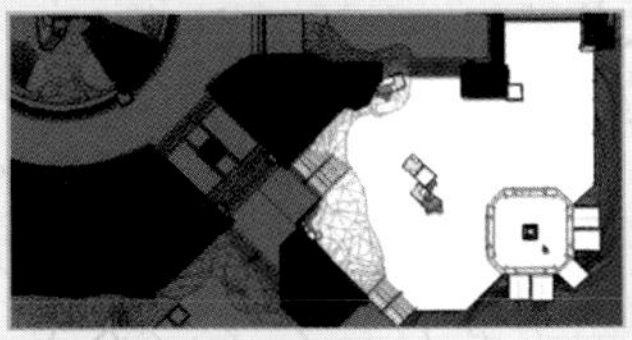

Pad is a large exterior location that typically serves as a team starting area. While there is a bit of cover in the center of the area, this space features a fairly open layout surrounded by some very effective vantage points. During games of Clash and Supremacy, **Pad** also serves as a source of Power Ammo. During Control, this location contains Capture Point C.

Director

Introduction and Overview

Exploring the worlds across the solar system is both thrilling and time-consuming, so it's worth having a complete run-down of what to expect to find in every World, Region, Sector, and Area you can access. This chapter is more than a mere atlas; it shows how the larger elements of the game are unlocked, the activities you can undertake, and the collectibles you can gather.

The Director Menu

As you progress through your explorations and the Campaign missions, you begin to access a number of locations and planets across the solar system, until your Director Menu screen looks a little like the one shown previously. It is here you can take your ship and fly to a different exploration element, as listed below:

1. **Earth: European Dead Zone:** The initial region to explore, once you've completed the first few Campaign missions. You also return here later into the Campaign to unlock further content. A complete list of all Sectors is shown in this guide. The social Sector of the Farm is also included in this content.

2. **Titan: Pacific Arcology:** The moon of Saturn becomes available to explore during the Campaign. A complete list of all Sectors is shown in this guide.

3. **Nessus: Arcadian Valley:** A machine world with an irregular orbit, this becomes available to explore during the Campaign (after Titan). A complete list of all Sectors is shown in this guide.

4. **Io: Echo Mesa:** The moon of Jupiter is the last main region to open up (after Nessus), during the latter half of the Campaign. A complete list of all Sectors is shown in this guide.

5. **The Tower:** Once the Campaign is over, humanity (led by the Vanguard) begins to rebuild, and the Social Sector is the epicenter of activities. It is detailed in this guide.

6. **Strikes:** The six available Strikes (and the even crazier Nightfall variants) are accessed here. The Director chapter flags where these Strikes take place, but actual strategies are covered in their own chapter.

7. **Crucible:** This is where you prove your worth to Lord Shaxx and attempt Player versus Player matches. An entire chapter of this guide is devoted to this game mode.

8. **The Almighty:** A colossal Cabal vessel attempting to destroy the solar system. This is part of the Campaign and not subsequently visited.

Other Worlds aren't Off Limits

The Almighty is a location that is accessible during the Campaign Mission: 1AU, and the maps and tactics to see all of this Cabal ship are included there.

How to Use this Atlas

Each of the four main worlds (AKA regions) are divided into different Sectors, and the guide's atlas is no different. Content is listed in the expected order you are likely to encounter it, or if a Sector is linked in some way to another. This allows for a more organic exploration of the world around you. For each area under examination, expect a brief synopsis, some statistical data, an icon-driven map, and additional explanation and pictures.

Sector Hierarchy

At a very general level, each "hub" or exploration area with a defined boundary is known as a "Sector". The guide and game both divide and name these. There are many types of Sectors:

Social: These are self-contained locations (that can only be accessed from Orbit) without any foes, where you appear in third-person view, and only vendors are available to interact with. Expect a vault, and other players to chat to. The Farm and the Tower are the only two Social Sectors.

Public: These are large-scale locations, where multitudes of like-minded Guardians gather. Enemies are roaming these Sectors, and a variety of activities are possible. Certain Public Sectors may have a vendor. Public Sectors also link to other Sectors of every type (except Social).

Activity or Enemy-Based: These are smaller Sectors. Sometimes they are partially, or completely inaccessible.

You'll know if an area is inaccessible as a barrier (usually a blue energy wall) prevents you from progressing. Such Sectors become active during certain missions (usually Campaign, Strikes, Adventures, or World Quests).

Lost: These occur as small, branching interior Sectors off a main Public Sector. They contain foes and a chest to unlock, once the Elite inside the Sector has been neutralized. Each Public Sector may have up to three of these.

This guide's atlas flowcharts (shown at the start of the sections on EDZ, Titan, Nessus, and Io) show the Sector types in iconographical form.

Atlas Content and Legend

Each time you read up on a specific Sector you're interested in, you're greeted with a variety of content, both text and icon-based. It's worth pointing out what all the icons mean, what the associated text is likely to indicate, and thus in turn, what this guide's atlas is keeping a track of throughout this chapter:

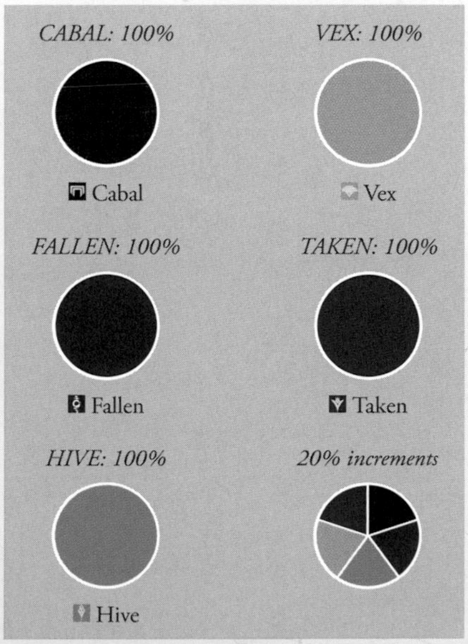

Expected Enemy(s): Each Sector receives a small pie-chart giving you an at-a-glance visual representation of what group dominates the Sector you are in. This takes into account enemies appearing in clusters, and during Public Events and in Lost Sectors.

Area of Interest: Some Sectors are large, so it's worth segmenting them up into smaller sections for easy visual digestion. Areas of Interest are parts of a Sector with something notable to be aware of; such as an exit, a landmark, or other piece of topographical content.

Adventure: This shows the expected location of an Adventure beacon within the Sector in question. If the beacon is not there, consult the flowchart. You may not have progressed far enough to unlock an activity.

Barriers: Walls of energy, or sometimes wreckage, preventing progress into parts of this sector, usually until a mission is active. Some Activity sectors may be Partially or Completely Inaccessible, with barriers erected.

Campaign: If a mission is accessible from a Sector, it is shown. This is mainly to show where you begin a Campaign mission after dropping in from Orbit, and is mainly shown in the flowchart.

Lost Sector: The cave icon of the Lost Sector signifies one is close to the indicated map location, so head there and explore within. A brief synopsis of what to expect inside the Lost Sector, including the enemy and Elite types, are included.

Material Node: Each world has its own material node; a strange, naturally-occurring object to harvest and exchange with vendors. There are dozens of possible locations where these might appear, but only around a tenth of the locations are active at any one time. Use the maps as a general guide only (as nine times out of ten, the item won't have appeared!). Use the guide map as a very approximate overview. Note that Lost Sectors also have these items, but are not tracked on the guide maps.

Public Events (Secret): This is the location of a minor Public Event that isn't announced (except for certain types which have a text clue in the bottom-left corner of your screen. These involve entering skirmishes, flying through Vex cannons, or hunting down Elites for loot. The exact nature of each event is revealed. Consult the chapter on Public Events for full details.

 CABAL **FALLEN** **HIVE**

 VEX **TAKEN**

Enemy Cluster(s): This indicates where an expected cluster of foes of a particular enemy group are roaming. Note there are additional areas too, but they are usually active during Public Events or other activities. This indicates enemies you should expect under normal, non-mission circumstance.

Patrols: Public Sectors have Patrol beacons that become active once you complete Campaign missions on Io and speak to Cayde-6 at the Farm. These beacons allow you to begin a (random) Patrol from a set number. Not all beacons are active at the same time. This map shows all available beacons. Consult the chapter on Patrols for full details.

Enemy Chests: These are chests that (randomly) appear across the Sector you are in. They are usually related in style to the dominant group of the Sector. The guide maps show (pretty much) every possible location a Enemy Chest could appear at. But only around a tenth of them are active at any one time. Use the guide map as a very approximate overview. Note that Lost Sectors also have this item, but are not tracked on the guide maps.

 Landing Zone: This pinpoints the likely landing spot of your ship if you access the Director menu from Orbit. If the Landing Zone (or LZ) isn't available, consult the flowchart; you may need to complete more activities first.

 Public Events (Full): This is the location of a specific Public Event, which is randomly (but frequently) triggered. Although you can see where the event will start, you must wait for the game to announce and begin this activity. The type of event, and brief tactics, are mentioned. Consult the chapter on Public Events for full details.

 Lost Sector Chests: Every Lost Sector has a chest that can only be opened with a key you loot from the Elite within the Lost Sector. The smaller, Lost Sector maps (shown within the Sector they link to) show you where each one is. There is always one of these per Lost Sector.

BE SURE TO CLAIM YOUR FREE eGUIDE!

Enter your eGuide code at primagames.com/code.

Additional coverage includes:
▶ Adventures
▶ Lost Sectors
▶ World Quests
▶ Patrols
▶ Public Events
▶ Challenges
▶ PS4 Exclusive Content

Region Chests: Each Public Sector usually has around three of these golden-hued chests hidden away, sometimes in ludicrously-placed locations. This guide shows you where each one is.

Strikes: If a Strike is available at a location, it is mentioned along with this icon. Note this is illustrated in the flowchart, as you drop into a Sector from Orbit once you start a Strike from the Strike Menu, rather than beginning it on the planet itself.

World Quest: Each of the four main worlds has a multi-stage World Quest to complete. The starting location of this quest is shown on the main maps of a particular Sector. The flowchart shows where that, and subsequent stages of the World Quest begin.

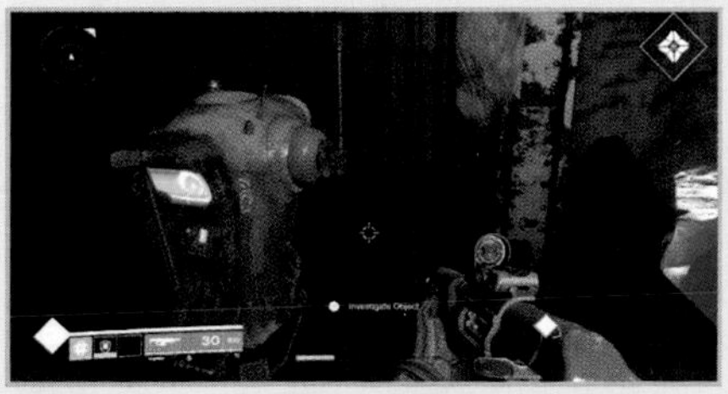

Scannable Objects: There is a wide variety of oddities across the regions and all four worlds (and within the two Social Sectors). This offers an approximate location, and a hint of what to expect. These are the Lore objects that Ghost scans when you find them.

Vendor: The two Social Sectors have a wealth of vendors. Otherwise, expect to find one vendor for each of the four worlds, not including Xur (who shows up randomly).

Our Maps are All-Encompassing

Although your in-game HUD has no compass bearing, you may find references to map directions (north, south, east, west) within this chapter. This presupposes that your in-game map, and all the guide maps, are showing "north" as "up" (and therefore east as right, south as down, and west as left). This helps situate yourself within a Sector, when comparing it to an in-game landmark or other area of interest.

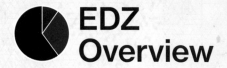

EDZ Overview

Enemy Control

⬚ **CABAL**
⬚ **FALLEN**
⬚ **TAKEN**

After the destruction of the Last City, the survivors of humanity fled to the forests and caves in order to recover. Keen to crush any possible insurrection, Dominus Ghaul has established a sprawling base of operations on the western side of this region, away from the pre-Golden Age structures and old settlements that dot the landscape. Hidden away within the woods are remains of the Traveler's might, Shards that help restore a Guardian's power. Other enemies also fight for dominance. Expect incursions of Fallen throughout the region and the odd (and terrifying) appearance of the Taken from time to time.

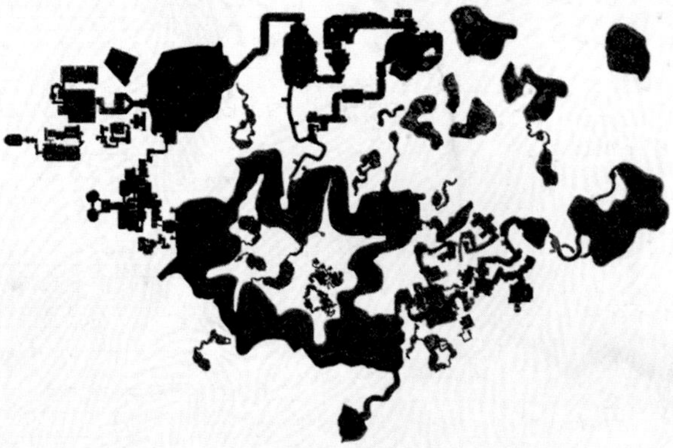

Progression (Initial Activities)

You first access the EDZ after the Campaign Mission: Spark. At this point, when you touch down in Trostland, you have a variety of activities to attempt, generally in the southeast part of the region. (However, you can explore the Cabal base to the west if you're feeling foolhardy or brave.) The following flowchart details the activities and their progression.

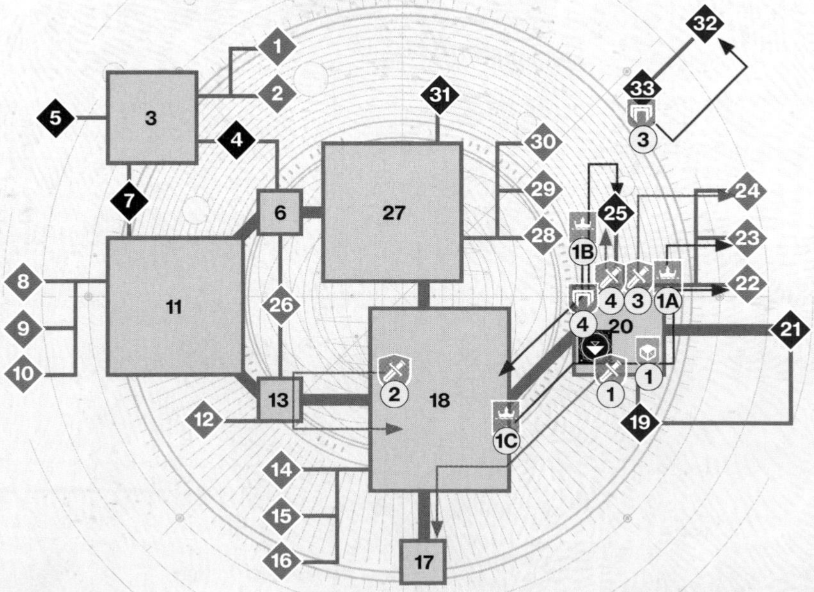

1. Skydock IV	12. The Weep	23. Terminus East
2. The Quarry	13. Winding Cove	24. Atrium
3. Sunken Isles	14. Whispered Falls	25. Salt Mines
4. The Tunnels	15. The Drain	26. Flooded Chasm
5. Legion's Hold	16. Scavenger's Den	27. The Sludge
6. The Gulch	17. Sojourner's Camp	28. Shaft 13
7. Legion's Anchor	18. Outskirts	29. Terminus West
8. The Pit	19. The Reservoir	30. Cavern of Souls
9. Pathfinder's Crash	20. Trostland	31. The Dark Forest
10. Excavation Site XII	21. Maevic Square	32. Blackened Forest
11. Firebase Hades	22. Widow's Walk	33. Quarantine Sector 236

Legend

⬣ Landing Zone

◆ Campaign Sector (Cabal-Related)

◆ Campaign Sector (Fallen-Related)

◆ Activity (Taken-Related)

◆ Lost Sector

⬛ Public Space

⚔1 Adventures: Calling Them Home

⚔2 Adventures: Poor Reception

⚔3 Adventures: A New Frontier

⚔4 Adventures: Frame Job

⛊3 Campaign: Spark

⛊4 Campaign: Combustion

♛1 World Quest: Enhance!

♛1A World Quest: Odd Symptoms

♛1B World Quest: Differential Diagnosis

♛1C World Quest: Experimental Treatment

Progression

⛊3 Campaign: Spark

⬣ Landing Zone (Trostland)

◈1 Devrim

⚔1 Adventures: Calling Them Home

⚔2 Adventures: Poor Reception

⚔3 Adventures: A New Frontier

⛊4 Campaign: Combustion

♛1 World Quest: Enhance!

⚔4 Adventures: Frame Job

To Titan

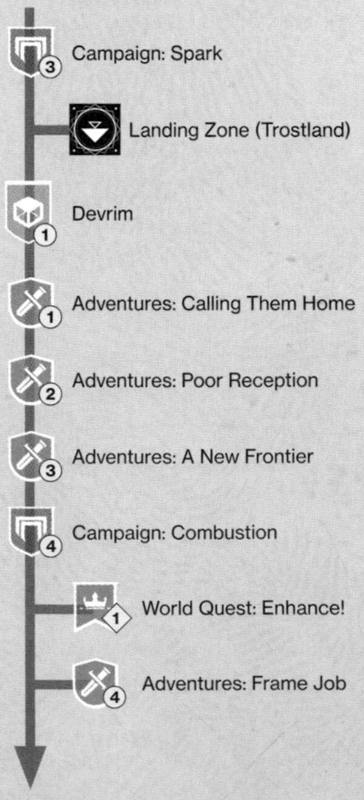

European Dead Zone: Initial Activities

Progression (Return Visit Activities)

As you complete the Campaign, you leave the EDZ, visiting Titan, Nessus, and Io. Then, you make a return visit to the EDZ, mainly focusing on the annihilation of as many Cabal as you can within the various Sectors of the main western base in this region. After that, you continue to complete the Campaign off-world as you visit the Almighty. Here's what becomes accessible between these two points.

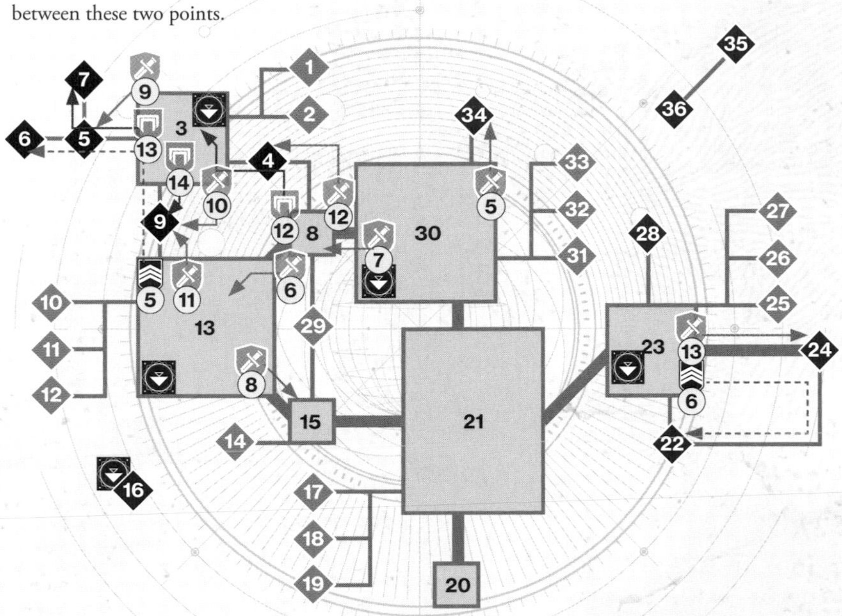

1. Skydock IV
2. The Quarry
3. Sunken Isles
4. The Tunnels
5. Legion's Hold
6. Echion Vae
7. Legion's Watch
8. The Gulch
9. Legion's Anchor
10. The Pit
11. Pathfinder's Crash
12. Excavation Site XII
13. Firebase Hades
14. The Weep
15. Winding Cove
16. The Farm
17. Whispered Falls
18. The Drain
19. Scavenger's Den
20. Sojourner's Camp
21. Outskirts
22. The Reservoir
23. Trostland
24. Maevic Square
25. Widow's Walk
26. Terminus East
27. Atrium
28. Salt Mines
29. Flooded Chasm
30. The Sludge
31. Shaft 13
32. Terminus West
33. Cavern of Souls
34. The Dark Forest
35. Blackened Forest
36. Quarantine Sector 236

Legend

- Landing Zone
- Campaign Sector (Cabal-Related)
- Campaign Sector (Fallen-Related)
- Activity (Taken-Related)
- The Farm
- Lost Sector
- Public Space
- Campaign: Paypack
- Campaign: Unbroken
- Campaign: Larceny
- Strike: The Arms Dealer
- Strike: Lake of Shadows
- Adventures: Dark Alliance
- Adventures: Reverse the Polarity
- Adventures: Getting Your Hands Dirty
- Adventures: Unsafe at any Speed
- Adventures: Red Legion, Black Oil
- Adventures: No Safe Distance
- Adventures: Anti-Anti_Air
- Adventures: Stop and Go
- Adventures: Supply and Demand

Progression

- Patrols Access (All Worlds)
- Landing Zone: Firebase Hades
- Adventures: Dark Alliance
- Adventures: Reverse the Polarity
- Adventures: Getting Your Hands Dirty
- Adventures: Unsafe at any Speed
- Campaign: Paypack
- Landing Zone: Sunken Isles
- Campaign: Unbroken
- Landing Zone: The Sludge
- Adventures: Red Legion, Black Oil
- Adventures: No Safe Distance
- Adventures: Anti-Anti_Air
- Adventures: Stop and Go
- Strike: The Arms Dealer
- Strike: Lake of Shadows
- Campaign: Larceny
- Adventures: Supply and Demand

To the Almighty, Campaign Mission: 1AU, and Campaign Conclusion

European Dead Zone: Initial and Return Visit Activities

The following table shows the available activities, entities, Side Missions, and other pertinent data for every Sector within this region. Note that some activities (for example, Landing Zones) are not immediately available, but appear through progression.

Name	Type	Adventures	Lost Sectors	Landing Zone	Material Nodes	Patrols	Public Events (Full)
The Farm	Social	–	–	Available	–	–	–
Sojourner's Camp	Public	–	–	–	Available	–	–
Outskirts	Public	1	3	–	Available	9	3
Trostland	Public	4	3	Available	Available	8	1
Salt Mines	Activity (Fallen)	–	–	–	–	–	–
Maevic Square	Activity (Fallen)	–	–	–	Available	–	–
The Reservoir	Activity (Taken)	–	–	–	–	–	–
The Sludge	Public	2	3	Available	Available	8	2
The Dark Forest	Activity (Fallen)	–	–	–	–	–	–
Quarantine Sector 236	Activity (Fallen)	–	–	–	–	–	–
Blackened Forest	Activity (Taken)	–	–	–	–	–	–
Winding Cove	Public	–	1	–	Available	5	1
The Gulch	Public	2	1	–	Available	7	2
The Tunnels	Activity (Cabal)	–	–	–	Available	–	–
Firebase Hades	Public	2	3	Available	Available	8	2
Sunken Isles	Public	2	2	Available	Available	7	2
Legion's Anchor	Activity (Cabal)	–	–	–	–	–	–
Legion's Hold	Activity (Cabal)	–	–	–	–	–	–
Legion's Watch	Activity (Cabal)	–	–	–	–	–	–
Echion Vae	Activity (Cabal)	–	–	–	–	–	–
Totals	8 (Public)	13	16	5	10 (Sectors)	52	13

	Public Events (Secret)	Enemy Chests	Region Chests	Lost Sector Chests	Scannable Objects	Vendors	Strikes	World Quests
	–	–	–	–	4	Darbi 55-30, Tess, Tyra, Lord Shaxx, Arcite 99-40, Cayde-6, Ikora, Zavala	–	–
	–	–	–	–	3	–	–	–
	3	Available	3	3	5	–	–	–
	7	Available	2	3	4	Devrim Kay	Available	Available
	–	–	–	–	3	–	–	–
	–	–	–	–	3	–	–	–
	–	–	–	–	–	–	–	–
	5	Available	3	3	3	–	–	–
	–	–	–	–	–	–	–	–
	–	–	–	–	–	–	–	–
	–	–	–	–	–	–	–	–
	3	Available	3	1	2	–	–	–
	5	Available	3	1	3	–	–	–
	–	–	–	–	2	–	–	–
	4	Available	3	3	4	–	Available	–
	8	Available	3	2	3	–	–	–
	–	–	–	–	1	–	–	–
	–	–	–	–	1	–	–	–
	–	–	–	–	–	–	–	–
	–	–	–	–	–	–	–	–
	35	7 (Sectors)	20	16	41	10	2	1

The Farm

Sector Notes: Landing Zone: Available | Scannable Objects: 4
Vendor: (Up to) 9

OVERVIEW MAP

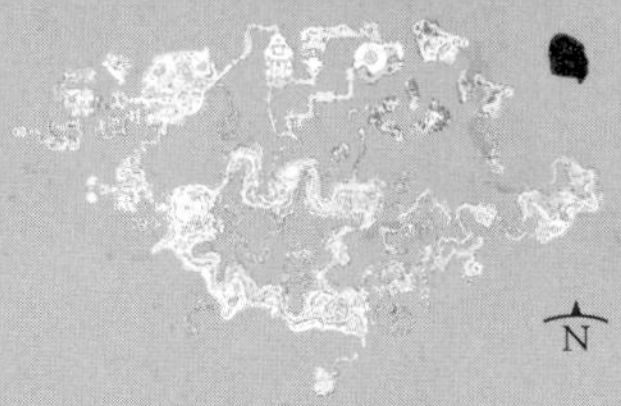

Welcome to the EDZ Resistance! This social sector has no enemies to worry about. It is a hub where you can meet up with friends, make purchases from an increasing number of merchants (until the conclusion of the Campaign) number of merchants, store items in your vault, find scannable objects, and welcome new vendors as you progress through the Campaign. Hone your character's prowess by changing armor and weapon loadouts, decrypting engrams for the items within, purchasing Eververse items, and gaining reputation with certain Vanguard members.

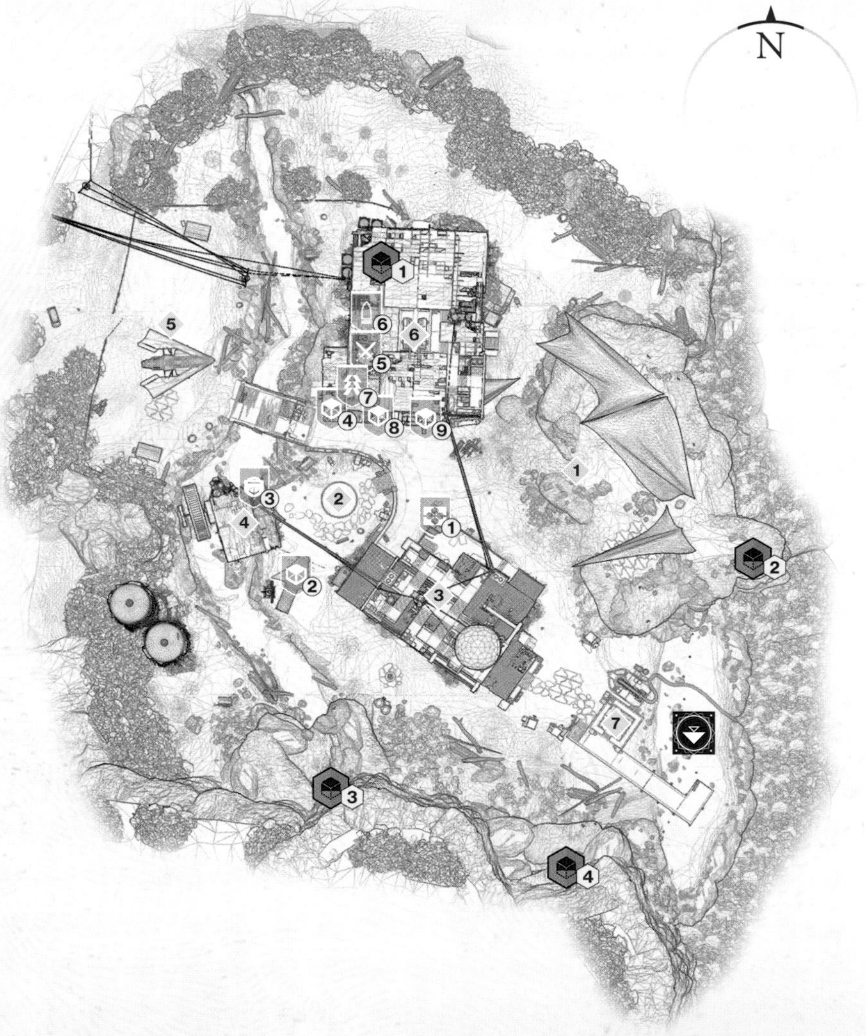

Down on The Farm

Once the Campaign concludes, the majority of the vendors move to the Tower, and you are encouraged to join them as the Farm's usefulness winds down.

Note that the perspective during the time here changes; you are in a third-person view and cannot execute your Movement Mode.

That Glowing Feeling

In addition to locating scannable objects, there's a good deal of larking around you can accomplish. Top of the list is earning the Scout Commander Aura! This glowing embodiment of awesomeness makes you stand out from the crowd. It requires you to complete four different activities:

Sentry Ranks (4): Scale heights and thoroughly explore around the Farm.

Vertigo: Wobbly tightrope walking is necessary.

A Wheel Boost: A swift jog on a rickety wheel.

On Scout Patrol: Visit a number of light columns before they blink out of existence.

Areas of Interest

1 Low Hill (Starting Point)

This is where you appear after dropping in rom Orbit.

2 Fountain Courtyard and Vaults

Access your vault in this serene fountain area.

3 Farmhouse

Visit some tinkerers inside the house, and scale the roof for a better view and some precarious wire walking.

4 Water Mill

An old rickety water mill where Tyra resides. Did you find the small watery tunnel under the building yet?

5 Soccer Pitch

Play a little football between the two nets in the northwestern field.

6 The Barn

The resistance members are busy building machines, and the majority of the later-visiting vendors and mentors appear here.

7 Harbor and Fire Pit

You might want to inspect the fire pit. There's some nearby lighting to flick on and off, too.

Landing Zone

The Farm LZ

Land your craft on the eastern side of this sector, which is the only way in or out of the Farm (since this doesn't have a direct pathway link to the rest of the EDZ).

Scannable Objects

What's this box of tricks on the rickety roof? My, that's a big gun.

"Look out" for this collection of goods on a rocky outcrop, overlooking water.

A southwest perimeter check is needed for this cluster of goods.

Do you enjoy sacks on the rocks? Check the southern perimeter.

Vendors

1 Darbi 55-30 (Postmaster)

Visit Darbi to gather items and objects of importance that you found (from dead enemies or chests) during missions or other explorations, but didn't pick up. Messages from other players are also accessed here.

Darbi 55-30 is available from the first time you visit the Farm.

2 Tess Everis (Eververse)

Tess Everis is a shopkeeper representing the Eververse Trading Company who grants you special free promotions (engram gifts and gear, for example). She also sells these items, provided you have enough Silver (which is currency you appropriate through the expenditure of real-world rather than in-game funds). Real-world purchases are purely optional.

3 Tyra Karn (Archivist)

Tyra Karn is a crypto-archeologist (or "cryptarch") who can decode any engrams you may have gathered on your travels. She also sells engrams from time to time and may be interested in artifacts you have collected, exchanging them for Glimmer.

Tyra is available from the first time you visit the Farm. She remains here once others leave at the end of the Campaign, so revisit her after the Campaign conclusion for some impressive loot!

4 Hawthorne (Farm Overseer)

Hawthorne is the leader of the resistance in the EDZ, and she sells both Leveling Gear. As you are already in good standing with her, you do not need to prove your loyalty (EDZ Tokens are given to Devrim in the Town Sector in Trostland). She also informs you about clans.

Present in the Farm from the beginning but leaves for the Tower once the Campaign is finished.

6 Arcite 99-40 (Crucible Gunsmith)

Arcite 99-40 is a gunsmith for the Crucible. He takes any Tokens you have acquired from breaking down weapons or armor; trade them in, bringing him groups of 10, five, or one. In return, you receive an increased Reputation (or "standing") with him. He awards you items from the Gunsmith Arsenal. Additionally, he has gear for sale.

8 Ikora Rey (Warlock Vanguard)

Ikora Rey is the Warlock Vanguard. She gladly accepts any Tokens you have acquired. Trade with her, depositing groups of 10, five, or one Tokens, and in return, you receive increased Reputation (or "standing") with her. Special Gear Sets are accessed from her. She also sometimes sells gear.

Arrives after the completion of Mission Fury and leaves for the Tower once the Campaign is finished.

5 Lord Shaxx (Crucible Overseer)

Lord Shaxx is an imposing, horned-helmeted combat veteran, as well as the Crucible Overseer. You can access Crucible events from here. He takes any Tokens you have acquired from the Crucible; trade them in, bringing him groups of 10, five, or one. In return, you receive an increased Reputation (or "standing") with him. Special Crucible Armor and Crucible Arsenal (Gear Sets) are accessed from him.

Arrives after the completion of Mission Spark and leaves for the Tower once the Campaign is finished.

7 Cayde-6 (Hunter Vanguard)

Cayde-6 is the Hunter Vanguard. He grabs any Tokens you have acquired. Trade with him, depositing groups of 10, five, or one Tokens, and in return, you receive increased Reputation (or "standing") with him. Scouting reports for EDZ, Titan, Nessus, and Io are available (which highlight nearby loot caches for you and your fireteam). He also sometimes sells gear.

Arrives after the completion of Mission Fury and leaves for the Tower once the Campaign is finished.

9 Commander Zavala (Titan Vanguard)

Commander Zavala is the Titan Vanguard. He gathers any Tokens you have acquired. Trade them in, bringing him groups of 10, five, or one. In return, you receive an increased Reputation (or "standing") with him. Special Vanguard Armor and Vanguard Arsenal (Gear Sets) are accessed from him. In addition, he sometimes has gear for sale.

Arrives after the completion of Mission Fury and leaves for the Tower once the Campaign is finished.

Sojourner's Camp

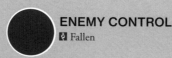

ENEMY CONTROL
Fallen

Sector Notes: Enemy Clusters: Fallen: 2 | Material Nodes: Available
Scannable Objects: 3

OVERVIEW MAP

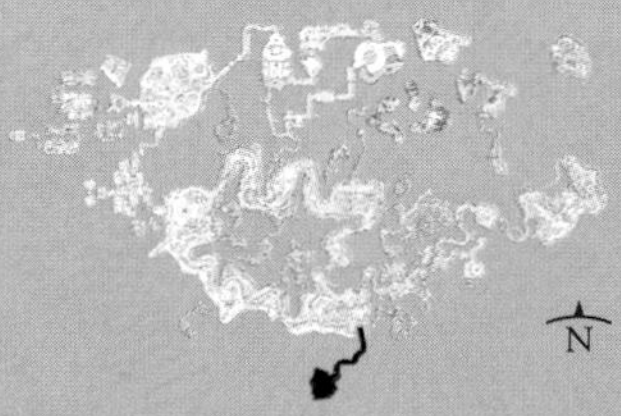

A small cliff peninsula with the crates and tent from a landing party. Now a small band of Fallen is staking claim to this territory. Mostly, this is an out-of-the-way location to get your bearings, tool up, and access the more populated Sector of Outskirts along the winding cliff road to the north.

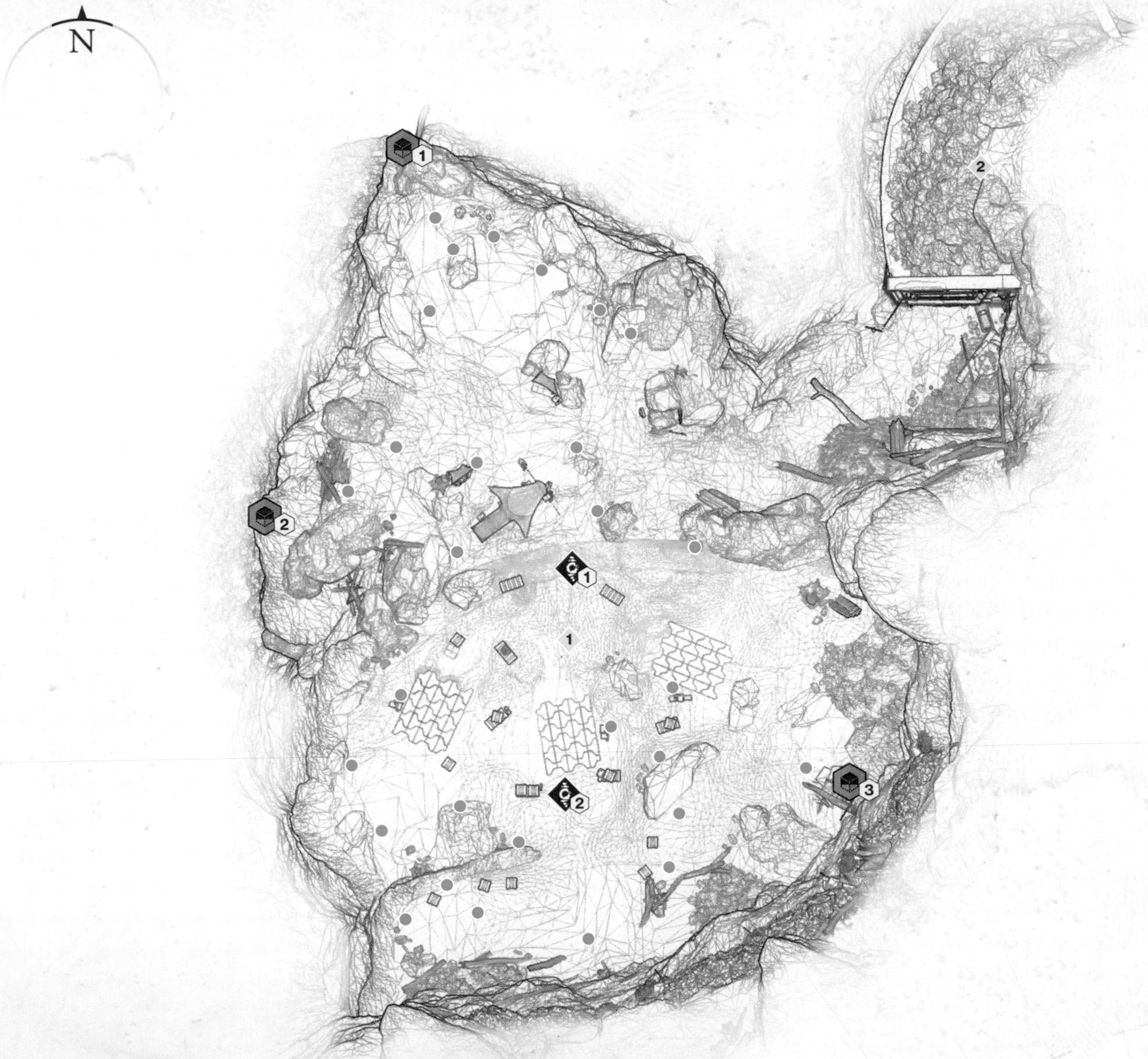

Areas of Interest

1 Camp Site

The main plateau with wooded areas surrounding it and a cliff to the west and north. It has a small contingent of Fallen to worry about.

2 Exit to Outskirts

This winding road, with a rusting open container you can use as a Sparrow ramp, is the only way in and out of here.

Enemy Clusters

1 Fallen

Expect Dregs and a few Shanks in this clearing by the tent.

2 Fallen

Dregs and a roaming Captain appear frequently by the remains of a small camp.

Scannable Objects

A globe-shaped oddity after a clifftop ramble.

Hidden between the rocks is a tarp-covered treasure.

Find a thin beacon on the edge of a precipice.

Outskirts

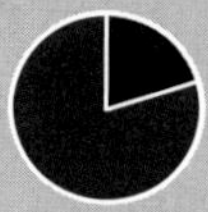

ENEMY CONTROL
Fallen Cabal

OVERVIEW MAP

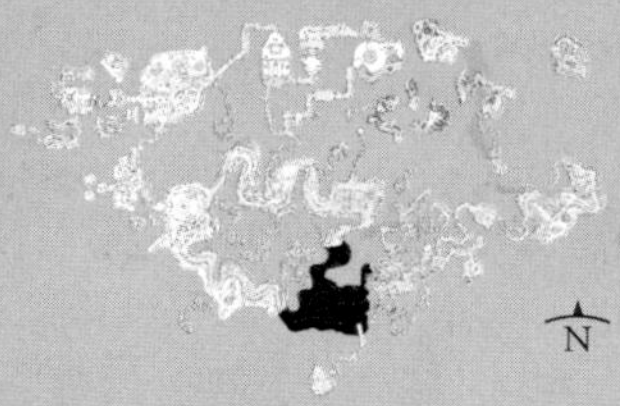

Sector Notes:

Lost Sectors: 3 | Enemy Clusters: Fallen: 3 | Enemy Chests: Available

Material Nodes: Available | Patrol Beacons: 9 | Public Event (Full): 3

Public Event (Secret): 3 | Region Chests: 5 | Scannable Objects: 5

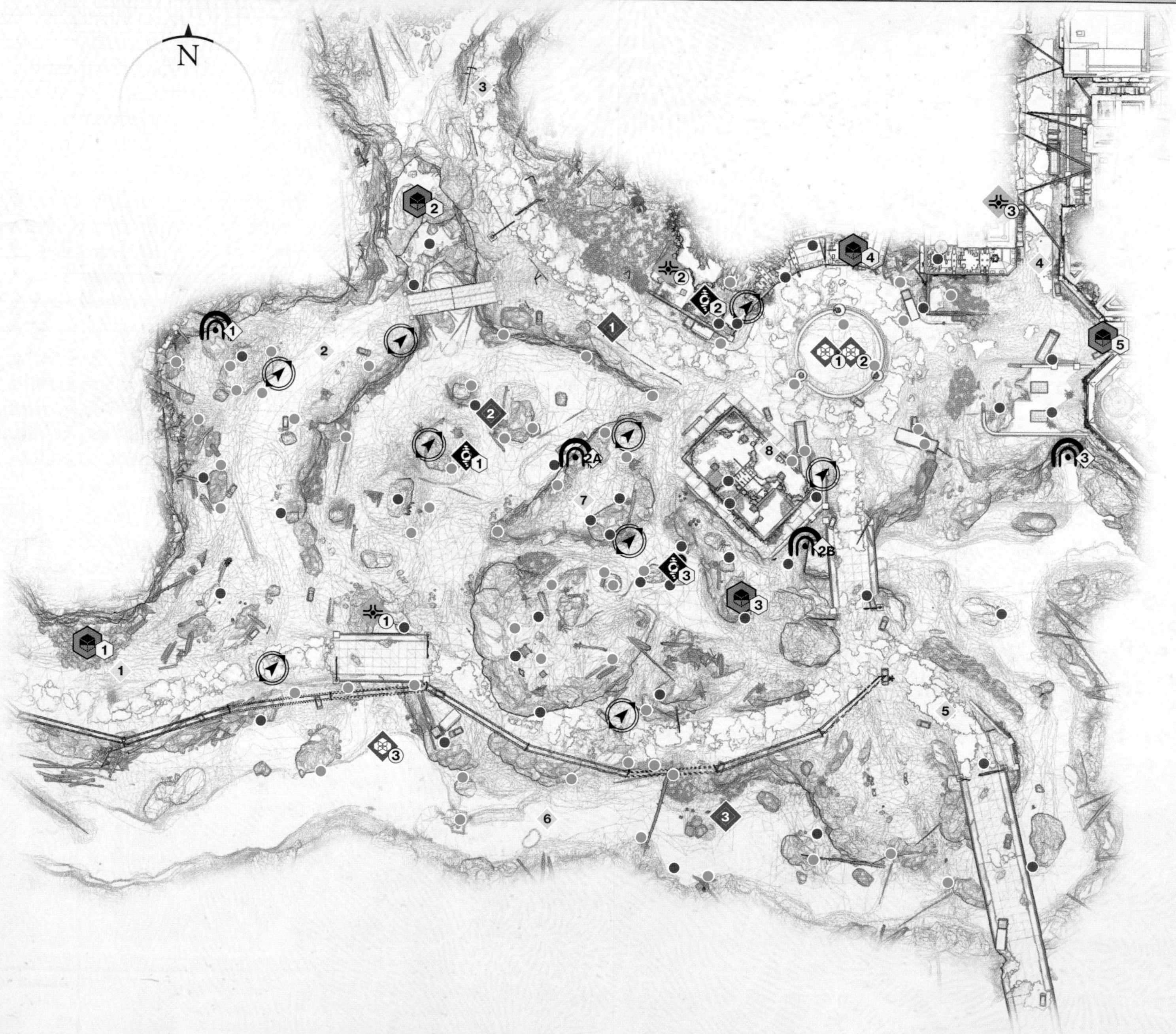

The ruins of an old town, linked to the Trostland Sector to the east, cover part of this junction Sector, where roads from more remote EDZ locations converge in all four compass directions. Fallen have made their presence felt here. Away from the central plaza is a beach dotted with foes, some hidden caves (and Lost Sectors), and a wooded area to the northwest where more pockets of Fallen resistance can be found. Expect to encounter three Lost Sectors (one with two entrances) here, along with intermittent Public Events (as you engage Spider Tanks or large Servitors), Skirmishes against the Cabal, and an encounter with a notorious Dreg Pike gang.

Areas of Interest

1 Road to Winding Cove (West)

The access road to the Winding Cove has minimal threats. You can approach it via the road, the beach to the south, or a trail from Lost Sector 1, to the north. Have you ridden your Sparrow all the way up a fallen log without falling off?

2 High Hills (Northwest)

The main circular road bisects this wooded area with numerous boulders and a small contingent of Fallen (mainly Vandals and Shanks) to tackle. The waterfall to the northeast holds some items of interest, and there's also a Lost Sector here to find.

3 Road to The Sludge (North)

If you find yourself racing up this hill, usually away from the main plaza or lower pond area, you'll end up at the Sludge, which has a Cabal presence to contend with.

4 Road to Trostland (Northeast)

Access this road from the plaza area (passing a store interior where you can find a Region Chest), and head up this U-shaped road with ruined buildings on either side of it. Note the pedestrian shortcut on the right side of this exit road.

5 Road to Sojourner's Camp (Southeast)

The road south is over a bridge that you can drop off, landing on the beach area where minor battles with Fallen are possible. Note the two nearby Lost Sector entrances to the north.

6 Southern Beach

Later Public Events cause havoc on this stretch of sand, which has dotted rocks and boulders and features minor Fallen incursions toward the eastern edge.

7 Fallen Hilltop

The area directly above Lost Sector 2 (with the circular drain hole you can see down and up from the interior) always has Fallen to face: Dregs, Vandals, Shanks, and a Captain who usually moves about in the lower pond to the northeast. Head here for the shortcut to and from the Sludge or Winding Cove.

8 Fountain Plaza

The majority of the fighting, especially when your first Public Event commences, is done in the main plaza. The area consists of a large circular fountain, a curved section of old apartment housing (which has Fallen to face), a store front to the northeast with a small interior to explore, and a three-story ruin near a rusting bus where Fallen (Dregs, Vandals, Marauders, and a Captain) reside.

Lost Sectors

1 The Drain

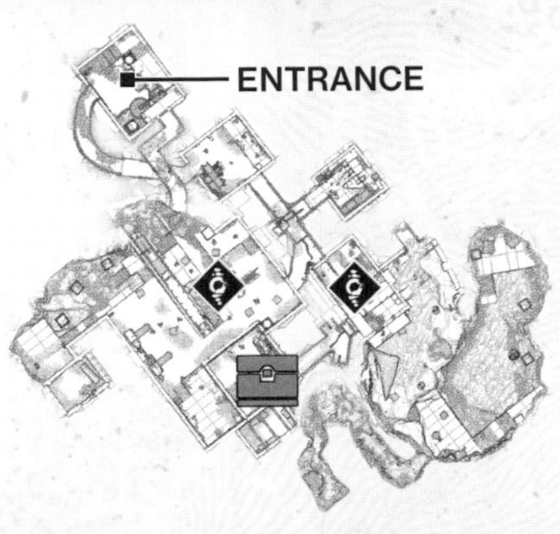

Access this in the high wooded hills northeast of the low pond and west of the waterfall. Inside is a compact grotto with ledges and a secondary cavern to explore. Fallen Dregs, Vandals, and a few Shanks are your main concerns.

2 Whispered Falls

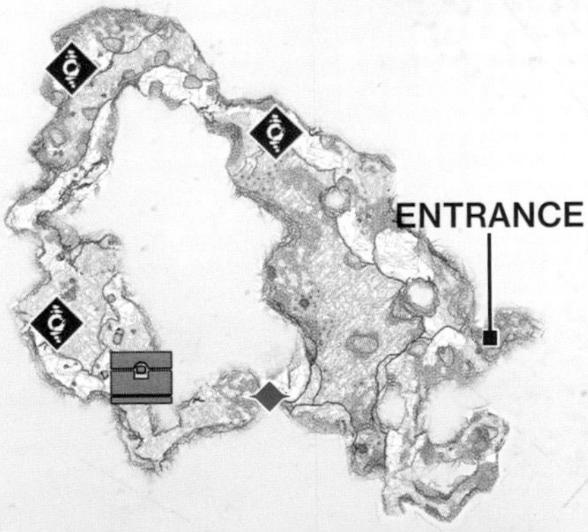

This Lost Sector is centrally located, with the distinction of having two separate entrances on the waterlogged pond or beach either side of the hilltop area. Take either entrance; with careful exploration, you can find passages down to a series of water treatment rooms where the Fallen, led by a toughened Captain, are residing.

3 Scavenger's Den

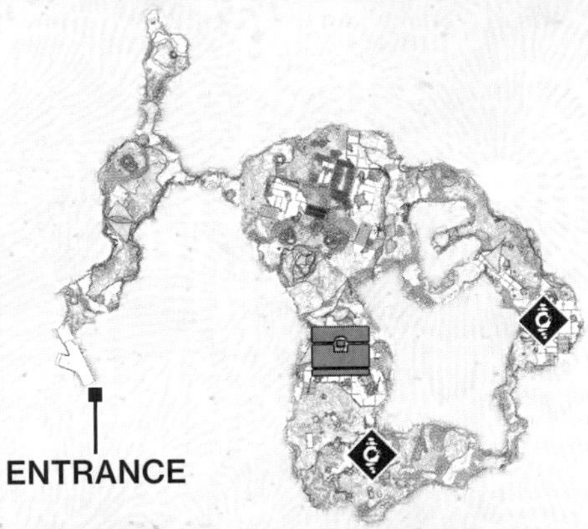

Find the entrance at sea level at the far eastern edge of the beach, south of the road to Town. Enter a series of caverns with evidence of a main Fallen command post, which ends in a sunlit grotto where a ruined human structure has fallen through into the cavern. Here, you'll find the Boss Chest and a Fallen Captain to tackle.

Outskirts

	Name	Sub-Boss	Reward
1	The Drain	Fallen Captain	Boss Chest
2	Whispered Falls	Fallen Captain	Boss Chest
3	Scavenger's Den	Fallen Captain	Boss Chest

Patrols

Outskirts (9)

There are a large number of Patrol beacons dotted around this Sector, though only three or four are active at a time.

Region Chests

① Region Chest 1

Underground, inside a cave, accessed under the south bridge from the beach.

② Region Chest 2

On the ruined wooden top floor of the partly demolished apartment structure teeming with Fallen, northwest of the plaza.

③ Region Chest 3

Located in a back room that's easily overlooked, inside the storefront area by the road to Trostland.

Public Events

Public Events (Full)

There are three randomly occurring Public Events, with the plaza spawning either the Servitor Resupply or the Weapons Exchange combat opportunities. The third event takes place on the beach.

Servitor Resupply: This takes place at the plaza. There are plenty of Fallen foes to tackle, multiple waves of lesser Servitors, and the usual Fallen adversaries to ignore so you aren't overwhelmed.

Weapons Exchange (both variants): Fallen forces are attempting to bolster one of the two indicated map areas (the plaza or beach), and they have dropped in an Walker. Destroy it, ideally with the Scorch Cannons you can unlock.

Event Number	Event Type	Target	Other Enemies	Reward
1	Servitor Resupply	Fallen Servitor	Shanks, Dregs, Vandals, Servitors	Boss Chest
2	Weapons Exchange (Walker)	Fallen Walker	Dregs, Vandals, Shanks, Marauders, Captain	Boss Chest
3	Weapons Exchange (Walker)	Fallen Walker	Dregs, Vandals, Shanks, Marauders, Captain	Boss Chest

Public Events (Secret)

Pike Gang: The Pike Gang takes a counterclockwise route around the main circular road in this Sector. Shoot the rider with accurate headshots so you can utilize the Pikes, not destroy them.

Skirmishes: The two Skirmishes take place in different locations, but the battles are similar, involving a full-on war between Cabal and Fallen forces. Expect all major enemy types to arrive: not only the infantry you're used to battling, but also Cabal Centurions, as well as Fallen Captains and Servitors!

Event Number	Event Type	Target	Other Enemies	Reward
1	Pike Gang	Four Dreg Pike Riders (around the main road)	–	Any Pikes you didn't destroy
2	Skirmish	Fallen and Cabal dropships (Caution! High-ranking foes!)	–	Random Loot
3	Skirmish	Fallen and Cabal dropships (Caution! High-ranking foes!)	–	Random Loot

Enemy Clusters

① Fallen

Dregs, Vandals, Shanks, and a Fallen Captain lurk in this shallow pond between the two road bridges (north and south), one of the entrances to Lost Sector 2, and the hilltop (Enemy Cluster 3). Later on, when random Secret Public Events begin, a Skirmish with high-ranking Cabal turns this area into a bloodbath.

② Fallen

Although there's a Vandal sniper on the open ruins to the east of here, and Marauders and Dregs in the open storefront near the road to Trostland, the majority of the foes congregate here, by the road (Dregs and Vandals are your main threats). Also expect a number of Fallen in the ruined building directly south of here (including Marauders and a Captain).

③ Fallen

Scurrying around the Hilltop area are Dregs, Vandals, and sometimes Shanks. This is a good spot for Fallen target practice, or if you feel the need to run foes over with your Sparrow or stolen Pike.

Scannable Objects

Find the tarp-covered crates in the western woods.

An "aerial" view, among the hilltop paths.

Tucked away near the rusting bus. No, the other one.

North of the pond, where the water used to fall.

A Vandal's handiwork: globes caught in a net.

Trostland

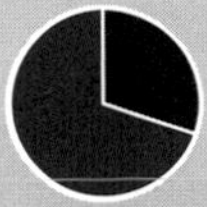

ENEMY CONTROL
Fallen Cabal

OVERVIEW MAP

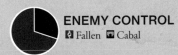

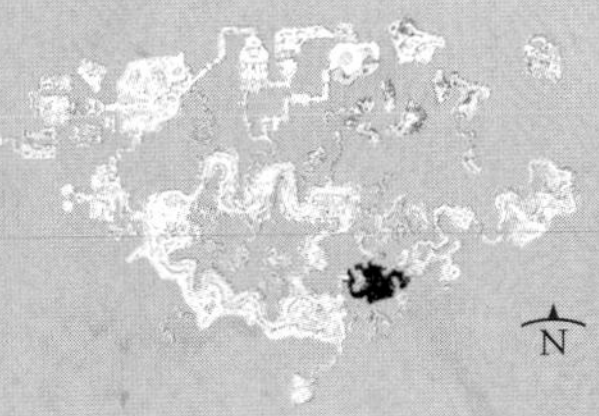

Sector Notes:

Adventure: Frame Job | Adventure: Stealing from Thieves
Campaign Mission: Combustion | Lost Sectors: 3 | Enemy Clusters: Fallen: 4
Enemy Chests: Available | Landing Zone: Available | Material Nodes: Available
Landing Zone: Available | Material Nodes: Available | Patrol Beacons: 8
Public Events (Full): 1 | Public Events (Secret): 7 | Region Chests: 4
Scannable Objects: 4 | Vendor: Devrim Kay (Dead Zone Scout) | World Quest: A Gift from the Gods

Trostland is a hub of activity centered on the EDZ vendor Devrim Kay, who is sniping from the central landmark: the ruined Church. Expect Fallen forces all around his location, as well as the only available access to both Maevic Square and Salt Mines. Note the Landing Zone, which is helpful for a quick rendezvous with Devrim, as well as the road link westward back down to Outskirts.

Areas of Interest

1 West Entrance / Road to Outskirts

A U-shaped ascent from Outskirts (with a pedestrian shortcut through a building prior to you accessing the Sparrow) ends at a building marked "Wausser." Think of this as the main west entrance into Trostland. Check inside for a Region Chest. The ruined tenement building just east of here, on the raised ground, has Fallen Dregs and Vandals, along with another Region Chest.

2 Graveyard

Fallen congregate in this general area that comprises an overgrown ruin (west) and the main graveyard south of the Church (east). A deadly chasm runs along the southern perimeter. Expect to fight mainly Fallen but occasionally Cabal forces (during Secret Public Event Skirmishes) here.

3 Church

The central landmark of Trostland, this shell of an old church houses Devrim in the steeple (south) and has a basement entrance to a Lost Sector. The Church is open, allowing access to and from the alleyways around the structure. This is a good spot to hide in if combat is taking its toll.

4 Salt Mines Entrance

Clusters of Fallen guard the entrance to the Salt Mines Sector, along the northern perimeter of Trostland. On the northwest and northeast sides are interior and Lost Sector entrances.

5 East Entrance / Road to Maevic Square

Don't overlook the winding street that allows access (via the debris-filled remains of a tenement block) to and from Maevic Square. Expect pockets of Fallen resistance on either side of this street.

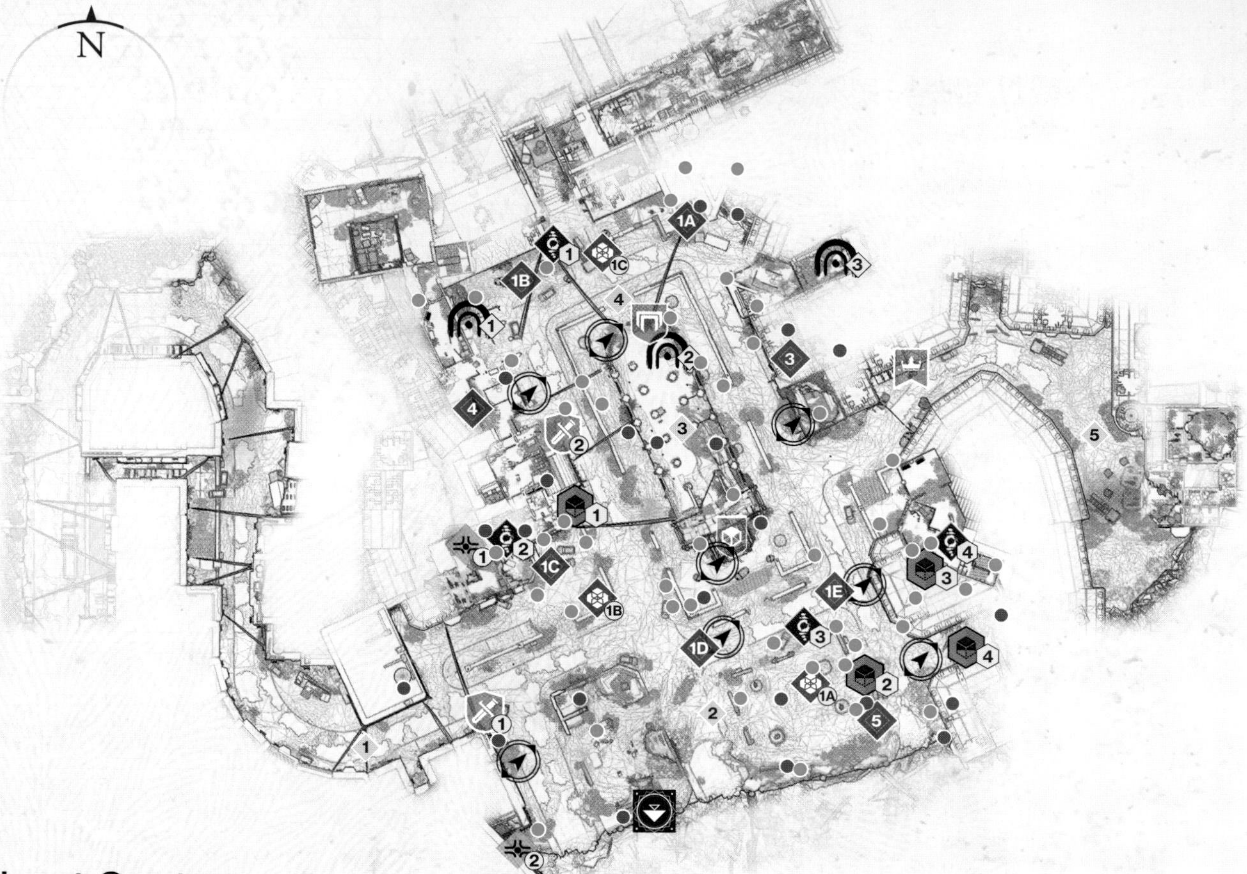

Lost Sectors

Widow's Walk

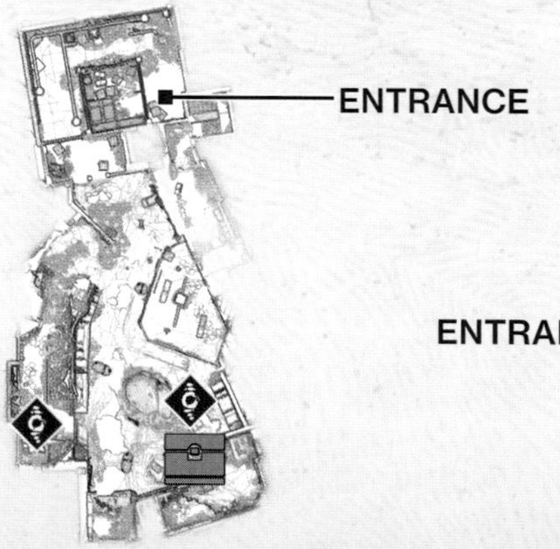

Head inside the compact rooms of the structure west of the Church to the rusting stairwell. This leads to an exterior, rubble-filled alleyway with a tenement block you can access the interior of. Dregs are your main problems here. Watch for (or use) explosive barrels, and face the Fallen Captain to claim the chest.

Atrium

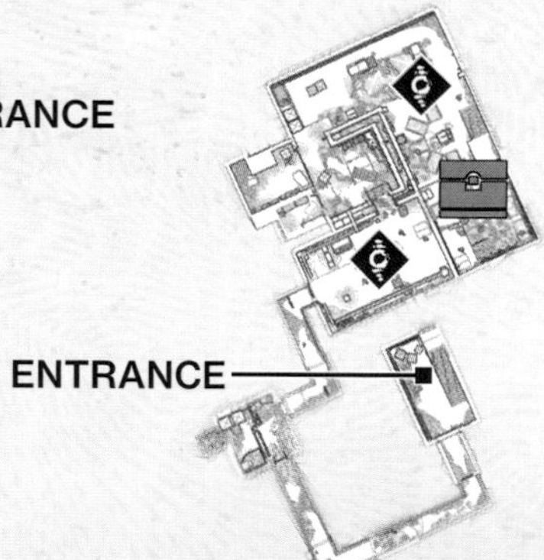

Under the Church is a series of corridors to a waterlogged and rusting underground storage area. Battle against Fallen here, who are mainly Dregs and Vandals (aside from the sub-boss Captain).

Terminus East

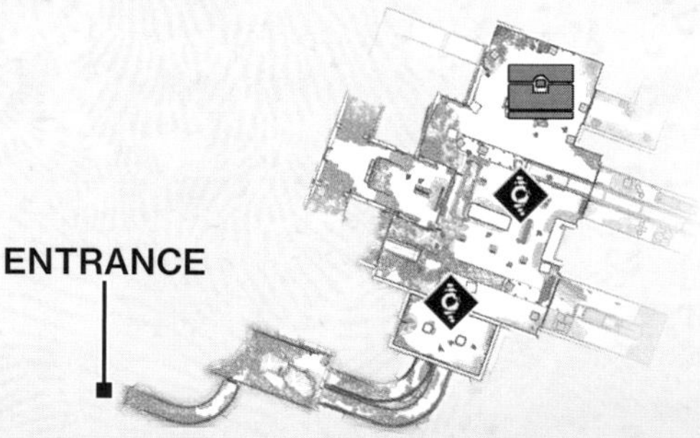

In the northeast corner outside the north end of the Church are the remains of a tube station. Slide under the entrance, drop down the hole, and battle Fallen (Dregs, Vandals, Marauders, and Shanks) in and around the main train station. The sub-boss is a Captain.

Trostland

	Guide Name	Sub-Boss	Reward
1	Widow's Walk	Fallen Captain	Boss Chest
2	Atrium	Fallen Captain	Boss Chest
3	Terminus East	Fallen Captain	Boss Chest

Enemy Clusters

1 Fallen

A scattering of Dregs, a Vandal, and occasional additional Shanks are roaming the overgrown roadway by the entrance to Salt Mines. Check the interior on the west side and expect Marauders inside here, as well as the entrance to Lost Sector 1.

2 Fallen

The ruined tenement block on the west side of Trostland houses Dregs and Wretches, but Shanks appear occasionally. Check the interior, since there are two small upper floors to explore. Note the interior entrance in the raised ground area (leading to Lost Sector 1 and the second Enemy Cluster), near the sign marked "Amsel" by the burned-out car.

3 Fallen

The main graveyard exterior is where you can expect to fight a small number of Fallen.

4 Fallen

The ruined buildings just east of the Church have foes (usually Dregs and Vandals) roaming the interiors of these structures.

Adventures

1 Frame Job

Accessed just inside the rusting bus.

2 Stealing from Thieves

On the ivy-covered wall on the cobblestone street by the Church.

Campaign Mission

Combustion

Start this close to the Lost Sector entrance, inside the Church.

World Quests

1 Gift of the Gods

Once certain prerequisites have been completed, begin this world-spanning quest at the street entrance to the Maevic Square.

Public Events

Public Events (Full)

Glimmer Extraction: The Fallen are mining Glimmer in this area. Follow the overview tactics for this Public Event. The map shows the three locations where the Glimmer machinery is activated (1A, 1B, and 1C) throughout the event.

Event Number	Event Type	Target	Other Enemies	Reward
1	Glimmer Extraction	Fallen Extractors	Fallen forces	Glimmer, Boss Chest

Public Events (Secret): High-Value Targets

HVTs #1 and #2: A Fallen Vandal or a Servitor (25% of the time) appears at one of the five indicated points (1A, 1B, 1C, 1D, or 1E). Defeat it!

HVT #3 (Tactician): A Fallen Captain is lurking in the small shop front. Defeat him and his explosive Shank entourage!

Skirmishes: There are two Secret Public Event Skirmishes within the area shown on the guide map. These take the form of combat events against Fallen or Cabal forces (or both) that descend from dropships or Cabal pods. Expect usual forces (Dregs, Vandals, Captains, Marauders; Cabal Legionaries). The number of foes depends on the level and the number of Guardians in the vicinity.

Event Number	Event Type	Target	Other Enemies	Reward
1*	High-Value Target	Fallen Vandal	Dregs, Marauders, Shanks	Boss Chest
1*	High-Value Target	Fallen Servitor	None	Boss Chest
3	High-Value Target	Fallen Captain	Shanks, Exploder Shanks	Boss Chest
4	High-Value Target	Fallen Captain	Dregs, Marauders, Vandals	Boss Chest
5	Skirmishes (two variations)	Fallen and Cabal dropships (within area shown)	–	Random Loot

(* High-Value Targets 1 and 2 spawn in one of the five same areas)

Region Chests

1 Region Chest 1

On the ruined upper floor interior, in a dark alcove.

2 Region Chest 2

On an ivy-covered alcove at the far western edge of the cliff.

Vendors

Devrim Kay

Devrim is one of the Haven Holdouts, who takes any Tokens you find throughout the EDZ. Bring him these in groups of 10, five, or one. In return, you'll receive an increase in your Reputation with him, allowing you to purchase unique EDZ armor and weaponry. Devrim also decrypts engrams.

Patrols

Trostland (8)

Once these become available, you can access a (random) Patrol from one of these beacons. Not all are active simultaneously; expect three or four of these to be accessible at any one time.

Scannable Objects

The Fallen's attempt at a hanging basket.

Up inside a structure, tucked away from Dregs.

A box sitting in the passenger seat, not going anywhere.

Daubed faction signage of the cloth variety.

Landing Zone

Trostland LZ

Only a few Sectors in the EDZ have a Landing Zone, so make use of this one when you want quick access to Outskirts, Salt Mines, or Maevic Square. You can also reach the areas of interest in Trostland. Most importantly, you have a quick route to get to the Vendor Devrim Kay in the Church.

Salt Mines

ENEMY CONTROL
Fallen

Sector Notes:

Campaign Mission: Combustion | Enemy Clusters: Fallen: 3
Partially Inaccessible | Scannable Objects: 3

OVERVIEW MAP

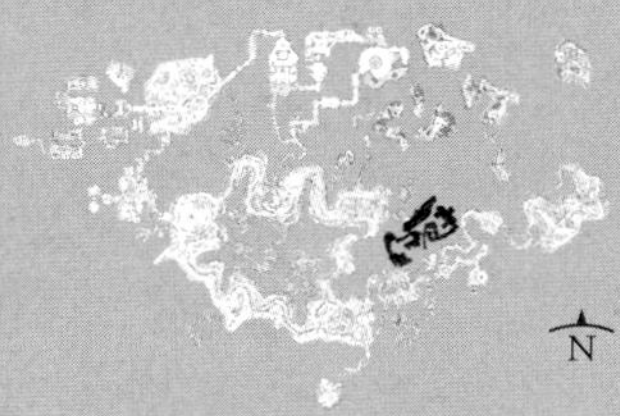

The "Salzwerk" Mine complex is only accessible via a Fallen-heavy entrance in the northern part of Trostland. It provides some interesting exploration options, but around half of the complex is inaccessible unless a mission is in play. Otherwise, you can entertain yourself by hunting Fallen throughout, as well as utilizing a Transmat to teleport to an otherwise inaccessible cliff with a view of the Shard.

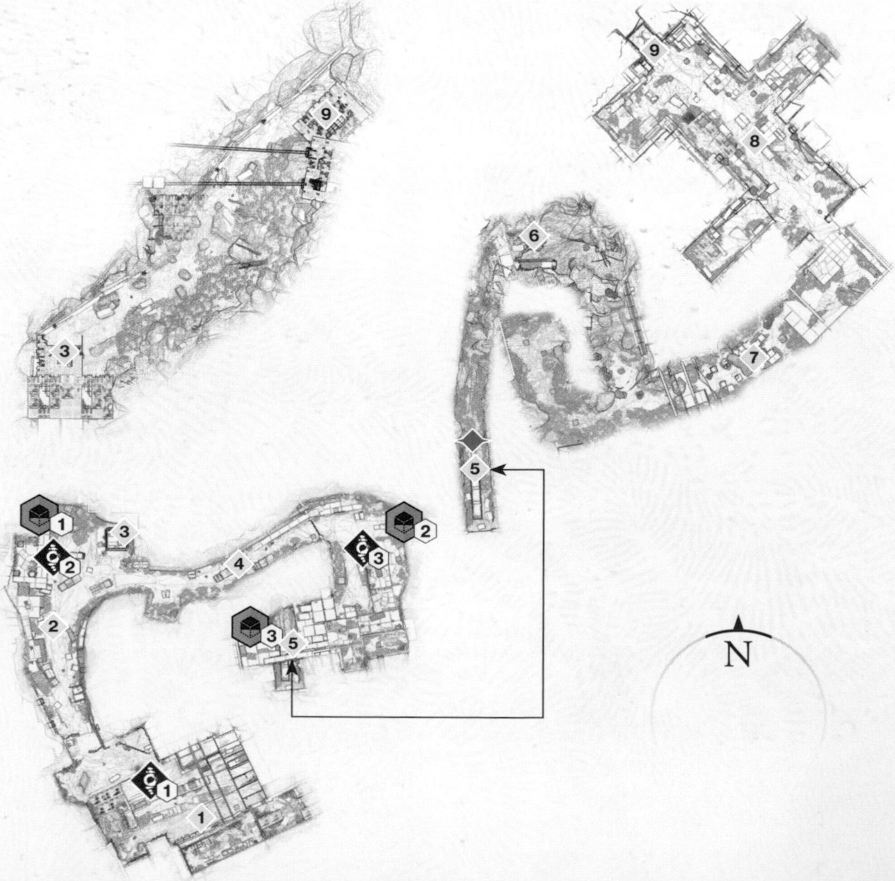

Areas of Interest

1 Salzwerk Mine Entrance

Enter here via the north entrance in Trostland. Expect a few Fallen (Dregs, Vandals, and Shanks) in this exterior area of rusting industrial buildings, now overtaken by nature. The mine entrance is through the "Salzwerk" sign.

2 Outer Depot

A roughly L-shaped storage depot with a rusting elevator at the far end, next to a Transmat. There's Fallen to contend with here as you maneuver farther into the depths of the mine itself.

3 Transmat

This is accessible once you've completed the Campaign Mission. It teleports you to the grassy cliff (the second map shown), where there's a view of the Shard. The cliff area is used in an Adventure, but it's otherwise mostly deserted.

4 Inner Yard

A second yard of rusting crates and a gantry platform to the left has a cluster of Fallen to easily tackle. Head across the far platforms to reach the old mine tunnel.

5 Tunnel

Drop from the rusting gantry to reach an old mine cart tunnel and barricade (if the Campaign Mission is inactive). Note the nearby Scannable Object. Progress from this point onward is not possible due to an energy barrier. This barrier is only inactive during the Campaign Mission.

6 Sinkhole (Inaccessible)

A sinkhole leading to the lower depths of the mine, this area is inaccessible unless the mission is active.

7 Laser Trap Tunnel (Inaccessible)

This area is inaccessible unless the mission is active. It's a series of fiendish laser traps designed to waylay the wary and kill the impatient.

8 Main Quarry (Inaccessible)

This area is inaccessible unless the mission is active. In this large, hall-like quarry area, you face multiple Servitor threats during the Campaign Mission.

9 Elevator to Grassy Cliff (Inaccessible)

This area is inaccessible unless the mission is active. Once you power on the elevator (Campaign only), you can ride the elevator to the grassy cliff exterior.

Campaign Mission

Combustion

The inaccessible areas within the mine complex are maneuvered through during Campaign Mission: Combustion (which starts inside the Church in Trostland). Refer to that mission for enemies and tactics. There are no collectibles within the inaccessible areas to worry about.

Enemy Clusters

1 Fallen

A small squad of Vandals, Dregs, and Shanks guards the exterior entrance to the mine.

2 Fallen

Expect around half a dozen Vandals and a few Dregs guarding the Transmat in this depot area.

3 Fallen

Shanks, Dregs, Vandals, and a Fallen Captain put up more of a fight in this inner yard.

Scannable Objects

This banner flies high in the Outer Depot.

What's that in the darkest, rubble-filled corner behind the half-buried container?

A rusty gantry and an old computer; look before you drop.

Maevic Square

ENEMY CONTROL

Fallen

Sector Notes:

Enemy Clusters: Fallen: 1 | Material Nodes: Available

Partially Inaccessible | Scannable Objects: 3

OVERVIEW MAP

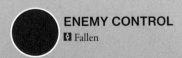

A once-thriving settlement to the northeast of Trostland has been reduced to ghostly graveyard of ruined buildings, overgrown streets, rusting vehicles, and tumbledown plazas. Normally, this place is sealed with a number of barriers, but you can tackle these during the World Quest (Gift from the Gods: Cutting off the Supply), an Adventure (Stealing from Thieves), and a Strike (Lake of Shadows). However, all these quests start in Trostland, so they aren't labeled on the adjacent map. Come here to tackle a small band of Fallen, but return here for more violent confrontations during the aforementioned quests. This Sector is also the only access point into the Reservoir Sector.

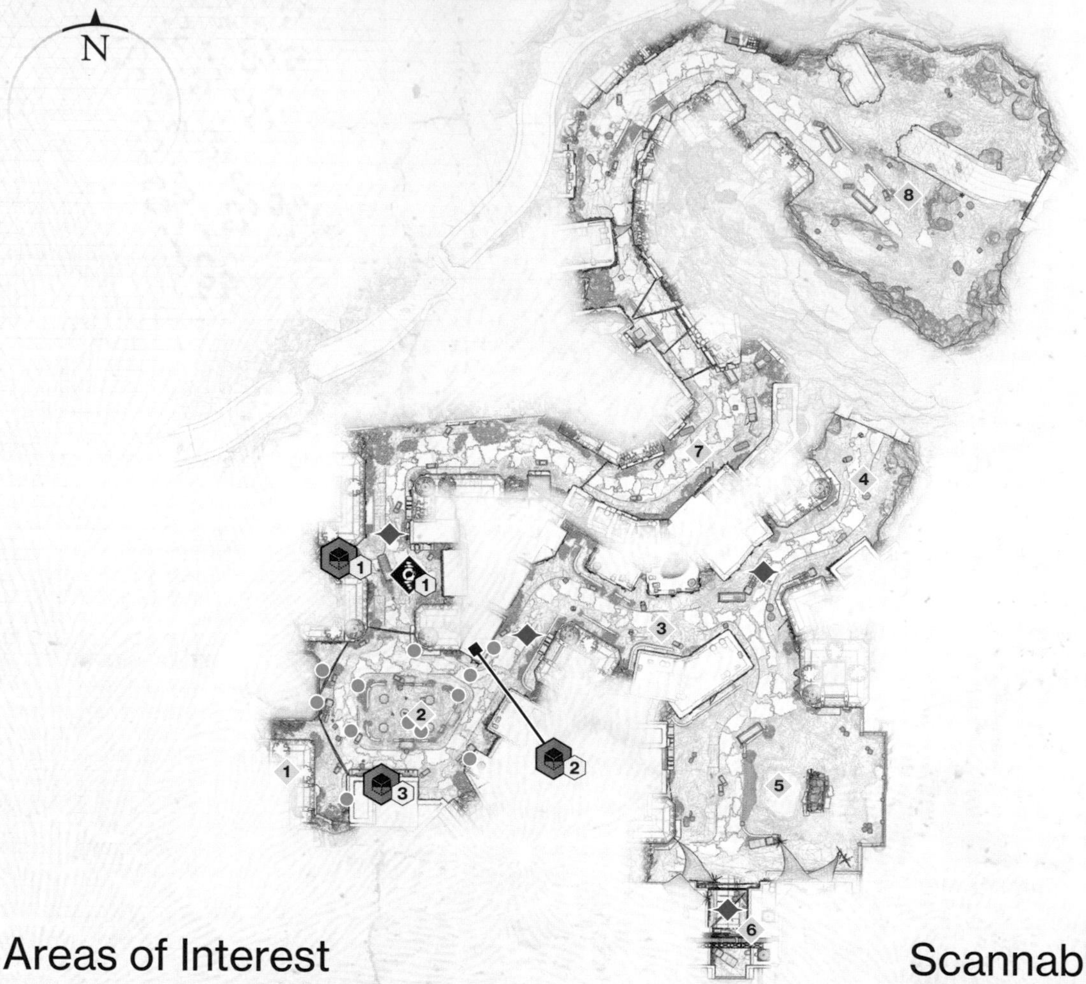

Areas of Interest

1 Exit to Trostland (Southwest)

The only way in and out of this Sector is via the blown-out remains of an old apartment building, which allows access to the eastern side of Trostland.

2 Plaza

A cluster of material nodes is available here, along with three scannable items. This overgrown plaza surrounded by derelict buildings has barricades stopping you from progressing too far north and northeast. Note the small Fallen contingent, which increases to a modest army during the World Quest.

3 East Street (Inaccessible)

Inaccessible unless a mission is active. This links you from the plaza to the outer East Tunnel and Coastal Plaza.

4 East Tunnel (Inaccessible)

Inaccessible unless a mission is active. You spend a brief period of time in this dead-end tunnel structure.

5 Coastal Plaza (Inaccessible)

Inaccessible unless a mission is active. This is a larger overgrown plaza overlooking a body of water, with an entrance to the Trostland hydroelectric station (the Reservoir Sector).

6 The Reservoir (Inaccessible)

Inaccessible unless a mission is active. Accessed during the Strike: Lake of Shadows, there's a hole in the inside wall of the left building, just below the "Trostland" sign. This leads to the Reservoir Sector.

7 Long Street (Inaccessible)

Inaccessible unless a mission is active. A long and uphill climb as you ascend an overgrown thoroughfare.

8 Collapsed Bridge Clearing (Inaccessible)

Inaccessible unless a mission is active. The remains of a freeway bridge and an impassable tunnel are located in the northeastern part of this Sector.

Enemy Cluster

1 Fallen

Expect a motley crew of Dregs, Vandals, and Shanks roaming the northern street near the barrier, off the plaza area.

Scannable Objects

1

Hidden in the leafy alcove, near the rusted bus.

2

A covered crate in the undergrowth.

3

Is it a weapon? Is it a pole? Only Ghost knows.

The Reservoir

ENEMY CONTROL
Taken

Sector Notes:

Usually Inaccessible | Strike: Lake of Shadows

OVERVIEW MAP

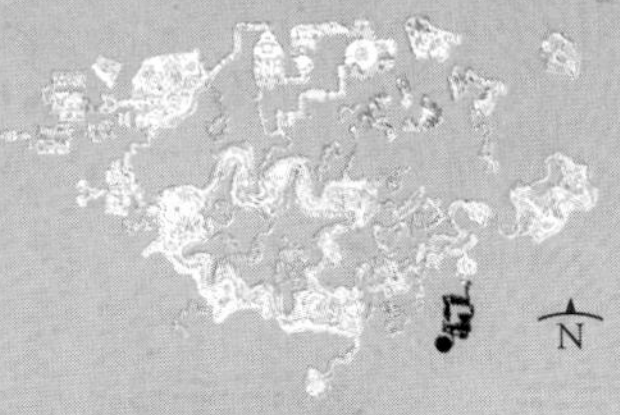

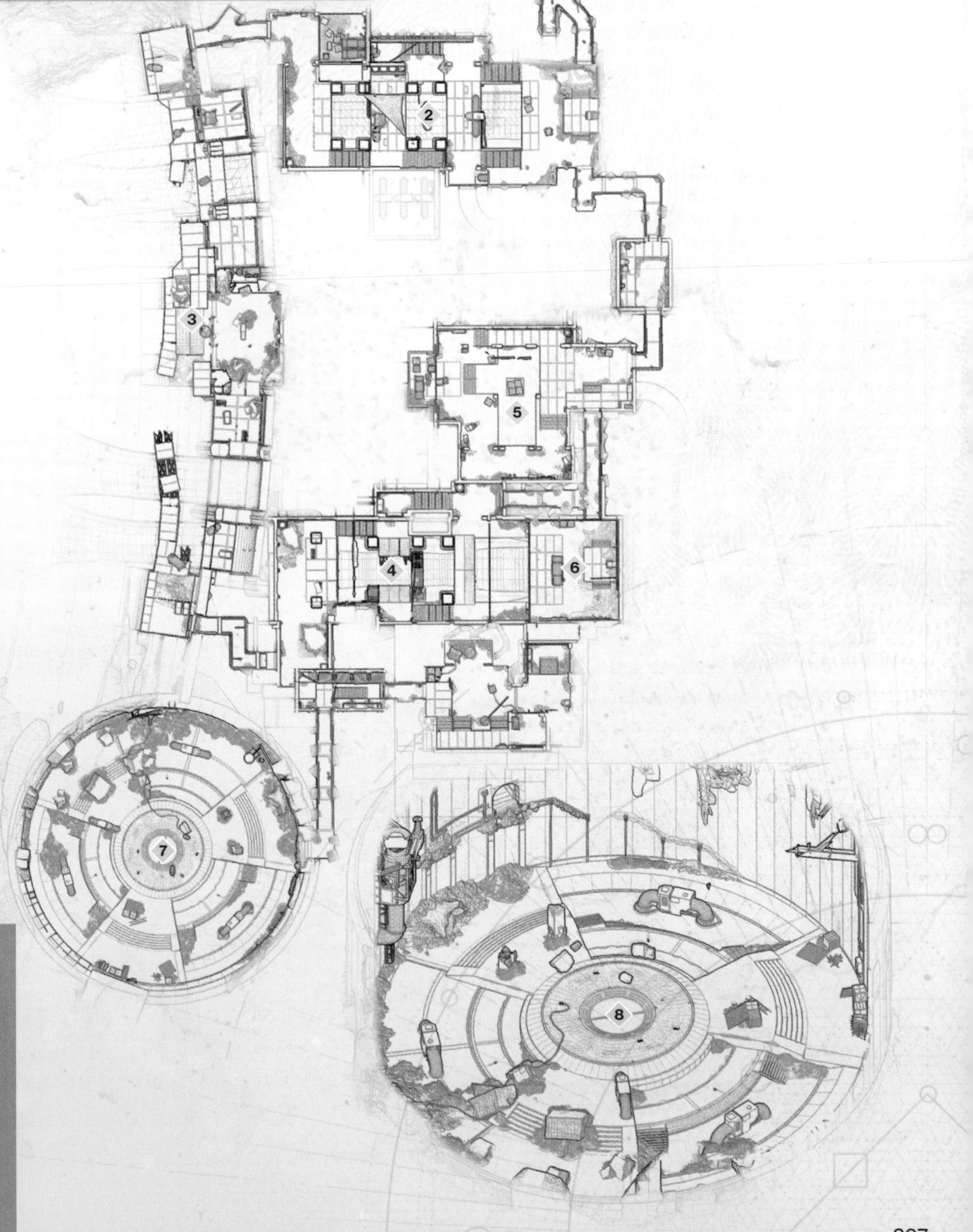

The ruins of a large hydroelectric dam overlook Trostland, and the gushing waters drain into the lake to the south of Outskirts, Winding Cove, and Firebase Hades. This mainly interior location is inaccessible unless you're battling through here during a Strike. The Reservoir is accessed via a hole in the wall of the Trostland building, which is in an inaccessible part of Maevic Square. You're not getting here without a fight!

Areas of Interest

1 Trostland and Entrance Corridor (Inaccessible)

This is inaccessible unless the Strike is active. The exterior Trostland sign is shown; the entrance to the Reservoir is via a hole in the left side of the building, behind the barrier. A single dark corridor with a couple of dead ends is mainly free from Taken, until you reach the area close to the Dam Chamber.

2 Dam Chamber North (Inaccessible)

This is inaccessible unless the Strike is active. Roaring water gushes through this sloped chamber, with gantries to fight down and plenty of Taken to worry about.

3 Dam Exterior Gantryway (Inaccessible)

This is inaccessible unless the Strike is active. Multiple precarious and ruined gantry platforms run the length of the exterior dam wall. Expect heavy Taken presence and a great view of the lake!

4 Dam Chamber South (Inaccessible)

This is inaccessible unless the Strike is active. During the Strike, you battle up the rusting platforms, fighting Taken as you go. There are gaps to leap as roaring water rushes under you.

5 Loading Bay (Inaccessible)

This is inaccessible unless the Strike is active. A waterlogged loading bay, with access to and from the Dam Chambers (which is optional but unnecessary).

6 Generator Room (Inaccessible)

This is inaccessible unless the Strike is active. A generator and a wire mesh wall prevent access directly from the southern Dam Chamber. Expect heavy Taken resistance when pushing through here.

7 Main Vat (Inaccessible)

This is inaccessible unless the Strike is active. A gigantic ruin of the dam's former vat, this is now the setting for a ferocious battle against a Taken Boss (Phalanx) named Grask, The Consumed.

Strikes

Lake of Shadows

As previously stated, this entire map is inaccessible unless the named Strike is active. The latter half of the Strike takes place through here (following the route of the Areas of Interest). The Strike begins in Trostland but moves to Maevic Square before you can enter the Reservoir.

The Sludge

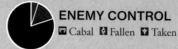

ENEMY CONTROL
Cabal | Fallen | Taken

OVERVIEW MAP

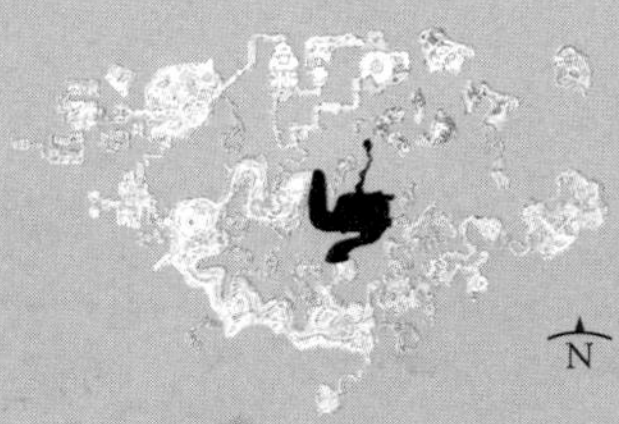

Sector Notes:

Adventure: Getting Your Hands Dirty | Adventure: Taken to Extremes
Lost Sectors: 3 | Enemy Clusters: Cabal: 6 | Enemy Chests: Available
Landing Zone: Available | Material Nodes: Available | Patrol Beacons: 8
Public Event (Full): 2 | Public Event (Secret): 6 | Region Chests: 3
Scannable Objects: 3

A river winds from east to west along the northern part of this old saw mill facility. It is now a cluster of rotting and rusting buildings, with a small contingent of Cabal forces attempting to battle intermittent attacks from Fallen, Taken, and Guardians. This offers a Landing Zone, entrances to three Lost Sectors, and a variety of Public Events (both Full and Secret). It also grants access deeper into the EDZ, toward the Gulch (to the west), and back to Outskirts (to the south). Note the secondary waterfall and stream (north), leading to a strange location known as the Dark Forest.

Areas of Interest

1 Road to The Gulch (West)

If you're just passing through between Outskirts and the Gulch, the western overpass and River provide access in a north loop toward the Gulch.

2 Road to Outskirts (South)

This is likely to be the first entrance you come through when exploring the Sludge. Note the small clusters of Cabal forces in the vicinity. Head southeast, along a winding river and road back to Outskirts.

3 East Yard

This expansive open area has rusting buildings to the northwest, north, and along the eastern perimeter. The main building ahead has a covered thoroughfare, allowing quick access down to the River. Note that the overgrown structure has a Region Chest nestled up in some rotting rafters. Along the eastern side is a Lost Sector and other warehouse openings you can hide in during Public Events, or as you clear out nearby Cabal forces.

4 Central Gully

This offers a straight shot to and from the River, and there's almost always enemy activity here, even if a Public Event isn't underway. West is a small rusting facility centrally located, with a small rail yard on the western side and a Lost Sector to explore. East of the gully is another rail yard, and both have Cabal forces.

5 North River

A low expanse of shallow water, with a Lost Sector to the northwest, various small caves, the entrance to the Dark Forest, and a waterfall around the Landing Zone with a Hidden Chest. Along the south side of the River is a cliff you can jump up and down when maneuvering to and from the buildings.

Lost Sectors

Hallowed Grove

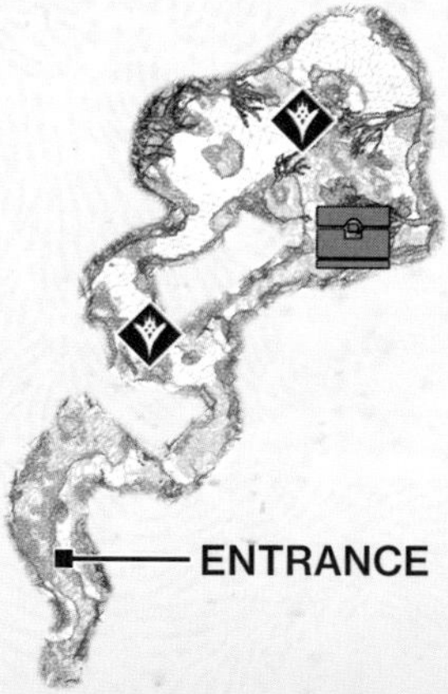

Enter the cave to the northeast of the River, and work your way through a grotto and into a once-idyllic sunlit glade, now teeming with Taken. Ascend to the upper pool, where you'll face a Taken Captain and his minions.

Cavern of Souls

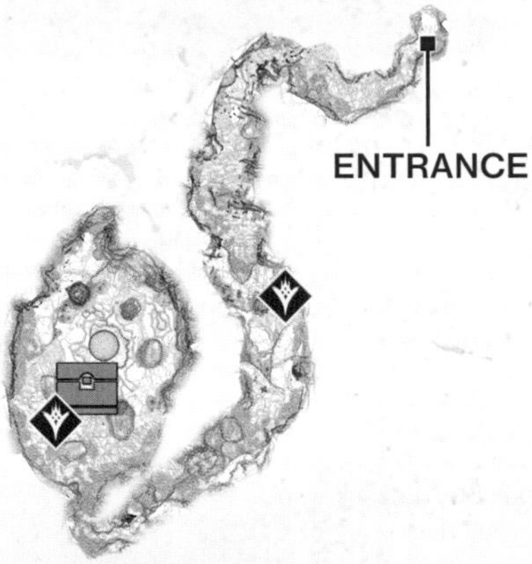

Head down below the central derelict structure (guarded by a small band of Cabal) into a rocky passageway that eventually leads to an oval-shaped cavern. Masses of Taken are active here, drawn by a Taken Minotaur Sub-Boss.

Shaft 13

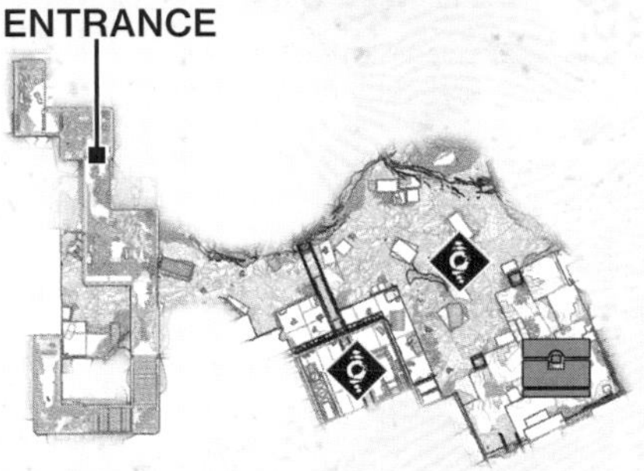

Navigate past some Cabal on the eastern warehouse perimeter, then negotiate some corrugated metal corridors, and you'll discover a hidden mine quarry with Fallen foes to battle. Grab the loot once you've slain the Fallen Captain situated here.

Lost Sectors: The Sludge

	Guide Name	Sub-Boss	Reward
1	Hallowed Grove	Taken Captain	Boss Chest
2	Cavern of Souls	Taken Minotaur	Boss Chest
3	Shaft 13	Fallen Captain	Boss Chest

Adventures

1 Getting Your Hands Dirty

Accessed along the steep riverbank, below the rusting cylinder tank.

2 Taken to Extremes

Accessed just inside one of the warehouse doors, on the eastern perimeter.

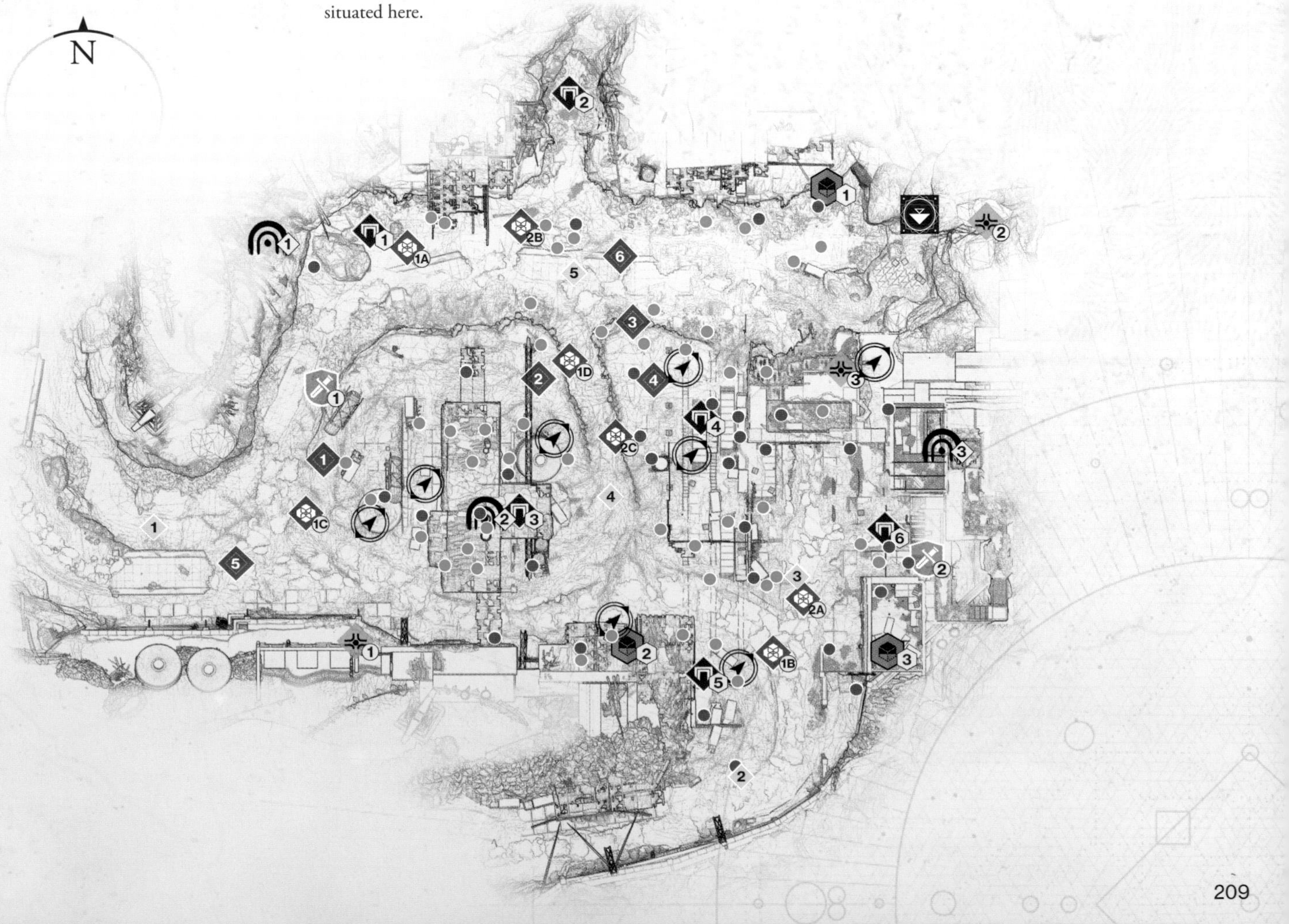

Enemy Clusters

❶ Cabal

A few Legionaries and Psions are getting their feet wet close to the Lost Sector entrance in the northeast River area.

❷ Cabal

Expect a Centurion and periodically other Cabal foes in front of the waterfall north of the River, by the Forest entrance.

❸ Cabal

Expect Psions, Legionaries, Phalanxes, and a Centurion (on the western rail yard side). These forces are on either side of the building. The ones on the east side guard a Lost Sector.

❹ Cabal

A Centurion and his Psion and Legionary underlings are guarding a rusting train yard just east of the central gully.

❺ Cabal

A small band of Psions and Legionaries, with possible Phalanx reinforcements, mooch about near some rusting containers.

❻ Cabal

Psions and Legionaries are your main concern in the vicinity of the third Lost Sector entrance.

Landing Zone

The Sludge

Drop in from Orbit and land in the northeastern corner of this Sector, close to the River and a small camp by a waterfall.

Patrols

The Sludge (8)

These scattered beacons aren't all available at one time. Each allows you to start a short, random Patrol.

Public Events

Public Events (Full)

Glimmer Extraction: This involves destroying three of the four Fallen extraction sites (1A, 1B, 1C, and 1D) dotted around the map.

Taken Blight: This involves removing Taken forces and three Blight locations (2A, 2B, and 2C) throughout the map.

Event Number	Event Type	Target	Other Enemies	Reward
1	Glimmer Extraction	Fallen Extractors	Fallen forces	Glimmer, Boss Chest
2	Taken Blight	Blight locations	Taken forces	Boss Chest

Public Events (Secret)

High-Value Targets: These four foes are easy to spot (they have yellow-orange health bars). The HVT#3 is hidden away inside a cave by the River. The Pike Gang event is easily concluded.

Skirmish: This is a protracted battle in the area shown on the guide map. It involves Cabal and Taken forces battling each other, and almost every enemy type makes an appearance! Expect a great deal of fighting here, and note that the Skirmish area extends to the cliff on the east side of the gully.

Event Number	Event Type	Target	Other Enemies	Reward
1	High-Value Target	Cabal Centurion	None	Boss Chest
2	High-Value Target	Fallen Captain	None	Boss Chest
3	HVT (Tactician)	Fallen Captain	Shanks	Boss Chest
4	High-Value Target	Cabal Centurion	None	Boss Chest
5	Pike Gang	Four Dreg Pike Riders (around the main road)	Any Pikes you didn't destroy	–
6	Skirmish	Fallen and Cabal dropships (Caution! High-ranking foes!)	–	Random Loot

Region Chests

① Region Chest 1

By a crate in the southwest perimeter wall: head down an interior waterlogged ramp to reach it.

② Region Chest 2

Leap to the raised camp near the LZ, in the far northeast corner, and investigate behind the waterfall.

③ Region Chest 3

Explore the interior of the derelict factory building; check the narrow passage overgrown with plant life. The chest is on the upper rafters.

Scannable Objects

What's blue and behind a tree? This glowing Shard splinter.

Tucked away below a series of structural pillars, in the rubble.

Clamped to a warehouse wall. That is all.

The Dark Forest

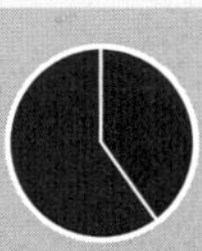

ENEMY CONTROL
Taken Fallen

OVERVIEW MAP

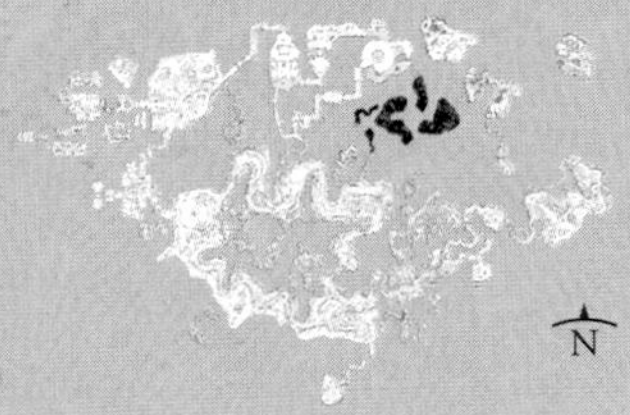

Sector Notes:

Campaign Mission: Spark – Pt. 2 | Usually Inaccessible

Can't see the forest for the trees? That's because the inner Sectors of this strange, foreboding, and sacred area is only accessible during Campaign Mission: Spark—Pt. 2. You revisit this location twice. Each time, you locate an Artifact randomly dropped by enemies that allows you to unlock the remaining two Subclasses of your Guardian. This is achieved by fighting the denizens of the Dark Forest and communing with the Shard itself. To enter the Dark Forest, approach it via the small sunken stream and waterfall, along the northern perimeter of the Sludge.

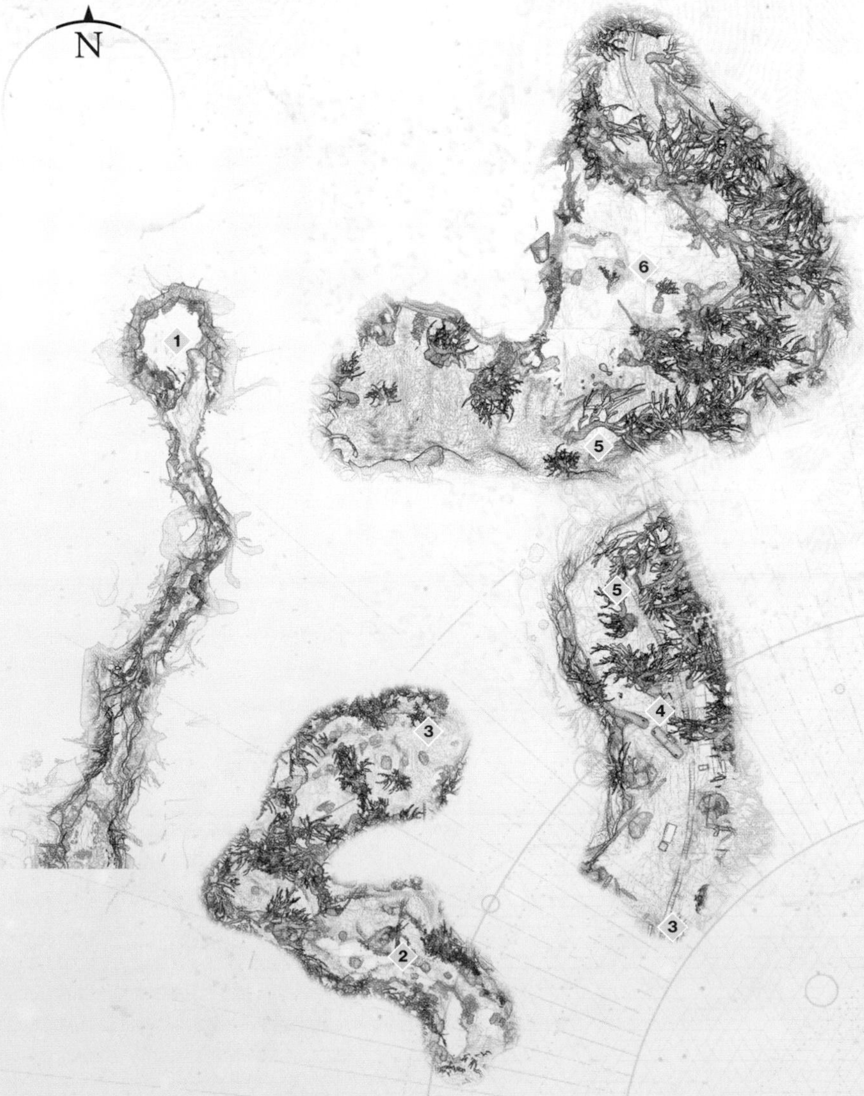

Areas of Interest

1 Pool and Portal

Once you enter from the Sludge (to the south), unless a Patrol is active, this area is deserted. If the Mission: Spark—Pt. 2 is active, a Taken portal appears in the middle of the shallow pool at the north end of the Dark Forest. This is the only way into the Dark Forest area.

The portal transports you to a rocky gully in the Dark Forest Sector, which is made up of three separate exploration areas you access via portals.

2 The Dark Forest Glade and Lake (Inaccessible)

Inaccessible unless the mission is active. Several ethereal statues greet you during the mission while you are en route to a confrontation with Fallen (visit #1) or Taken (visit #2).

3 Portal (Inaccessible)

Inaccessible unless the mission is active. Once you defeat a group of Fallen (visit #1) or Taken (visit #2) in this rocky pool of shallow water, a portal opens, depositing you inside a railroad tunnel.

4 Railroad Tunnel and Forest Floor (Inaccessible)

Inaccessible unless the mission is active. Exit the tunnel, seeking more answers from ethereal statues of Guardian mentors. On your way back from the Shard, expect combat during both trips.

5 Portal (Inaccessible)

Inaccessible unless the mission is active. A portal at the end of the Forest Floor section deposits you in the final location of the Dark Forest: a large lake where the Shard is.

6 The Traveler's Shard (Inaccessible)

Inaccessible unless the mission is active. This is where you commune with the Traveler's Shard and gather your lost power. This is done after you defeat any Fallen foes (visit #1) or Taken enemies (visit #2). Then, you must retrace your steps all the way back to the different portals before you exit. Along the way, expect fierce resistance from the enemies you've previously faced.

Campaign Mission

Spark

Although this mission doesn't start here, it is the only quest that allows access deeper into the Dark Forest Sector. Commune with the Shard here to receive your Guardian's other two Subclass powers.

Quarantine Sector 236
Blackened Forest

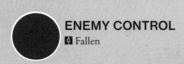

ENEMY CONTROL
Fallen

Sector Notes:

Campaign Mission: Spark | Usually Inaccessible

OVERVIEW MAP

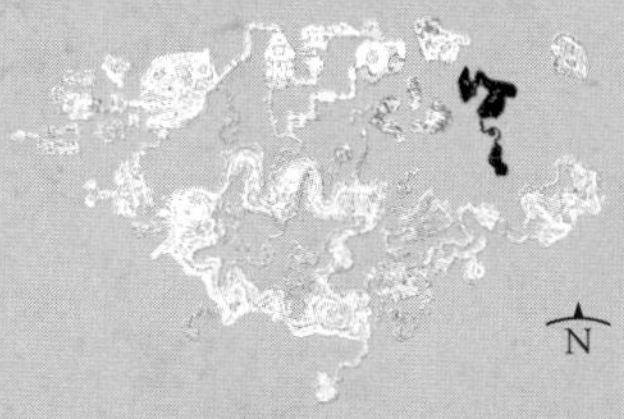

This self-contained area within the European Dead Zone is only accessible during the Campaign Mission: Spark. It involves a hike from a deserted road barricade through a tunnel and grotto (where Fallen Marauders are first encountered). Then, you head out from some old mine workings and down to the Forest Floor area. You pass a ship's crash site before finally reaching the site of the main piece of Shard itself. It is here that you regain your first Guardian Class Abilities.

Shard Facts

Even though you can't reach this area under normal circumstances, you can enter the Salt Mines, use the Transmat inside the mines, and appear on a grassy cliff with a view of this Shard.

Also, there is a second large piece of the Traveler's Shard located deep within the Dark Forest – a usually inaccessible Sector only reachable during Mission: Spark – Pt. 2.

Areas of Interest

1 Deployment Zone and Road Barricade (Inaccessible)

This is inaccessible unless the mission is active. You begin the mission here, on a grassy bank close to the remains of a road into a tunnel, now barricaded.

2 Overgrown Forest (Inaccessible)

This is inaccessible unless the mission is active. Leap the gap in the road here, or face a climb up the large hole.

3 Marauders' Grotto (Inaccessible)

This is inaccessible unless the mission is active. A dark cave tunnel leads to a grotto, where you face Fallen Marauders for the first time.

4 Abandoned Mine (Inaccessible)

This is inaccessible unless the mission is active. This is where the two Sectors merge; you access your first chest, and gaze out from a balcony overlooking the Shard itself.

5 Ship Crash Site (Inaccessible)

This is inaccessible unless the mission is active. This entire wooded area has a host of Fallen to contend with, and the majority of the Dregs you encounter scurry out of a hole in front of a crashed ship. Expect further incursions with Marauders, Wretches, and Captains as you progress through the murky forest path.

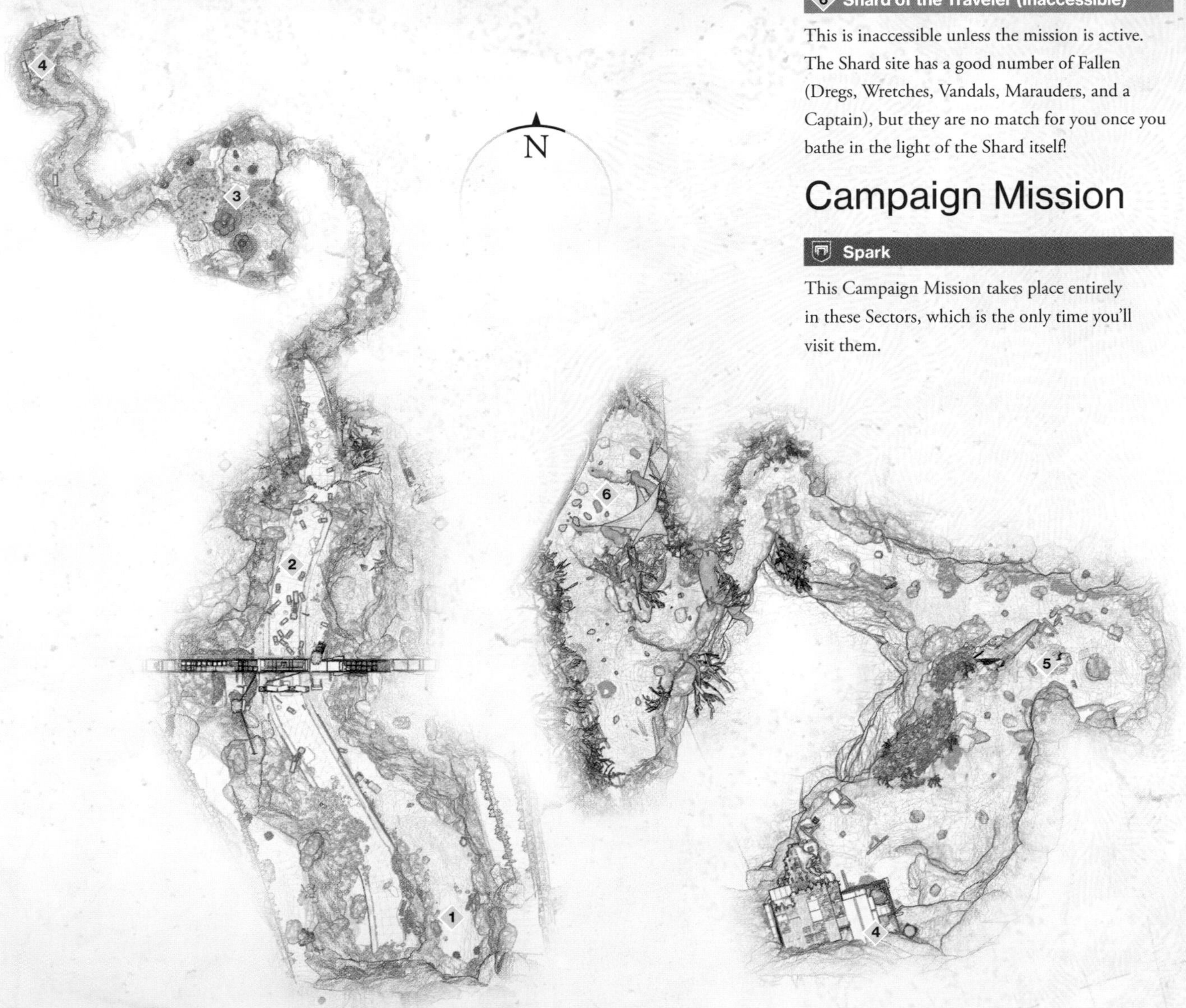

6 Shard of the Traveler (Inaccessible)

This is inaccessible unless the mission is active. The Shard site has a good number of Fallen (Dregs, Wretches, Vandals, Marauders, and a Captain), but they are no match for you once you bathe in the light of the Shard itself!

Campaign Mission

Spark

This Campaign Mission takes place entirely in these Sectors, which is the only time you'll visit them.

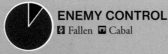

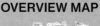

Winding Cove

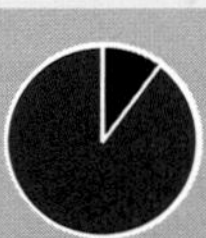

ENEMY CONTROL
Fallen Cabal

Sector Notes:

Lost Sectors: 1 (2 accessible) | Enemy Clusters: Fallen: 2

Enemy Chests: Available | Material Nodes: Available | Patrol Beacons: 5

Public Event (Full): 1 | Public Event (Secret): 3 | Region Chests: 3

Scannable Objects: 2

OVERVIEW MAP

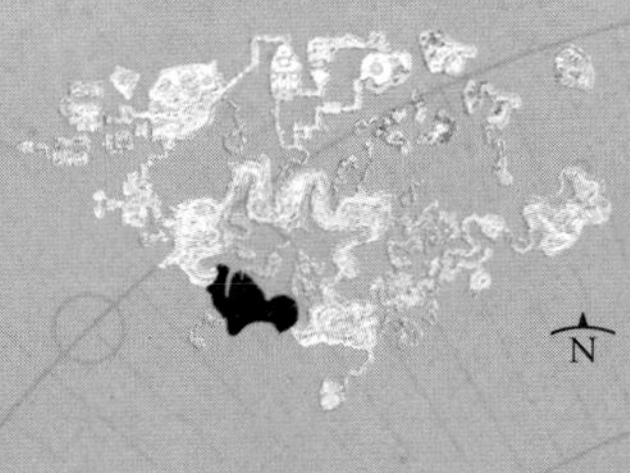

If landing parties of Fallen and a crashed Fallen craft on the upper wooded ledges didn't constantly spawn Dregs, Vandals, and other enemy infantry, this would be a somewhat idyllic Sector. It is comprised of a winding main road that follows the coast (to the south), allowing access to the Cabal Firebase Hades (to the west) and Outskirts (to the east). More cunningly, there's also access northwards via an underground Lost Sector to the Gulch. It's a relatively compact Sector but one with a lot to discover, including three Region Chests and two scannable objects.

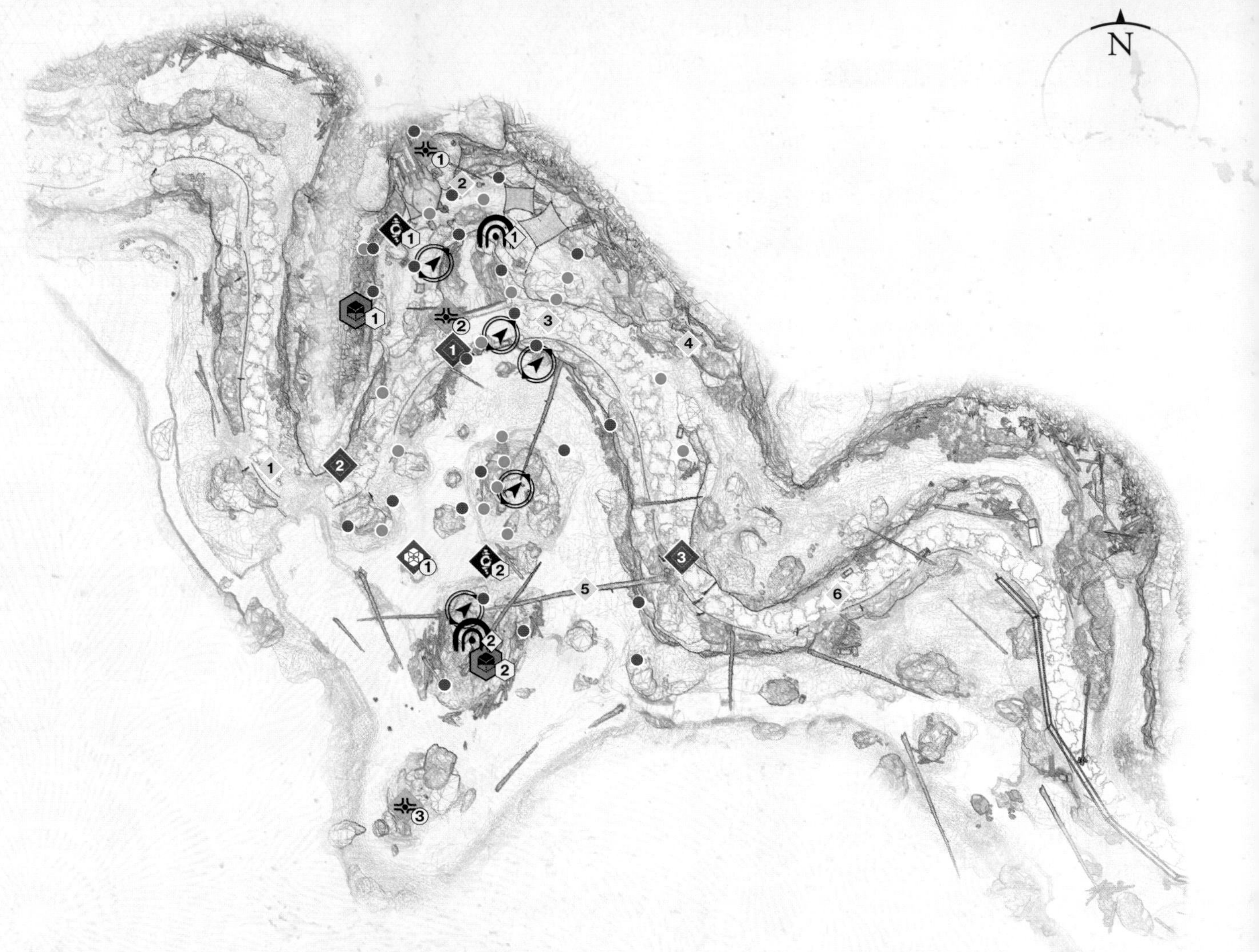

Areas of Interest

1 Road to Firebase Hades (West)

Make the sharp turn at the far western edge of this Sector and you're soon heading straight into a large-scale Cabal satellite array and base. Note you can drive or dash along the road or the sandy beach.

2 Wooded Ledge (Fallen Alcove)

The narrow U-shaped trail above the main road in the northern wooded area houses a couple of alcoves (including a cave you can move into to reach an upper vantage point). Fallen are always present here, along with a Region Chest and a nearby scannable object.

3 Main Road

A U-shaped thoroughfare that's in reasonable shape, featuring a bridge (with a Region Chest and entrance to the Gulch's Lost Sector below it). It also has numerous access points to and from the beach, as well as a secondary U-shaped trail up to the Fallen Alcove.

4 Rusting Door

This odd-looking door is completely sealed from the roadside. It is actually the exit to the Lost Sector (#2), and it's only accessible once you maneuver through that underground area.

5 The Beach

Expect light Fallen resistance throughout the beach cove itself. There are two main islands (note the Lost Sector you drop into on the south island) and a scattering of smaller protrusions. The main Public Event takes place here. Use this as a shortcut when traveling through this Sector.

6 Road to Outskirts (East)

This offers quick access back to Outskirts, either via the main road or along the sandy coast. If you have the skill, you can try driving up the fallen tree logs to move between the road and the beach.

Enemy Clusters

1 Fallen

Though you may find Fallen on the beach from time to time, the majority of the enemies, including the bigger threats like Vandals, Marauders, and a Captain, appear around a crashed craft on the upper wooden area above the exit to the Gulch Lost Sector.

2 Fallen

Expect a few Fallen foes wandering around the beach, usually consisting of Dregs and a Vandal or two.

Patrols

Winding Cove (5)

There are only five patrol beacons available here, and between three and four are active at one time. Leave the Sector after completing all available Patrols, then return. At that point, the other beacons may be active.

Lost Sectors

Flooded Chasm (The Gulch)

This Lost Sector is actually the exit from the Gulch Lost Sector, though it can be approached from this direction, too. Inside is a large cavern where Cabal and Fallen troops are battling. Consult the Gulch portion of this guide for the map and more info.

The Weep

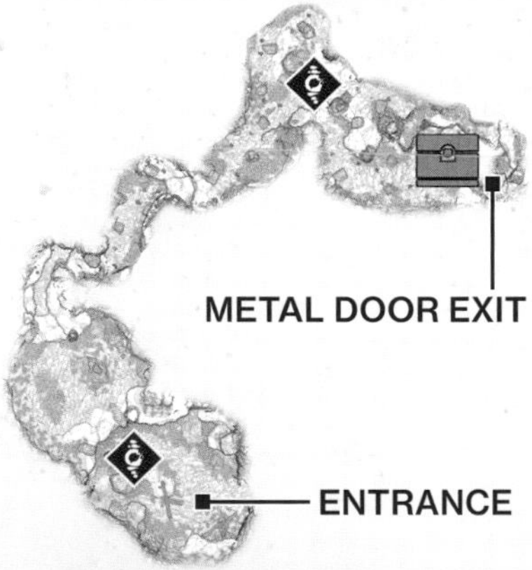

Drop down into the crevasse in the middle of the largest island on the beach, and explore two narrow, rocky caverns overgrown with ivy. Defeat some Fallen infantry and a Captain to claim your loot. Exit via the rusting door (Area of Interest location #4).

Winding Cove

	Guide Name	Sub-Boss	Reward
1*	Flooded Chasm (The Gulch)	Fallen Captain	Boss Chest
1*	The Weep	Fallen Captain	Boss Chest

(* The Gulch Lost Sector)

Region Chests

1 Region Chest 1

On a high ledge, adjacent to the crashed Fallen craft, in the northern wooded ledge and Fallen alcove.

2 Region Chest 2

Below the main road bridge, in the small gully to the Gulch Lost Sector exit.

3 Region Chest 3

On the tiny southernmost island.

Scannable Objects

Look up and watch for logs when scanning this strange crate.

Scan this pole without falling into a Lost Sector.

Public Events

Public Events (Full)

Cabal Excavation: This event takes place on the beach. You attempt to override a Cabal mining laser while dodging any incoming laser-guided missiles and the Cabal infantry waves that drop in from above.

Event Number	Event Type	Target	Other Enemies	Reward
1	Cabal Excavation	Mining Lander	Cabal infantry	Boss Chest

Public Events (Secret)

HVT: This is a floating globe of horror: the Fallen Servitor. It is usually relatively easy to defeat. There are also two Dreg Pike gangs active in this area. One starts on the western side of the road, and the other starts at the eastern side of the road. They are not active simultaneously, but they move back and forth between these points.

Event Number	Event Type	Target	Other Enemies	Reward
1	High-Value Target	Servitor	Fallen infantry	Boss Chest
2	Pike Gang	Three to four Dreg Pike Riders (along the main road)	–	Any Pikes you didn't destroy
3	Pike Gang	Three to four Dreg Pike Riders (along the main road)	–	Any Pikes you didn't destroy

The Gulch

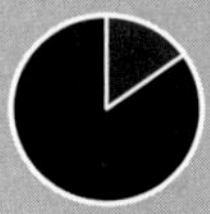

ENEMY CONTROL
Cabal Fallen

OVERVIEW MAP

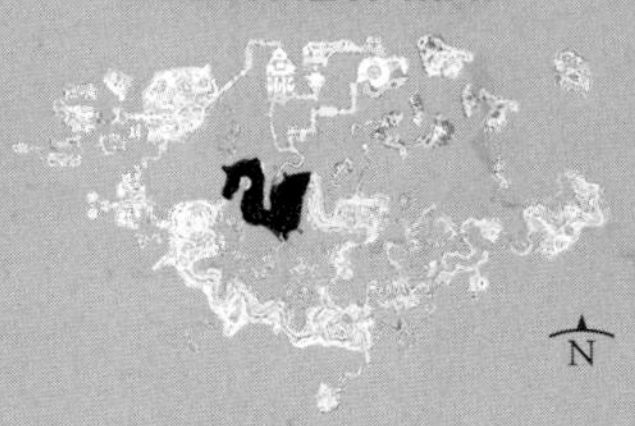

Sector Notes:

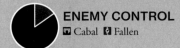

Adventure: Reversing the Polarity | Adventure: Stop and Go and Stop and Go

Lost Sectors: 1 | Enemy Clusters: Cabal: 6 | Enemy Chests: Available

Material Nodes: Available | Patrol Beacons: 7 | Public Event (Full): 2

Public Event (Secret): 5 | Region Chests: 3 | Scannable Objects: 3

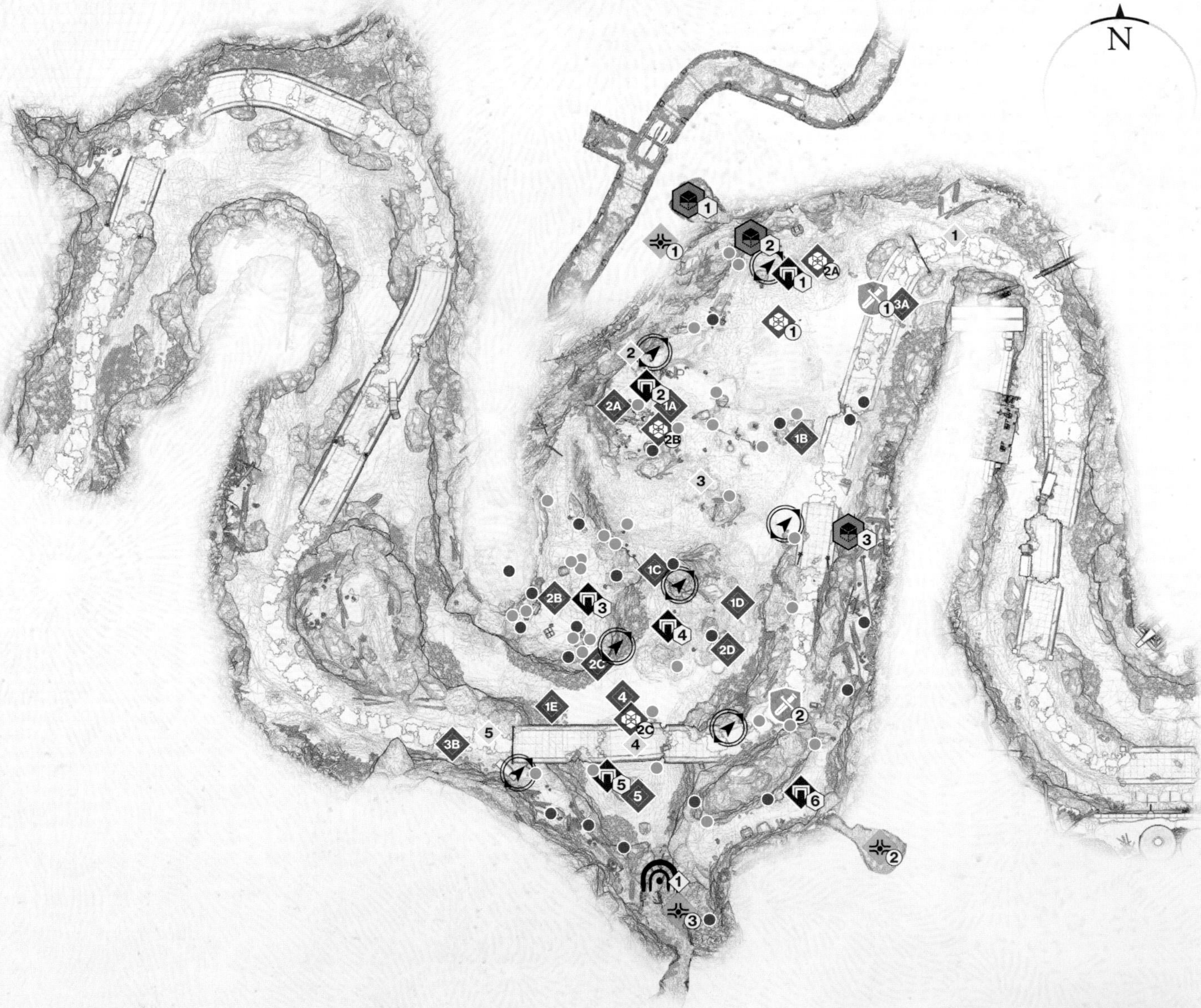

This is a relatively easy Sector to understand geographically, as it features a large, partly flooded floor that takes up most of the accessible room. The Cabal has a heavy presence here because this Sector is adjacent to Firebase Hades and provides access via the Tunnels section to their sprawling inner spaceport (Sunken Isles). To the south are some dotted boulders, a small upper plateau with foes, and the remains of an overpass. This Sector is possibly the most accessible, with access to Firebase Hades, the Tunnels, the Sludge, and Winding Cove (via the Lost Sector to the south).

Areas of Interest

1 Road to The Sludge (Northeast)

A winding forest road in various broken pieces allows access to and from the Sludge. Enter from here to get an excellent view of most of the Sector.

2 The Tunnels Entrance (North)

There's usually some Cabal combat to overcome in this area, close to the burned-out remains of a Fallen Walker. This is the entrance to the Tunnels, a Cabal-controlled interior that allows access to their main spaceport on EDZ (Sunken Isles).

3 The Gulch Floor

A wide expanse of shallow water that gives you little cover but makes long-range enemy takedowns a breeze. Various Public Events, both small and large in scale, occur here.

4 Ruined Overpass (South)

Use this or the lower river when maneuvering to Firebase Hades. You can also stop by the rusting truck at the overpass bridge to reconnoiter the narrow trail leading to two hidden caves and the Lost Sector down below. Note the Cabal-heavy plateau just northwest of here, as well as a frequently overlooked trail behind some boulders on the east side of the overpass.

5 Road to Firebase Hades (Southwest)

The main road to Firebase Hades offers alternate trails via the river. Note the rusting truck on the bridge; if you're heading in from Firebase Hades, use it as a ramp. There's a trail on the western side of the plateau you can use to sneak up and onto the plateau and surprise the Cabal forces up there, too.

Adventures

1 Reversing the Polarity

On a grassy bank at the northern end of the ruined roadway.

2 Stop and Go and Stop and Go

By some boulders near a trail and the overpass bridge.

Patrols

The Gulch (7)

Expect up to four active patrol beacons from the seven available. Note that some may be above or below the broken overpass section.

Public Events

Public Events (Full)

Injection Rig: This lands at the point shown on the map, in the large shallow waterlogged area north of the Tunnels entrance. Expect a hard fight with a sub-boss Psion to defeat multiple times, Gladiators toward the end of the battle, and a Centurion (in addition to normal Cabal forces) during the last wave.

Glimmer Extraction: This involves destroying three Fallen extraction sites (2A, 2B, and 2C) dotted around the map.

Event Number	Event Type	Target	Other Enemies	Reward
1	Injection Rig	Psion Sub-Boss	Cabal forces	Boss Chest
2	Glimmer Extraction	Fallen Extractors	Fallen forces	Glimmer, Boss Chest

Public Events (Secret)

HVT #1: A Cabal Centurion descends from a dropship at one of the five indicated points (1A, 1B, 1C, 1D, or 1E).

HVT #2: A Fallen Captain drops in via a Fallen spacecraft at one of the four indicated points (2A, 2B, 2C, or 2D).

Pike Gang and Interceptor: These events are both easily concluded by destroying these foes.

Skirmish: The Skirmish is a protracted battle in the area shown on the guide map. It involves Cabal and Taken forces battling each other. Almost every enemy type makes an appearance! Expect a great deal of fighting here, and note that the surrounding cliffs and overpass make good firing positions.

Event Number	Event Type	Target	Other Enemies	Reward
1	High-Value Target	Cabal Centurion	–	Boss Chest
2	High-Value Target	Fallen Captain	–	Boss Chest
3	Pike Gang	Three to four Dreg Pike Riders (along the main road)	–	Any Pikes you didn't destroy
4	Interceptor	One Psion pilot	–	The Interceptor if it wasn't destroyed
5	Skirmish	Fallen and Cabal dropships (Caution! High-ranking foes!)	–	Random Loot

Lost Sectors

Flooded Chasm

You can approach this Lost Sector either via the waterlogged cave entrance south of the overpass, or from the Winding Cove Sector directly south of here, which this Lost Sector links to. Inside is a large cavern where Cabal and Fallen troops are battling. Expect to face a larger contingent of Fallen as you progress farther into the cavern. The Cabal presence is minimal and exploratory (mainly Psions and Legionaries), but the Fallen have Dregs, Vandals, Shanks, and a Captain to tackle.

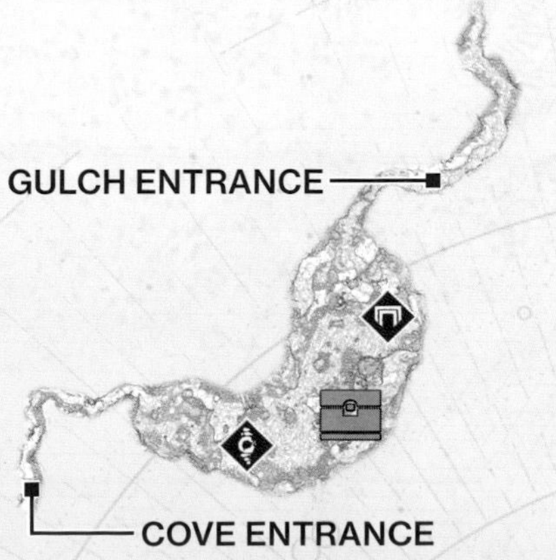

Lost Sectors: The Gulch

	Guide Name	Sub-Boss	Reward
1*	Flooded Chasm	Fallen Captain	Boss Chest

(* Exits into Winding Cove Sector)

Enemy Clusters

1 Fallen

A small Cabal presence is located in the northern part of the waterlogged floor of the Gulch. They are guarding multiple collectibles, so check the perimeter behind them.

2 Fallen

This is a large contingent of foes, including occasional Incendiors, guarding the Tunnels entrance.

3 Fallen

Up on a grassy plateau overlooking the river and overpass is the strongest selection of Cabal forces, led by a Centurion.

4 Fallen

A small cluster of foes in the shallow riverbed surrounded by low cliffs and boulders. Expect Legionaries and Psions here.

5 Fallen

A few Cabal congregate under the overpass, close to the Lost Sector entrance.

6 Fallen

A raiding party of Legionaries is checking the curved trail in the upper southeastern part of this Sector. Note the two nearby cave entrances.

Region Chests

1 Region Chest 1

Above Cabal Enemy Cluster #1 and the ground-level cave is a second cave almost directly above; this hidey-hole has a chest inside.

2 Region Chest 2

When moving along the curved trail by Enemy Cluster #6 in the southeast edge of this Sector, check an easily overlooked small cave.

3 Region Chest 3

Above the entrance to the Lost Sector, accessed from the curved trail near Enemy Cluster #6, is a scree slope with fallen logs and other detritus. Find a cave here with the chest inside.

Scannable Objects

A Shard piece inside a small ground-level Cabal cave.

A globe-shaped object, hidden along the north Gorge wall.

The smallest radar you've seen, up on an east perimeter rock.

The Tunnels

ENEMY CONTROL

Cabal

Sector Notes:

Campaign Mission: Payback | Enemy Clusters: Cabal: 4

Material Nodes: Available | Partially Inaccessible | Scannable Objects: 2

OVERVIEW MAP

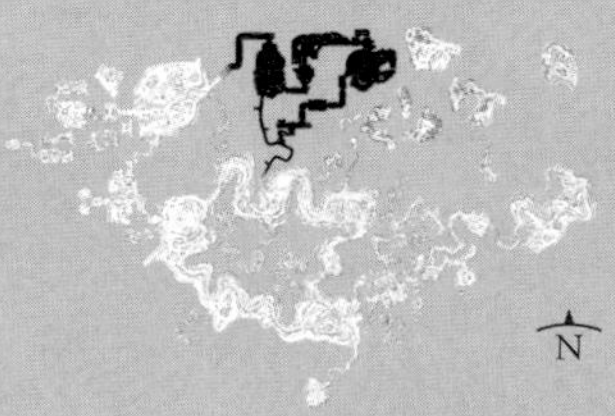

Once you feel confident enough to assault a sprawling Cabal spaceport (known as Sunken Isles), this is one of the two Sectors you can use to reach it (the other is Firebase Hades). This Sector is unique in being completely underground. You can access it via the tunnel entrance in the Gulch. Simply head north along the winding tunnel, ignoring the cavern and small interior Cabal base (unless you're here for collectibles), and maneuver north into a giant cavern with two parallel bridges. The exit to Sunken Isles is on the opposite side of the bridge. The rest of the Tunnels (a series of huge corridors and a landing platform) is only accessible during Campaign Mission: Payback.

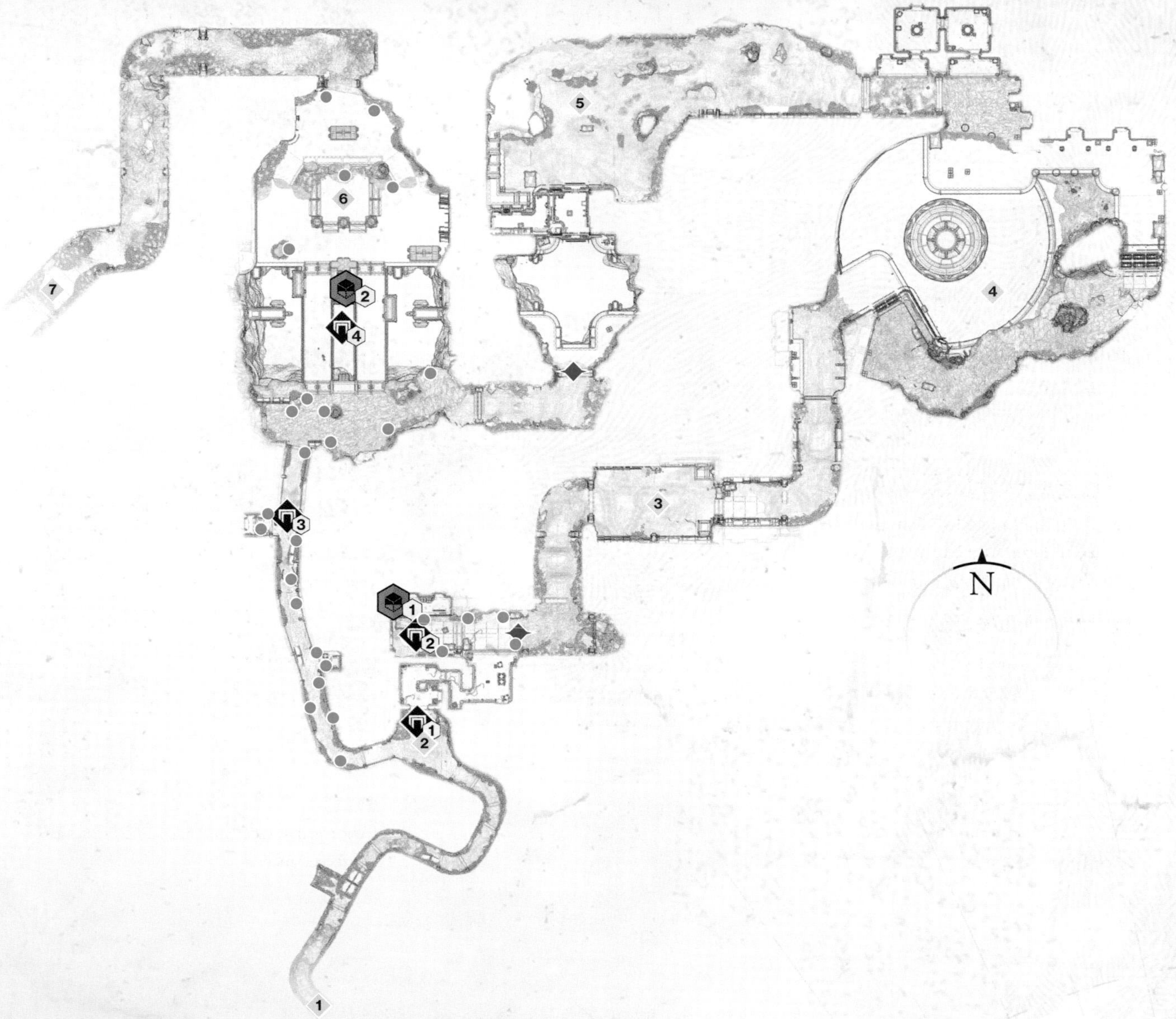

Areas of Interest

1 Tunnel to The Gulch (South)

Head into this tunnel from the Gulch, and check the map. Take this narrow, snaking tunnel with intermittent Sparrow ramps (you can boost off these for fun) all the way into the Bridge Cavern (Area of Interest #6). Exploring the small Cabal base is optional.

2 Cabal Underground Base

Halfway along the narrow tunnel is a small Cabal base with Legionaries, Psions, and a Centurion to worry about once you pass through into a giant corridor entrance. A huge circular door to the east (indicated by the barrier on the guide map) prevents progress. Stay here for the materials and scannable object.

3 Wide Tunnel (Inaccessible)

This is inaccessible unless the mission is active. Expect heavy Cabal presence as you drive your tank along here.

4 Cabal Cavern and Landing Platform (Inaccessible)

This is inaccessible unless the mission is active. An expansive cavern with a large circular landing and loading areas, the place is teeming with Cabals and enemy vehicles.

5 Rocky Tunnel and Bridge (Inaccessible)

This is inaccessible unless the mission is active. Engage your first enemy tank in this rocky tunnel, then pause to release the bridge controls. This allows access into the Bridge Cavern (mission only).

6 Bridge Cavern

Accessible at any time, expect the largest Cabal presence here. Outside of the mission, there's likely to be infantry and a possible Centurion here. The Sparrow helps you easily and quickly negotiate either parallel bridge. Stop to collect materials and scan an object.

7 Tunnel to Sunken Isles

The exit tunnel leading to and from the main Cabal spaceport known as Sunken Isles, where a gigantic carrier is moored. Remember that you can return from Sunken Isles to the Gulch when you're traveling in the opposite direction!

Enemy Clusters

1 Cabal

A small cluster of Legionaries, Psions, and a Phalanx or two guard this base.

2 Cabal

Additional enemies are in this large corridor cavern with two giant circular doors preventing progress. This dead end has a Centurion to tackle, too.

3 Cabal

Psions and Legionaries are expected enemies in the northern part of the narrow access tunnel.

4 Cabal

A Centurion leads the bridge enemies, and the wide expanse of ground makes dropping them from range easier than normal.

Scannable Objects

Clamped to the ceiling, close to the furious Centurion.

A bridge too far? Try the other one.

Campaign Mission

Payback

Around half of this Sector is inaccessible unless Campaign Mission: Payback is underway. In that case, you're trundling through the massive corridors in a Drake tank. This covers Areas of Interest points #3, #4, and #5.

Firebase Hades

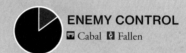

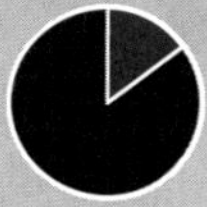

ENEMY CONTROL
Cabal Fallen

Sector Notes:

Adventure: Unsafe at Any Speed | Adventure: Anti Anti-Air | Lost Sectors: 3 | Enemy Clusters: Cabal: 6 | Enemy Clusters: Fallen: 1 | Enemy Chests: Available

Landing Zone: Available | Material Nodes: Available | Patrol Beacons: 8

Public Event (Full): 2 | Public Event (Secret): 4 | Region Chests: 3

Scannable Objects: 4

OVERVIEW MAP

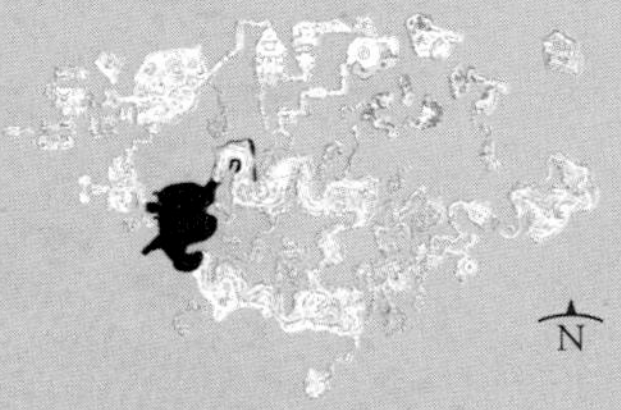

This may be the first evidence of the massive power that the Cabal Red Legion wields on the remains of this planet. A gigantic dish structure has been constructed on the southwestern edge of the EDZ, and all life (including pockets of Fallen foes) has been pushed east into the forest. A large-scale sunken dish arena dominates the ground, with a difficult-to-find entrance into the Legion's Anchor Sector through the west cargo bay, which is above a Lost Sector. There are two other Lost Sectors on the eastern woods, where the remains of the road skirt the base. Northeast is access to the Gulch; southeast is access to Winding Cove. Don't forget the Landing Zone if you need access to the western side of the EDZ.

Areas of Interest

1 Road to The Gulch (Northeast)

Close to the Landing Zone and offering access to the dirt terrain around the northern perimeter of the dish arena, this road eventually takes you to the Gulch. If you don't want to start a battle with the Cabal, stay on this road, heading through the Roads and Woods (East: #7) to the Road to Winding Cove (#8).

2 Firebase Hades Pillar Cargo Bay (North)

A massive pillar so big it comprises a two-level cargo area with a short tunnel underneath. Cabal foes are active in this area.

3 Firebase Hades Pillar Cargo Bay (West)

This is the main cargo bay for this Sector, and it offers access to the Legion's Anchor Sector itself. There are also some ramps to check out: one north and south allowing access through the opening around the perimeter of the arena, and a second north and south ramp heading down to Lost Sector 1. Expect a heavy Cabal presence here.

4 Ducts to Legion's Anchor Sector (Northwest)

Often overlooked, if you wish to investigate deeper into this sprawling Cabal base, find the open hatch tunnel at the western perimeter of the cargo bay. This takes you through some loading ducts and eventually into Legion's Anchor Sector.

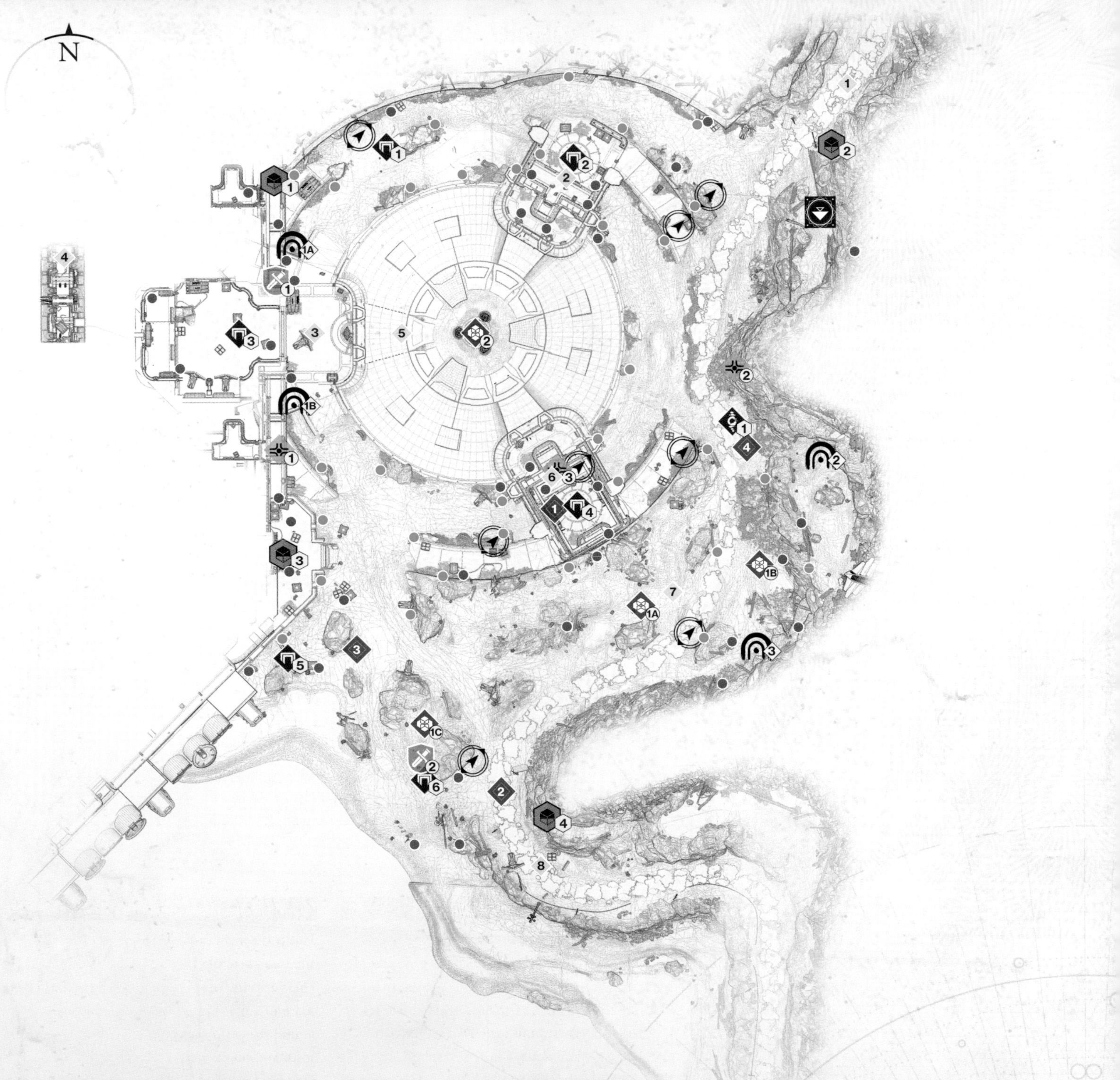

5 Sunken Dish Arena

Think of this as a large circular arena where one of the main Full Public Events takes place. At all other times, use it as a shortcut. You can jump up to either of the north or south dish pillars, too.

6 Firebase Hades Pillar Control Room

The third of the three main dish pillars has a ledge overlooking the arena, accessed via the arena (jump) or an interior control room. Below that is a short access tunnel. As always, Cabal are guarding this area.

7 Road and Woods (East)

Contact with the Fallen occurs along this stretch of ruined roadway, with a number of scorched boulders and trees indicating the deforestation the Cabal completed recently. There are some trees, rocky ledges, and two Lost Sector entrances to find here.

8 Road to Winding Cove (Southeast)

Take this to and from the Winding Cove Sector. West of here is the end of the coastal waters, now set alight from the Cabal's pollutants poisoning the water. Cabal forces roam the nearby dirt beach.

Adventures

1 Unsafe at Any Speed

Begin this adventure just above the Lost Sector ramped entrance, on the western side of the sunken dish arena.

2 Anti Anti-Air

Start this mission on the rocky southeastern shores.

Enemy Clusters

1 Cabal

Legionaries and Psions are roaming the northwestern part of the ground dish arena.

Lost Sectors

The Pit

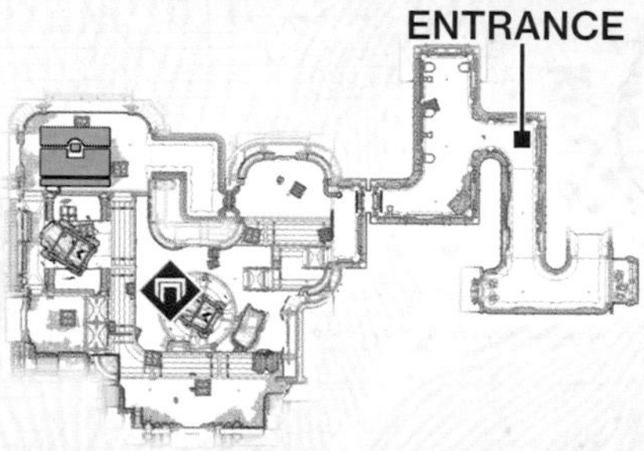

A connecting corridor leads to a large two-tiered storage bay with a number of Cabal infantry threats, led by a Sub-Boss Centurion.

Excavation Site XII

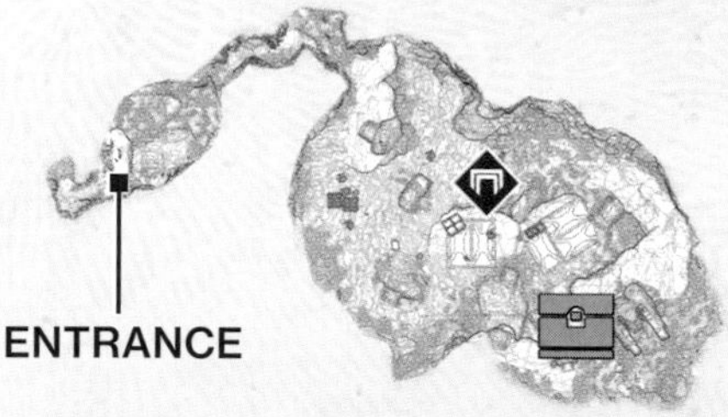

This entrance is on the upper grassy ledge of the eastern wooded area. Inside, you must cross a bottomless chasm (via jumping or the bridge) and face a dozen or so Cabal infantry and a fearsome Sub-Boss Centurion.

Pathfinder's Crash

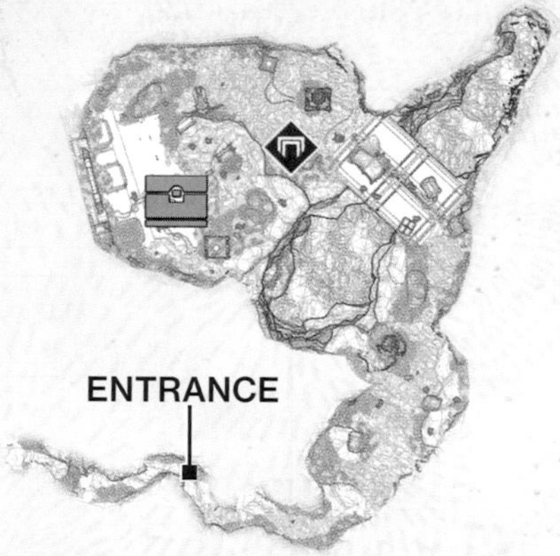

Accessed at ground level on the eastern wooded side of the Sector, this leads to a large cavern with a stream, and Cabal infantry forces led by a Sub-Boss Incendior.

Lost Sectors: Firebase Hades

	Guide Name	Sub-Boss	Reward
1	The Pit	Cabal Centurion	Boss Chest
2	Excavation Site XII	Cabal Centurion	Boss Chest
3	Pathfinder's Crash	Cabal Incendior	Boss Chest

Landing Zones

Firebase Hades LZ

Land your craft here if you wish to proficiently storm the Cabal stronghold, with access to the main port through the Legion's Anchor Sector. You land in the northeastern wooded perimeter of this area.

Patrols

Firebase Hades (8)

Up to eight Patrol locations are available, dotted through this Sector.

2 Cabal

Led by a Centurion, Cabal infantry forces are mainly congregated on the roof of this storage area.

3 Cabal

Cabal infantry, including Phalanxes, Psions, and Legionaries, are inside the western cargo bay (and entrance to Legion's Anchor Sector). Sometimes, a Centurion is present.

4 Cabal

Legionaries and Phalanxes are active, mainly on the ledges and the small tunnel under the control room of the massive pillar.

5 Cabal

Expect minor incursions with Legionaries, Psions, and Phalanxes along the southwest barricaded exterior storage area.

6 Cabal

Legionaries and a Phalanx patrol the burning waters of the southwest perimeter.

1 Fallen

A small Fallen base in the wooded area along the eastern side of Firebase Hades, with Vandals, Shanks, and Dregs to worry about.

Region Chests

1 Region Chest 1

Look up on the south side of the western pillar, by the ramped cargo bay entrance. Jump to a small overhang gantry platform close to the ramp down to Lost Sector 1, and secure a chest up here.

1 Region Chest 2

Farther north along from the Fallen enemy cluster, on the edge of the forested area.

Region Chest 3

Inside the control room pillar. Enter the room with the hologram in the middle of it, then jump up to the upper platform surrounding the room. The chest is in an alcove up here.

Scannable Objects

Tucked away, north of the ramps, near the stack of missiles.

Take time to explore the roadside detritus around the LZ.

What's clamped to the tiny platform above the southwest barriers?

Above the Winding Cove road, nestled at the edge of the trees.

Public Events

Public Events (Full)

Glimmer Extraction: This involves destroying three Fallen extraction sites (1A, 1B, and 1C) dotted around the map.

Servitor Resupply: This takes place below the gigantic dish, in the sunken arena area. There are plenty of Fallen foes to tackle, multiple waves of lesser Servitors, and the usual Cabal crowd to ignore so you aren't overwhelmed.

Event Number	Event Type	Target	Other Enemies	Reward
1	Glimmer Extraction	Fallen Extractors	Fallen forces	Glimmer, Boss Chest
2	Servitor Resupply	Fallen Servitor	Shanks, Dregs, Vandals, Servitors	Boss Chest

Public Events (Secret)

Interceptor and Pike Gang: Destroy these foes to conclude this event.

Skirmish: This is a fight against consecutive waves of Cabal infantry, including some behind the walls and barriers of the southwestern corner of the western base, near the water's edge.

Skirmish: This is a relatively easy massacre, with Fallen dropships mainly depositing Dregs and Vandals onto the grassy ledges on the upper wooded side of the Sector.

Event Number	Event Type	Target	Other Enemies	Reward
1	Interceptor	One Psion pilot	–	The Interceptor if it wasn't destroyed
2	Pike Gang	Three to four Dreg Pike Riders	–	Any Pikes you didn't destroy
3	Skirmish	Cabal dropships (Caution! High-ranking foes!)	–	Random Loot
4	Skirmish	Fallen dropships (Caution! High-ranking foes!)	–	Random Loot

Sunken Isles

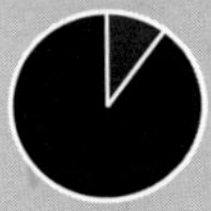

ENEMY CONTROL
Cabal Fallen

OVERVIEW MAP

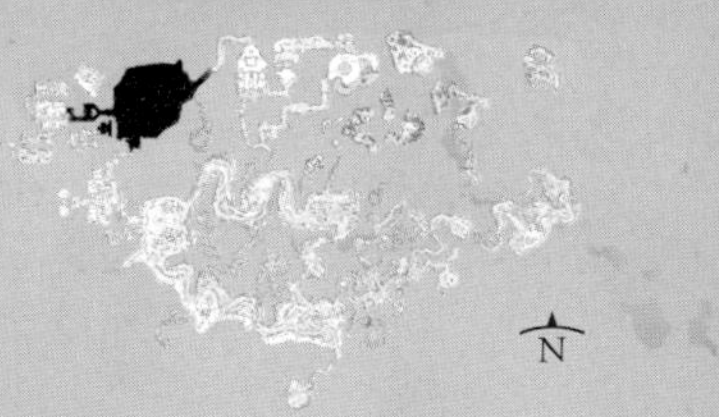

Sector Notes:

Adventure: No Safe Distance | Adventure: Red Legion, Black Oil

Lost Sectors: 2 | Enemy Clusters: Cabal: 10 | Enemy Clusters: Fallen: 1

Enemy Chests: Available | Landing Zone: Available

Material Nodes: Available | Patrol Beacons: 7 | Public Event (Full): 2

Public Event (Secret): 8 | Region Chests: 3 | Scannable Objects: 3

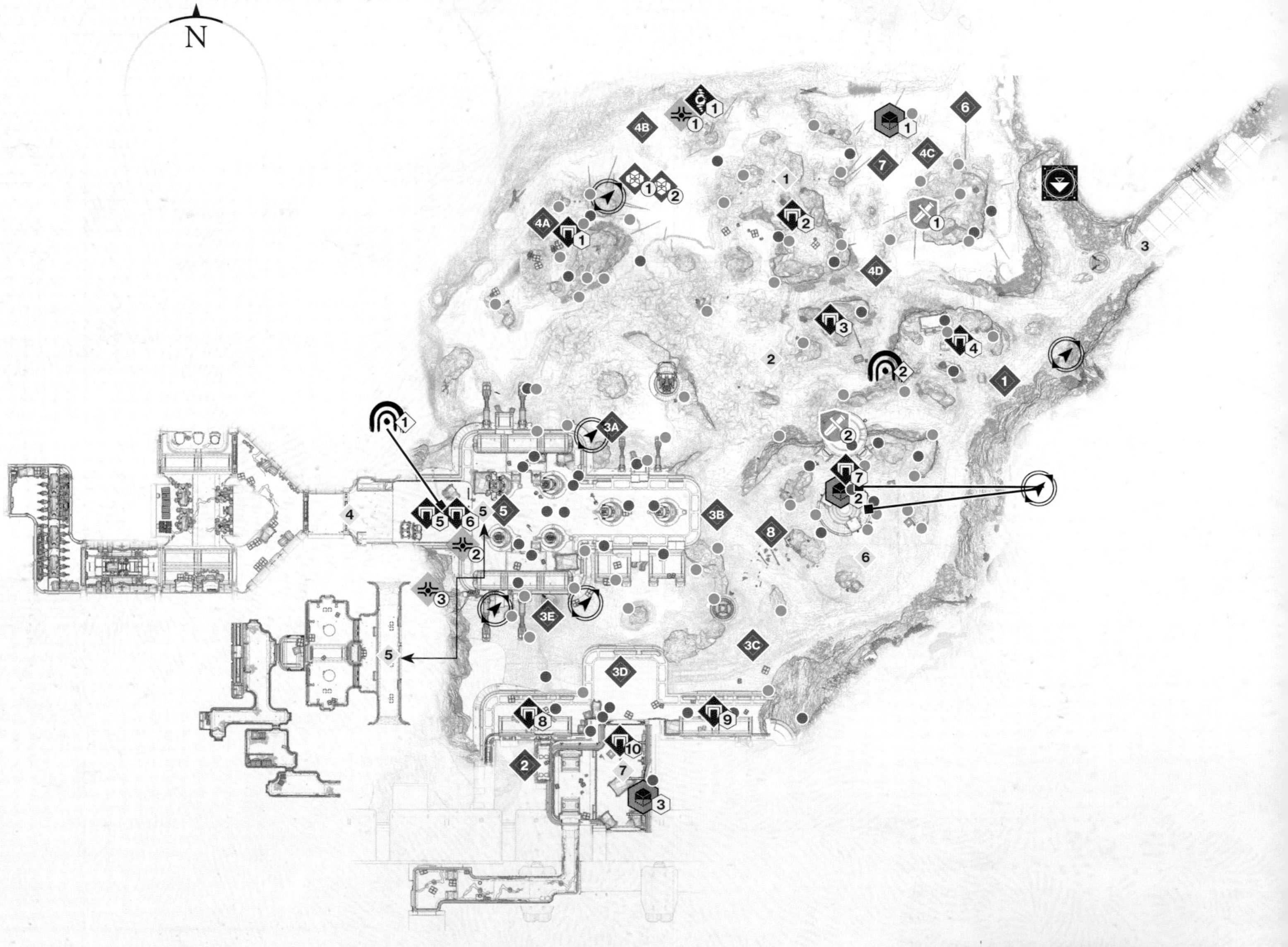

A mighty Red Legion Carrier is docked in this lakefront Sector, on the northwestern edge of the EDZ. This massive ship can be disabled (during Campaign Mission: Payback), but under most other circumstances, it is here to show the immense power the Cabal possesses. The Sunken Isles the Sector is named after are clustered throughout the north and central part of the Sector, close to a northwest access point from the Tunnels. Further south, the Cabal presence is more significantly felt, with the Carrier Bay offering access to the west into the Legion's Hold Sector. Under the bay is a tunnel that leads to a Lost Sector (the other is a rock opening in the eastern part of the outdoors). To the south is a large Cabal structure and cargo bay leading to the aptly named Legion's Anchor Sector, a good way to get back to the Firebase Hades Sector. Finally, note the Landing Zone, if you need to get here in a hurry.

Areas of Interest

1 North Islands

The north perimeter has a line of logs, branches, and reeds to signify that progress beyond this point isn't possible. Instead, inspect the scattered islands for foes and collectibles, and wait for a Public Event in the largest expanse of shallow water.

2 Central Islands

Expect intermittent violence from the various clusters of Cabal that are patrolling the Central Islands, with a circular vehicle route to the north and south.

3 The Tunnels Entrance (Northeast)

This is one way to arrive: take the Tunnels Sector from the Gulch, and you eventually emerge at this point. This is one of two possible exits to other EDZ Sectors.

4 Carrier Bay (Transport) Entrance (West)

Normally accessible during the Campaign and a Strike, this giant ramp is very well-guarded by Cabal. It leads to a dead end (the Legion's Hold Sector).

5 Carrier Bay Tunnel and Lost Sector

This underpass offers quick access to and from the northern and southern parts of this Sector, which is helpful when encountering a foe some distance away. Leap to the Cabal-controlled underground platform along the western side of the tunnel, and you can access an entrance corridor down to one of the Lost Sectors.

6 Control Pod and Landing Pad (Southeast)

A circular landing pad and control pod structure dominate the southeastern exterior of Sunken Isles. Here, Cabal foes are positioned, and a Skirmish may break out. Farther west is the Carrier Bay entrance, along with the south exit from the Carrier Bay Tunnel.

7 Cargo Bay (South)

Always guarded by a variety of Cabal infantry, this sizable cargo bay offers a duct-sized access route back to Legion's Anchor Sector, enabling you to complete a full loop of the EDZ in either direction.

Adventures

1 No Safe Distance

Commence this Adventure by locating the starting point on the northeastern island.

2 Red Legion, Black Oil

This starts when you access the marker under the landing pad, in the central-eastern part of the map.

Lost Sectors

1 Skydock IV

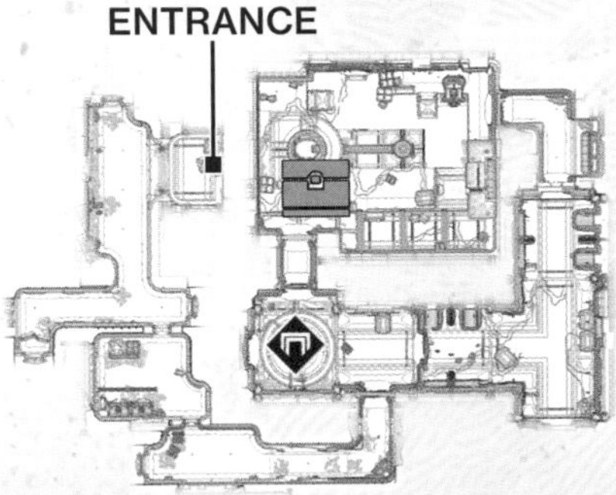

Enter from the Carrier Bay Tunnel. After some corridor navigation, Cabal infantry battling, and a drop down a tube-like hole, you reach a two-tiered generator room that Cabal forces and a Sub-Boss Centurion guard. Note the exit up on the platform level so you don't need to retrace your steps after the Boss Chest is purloined.

2 The Quarry

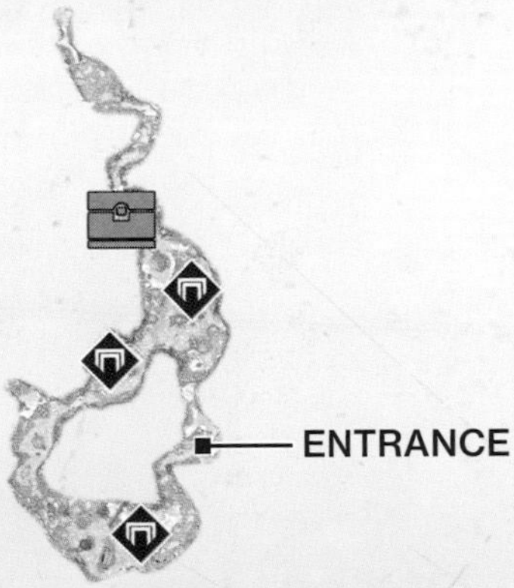

Enter the slit in the rocky outcrop on the east side of the sector, and begin to explore a tunnel that widens into a series of four adjacent caverns. The last of these caverns has a toughened Cabal Centurion and his minions, infantry you've been ridding the caverns of along the way.

Sunken Isles

	Guide Name	Sub-Boss	Reward
1	Skydock IV	Cabal Centurion	Boss Chest
2	The Quarry	Cabal Centurion	Boss Chest

Enemy Clusters

1 Cabal

The northwest island, almost due north of the Carrier Bay Tunnel, is guarded by Psions and Legionaries.

2 Cabal

Legionaries and Incendiors are attempting to maintain domination of the largest inlet island.

3 Cabal

This rocky outcrop (across from the Lost Sector graffiti hint) has Legionaries and usually a Centurion to worry about.

4 Cabal

A rock outcrop above the Lost Sector entrance, with views of the Tunnels entrance and inlet islands, has a few Legionaries and Psions to worry about.

5 Cabal

A fearsome display of power greets you on the Carrier Bay ramp itself, which leads to the Legion's Hold Sector. Expect Legionaries, Phalanxes, Psions, Incendiors, and a possible Centurion incursion.

6 Cabal

Legionaries and Phalanxes are active in the Carrier Bay Tunnel along the raised western side (underground), at the entrance to the Lost Sector.

7 Cabal

The control pod area (with the landing pad and circular construction) houses some minor infantry when a Skirmish isn't active. Expect Legionaries and Psions.

8 Cabal

A small pack of War Beasts roams the right side of the raised entrance into the Cargo Bay when the High-Value Target is active. Note the small T-shaped corridor where the HVT likes to hide. Normally, expect Legionaries and Psions here.

9 Cabal

Legionaries and Psions are behind the crates to the left of the raised entrance into the Cargo Bay.

Cabal

Legionaries and Phalanxes are active in the Carrier Bay Tunne A small group of infantry (Legionaries) guards the Cargo Bay that leads to the Legion's Anchor Sector. l along the raised western side (underground), at the entrance to the Lost Sector.

Fallen

A particularly vicious Vandal with Shanks is guarding a lone Region Chest on a small island along the northern watery border.

Region Chests

Region Chest 1

Sitting on the northernmost island and guarded by a nasty Reaver Vandal with a Shank backup. Don't underestimate this foe!

Region Chest 2

Check the underground entrance to the Lost Sector. On the tunnel platform, the chest is behind some cargo scenery.

Region Chest 3

Difficult to spot, this is lodged at the very back of the rocky terrain to the south side of the main carrier ramp.

Public Events

Public Events (Full)

Injection Rig: The Injection Rig lands at the point shown on the map in the large shallow water area north of the Carrier. Expect a hard fight with a Sub-Boss Psion to defeat multiple times, Gladiators toward the end of the battle, and a Centurion (in addition to normal Cabal forces) during the last wave.

Weapons Exchange: Fallen forces are attempting to attack the North Islands area and have dropped in an Walker. Destroy it, ideally with the Scorch Cannons you can unlock.

	Event Type	Target	Other Enemies	Reward
1	Injection Rig	Psion Sub-Boss	Cabal forces	Boss Chest
2	Weapons Exchange (Walker)	Fallen Walker	Dregs, Vandals, Shanks, Marauders, Captain	Boss Chest

Public Events (Secret)

Ambush: You're attacked by a Sub-Boss Centurion on the outer road.

HVT #1: This is a hiding sub-boss Incendior that sends out his pack of War Beasts before making an appearance. He hides in the small corridor alcove to the north of the main Cargo Bay entrance.

HVT #2: A toughened sub-boss Psion drops in at one of the five marked locations on the guide map (3A, 3B, 3C, 3D, or 3E).

HVT #3: A devious Reaver Captain has landed somewhere in the North Islands. Battle him close to where he appears (4A, 4B, 4C, or 4D).

Interceptor and Pike Gang: These events are both easily concluded by destroying these foes.

Refinery: This involves destroying the single Fallen extraction site shown around the map.

Skirmish: Repel enemy threats in the small hillock of dirt ground between the Cargo Bay (south) and the landing pad hill (northeast). Fallen are landing at the latter location. Expect a steady stream of infantry on both sides, with the most difficult foe being a Centurion.

Event Number	Event Type	Target	Other Enemies	Reward
1	Ambush	Cabal Sub-Boss Centurion	None	Boss Chest
2	HVT (Tactician)	Cabal Sub-Boss Incendior	War Beasts	Boss Chest
3	High-Value Target	Cabal Sub-Boss Psion	None	Boss Chest
4	High-Value Target	Fallen Captain	None	Boss Chest
5	Interceptor Gang	Up to three Psion pilots	–	Interceptors if they weren't destroyed
6	Pike Gang	Three to four Dreg Pike Riders	–	Any Pikes you didn't destroy
7	Refinery	Fallen Extractor	Fallen forces	Glimmer, Boss Chest
8	Skirmish	Cabal ground forces and Fallen dropships	Random Loot	–

Landing Zone

Sunken Isles LZ

This puts you slightly away from the thick of the action, near the dotted islands half-submerged in lake water and close to the Tunnels entrance.

Patrols

Sunken Isles (7)

There are seven Patrol beacons you can access here, though up to four are active at any one time. Once the first are completed, you can return to Sunken Isles to have the other locations appear.

Scannable Objects

A quick wade to a tiny northeastern island is necessary.

Make sure that the circular hut is screened.

This Cargo Bay object needs strong wall clamps.

Legion's Anchor

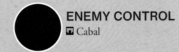

ENEMY CONTROL
Cabal

Sector Notes:

Campaign Mission: Larceny | Enemy Clusters: Cabal: 6 | Partially Inaccessible

Scannable Objects: 1 | Strike: The Arms Dealer

OVERVIEW MAP

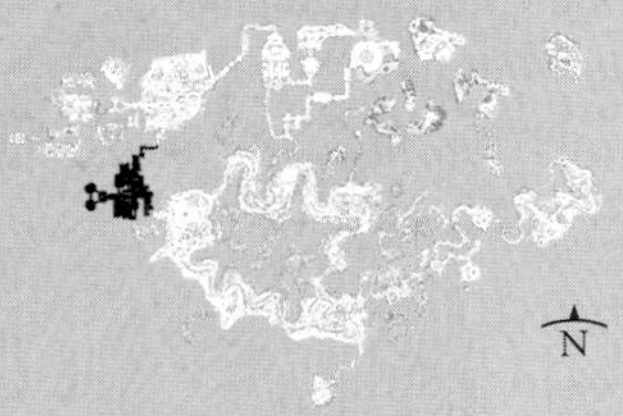

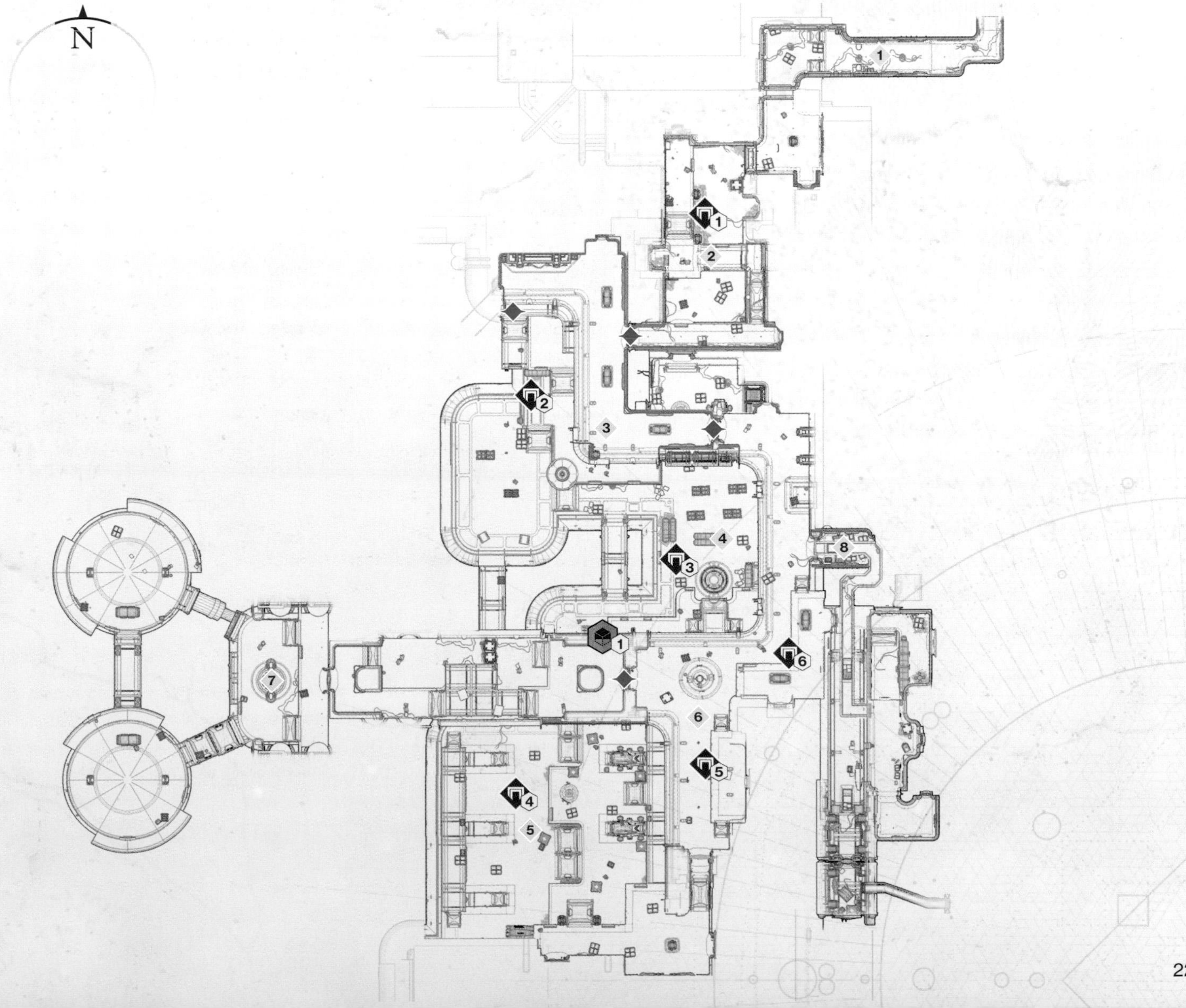

Legion's Anchor is a small Sector that's more of a maze-like thoroughfare, linking Firebase Hades and the Sunken Isles Sectors together. This allows navigation around the entirety of the EDZ. Only some of Legion's Anchor is accessible at all times; some sections are only maneuverable through during a Campaign and Strike Mission. Note the single scannable object as you head through a Cargo Bay, through two exterior yards, and back into a windowed corridor. Small pockets of Cabal resistance are found throughout.

Areas of Interest

1 Corridors to Sunken Isles (Northeast)

Take the Cargo Bay entrance on the southern perimeter of the Sunken Isles, and you end up in this connecting corridor, which leads to a Loading Bay.

2 Loading Bay

This tiered Loading Bay has a bridge and a ledge along its southern perimeter. During Campaign Mission: Larceny, this allows access to a windowed thoroughfare (#3), but a door you can't open blocks it otherwise. Instead, head out of the hangar exit into the exterior area. Legionaries and Psions make up the bulk of the foes stopping your progress.

3 Windowed Thoroughfare (Inaccessible)

This is inaccessible unless a mission is active. A Z-shaped area of windowed corridor provides mission-only access farther south along the thoroughfare, or outside to an exterior ramp area.

4 North Legion's Anchor Docks

A large exterior cargo bay with a Centurion and other scattered foes to face, along with a scannable object to find. Note that the access to the south cargo dock is via the support pillars between the two docks.

5 South Legion's Anchor Docks

Another sizable dock. Don't overlook the exit ramp (to #6), which is in the southwestern raised platform area with an overhang and easily missed. The multi-tiered bay has a few foes to dispatch, including an Incendior.

6 Windowed Thoroughfare (South)

A large upper interior corridor with windows on the eastern side, this has a circular computer hologram terminal in the middle and an (inaccessible) door to the main Cabal Landing Zone.

7 Cabal Landing Zone (Inaccessible)

This is inaccessible unless a mission is active. This long cargo corridor can't be breached. It leads to a Landing Zone with two exterior circular landing pads that are only accessed during the Campaign.

8 Ducts to Firebase Hades (East)

Don't overlook the easily missed exit back into the ducts that take you to the western cargo bay at Firebase Hades.

Scannable Objects

You need to ramp up your investigative capabilities for this item.

Enemy Clusters

1 Cabal

Expect the usual Psions, Legionaries, and a Centurion on the platforms of this tiered Loading Bay.

2 Cabal

The exterior ramped area of the north cargo docks has Legionaries, Phalanxes, and Incendiors to face.

3 Cabal

Expect a Centurion, Psions, Incendiors, and Legionaries dotted around this exterior dock.

4 Cabal

The south loading docks have Legionaries and Incendiors to thwart or avoid.

5 Cabal

Psions and Phalanxes are guarding this windowed corridor section.

6 Cabal

A light Psion presence is patrolling this windowed corridor section.

Campaign Missions

Larceny

The inaccessible areas of this Sector can be maneuvered through during this mission.

Strikes

The Arms Dealer

The mayhem of The Arms Dealer Strike partly takes place in this Sector, though the action soon moves to Sunken Isles, Legion's Hold, and finally, The Arms Dealer itself.

Legion's Hold

ENEMY CONTROL

Cabal

Sector Notes:

Campaign Mission: Unbroken | Enemy Clusters: Cabal: 4 | Partially Inaccessible

Scannable Objects: 1 | Strike Mission: The Arms Dealer

OVERVIEW MAP

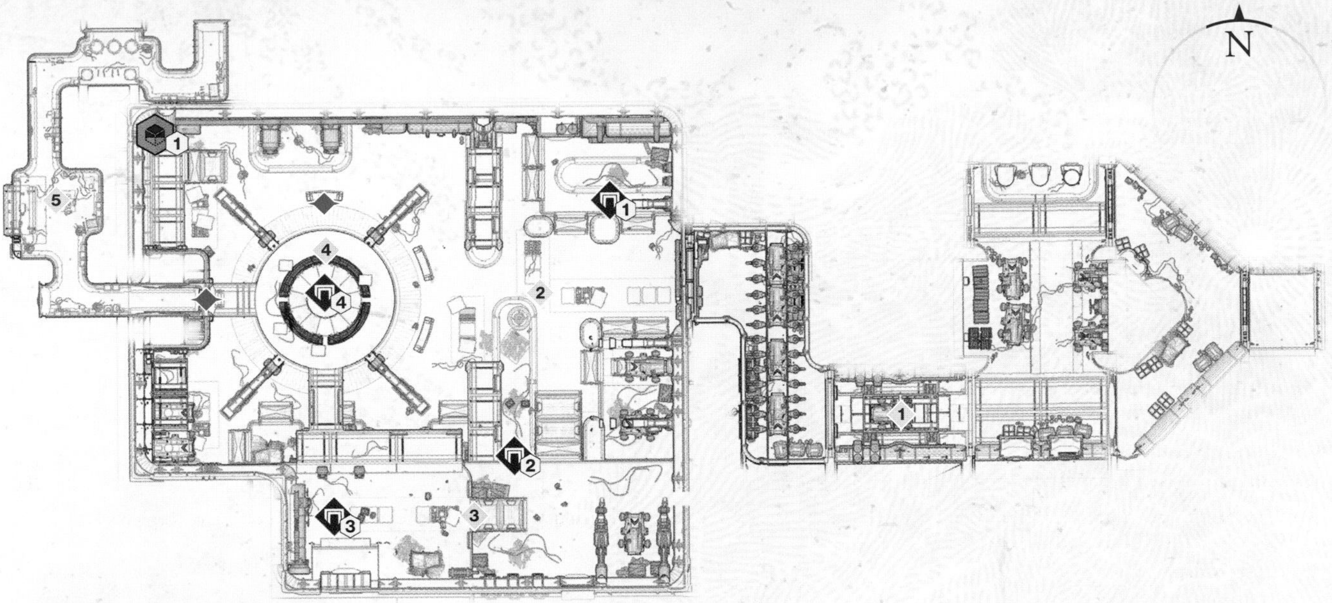

The giant Legion's Hold hangar accessed via the Carrier ramp in Sunken Isles offers an interior to battle through once you've navigated your way through the tank workshop. You must ascend the main hangar up a couple of ramped platform sections to an elevated circular lift. Here, there are two exits, and both are only available in a particular mission (Campaign or Strike). Otherwise, consider this a dead end.

Areas of Interest

1 Tank Workshop (from Sunken Isles)

Take the right diagonal corridor, working your way through a tank maintenance bay and under a hoisted tank until you reach the hangar entrance. This is the only way into and out of Legion's Hold.

2 Main Hangar

This huge hangar has Cabal forces in various locations, and many more to worry about if a mission is active! The area is large, but to progress, you need to work your way in a clockwise manner up the ramped area. Don't forget the scannable object in the far northwest corner.

3 Raised Ramps

You can use the parked tank in the southeast corner as cover. Otherwise, you're exposed as you move up two ramps or leap across to a platform and storm the upper reaches of the hangar.

4 Circular Lift

The door to Legion's Watch is out of reach unless the Campaign Mission is active. Access the gantry to the circular lift platform, and jump up to the Legion's Watch door (above and north of the lift) or head west to The Arms Dealer door (inaccessible).

5 Door to The Arms Dealer (Inaccessible)

This area beyond the door is inaccessible unless the Strike is active. If you're battling through here during a Strike, there is a brief respite as you ascend to the computer-controlled door.

Enemy Clusters

1 Cabal

A small group of Psions and Legionaries patrolling the northwestern corner of the massive hangar.

2 Cabal

Psions and Legionaries are atop the large ramp and the jutting platform.

3 Cabal

The upper platform and control console (mission only) has an Incendior and other foes, depending on where you've previously fought the enemy (they may have intercepted you on the hangar floor).

4 Cabal

The circular platform has a Centurion and underlings (including Phalanxes and Legionaries), who usually drop down to the hangar floor to engage you.

Scannable Objects

One hangar corner has a cylinder you won't want to overlook.

Campaign Missions

Unbroken

Once you enter from the Sunken Isles Sector, you must assault this hangar all the way to the circular lift and up into the access door to Legion's Watch.

Strikes

The Arms Dealer

After storming through Legion's Anchor and the Sunken Isles Sectors, you must assault Legion's Hold before challenging the main Cabal Boss (yet again) on the circular platform lift. Your Strike continues on to face The Arms Dealer.

Legion's Watch

ENEMY CONTROL
Cabal

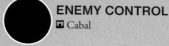

Sector Notes:

Campaign Mission: Unbroken | Usually Inaccessible

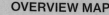

OVERVIEW MAP

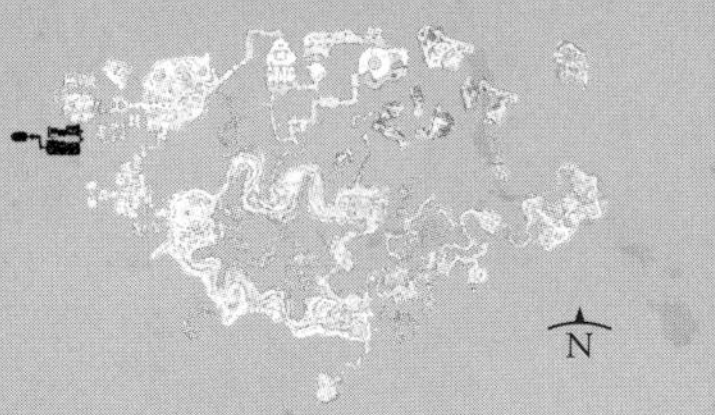

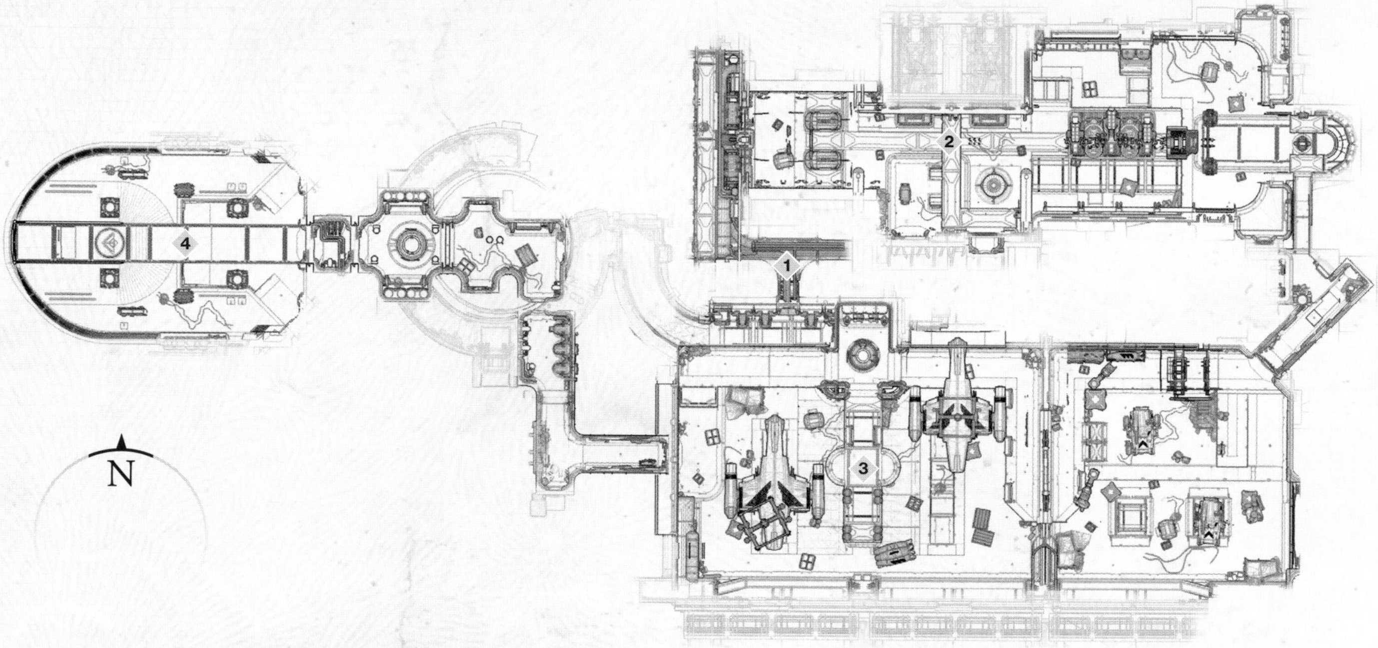

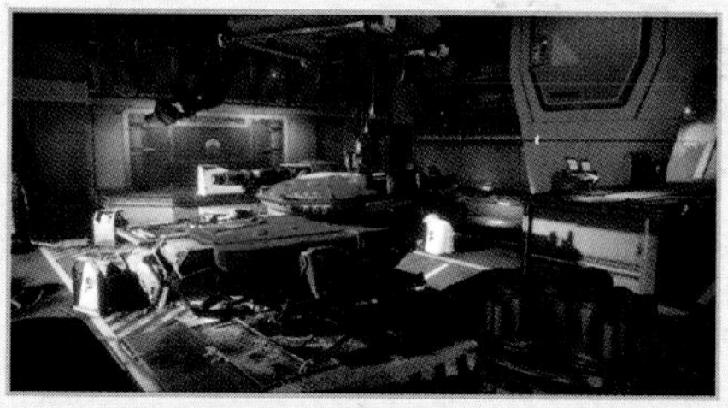

Legion's Watch is an inaccessible Sector that can only be breached during the Campaign Mission: Unbroken. It is entered via a corridor above the circular lift in the Legion's Hold hangar. You must battle a host of Cabal foes as you cross a long Machine Room, through two huge Docking Bays, and through a Bridging Corridor before your final destination: the bridge of Thumos the Unbroken's space craft! Note that the enemies are not listed here; consult the Campaign for the Cabal you're set to face.

Areas of Interest

1 Ducts from Legion's Hold (Inaccessible)

This area is inaccessible unless the mission is active. Head here from the Legion's Hold hangar; it is the only way in or out.

2 Machine Room (Inaccessible)

This area is inaccessible unless the mission is active. It features a long chamber of rotating pistons, Cabal infantry (including some fearsome Gladiators), and a Sub-Boss Incendior at the far end.

3 Docking Bays (Inaccessible)

This area is inaccessible unless the mission is active. Two sprawling Docking Bays have every Cabal infantry type imaginable, as well as plenty of Sub-Bosses. You are fortunate, then, to have additional firepower as Amanda Holliday provides support to your assault.

4 Bridge of Thumos the Unbroken (Inaccessible)

This area is inaccessible unless the mission is active. The bridge of this spacecraft features a high-ranking Cabal commander, whom you must defeat to complete the mission.

Campaign Missions

Unbroken

Legion's Watch is only accessible during this Campaign. Otherwise, it is off-limits and cannot be entered.

Echion Vae

ENEMY CONTROL
Cabal Fallen

OVERVIEW MAP

Sector Notes:

Usually Inaccessible | Strike: The Arms Dealer

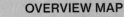

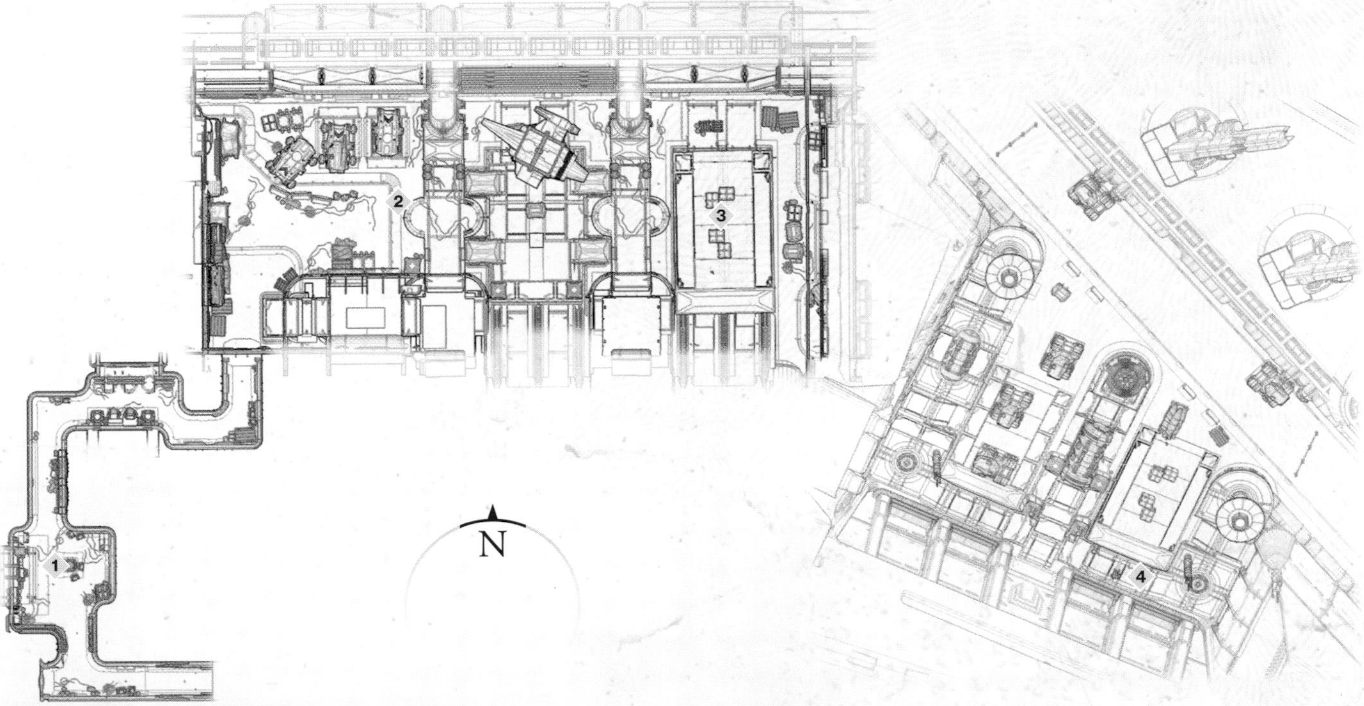

The entirety of Echion Vae is inaccessible unless you're completing the Strike. This is a large-scale loading dock, complete with a small army of Cabal forces led by the ferocious Legionary Boss Valus Zahn. You enter the area via a door on the western side of Legion's Hold, at the circular lift. Once you're through the loading dock, there's a huge winch platform elevator that ascends to a superstructure cargo deck, where the final part of this insane Strike takes place. Note that the enemies are not listed here; consult the Strike for the Cabal you're set to face.

Areas of Interest

1 Corridor from Legion's Hold (Inaccessible)

This location is inaccessible unless the Strike is active. Enter this corridor from the west side of Legion's Hold (via the circular elevated lift where you face Valus Zahn).

2 Loading Dock (Inaccessible)

This location is inaccessible unless the Strike is active. There is a lengthy battle here as you cross over two platforms to the huge platform elevator.

3 Platform Elevator (Inaccessible)

This location is inaccessible unless the Strike is active. Ride this elevator up once you've defeated all of the foes.

4 Superstructure Cargo Deck (Inaccessible)

This location is inaccessible unless the Strike is active. The culmination of the Strike concludes on this exterior deck.

Strikes

The Arms Dealer

Are you ready to deal death to dozens of Cabal forces? This fight takes you all the way from Legion's Anchor, through Sunken Isles and Legion's Hold, and into Echion Vae to defeat the Legionary (and legendary) Cabal boss Valus Zahn.

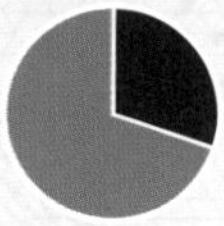

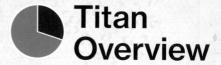

Titan Overview

Enemy Control

FALLEN
HIVE

Orbiting the planet of Saturn and nearly 50% larger than Earth's moon, this planetoid has been colonized somewhat. The choppy methane oceans have been harvested despite the inclement weather conditions, including almost continuous violent storms. Currently, the shipyard is in disrepair, with Fallen incursions but a prelude to the real threats aboard the methane rig platforms and an Arcology facility that was once a luxury residential complex. The Hive are here, and they have clawed deep into this place, secreted their nests around the rusting platforms and chambers, and turned this remote outpost into a festering hellhole.

Progression (Activities)

You access Titan for the first time once you complete Campaign Mission: Combustion in EDZ. This enables you to travel to Titan and begin Campaign Mission: Hope. Once this occurs, you are gradually granted access to more Landing Zones, Sloane, and Adventures, more Campaign Missions, and the World Quest. The Strike is the last activity to be unlocked. As soon as Campaign Mission: Utopia is concluded, you can access Nessus (or head back to EDZ, or continue to explore Titan).

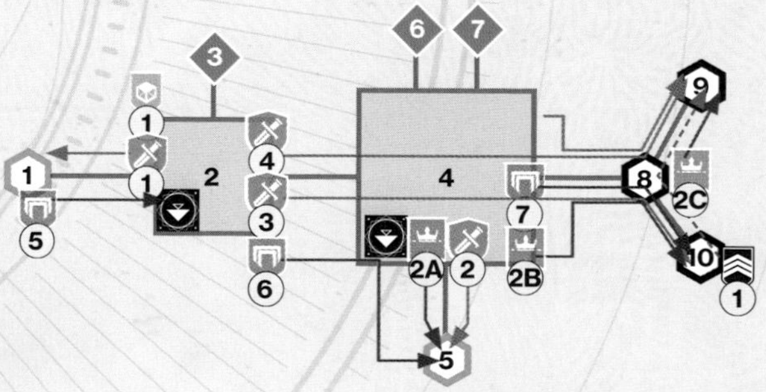

1. Sinking Docks
2. Siren's Watch
3. Methane Flush
4. The Rig
5. Tidal Anchor
6. Cargo Bay 3
7. DS Quarters-2
8. Solarium
9. Arboretum
10. Festering Halls

Legend

- Landing Zone
- Campaign Sector (The Rig Related)
- Campaign Sector (Festering Halls Related)
- Lost Sector
- Public Space
- Campaign: Hope
- Campaign: Riptide
- Campaign: Utopia
- Strike: Savathun's Song
- Adventures: Thief of Thieves
- Adventures: Bad Neighbors
- Adventures: Deathless
- Adventures: Siren Song
- World Quest: Enemy of My Enemy
- World Quest: Data Acquisition
- World Quest: Lighting the Dark
- World Quest: Chances and Choices

Progression

- Campaign: Hope
- Campaign: Riptide
  - Landing Zone (Siren's Watch)
  - Landing Zone (The Rig)
- Sloane
  - Adventures: Thief of Thieves
  - Adventures: Bad Neighbors
- Campaign: Utopia
  - Adventures: Deathless
  - Adventures: Siren Song
  - World Quest: Enemy of My Enemy
  - Strike: Savathun's Song

To Nessus

Titan: Activities

The following table shows the available activities, entities, Side Missions, and other pertinent data for every Sector within this region. Note that some activities (for example, Landing Zones) are not immediately available, but appear through progression.

Name	Type	Adventures	Lost Sectors	Landing Zone	Patrols	Public Events (Full)	Public Events (Secret)
Sinking Docks	Activity (Rig Related)	–	–	–	–	–	–
Siren's Watch	Public	3	1	Available	7	1	4
The Rig	Public	2	2	Available	9	2	4
Tidal Anchor	Activity (Rig Related)	–	–	–	–	–	–
Solarium	Activity (Festering Halls Related)	–	–	–	–	–	–
Festering Halls	Activity (Festering Halls Related)	–	–	–	–	–	–
Arboretum	Activity (Festering Halls Related)	–	–	–	–	–	–
Chasm of Screams	Activity (Festering Halls Related)	–	–	–	–	–	–
Total	2 (Public)	5	3	2	16	3	8

Name	Material Nodes	Enemy Chests	Region Chests	Lost Sector Chests	Scannable Objects	Vendors	Strikes	World Quests
Sinking Docks	Available	–	–	–	5	–	–	–
Siren's Watch	Available	Available	3	1	5	Sloane	–	Available
The Rig	Available	Available	3	2	5	–	Available	–
Tidal Anchor	Available	–	–	–	1	–	–	–
Solarium	Available	–	–	–	1	–	–	–
Festering Halls	Available	–	–	–	3	–	–	–
Arboretum	Available	–	–	–	3	–	–	–
Chasm of Screams	–	–	–	–	–	–	–	–
Total	7 (Sectors)	2 (Sectors)	6	3	23	1	1	1

Sinking Docks

Sector Notes:

ENEMY CONTROL
Hive

Campaign Mission: Hope | Enemy Clusters: Hive: 5

Material Nodes: Available | Scannable Objects: 5

OVERVIEW MAP

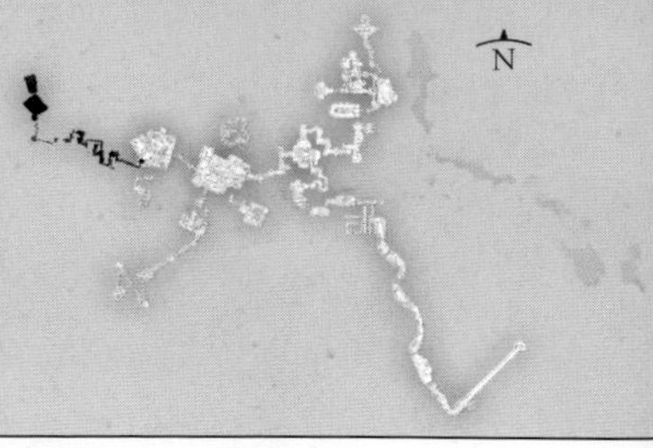

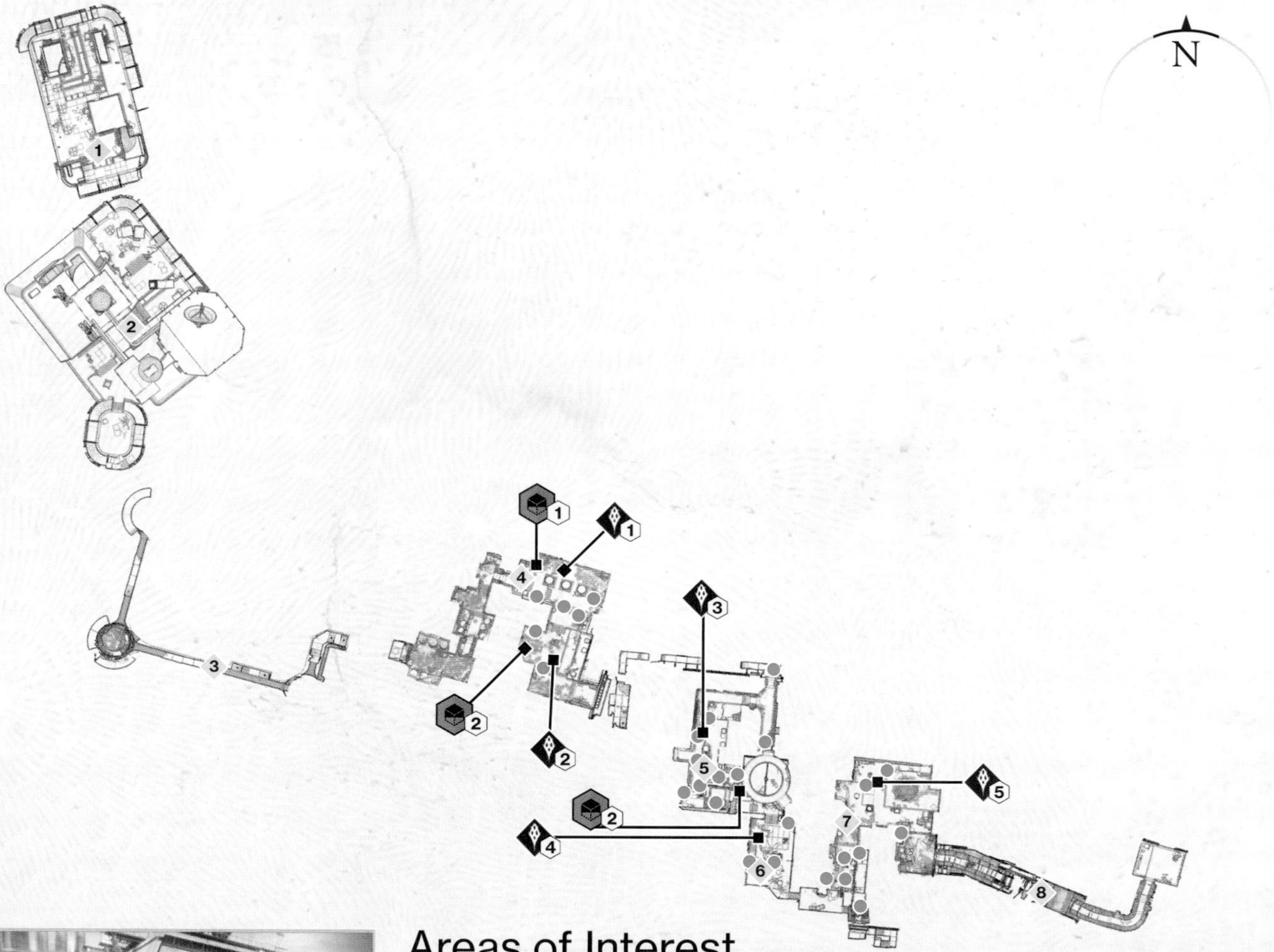

Sinking Docks is the first-seen (but not often explored) initial series of rig superstructures on the seas of Titan. It is the first set of rig islands you must navigate during Campaign Mission: Hope, but once you have secured this moon, there's little need to return here, unless you're hunting for Hive and the three collectible objects. Sinking Docks is then accessed via Siren's Watch, using the alarmingly dilapidated covered bridge.

Areas of Interest

1 Rig: Poelruiter (Entrance)

This is the initial rig you maneuver across during the Campaign Mission. There's nothing but wind and the splash of liquid methane if you return here.

2 Rig: 02 Stormvogel

This is the second main rig to navigate across, with no interiors to access. Though you can reach it after the mission, it is simply a stepping stone.

3 Pipe Platforms

A set of pipe platforms on the underside of an inaccessible rig island allows you to practice your jumping, or die in the process!

4 Rig: Kemphaan

This is the first rig you can enter the interior of, which is a series of small chambers and corridors that the Hive are using as a disgusting nest. There are Thralls, Acolytes, and a Knight to concern yourself with, and limited maneuverability. Don't leave the area without checking the two scannable objects.

5 Rig: Poelruiter (Bay 03 Northwest)

After a series of precise jumps from the Kemphaan rig to the interior door of Poelruiter, you can enter "Bay 03" and battle Acolytes and Thralls in the computer room. This leads to a circular fan you can drop through (it is spinning during the mission and must be shot to deactivate it). There's also a side chamber you can use to maneuver down to the next area, but only if the mission is inactive.

6 Rig: Poelruiter (Bay 03 South)

This exterior of the superstructure is a cargo area with a roaming Wizard and Acolytes to worry about. Note the scannable object (a computer terminal) in the vicinity, along with a precarious gantryway staircase you must carefully climb to reach the last part of this rig.

7 Rig: Poelruiter (Bay 03 East)

A U-shaped cargo bay and site of your first main Hive nest, guarded by Acolytes and a Knight.

8 Covered Bridge to Siren's Watch (East)

Carefully move and leap across the gap in the gantry of this covered bridge, which links the Sinking Docks and Siren's Watch Sectors.

Campaign Missions

Hope

The entirety of this Sector is first navigated from west to east during the Campaign Mission. Afterward, it is fully accessible. That includes a small additional corridor just southwest of the large circular fan, so you can access the western side of this map without trying to ascend between the fan blades.

Enemy Clusters

1 Hive

Expect Acolytes in the darkness of the corridor where the three vertical pipes are located.

2 Hive

A Knight and Acolytes are guarding the scannable object in this cargo area.

3 Hive

Thralls and Cursed Thralls can cause you problems in this enclosed space, so prepare to backpedal to avoid being overwhelmed.

4 Hive

The exterior red gantry features a Hive Wizard and some Acolyte underlings.

5 Hive

A Knight and Acolytes are guarding the nest chamber on the eastern side of the main rig.

Scannable Objects

Is that something strange hanging down in the darkness near those vertical pipes?

Check this small cargo bay for more than just crates.

You'll become a "big fan" of this computer terminal.

Siren's Watch

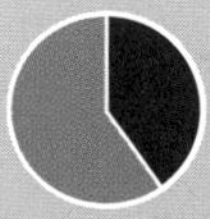

Sector Notes:

Adventure: Thief of Thieves | Lost Sectors: 1 | Enemy Clusters: Fallen: 4
Enemy Clusters: Hive: 4 | Enemy Chests: Available | Landing Zone: Available
Material Nodes: Available | Patrol Beacons: 7 | Public Event (Full): 1
Public Event (Secret): 4 | Region Chests: 3 | Scannable Objects: 5
Vendor: Sloane | World Quest: O Captain

OVERVIEW MAP

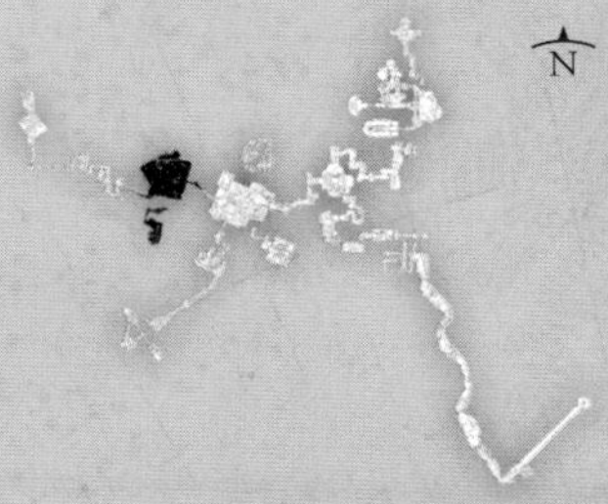

One of the main rigs of Titan, this Sector can be a confusing maze of exterior corridors and interior chambers, as well as Hive infestations and Fallen clusters to deal with. Think of the Sector as having two main levels. There's a "ground" level around a central interior "nest" where the main Hive presence is located. There's also an "upper" level of mainly exterior platforms and rooftops leading to the Command Center (and Sloane the Fleet Tactician) in the northern part of the map, where the Landing Zone is established. But there are still small interiors on the ground level to inspect for collectibles, along with an easily overlooked Lost Sector to find.

Look Up. Look Down. Look Out!

The following map pinpoints Areas of Interest, enemy clusters, and collectibles that may be "under" the visible part of the map that you can see. To ensure that you find the icon in question, check both below and above the indicated location.

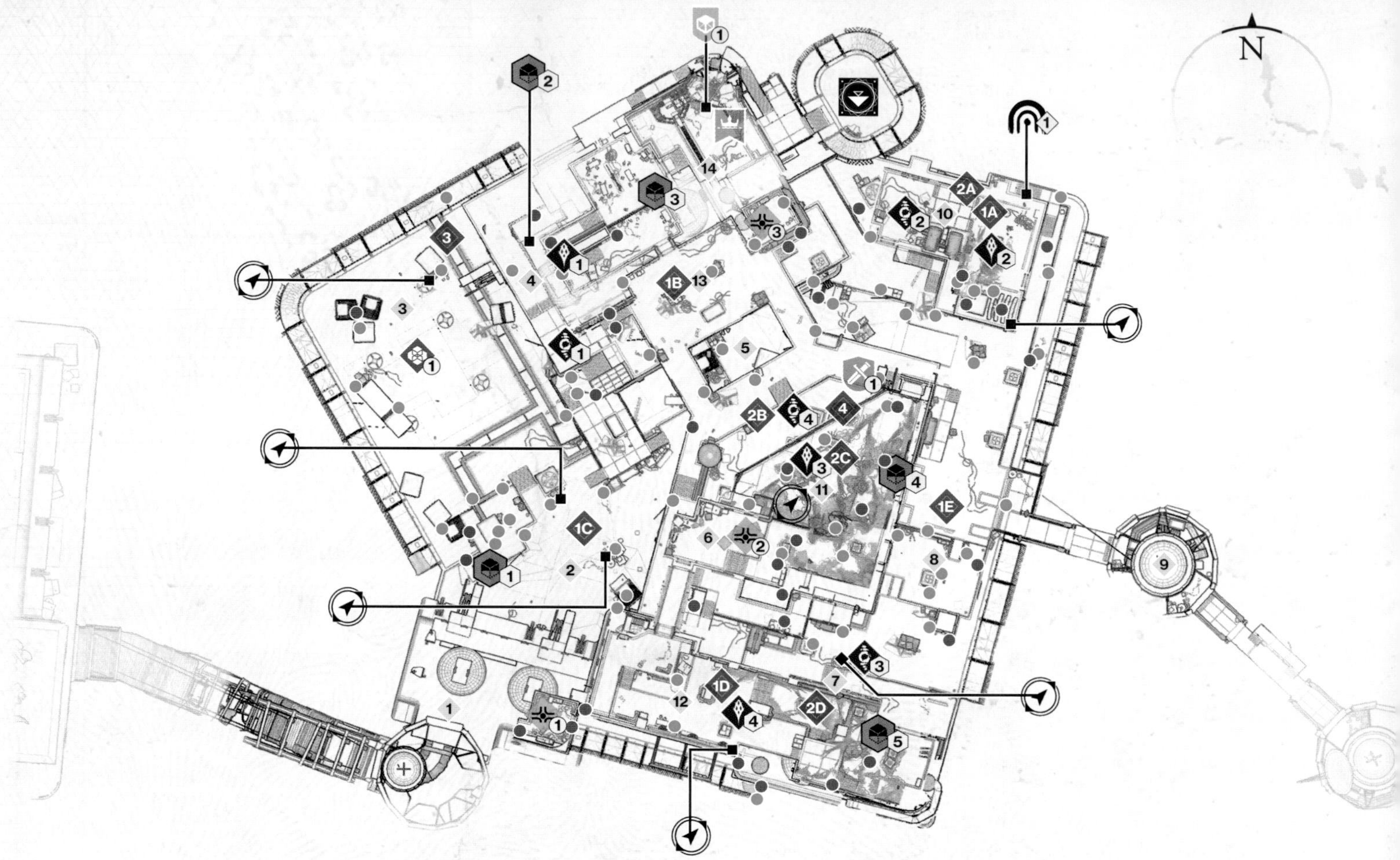

Areas of Interest

1 Bridge to Sinking Docks

The covered yellow tube-like bridge with the worryingly large broken section to jump across allows access back to the Sinking Docks. This is usually the way you enter Siren's Watch for the first time during the Campaign Mission: Hope.

2 Exterior Forecourt

A flat expanse of ground with scattered crates and a number of directions to investigate.

3 Open Cargo Platform (Exterior)

This entire area is completely open to the elements, with dotted cargo containers around the perimeter that you can use for cover, as well as quick access eastward into the Interior Cargo Room.

4 Interior Cargo Room (Ground Floor Interior)

This chamber with two entrances (south to the main cargo thoroughfare (#5) and west to the open cargo platform (#3)) has Acolytes guarding a scannable object. This room layout is not shown on the guide map (it is underneath the staircase you can see on this map).

5 Main Thoroughfare (Exterior)

This area features scattered cargo crates and is the main ground-level exterior route between the forecourt and the northeastern corner of the Sector where Comms Tower 02 (#10) is located. Unlike the Campaign, there are very few foes to thwart your progress, just some Shanks and Dregs at the northeast end of the route. This layout is not fully shown on the guide map (it is underneath the Command Center platform (#13) you can see on this map).

6 Terminal Side Chamber (Interior)

This room is accessed from the outside via the metal steps and low gantry platform and Side Walkway running east to west from Areas of Interest #2 to #7. The wall structure (but not the interior) is shown on the guide map, as it is directly below the Spawn Pod Chamber exit to the Computer Room. Offering quick access into the Spawn Pod Chamber itself, this small room has an even smaller antechamber where the remains of a skeleton clutch a "help" sign. There's a Region Chest up for grabs in here, too.

7 Side Walkway (Exterior)

There is an exterior walkway and a gantry just above it that follow the perimeter of the Spawn Pod Chamber in the middle of this Sector. To the south and upstairs (usually accessed via the Spawn Pod Chamber) is the Computer Room. This room's exit is at the far eastern corner of this area. Expect a few Fallen roaming this area, as it connects to the long stepped area and wraps around to the Comms Tower 02. Note an often-ignored path to a tiny antechamber, where Region Chest #1 is located.

8 Stepped Cargo Area (Exterior)

The eastern edge of this Siren's Watch rig connects from the Side Walkway (to the south; #7) to the Comms Tower 02 (to the north; #10). It offers quick access to the Rig Sector, and it has less traffic than the main thoroughfare (#5).

9 Gantry Towers to The Rig (Exterior)

Head east toward two connected gantry towers, and you access the next Sector on Titan: the Rig. Just look for the two towers between the rig islands.

10 Comms Tower 02 (Exterior and Interior)

This area offers a great deal of investigative opportunities. First, there is a Lost Sector on the northeast gantryway. Second, you can leap to the roof of this area, and then you can jump across heading west, landing on the Command Center exterior platforms (#13). Back at ground level, the entrance to the Spawn Pod Chamber is just south of the Comms Tower. There are also a couple of interior rooms accessed at the east and west sides of the building, with Hive foes inside. Finally, on the western edge of this area, below the LZ platform, is an open door into a tiny room with a Region Chest (#3).

11 Spawn Pod Chamber (Interior)

A mess of Hive secretions, and a mass of Hive activity, this is the central interior chamber of this Sector. It is on three tiered levels and also features a scannable item. Entrances and exits are via the southwest corner (#6), north end (#10), and an upper interior corridor (from #12).

12 Computer Room (Interior)

This links to the Spawn Pod Chamber (#11) and the outside Side Walkway (#7). It features a relatively intact computer room with a light blue floor. Further east, the room dissolves into an orange-lit nightmare of Hive secretions, Thralls, and the Side Walkway exit.

13 Command Room Platform (Exterior)

This relatively flat upper area above the main thoroughfare (#5) features crates, a raised platform to the southeast above the Spawn Pod Chamber, and a number of Fallen foes. It's also the entrance (in the north wall) to the Command Room itself. Access here by the gantry stairs to the southwest, or by jumping from the Comms Tower roof (northeast).

14 Command Room (Interior)

Head up into here to visit Sloane, start the World Quest (from Sloane), and access a scannable object. This northern interior, linked to the exterior LZ, is the highest point on Siren's Watch.

Adventures

1 Thief of Thieves

Access this Adventure on the upper Command Room platform opposite the room door, near some metal steps to the raised area (exterior).

Lost Sectors

1 Methane Flush

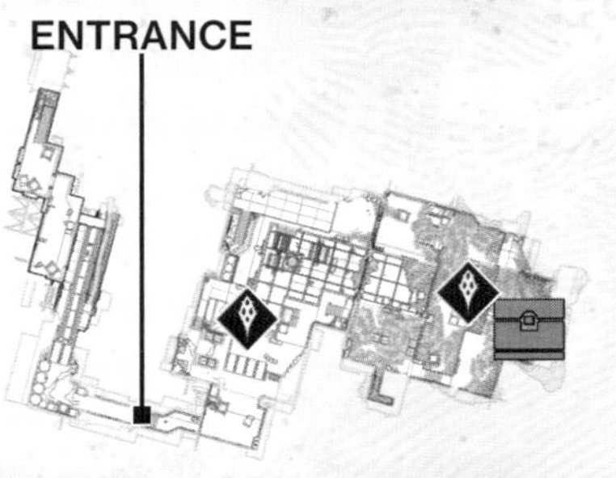

Deeper down in the superstructure of Siren's Watch is a series of storage and cargo bays, partly eaten away by Hive activity. Here, you'll find a large number of foes, including Knights, Acolytes, and two screaming Shriekers. The biggest problem is the Sub-Boss Wizard; he must be stopped before you can claim the chest contents.

Siren's Watch

	Guide Name	Sub-Boss	Reward
1	Methane Flush	Wizard	Boss Chest

Patrols

Siren's Watch (7)

There are six other Patrol beacons you can locate and start a (random) Patrol from. Leave and return to this Sector to reveal additional beacons.

Landing Zones

Available LZ

Once you've completed the Campaign Mission on this Sector (Campaign Mission: Hope), the LZ is established on the platform attached to the Command Center where Sloane is located.

World Quests

1 O Captain

Once certain prerequisites have been made, start this quest spanning the length and breadth of Titan by speaking to Sloane.

Enemy Clusters

1 Fallen

Check the exterior gantry stairs and open cargo platform for Dregs, Shanks, and Vandals.

2 Fallen

Dregs and Shanks are the main problem foes in and around (and on the roof of) the Comms Tower 02. Note that the nearby interior of the tower houses Hive foes.

3 Fallen

The usual Fallen infantry are roaming and sniping along the southeastern Side Walkway and tiered cargo area; expect Dregs and Vandals, along with Shanks.

4 Fallen

Up on the Command Room platform upper level, Vandals and Dregs are the foes to contend with.

1 Hive

The lower chamber to the east of the open cargo platform houses a cluster of Acolytes guarding a scannable object.

2 Hive

Acolytes and a Knight are the problem foes inside the Comms Tower 02 room.

3 Hive

Acolytes and a Hive Wizard are active within the Spawn Pod Chamber.

4 Hive

The Computer Room houses Acolytes and a Knight, with Thralls darting about the eastern secretion-filled area.

Vendors

Sloane

Sloane is the Fleet technician and an impressive ally. She takes any Tokens that you find across Titan. Bring her these in groups of 10, five, or one. In return, you'll receive an increase in your Reputation with her, allowing you to purchase unique Titan armor and weaponry. Sloane also decrypts engrams.

Public Events

Public Events (Full)

Weapons Exchange: Fallen forces are attempting to command the open platform area (west) and have dropped in an Arsenal Walker. Destroy it, ideally with the Scorch Cannons you can unlock.

Event Number	Event Type	Target	Other Enemies	Reward
1	Weapons Exchange (Arsenal Walker)	Fallen Arsenal Walker	Dregs, Vandals, Shanks, Marauders, Captain	Boss Chest

Public Events (Secret)

HVT #1: A toughened Sub-Boss Fallen Captain drops in at one of the five marked locations on the guide map (1A, 1B, 1C, 1D, or 1E).

HVT #2: A devious Sub-Boss Hive Knight has landed somewhere in this Sector. Battle him close to where he appears (2A, 2B, 2C, or 2D).

HVT #3: A Hive Knight summons a horde of Thrall, then lurks in the northeastern corner of the open cargo platform.

Scavengers: When Fallen scavengers arrive at the Spawn Pod Chamber, all hell breaks loose, and you're here to help mop up the mayhem. Expect large numbers of Hive and Fallen foes inside the Spawn Pod Chamber. Two Servitors guard a Fallen treasure chest while attacking nearby Hive. Defeat the Servitors and the chest unlocks.

Event Number	Event Type	Target	Other Enemies	Reward
1	High-Value Target	Fallen Captain	None	Boss Chest
2	High-Value Target	Hive Knight	None	Boss Chest
3	HVT (Tactician)	Hive Knight	Hive Thrall	Boss Chest
4	Scavengers	Spawn Pod Chamber	Fallen and Hive foes	Random Loot

Region Chests

① Region Chest 1

Inside a tiny maintenance room accessed via a U-shaped route down the Side Walkway to the very southern exterior of the Sector.

② Region Chest 2

Inside the Terminal Side Chamber (lower area) off the Spawn Pod Chamber.

③ Region Chest 3

Inside a small maintenance room (just above ground level) accessed from the dead-end path (exterior) just west of the Comms Tower 02 area.

Scannable Objects

An odd little device, perched at the scattered cargo forecourt.

Clamped to a wall, in the least visited room of all.

You can see Sloane from here!

This Servitor shell may have stopped working due to the revolting secretions everywhere.

Take "control" from this location, in the southeast corner.

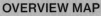

The Rig

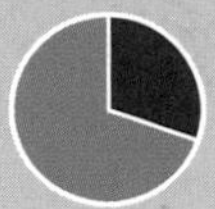

ENEMY CONTROL

Hive Fallen

Sector Notes:

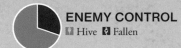

Adventure: Siren Song | Adventure: Bad Neighbors | Adventure: Deathless

Lost Sectors: 2 | Enemy Clusters: Fallen: 3 | Enemy Clusters: Hive: 4

Chests: Available | Landing Zone: Available | Material Nodes: Available

Patrol Beacons: 9 | Public Event (Full): 2 | Public Event (Secret): 4

Region Chests: 3 | Scannable Objects: 5

OVERVIEW MAP

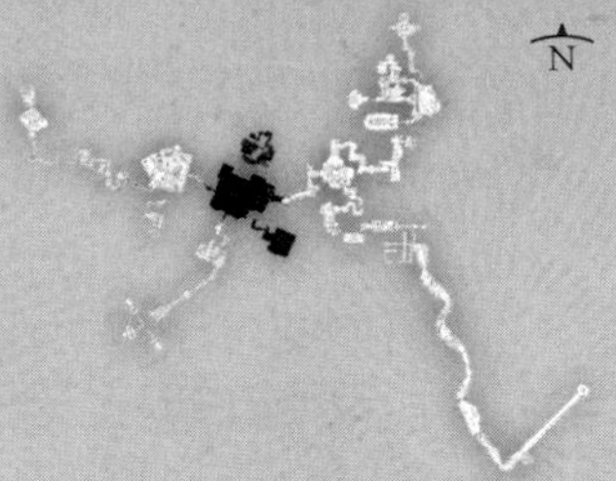

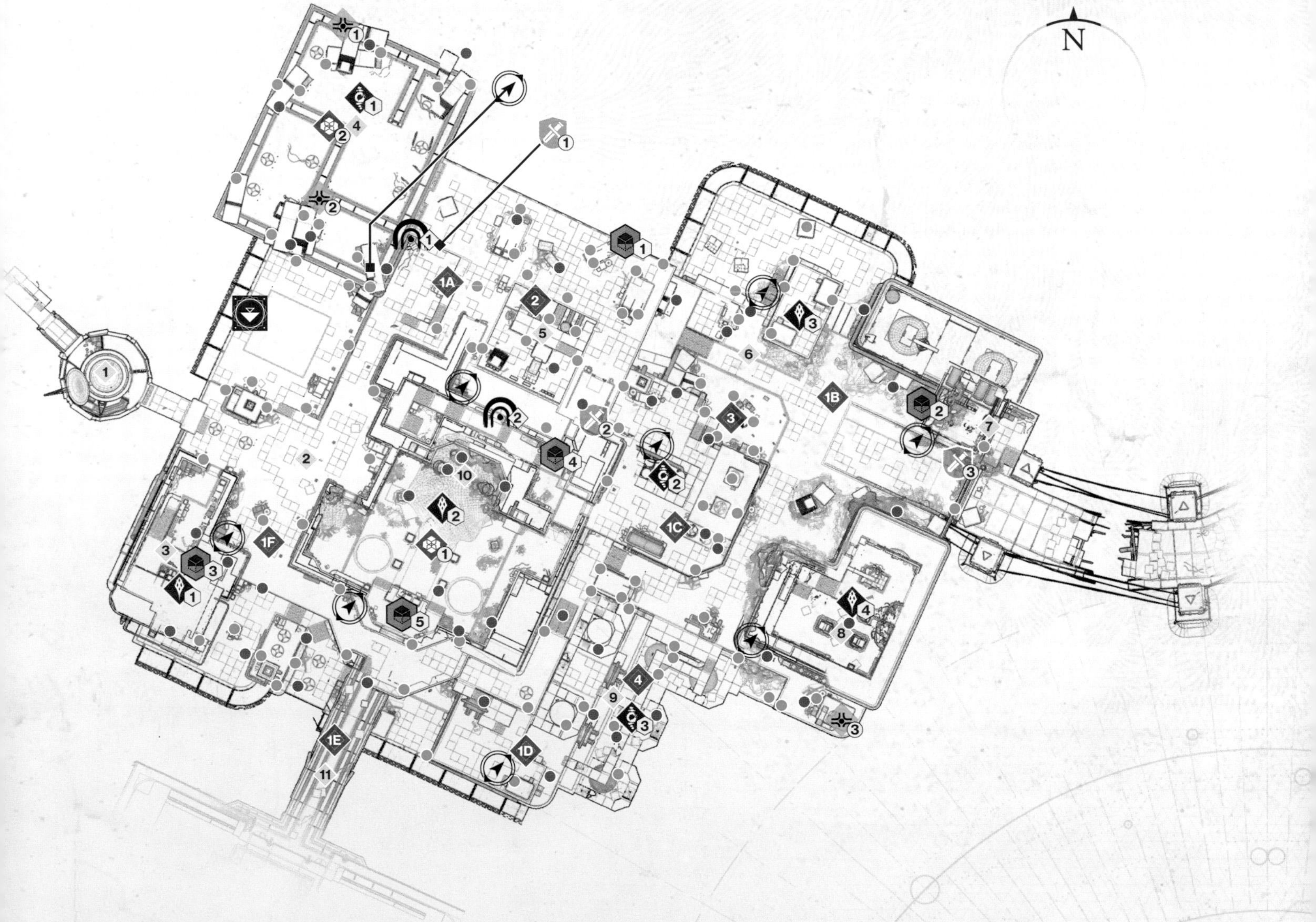

This gigantic platform around a central (and Hive-filled) chamber is the hub of the rig islands on Titan. Here, you can reach the Festering Halls to the east, Siren's Watch and the Sinking Docks to the west, and the Solarium Sector to the south. Recent Hive activity has intensified in the area as incursions from other dimensions threaten both Guardians, and pockets of Fallen also on this rig. Expect a constant battle between both enemy groups as you continue to explore, and watch for some precariously positioned collectibles and entrances.

Areas of Interest

1 Gantry Towers to Siren's Watch (Exterior)

Note the two cylindrical towers marked "01" and "02"; use these landmarks to navigate your way to and from Siren's Watch to the west.

2 West Thoroughfare (Exterior)

This T-junction offers quick access around the perimeter of the Rig Sector to the north decks, the south Computer Room, and Bridge to the Tidal Anchor. Or, use a circular doorway to the southeast to go into the Hive Chamber. You can also head back to Siren's Watch, if you want.

3 Computer Room and Storage (Interior)

A two-floor, L-shaped room with computer banks, scattered storage scenery, and unpleasant Hive foes to slay. This offers an alternate route around the Sector's southwestern perimeter.

4 Upper Deck Platform (Exterior)

This raised deck platform to the north of the Landing Zone offers good hiding potential, especially during the Public Event that sometimes spawns here. Note that the Region Chest and Lost Sector entrance are directly below the platform, requiring some deft jumping to reach them from the northeastern corner of the map.

5 North Thoroughfare (Exterior)

A covered deck running from the Upper Deck Platform (North) to the Northeast Courtyard. Note there's a very narrow lip ledge directly under this thoroughfare, entered via the protruding deck to the northeast, which allows access to a Lost Sector and Region Chest. In the middle of the thoroughfare are metal steps down to a small courtyard, which is usually filled with foes. This offers access to the other Lost Sector, as well as the Hive Chamber (Area of Interest #10).

6 Northeast Courtyard (Exterior)

This open area usually features warring incursions between Hive and Fallen forces, which take place on the exterior of the superstructure. The main north thoroughfare reaches this point, with a long ramp down to the exit bridge to the Solarium Sector (to the east) and a courtyard with a small building to the north (usually with Hive on top of it). The Fallen are swarming around a cluster of fuel tanks and rooftop AC units just south of the Hive.

7 Exit to Solarium Bridge (Interior and Exterior)

Pass the Patrol and Adventure beacons, and weave through a small interior bridge control room to reach a large but partially destroyed bridge that links the Rig to the Solarium (and the Festering Halls). This bridge is used frequently, so note the slightly indirect route through the small room to reach it.

8 Control Room and Storage (Interior)

The eastern perimeter has a small control building that you can enter, offering a respite from the battle raging in the Northeast Courtyard. That is, once you clear this two-room interior of a Knight and Acolytes.

9 Low Gantry Vats (Exterior)

Small cylindrical vats are sitting below some metal gantries in the southeastern part of this Sector. This offers quick jumping access around the perimeter of the map, though there are higher decks and stairs adjacent to this area, too. Expect a modicum of Fallen resistance, with more if a Skirmish is active.

10 Hive Chamber (Interior)

With access doors from all directions (north, south, east, and west), the central chamber is a waterlogged mess of Hive secretions and foes. The room glows orange, and a fearsome rift sometimes opens up, summoning additional foes and deadly Hive Wizards. This is an area to be wary of, but it's one with access to both a Lost Sector and collectibles.

11 Lower South Perimeter and Bridge (Exterior and Interior)

The most obvious landmark here is the bridge (with cargo on it) that links the Rig to a rig to the south (Tidal Anchor Sector). There's also a balcony and access into the Hive Chamber (to the north), along with a lower deck enabling you to quickly head west to east or vice versa. Cross the bridge, and you enter a connecting ramp room and gantry area covered in Hive secretions. Just follow the gantry to the Tidal Anchor.

Patrols

The Rig (9)

There are nine Patrols across the Rig Sector. Once you complete the first set of Patrols, leave here and then return, and more beacons should appear.

Lost Sectors

1 Cargo Bay 3

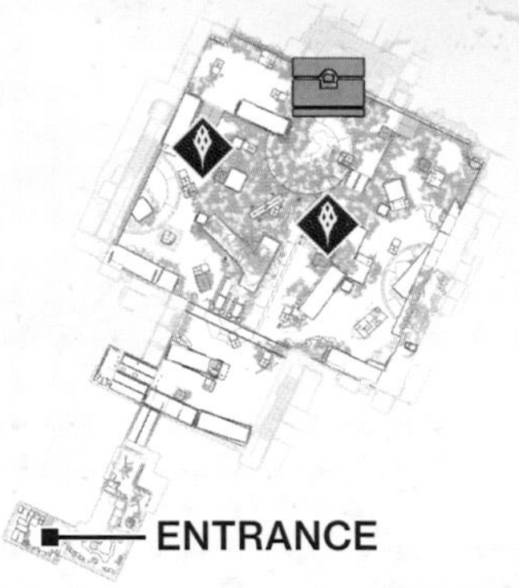

Accessing this entrance is tricky because it's directly below the Upper Deck Platform. It requires you to move around the lip of a very narrow gantry ledge and across to a broken gantry from the jutting lower platform area in the northeast area of the map. Look west to spot the entrance. Don't forget to check the Region Chest just beyond the entrance doorway, continuing along the gantry. Then, head down an interior stairwell to a huge lower cargo bay. You'll need the room to avoid the piercing gaze of Golmuut the Ogre and his Knight and Acolyte minions!

2 DS Quarters-2

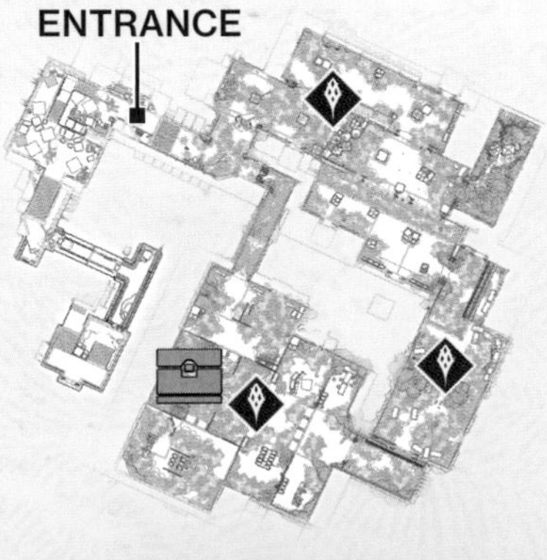

Enter this from the north wall of the main central chamber, accessed via the Hive Chamber itself or the northern thoroughfare (the lower platform area near the metal gantry stairs). After a descent, you reach the frightening, Hive-filled catacombs that used to be Cargo Bay 7 and the main mess hall. Now it's just a mess; wade through the Hive infantry (especially Thralls) to a final confrontation with Thann'Hul, a sub-boss Knight.

The Rig

	Guide Name	Sub-Boss	Reward
1	Cargo Bay 3	Hive Ogre	Boss Chest
2	DS Quarters-2	Hive Knight	Boss Chest

Region Chests

① Region Chest 1

Sat on the edge of a cargo container in the northern corner of the Upper Deck Platform.

② Region Chest 2

Directly below the Upper Deck Platform, through the doorway entrance to Lost Sector #1. Accessed via the Lower Deck Platform to the northeast, northwest of Hive Enemy Cluster #3.

③ Region Chest 3

On top of a small hut building in the northeast corner of the map.

Public Events

Public Events (Full)

Witches' Ritual: Defeat the Wizards as priority targets while capturing the Hex Circles that appear in this chamber. Continue until you face and defeat the Abyssal Sorcerer, a Boss Wizard.

Weapons Exchange: Fallen forces are attempting to bolster the northern cargo deck area and have dropped in an Arsenal Walker. Destroy it, ideally with the Scorch Cannons you can unlock.

Event Number	Event Type	Target	Other Enemies	Reward
1	Witches' Ritual	Boss Ritual Wizard	Sub-Boss Ritual Wizards, Hive infantry	Boss Chest
2	Weapons Exchange (Arsenal Walker)	Fallen Arsenal Walker	Dregs, Vandals, Shanks, Marauders, Captain	Boss Chest

Public Events (Secret)

HVT #1: A toughened sub-boss Fallen Captain drops in at one of the six marked locations on the guide map (1A, 1B, 1C, 1D, 1E, or 1F).

Scavengers (both battles): A Servitor and Fallen infantry appear at the indicated location, bolstering other Fallen foes in the vicinity and attacking Hive (or you, if you're close). Defeat them.

Skirmish: Repel enemy threats in the northern covered cargo deck area near the metal stairs and landing by the entrance to Lost Sector #2. Fallen are landing at the latter location. Expect a steady stream of infantry on both sides.

Skirmish: This takes place on the gas storage gantryway, with Fallen appearing (including Captains) and being repelled by Hive forces (including Knights). Watch or take a stand; it's your call.

Event Number	Event Type	Target	Other Enemies	Reward
1	High-Value Target	Fallen Captain	Dregs, Marauders, Shanks	Boss Chest
2	Scavengers	Sub-Boss Servitor	–	Fallen Infantry Random Loot
3	Scavengers	Sub-Boss Servitor	–	Fallen Infantry Random Loot
4	Skirmish	Fallen and Hive ground forces	–	Random Loot

Enemy Clusters

① Hive

The interior of the L-shaped Computer Room usually has Acolytes and a Knight.

② Hive

There are usually a Knight and several Acolytes in the Hive Chamber, which increases to Wizards, Thralls, and additional Knights and Acolytes if the Public Event is underway. This is the largest concentration of Hive forces in the Sector.

③ Hive

The Northeast Courtyard usually has Acolytes and a Wizard.

④ Hive

Expect a Knight commanding a small squad of Acolytes inside the interior of this command and storage room.

① Fallen

The high deck platform has your expected cluster of Fallen infantry: Dregs, Vandals, and Shanks are active.

② Fallen

Expect Dregs and Vandals to be battling across the courtyard against the Hive.

③ Fallen

Several Vandals and Dregs are likely to be roaming the vat gantries, and many more arrive if a Skirmish is underway.

Scannable Objects

Something scannable is sitting at the edge of this open cargo container.

Check the wall-mounted terminal near the Lost Sector entrance, off the Hive Wizards' lair.

What's this among the revolting secretions, close to that Adventure marker?

Something roughly ball-shaped is slowly rusting, near the bridge.

Dodge the Hive as you "monitor" an interior wall in a two-tiered room.

Adventures

1 Siren Song

Access this from the end of an upper deck thoroughfare, in the northern part of the Sector.

2 Bad Neighbors

This is positioned by a wall, just east of the northern thoroughfare, on the upper level by the fuel tank cluster.

3 Deathless

This is at the bottom of the courtyard ramp, by the exit room to the bridge to Solarium.

Landing Zones

The Rig LZ

Instant access to this Sector is available from Orbit; you land on the cargo deck just north of the entrance from Siren's Watch.

Tidal Anchor

ENEMY CONTROL
Hive

Sector Notes:

Campaign Mission: Riptide | Enemy Clusters: Hive: 3 | Material Nodes: Available
Partially Inaccessible | Scannable Objects: 1

OVERVIEW MAP

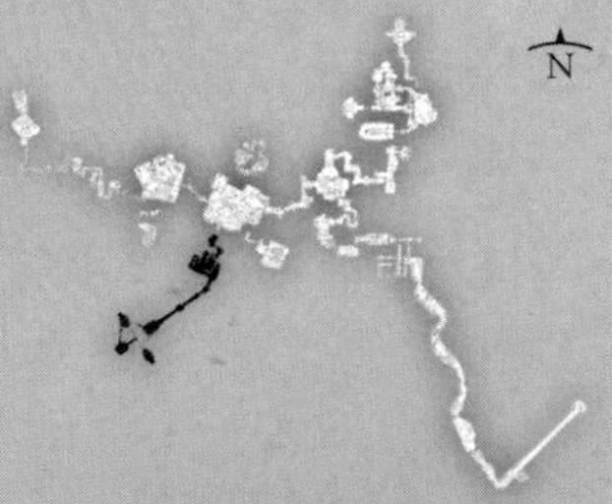

The rig where you first begin exploring this Sector is informally known as the "Sunburst" rig. It's named for the insignia on the exterior walls of the structure as you cross from the southern bridge of the Rig Sector (the only way in and out). The Hive presence is strong here, with secretion-filled corridors and a Wave Converter Control Room you can interact with (mission only). There's a lower Machine Corridor leading to a sealed pair of doors. Further investigations are only possible during the mission. Head outside to a red-colored deck before maneuvering across two connected bridges and towers and two Converter Towers (which must be fixed during the mission), after which there's a tricky rooftop battle on Tower 02. At all other times, this is a place to hone your Hive-culling talents.

Enemy Clusters

1 Hive

The Wave Converter Control Room has a Knight and Acolytes close to the windowed area.

2 Hive

Expect Acolytes on the stairwell area.

3 Hive

Acolytes, Thralls, and a Wizard are your main concerns along the lower windowed Machine Room.

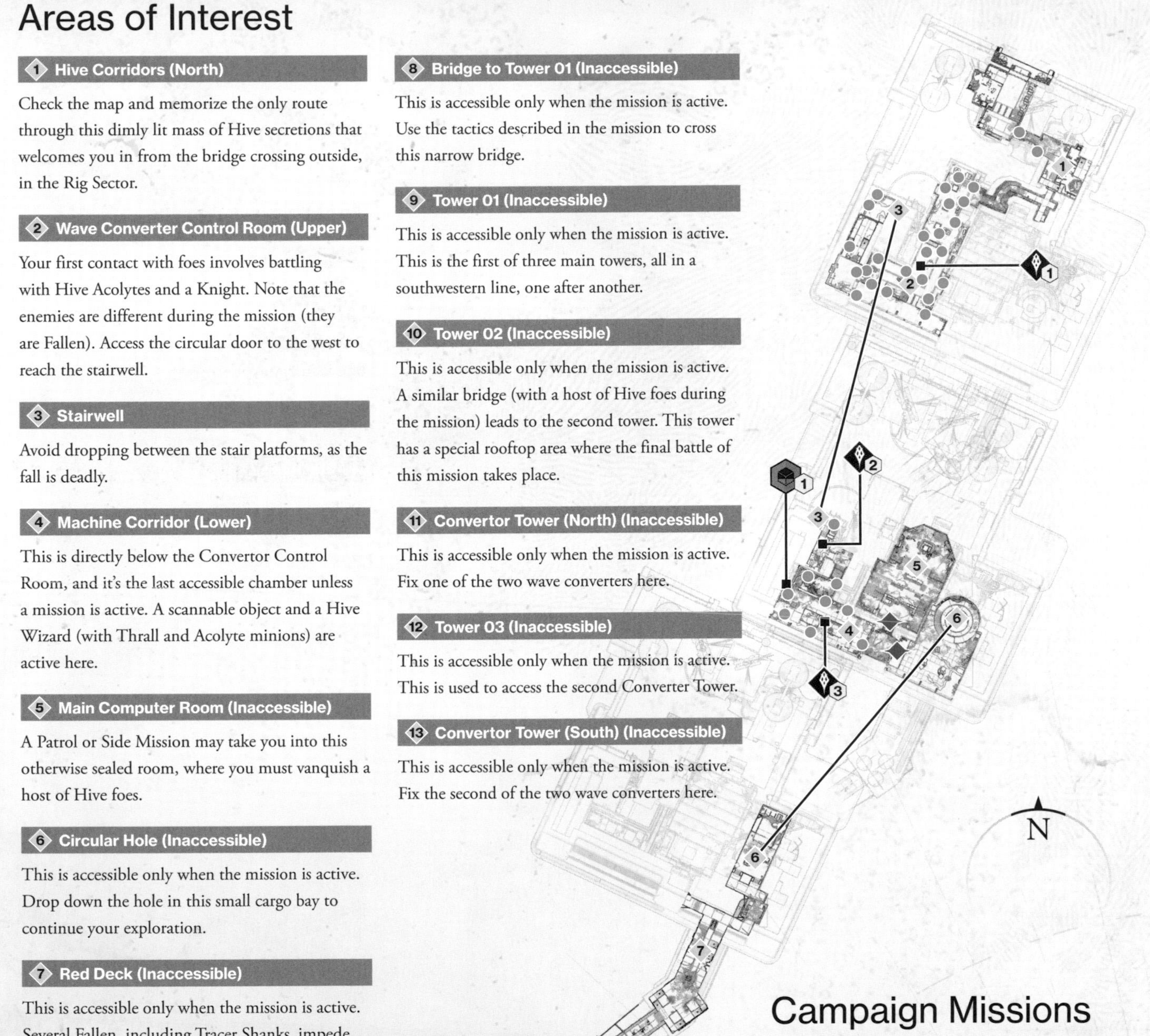

Areas of Interest

1 Hive Corridors (North)

Check the map and memorize the only route through this dimly lit mass of Hive secretions that welcomes you in from the bridge crossing outside, in the Rig Sector.

2 Wave Converter Control Room (Upper)

Your first contact with foes involves battling with Hive Acolytes and a Knight. Note that the enemies are different during the mission (they are Fallen). Access the circular door to the west to reach the stairwell.

3 Stairwell

Avoid dropping between the stair platforms, as the fall is deadly.

4 Machine Corridor (Lower)

This is directly below the Convertor Control Room, and it's the last accessible chamber unless a mission is active. A scannable object and a Hive Wizard (with Thrall and Acolyte minions) are active here.

5 Main Computer Room (Inaccessible)

A Patrol or Side Mission may take you into this otherwise sealed room, where you must vanquish a host of Hive foes.

6 Circular Hole (Inaccessible)

This is accessible only when the mission is active. Drop down the hole in this small cargo bay to continue your exploration.

7 Red Deck (Inaccessible)

This is accessible only when the mission is active. Several Fallen, including Tracer Shanks, impede your progress during the mission.

8 Bridge to Tower 01 (Inaccessible)

This is accessible only when the mission is active. Use the tactics described in the mission to cross this narrow bridge.

9 Tower 01 (Inaccessible)

This is accessible only when the mission is active. This is the first of three main towers, all in a southwestern line, one after another.

10 Tower 02 (Inaccessible)

This is accessible only when the mission is active. A similar bridge (with a host of Hive foes during the mission) leads to the second tower. This tower has a special rooftop area where the final battle of this mission takes place.

11 Convertor Tower (North) (Inaccessible)

This is accessible only when the mission is active. Fix one of the two wave converters here.

12 Tower 03 (Inaccessible)

This is accessible only when the mission is active. This is used to access the second Converter Tower.

13 Convertor Tower (South) (Inaccessible)

This is accessible only when the mission is active. Fix the second of the two wave converters here.

Campaign Missions

Riptide

The majority of this Sector is inaccessible unless this Campaign Mission is active. Note that enemy types in accessible chambers are different during the mission, too.

Scannable Objects

"Wrap up" your searching for this strange item of lore.

Solarium

ENEMY CONTROL
Hive Fallen

OVERVIEW MAP

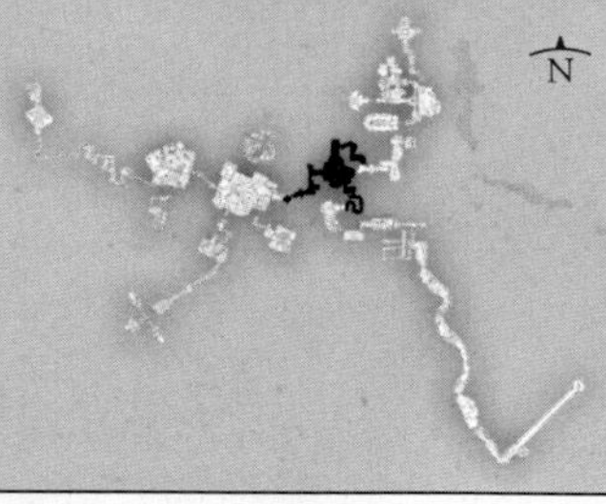

Sector Notes:

Enemy Clusters: Hive: 3 | Material Nodes: Available | Scannable Objects: 1

A botanist's dream, this experiment into growing plant life on Titan can be seen as a sterling success, though there are no humans around and nature has been allowed to run rampant. The main lobby forecourt of this tourist attraction, with a waterlogged sunken central area, acts as a hub allowing you to progress either to the Arboretum (north) or Festering Halls areas (south). Both locations are spawning grounds for Hive forces. Head deeper into either of these other Sectors to discover greater danger. Aside from clearing Hive forces, this area is used as a pass-through point during missions (usually Campaign and Strike-related), where there are more Fallen active in the vicinity.

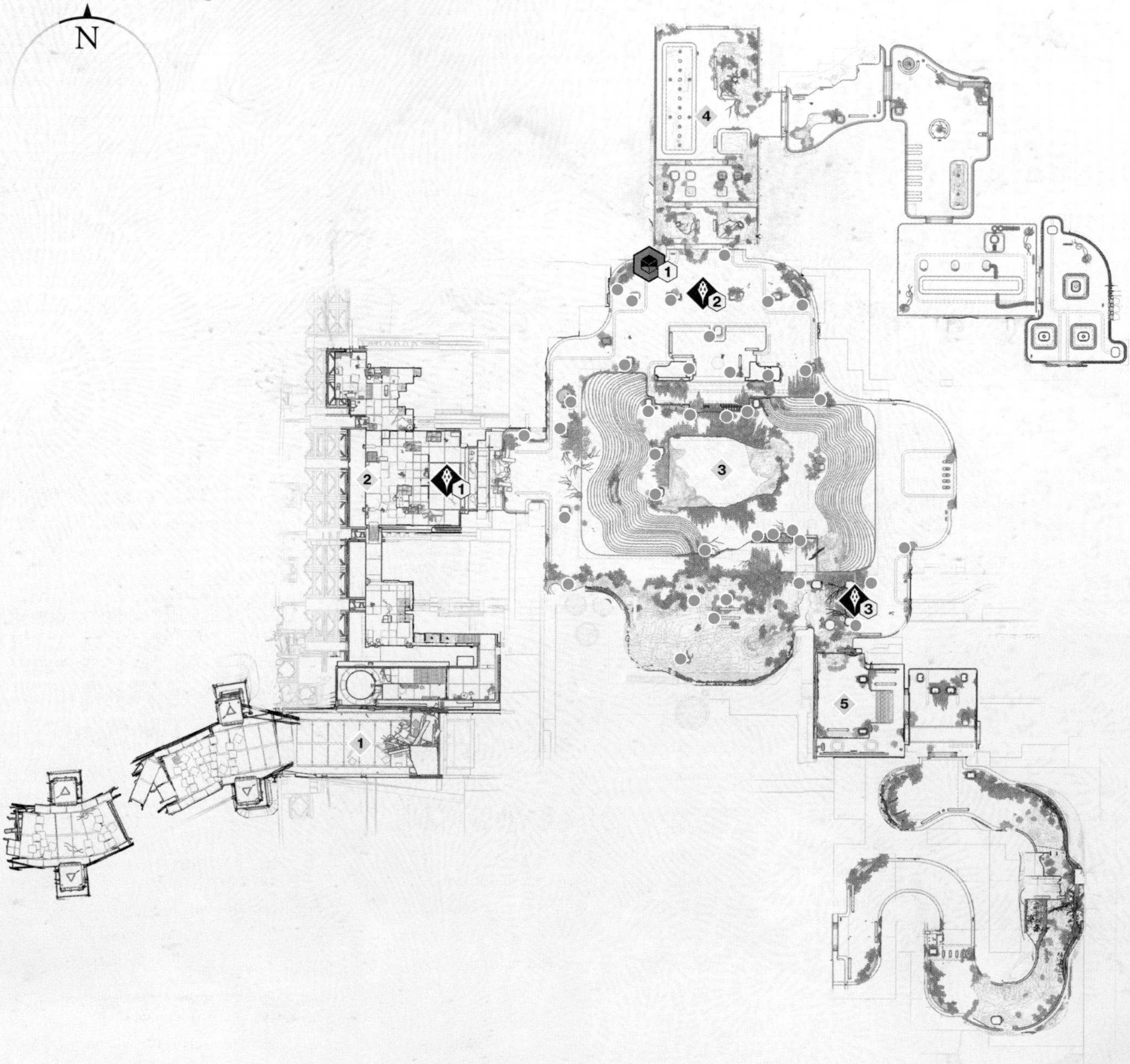

Areas of Interest

1 Exit to The Rig

This is where you first explore from. Head in from the west, proceeding east across the badly damaged exterior bridge to reach a cargo bay and gantry stairs.

2 Gantry Platforms

The drops around the sides of these platforms can't be survived, so bear this in mind when leaping around. A fissure in the LED lighting wall (part of a giant monitor) allows access into the main lobby area.

3 Forecourt and Lobby

This huge central section features a sunken central area, now waterlogged. To the north is a relatively clean entrance to the Arboretum. South is a jungle of plant and Hive life, as well as access to the Festering Halls Sector itself.

4 Arboretum Entrance (North)

Note the vivid green color and the displays of plant life at the entrance to the Arboretum; use this to situate yourself so you don't head in the wrong direction.

5 Festering Halls Entrance (South)

This is much more overgrown, with a subsequent large corridor that winds down to the Festering Halls after a turnstile.

Enemy Clusters

1 Hive

Acolytes led by a Knight are guarding the gantryway platforms that lead to the LED opening into the main part of this Sector. Note that during missions, Fallen are usually operating in this area.

2 Hive

The left (northern) doorway into the green-lit arboretum features a small group of Acolytes. Bring your best weaponry, and make that group even smaller.

3 Hive

A few Acolytes are milling around near the southwest exit of the main forecourt.

Scannable Objects

It's worth "monitoring" the situation at this point.

Festering Halls

ENEMY CONTROL
Hive

OVERVIEW MAP

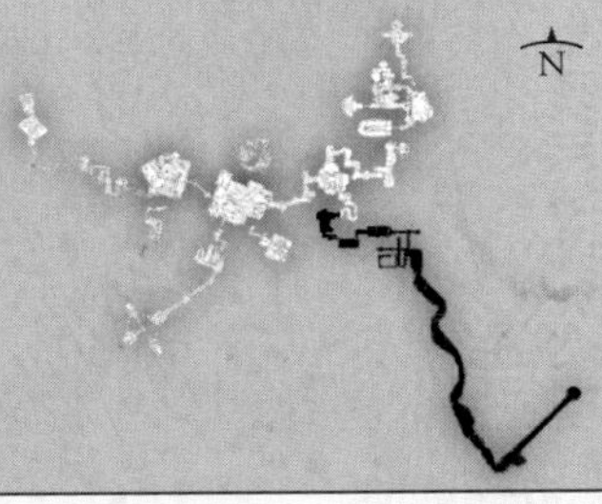

Sector Notes:

Campaign Mission: Utopia | Enemy Clusters: Hive: 3 | Material Nodes: Available
Partially Inaccessible | Scannable Objects: 3

Seen as an example of harmonious design of man and nature, this facility is now an overgrown, dilapidated mess of Hive secretions, nests, and flooded hallways. Navigating your way through here requires quick reflexes because the lights and power are mostly out, and the Hive presence is always there. Negotiate to the flooded eastern side of the main hall, and your progress is halted. A barrier prevents progress down an elevator shaft to the long descent down ducts and service passageways to an APC hangar and a vehicular escape.

Areas of Interest

1 Forecourts and Lobby (from Solarium)

An overgrown mass of vegetation clashes with Hive secretions. Several Hive foes are active in this sunken forecourt, with steps up to a lobby that ends in a hole down to the lower corridor.

2 Lower Corridor

The darkness can be a problem because the foes here can quickly swarm you, so take extra care when exploring this area. If you're here and haven't found the scannable objects, you've explored too far.

3 Main Hall

This crusty Hive hub has a Wizard and Acolytes to worry about. There's a raised walkway across the middle of the room (where you fight Knights during the mission only) and a water-filled eastern area where an Ogre appears. Normal exploration stops at this point.

4 Elevator Shaft (Inaccessible)

This area is accessible only if the mission is active. To progress deeper into this Sector, navigate a series of narrow vertical drops.

5 Descent (Inaccessible)

This area is accessible only if the mission is active. Explore ductwork and service passageways.

6 Core Chamber (Inaccessible)

This area is accessible only if the mission is active. The core itself is a fusion ball you carry out of here to a waiting APC.

7 APC Hangar (Inaccessible)

This area is accessible only if the mission is active. Choose an APC, and use it to drive your way out of the massive Hive tunnels under the facility.

8 Landing Pad (Inaccessible)

This area is accessible only if the mission is active. Amanda Holliday picks you up from this point to conclude the mission.

Campaign Mission

Utopia

An attack on this Hive base takes place during the aforementioned Campaign Mission. Note the increased Hive presence and full access to all chambers, including a vehicular escape.

Enemy Clusters

1 Hive

Expect Acolytes and possibly a Knight in the initial overgrown lobby chambers.

2 Hive

Acolytes clutter up the darkness of the lower corridor.

3 Hive

The main hall houses a number of Acolytes under the watchful gaze of a Wizard. Note that the enemy types are different during the mission.

Scannable Objects

Monitor the situation from this object, in the sunken entrance chamber.

Something sharp is protruding near this overgrown sign.

No entry to this door, but what's in front of it?

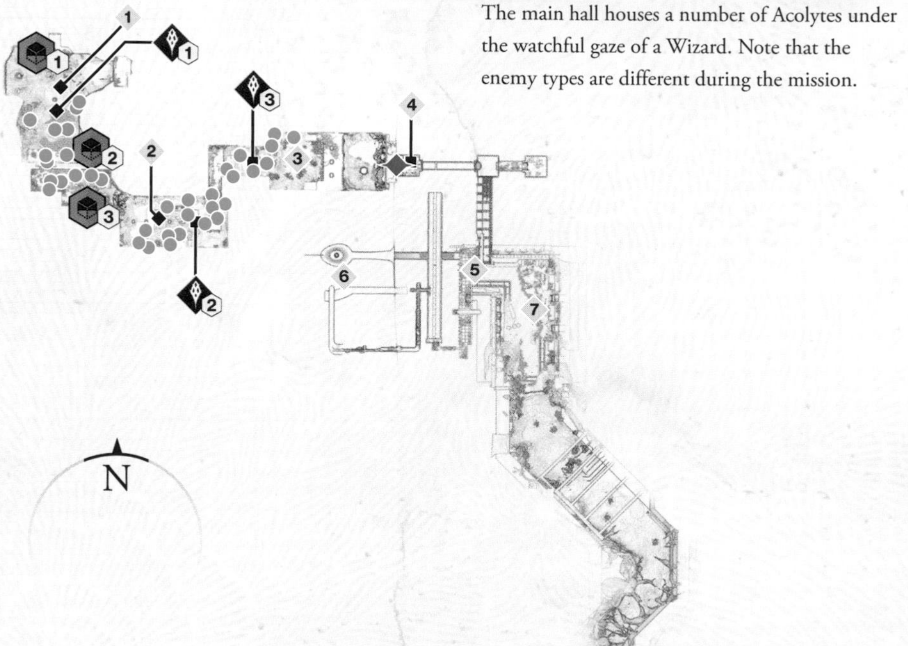
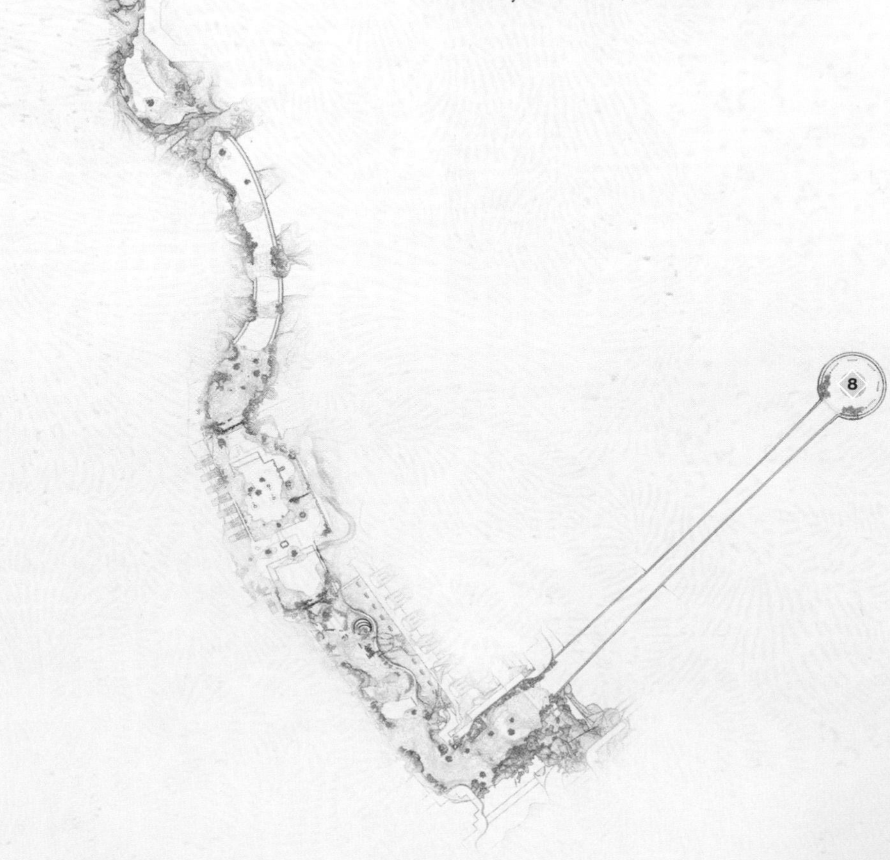

Arboretum

ENEMY CONTROL
Hive

Sector Notes:

Enemy Clusters: Hive: 1 | Material Nodes: Available | Partially Inaccessible

Scannable Objects: 3 | Strike Mission: Savathûn's Song

OVERVIEW MAP

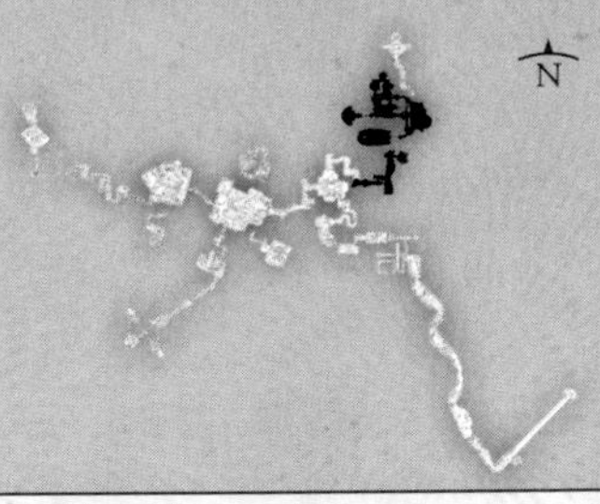

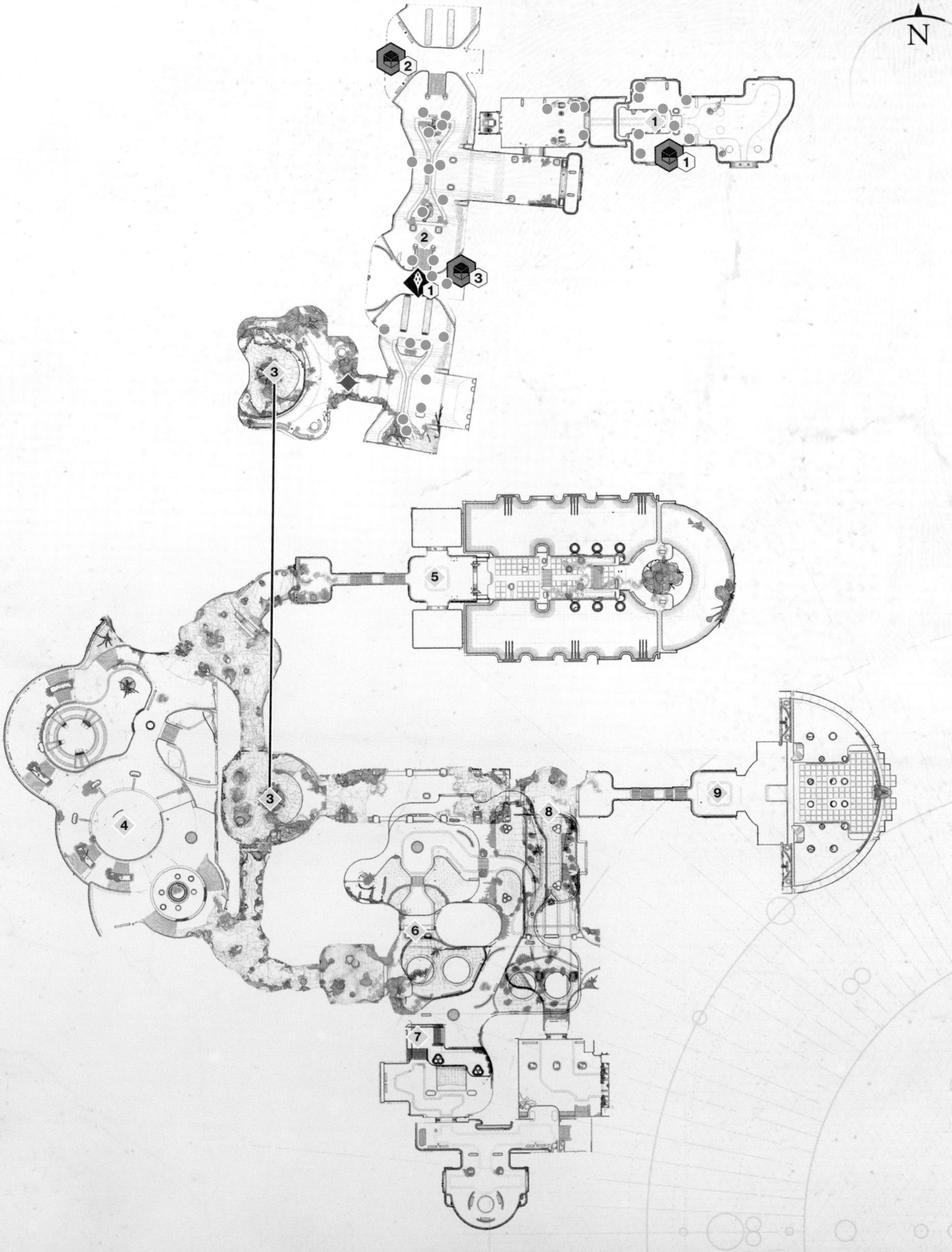

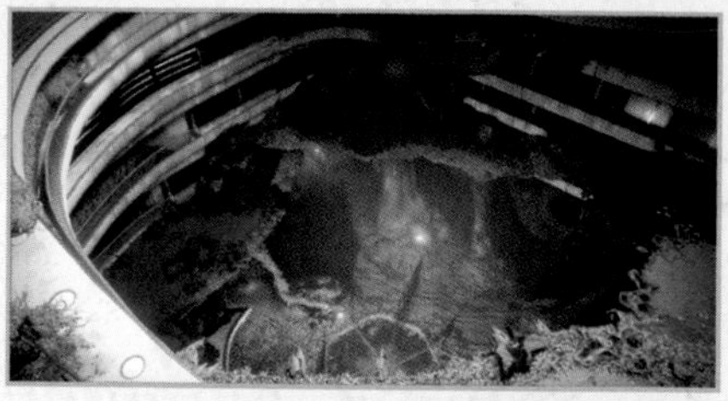

The main mezzanines and vast hallways showing the plant life that could grow on Titan have been left to fester. Now the Hive forces have spread through these hallways like a virus. Accessed from Solarium, most of this Sector (aside from some initial hallways) is inaccessible unless the Strike: Savathûn's Song is active. Should this occur, you have a massive number of Hive foes to tackle, including Wizards and Ogres, as you battle through the various chambers of Arboretum, destroying strange Hive crystals as you go. Only then can you drop down into the Chasm of Screams, where you face the biggest Hive foe. Under normal conditions, spend time here locating scannable objects and honing your Hive-culling talents. Note that one of the locations (the Reactor Core) is only available during the World Quest: Enemy of My Enemy.

Areas of Interest

1 Exit to Solarium (North)

Several smooth-floored and relatively clean corridors are accessible should you venture here from the Solarium. A scattering of Hive foes and a scannable object are likely in this area.

2 Main Hall

A long and impressive main hallway with a giant pink-colored LED wall visible as you arrive and look left (south). Look out, as the place is teeming with Hive (even more so during the Strike). Come here to clear the area, and progress no farther if the Strike is active.

3 The Pit to Chasm of Screams (Inaccessible)

This is inaccessible unless the Strike is active. This is the central hub to the lower expansive part of this Sector. The only way to reach the Chasm of Screams (during the Strike) is by destroying the chained crystal. Note the north and south Hive tunnels and the main corridor to the east.

4 Bio Dome Mezzanine (Inaccessible)

This is inaccessible unless the Strike is active. This huge, impressive series of open-air platforms is filled with Hive foes during the Strike.

5 Crystal Chamber (Inaccessible)

This is inaccessible unless the Strike is active. Accessed after negotiating your way through the Bio Dome Mezzanine, this dead-end platform is bathed in reddish light, with a large crystal at one end. As always, plenty of Hive are here.

6 Interior Mezzanine Entrance (Inaccessible)

This is inaccessible unless the Strike is active. Enter the area after maneuvering through the Hive tunnel on the south side of the Pit.

7 Lower Mezzanine Entrance (Inaccessible)

This is inaccessible unless the Strike is active. After fighting the Hive across the Interior Mezzanine, there's a lower area connected to the Main Corridors. Once again, Hive foes are plentiful.

8 Main Corridors (Inaccessible)

This is inaccessible unless the Strike is active. A large L-shaped corridor section leads from the Lower Mezzanine back to the Pit. Note that the reactor room to the east is inaccessible, even during the Strike.

9 Reactor Core (Inaccessible)

This is inaccessible unless the World Quest is active. Reaching this reactor chamber is the culmination of the World Quest on Titan. Face down a Fallen Captain, and complete the mission. This is the only time this chamber is accessible.

Scannable Objects

Check the terminal at the exit back to the Solarium Sector.

All signs (well, arrows, at least) point to this wall circuit.

Keep "monitoring" the situation in the main hall.

Strikes

Savathûn's Song

Almost the entirety of Arboretum opens up during this Strike. You'll encounter a huge number of Hive foes, including Wizards and Ogres, which are simply a prelude to the really nasty foes deeper down in the Chasm of Screams!

Chasm of Screams

Sector Notes:

Usually Inaccessible | Strike Mission: Savathûn's Song

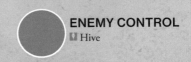

ENEMY CONTROL
Hive

OVERVIEW MAP

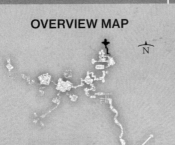

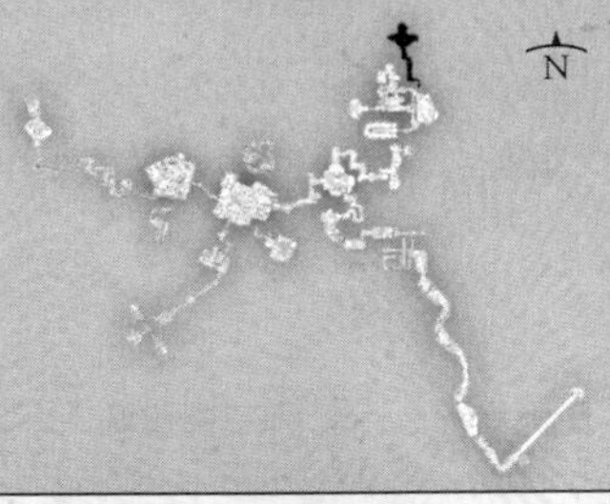

Beneath the Arboretum are several connected burrow-like tunnels that the Hive have constructed. They lead to a large ledge-like chamber where the main host of Hive on this planetoid reside under the watchful and terrible gaze of the Dark Heart. Head here to conclude the Strike: Savathûn's Song. Otherwise, this is not an accessible area.

Areas of Interest

1 Hive Burrows (Inaccessible)

This is inaccessible unless the Strike is active. The ground of the Pit in the central part of the Arboretum falls away once a crystal is destroyed, allowing you to progress through a series of revolting, secretion-filled Hive burrows.

2 Chamber of the Dark Heart (Inaccessible)

This is inaccessible unless the Strike is active. The epicenter of Hive activity on Titan, this large ledge has been extensively burrowed. It's also the place where the Dark Heart (a giant Shrieker) resides. Conclude your Strike here.

Strikes

Savathûn's Song

Battle through Arboretum to finish your Strike at the Chasm of Screams, and face the terrible eye of the Dark Heart itself. Beware of Ogres! This is the only time the Chasm of Screams is accessible.

Overview

Enemy Control

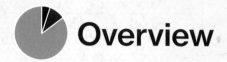

- CABAL
- FALLEN
- VEX

A minor Centaur planet changed into a machine planetoid by the Vex, the Red Legion have recently landed on this world, ostensibly to start an impressively large strip-mining operation. Vex entities were subsequently awoken to this invasion, and the region is now overrun with Vex forces, who are adeptly battling the remnants of the Cabal and some rag-tag Fallen exploratory forces also on the world. Nessus would be strange and wonderful to explore, with breathtaking block-like architecture, massive lakes of white fluid, and grand vistas. There are interior Sectors that offer a glimpse into the very core of this planet. But the architecture is swarming with Vex, the water is deadly Radiolarian Fluid, and the grand vistas lead to deadly drops.

Progression (Activities)

You begin your investigation of this world at the start of Campaign Mission: Looped, when you arrive at Artifact's Edge. Aside from the mission, you can optionally complete a variety of activities, including an exploration, Adventures, and a World Quest. The following flowchart details the activities and their progression.

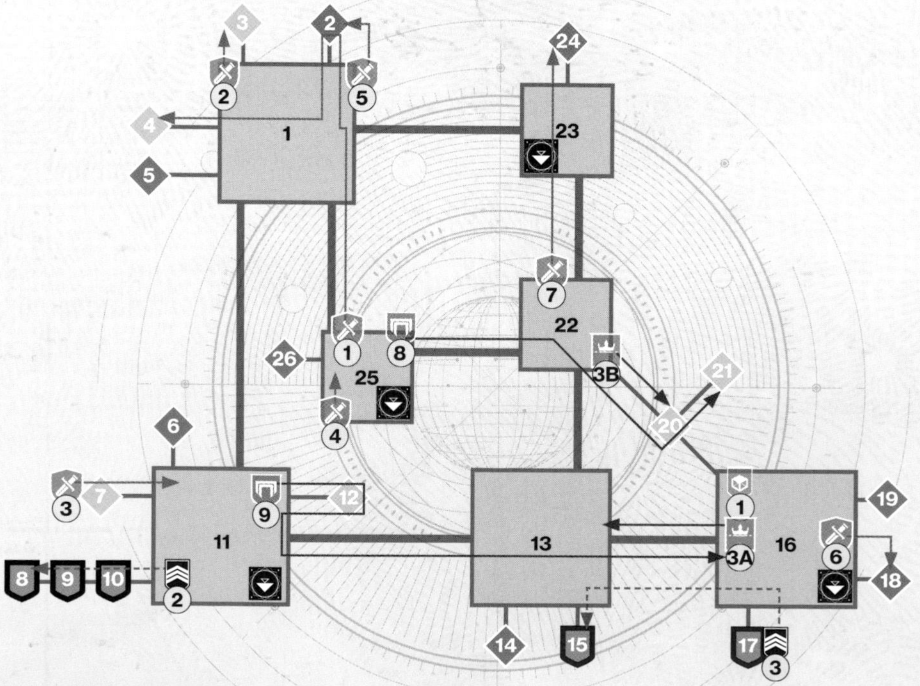

1. The Tangle
2. Chamber of Stone
3. The Mists
4. Well of Echoes
5. Ancient's Haunt
6. The Conflux
7. Well of Flame
8. The Inverted Spire
9. Excavation Site VII
10. The Anchor
11. The Cistern
12. The Shimmering Pools
13. Glade of Echoes
14. The Carrion Pit
15. EX-077 Command
16. Exodus Black
17. Prodromus Down
18. Chamber of Sky
19. The Rift
20. Sunken Cavern
21. Well of Giants
22. Hallows
23. Watcher's Grave
24. Chamber of Water
25. Artifact's Edge
26. The Orrery

Legend

- Landing Zone
- Activities: Wells
- Activities: Chambers
- Strike: Fallen and Vex
- Strike: Cabal and Vex
- Lost Sector
- Public Space
- Campaign: Looped
- Campaign: Six
- Strike: The Inverted Spire
- Strike: Exodus Crash
- Adventures: Unbreakable
- Adventures: Release
- Adventures: Invitation
- Adventures: Exodus Siege
- Adventures: Hack the Planet
- Adventures: Deep Conversation
- Adventures: Lost Crew
- World Quest: Exodus Black
- World Quest: O Captain!
- World Quest: My Captain!

Progression

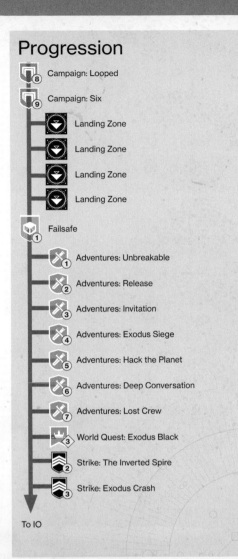

- Campaign: Looped (8)
- Campaign: Six (9)
  - Landing Zone
  - Landing Zone
  - Landing Zone
  - Landing Zone
- Failsafe (1)
  - Adventures: Unbreakable (1)
  - Adventures: Release (2)
  - Adventures: Invitation (3)
  - Adventures: Exodus Siege (4)
  - Adventures: Hack the Planet (5)
  - Adventures: Deep Conversation (6)
  - Adventures: Lost Crew (7)
  - World Quest: Exodus Black (3)
  - Strike: The Inverted Spire (2)
  - Strike: Exodus Crash (3)
- To IO

Nessus: Activities

Nessus: Activities Table

The following table shows the available activities, entities, Side Missions, and other pertinent data for every Sector within this region. Note that some activities (for example, Landing Zones) are not immediately available, but appear through progression.

Name	Type	Adventures	Lost Sectors	Landing Zone	Material Nodes
Artifact's Edge	Public	2	1	Available	Available
The Tangle	Public	2	1	–	Available
Chamber of Stone	Activity (Chamber)	–	–	–	Available
The Mists	Activity (Well)	–	–	–	Available
Well of Echoes	Activity (Well)	–	–	–	–
Watcher's Grave	Public	–	–	Available	Available
Chamber of Water	Activity (Chamber)	–	–	–	Available
The Cistern	Public	1	1	Available	Available
The Shimmering Pools	Activity (Well)	–	–	–	Available
Well of Flame	Activity (Well)	–	–	–	–
The Anchor	Activity (Strike)	–	–	–	–
Excavation Site VII	Activity (Strike)	–	–	–	–
The Inverted Spire	Activity (Strike)	–	–	–	–
Hallows	Public	1	–	–	Available
Glade of Echoes	Public	–	1	–	Available
EX-077 Command	Activity (Strike)	–	–	–	–
Sunken Cavern	Public	–	–	–	–
Well of Giants	Activity (Well)	–	–	–	–
Exodus Black	Public	1	1	Available	Available
Chamber of Sky	Activity (Chamber)	–	–	–	Available
Prodromus Down	Activity (Strike)	–	–	–	–
Total	8 (Public)	7	5	4	12 (Sectors)

Name	Patrols	Public Events (Full)	Public Events (Secret)	Enemy Chests	Region Chests	Lost Sector Chests	Scannable Objects	Vendors	Strikes	World Quests
Artifact's Edge	4	1	2	Available	3	1	1	–	–	–
The Tangle	11	3	4	Available	3	1	5	–	–	–
Chamber of Stone	–	–	–	–	–	–	1	–	–	–
The Mists	–	–	–	–	–	–	2	–	–	–
Well of Echoes	–	–	–	–	–	–	–	–	–	–
Watcher's Grave	7	2	6	Available	3	–	3	1 (Xur)	–	–
Chamber of Water	–	–	–	–	–	–	1	–	–	–
The Cistern	9	2	6	Available	3	1	5	–	Available	–
The Shimmering Pools	–	–	–	–	–	–	2	–	–	–
Well of Flame	–	–	–	–	–	–	–	–	–	–
The Anchor	–	–	–	–	–	–	–	–	–	–
Excavation Site VII	–	–	–	–	–	–	–	–	–	–
The Inverted Spire	–	–	–	–	–	–	–	–	–	–
Hallows	7	1	3	Available	3	–	3	–	–	–
Glade of Echoes	5	2	7	Available	3	1	5	–	–	–
EX-077 Command	–	–	–	–	–	–	1	–	–	–
Sunken Cavern	–	–	–	–	–	–	2	–	–	–
Well of Giants	–	–	–	–	–	–	–	–	–	–
Exodus Black	7	2	5	Available	3	1	5	1 (Failsafe)	–	Available
Chamber of Sky	–	–	–	–	–	–	1	–	–	–
Prodromus Down	–	–	–	–	–	–	–	–	Available	–
Total	50	13	33	7 (Sectors)	21	5	37	2	2	1

Artifact's Edge

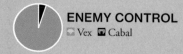

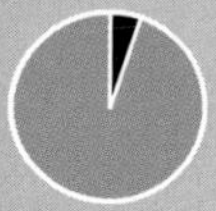

Sector Notes:

Adventure: The Disruptor Core | Adventure: Ghost in the Machine
Lost Sectors: 1 | Enemy Clusters: Vex: 2 | Landing Zone: Available
Material Nodes: Available | Patrol Beacons: 4 | Public Event (Full): 1
Public Event (Secret): 2 | Region Chests: 3 | Scannable Objects: 1

OVERVIEW MAP

Aside from the two large exit roadways, this is a short thoroughfare with a dead-end crash site to the south and your first clue (during the Campaign) regarding the whereabouts of Cayde-6. Under regular circumstances, this Sector offers good access to the upper entrance into Hallows (to the east) and a main road entrance into the Tangle (to the west). Expect light Vex activity, mainly clustered on the upper plateau above the Lost Sector entrance.

Areas of Interest

1 Exit to The Tangle (West)

A winding road, gradually filling in with trees and other plant life.

2 Energy Elevator

You can drop down here using the energy chute. Otherwise, use this as a landmark so you know that an uphill run leads to the Tangle (west).

3 Upper Plateau and Curved Alcove

Expect the largest concentration of Vex foes on the plateau area above the Lost Sector entrance across from the energy elevator.

4 Rocky Junction

Head south to the Crash Site, or remain on this thoroughfare when exiting to either of the adjacent Sectors.

5 Crash Site

The remains of a crashed spacecraft mark this dead-end area, though you can find a scannable object and Region Chest.

6 Exit to Hallows (East)

A sharp right followed by a left turn past the Adventure beacon lets you reach the large circular hole that marks the upper entrance into Hallows.

Adventures

1 The Disruptor Core

Access this marker on the edge of the rock clump under the energy elevator.

Adventures

2 Ghost in the Machine

Stuck into a cluster of rocks at the entrance to the Hallows exit.

Enemy Clusters

1 Vex

The northwest plateau has a group of Goblins, two Hobgoblins (one guarding the rock wall above the Lost Sector entrance), and a Minotaur in the curved alcove.

2 Vex

Harpies cluster on the rocks in the central junction area.

Landing Zone

Artifact's Edge

Drop in from Orbit to this reasonably central location, landing close to the energy elevator with quick access to both the Tangle (west) and Hallows (east).

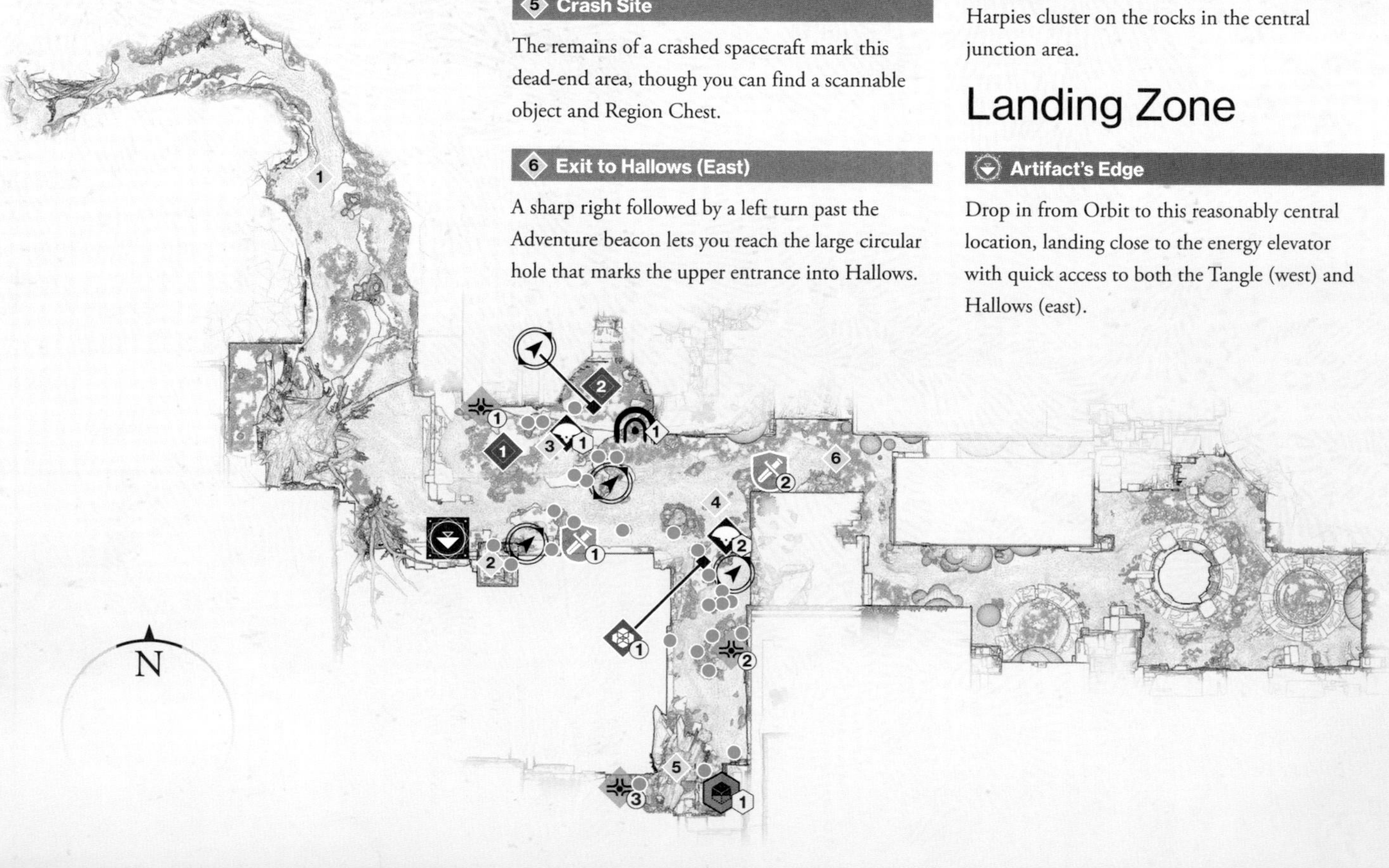

Lost Sectors

The Orrery

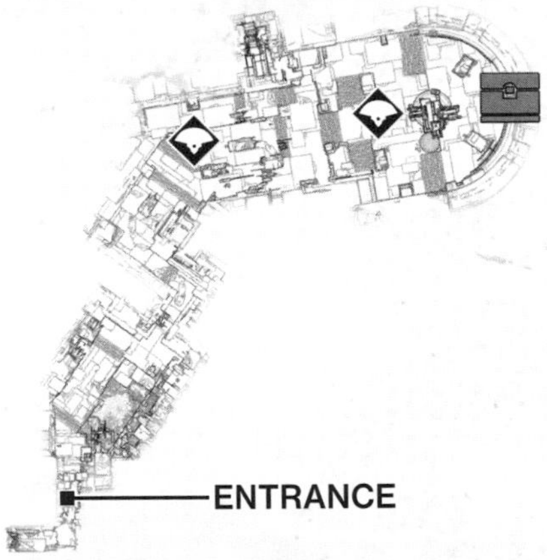

An opening in the northern perimeter, guarded by a Hobgoblin, leads beyond an earthen pit and into a Vex chamber with an altar-like structure at the far end. Goblins, Hobgoblins, and a toughened Minotaur are ready to repel intruders.

Artifact's Edge

	Guide Name	Sub-Boss	Reward
1	The Orrery	Vex Minotaur	Boss Chest

Patrols

Artifact's Edge (4)

There are only four available Patrols in this relatively diminutive Sector.

Scannable Objects

Head south, Guardian! Deft jumping to this tiny alcove is required.

Public Events

Public Events (Full)

Cabal Excavation: This takes place on the raised central rock formation. It has you attempt to override a Cabal mining laser while dodging incoming laser fire and the Cabal infantry waves that drop in from above, as well as any nearby Vex.

Event Number	Event Type	Target	Other Enemies	Reward
1	Cabal Excavation	Mining Lander	Cabal Infantry	Boss Chest

Public Events (Secret)

Ambush: While you're in the flat pond area to the northwest where Vex Enemy Cluster #1 is located, a Storm Minotaur warps in to bolster the enemy's forces. Defeat it, along with any other hostiles.

Jailbreak: Fallen Captain or Cabal Centurion is being held in an energy cell in the curved north alcove. Tackle the Vex Goblins and guard Minotaurs. Then, the cell disappears, leaving you to deal with the remaining foe!

Event Number	Event Type	Target	Other Enemies	Reward
1	Ambush	Storm Minotaur	Vex Goblins, Hobgoblins, Harpies	Random Loot
2	Jailbreak	Fallen Captain or Cabal Centurion	Guard Minotaurs, Vex forces	Boss Chest

Region Chests

1 Region Chest 1

Up on the northwest perimeter, behind a low plateau rock.

2 Region Chest 2

Partially hidden below a large chunk of white, cubic rock.

3 Region Chest 3

On the Vex-like golden structure to the west of the crashed craft.

The Tangle

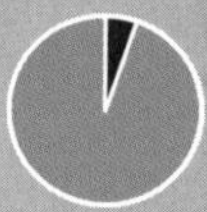

ENEMY CONTROL
Vex | Fallen

Sector Notes:

Adventure: Release | Adventure: The Vex Trial | Lost Sectors: 1

Enemy Clusters: Vex: 7 | Enemy Chests: Available | Material Nodes: Available

Patrol Beacons: 11 | Public Event (Full): 3 | Public Event (Secret): 4

Region Chests: 3 | Scannable Objects: 5

OVERVIEW MAP

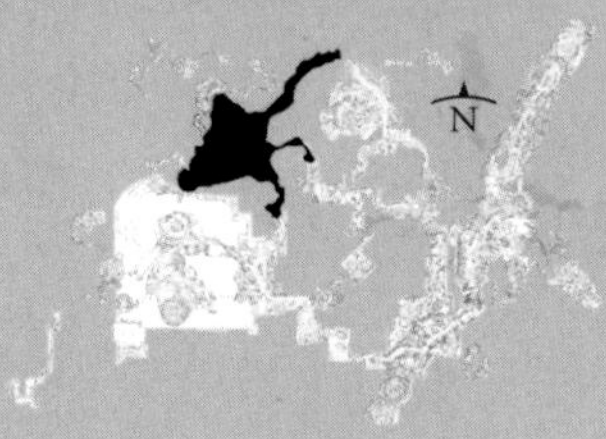

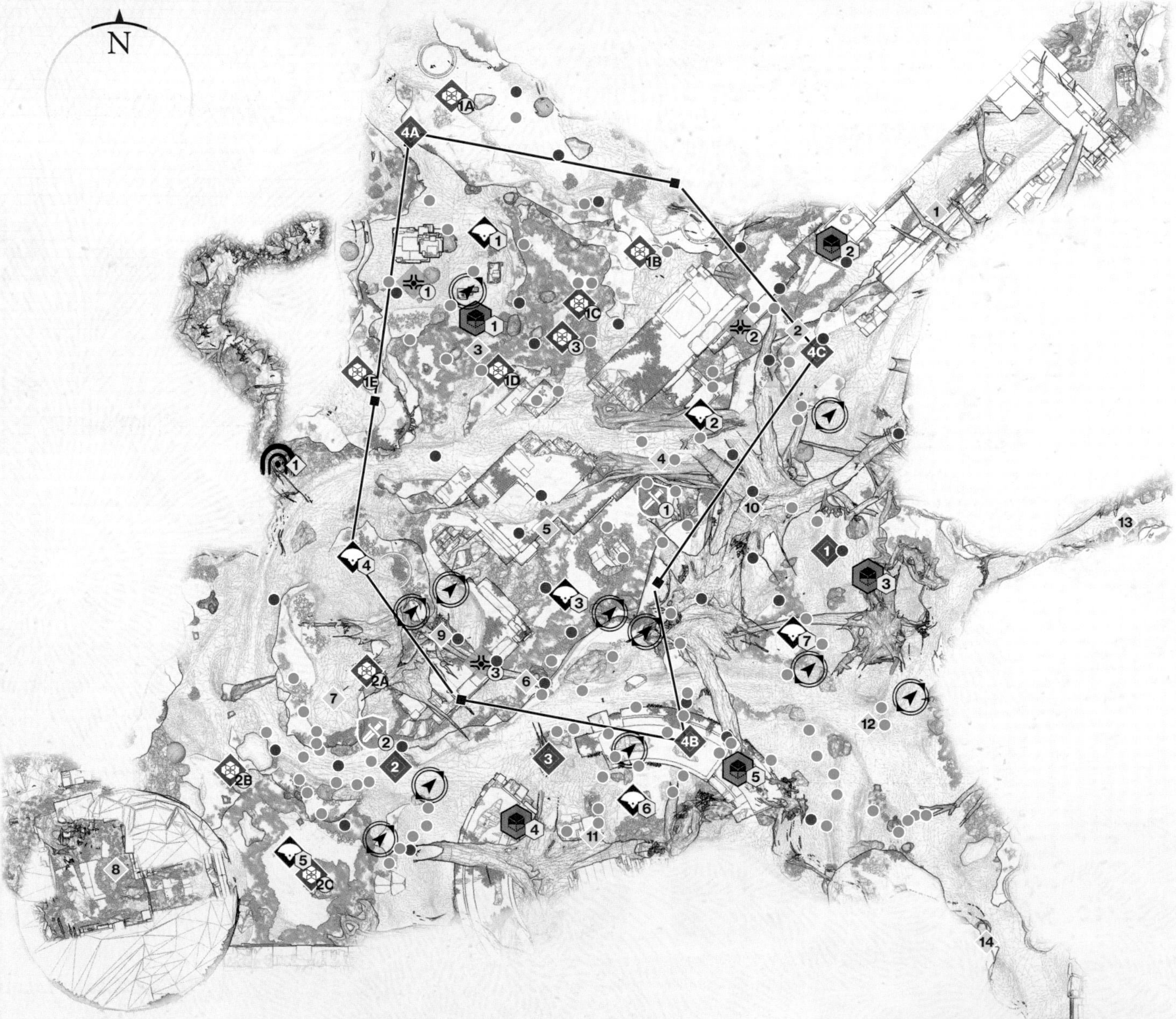

An initially confusing maze of branches, Vex architecture, and plateau rock formations bisected by a cutting crevasse that runs southwest to northeast, this Sector takes a little time to learn. This isn't helped by the number of Vex clusters to combat as you check the winding, roughly U-shaped road that runs the perimeter. There are also a good number of exits: Watcher's Grave (northeast), Artifact's Edge (east), and the Conflux (southeast). All of them are on the eastern perimeter of the map, so head in this direction if you need to be elsewhere. Otherwise, stay to find the Lost Sector, as well as three additional entrances to interiors. This is the only Sector where you can access the Well of Echoes, the Mists, and the Chamber of Stone.

Areas of Interest

1 Exit to Watcher's Grave (Northeast)

This offers immediate access to Watcher's Grave. Just remember that the road almost immediately gives you access to the crevasse and tree bridge, so you can find your bearings.

2 Crevasse Entrance (Northeast)

You can head southwest down into the crevasse at this point (or jump down at any point along the crevasse on either side). Note the road that continues along the eastern perimeter to the junction (#12).

3 Hydra's Lair (North)

A Vex Hydra dominates this dried-up sunken riverbed and surrounding plateau of flat rock where Goblins like to congregate. Come here if you need to kill one.

4 Tree Bridge

This runs atop the crevasse, allowing quick access around the looping perimeter road toward the Lost Sector.

5 Entrance to The Mists (Crevasse)

Head down into the crevasse and find the orange-hued Vex wall, which has an opening here. This is the only entrance to (and exit from) the Mists.

6 Entrance to Crevasse (South)

Head down (or out) of the crevasse at this point by the Adventure marker and under the large southwest tree.

7 Southwest Road and Pond

The road sweeps around at this point. Watch for multiple foes in the vicinity.

8 Entrance to Well of Echoes (Southwest)

A sunken pond with plenty of Vex foes allows you to reach a strange pyramidal entrance to (and exit from) the Well of Echoes. This is the only access point.

9 Mighty Tree (Southwest)

Aside from foes in the vicinity, check this area for the tree you can climb and the branches you can navigate, allowing easier access to elevated areas around the edge of the Sector.

10 Mighty Trees (Northeast)

There are two huge trees in this area, and you can use their branches to reach upper areas around the perimeter of the map. Or, use them as cover.

11 Entrance to Chamber of Stone (South)

A cluster of Vex foes is always around this circular Vex teleport. This is the only entrance to (and exit from) the Chamber of Stone.

12 Road Junction (Southeast)

Use this as a landmark; a small patch of grass and rough dirt roads merge here. Remember to check which exit you want to maneuver to!

13 Exit to Artifact's Edge (East)

Head east to reach the Artifact's Edge. Note that the road heads down to the junction. It also sharply turns north to link to the rest of the thoroughfare.

14 Exit to The Conflux (Southeast)

Study the turns and environment at this exit so you don't confuse it with the one to Artifact's Edge. This takes you south to the Conflux Sector.

Enemy Clusters

1 Vex

Goblins, Harpies, and a Hydra are possible foes to face in the lair of the Hydra, up in the northern part of the map.

2 Vex

Enter the crevasses, and prepare for Harpy combat. There may be additional Goblins in the vicinity, too.

3 Vex

Expect Harpies and possibly Goblins in the crevasse, close to the entrance to an interior known as the Mists.

4 Vex

The raised rocky area around the southwestern tree usually has patrols of Goblins, Harpies, and Hobgoblins.

5 Vex

A Minotaur, Goblins, and possible Hobgoblins are splashing around in the waterlogged sunken pond area close to the entrance to the Well of Echoes.

6 Vex

The entrance to the Chamber of Stone has a number of Goblins and Hobgoblins to worry about. If a Skirmish is active, there are more enemies.

7 Vex

Expect Goblins and Minotaurs under the canopy of the two large trees near the road junction, on the east side of the map.

Adventures

1 Release

Find the marker in the base of the crevasse, opposite the entrance to the Mists Sector, on the rocky outcrop.

2 The Vex Trial

Locate this marker on the main thoroughfare, close to the southwest pond and entrance to Well of Echoes.

Lost Sectors

Ancient's Haunt

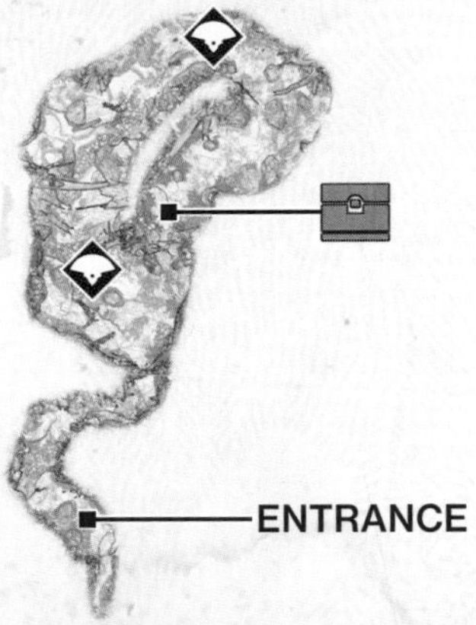

A narrow rocky tunnel opens up into an exotic glade with various red-hued trees and plant life. A sizable Vex presence is here, with Goblins, Hobgoblins, Harpies, and a Sub-Boss Hydra to punish.

The Tangle

	Guide Name	Sub-Boss	Reward
1	Ancient's Haunt	Hydra	Boss Chest

The Tangle (11)

There are a good number of Patrol beacons (11) available. Find a few of them at a time on each visit to this Sector.

Region Chests

① Region Chest 1

On a ledge halfway up the Vex tower that the Hydra guards.

② Region Chest 2

Above the northern entrance to the crevasse.

③ Region Chest 3

On one of the branches of the mighty tree (southeast).

Public Events

Public Events (Full)

Glimmer Extraction: Involves destroying three of the five Fallen extraction sites (1A, 1B, 1C, 1D, and 1E) dotted around the map or three (2A, 2B, and 2C), depending on which Full Event is active.

Spire Integration: Vex are attempting to fortify their nearby structures. Simply hold off waves of Vex at the indicated spot. They approach from different directions (which appear around the indicated guide map area); to complete this event, defeat them all without letting the integrations total reach zero.

Event Number	Event Type	Target	Other Enemies	Reward
1	Glimmer Extraction	Fallen Extractors	Fallen forces	Glimmer, Boss Chest
2	Glimmer Extraction	Fallen Extractors	Fallen forces	Glimmer, Boss Chest
3	Spire Integration	Integration points	Vex infantry	Boss Chest

Public Events (Secret)

Skirmish 1: A Fallen Captain, Dregs, and Tracer Shanks face off against a Hydra, Goblins, and Hobgoblins, with more waves of these foe types continuously appearing in the area shown.

Skirmish 2: Features Fallen dropships and a variety of foes (mainly Dregs and a Captain) fighting against an increased Vex presence (additional Goblins, Hobgoblins, and a Hydra) in the area shown.

Skirmish 3: Features teleporting Vex infantry (including Goblins and Hobgoblins) and multiple Hydras in the area shown. Fallen approach from the road to engage them, including Dregs and Tracer Shanks.

Launchers: Defeat the Vex Hobgoblins at each of the indicated cannon positions. Remove threats at 4A, then leap through the cannon to reach 4B, and continue to 4C. Then, mow down the Vex Minotaurs as you work your way around 4A, 4B, and 4C once more (using the cannons each time). Defeat all foes around the cannons before they disappear to claim each chest.

Event Number	Event Type	Target	Other Enemies	Reward
1	Skirmish	Vex incursions and Fallen infantry	–	Random Loot
2	Skirmish	Fallen dropships and Vex infantry	–	Random Loot
3	Skirmish	Vex incursions and Fallen infantry	–	Random Loot
4	Launchers	Three cannons	Hobgoblins and Minotaurs	Boss Chest (x3)

Scannable Objects

Something is sitting on a Vex stalagmite. Beware the Hydra!

Shimmering white column? Close to a chest.

Half a Goblin, sitting on a column near two mighty trees.

Scan this wall after a climb near a circular teleport.

Something blue is shimmering up here. Can you find it?

Chamber of Stone

ENEMY CONTROL
Vex

Sector Notes:

Enemy Clusters: Vex: 2 | Material Nodes: Available | Scannable Objects: 1

OVERVIEW MAP

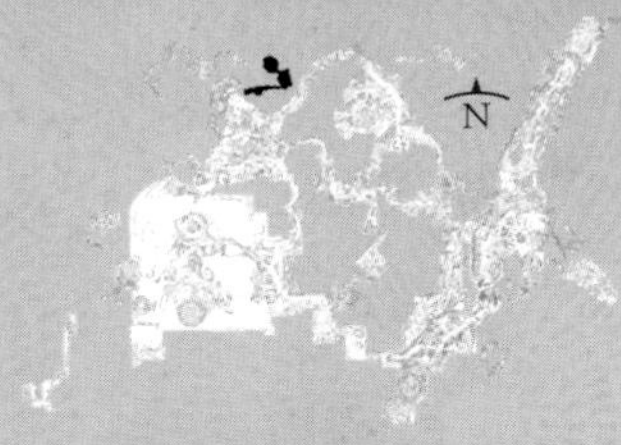

This small secondary Sector is only accessible via the Tangle. It features a narrow entrance tunnel (after the portal) leading to a pair of partially natural, partially Vex-constructed caverns, each with a cluster of foes to worry about. Aside from secondary questing (Adventure: The Vex Trial concludes here, with many more foes than those listed during normal activities), you're here for the exploration and the scannable object.

Areas of Interest

1 Portal to The Tangle

This drops you back in the Tangle (the only way to reach this place), in the southern part of that Sector. There is a tight tunnel corridor leading toward the first cavern.

2 First Cavern

Expect Vex activity in this area, along with scattered materials to gather. Note the red Vex teleport, which is an exit (from #3).

3 Second Cavern

Push through the narrow gap into a second almost identically sized cavern, with further foes, a scannable object, and a teleport dropping you back in the first cavern.

Enemy Clusters

1 Vex

The first cavern has Goblins and other Vex infantry that turn hostile as you enter. Expect Hobgoblins and Harpies, as well.

2 Vex

The second cavern has additional Vex infantry. Around six enemies are expected, including a possible Minotaur.

Scannable Objects

This portal has seen better days.

The Mists

ENEMY CONTROL

Vex

Sector Notes:

Enemy Clusters: Vex: 4 | Material Nodes: Available | Scannable Objects: 2

OVERVIEW MAP

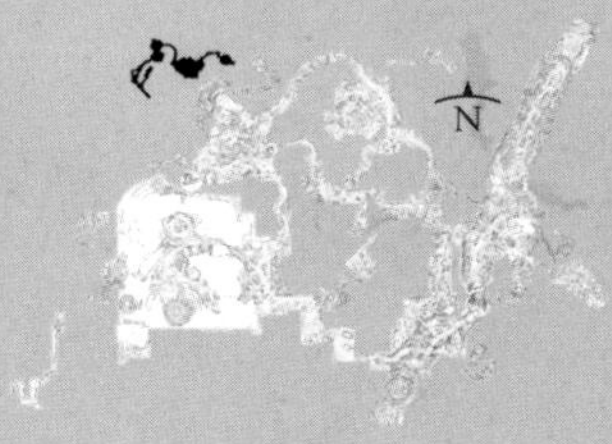

Investigate this underground Vex shrine by accessing the lower crevasse area in the Tangle. Locate the opening (with a glowing orange hue) along the northwestern side of the crevasse wall. Inside is a winding tunnel to a couple of caverns, a curved passage around to a large underground chasm, and two promontories separated by a bottomless drop. Leap across to find a final corridor to an altar chamber, along with a teleport back close to the entrance/exit. Head here for the Vex culling and collectibles.

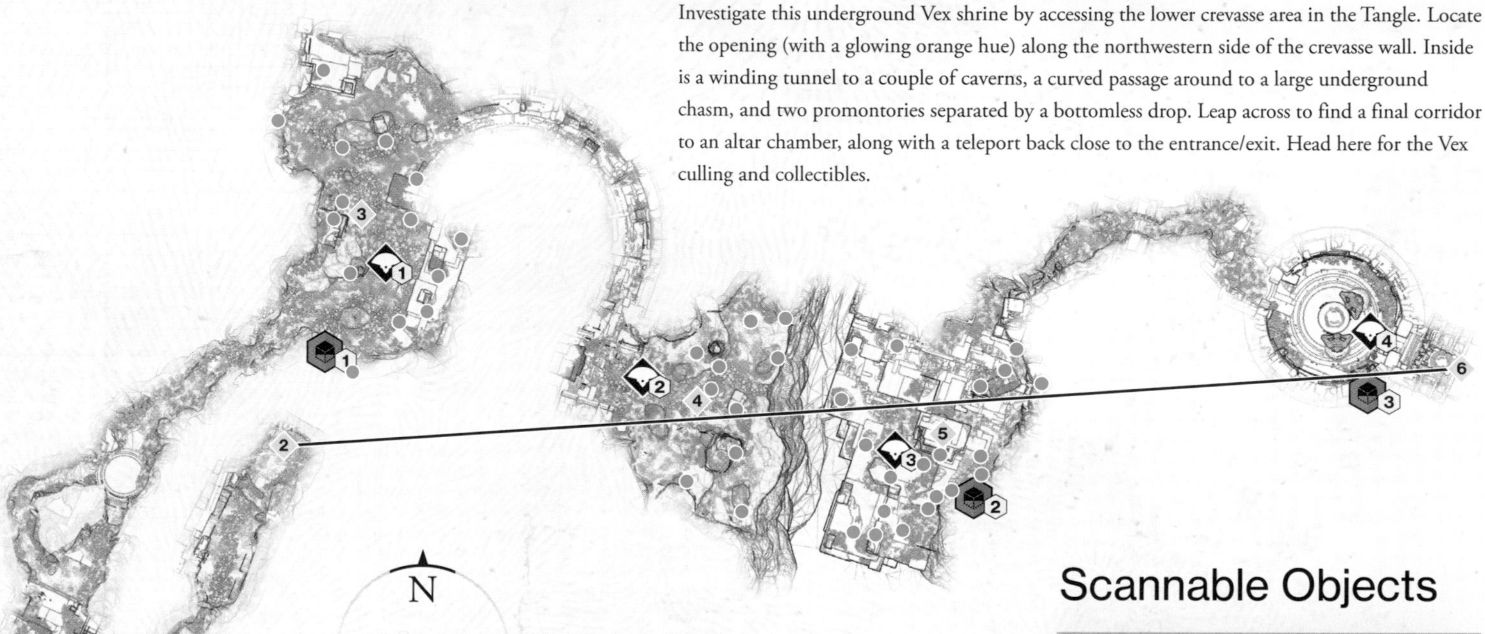

Areas of Interest

1 Entrance and Exit (to The Tangle)

The continuation of this tunnel leads to and from the lower crevasse area of the Tangle. Look for the orange glow. Inside, a narrow and mostly natural-looking rock tunnel leads you deeper.

2 Circular Floor and Teleport Exit

A slightly wet tunnel area, with a branching passage leading to a red teleport exit (where you appear from after completing this exploration). Head onward across a circular stone floor, and wind through another narrow tunnel.

3 Vex Cavern

A group of Vex infantry guards this rocky cavern, with Vex carved stone to the right (east) side. Access the narrow curved opening ahead and right (east), working your way around it and battling Harpies as you go.

4 West Promontory

The western side of the main chamber, bisected by a misty chasm you must jump across, has more naturally occurring rock formations, as well as Vex to dispatch.

5 East Promontory

The eastern side of this map features more block-based Vex carvings, with infantry (Goblins and Hobgoblins) guarding the many small ledges and pillars. Leap across to engage them. Note the scannable object in this area.

6 Altar and Teleport Room

The final chamber features a scannable object and the last set of foes to face, including a Minotaur. Take the teleport back to #2 if you don't want to trudge back the way you came.

Scannable Objects

This Lore object is a "dish" best served in the Vex Cavern.

Look for the orange, under the eastern promontory.

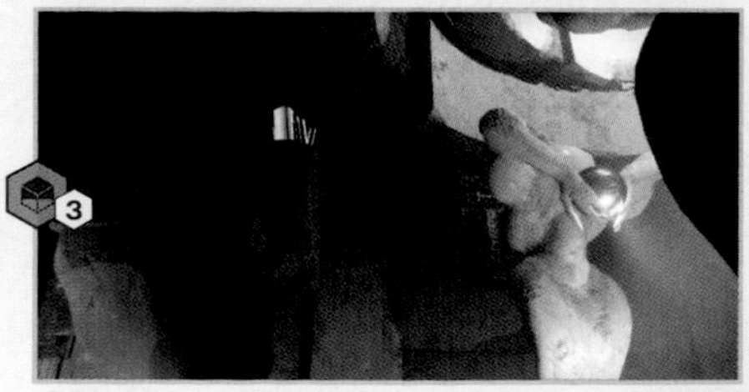

Something is showing up on the scanner above the altar room.

Well of Echoes

Sector Notes:

Partially Inaccessible

ENEMY CONTROL

Vex

OVERVIEW MAP

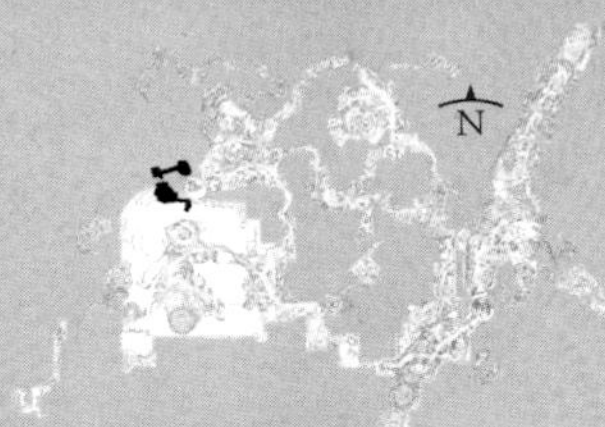

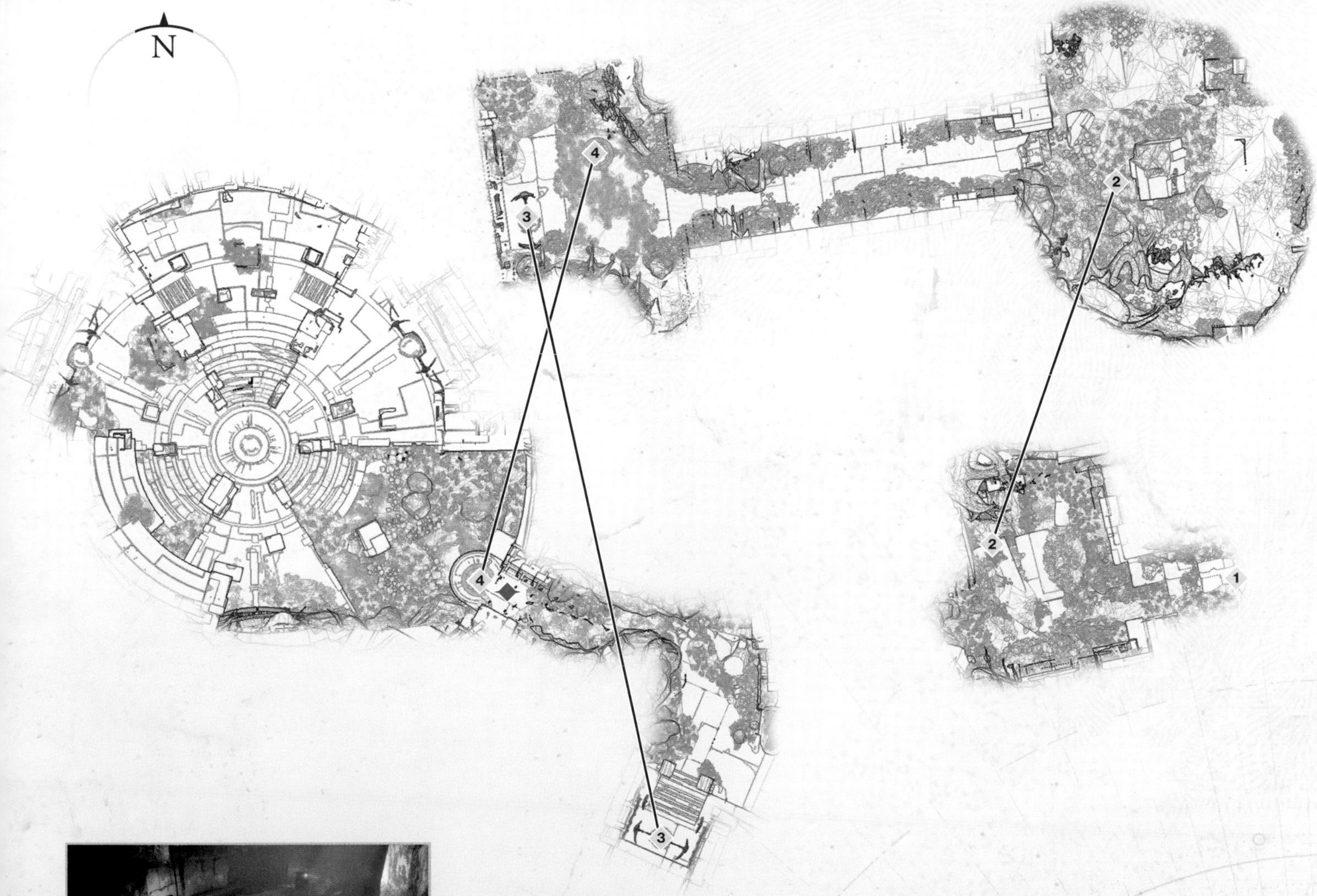

This large single chamber with an entrance tunnel is accessed via the shallow pool in the southwestern corner of the Tangle Sector. It is normally sealed, opening only one of the Adventures that begins in the Tangle.

Areas of Interest

1 Exit to The Tangle

This is the only entrance and exit to this Sector. Reach it via the pyramid-shaped entrance in the southwestern corner of the Tangle.

2 Cave Drop

A hole in the upper cave leads down to the Well of Echoes entrance corridor.

3 Portal to Well Chamber

Accessed at the end of the entrance corridor. Note the red teleport allows you to return here once your exploration of the Well Chamber is complete, though that chamber is inaccessible. Enter the portal, and there's a small rocky tunnel leading to an energy barrier.

4 The Well Chamber (Inaccessible)

The cylindrical Well Chamber itself is devoid of life and cannot be accessed unless the specific Adventure is active. Then, expect a host of Vex to be here, ready to receive your firepower.

Watcher's Grave

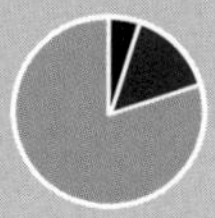

ENEMY CONTROL
Cabal | Fallen | Vex

Sector Notes:

Enemy Clusters: Vex: 6 | Enemy Chests: Available | Landing Zone: Available
Material Nodes: Available | Patrol Beacons: 7 | Public Event (Full): 2
Public Event (Secret): 6 | Region Chests: 3 | Scannable Objects: 3
Vendor: Xur

OVERVIEW MAP

Even though you can skirt the majority of this Sector by passing along the northeastern perimeter thoroughfare between the Tangle and Hallows, investigate the large circular arena to discover multiple Vex patrolling, as well as two areas where a careless maneuver can cost you your life. Although there are no Lost Sectors, there is an entrance to the Chamber of Water, along with an alcove along the northern edge of the sunken arena where a host of Vex may appear. Fallen are also active in this area, and there's even a captured Cabal prisoner to face, should one of the three Secret Public Events activate. Finally, note the Landing Zone: it's an excellent way to reach the two larger adjacent Sectors, as well as this one.

Landing Zone

Watcher's Grave LZ

An LZ is accessible in this Sector; you land over on the eastern perimeter of the map, close to the road and equidistant to both exits. Head here for quick access to the Tangle or Hallows.

Patrols

Watcher's Grave (7)

A total of seven Patrol beacons eventually become available here. Note that one of the beacons is below ground, in the alcove cave.

Areas of Interest

1 Road to The Tangle (North)

The northern exit heading west enables you to quickly reach the northern part of the Tangle.

2 Entrance to Chamber of Water

This side alcove in the northern exterior has numerous Vex infantry guarding a circular teleport, which whisks you to the Chamber of Water Sector. This is the only access point to this Sector.

3 North Ruins

Expect a light enemy presence (or a cluster of Fallen during a Skirmish) in the vicinity of the protruding low cubed ruins around the northern perimeter of the arena.

4 Northwest Plateaus

The naturally occurring rock plateaus have Vex foes to concern yourself with, and an arena cave alcove beneath your feet.

5 Arena Alcove (North Central)

Don't overlook the opening in the arena wall in the sunken north-central part of this Sector. There's a Vex cluster and some interesting discoveries inside.

6 Watcher's Arena

The majority of this Sector consists of this large circular arena. Southwest is the "eye," part of the huge perimeter wall. Watch for bottomless drops to the west and southeast.

7 Arena Eye (Southwest)

The floor below the arena eye is bathed in orange light. Note the three pillars (one with a Region Chest), a scannable object on the left (eastern) corner of the numerous wall ledges, and a Hydra roaming the lower floor.

8 Mist Pillars

A frightening part of this Sector, this area below a massive Vex construction overhang features a smattering of rock pillars and a bottomless drop into mist. One of the pillars has a chest to find.

9 East Promontory

This offers good views of the arena below and is a reasonable sniping point. Beware of the Minotaur and Goblins patrolling here, and check around the narrow ledge to the south for a chest.

10 Road to Hallows (Southeast)

The curved roadway skirts around the northeastern side of this Sector, weaving southeastward to Hallows.

Enemy Clusters

1 Vex

Expect Goblins and Hobgoblins to be guarding the entrance to the Chamber of Water in the northeastern perimeter.

2 Vex

The upper ruins along the northern edge of the arena have roaming Goblins for you to contend with.

3 Vex

The northwestern plateaus have Harpies to tackle, as well as Goblins (plus a sniping Hobgoblin) to watch for.

4 Vex

The underside of the northern plateau area features a wide but short alcove cave, with Harpies, Goblins, and a Minotaur inside.

5 Vex

The eastern promontory features a Minotaur roaming the area, along with its Goblin brethren.

6 Vex

Goblins, Hobgoblins, and a fearsome Hydra are patrolling the area under the orange-lit arena eye.

Public Events

Public Events (Full)

Servitor Resupply: This takes place in the sunken arena area. There are plenty of Fallen foes to tackle, multiple waves of lesser Servitors, and the usual Vex foes to ignore so you aren't overwhelmed.

Spire Integration: Vex are attempting to fortify their nearby structures. Simply hold off waves of Vex at the indicated spot. They are approaching from different directions (which appear around the indicated guide map area); to complete this event, defeat them all without letting the integrations total reach zero.

Event Number	Event Type	Target	Other Enemies	Reward
1	Servitor Resupply	Fallen Servitor	Shanks, Dregs, Vandals, Servitors	Boss Chest
2	Spire Integration	Integration points	Vex infantry	Boss Chest

Public Events (Secret)

HVT #1: A Vex Storm Minotaur appears at one of the indicated guide map locations (1A, 1B, 1C, or 1D). Defeat it immediately!

HVT #2: A Fallen Captain appears at one of the indicated guide map locations (2A, 2B, 2C, 2D or 2E). Remove it at once!

Jailbreak (three locations): A captured enemy (a Cabal Centurion, Fallen Captain, or Fallen Servitor, depending on the location) is being held in an energy cell. Tackle the Vex Goblins and Minotaur guards. Then, the cell disappears, leaving you to deal with the prisoner foe!

Skirmish: This is a fight against consecutive waves of Fallen infantry throughout the indicated area, close to the main thoroughfare.

Event Number	Event Type	Target	Other Enemies	Reward
1	High-Value Target	Storm Minotaur	Goblins, Hobgoblins, Harpies	Boss Chest
2	High-Value Target	Fallen Captain	None	Boss Chest
3	Jailbreak	Cabal Centurion (Brawn Gladiator)	Guard Minotaurs, Vex forces	Boss Chest
4	Jailbreak	Fallen Captain	Guard Minotaurs, Vex forces, two Hydras	Boss Chest
5	Jailbreak	Fallen Servitor	Guard Minotaurs, Vex forces	Boss Chest
6	Skirmishes Fallen infantry	–	–	Random Loot

Region Chests

① Region Chest 1

Below the arena eye, atop one of the stone-like Vex pillars.

② Region Chest 2

On a narrow corner of the ledge, around and south from the eastern promontory.

③ Region Chest 3

On the rear mist pillar, requiring deft jumping across the bottomless chasm.

Scannable Objects

This Goblin is half the robot it used to be. Now it's branching out.

There's something interesting to scan below the surface.

A rusting globe of machinery on a high corner ledge, bathed in orange.

Vendor

① Xur

Have you spotted the Agent of the Nine? He occasionally appears on the branch of the large tree on the north side of the main thoroughfare, if you're lucky! Xur offers special items to those who can find him. He can appear other places as well.

Chamber of Water

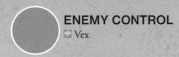

ENEMY CONTROL
Vex

OVERVIEW MAP

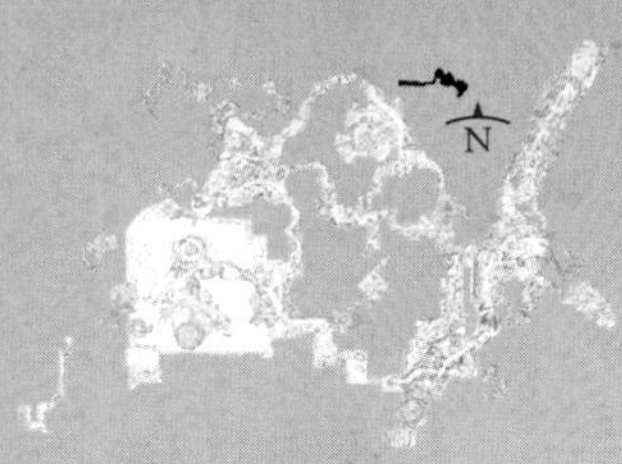

Sector Notes:

Enemy Clusters: Vex: 2 | Material Nodes: Available | Scannable Objects: 1

Those Guardians investigating the Vex portal along the northern perimeter of Watcher's Grave find themselves in a tight and precarious position: a corridor leading to a Vex chamber overlooking a death plummet into the white mists. You're here for the scannable object and to slaughter Vex. This location is also visited during Adventure: Key to the Network, where the Sector is much more populated.

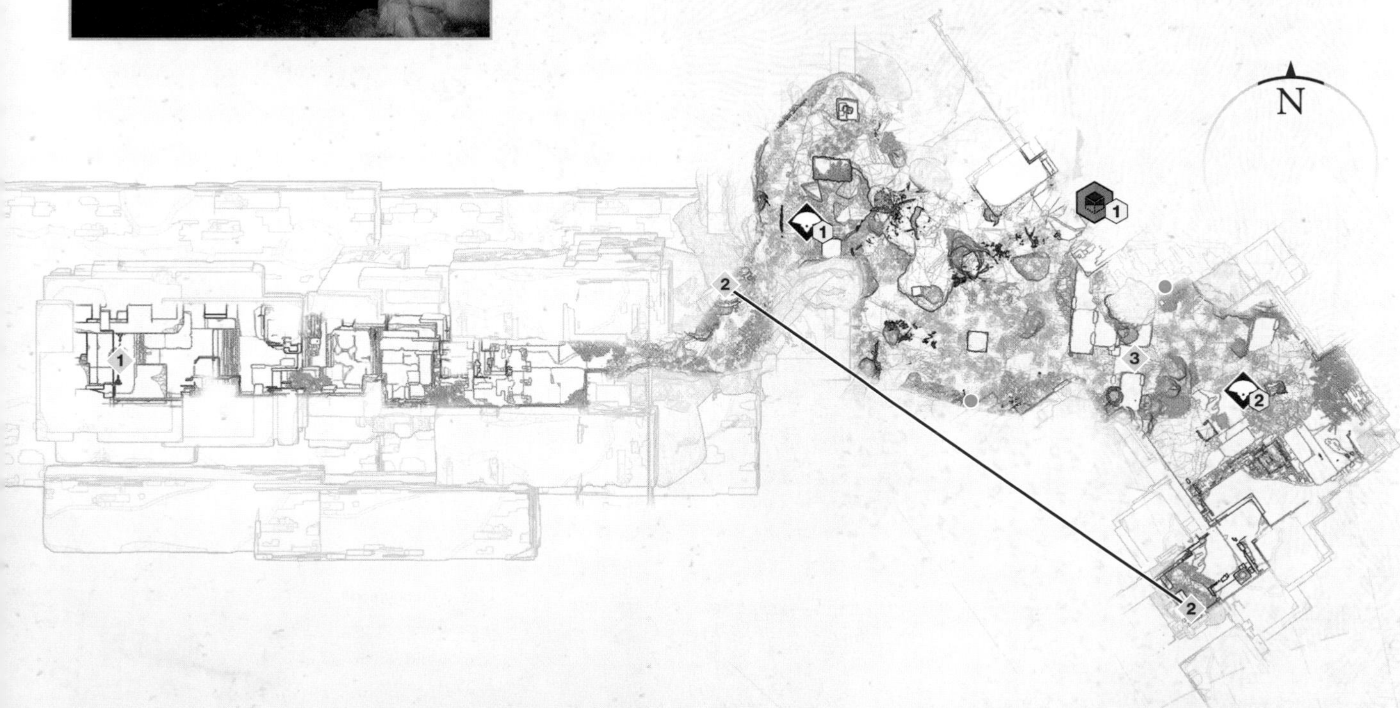

Areas of Interest

1 Exit to Watcher's Grave

This is the only entrance and exit to this Sector. It leads back to Watcher's Grave and the waterlogged portal area along the northern perimeter of that map. The entrance tunnel is narrow and slopes to the right.

2 Cavern Chamber

A small contingent of Vex is in the initial chamber, along with a red teleport (where you exit after discovering the main chamber).

3 Main Chamber

The bulk of the Vex combat occurs throughout this partially ruined Vex level. Openings along the north and eastern sides lead to a death plummet. The teleport returning you close to the exit is in a high south corner.

Enemy Clusters

1 Vex

In this initial cavern, be wary of Hobgoblins sniping you from the upper rocks, as well as Goblins.

2 Vex

Harpies, Minotaurs, Goblins, and Hobgoblins are active in the main chamber.

Scannable Objects

A thin, white crackle that's sure to Vex you.

The Cistern

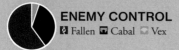

OVERVIEW MAP

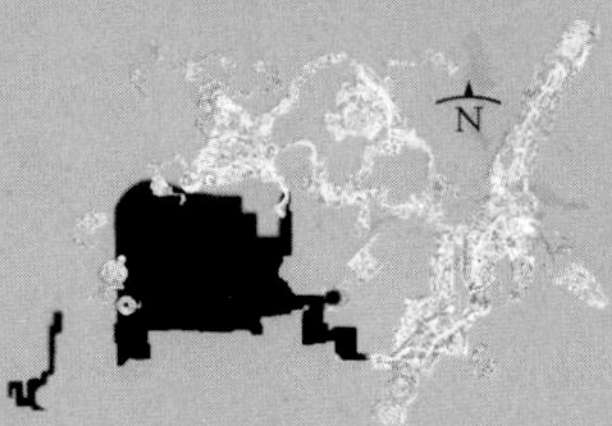

Sector Notes:

Adventure: A Tale of Two Confluxes | Lost Sectors: 1 | Enemy Clusters: Cabal: 2
Enemy Clusters: Fallen: 5 | Enemy Chests: Available | Landing Zone: Available
Material Nodes: Available | Patrol Beacons: 9 | Public Event (Full): 2
Public Event (Secret): 6 | Region Chests: 3 | Scannable Objects: 5

Perhaps the largest of all the Sectors on this planetoid, it's one with numerous secrets to uncover. The Cistern features a vast expanse of Radiolarian Fluid, harmful to the touch and deadly if you ride your Sparrow over the waterfall to the south. Instead, search along the winding and open thoroughfare for a Lost Sector and entrance to the Well of Flame at the top of the large cylindrical tower that dominates the southwestern edge of the map. Even farther across the white void to the southwest is the entrance to the Anchor, a Sector you can't fully explore unless a Strike is active. To the east are main exits to other major Sectors (northeast and southeast), as well as a wall slit to the Pools of Luminance (southeast). Come here for the Fallen and Cabal to cull, and stay for the Public Events.

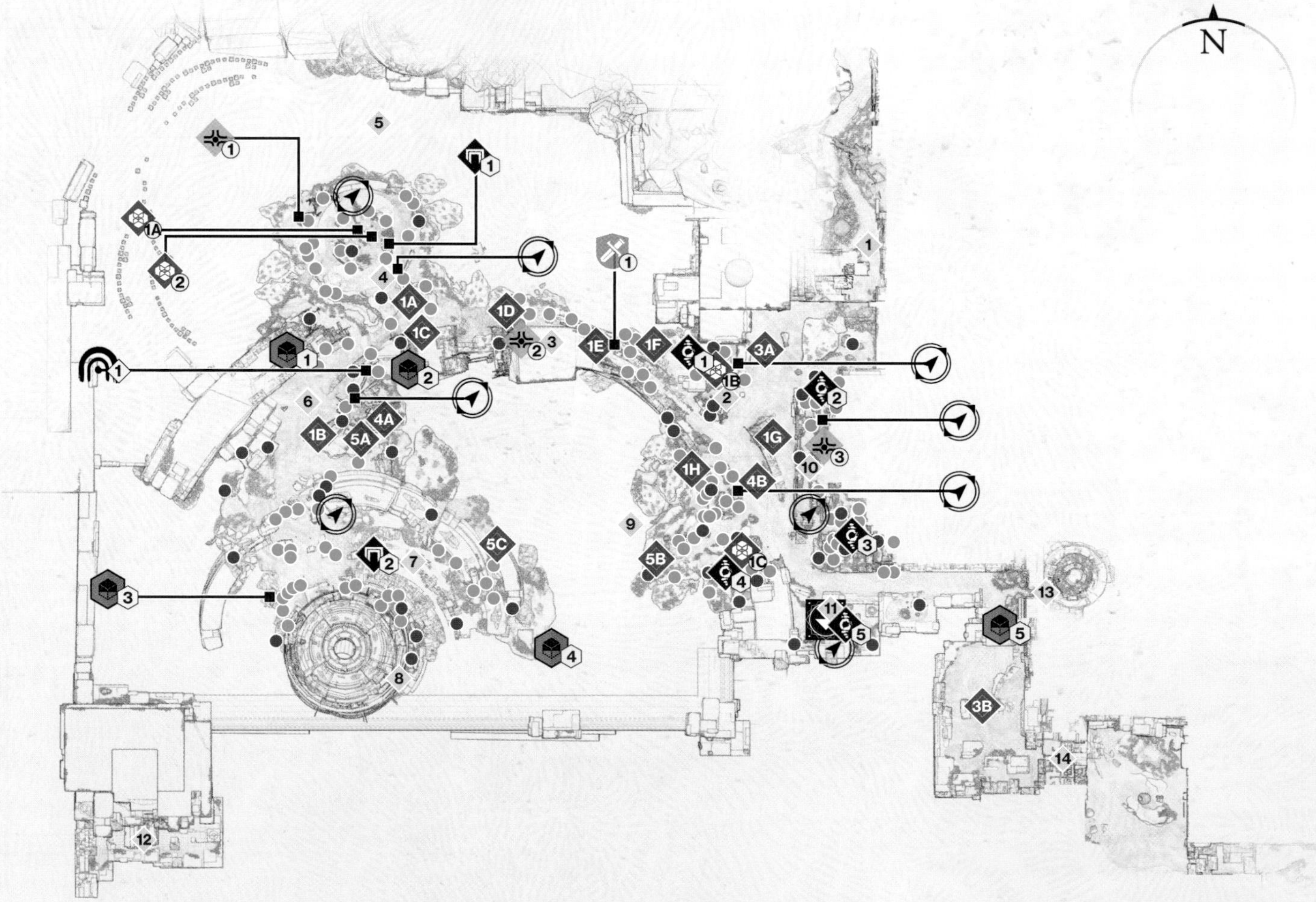

Areas of Interest

1 Exit to The Tangle (Northeast)

If you want to simply maneuver from Sector to Sector, just travel south and then southeast from the Tangle to Glade of Echoes, or vice versa. The large, cube-like Vex architecture and top of the hill indicate this exit.

2 Northeast Junction

This marks the spot where the road continues north (to the Tangle), south (to Glade of Echoes), and west to the remainder of this Sector. Pike Gangs frequent this sloped area, as do Fallen foes.

3 Main Thoroughfare (East to West)

A long, raised, curved road bisects the two sections of the white lake, with a block-like Vex ruin on the southern side of the path. Note the Region Chest in the vicinity and the road into the northwest promontory.

4 Northwest Promontory

A circular spit of ground where the Cabal like to summon their injector rig. Cabal are here, and so are several low Vex ruins and a Region Chest.

5 White Lake (North)

Although your Sparrow can take you to the perimeter of this Sector, there's little to find that's north of the promontory.

6 Mighty Tree (West)

Use this huge red-leafed tree as a landmark as you enter from the main thoroughfare. The tree marks a Secret Public Event, as well as a Lost Sector. Two scannable objects are in the vicinity here.

7 Tower Pools

The base of the tower has a small squad of Cabal to cull, including Psions and Phalanxes. The area has obstacles and stepping stones, so watch your Sparrow maneuvers. Note the two scannable objects in the vicinity.

8 Well of Flame Entrance (Southwest)

After you navigate through the Cabal cluster and jump up the huge cube-like Vex architecture to the top of the "steps," an opening inside this cylindrical tower allows access to the mysterious Well of Flame.

9 White Lake and Shore (South)

Although the Radiolarian Fluid is dangerous to the touch, you can ride a Sparrow (or Pike) across here with minimal harm. Investigate this shoreline for Fallen foes and a possible Public Event or two. To the south is a rushing waterfall into a white void; don't head over the edge!

10 Overhang (East)

A partially covered perimeter section with a well-hidden Region Chest and two clusters of Fallen foes, including invisible Marauders and a Captain to the north. It is parallel to the main road just west of this area.

11 Pedestal Platforms (Southeast)

This is the Landing Zone for the Sector, where a group of Fallen is milling about. Normally, you'd head here for a possible Patrol beacon. During Strike: The Inverted Spire, though, this is where a series of floating platforms is summoned, leading westward to the Anchor Sector.

12 Exit to The Anchor (Southeast)

When the Strike: The Inverted Spire is active, an interaction with Vex technology allows you to reach a series of Vex cannons via some floating stepping stones at #11. During normal action, you can drive your Sparrow south from #9 to the corner section of the waterfall and reach a Vex cannon. Then, you propel yourself westward across the waterfall chasm to this ledge. The exit to the Anchor Sector is via another Vex cannon west of this position.

13 Entrance to Pools of Luminance (Southeast)

This slit in the perimeter wall (with a nearby scannable object you must climb to) allows access into the Pools of Luminance. This is fully accessed during Campaign Mission: Six.

14 Exit to Glade of Echoes

The far southeastern corner of this Sector features a cliff-top road leading eastward into the Glade of Echoes Sector.

Region Chests

1 Region Chest 1

Inside the shell of the Vex globe, in the circular promontory.

2 Region Chest 2

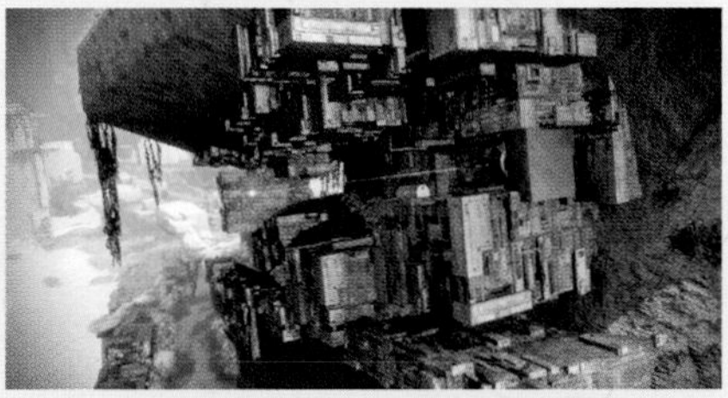

High atop the Vex structure along the main thoroughfare.

3 Region Chest 3

Tucked in a high alcove along the sloped overhang.

Lost Sectors

The Conflux

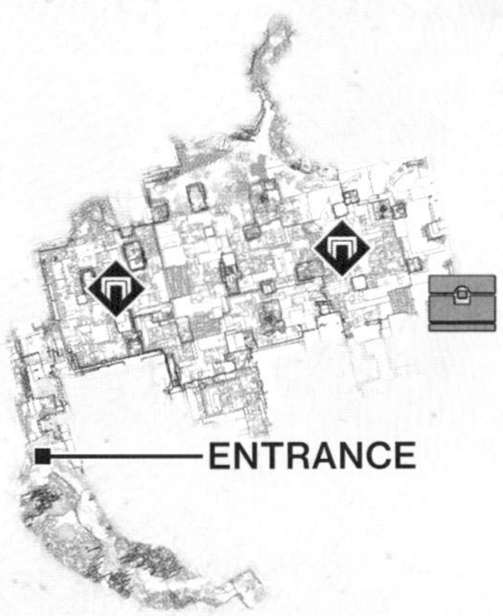

Enter this Lost Sector under the large tree on the western side of the Sector. Inside is a large Vex-built chamber hosting a group of Cabal to fight. Their leader is a Sub-Boss Centurion.

The Cistern

	Guide Name	Sub-Boss	Reward
1	The Conflux	Cabal Centurion	Boss Chest

Adventures

1 A Tale of Two Confluxes

The marker is on the side of the main thoroughfare, centrally located.

Landing Zone

The Cistern LZ

Drop in on a group of Fallen in the southeastern part of this Sector, close to the exit to Glade of Echoes.

Patrols

The Cistern (9)

There are up to nine Patrol beacons in this Sector. Return here again to access additional beacons.

Public Events

Public Events (Full)

Glimmer Extraction: This involves destroying three Fallen extraction sites (1A, 1B, and 1C) dotted around the map.

Injection Rig: This lands at the point shown on the map in the large circular promontory (northwest). Expect a hard fight with a Sub-Boss Psion to defeat multiple times, Gladiators toward the end of the battle, and a Centurion (in addition to normal Cabal forces) during the last wave.

Event Number	Event Type	Target	Other Enemies	Reward
1	Glimmer Extraction	Fallen Extractors	Fallen forces	Glimmer, Boss Chest
2	Injection Rig	Psion Sub-Boss	Cabal forces	Boss Chest

Public Events (Secret)

HVT #1 and #2: A Cabal Centurion or a Vex Storm Minotaur appears at one of the eight indicated points (1A, 1B, 1C, 1D, 1E, 1F, 1G, or 1H).

Pike Gangs: These events are both easily concluded. They each start and finish at the indicated route points.

Launchers: Defeat the Vex Hobgoblins at each of the indicated cannon positions. Remove threats at 5A, then leap through the cannon to reach 5B, and continue to 5C. Then, mow down the Vex Minotaurs as you work your way around 5A, 5B, and 5C once more (using the cannons each time). Defeat all foes around the cannons before they disappear to claim each chest.

Skirmish: Not shown on the map, this Fallen versus Cabal skirmish is lengthy and features tough targets from both groups.

Event Number	Event Type	Target	Other Enemies	Reward
1*	High-Value Target	Cabal Centurion	None	Boss Chest
1*	High-Value Target	Vex Storm Minotaur	None	Boss Chest
3	Pike Gang	Three to four Dreg Pike Riders (along the main road)	Any Pikes you didn't destroy	–
4	Pike Gang	Three to four Dreg Pike Riders (along the main road)	Any Pikes you didn't destroy	–
5	Launchers	Three cannons	Hobgoblins and Minotaurs	Boss Chest (x3)
6	Skirmish	Fallen versus Cabal	High-ranking targets	–

(* Both High-Value Targets appear in one of the same locations across this map)

Enemy Clusters

1 Cabal

The circular promontory north of the main thoroughfare houses Legionaries, Phalanxes, and Incendiors when there's not a Full Event active.

2 Cabal

The shallow pool and ramparts below the Well of Flame tower have Legionaries, Phalanxes, Incendiors, and sniping Psions.

1 Fallen

The large, white blocks by the main road junction have Dregs and Vandals for you to worry about.

2 Fallen

A Captain and some stealthy Marauders are hiding in the northern part of the overhang on the eastern perimeter.

3 Fallen

Expect Vandals, Shanks, and Dregs at the southern end of the overhang on the eastern perimeter.

4 Fallen

The shoreline of the southern white lake features Shanks, Dregs, and a Servitor.

5 Fallen

Led by a Captain, Vandals, Shanks, and Dregs have invaded the Landing Zone.

Scannable Objects

Something sharp is sticking out of this Vex ruin. It's near the big tree.

What's red and monitors Vex architecture? This lore item.

Shimmering white; an archaic Vex pedestal, "well" hidden.

A spear on the edge of a great Radiolarian Fluid lake.

Horizontal energy beam atop a "luminous" entrance.

Pools of Luminance

ENEMY CONTROL
Vex

Sector Notes:

Enemy Clusters: Vex: 2 | Material Nodes: Available | Scannable Objects: 2

OVERVIEW MAP

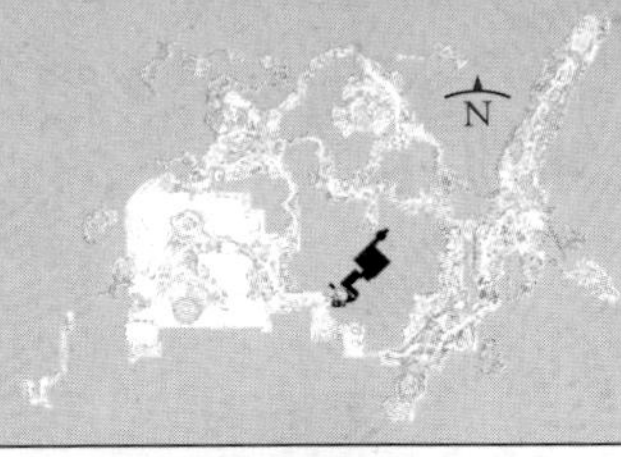

The pools that this Sector is infamous for consist of pure Radiolarian Fluid, the lifeblood of the Vex. It is harmful to stand on, making accurate jumping more important than normal as you investigate this interior area, accessed via the Vex fissure in the southeastern corner of the Cistern Sector. Inside are several uphill caverns leading to a Luminance Arena where you must face a large cluster of Vex foes. Note that this area is visited (with even more Vex threats) during Campaign Mission: Six. During normal circumstances, hone your Vex-culling talents and gather data on two scannable objects when checking this Sector out.

Areas of Interest

1 Exit to The Cistern

A metal block corridor enables you to reach this Sector from the Cistern. This is the only way in or out, assuming the Campaign Mission is not active. Note that the initial circular room, which has an upper alcove and a teleport return, leads to a stream.

2 Radiolarian Stream

A winding stream offers you a chance to perfect your jumping, landing on the rocks rather than the fluid itself. Note the golden alcove to the south that leads to a scannable object.

3 Radiolarian Cavern

Your first Vex encounter occurs here as you ascend a rocky cavern embankment and old ruins.

4 Luminance Arena

The majority of your time here is spent battling almost every Vex enemy type, including a Hydra. Note the stepping stones around the base of this arena and the raised platforms across and north, with a scannable object below.

5 Vex Teleport

The exit corridor usually has Harpies to shoot. It ends at a teleport, which sends you back to the entrance room.

Scannable Objects

A solid gold corridor leads to this scannable prize.

Something is sticking out of that arena chamber Radiolarian Fluid.

Enemy Clusters

1 Vex

The initial cavern has Goblins, Hobgoblins, Harpies, and a Minotaur for you to contend with.

2 Vex

The Luminance Arena is filled with foes, though not quite as many as during the Campaign Mission. Expect the usual Goblins and Hobgoblins, along with Harpies and Minotaurs. A Hydra is also active in this area. Note that the white Radiolarian Fluid is harmful, as always. Watch for Harpies as you exit to the teleport chamber.

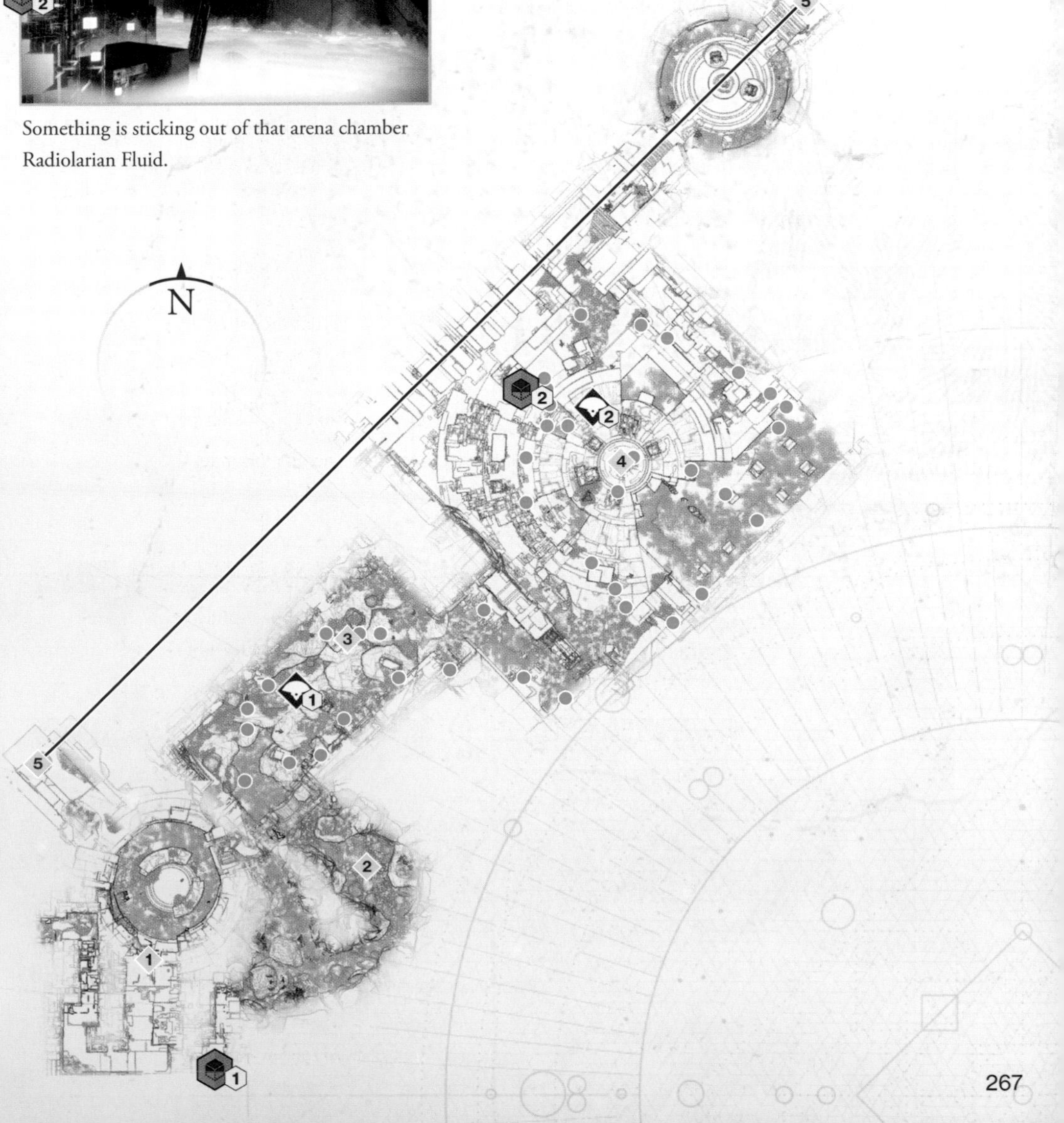

Well of Flame

Sector Notes:

Partially Inaccessible

ENEMY CONTROL

Vex

OVERVIEW MAP

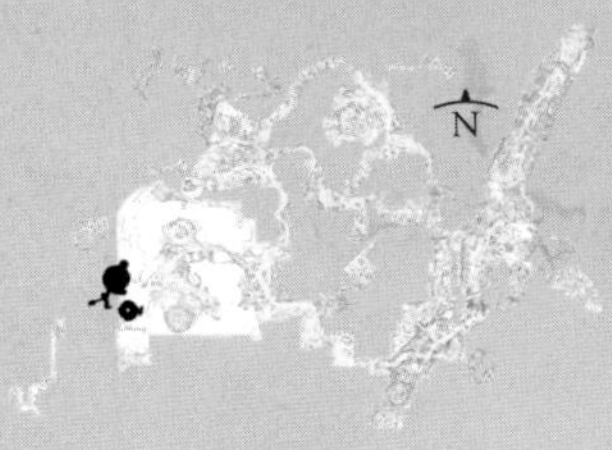

The dominant structure in the southeastern part of the Cistern is a large cylindrical tower. Bound up the side of it to enter the Wall of Flame. This is a Vex temple of some description, but the main arena chamber is inaccessible under normal conditions (only during the Adventure: A Tale of Two Confluxes is it available to enter). There's a slightly convoluted method of getting in and out of this place (which is only accessible via the Cistern), with multiple chances to use Vex teleports depending on how far into the well you want to descend.

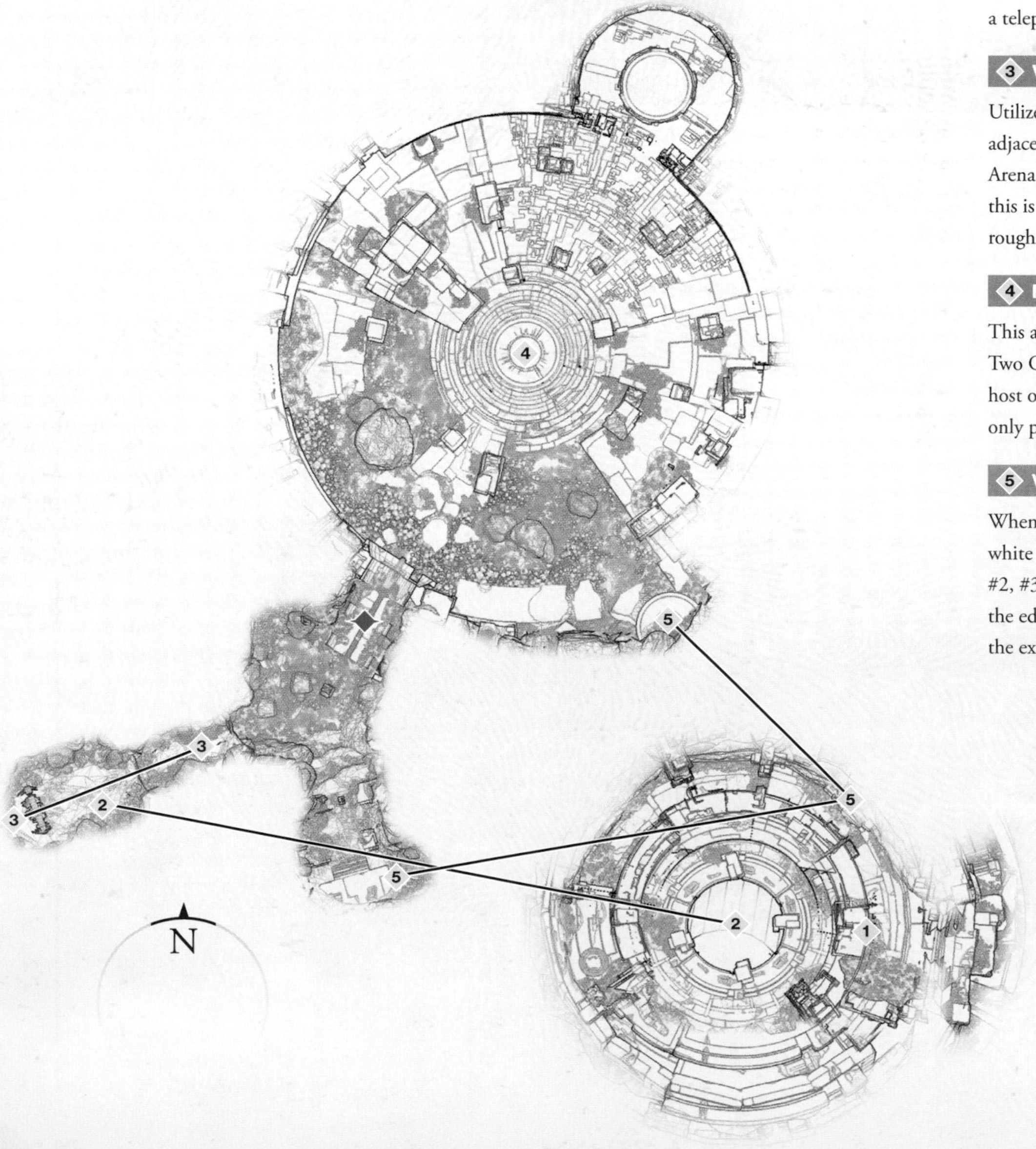

Areas of Interest

1 Exit to The Cistern

This shining Vex entrance is atop a series of large block steps around the exterior of the structure, accessed in The Cistern. This is the only way in or out.

2 Initial Well Drop

The initial chamber is circular, with a deep well hole in the middle. Drop down to reach a small lower dead-end cavern with a Vex portal (#3) and a teleport back to the surface (#5).

3 Vex Portal

Utilize the Vex portal, and you warp into an adjacent chamber with access down to the Flame Arena entrance itself. Under normal circumstances, this is sealed with a barrier, forcing you up some rough steps to another Vex teleport (#5).

4 Flame Arena (Inaccessible)

This area is inaccessible unless Adventure: A Tale of Two Confluxes is active. This is where you battle a host of foes, but under normal conditions, you can only peer into this place from the energy barrier.

5 Vex Teleports and Exit

When you want to leave, use any of the three white glowing teleports on the ground in areas #2, #3, or #4. All warp you to an upper alcove on the edge of the initial drop chamber, just north of the exit.

The Anchor

ENEMY CONTROL
Vex

Sector Notes:

Strike Mission: The Inverted Spire | Usually Inaccessible

OVERVIEW MAP

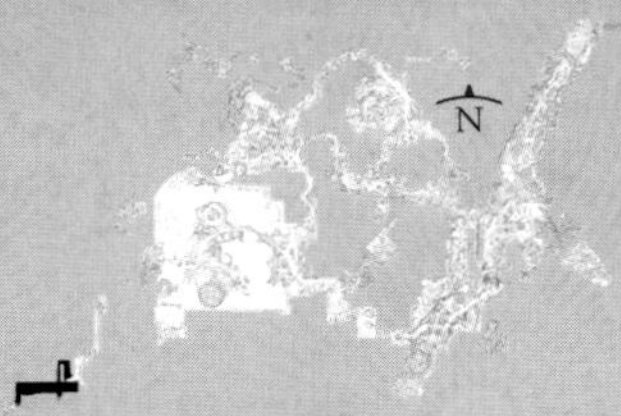

A small connecting chasm that allows access from the Cistern's Vex cannon route (in the far southwestern area of that Sector) into the main Cabal Drill Site Sector. Even though you can reach the entrance at any time, an energy barrier blocks the narrow fissure entrance. This is only removed during the Strike: The Inverted Spire. At all other times, this is impassable.

Areas of Interest

1 Entrance from The Cistern (Northeast)

Head in here from the Cistern after flying across using the Vex cannons.

2 Anchor Chasm (Inaccessible)

This area is only accessible during the Strike. In this chasm, a careful descent and landing is advisable as you and your team fight against Vex forces dotted around the high ledges and lower western platforms. Note the Vex catapult you can use from a lower ledge to reach the exit area.

3 Exit to Cabal Drill Site (Southwest) (Inaccessible)

This area is only accessible during the Strike. The exit brings you out on a tall precipice overlooking the gigantic Cabal Drill Site.

Strikes

The Inverted Spire

To ensure complete access to this area, the aforementioned Strike must be underway.

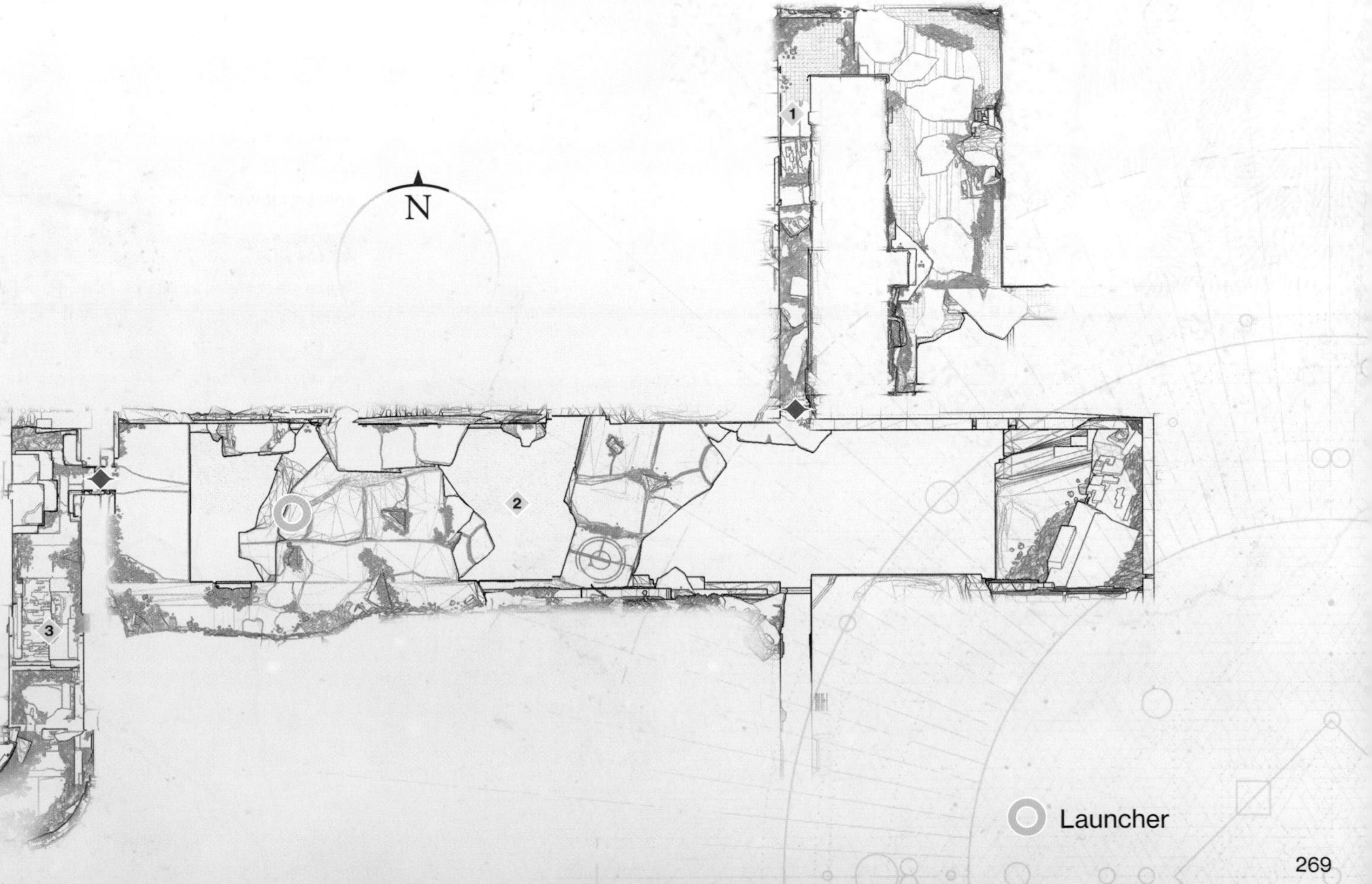

Excavation Site VII

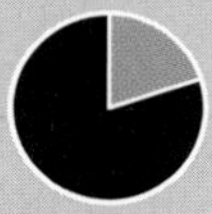

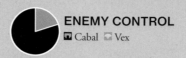

ENEMY CONTROL

Cabal Vex

OVERVIEW MAP

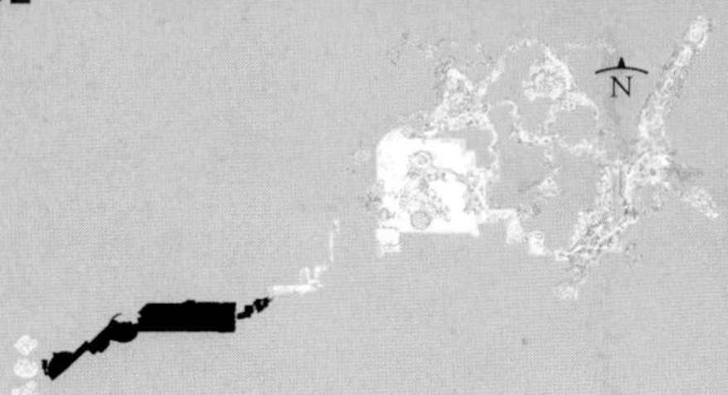

Sector Notes:

Strike Mission: The Inverted Spire | Usually Inaccessible

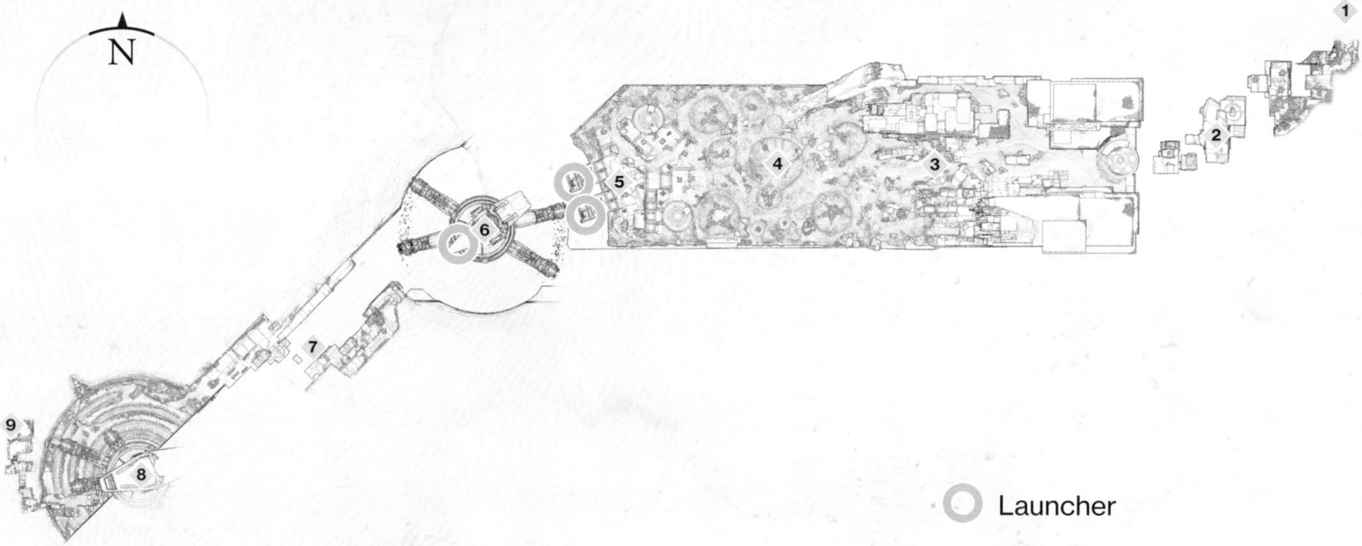

Launcher

This entire Sector is a huge expanse of exterior ground, deadly bottomless mist chasms, and a massive drilling operation undertaken by the Cabal. It is out of bounds unless you are attempting to complete the Strike: The Inverted Spire.

Areas of Interest

1 Exit to The Anchor (Inaccessible)

This area is inaccessible unless the Strike is active. The exit from the Anchor leads you to a spectacular vista overlooking the main drilling operation on Nessus.

2 Stepping Stones (Inaccessible)

This area is inaccessible unless the Strike is active. A series of giant pillars and islands stretch up from the bottomless chasm below. Expect Cabal at every island you land on as you double-jump to the circular promontory at ground level.

3 Vex Paths (Inaccessible)

This area is inaccessible unless the Strike is active. Ride your Sparrow and navigate any of the pathways (there are around four) that are reasonably parallel to one another, all leading to the crater field. The Vex are active in this area.

4 Crater Field (Inaccessible)

This area is inaccessible unless the Strike is active. This open field of craters has received recent bombardment. Cabal are attempting to thwart you; push on to the base.

5 Cabal Mining Base (Inaccessible)

This area is inaccessible unless the Strike is active. This base has a couple of sub-bosses to neutralize. Charge either of the energy cannons before you can catapult yourself at the drill rig to the west.

6 Drill Rig (Inaccessible)

This area is inaccessible unless the Strike is active. Descend into the circular platform below the rig tower, and prepare to repel a wide variety of dangerous Cabal until the energy cannon you programmed to move reaches its position. Then, you can catapult yourself southwest.

7 Vex Gorge (Inaccessible)

This area is inaccessible unless the Strike is active. Work your way along this massive gorge with a deadly drop between two ledge sections. Cross at the islands as you continue heading southwest.

8 Quarry (Inaccessible)

This area is inaccessible unless the Strike is active. Work your way counterclockwise around the grooves the massive digging arms have made, optionally darting into the alcoves to avoid being slain as the arms continue to spin around. You're heading to the exit on the western side of the quarry.

9 Exit to The Inverted Spire (Inaccessible)

This area is inaccessible unless the Strike is active. A narrow Vex passageway connects to the final chamber of the Strike: The Inverted Spire.

Strikes

The Inverted Spire

This entire map is only accessible during this Strike, so learn the more precise troop types you should expect by consulting that section of this guide.

The Inverted Spire

ENEMY CONTROL

Vex

Sector Notes:

Strike Mission: The Inverted Spire | Usually Inaccessible

OVERVIEW MAP

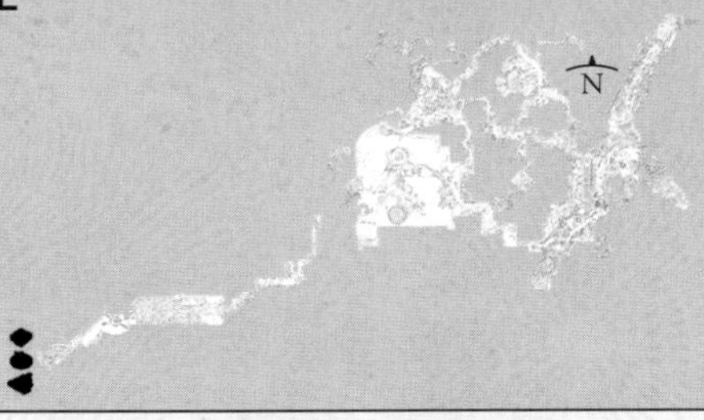

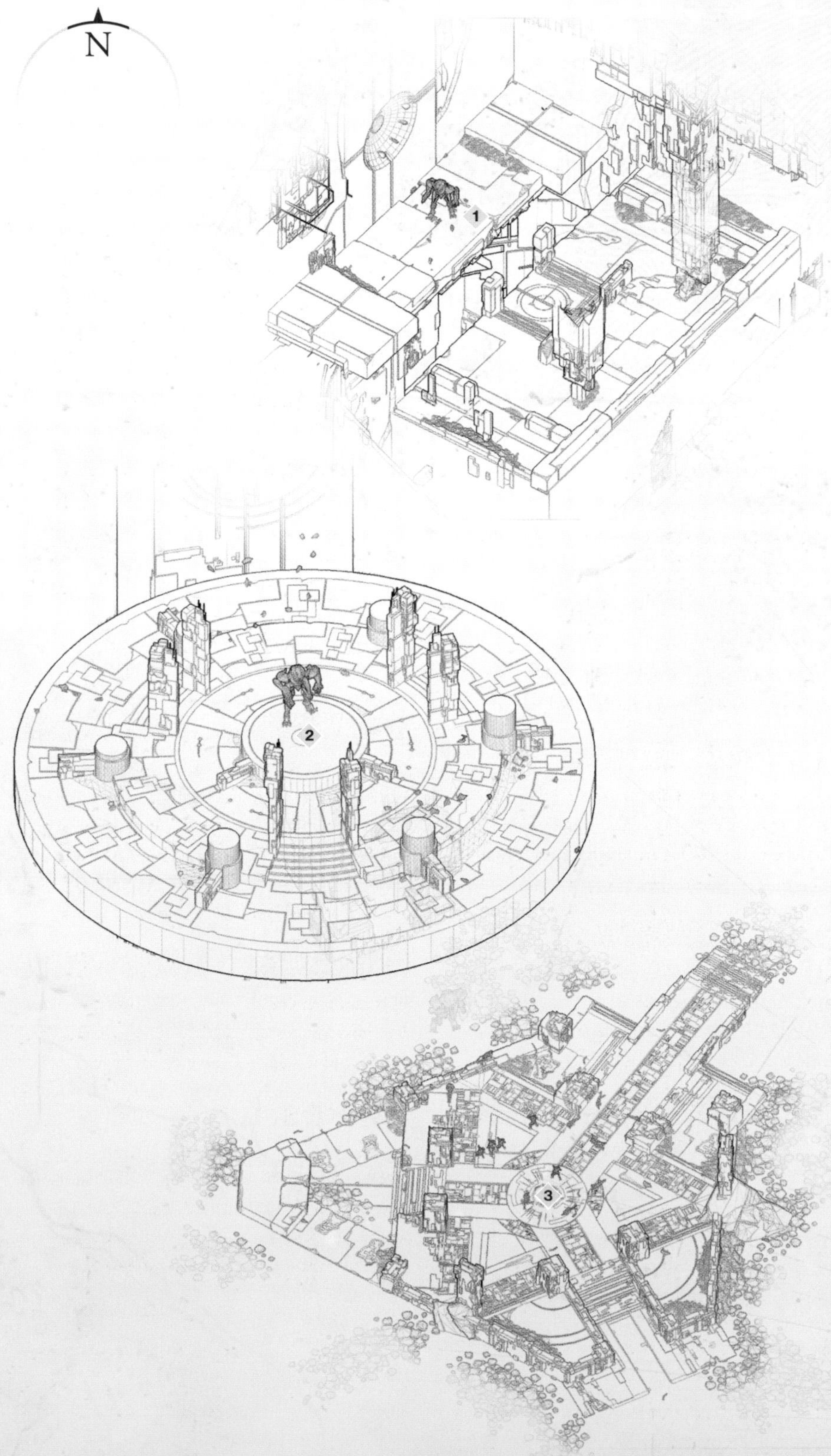

The end of the inaccessible Sectors that you utilize the Cistern to reach concludes with The Inverted Spire, a massive, three-level drop into the core of Nessus. You're also battling a huge and devastatingly powerful Vex Boss known as the Modular Mind. The area is inaccessible unless you are attempting to complete the Strike: The Inverted Spire.

Areas of Interest

1 Guardian Platform (Inaccessible)

This area is inaccessible unless the Strike is active. Enter from the massive circular Cabal Quarry in the Cabal Drill Site Sector. With the Vex Boss woken, you fight the first part of the battle here, in a stone platform of giant floating blocks with a central gap you can't fall through. That is, until the Modular Mind removes this entire ground, and you plummet down to Area #2!

2 Radiolarian Circle (Inaccessible)

This area is inaccessible unless the Strike is active. This circular platform hovers halfway down the spire until the Modular Mind heats up the vicinity and ultimately removes the platform entirely.

3 Tower Base (Inaccessible)

This area is inaccessible unless the Strike is active. The final part of the battle takes place here on the surface of a great lake of fluid. Note the platforms and small pillars you can take a stand on—literally.

Strikes

The Inverted Spire

This entire map is only accessible during this Strike, so learn the recommended methods of slaying the massive Vex Modular Mind by checking that section of this guide.

Hallows

ENEMY CONTROL
Fallen Vex

Sector Notes:

Adventure: Key to the Network | Enemy Clusters: Vex: 3
Enemy Chests: Available | Material Nodes: Available
Patrol Beacons: 7 | Public Event (Full): 1 | Public Event (Secret): 3
Region Chests: 3 | Scannable Objects: 3

OVERVIEW MAP

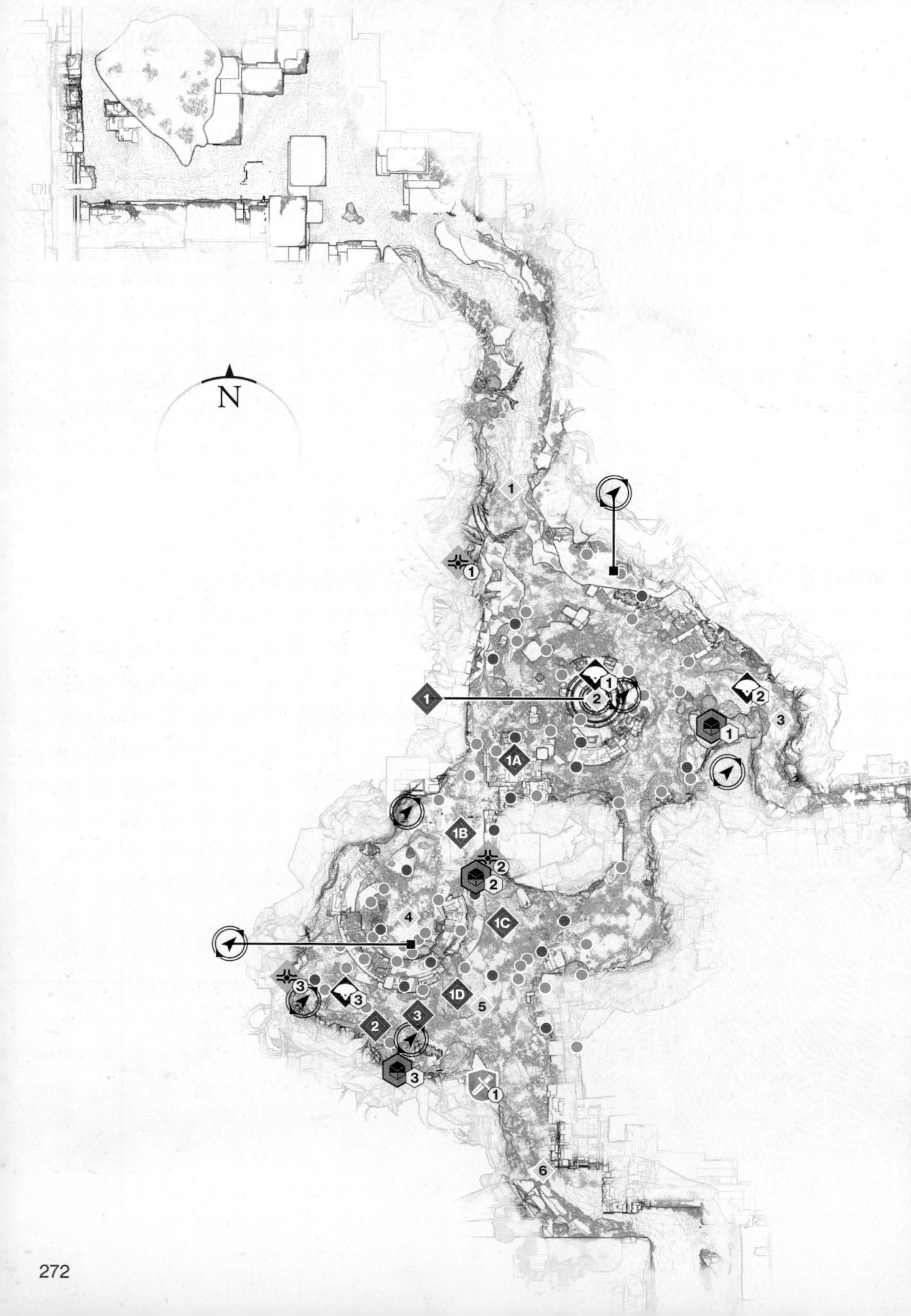

Hallows is an interesting Sector because it has a lot of verticality to it. The usual method of entering is via the surface "hole" from the Artifact's Edge Sector (during Campaign Mission: Looped). Before you descend into the underground (and main) portion of the Sector, note the large Vex courtyard that's overgrown with plants. It features additional materials, a Region Chest, and a scannable object. The subterranean cavern has a main winding thoroughfare running north (from Watcher's Grave) to south (to Glade of Echoes).

Aside from the main cluster of Vex in the portal area, there's a side passage to the east, leading down into the underworld of this planetoid (Sunken Cavern). Learn the geography of this place quickly, and it becomes a lot less confusing to navigate around.

Look Up. Look Down. Look Out!

The following map pinpoints Areas of Interest, enemy clusters, and collectibles that may be "over" the visible part of the map. To ensure that you find the icon in question, check both below and above the indicated location.

Areas of Interest

1 Exit to Watcher's Grave (North)

Look for the tangle of tree branches overhanging the tunnel exit to the Watcher's Grave, which is just north of the main Vex portal area.

2 Vex Summoning Portal

Expect the largest concentration of Vex foes (including a Hydra) here. This is where the only Public Event (aside from the Secret ones) occurs. Check the perimeter area for a chest and scannable object.

3 Exit to Sunken Cavern (East)

Head up the rocky tunnel. Should you wish to explore this moon's interior core, you can proceed through the narrowing entrance of Vex construction that leads into the great void of the Sunken Cavern.

4 Exit to Artifact's Edge (Upper Southeast)

Note the two pictures. The first is the exterior courtyard area, complete with a number of material nodes, as well as a chest and scannable object. Drop down here from Artifact's Edge. Or, climb up the curved ledge perimeter from down below. The second picture shows the base of the hole: a mound with natural light and easy access to the north and south interior areas.

5 Rocky Alcove and Thoroughfare

Just past the Adventure marker is a southwestern alcove, behind the curved foundations of the hole up to the surface. Expect foes and a Skirmish to occur here. This is adjacent to the main thoroughfare; simply follow the winding path northward to investigate the majority of this Sector.

6 Exit to Glade of Echoes (South)

Head south to Glade of Echoes by accessing this exit, which has several gigantic blocks of Vex origin. Use these as recognizable landmarks so you're heading out of the correct exit.

Patrols

Hallows (7)

There are up to seven Patrol beacons, with three or four active at a time.

Region Chests

1 Region Chest 1

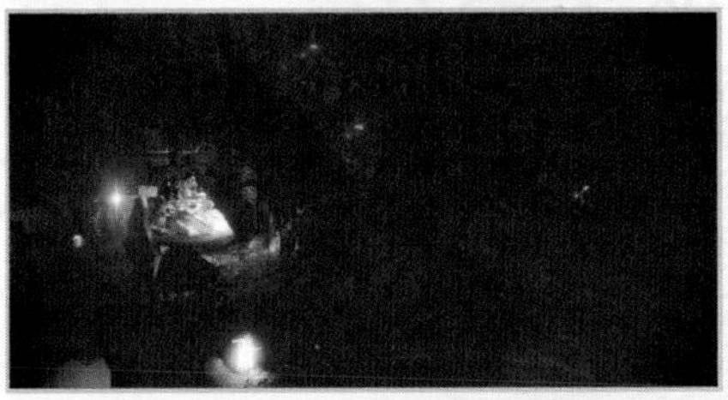

Hidden in the tangle of branches of the old tree, at the northern exit (underground).

2 Region Chest 2

On a ceiling alcove just northeast of the circular hole to the surface (underground).

3 Region Chest 3

On an exterior ledge on the southern perimeter of the entrance to the circular hole (surface).

Enemy Clusters

1 Vex

The main Vex presence around the circular summoning portal includes Goblins, Hobgoblins, Minotaurs, and a Hydra. This is the largest concentration of foes in the vicinity. Expect Goblins to encroach on areas to the south of here. Occasionally, you also encounter Harpies.

2 Vex

The exit tunnel to the east has Goblins and Hobgoblins to worry about.

3 Vex

The alcove cluster features Goblins, Hobgoblins, and a Minotaur.

Public Events

Public Events (Full)

Spire Integration: Vex are attempting to fortify their nearby structures. Simply hold off waves of Vex at the indicated spot. They are approaching from different directions (which appear around the indicated guide map area); to complete this event, defeat them all without letting the integrations total reach zero.

Event Number	Event Type	Target	Other Enemies	Reward
1	Spire Integration	Integration points	Vex infantry	Boss Chest

Public Events (Secret)

HVT #1: A Vex Storm Minotaur appears at one of the indicated guide map locations (1A, 1B, 1C, or 1D). Defeat it immediately!

HVT #2: A Vex Storm Minotaur is hiding on the southern side of the circular drop. Attack it!

Skirmish: This is a fight against consecutive waves of Fallen and Vex infantry throughout the indicated area, close to the main thoroughfare.

Event Number	Event Type	Target	Other Enemies	Reward
1	High-Value Target	Storm Minotaur	None	Boss Chest
2	High-Value Target	Storm Minotaur	Goblins, Hobgoblins, Harpies	Boss Chest
3	Skirmish	Fallen and Vex infantry attack each other	–	Random Loot

Scannable Objects

You get a good view of the summoning portal from here.

Something is glowing red up on the ceiling, near that chest.

This Goblin is half the Vex it used to be. Check outside?

Adventures

1 Key to the Network

The marker is located by a rock near the southern exit of this Sector, below ground.

Glade of Echoes

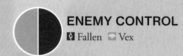

ENEMY CONTROL

Fallen Vex

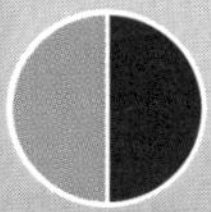

OVERVIEW MAP

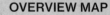

Sector Notes:

Lost Sectors: 1 | Enemy Clusters: Fallen: 4 | Enemy Clusters: Vex: 3

Enemy Chests: Available | Material Nodes: Available | Patrol Beacons: 5

Public Event (Full): 2 | Public Event (Secret): 7 | Region Chests: 3

Scannable Objects: 5

The command section of the EX-077 has crashed to the south of this scorched plateau, which also features access roads westward to the Cistern, northward to Hallows, and northeastward, should you wish to visit the ship Exodus Black itself. The area has scattered clusters of both foe types (Fallen in the middle and Vex around the edges) and cargo containers, pieces of broken fuselage and ship parts, and other debris.

Areas of Interest

1 Exit to Hallows

Towering Vex block walls on either side of the thoroughfare road, and ground-level plateaus mark this exit.

2 Upper Plateau and Road (Northwest)

The relatively flat upper plateau to the northwest has minor Fallen inconveniences (unless a Public Event is active). The road sweeps down below the plateau rocks in a brief natural tunnel.

3 Upper Plateau (West)

The main Vex presence is felt here, especially if a Skirmish is active. Note the globe-like Vex ruins in the vicinity and a side path allowing quicker access to and from the Cistern (to the south).

4 Fuselage and Rock Wall

The remains of a ship fuselage and the base of the plateau rocks have created a narrow gorge in this vicinity. Aside from a scannable object, Fallen are active here in makeshift bases constructed of scavenged ship materials.

5 Crates and Wreckage

The central part of this Sector has areas of wreckage recently constructed into protective platforms and bases by the Fallen. Note the often-overlooked Lost Sector entrance in the middle of it, and the roads bisecting the area.

6 Main Thoroughfare

If you want to get to any of the perimeter exits, take this road that slopes northward. This pinpoints a junction where you can take a sweeping curved road to the northwest, running under the plateau rocks. Or, continue northeast toward Exodus Black Sector.

7 Fuselage and Rocks

A covered shell of fuselage half-hides the Fallen milling around in this area. This is a shortcut to the north exit and a Skirmish area.

8 Exit to Exodus Black

Drive or run up the metal ramp, and you're through to the massive debris piles and ship skeleton that runs all the way into Exodus Black Sector.

9 Southeast Blocks

The raised rocky ground to the southeast has active Vex, along with a number of protruding white cubed ruins. This general area has multiple chests and scannable objects to gather.

10 Exit to The Cistern

A lengthy run along a cliffside road (the bottomless drop is to the south), with access to the southeastern corner of the Cistern near that Sector's LZ.

11 Entrance to EX-077 Command

Access the remains of the command module of the doomed craft by heading through the giant circular fuselage section at the southern and lowest point of the map.

Lost Sectors

1 The Carrion Pit

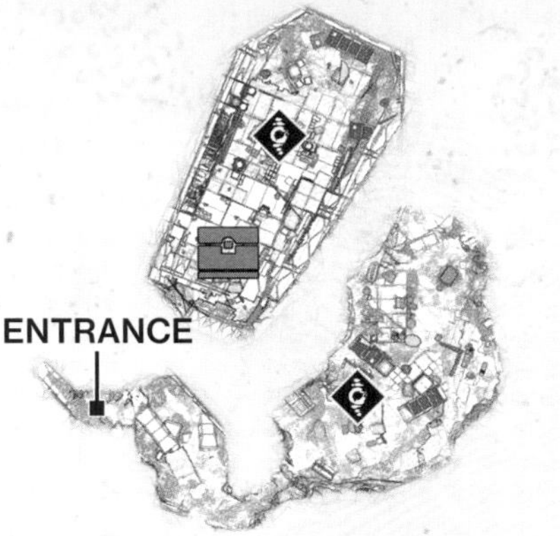

Enter via the entrance among the wreckage of the Fallen-controlled platforms in the center of this Sector. Expect a Shank welcoming committee (Shanks, Tracer Shanks, and a large Shank) at the entrance. Dregs and Vandals appear as you venture farther into this deep blue cargo bay, where you must destroy a named Servitor before the chest is acquired.

Glade of Echoes

	Guide Name	Sub-Boss	Reward
1	The Carrion Pit	Fallen Servitor	Boss Chest

Enemy Clusters

1 Fallen

The upper plateau area has Dregs, Vandals, and Shanks to contend with. Other Fallen infantry types may be present, too.

2 Fallen

The small roadside ambush point is Dreg-heavy, with Vandals and other infantry also a possible threat.

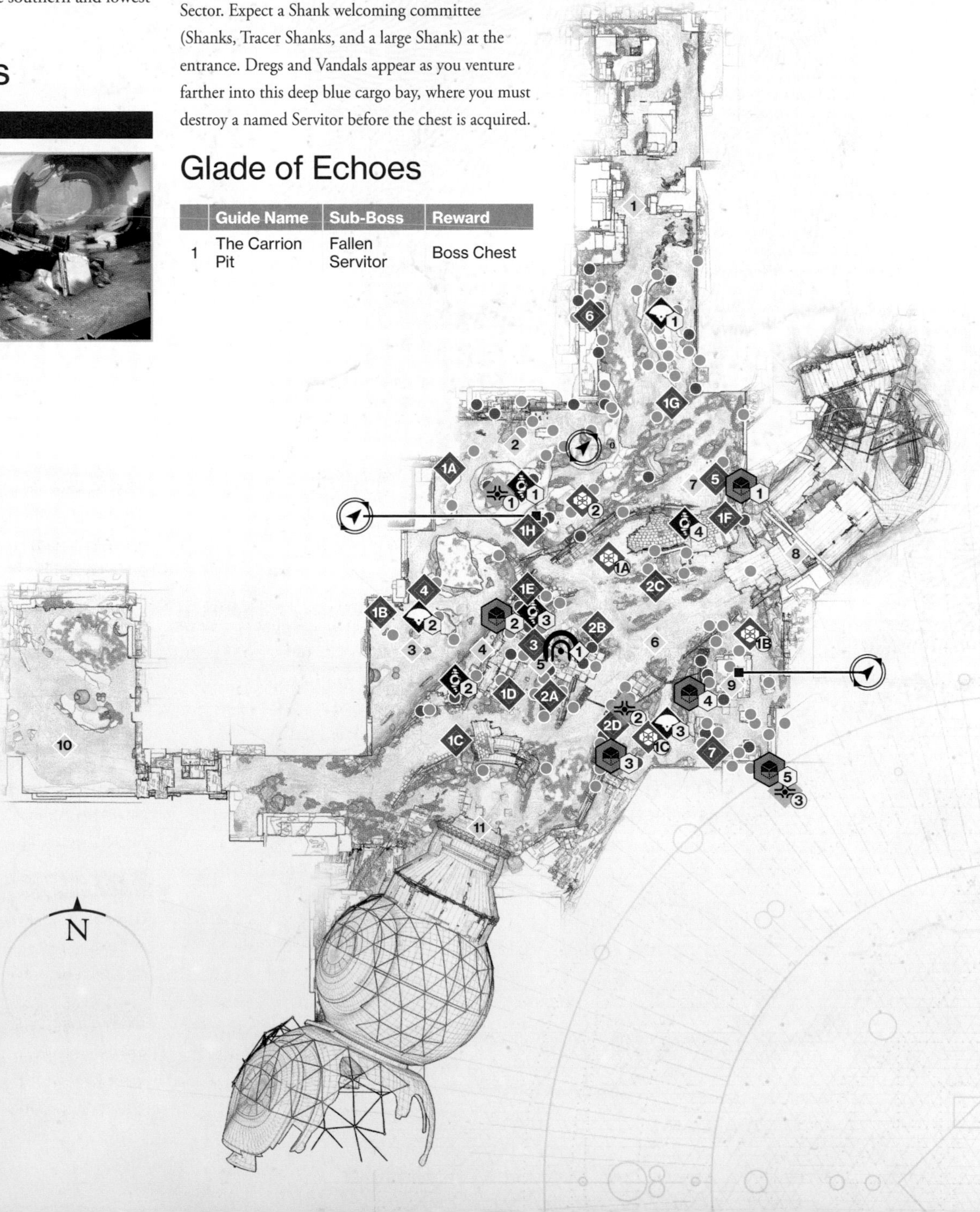

3 Fallen

The majority of the foes among the wreckage in the central part of the Sector are Dregs, with Vandals also active.

4 Fallen

Expect Vandals, Dregs, and a possible Marauder and Shank presence among the fuselage debris just north of the Exodus Black exit.

1 Vex

The low rocks close to the northern exit have Harpies, with additional Goblins in the general vicinity.

2 Vex

Goblins, Hobgoblins, Harpies, and a Minotaur are all expected foes along the western edge of the map, where the greatest Vex presence is felt.

3 Vex

Goblins, Hobgoblins, and possibly a Minotaur and Harpy incursion are likely in the southeastern cube plateau.

Scannable Objects

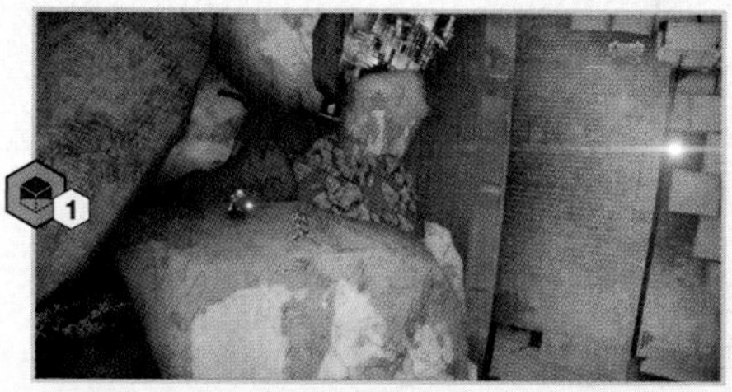

The Goblin has seen better days. You can see an engine fan from here.

Stuck in the wedge between fuselage and a rock wall.

Public Events

Public Events (Full)

Glimmer Extraction: This involves destroying three Fallen extraction sites (1A, 1B, and 1C) dotted around the map.

Spire Integration: Vex are attempting to fortify their nearby structures. Simply hold off waves of Vex at the indicated spot. They are approaching from different directions (which appear around the indicated guide map area); to complete this event, defeat them all without letting the integrations total reach zero.

Event Number	Event Type	Target	Other Enemies	Reward
1	Glimmer Extraction	Fallen Extractors	Fallen forces	Glimmer, Boss Chest
2	Spire Integration	Integration points	Vex infantry	Boss Chest

Public Events (Secret)

HVT #1: A Fallen Captain appears at one of the indicated guide map locations (1A, 1B, 1C, 1D, 1E, 1F, 1G, or 1H). Remove it at once!

HVT #2: A Vex Storm Minotaur appears at one of the indicated guide map locations (2A, 2B, 2C, or 2D) and may be battling Fallen forces. Defeat everything immediately!

Pike Gang: This event is easily concluded with the destruction of these foes.

Skirmish: The first Skirmish features Fallen foes (mainly Dregs and a Captain) fighting against an increased Vex presence (additional Goblins, Hobgoblins, Harpies, Minotaurs, and a Hydra) in the area shown. The top of the plateau rocks is a good place to snipe from.

Skirmish: This second battle has similar foes. Fallen are fighting against Vex, with all infantry types eventually making appearances, including Captains and Servitors (Fallen) and Minotaurs and a Hydra (Vex).

Jailbreak (two locations): A captured enemy (a Fallen Captain or Fallen Servitor, depending on the location) is being held in an energy cell. Tackle the Vex Goblins and Guard Minotaurs. Then, the cell disappears, leaving you to deal with the prisoner foe!

Event Number	Event Type	Target	Other Enemies	Reward
1	High-Value Target	Fallen Captain	None	Boss Chest
2	High-Value Target	Storm Minotaur	Fallen or Vex infantry	Boss Chest
3	Pike Gang	Three to four Dreg Pike Riders	–	Any Pikes you didn't destroy
4	Skirmish	Fallen and Vex infantry	–	Random Loot
5	Skirmish	Fallen and Vex infantry	–	Random Loot
6	Jailbreak	Fallen Captain	Guard Minotaurs, Vex forces, two Hydras	Boss Chest
7	Jailbreak	Fallen Servitor	Guard Minotaurs, Vex forces	Boss Chest

Is it a spear? Is it hidden in a cargo container? Yes.

Coil-shaped and stuck in the southeast rocky outcrop.

Head southeast; it's tucked away up there.

Region Chests

① Region Chest 1

Atop the northwest plateau platform, which you can run under.

② Region Chest 2

Hidden inside one of the stacked cargo containers on the east side of the main thoroughfare.

③ Region Chest 3

In the dark overhang in the very southeastern corner of the Sector (ground level).

Patrols

Glade of Echoes (5)

Despite the size of this Sector, there are only five total Patrol beacons.

EX-077 Command

ENEMY CONTROL
Fallen

Sector Notes:

Strike Mission: Exodus Crash | Scannable Objects: 1 | Usually Inaccessible

OVERVIEW MAP

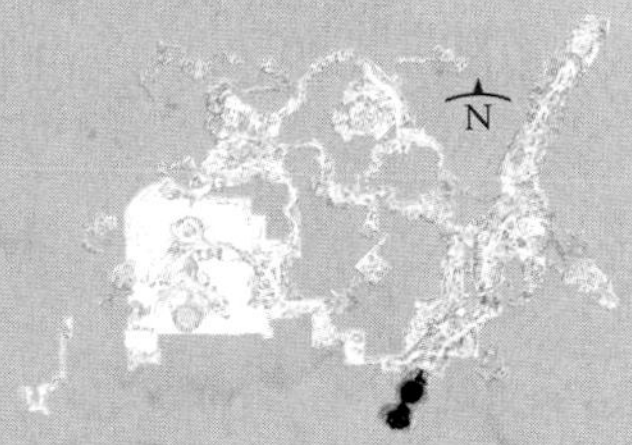

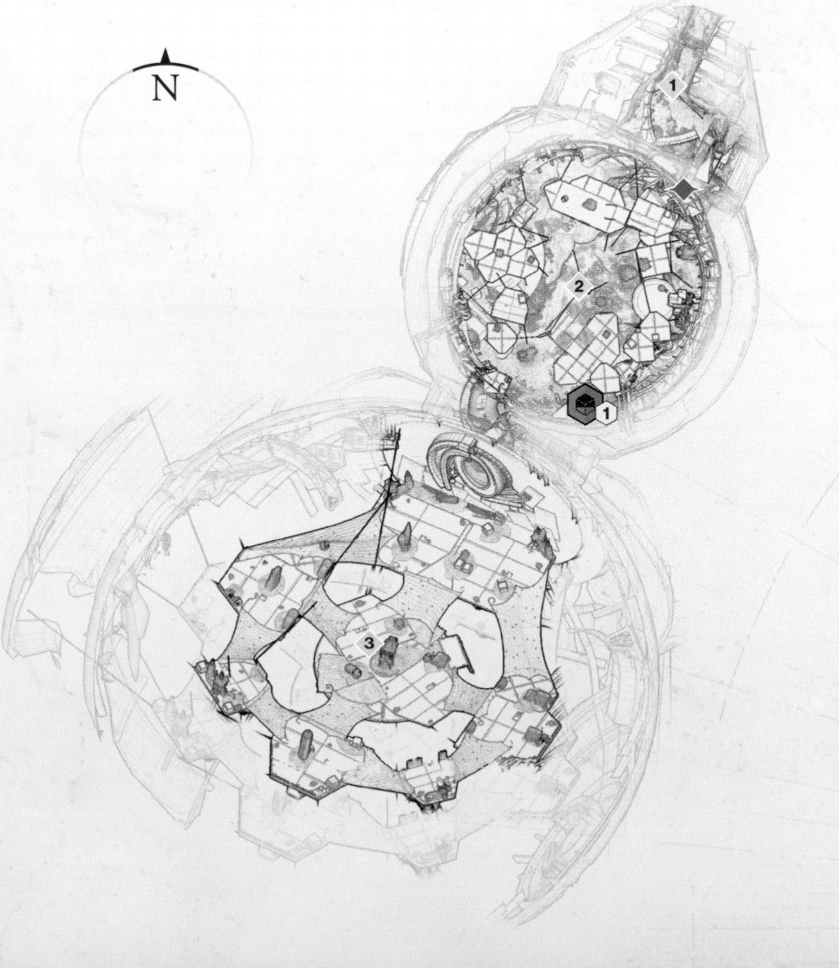

The Command module of the EX-077 departed from the rest of its ship and crash-landed in the southern edge of Glade of Echoes. Currently, the interior of the module is off-limits unless a Strike is active. The interior comprises two large globular chambers. The first features a series of stepping stones. The second is several makeshift platforms connected by ramps, made from both tarp and metal. Conclude your Strike here, and don't forget the scannable object!

Areas of Interest

1 Exit to Glade of Echoes

The patches of burning debris and the steep narrow passage to and from the southern part of Glade of Echoes allow you to reach the lower of the two interior chambers. Under normal circumstances, there is an energy barrier preventing progress.

2 Dark Platforms (Inaccessible)

This area is inaccessible unless the Strike is active. Enter an almost pitch-black interior area, where Fallen have commandeered a makeshift camp. There are several floating platforms, each with a section of scenery on it to make it easier to spot. Simply ascend the platforms to reach the opening into the boss chamber. Did you spot the scannable object along the way?

3 Chasm Platforms (Inaccessible)

This area is inaccessible unless the Strike is active. You must defeat the Fallen Captain Thaviks on a series of ramps connected to platforms above a vertigo-inducing death plummet. Note the Shank intrusion areas dotted about the perimeter of this map.

Strikes

Exodus Crash

Aside from the initial passageway in from the outside (Glade of Echoes), this entire Sector is not accessible unless the Strike: Exodus Crash is active. The Strike culminates here with an assault on a major Fallen force led by Thaviks (a depraved Captain) and his explosive Shank comrades.

Scannable Objects

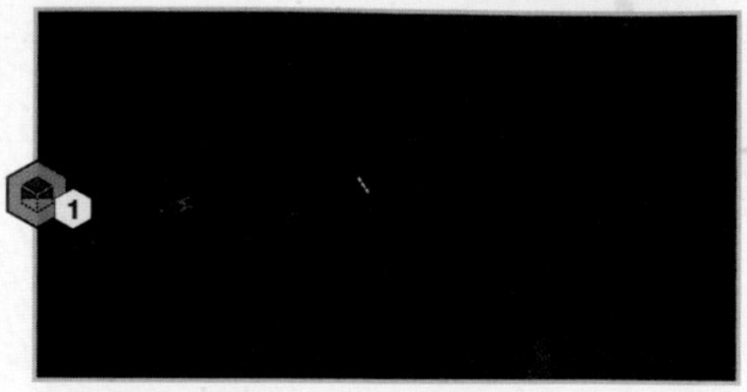

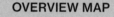

There's an exception to every rule; naturally, there's a scannable object in an inaccessible area! Scan it during the Strike. Try behind the platforms and steps.

Sunken Cavern

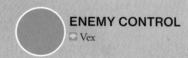

ENEMY CONTROL
Vex

Sector Notes:

Enemy Clusters: Vex: 3 | Material Nodes: Available | Scannable Objects: 2

OVERVIEW MAP

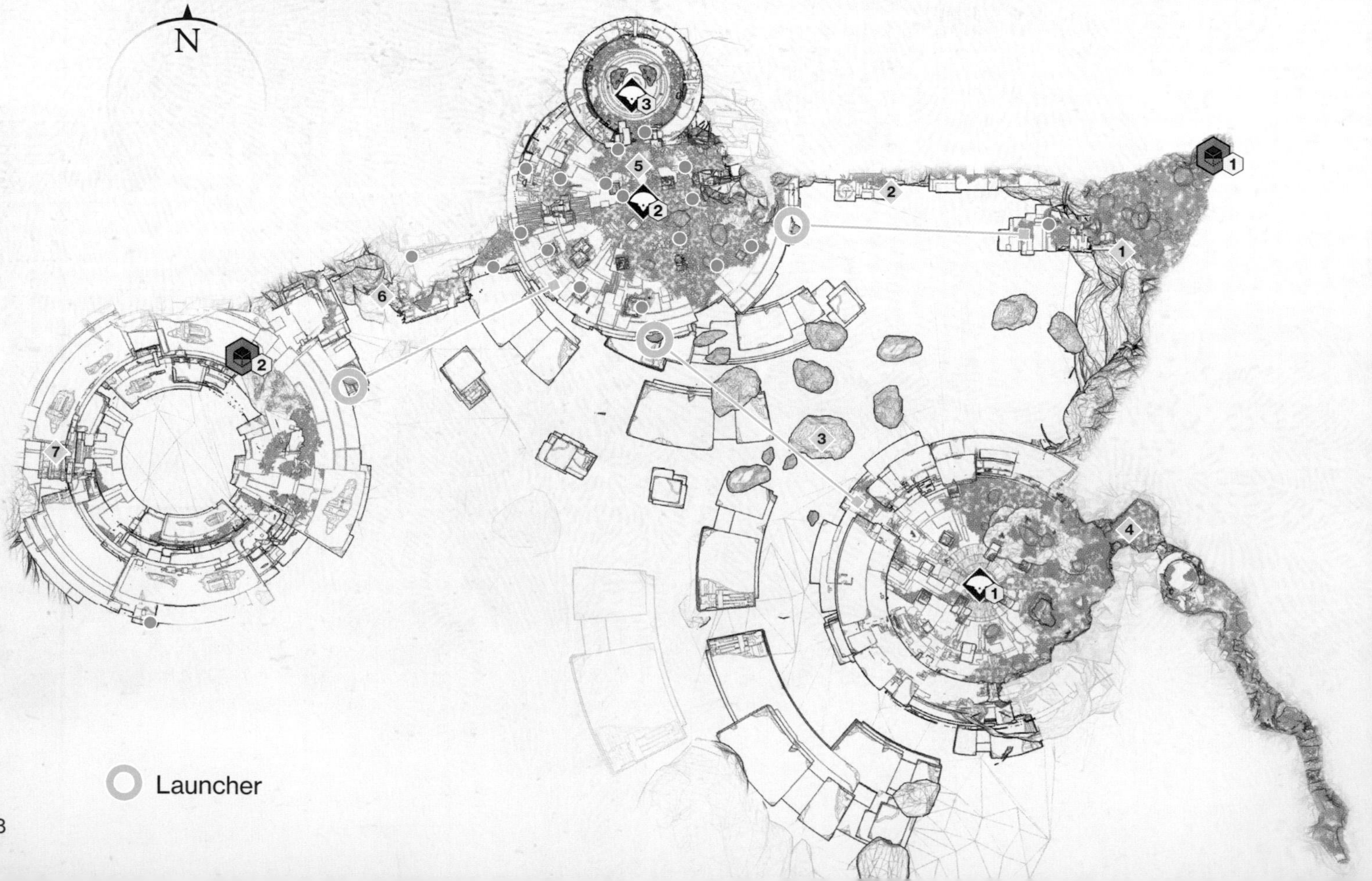

Deep into the bowels of Nessus is a Sector with an understated name: the Sunken Cavern. This is actually three anti-gravity well islands with numerous floating rock and cubic formations surrounding each of them. The deepest Sector (aside from the Well of Giants), this is the most precarious of Sectors you'll visit. That's because of the sheer number of small platforms you need to correctly land on, or you'll face a death plummet into the core of Nessus itself! There is an easily found entrance from Hallows and a lesser-known entrance to Exodus Black from here, but the real reason you're here is to find a couple of scannable objects. One is hidden in an exceedingly cunning location!

Areas of Interest

1 Entrance from Hallows (Upper Northeast)

Head in from the subterranean tunnel linking Hallows to here, and you appear at the top of the glowing void. From here, you can use the Vex ledges or floating boulders to reach the other areas.

2 Vex Ledges (Upper North)

The safer way to reach the mid-level circular chamber is via a descent along the narrow jutting Vex block ledges.

3 Floating Boulders

This is a great way to fall to your death, but it's also a reasonable method of improving your precision jumping. If you're careful, you can reach the upper gold chamber or the mid-level circular chamber from here.

4 Upper Gold Chamber (Exit to Exodus Black)

Accessed via the floating boulders or the Vex catapult attached to the mid-level circular chamber (the one pointing to the upper entrance), expect a Vex presence in this circular room, with a tunnel exit on the eastern wall. This leads you to the Exodus Black Tunnels Sector.

5 Mid-Level Circular Chamber and Vex Altar

A cluster of Vex is present in this north-central circular chamber platform that has a smaller enclosed altar room attached to it. Use the pillars as cover or snipe from them. Note the two Vex catapults; use either to ascend to the Sector exit of your choosing (Hallows or Exodus Black).

6 Northwest Vex Ledges

Use these for a more careful, less "plummet-based" descent from the mid-level chamber. Note the Vex catapult that can deposit you back at the mid-level chamber, allowing for a quick exit.

7 Hovering Well (Exit to Well of Giants)

The lowest point in the Sunken Cavern is this large floating well section, with a series of sizable blocks to drop down in a clockwise maneuver to a Vex portal. The portal warps you to the Well of Giants, but not before you've looked around for a ludicrously positioned scannable object!

Enemy Clusters

1 Vex

There are a number of foes in the upper gold chamber and entrance tunnel to Exodus Black. Most worrisome is a Minotaur, but expect Goblins, Hobgoblins, and Harpies, too.

2 Vex

A sizable Vex presence guards the mid-level circular chamber. Expect the usual smattering of Goblins, Hobgoblins, Harpies, and a Minotaur.

3 Vex

The altar chamber has Goblins and Harpies for you to contend with.

Scannable Objects

In a tiny alcove, near one of the entrances. Don't miss it!

It's a shame you can't float to this yellow Vex conduit near the portal.

Well of Giants

ENEMY CONTROL

Vex

Sector Notes:

Campaign Mission: Looped | Usually Inaccessible

OVERVIEW MAP

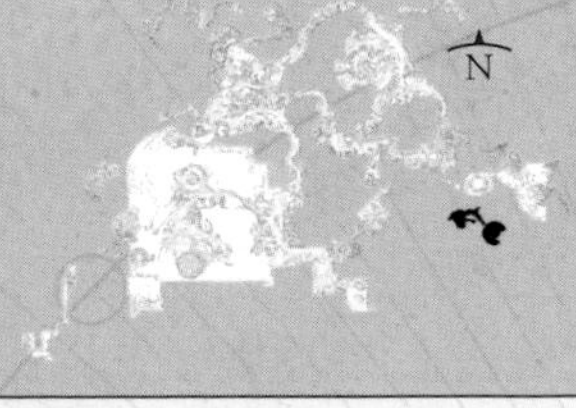

Perhaps the most awe-inspiring of all the Wells on Nessus, this deep opening into the core of the world is normally only accessible during Campaign Mission: Looped. You reach a strange pyramid-shaped opening from the Sunken Cavern, which in turn leads to a sizable energy elevator, dropping you at a large floating arena. Here, you encounter a large Hydra, and you also attempt to save Cayde-6 for the first time.

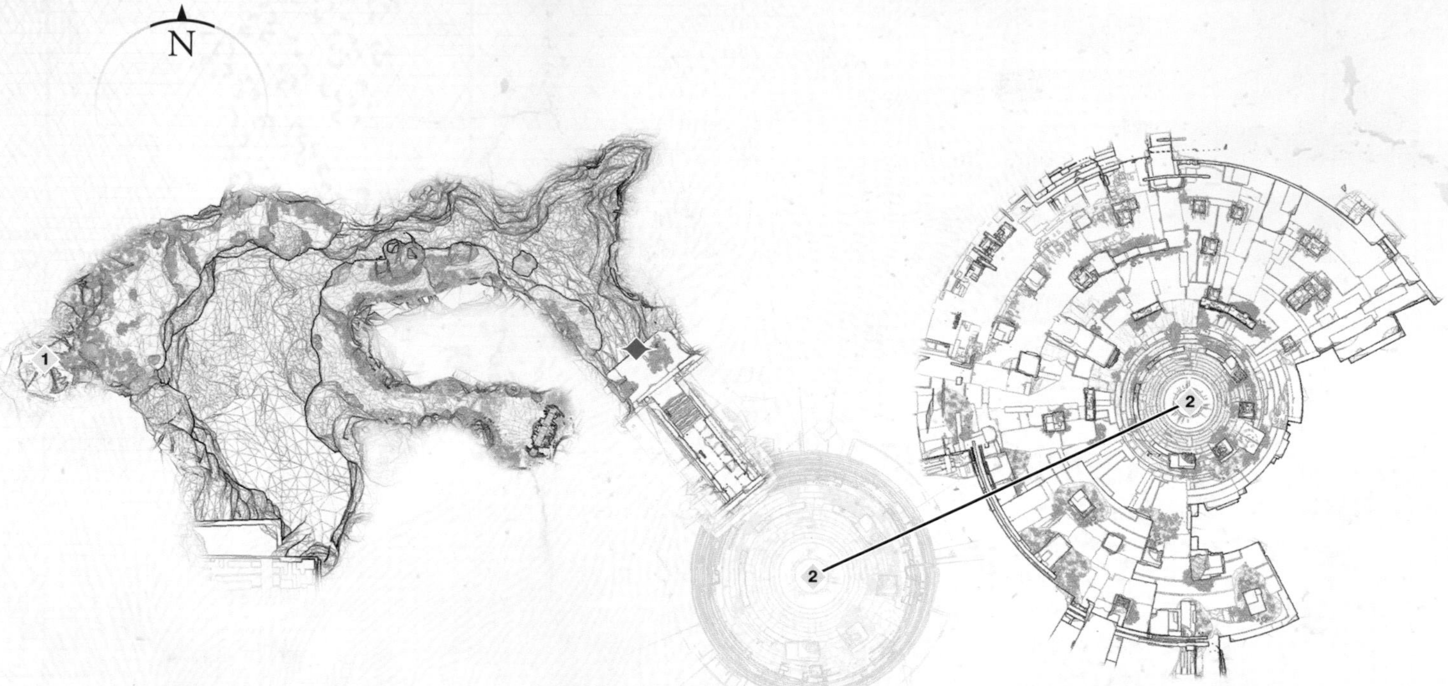

Areas of Interest

① Exit to Sunken Cavern

Enter via careful jumping across some small ledges and islands above a bottomless void. The entrance is a pyramid-shaped connecting passage.

② Well Arena (Inaccessible)

This area is only accessible during the mission. Drop down the energy elevator to the arena itself. Use the many walls and upper platforms on the western side of the arena as your fight with the Hydra progresses. Beware of a large influx of Vex during this battle.

Campaign Mission

Prospect

Battle a Hydra (and completely fail to save Cayde-6) in this chamber. It usually isn't accessible at any other time.

Exodus Black

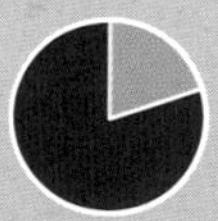

ENEMY CONTROL

Fallen Vex

OVERVIEW MAP

Sector Notes:

Adventure: Assault of Black | Lost Sectors: 1 | Enemy Clusters: Fallen: 4
Enemy Clusters: Vex: 1 | Enemy Chests: Available | Landing Zone: Available
Material Nodes: Available | Patrol Beacons: 7 | Public Event (Full): 2
Public Event (Secret): 5 | Region Chests: 3 | Scannable Objects: 5
Vendor: Failsafe | World Quest: The Exodus Black

The resting place of the Exodus Black and location of the A.I. Failsafe looks to be a dead end. But appearances can be deceiving. This expansive Sector of water surrounded by spacecraft wreckage, with a makeshift Fallen base to the northwest, has a few surprise exits that aren't immediately obvious. When you enter from Glade of Echoes or land here from Orbit, be sure to check the Lost Sector, the (blocked) entrance to Prodromus Down (north), and most importantly, the narrow crag under a huge tree just east of the Fallen base. This leads to an underground tunnel area with the only portal to the Chamber of Sky, as well as a secondary entrance to the Sunken Cavern. If you plan on a deeper exploration of Nessus, this is a good place to start.

Areas of Interest

1 Exit to Prodromus Down (Inaccessible)

This passageway is inaccessible, as an energy barrier prevents you from entering a giant trench-like area where the ship Prodromus has crash-landed. Enter this Sector, navigating its electrical fields, during Strike: Exodus Black.

2 Entrance to Exodus Black (Northwest)

The entrance to the doomed ship is under the giant circular canopy. Enter this to reach Failsafe and start the World Quest.

3 Fallen Base (Northeast)

Bisected by roads, there are two main base structures built from wreckage, where a large portion of the Fallen enemies is lurking. Note the numerous chests, scannable objects, and Secret Public Events that occur around these structures.

4 Tunnel Entrance (Northeast)

A large tree wraps its roots above this sunken entrance down into some narrow crags, which lead to a narrow tunnel interior.

5 Entrance to Chamber of Sky (Tunnel)

The tunnel widens to a cavern with Vex enemies in the vicinity. Choose to enter the Vex portal, and you're transported to the Chamber of Sky. This is the only access point.

6 Entrance to Sunken Cavern (Tunnel)

This is the alternate entrance to and from the Sunken Cavern Sector (the other is via Hallows). Simply maneuver to the opposite end of the Tunnel area.

7 Lake and West Wreckage Zone

The middle of this map is a wide expanse of water dotted with wreckage and boulders that become more numerous as you head north and south along the western perimeter, where the Lost Sector entrance and a scannable object are. Expect periodic Fallen battles in this area.

8 Southeast Wreckage Zone

Fallen enemies lurk among the pathway and scattered wreckage along the southeastern side of this map. Note the scannable object at the southern end.

9 Exit to Glade of Echoes

The southern part of the map is a large thoroughfare that connects this Sector to Glade of Echoes. Feel free to use the elevated cylindrical chassis of a spacecraft as an alternate entrance when driving a Sparrow.

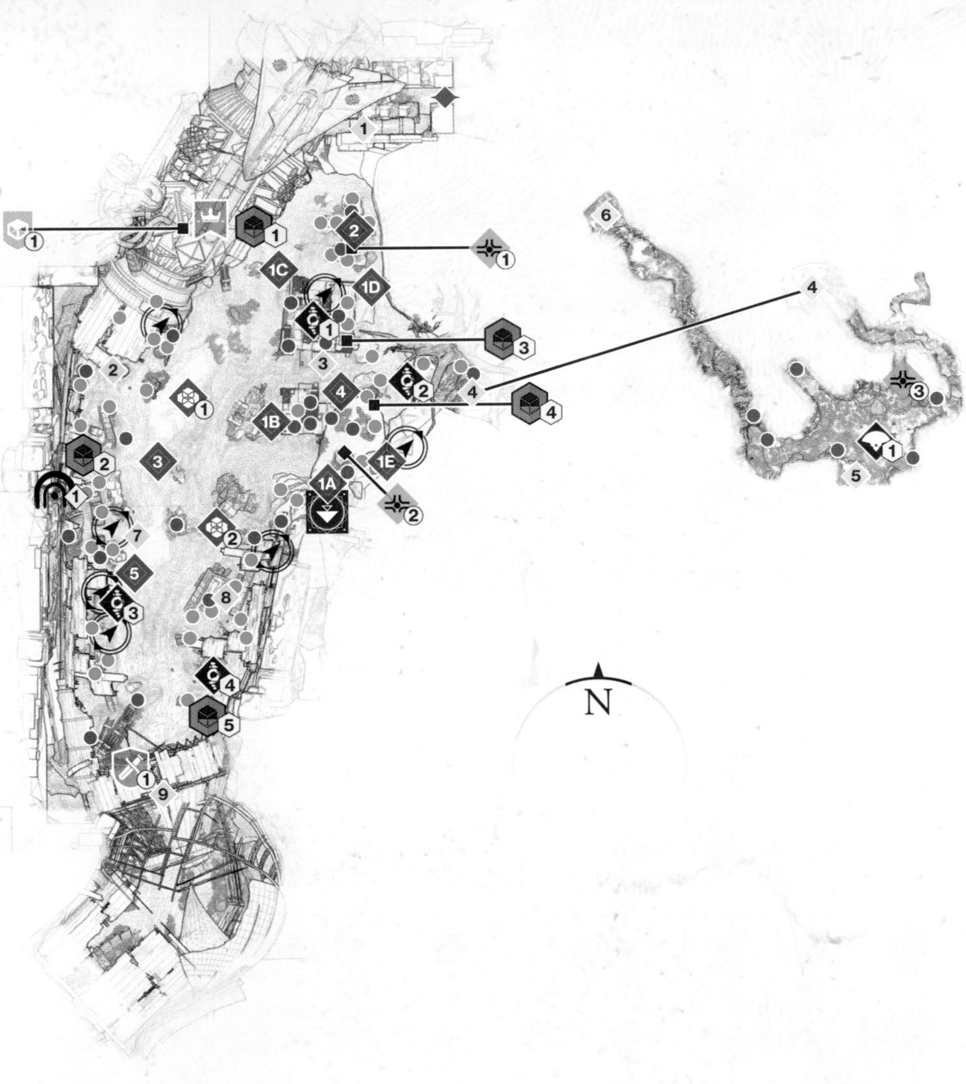

Lost Sectors

The Void

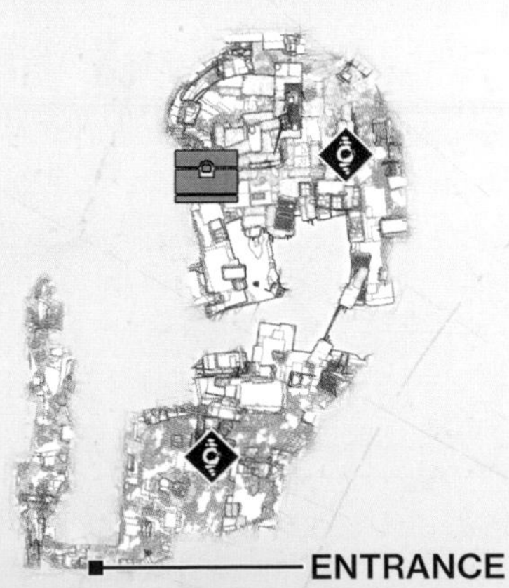

Enter the opening in the western perimeter wall to reach an underground block construction of Vex origin. This is now a Fallen base, complete with Dregs, Servitors, other infantry types, and a Fallen Captain across the bridge, which spans a bottomless void.

Exodus Black

	Guide Name	Sub-Boss	Reward
1	The Void	Fallen Captain	Boss Chest

Adventures

1 Assault of Black

Begin this Adventure by locating the marker at the threshold of this Sector, at the southern entrance.

Region Chests

① Region Chest 1

Check the collection of natural rock formations just north of the Fallen base.

② Region Chest 2

This sits atop the very high flat rock plateau above and southeast of the Fallen base.

③ Region Chest 3

Check a narrow alcove in the northern edge of the main cavern, across from the Vex portal in the Tunnel area.

Landing Zone

Exodus Black LZ

Descend from Orbit and disembark on the top of a rock formation, close to the Fallen base and high rock plateau. Use this LZ if you need quick access to Failsafe.

Patrols

Exodus Black (7)

There are seven total Patrol beacons you can interact with in this Sector. Return to access any that aren't active.

Public Events

Public Events (Full)

Servitor Resupply: This takes place in the central lake area. There are multiple waves of lesser Servitors and Fallen foes can overwhelm you if you aren't careful.

Spire Integration: Vex are attempting to consolidate to this position. Simply hold off waves of Vex at the indicated spot. They are approaching from different directions (which appear around the indicated guide map area); to complete this event, defeat them all without letting the integrations total reach zero.

Event Number	Event Type	Target	Other Enemies	Reward
1	Servitor Resupply	Fallen Servitor	Shanks, Dregs, Vandals, Servitors	Boss Chest
2	Spire Integration	Integration points	Vex infantry	Boss Chest

Public Events (Secret)

HVT #1: A Fallen Captain appears at one of the indicated guide map locations (1A, 1B, 1C, 1D, or 1E). Remove him at once!

Ambush: A Fallen Captain and a group of Fallen infantry are lurking among the rock formations north of the Fallen base. Defeat all of them!

Pike Gang: This event is easily concluded by eliminating these foes on vehicles.

Skirmish: The first battle features Fallen foes (Dregs, Vandals, Shanks, and a Captain) defending their base against an increased Vex presence (Goblins, Hobgoblins, Harpies, Minotaurs, and a Hydra) in the area shown.

Skirmish: This second battle (by the water's edge) has Vex attacking Fallen forces from the south. Vex infantry teleport in, while Fallen descend from dropships. The full range of enemy types isn't incoming for this Skirmish, making it slightly easier.

Event Number	Event Type	Target	Other Enemies	Reward
1	High-Value Target	Fallen Captain	Fallen infantry	Boss Chest
2	Ambush	Fallen Captain	Fallen infantry	Boss Chest
3	Pike Gang	Three to four Dreg Pike Riders	–	Any Pikes you didn't destroy
4	Skirmish	Fallen and Vex infantry	–	Random Loot
5	Skirmish	Fallen and Vex infantry	–	Random Loot

Enemy Clusters

① Fallen

The base itself has a fair number of Dregs, Vandals, and Shanks, along with the possibility of a Captain (especially if an ambush or High-Value Target is active).

② Fallen

Mainly Shanks and Dregs guard the tree root entrance to the Tunnel.

③ Fallen

Expect periodic battles with lesser Fallen along the wreckage-strewn western edge. Shanks are common here.

④ Fallen

Expect Vandals, Dregs, and a Captain to be lurking from time to time in the southeastern wreckage zone.

① Vex

If you want to face down Fanatics, Goblins, and a Minotaur, head into the Tunnel.

Scannable Objects

What's inside this Fallen bag of tricks? Hanging closer to Failsafe than she thinks.

If you're looking for a transmitter, it's got to be on a high plateau, right?

Small fuselage sections have more than just inaccessible cargo crates inside them.

The shape of a pot, in a small copse of saplings. Easy to find for those seeking "Adventure."

A computer terminal, forgotten by the Fallen.

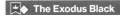

Vendor

Failsafe

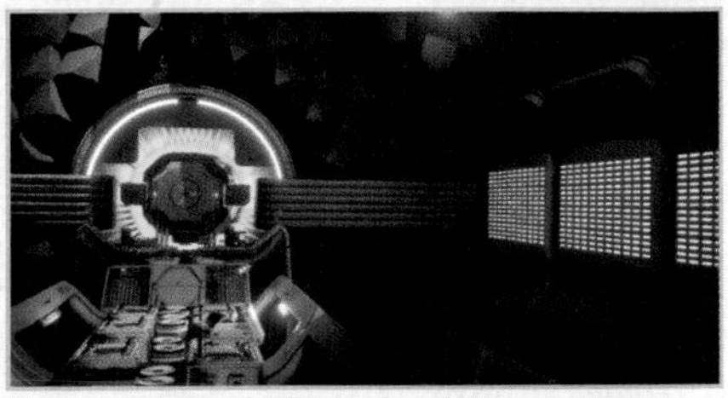

The slightly unhinged artificial intelligence of the Exodus Black could be considered an ally. She takes any Tokens you find across Nessus. Bring her these in groups of 10, five, or one. In return, you'll receive an increase in your Reputation with her, allowing you to purchase unique Nessus armor and weaponry. Failsafe also decrypts engrams.

World Quest

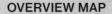

The Exodus Black

Once certain prerequisites have been made, start this quest spanning much of the entirety of Nessus by speaking to Failsafe.

Chamber of Sky

ENEMY CONTROL
Vex

Sector Notes:

Enemy Clusters: Vex: 2 | Material Nodes: Available | Scannable Objects: 1

OVERVIEW MAP

This chamber is only accessible if you're exploring the tunnel system beneath Exodus Black that runs to Sunken Cavern Sector. Mid-way through the tunnel is a small Vex-guarded cavern with a portal on a ledge. Step into the portal to appear here. This is a giant cavern, with elements of nature and Vex melded together. The initial part of the cavern has a rocky feel, whereas the far cavern has the block-like architecture you'd expect from the Vex. As expected, the Vex are out in force here (especially sniping Hobgoblins), so clear this Sector by finding the scannable object and teleporting back to the entrance tunnel. This chamber is also accessed during Adventure: Assault of the Black.

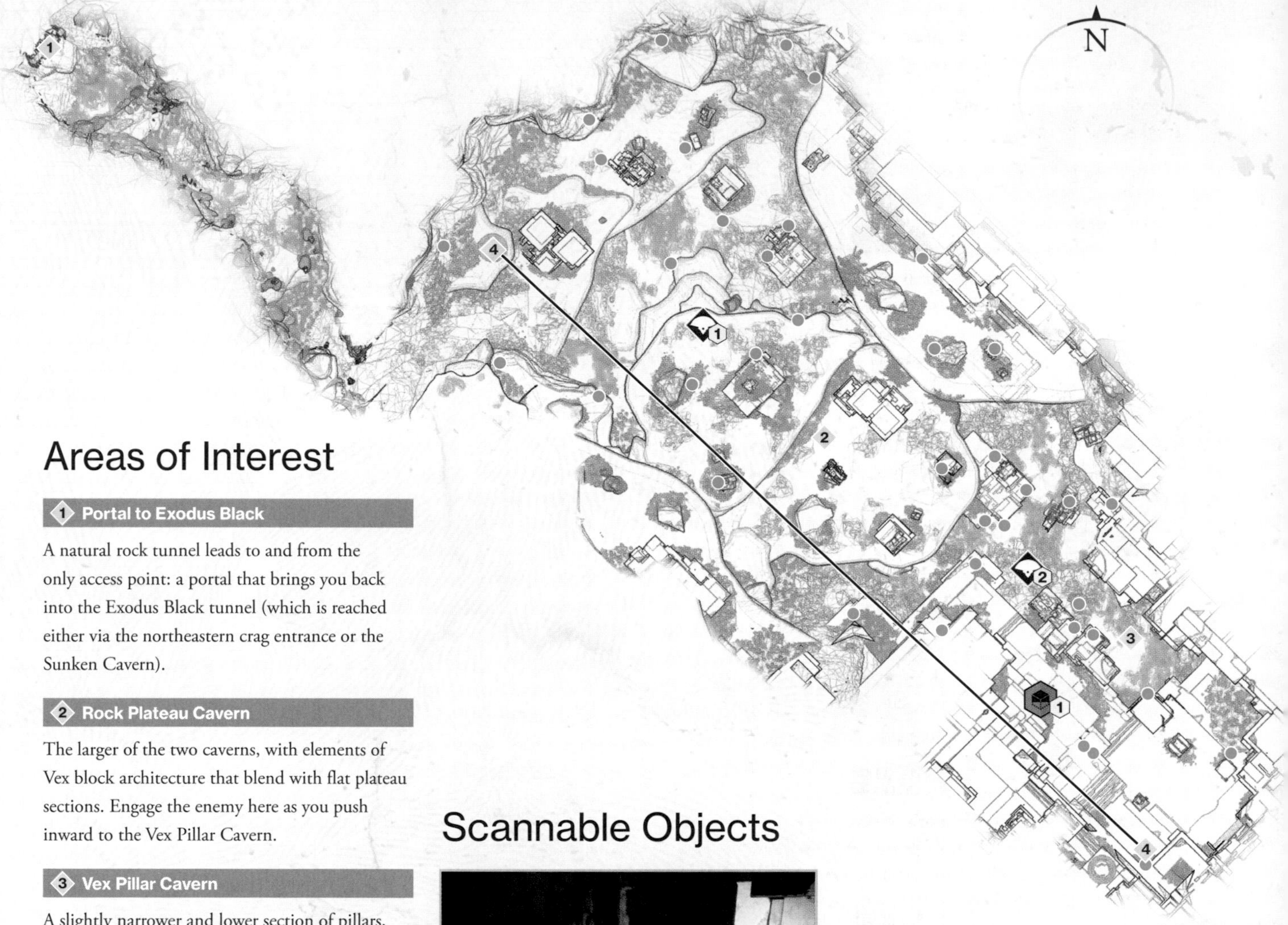

Areas of Interest

1 Portal to Exodus Black

A natural rock tunnel leads to and from the only access point: a portal that brings you back into the Exodus Black tunnel (which is reached either via the northeastern crag entrance or the Sunken Cavern).

2 Rock Plateau Cavern

The larger of the two caverns, with elements of Vex block architecture that blend with flat plateau sections. Engage the enemy here as you push inward to the Vex Pillar Cavern.

3 Vex Pillar Cavern

A slightly narrower and lower section of pillars, where you and Vex forces play a game of hide and seek. Note the scannable object in the vicinity.

4 Teleport

The dead end here means you can either retrace your steps or use the teleport to reach the initial ledge area close to the exit tunnel.

Scannable Objects

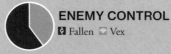

Something is slowly pulsing and clamped to a block wall. Found it yet?

Prodromus Down

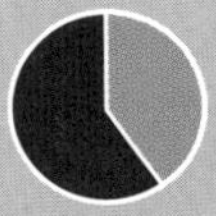

ENEMY CONTROL

Fallen / Vex

OVERVIEW MAP

Sector Notes:

Strike Mission: Exodus Crash | Usually Inaccessible

This is a vast trench with scattered debris, crashed craft, and a turf war between Vex and Fallen forces, which you must deal with during the Strike: Exodus Crash. Otherwise, only the entrance passage from Exodus Black is accessible (which is where you exit if you're playing the Strike).

Areas of Interest

1 Exit to Exodus Black

This is the only accessible part of this Sector if the Strike is not active. You appear on the northern edge of the Exodus Black map. Head into this Sector, and an energy barrier prevents progress.

2 Transmitter Chamber (Inaccessible)

This area is inaccessible unless the Strike is active. It's a small Vex transmitter chamber with encroaching Fallen foes (the most dangerous are explosive Shanks and toughened Servitors). Stand your ground here and clear the area before continuing.

3 Cargo Storage Exit (Inaccessible)

This area is inaccessible unless the Strike is active. During the Strike, you work your way from the massive scarred trench through a low-ceiling cargo storage area to Area #2.

4 Trench (Inaccessible)

This area is inaccessible unless the Strike is active. This is a vast exterior area of Sparrow-suitable roads, a nasty bottomless chasm to the southwest, and a number of Vex foes to navigate around or nullify.

5 Side Cavern (Inaccessible)

This area is inaccessible unless the Strike is active. These are optional passages into a small interior cavern. They are usually not imperative to visit.

6 Strike Insertion Point (Inaccessible)

This area is inaccessible unless the Strike is active. The Radiolarian Fluid cascading into a bottomless pit serves as the starting point from Orbit during the initial stages of the Strike.

Strikes

Exodus Crash

This entire Sector is only accessible during this Strike. You and your team must pass through a number of electrical fields and gather data on the Fallen before moving on to Exodus Black.

Io Overview

Enemy Control
- CABAL
- VEX
- TAKEN

A partially terraformed planetoid orbiting Jupiter, Io was abandoned by the Traveler, though Ikora Rey and the Warlock Guardians consider the area around the Echo Mesa mountain to be sacred. Currently, this region has seen recent Cabal activity, though the Red Legion appear to be actively fleeing the world, rather than savaging it. The reason may involve some concerning anomalies detected by Asher Mir. Although this area has examples of impressive Vex architecture, the telltale signs of Taken activity are present throughout this place.

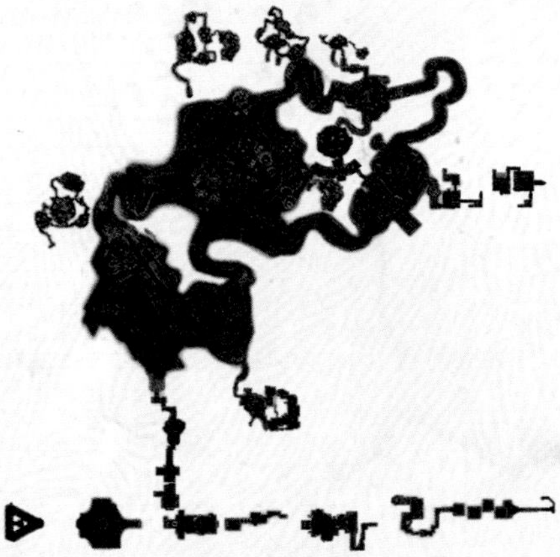

Progression (Activities)

Exploration on Io begins once you arrive at the beginning of Campaign Mission: Sacrilege. You stay here for a total of two Campaign Missions, after which you return to the EDZ. During this time and any time afterward, you are free to explore this region and complete any World Quests and Adventures you deem necessary. The following flowchart details this progression.

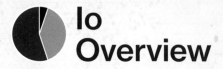

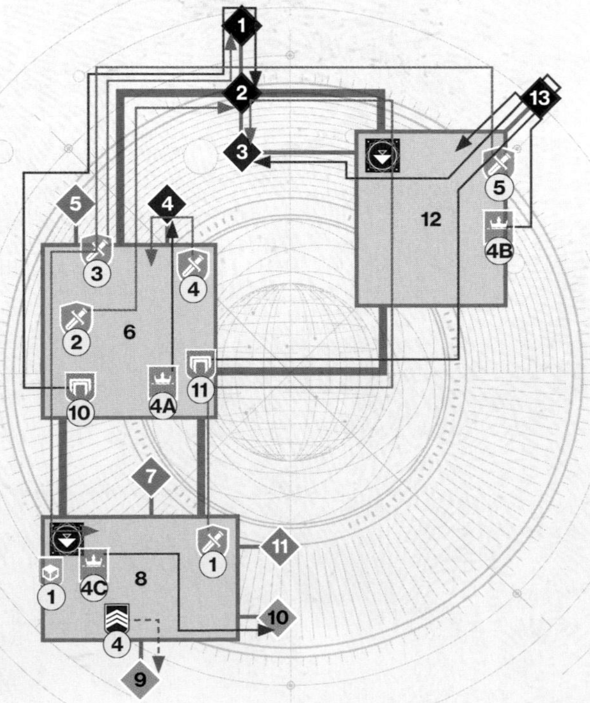

1. The Wraith Mines
2. Terrabase Charon
3. Warmind Vault JYS-2
4. Spine Burrows
5. Grove of Ulan-Tan
6. Lost Oasis
7. Sanctum of Bones
8. The Rupture
9. Pyramidion
10. The Endless Gate
11. Aphix Conduit
12. Giant's Scar
13. Excavation Site II

Legend

- Landing Zone
- Activities: Wells
- Activities: Chambers
- Strike: Fallen and Vex
- Lost Sector
- Public Space
- Campaign: Sacrilege (10)
- Campaign: Fury (11)
- Strike: The Pyramidion (4)
- Adventures: Stravinsky (1)
- Adventures: Experiment 7X (2)
- Adventures: Ascendant (3)
- Adventures: Conversion Process (4)
- Adventures: Road Rage (5)
- World Quest: King's Shadow (4)
- World Quest: The Hunt (4A)
- World Quest: The Conversion (4B)
- World Quest: Asher's Theory and The Army (4C)

Progression

- Campaign: Sacrilege (10)
- Campaign: Fury (11)
  - Landing Zone (The Rupture)
  - Landing Zone (Giant's Scar)
- Asher Mir (1)
  - Adventures: Stravinsky (1)
  - Adventures: Experiment 7X (2)
  - Adventures: Ascendant (3)
  - Adventures: Conversion Process (4)
  - Adventures: Road Rage (5)
  - World Quest: King's Shadow (4)
  - Strike: The Pyramidion (4)
- Back to EDZ

Io: Activities

Io: Activities Table

The following table shows the available activities, entities, Side Missions, and other pertinent data for every Sector within this region. Note that some activities (for example, Landing Zones) are not immediately available, but appear through progression.

Name	Type	Adventures	Lost Sectors	Landing Zone	Patrols	Public Events (Full)	Public Events (Secret)
Lost Oasis	Public	3	1	Available	6	2	5
Spine Burrows	Activity (Taken)	–	–	–	–	–	–
The Rupture	Public	1	2	Available	8	1	4
The Endless Gate	Activity (Vex)	–	–	–	–	–	–
Pyramidion	Activity (Vex)	–	–	–	–	–	–
Terrabase Charon	Activity (Cabal and Taken)	–	–	–	–	–	–
The Wraith Mines	Activity (Cabal and Taken)	–	–	–	–	–	–
Warmind Vault JYS-2	Activity (Taken)	–	–	–	–	–	–
Giant's Scar	Public	1	–	Available	9	2	6
Excavation Site II	Activity (Cabal and Taken)	–	–	–	–	–	–
Total	3 (Public)	5	3	3	23	5	15

Name	Material Nodes	Enemy Chests	Region Chests	Lost Sector Chests	Scannable Objects	Vendors	Strikes	World Quests
Lost Oasis	Available	Available	3	1	4	–	–	Available
Spine Burrows	Available	–	–	–	2	–	–	–
The Rupture	Available	Available	3	2	5	1 (Asher Mir)	Available	–
The Endless Gate	Available	–	–	–	1	–	–	–
Pyramidion	–	–	–	–	–	–	–	–
Terrabase Charon	Available	–	–	–	5	–	–	–
The Wraith Mines	Available	–	–	–	3	–	–	–
Warmind Vault JYS-2	–	–	–	–	–	–	–	–
Giant's Scar	Available	Available	3	–	5	–	–	–
Excavation Site II	Available	–	–	–	3	–	–	–
Total	8 (Sectors)	3 (Sectors)	9	3	28	1	1	1

Lost Oasis

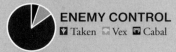

ENEMY CONTROL
Taken Vex Cabal

Sector Notes:

Adventure: Ascendant | Adventure: Experiment 7X | Adventure: Conversion Process

Lost Sectors: 1 | Enemy Clusters: Taken: 11 | Enemy Chests: Available

Landing Zone: Available | Material Nodes: Available | Patrol Beacons: 6

Public Event (Full): 2 | Public Event (Secret): 5 | Region Chests: 3

Scannable Objects: 4 | World Quest: King's Shadow

OVERVIEW MAP

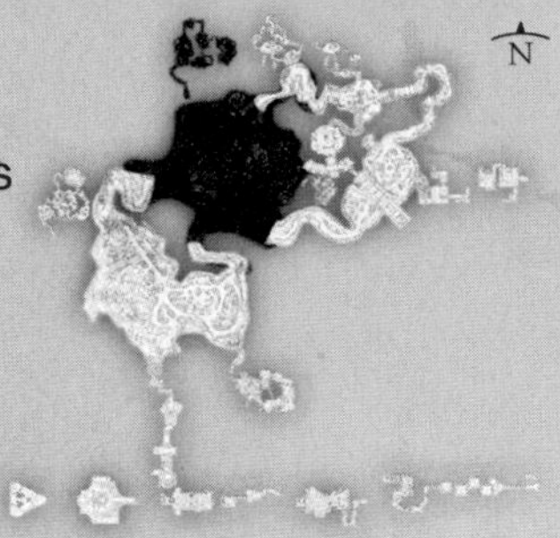

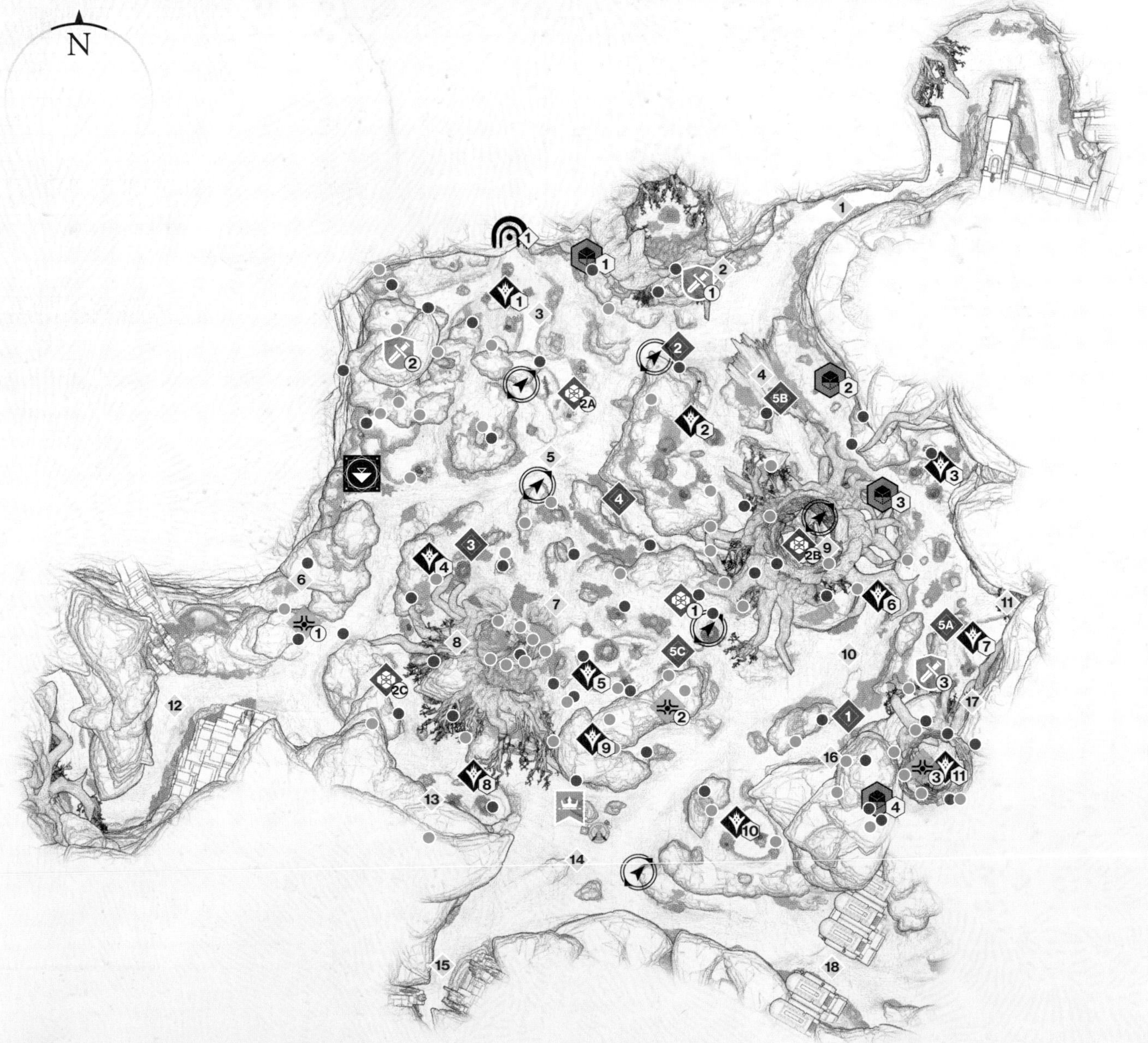

Lost Oasis is easily the largest Sector on this moon. It contains a good deal of tiny cave alcoves to find, Taken foes scattered across the open mesa plateaus, and a half-dozen ancient and gigantic trees, now frozen like stone. The two biggest have an underground tunnel linking them. There are roads around the perimeter and a river bisecting the general area. This is also the hub when you're maneuvering to all the other Sectors on Io.

Areas of Interest

1 Road to Terrabase Charon (Northeast)

The main road narrows and the cliffs close in as you attempt to head toward Terrabase Charon Sector. Go here mainly to access missions.

2 Giant Tree Hole (North)

There's a hole in the side of the rock wall allowing access into the ancient remains of a tree. There's little inside, but outside is an Adventure to access. An upper tunnel connects to a small ledge on the west side of the hole, where you can find a scannable object.

3 Waterlogged Gorge

Northeast of the plateau cluster near the Landing Zone is a waterlogged floor, close to the Lost Sector entrance.

4 Tree Log Ramp

It's easier to access heading from southeast to northwest, but this giant hollow log makes a great ramp if you're riding a Sparrow. It's also a good landmark to spot. Note the nearby plateau to the west, with a cluster of Taken foes and a scannable object to the east.

5 Main Mesa Road

The rough center of this Sector is a winding rough road that takes a diagonal path from one of the Rupture entrances (Area of Interest #12) all the way to the Terrabase Charon entrance (#1). There are plateaus on both side of this road.

6 West Cliffs

A small opening in the rock plateau to the east of this point takes you to a little ledge and into a cavern with a Region Chest inside. The entire western edge of this area is a death plummet: stay on solid ground!

7 Main Mesa Plateau

Between the two gigantic tree forms (#8 and #9) is a large plateau, where you'll always find Taken to battle. Also, there are usually other activities (typically Full Events) to attempt. You can use plenty of low rocks as cover.

8 Mesa Tunnel (West Entrance)

Amid the massive tangle of roots of an ancient dead tree is an entrance to a winding interior tunnel with Material Nodes, a Region Chest, and Taken to battle. Note the rough path of this tunnel shown on the guide map.

9 Mesa Tunnel and Stream (East Entrance)

The other entrance to the Mesa Tunnel is at the large tree stump on the eastern side of the Sector. This also marks the location of a gorge stream and a connecting road running along the eastern side of the map.

10 Eastern Road

This connects the Log Ramp and Terrabase Charon entrance and curves around to the south of the Sector. In addition to exploring the more rocky perimeter and hidden caves along the eastern perimeter, you can also access the main mesa plateau from here.

11 Entrance to Spine Burrows (East)

Close to a selection of Taken and an Adventure is the entrance to a small but significant secondary Sector, a cave tunnel to the Spine Burrows.

12 Entrance to The Rupture (Southwest)

This is one of two large gorge roads that winds its way to the Rupture Sector. It's usually the quickest way from the Landing Zone to reach Asher Mir (in the Rupture), though the road runs by some cliffs. Don't be overly enthusiastic with the Sparrow acceleration.

13 South Cave Alcove

Close to the World Quest start and other exit to the Rupture is a cluster of Taken foes guarding a small cave. You may find it devoid of items, or there may be a chest inside, ready to loot.

14 Vehicle Pad and Crossroads (South)

A small collection of boulders and a circular vehicle pad mark the crossroads of the main roads running along the southern and eastern edges of this Sector.

15 Entrance to The Rupture (South)

Just south of the Crossroads is your second exit to the Rupture. Depending on where you're headed to in the Rupture, pick this or Area of Interest #12.

16 17 Dead Tree Climb Entrance 1 and 2

Don't overlook a couple of strange holes in the eastern perimeter rock wall. Both lead to a vertical and hollowed out ancient tree trunk, with a small cavern at the top. You can jump up or down the trunk, watching for foes as you go. You're rewarded with a Region Chest and scannable object.

18 Entrance to Giant's Scar (Southeast)

Should you want to view the massive drilling operation occurring at Giant's Scar Sector, this southeast exit is the one to take.

Adventures

1 Ascendant

Positioned on the rock outcrop near the tree hole along the northern perimeter.

2 Experiment 7X

Atop a boulder plateau in the northwestern corner of the map.

3 Conversion Process

Adjacent to the glistening pool and entrance to the Spine Burrows, where Taken foes reside.

Lost Sectors

Grove of Ulan-Tan

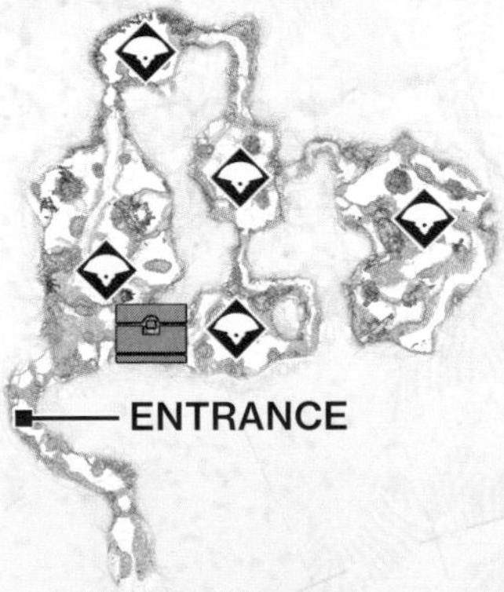

Accessed via a cave entrance in the northwest corner of Lost Oasis, this leads to a series of narrow caverns. Follow the glistening stream, battling Vex Harpies and Goblins, with a main battle against a Sub-Boss Minotaur.

Lost Oasis

	Guide Name	Sub-Boss	Reward
1	Grove of Ulan-Tan	Vex Minotaur	Boss Chest

Enemy Clusters

1 Taken

Expect a possible Taken incursion of four or five foes in the glistening pool at the entrance to the northwest (and only) Lost Sector.

2 Taken

A few Taken infantry guard the rocky mesa just northwest of the main dead tree.

3 Taken

Along the eastern perimeter of this Sector, an upper reflecting pool near the root tendrils of the massive dead tree has a Knight and two underlings to tackle.

4 Taken

A Taken Centurion and two Psions are the usual problems you encounter on this plateau above one of the main thoroughfares.

5 Taken

On top of the main mesa between the two gigantic dead trees are around five Taken, with Phalanxes being the main threat.

6 Taken

A couple of Taken (usually a Knight and a Psion) are guarding a rock close to the largest tree roots and underground exit on the east side. Behind them in the low rock wall is a cave entrance leading to a scannable object.

7 Taken

A Taken Knight and some other infantry are guarding the glistening pool to the southeast, where the entrance to Spine Burrows is located.

8 Taken

A small cluster of Taken infantry (usually a Knight and two Thralls) is near a tiny alcove cave against the southern perimeter.

9 Taken

Expect Taken Knights and sometimes other Taken entities inside the central cave system you enter at either of the tree root entrances (Areas of Interest #8 and #9).

10 Taken

A Taken Wizard and two underlings (usually Taken Psions) are guarding the strange glistening pool on the ledge above the exit to Giant's Scar.

11 Taken

A tortured Taken Knight is sometimes guarding the interior of this tree stump cave. Climb the interior of the "trunk" to an upper cave with Thralls to face.

Landing Zones

Lost Oasis

Land on the edge of the mesa at a small camp with strange fossilized bones on the rock formations nearby. This offers quick access to all major Sectors.

Patrols

Lost Oasis (6)

There are six Patrols that are accessible here (one is shown as an example); leave and return to unlock more beacons as you progress.

Public Events

Public Events (Full)

Cabal Excavation: This takes place on the flat central plateau. You attempt to override a Cabal mining laser while dodging incoming laser fire and Cabal infantry waves that drop in from above, as well as any nearby Taken.

Taken Blight: Large black sacs of rift material that oozes out new Taken are active in this area! Your job is to destroy the Blight's integrity until it explodes and then regenerates at a second position. Repeat the demolishing of the Blight, then move to a third regeneration (2A, 2B, and 2C locations on the guide map). Make sure that multiple Guardians are engaged in removing both Taken and Blight integrity, or this is impossible to finish.

Event Number	Event Type	Target	Other Enemies	Reward
1	Cabal Excavation	Mining Lander	Cabal infantry	Boss Chest
2	Taken Blight	Blight Integrity	Taken infantry	Boss Chest

Public Events (Secret)

HVT #1: A Vex Storm Hydra appears somewhere on the indicated guide map route. Neutralize it at once!

HVT #2: A Vex Storm Minotaur appears somewhere on the indicated guide map route. Defeat it immediately!

Skirmish: A clash between the Vex and Taken takes place on the slope of the main plateau. There are various troops from both sides, so remaining active and in cover is imperative.

Skirmish: A clash between the Vex and Taken occurs along the gorge stream close to the eastern tree trunk. The enclosed area and plethora of troops (including a Hydra and toughened Taken in the last waves) mean this is dangerous.

Launchers: Defeat the Vex Hobgoblins at each of the indicated cannon positions. Remove threats at 5A, then leap through the cannon to reach 5B, and continue to 5C. Then, mow down the Vex Minotaurs as you work your way around 5A, 5B, and 5C once more (using the cannons each time). To claim the three chests, defeat all foes around the cannons before they disappear.

Event Number	Event Type	Target	Other Enemies	Reward
1	High-Value Target	Storm Hydra (Vex)	None	Boss Chest
2	High-Value Target	Storm Minotaur (Vex)	None	Boss Chest
3	Skirmish	Vex versus Taken	Warning! Copious enemies!	Random Loot
4	Skirmish	Vex versus Taken	Warning! Copious enemies!	Random Loot
5	Launchers	Three cannons	Hobgoblins and Minotaurs	Boss Chest (x3)

Region Chests

① Region Chest 1

Inside a small cliff ledge chest to the west, close to the exit to the Rupture.

② Region Chest 2

Halfway along the main interior tunnel connecting both giant tree stumps, below the main mesa plateau.

③ Region Chest 3

Halfway up the inside of the hollow tree cave, southeast perimeter.

Scannable Objects

1

Head north, find a tiny ledge, and ignore a hollow tree.

2

An old Vex cannon, now slowly disintegrating near a giant fallen log.

3

Found the small cave along the main east road by the giant tree?

4

The climb up the hollowed-out tree with the Region Chest is worth it; this is at the top.

World Quest

① King's Shadow

Taken activity has increased on Ganymede, with an unusual focus on the Vex. You must find out what they're planning to do and put a stop to it. Begin this lengthy mission at the flag atop a large boulder at the south crossroads.

Spine Burrows

ENEMY CONTROL
Taken

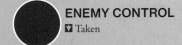

Sector Notes:

Enemy Clusters: Taken: 3 | Material Nodes: Available | Scannable Objects: 2

OVERVIEW MAP

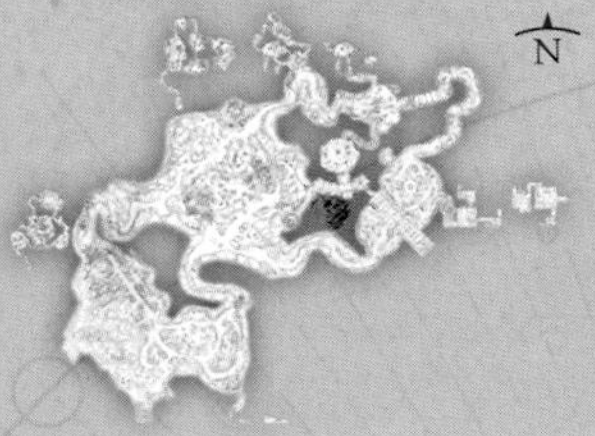

A secondary Sector that is accessed on the eastern perimeter of Lost Oasis, Spine Burrows is a once-tranquil cavern with some interesting and ancient fossilized remains embedded in the rock pillars and formations present here. Also present are three groups of Taken. Remove them as threats before gathering any data on the two scannable objects, grabbing any Material Nodes, and leaving.

Areas of Interest

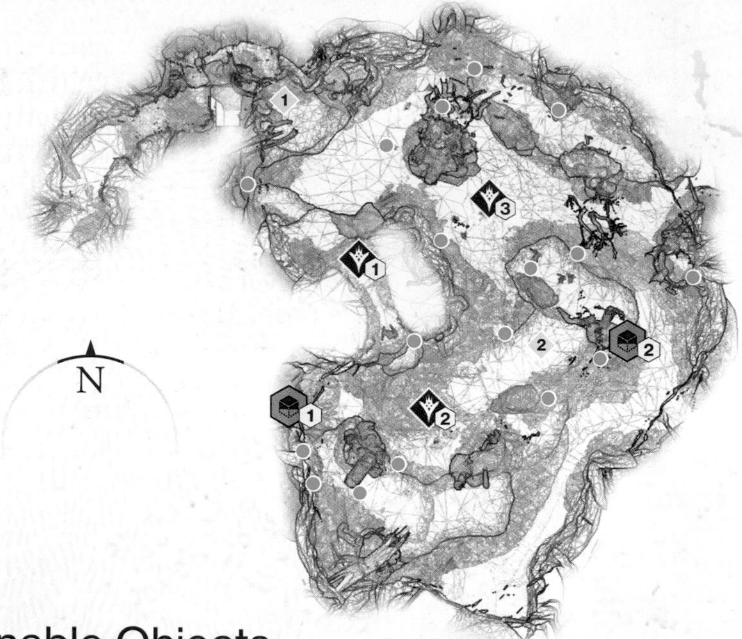

1 Exit to Lost Oasis

This allows access in and out of Lost Oasis; you appear at a glistening pool along the eastern rocky perimeter of that Sector.

2 Interior Cavern

Think of this as a Lost Sector, but well-lit and without a boss to challenge. Take a long circular route in either direction so you don't miss anything.

Enemy Clusters

1 Taken

A Phalanx on the small upper ledge tunnel makes initial traversing a little tricky.

2 Taken

The main gathering of Taken forces in the south part of the cavern involves Taken Goblins, Psions, and Phalanxes. Defeat the Goblins first, as they can keep others invulnerable with their energy link.

3 Taken

The northern cluster of foes has a Phalanx on the upper ledge and Psions, Goblins, and Phalanxes down below.

Scannable Objects

Half-buried Vex apparatus? Check!

This droid is half the robot it used to be.

The Rupture

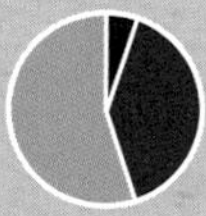

ENEMY CONTROL
Vex | Taken | Cabal

OVERVIEW MAP

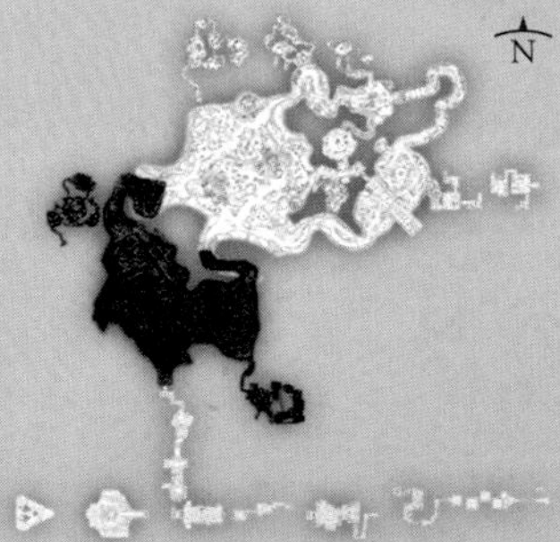

Sector Notes:

Adventure: Stravinsky | Lost Sectors: 2 | Enemy Clusters: Taken: 6
Enemy Clusters: Vex: 4 | Enemy Chests: Available | Landing Zone: Available
Material Nodes: Available | Patrol Beacons: 8 | Public Event (Full): 1
Public Event (Secret): 4 | Region Chests: 3 | Scannable Objects: 5
Vendor: Asher Mir

A sprawling plateau of interconnecting dirt roads, rocky outcroppings, and other interesting ancient formations (like skeletal remains and fossilized walls) is nothing compared to a massive Vex pyramid that takes up the entire western perimeter of this large Sector. The pyramid has two (usually inaccessible) Sectors you can enter during certain missions and a large Vex presence, alerted by the encroaching Taken. In the midst of all this is Asher Mir, a no-nonsense scientist and vendor for this world. Note the Landing Zone adjacent to his location. Also, note that there are only two exits to other major land Sectors: both along the north side, and both leading to Lost Oasis. Expect major battles between Vex and Taken forces as you search through Vex architecture and a natural mesa cave near the eastern perimeter.

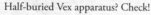

Areas of Interest

1 Exit to Lost Oasis (Northwest)

Take this cliff-top road to reach the western side of Lost Oasis, and return here for quickest access to Asher Mir.

2 North Road and Pyramid Trail

A relatively straight section of dirt road has a trail heading up and southwest into a Vex gorge and split in the pyramid. This is one route to climb the exterior of the pyramid (for collectibles).

3 Exit to Lost Oasis (Northeast)

This is the other exit out of the Rupture and winds its way to the southern crossroads area of Lost Oasis. If you need a quick route to Giant's Scar, take this exit instead.

4 Central Crossroads

Note the Adventure beacon as a landmark, and stop here the first time you're exploring the Rupture so you know how all the roads link together. This offers reasonable views of the circular paths here.

5 South Junction

This road junction bisects the main mesa "island" to the northeast and the Taken outcrop to the east. South is a larger Vex presence. Note the Vex architecture on either side, creating a short gorge-like road to the west.

6 Vex Pyramid

This immense structure has a sunken lower area where the entrance to Pyramidion (inaccessible) is located. Either side of that has cube-like ledges and platforms you can leap around, with foes on the ground below. To the southwest corner is a more natural ledge. Above are floating platforms and a teleport at the pyramid roof apex, which leads to a spectacular viewing ledge and collectibles.

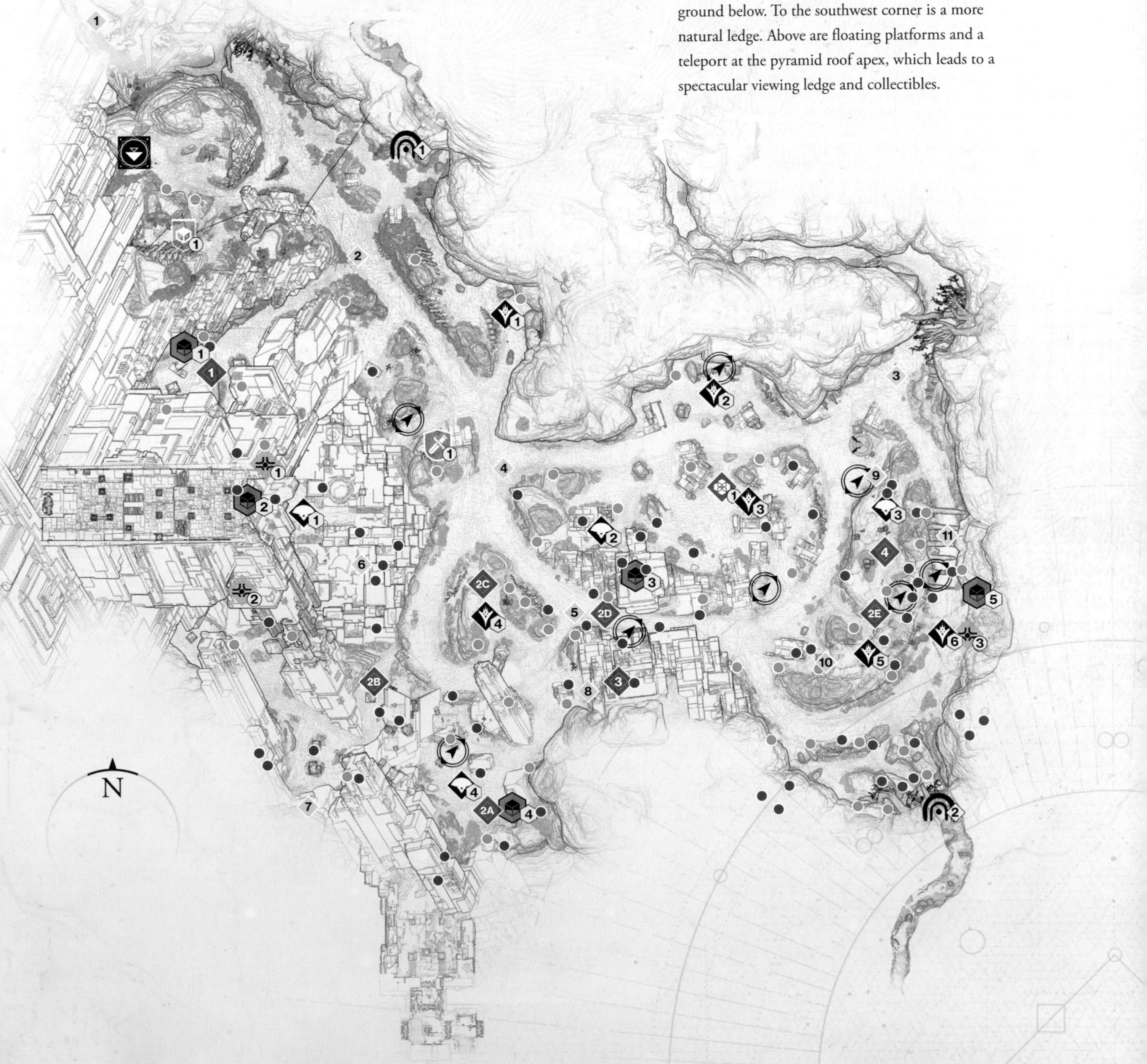

7 Entrance to The Endless Gate (Southwest)

A circular-like hole in the southwest wall, with tiered ground and sizable Vex presence (including a nearby Hydra) in the surrounding exterior area, leads to a small (and inaccessible) chamber, usually entered during an Adventure.

8 Vex Alcove

The black and shiny Vex architecture near the trail point has an easily overlooked alcove where a Storm Hydra appears during a Secret Public Event.

9 10 East Outcrop Tunnel (North and South)

The eastern mesa area has a large outcrop with both Vex and Taken vying for position. However, underneath it is a short tunnel and cavern with further Taken for you to tackle, as well as a couple of collectibles.

11 Ribcage Trail

The rarely used eastern perimeter road curves around, heading through the ribcage bones of an ancient beast of yore. Use this trail to avoid combat or to quickly get to the northeast exit or second Lost Sector.

Lost Sectors

1 Sanctum of Bones

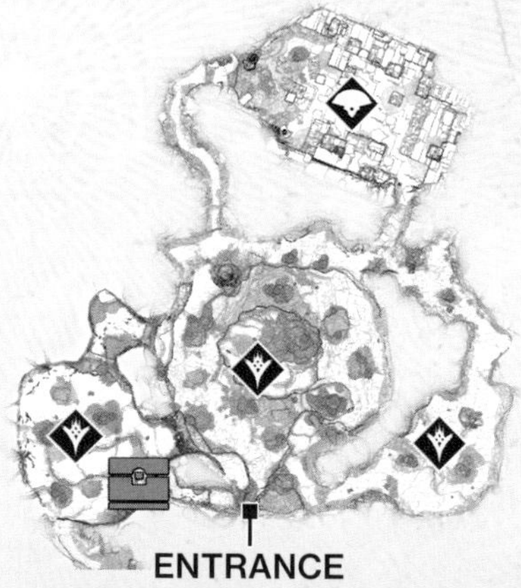

Enter this natural rocky grotto (the entrance is along the north road near Asher Mir) with some considerable height inside. The connecting tunnels ascend to some central platforms, where you can find a Sub-Boss Taken Knight.

2 Aphix Conduit

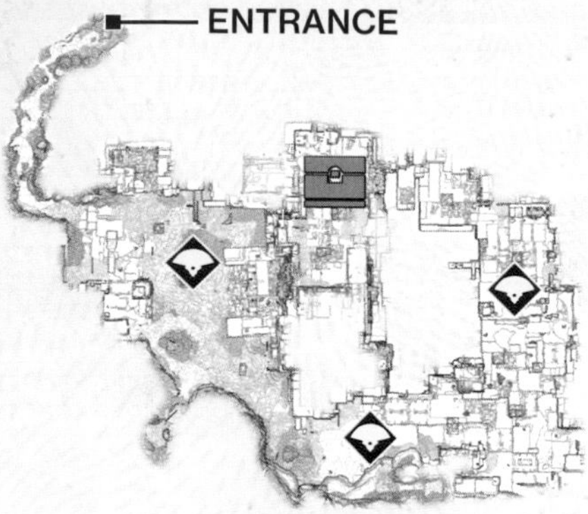

Enter the sunken gully entrance to this natural cavern in the southeast corner of the Sector, and access a rocky cavern filled with Goblins. The Vex presence continues into a sizable cube-shaped cavern with a central chasm and a deadly Hydra that you must defeat.

The Rupture

	Guide Name	Sub-Boss	Reward
1	Sanctum of Bones	Taken Knight	Boss Chest
2	Aphix Conduit	Hydra	Boss Chest

Enemy Clusters

1 Taken

Along the main road southeast of the first Lost Sector, a Taken Phalanx and other infantry are lurking in a small dell near the bones of an unknown creature.

2 Taken

Along the northern perimeter of the map by some strange box-like archeology are a Taken Phalanx and some other foes.

3 Taken

A Phalanx and two other Taken are roaming the area where a Public Event sometimes takes place in the cluster of large cubed and flat boulders.

4 Taken

The usual Phalanx and underlings are roaming the small hillock surrounded by pathways, overlooking the main Vex archeological site.

5 Taken

The top of the rock plateau with the tunnel running beneath it (east side of the map) has a Taken Centurion and other Taken for you to worry about.

6 Taken

The interior of the small cavern and tunnel running below the eastern mesa outcrop has a small host of Taken infantry for you to tackle as you reach the Region Chest and scannable object.

1 Vex

The Vex pyramid is guarded by Harpies and Goblins, with the occasional Hydra presence.

2 Vex

Goblins and a Harpy are checking the area for signs of a Taken infestation. They are on the Vex platform embedded into the main valley plateau, next to the small box-like Vex construction with the scannable object inside.

3 Vex

A small but powerful band of Vex is guarding their ancient construction in the southwestern corner of the map. Expect Goblins, a Minotaur, and a Hydra active on the clifftop mound in this vicinity.

Landing Zones

The Rupture LZ

You're fortunate that there's an LZ just north of where Asher Mir is located. You can then easily acquire or sell items before jetting off to Lost Oasis, which is just north of the Landing Zone.

Region Chests

1 Region Chest 1

This features an ascent up the darkened side of the pyramid, starting close to Area of Interest #2. Climb into the sharp smooth slopes and up the anti-gravity platforms of the pyramid until you see a Vex teleport wall. Check the first orange-hued anti-gravity platform across from the teleport; there's a narrow ledge behind and left of it with the chest.

Region Chest 2

This features an ascent up the darkened side of the pyramid, starting close to Area of Interest #2. Climb into the sharp smooth slopes and up the anti-gravity platforms of the pyramid across to a circular Vex teleport wall, then to a purple-hued chamber atop the pyramid exterior. The chest is on the outer edge of this exterior, along with a scannable object.

Region Chest 3

Enter the tunnel and cave system that runs below the eastern mesa area. There are Taken foes in here, along with the chest and scannable object.

Adventures

Stravinsky

Start the only available Adventure in this Sector by accessing the marker on the low rocky outcropping overlooking the pyramid.

Scannable Objects

Stay low while you're scrambling up the pyramid trail for this old piece of curved Vex architecture.

How high up the pyramid can you go?

Inside a Vex construction box, away from the main pyramid.

Guarded by a Hydra, adjacent to a cliff drop.

Look underground under the eastern mesa outcrop for this black globe.

Public Events

Public Events (Full)

Cabal Excavation: This takes place on the flat east-central plateau. It has you attempting to override a Cabal mining laser while dodging incoming laser fire and Cabal infantry waves that drop in from above, as well as any nearby Taken and Vex.

Event Number	Event Type	Target	Other Enemies	Reward
1	Cabal Excavation	Mining Lander	Cabal infantry	Boss Chest

Public Events (Secret)

HVT #1: A Storm Harpy appears in or around the pyramid area. Destroy it at once!

HVT #2: A Vex Storm Minotaur appears at one of the indicated guide map locations (2A, 2B, 2C, 2D, or 2E). Defeat it immediately!

HVT (Tactician): A Storm Hydra teleports in at the short Vex alcove (Area of Interest #8). Watch for the second Hydra at Enemy Cluster #4 as you defeat it.

Jailbreak: A Blighted Taken Centurion is being held in an energy cell on the long east outcropping. Tackle the Vex Goblins and Guard Minotaurs. Then, the cell disappears, leaving you to deal with the Centurion!

Event Number	Event Type	Target	Other Enemies	Reward
1	High-Value Target	Storm Harpy	None	Boss Chest
2	High-Value Target	Storm Minotaur	None	Boss Chest
3	HVT (Tactician)	Storm Hydra	None	Boss Chest
4	Jailbreak	Boss Taken Centurion	Guard Minotaurs, Vex and Taken forces	Boss Chest

Patrols

The Rupture (8)

Expect up to eight available Patrol beacons, with up to four active at a time.

Vendor

Asher Mir

Besides providing instructions and missions, the haughty scientist Asher Mir takes any Tokens you find across Echo Mesa. Bring him these in groups of 10, five, or one. In return, you'll receive an increase in your Reputation with him, allowing you to purchase unique Echo Mesa armor and weaponry. Asher also decrypts engrams.

The Endless Gate

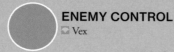

ENEMY CONTROL
Vex

Sector Notes:

Enemy Clusters: Vex: 1 | Material Nodes: Available | Scannable Objects: 1

OVERVIEW MAP

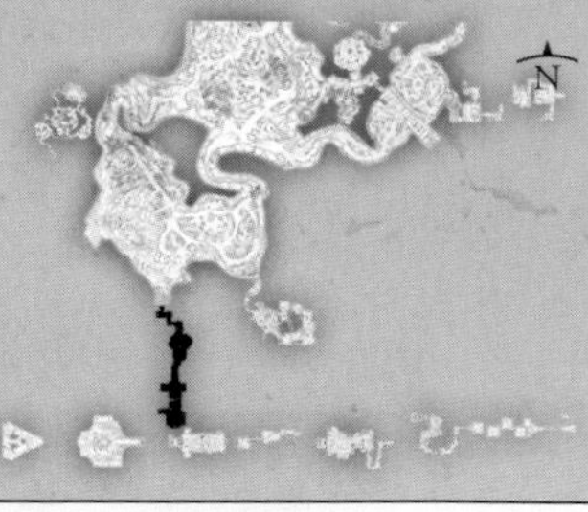

A small subterranean passageway of Vex construction leads to a gaping chasm chamber, with death on either side. There are Side Missions that have you accessing this otherwise remote location, which is entered in the southwestern corner of the Rupture.

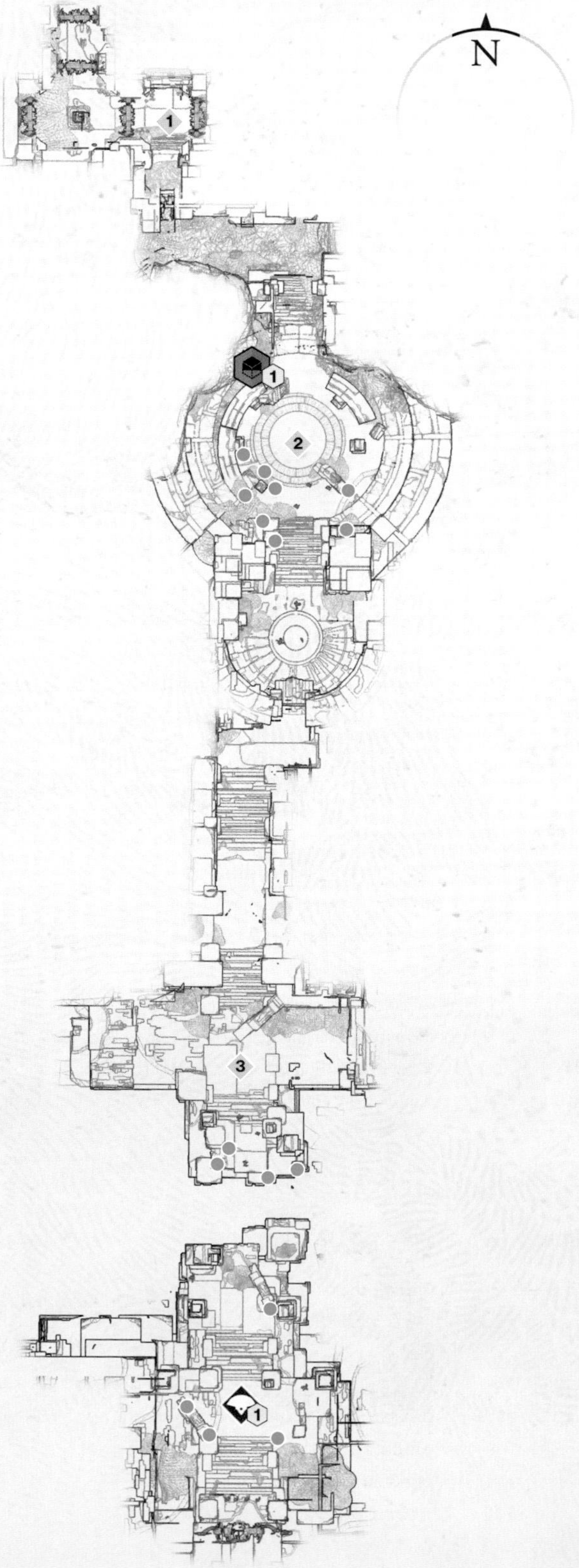

Areas of Interest

1 Entrance Tunnel

Head in here after navigating your way past the Vex guards (mainly Goblins, a Minotaur, and a Hydra) in the Rupture.

2 Curved Chamber

A scannable object is the main reason to visit this central chamber with a set of ruined monolith stones around the perimeter.

3 Chasm Chamber

Expect a small Vex presence (but sometimes, no foes at all) as you reach this chamber with bottomless drops on either side.

Enemy Clusters

1 Vex

The final chasm chamber may hold a few Vex entities. Otherwise, head here for materials to gather.

Scannable Objects

What's atop the monolith stones of Vex design?

Pyramidion

ENEMY CONTROL
Vex

Sector Notes:

Strike Mission: The Pyramidion | Usually Inaccessible

OVERVIEW MAP

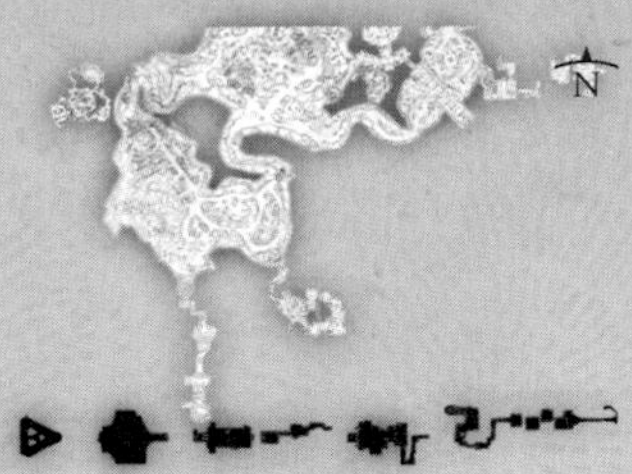

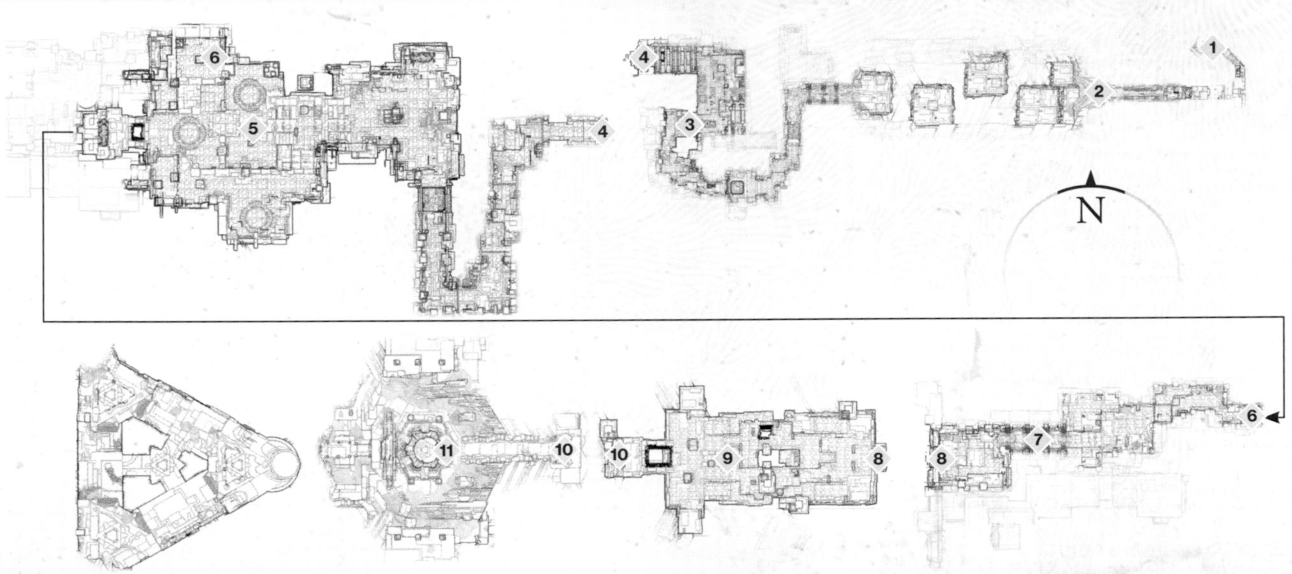

The interior of the great Vex Pyramid is only available to Guardians who attempt to complete the Strike: The Pyramidion. This marvel of Vex architecture is otherwise inaccessible. The following information gives a good overview of how to navigate through the series of gigantic Vex platforms floating in a void, but the Strike part of this guide provides more tactical knowledge. Pyramidion is entered via the opening in the sunken area of the pyramid in the Rupture (western perimeter).

Areas of Interest

1 Entrance from The Rupture

A compact passage from the surface that soon widens out into a spectacular look at the almost infinite architecture of the Vex.

2 Steps

A trio of three floating Vex platform steps, complete with Goblins and Minotaurs to tackle. Hobgoblins are on either side of the circular doorway with the laser traps.

3 Void Corridors

Avoid deadly laser traps on the walls and floors, drop down a long square-shaped hole, and navigate a winding corridor while attacking dozens of Goblins and Harpies.

4 First Warpgate

The end of this section features a warpgate. Note the map showing you where you exit.

5 Altar Room

Maneuver through more laser traps and into a chamber where you must activate three energy altars (large circular floor sections). Naturally, the Vex are throwing dozens of foes at you during this task. Beware of the Hydra!

6 Warpgate Teleports

The teleport at the end of the Altar Room deposits you in a new area almost directly below the Altar Room.

7 Second Warpgate

The entrance to the warpgate has you running through some rotating laser traps, which are particularly unforgiving.

8 Warpgate Teleport

Pass the warpgate and into the teleport, and you appear at the penultimate void island.

9 Tower Platform

This platform houses four energy towers that you must hack before progress can be made. Vex enemies are bountiful, including the rarely seen Cyclops.

10 Final Warpgate Teleport

Once activated, the warpgate at the end of the Tower Platform whisks you across to the gigantic final island.

11 Conduit and Final Altar

Drop down into the orange-lit conduit, landing in a roughly hexagonal Final Altar Room where you must face an Boss Hobgoblin and his Vex minions!

Strikes

The Pyramidion

This Strike begins outside the Pyramidion in the Rupture, but the assault soon enters the interior as you valiantly battle to the farthest void island and an audience with the largest Hobgoblin you've ever seen!

Terrabase Charon

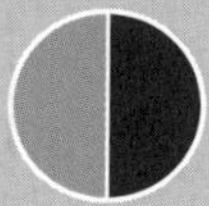

ENEMY CONTROL
Taken Vex

OVERVIEW MAP

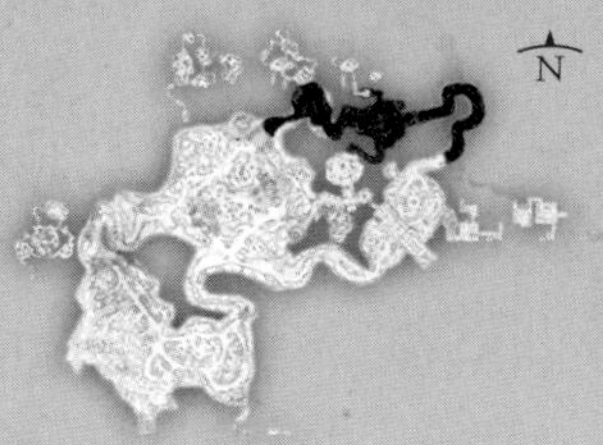

Sector Notes:

Enemy Clusters: Taken: 2 | Enemy Clusters: Vex: 2

Material Nodes: Available | Scannable Objects: 5

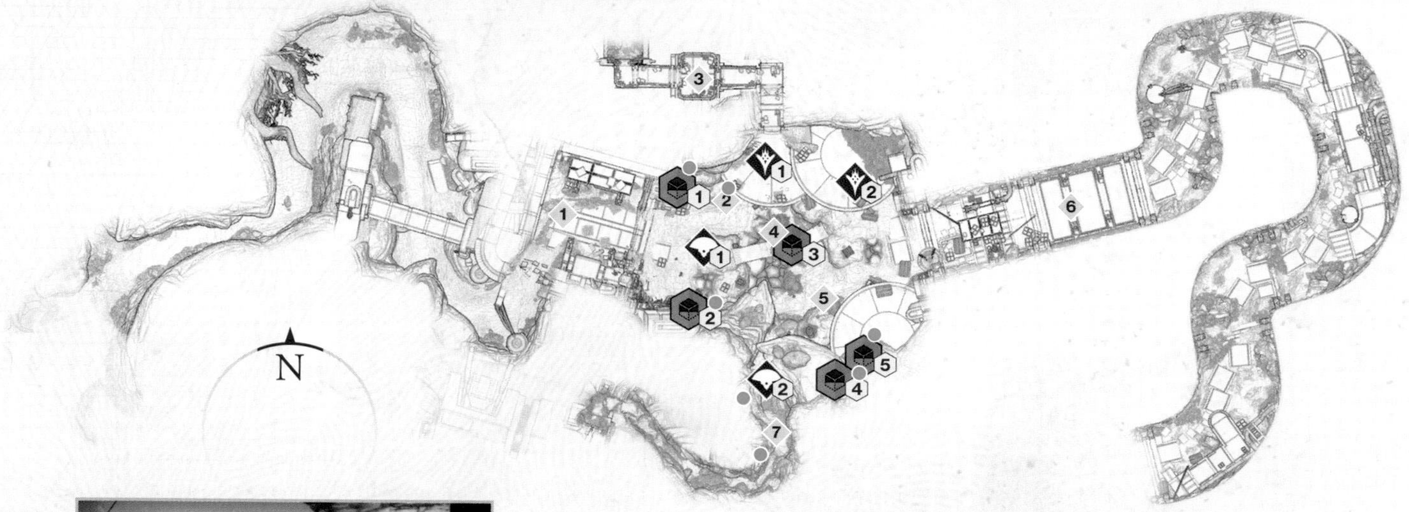

This is a small Sector, mainly comprised of a depot constructed and used by the Cabal until recently. Since their swift departure, Vex and Taken forces are warring to retake this junction-like Sector that links Lost Oasis and Giant's Scar together. Aside from these two main exits, there are routes to smaller Sectors: north to the Wraith Mines, and south to Warmind Vault JYS-2. This location is accessed during Campaign Mission: Sacrilege, though it is fully open under normal conditions.

Areas of Interest

1 Exit to Lost Oasis

This is usually the way you first enter this Sector, from the northwestern Lost Oasis exit through the winding ravine.

2 Depot Cave (Northwest)

Find a tiny cave left of the curved platform where the Taken are standing.

3 Exit to The Wraith Mines

Maneuver onto the platform overlooking the sunken arena, and head down the narrow cargo corridors into the Wraith Mines.

4 Sunken Arena

The main battles rage here, with two clusters of Taken and Vex each fighting both you and each other. Investigate the ramps, caves, and perimeter for five difficult scannable objects.

5 Depot Cave (Southeast)

Just to the right of the dirt slope toward the Giant's Scar tunnel is another small cave. Check it for a collectible.

6 Exit to Giant's Scar

A large-scale tunnel begins at this point on the eastern side of the Sector and winds east and then southward, enabling you to access Giant's Scar.

7 Exit to Warmind Vault JYS-2

A narrow crevasse on the southern perimeter of the main sunken arena leads to a Vex-controlled Sector known as Warmind Vault JYS-2.

Enemy Clusters

1 Vex

Aggressive Vex infantry is guarding the entrance to the central sunken area, with Goblins and Hobgoblins active.

2 Vex

Expect Harpies and a Minotaur in the upper rocky ground close to the tunnel down to Warmind Vault JYS-2.

1 Taken

A Taken Centurion and lesser Taken foes are on the loading bay platform, repelling Vex attacks.

2 Taken

A Taken Centurion and lesser Taken foes are on the loading bay platform, repelling Vex attacks.

Scannable Objects

A black globe, crackling with rift energy. Found the cave yet?

A thin energy laser, still active in one corner.

You'll need to "ramp" up your investigative capabilities to find this container.

Take a look along a rocky perimeter for a warpgate shell.

There's something odd in this cave. A Vex computer?

The Wraith Mines

ENEMY CONTROL
Taken

Sector Notes:

Enemy Clusters: Taken: 5 | Material Nodes: Available | Scannable Objects: 3

OVERVIEW MAP

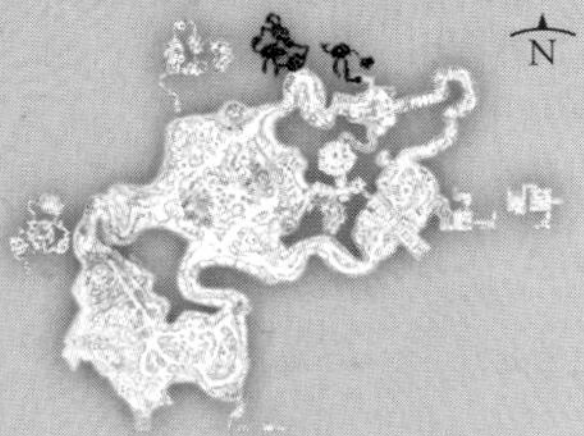

This interior digging site was appropriated by the Cabal, then recently left deserted. The reason why becomes clear as you descend down the cargo corridor from Terrabase Charon: this place is teeming with Taken because a rift has opened nearby. Aside from the danger involved in exploring this cave system, the confusing series of tunnels and caverns means that studying this map becomes more important than normal. Just remember this is essentially a dead end; you have to head back out the same way you came in. You're here for Taken takedowns and three scannable objects. Note that you fully explore this area (with more enemies to face) during Campaign Mission: Sacrilege.

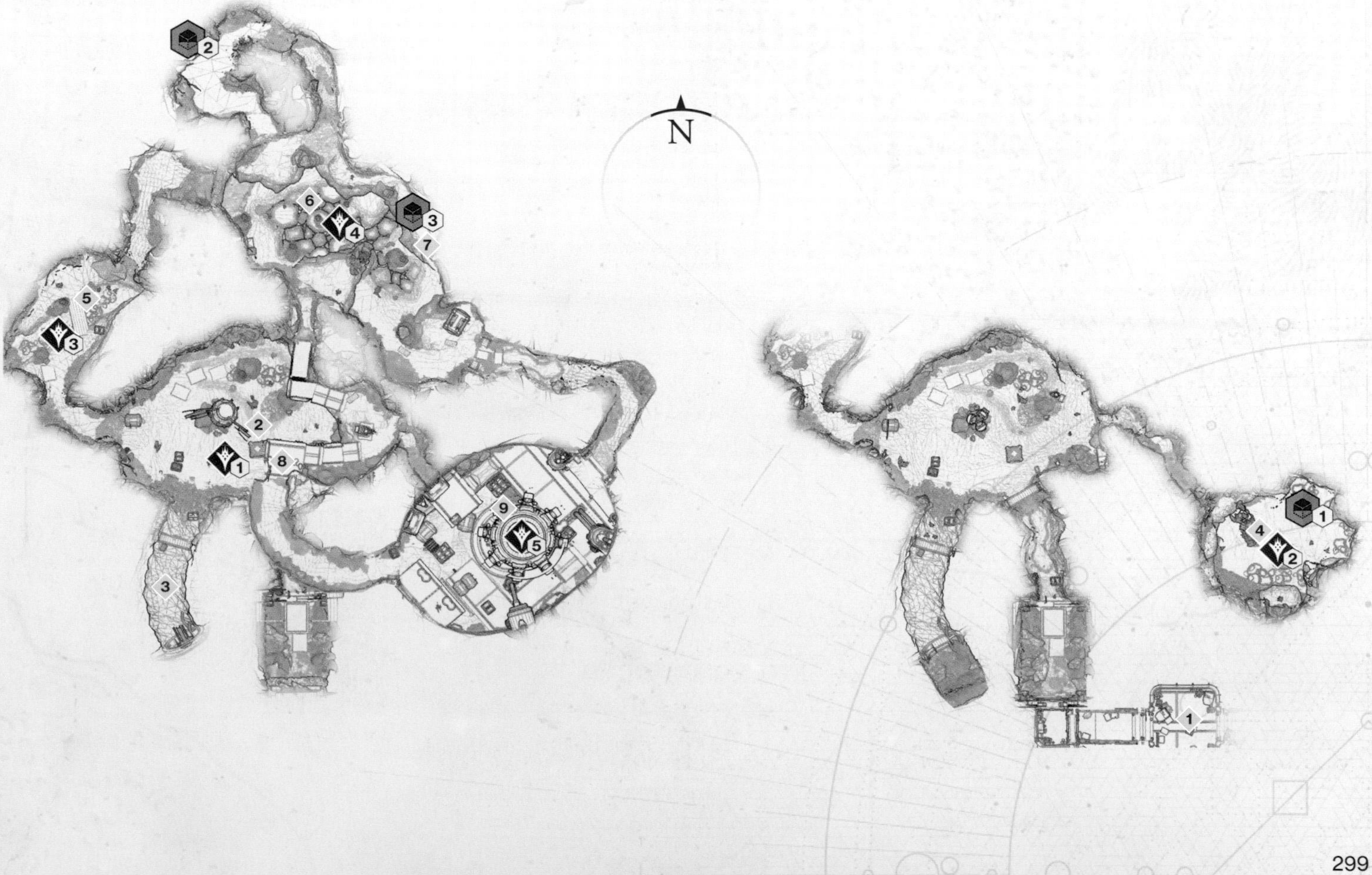

Areas of Interest

1 Entrance from Terrabase Charon

The northern cargo platform at Terrabase Charon is the exterior entrance, leading down a narrow set of cargo corridors.

2 Central Cavern

Lit with an orange glow, the central cavern features Taken (including Centurions). There are a total of six paths out of here on two levels (remember to look up). South is the corridor you came from. Southwest is a rift tunnel (Area of Interest #3). West is to a Taken cave (#5). North is an upper platform and stairs running north to south above you, exiting in the southwest corner and leading to an upper storage area (#9). East is a corridor to the Wizard's Grotto (#4).

3 Rift Tunnel

It seems that the largest concentration of rifts is located in this dead-end tunnel, which yields nothing of value.

4 Wizard's Grotto

A small dead-end grotto with a Taken Wizard and some underlings to face, and a scannable object to find.

5 Small Cave

A Taken Knight and lesser Taken foes are waiting in this small connecting cave with a glistening blue floor. It links the main chamber to the north Glowing Cavern.

6 Glowing Cavern

Expect the largest concentration of Taken enemies in this chamber, with orange walls and a blue glowing floor. Defeat the Psions and Thralls (of the Taken variety) while investigating a short north tunnel loop past a collectible. Then, check the south wall for an exit to the staircase above the entrance chamber. Southeast is a circular tunnel exit.

7 Circular Tunnel Exit

This connects the Glowing Cavern to a curved and large tunnel up to the Upper Storage Room. It is one of two routes and slightly safer to take.

8 Upper Steps Exit

Take some metal steps above the central cavern, and reach a connecting tunnel on the far (south) side.

9 Upper Storage Room

Accessed via the metal stairs on the upper floor of the central cavern or the circular tunnel from the Glowing Cavern, this uppermost chamber has Thralls to see off. Make a return journey from this point.

Enemy Clusters

1 Taken

Your first enemies to face include Phalanxes, Psions, and a Centurion in the central cavern.

2 Taken

The Wizard's Grotto is named for the Taken Wizard here, along with other infantry.

3 Taken

Expect a Knight and Thralls in this small western cave connecting the two larger caverns.

4 Taken

An abundance of foes, mainly Psions and Goblins, is warping into view across the Glowing Cavern.

5 Taken

Only Thralls seem active in this upper storage chamber.

Scannable Objects

Coax the Wizard's underlings away from this globe.

Just about everything in this cavern glows, except for this globe.

Same cavern, different globe.

Warmind Vault JYS-2

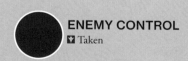

ENEMY CONTROL

Taken

Sector Notes:

Campaign Mission: Fury | Usually Inaccessible

OVERVIEW MAP

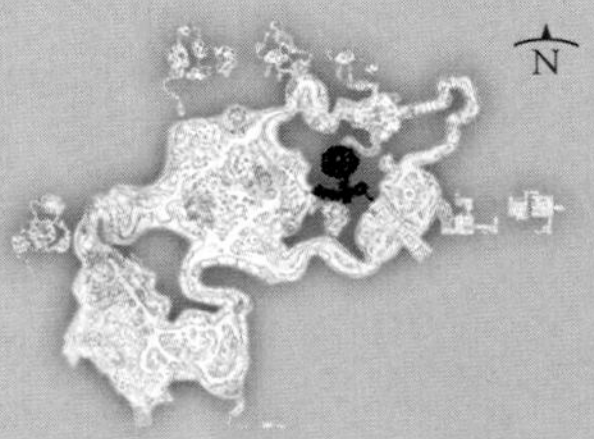

This inaccessible Sector is only entered during the Campaign Mission: Fury. It is the hidden Vex lair known as the Warmind Vault JYS-2, now completely overrun by the Taken. This leads to a mainframe arena where you battle one of the toughest foes on this planetoid: a gigantic Taken Boss known as Modular Upsilon and his energy-chaining partner Modular Sigma. The entrance from Terrabase Charon is usually sealed, and the only other route (during the mission) is via the hole the giant drill has made in the large mining area of that Sector.

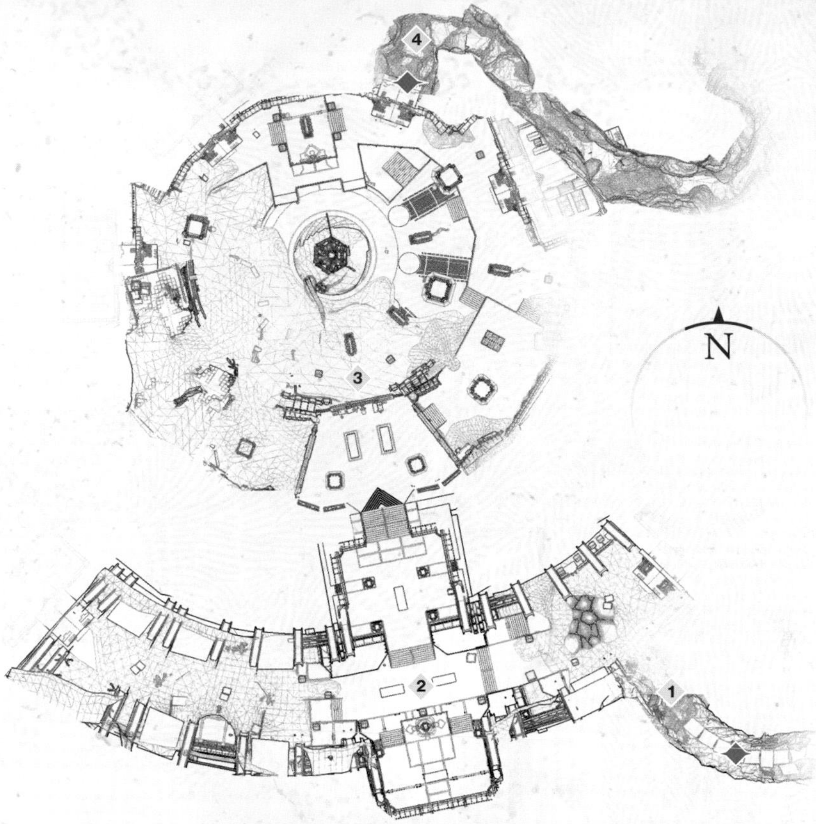

Areas of Interest

1 Entrance from Giant's Scar (Inaccessible)

This is inaccessible unless the mission is active. Once you've raised the colossal drill bit in Giant's Scar Sector during the mission, drop into this entrance tunnel via an opening on the massive circular side wall.

2 Warmind Vault (Inaccessible)

This is inaccessible unless the mission is active. Though a Vex vault, the Taken have a stronghold here now, and you fight numerous Goblins, Hobgoblins, and Minotaurs as you breach the mainframe chamber.

3 Mainframe Arena (Inaccessible)

This is inaccessible unless the mission is active. This location is where you fight the giant Taken Boss and his minion.

4 Exit to Terrabase Charon (Inaccessible)

This is inaccessible unless the mission is active. If open, a pair of blast doors allows access up the tunnel to the south side of Terrabase Charon.

Campaign Missions

Fury

The vast majority of the time spent in this Sector is during the aforementioned Campaign Mission, which is where the recommended tactics and enemy locations are detailed.

Giant's Scar

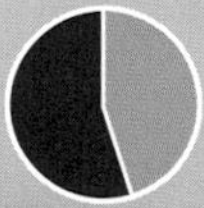

ENEMY CONTROL

Taken Vex

Sector Notes:

Adventure: Road Rage | Enemy Clusters: Taken: 5 | Enemy Clusters: Vex: 4
Enemy Chests: Available | Landing Zone: Available | Material Nodes: Available
Partially Inaccessible | Patrol Beacons: 9 | Public Event (Full): 2
Public Event (Secret): 6 | Region Chests: 3 | Scannable Objects: 5

OVERVIEW MAP

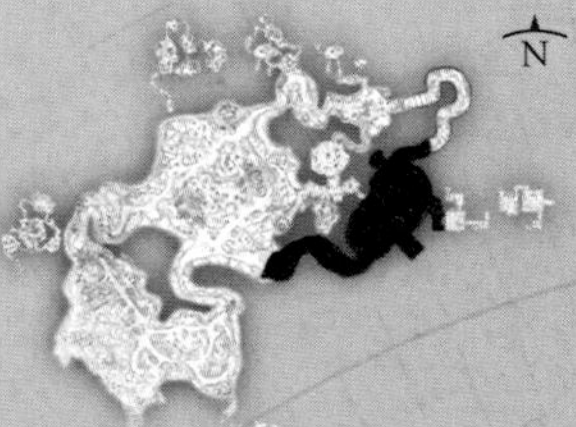

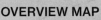

The remains of a Cabal mining operation exist in this Sector, formerly a natural rock formation known as Giant's Scar. Bisecting the two boulder-laden valley floors is a long mining operations center, with pedestrian and vehicular access to and from each main area. The majority of the battling occurs at the drill site, a roughly circular arena-like valley with a massive central mining drill. Around the perimeter are various exits to small caves and other Sectors. Note that the area below the massive central drill is inaccessible unless Campaign Mission: Fury is underway.

Areas of Interest

1 Exit to Terrabase Charon (North)

A very long and winding tunnel allows you to navigate the northern part of Echo Mesa, should you want a lengthier trip back to Lost Oasis via Terrabase Charon.

2 Small Cave (North)

A small crack in the canyon wall allows you into a tiny cave with a couple of collectibles, a possible Secret Public Event High-Value Target, and a Patrol beacon.

3 Small Cave (Northeast)

A small cave is sometimes worth hiding in or checking for regular chests. This one is across from the Hydra at Enemy Cluster (Vex) #1.

4 Drill Control Hut (Northwest)

Taken are controlling access to this hut. The area is raised above the main path, making it worth considering as a defensive position. Note the Region Chest above your head.

5 Giant's Scar: Drill Site

This massive northern area is the epicenter of the battle between Vex and Taken, so expect conflict at all times. There's a main circular road around the central drill. The drill itself can't be moved unless the Campaign Mission: Fury is active.

6 Entrance to Warmind Vault JYS-2 (Inaccessible)

This is inaccessible unless the mission is active. Under the massive drill bit is a tunnel with debris strewn about, along with access down into the Warmind Vault itself.

7 Entrance to Excavation Site II

Take this route during the Campaign Mission, or if you want to tackle more Taken in a confined space (Excavation Site II). The entrance is atop a small (and usually empty) cave directly below it.

8 Secondary Path

Taken congregate around this cluster of crates and a path up to the Excavation Site II entrance.

9 Vehicle Access Road

This offers quick access (usually via Sparrow) between the north and south areas.

10 Mining Control Center

A long interior structure offers windowed views of the drill site. There are pedestrian exits to the west (south side) and east (north side). The interior has enemies battling it out.

11 South Area

This is usually the area you first encounter, and it's where the Landing Zone is located. Pockets of Taken are active in this area. Note the large cylindrical tower to the north. Is there something on top of it?

12 Exit to Lost Oasis

The quickest way between Giant's Scar and the Rupture is to take the large south exit back to Lost Oasis. This is a frequently used thoroughfare.

Adventures

Road Rage

Access this Adventure at the base of one of the drill support pillars in the northeast corner of the map.

Region Chests

1 Region Chest 1

Inside the small northwest cave, behind the far right natural cave pillar. Don't open a regular chest instead!

2 Region Chest 2

Tucked on the drill support arm above the control hut. Deft jumping is required to access this chest.

③ Region Chest 3

Sitting atop the large cylindrical tower outside the pedestrian entrance to the mining control center. Use the connecting pipes to leap up to the top of the cylinder.

Campaign Mission

Fury

This mission is the only time you're allowed access into the underground tunnel off the drill site (Area of Interest #6). Also, the vehicular entrance under the mine control center (Area of Interest #9) is closed (mission only).

Enemy Clusters

① Taken

A group of Taken is guarding the control hut that lifts the massive drill from the central mining area. Expect a Phalanx, Knight, and some other Taken infantry.

② Taken

Several Taken are attempting to storm the west bridge and being stopped by Vex forces. Expect Taken Phalanxes and Knights, along with lesser foes.

③ Taken

A Taken Knight and some underlings are guarding the interior of the control room.

④ Taken

The entrance to the mine control center (southwest side) has a few Taken, including a Phalanx, for you to worry about. Note that there are many more foes if the Campaign Mission: Fury is active.

⑤ Taken

Expect additional Taken to warp in via a rift in this general area. Aside from Thralls, there's likely a Centurion here, so watch your step.

① Vex

A Vex Hydra is located in the northern part of this mining area, with a Minotaur and Goblins guarding the bridge to the west. Expect them to attack nearby Taken hostiles.

Public Events

Public Events (Full)

Spire Integration: Vex are attempting to fortify their underground structures. To complete this event, simply hold off waves of Vex at each of the 10 integration points (which appear anywhere in the indicated guide map area).

Taken Blight: Your job is to destroy the Blight's integrity until the Blight explodes and then regenerates at a second position. Repeat the demolishing of the Blight, then move to a third regeneration (2A, 2B, and 2C locations on the guide map). Make sure to engage multiple Guardians in removing both Taken foes and Blight integrity, or this is impossible to finish.

Event Number	Event Type	Target	Other Enemies	Reward
1	Spire Integration	Integration points (10)	Vex infantry	Boss Chest
2	Taken Blight	Blight integrity	Taken infantry	Boss Chest

Public Events (Secret)

HVT #1: A Vex Storm Minotaur appears somewhere on the indicated guide map route (1A, 1B, 1C, 1D, or 1E). Neutralize it at once!

HVT (Tactician): A Taken Wizard appears in the vicinity of the cave and sometimes moves to the control cabin area. Defeat it immediately!

Jailbreak: A Blighted Taken Centurion or Knight is being held in an energy cell. Tackle the Vex Goblins and Guard Minotaur. Then, the cell disappears, leaving you to deal with the Centurion!

Skirmish: A clash between the Vex and Taken occurs along the sunken drill site area southwest of the drill, by the control center building.

Skirmish: A battle between the Vex and Taken begins in the rocky area by the pedestrian entrance southwest of the control center building, and it continues part of the way into the structure.

Event Number	Event Type	Target	Other Enemies	Reward
1	High-Value Target	Storm Minotaur	Vex infantry	Boss Chest
2	HVT (Tactician)	Tortured Wizard	Taken infantry	Boss Chest
3	Jailbreak	Blighted Taken Centurion or Knight	Vex guards, Hydra	Boss Chest
4	Jailbreak	Blighted Taken Centurion or Knight	Vex guards	Boss Chest
5	Skirmish	Vex versus Taken	Warning! Copious enemies!	Random Loot
6	Skirmish	Vex versus Taken	Warning! Copious enemies!	Random Loot

② Vex

The trails in the southern part of the mining facility have a couple of Minotaurs and Goblins, but these foes are preoccupied with Taken foes in other parts of the arena.

③ Vex

Harpies and a cluster of Goblins are battling the Taken to the southeast, inside the mining control center. As you head in from the western stepped pedestrian entrance, expect three Goblins to the left of you.

Landing Zones

Giant's Scar LZ

Should you want to access the entirety of Giant's Scar with relative swiftness, the LZ is located on the western side of the initial rock gorge.

Patrols

Giant's Scar (9)

There are nine Patrol beacons located throughout this Sector. As always, only around four are active at a time.

Scannable Objects

What Vex wreckage is inside this tiny cave?

That Vex Hydra isn't happy you're encroaching on the object it's guarding.

Dish of the day, leaning on the mine center wall.

Mining cargo room upper corner? Rift globe accessed.

A Vex beacon, below bunker hill.

Excavation Site II

ENEMY CONTROL
Taken

Sector Notes:

Campaign Mission: Fury | Enemy Clusters: Taken: 4 | Material Nodes: Available
Partially Inaccessible | Scannable Objects: 3

OVERVIEW MAP

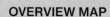

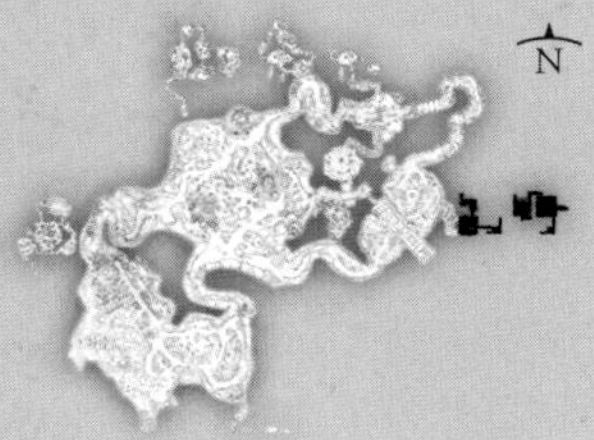

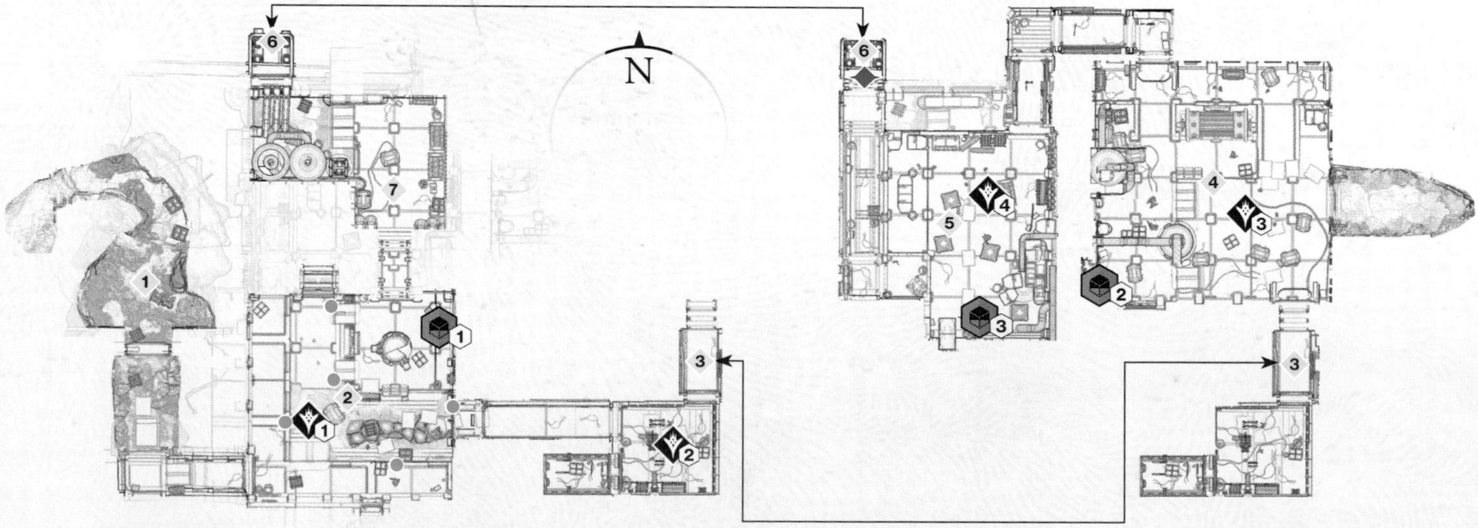

Accessed via the exterior entrance at the drill site in Giant's Scar, this small interior set of storage rooms and computer operations room must be exited the same way you came in. It features a series of square-shaped chambers, each with a half-dozen Taken to engage. Come for combat, leave after finding the three scannable objects.

Areas of Interest

1 Exit to Giant's Scar

This is the entrance in and out of Excavation Site II. It brings you out onto a raised perimeter area overlooking the main drill site in Giant's Scar.

2 Main Storage Room

This square-shaped storage area has blocked access from the rock floor storage room (north), along with a ramp to the east. You can see this room from the main Override Terminal Room above and north of you. Expect a heavy Taken presence here.

3 Ramped Corridor

This L-shaped area connects the lower and upper levels of this Sector. Expect a small Taken presence here.

4 Upper Storage Room

A similarly sized storage room to the one downstairs, with another scannable object and Taken to tackle. The exit door is on the raised ramp section to the northwest.

5 Override Terminal Room

The majority of the objectionable opponents you meet are clustered here in this chamber, with an override terminal that is only accessed during the mission. When you're done finding scannable objects and fighting foes, retrace your steps out of this Sector.

6 Elevator Shaft (Inaccessible)

This area is inaccessible unless the mission is active. You drop down here to reach the next area.

7 Rock Floor Storage Room (Inaccessible)

This area is inaccessible unless the mission is active. This leads you back to the initial storage room, but only during the mission.

Campaign Missions

Fury

The elevator shaft and small lower floor storage area are the only two locations that you can't access unless the mission is active.

Enemy Clusters

1 Taken

The main storage room has a Phalanx, Knight, and Wizard, as well as lesser Taken infantry for you to worry about.

2 Taken

A few Thralls are little match for your firepower as you ascend through this ramped corridor and past a small storage area.

3 Taken

Expect a similar crowd of foes to the storage room downstairs: Phalanxes and larger foes, with a few Thralls, as well.

4 Taken

Taken Centurions are the biggest threat in the Override Terminal Room, though other foe types are present.

Scannable Objects

There's one floating globe. Now, are there any more?

The corner of the first room upstairs. That's globe number two.

There's a good view downstairs from the final globe location.

The Tower

Sector Notes:

Landing Zone: Available | Scannable Objects: 22 | Vendor: Up to 10 initially

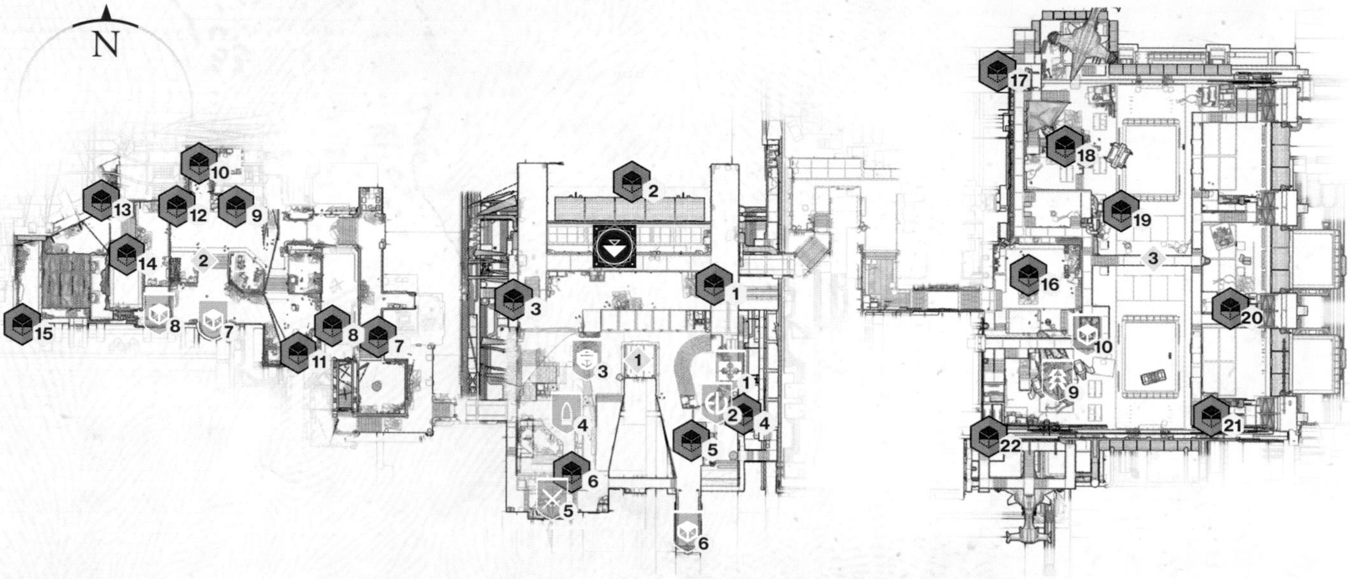

Welcome to the resistance! This social Sector has no enemies to concern yourself with. It becomes accessible once the Campaign Missions have concluded. Think of this as a hub of activity where you can meet fellow Guardians and clan-mates, store items in your vault, locate a wealth of scannable objects, and most importantly, trade with vendors. This is where you'll begin the end-game content: trading unwanted items for weapons and armor sets, receiving rare or exotic gear from engrams, and purchasing items from the Eververse merchant. You can continue to present Tokens to certain traders and gain Reputation with Vanguard members and others. Welcome to the rest of your game.

Down (and out) on The Farm

Now that the Campaign has concluded and the Tower becomes the active hub, the usefulness of the Farm winds down, though Tyra should be visited for some additional loot.

That Glowing Feeling

The perspective changes during the time in this social Sector. You are in third-person view and cannot execute your Movement Mode.

If you want to ensure a hot reception for your Guardian, why not pick up the object atop the courtyard gantryway near the purple ball that expressly tells you not to? You're in for a lava-ly time! Why not "fan" yourself to cool down?

You can play soccer games in the main hangar floor.

There are various controls to play with, such as light switches on the Bazaar stairwell, and hangar gantries to move.

There's also some hidden treasure, such as those requiring a Loot-a-Palooza Key (Hangar) and Dance Party Key (Bazaar).

Areas of Interest

1 Courtyard

This upper deck is the central part of the Tower wall, with two "wings" to the east (a large covered ship hangar) and the west (a stairwell leading to the Bazaar). Some key vendors are located here, along with your vault, and a small staircase behind Banshee's shop leads to the maintenance chasms between the Tower hangar and other areas. Zavala is here, surveying the recent destruction.

2 Bazaar

A relatively small stairwell area links the Bazaar to the courtyard. A connecting corridor to the north leads to the dangerous maintenance chasm between structures. Head there if you're keen on finding all scannable objects.

There's a festive atmosphere over in the western side of the Tower, with a plaza and a covered Bazaar area, as well as a small central staircase structure. There are vendors here, including Ikora.

3 Hangar (East)

The eastern side of this Sector, connected by a staircase, is a giant maintenance bay and hangar, where Cayde and Holliday like to hang out. Though there aren't scannable objects in this area, there's still plenty to do, including a game of soccer on the main hangar floor.

Landing Zones

Courtyard LZ

Fly in from Orbit and land your craft on the edge of the upper exterior courtyard area.

Scannable Objects (Courtyard)

On a high exterior AC duct in the chasm between the courtyard and hangar; hop over the railing from the mesh bridge while facing the hangar roof.

What's under the Landing Zone netting on a tiny lip ledge below the air traffic droid? This item.

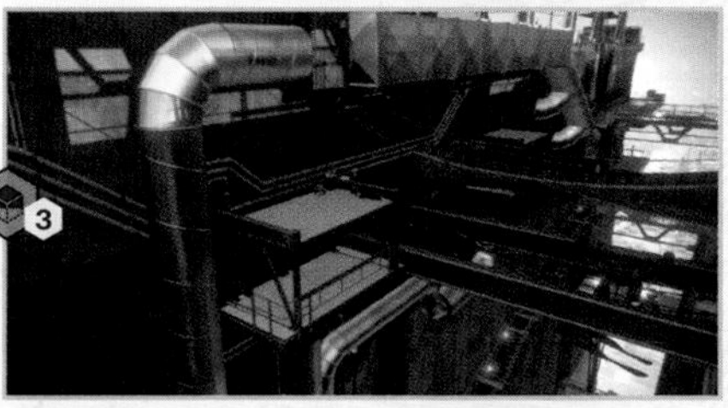

Time to climb some girders and pipes to get to this collection of hoarded debris. On the side of the courtyard structure, between it and the Bazaar. Don't miss a landing!

Careful jumping and a possible death plummet afterward? You must be finding this lore item, which is on the low yellow girders in the chasm between the courtyard and hangar.

The covered maintenance walkway under the courtyard has a prime item to scan, near those yellow railings.

Something's worth scanning in the small storage stairwell under Banshee's store.

Scannable Objects (Bazaar)

Time for some maintenance chasm extreme jumping to get to this collection of crates beyond the AC silver piping, on the outer girder.

Once you find the kitty at the window, the object becomes clear to see.

A blue crate of electronics. Cunningly hidden behind that pillar.

Some light reading. But you'll need to crouch under a gate to get to it.

This market stall has a box that's of particular interest.

Sitting on the curved corner of the AC duct, above the red shade cloth and north alley. Time to attempt some lengthy and cunning moves to get it!

Are you reading these notes by candlelight? My, that's a tiny balcony.

More light reading, near the comfy patio seating on the mezzanine.

A hidden tome on a stack of containers, with a great view and a narrow ledge lip.

Scannable Objects (Hangar)

These **are** the droids you're looking for.

Time to monitor the situation in the northwest yellow metal stairwell corner gantry.

Is that something sitting atop the cradle holding those two blue missiles?

Even the pipework in the hangar holds secrets to scan. These are close to an upper gantry stairwell and red girder column.

Hang out on the sturdy hydraulic pillar above the yellow gantry. Eastern side, as you watch the ships land.

Check the red metal landing dock gantry. Southeast and up.

Check the rarely used gantry outside the hangar, southwest corner near the moored ship. You'll be glad you did; there's some light reading on a crate stack.

Vendors

1 Darbi 55-30 (Postmaster)

Visit Darbi to gather items and objects of importance that you found (from dead enemies or chests) during missions or other explorations but didn't pick up. Messages from other players are also accessed here.

2 Tess Everis (Eververse Promotions)

Tess Everis is an accomplished broker of stylish and highly coveted items procured from the City and beyond. She grants you special free promotions (engram gifts and gear, for example) and also sells these items, provided you have enough Silver (which is currency you appropriate through the expenditure of real-world rather than in-game funds). Real-world purchases are purely optional.

3 Master Rahool (Archivist)

A senior representative of the Cryptarchy, Master Rahool decodes engrams and seeks the treasures of humanity's past. He also sells engrams from time to time and may be interested in Artifacts you have picked up, exchanging them for Glimmer.

4 Banshee-44 (Gunsmith)

Banshee-44 has lived many lives. As master weaponsmith for the Tower, he supplies Guardians with only the best. Show him proof of your enthusiasm for destruction by offering him Tokens you have acquired from breaking down weapons and armor. Trade them in, bringing him groups of ten, five, or one. In return, you receive an increased Reputation (which gradually gets you better items). He rewards you with items from his arsenal. You can also purchase gear mods from him, as well as gear for sale. Those wanting to continuously improve their Guardians will be visiting him countless times.

5 Lord Shaxx

The Crucible is the arena in which Guardians forge their light. Lord Shaxx is the Crucible. Complete matches and challenges within the Crucible to obtain Tokens. He takes any Tokens you have acquired; trade them in, bringing him groups of 10, five, or one. In return, you receive an increased Reputation (or "standing") with him. Special Crucible Armor and Crucible Arsenal (Gear Sets) are accessed from him.

6 Commander Zavala

The resolute Commander Zavala advises and outfits Titans as their Vanguard at the Tower. Purchase the Vanguard Tactician Arsenal once you return Tokens to gain Reputation with him.

7 Ikora Rey

The wise Ikora Rey advises and outfits Warlocks as their Vanguard at the Tower. Though she sells gear, she allows you to meditate on the Campaign Missions you have previously played. When available, you can replay any Campaign Mission to acquire Tokens and Reputation with her (to gain her gear). You can play Campaign Missions as a single Guardian or as part of a fireteam.

8 Suraya Hawthorne

Once a wanderer beyond the City, Suraya Hawthorne now acts as a liaison between humanity and the Guardians. She has items to sell and has a commanding view from a mezzanine balcony in the Bazaar area.

9 Cayde-6

Languishing near the entrance to the main maintenance hangar is the freewheeling Exo with both Scout Reports and Treasure Maps to impart to you (as well as some "Odds and Ends" you might want to check into). Part with some Glimmer, and you're able to purchase these references. For Scout Reports, these reveal Loot Caches that are active in a particular region. For Treasure Maps, you go on some minor end-game treasure hunts. The locations of treasure then appear on your in-game map of the associated region. Bring back the "treasure" to Cayde for more frivolity.

10 Amanda Holliday

Shipwright to the Tower, Holliday runs the hangar like a finely tuned engine. As you'd expect, she also sells things. These goods are attached to a variety of ships (which you use for traveling between Landing Zones) and vehicles (Sparrow variants). Purchase them and an assortment of mods with Glimmer.

The Bestiary

Overview

Five distinct enemy combatant races have occupied various locations in the solar system. All are considered hostile, and Guardians should prepare to engage every one of these as such. Visual evidence and generalized takedown strategies are presented here. Please note that tactics may vary depending on the topography of an area, along with the equipment and Abilities you use in a particular confrontation.

Unique Foes are Elsewhere

This chapter covers enemies you'll encounter more than once, usually with extreme frequency. If you're looking for information on a unique foe, such as a Boss Hobgoblin, or other Campaign or Strike Boss, consult the appropriate mission chapter.

Know Your Enemy

For each general foe you may face, there are several reference charts you can study. These charts impart some helpful data, and this section of the chapter explains what this data means.

Enemy Type

An example of a named enemy type: a Cabal Legionary.

This indicates the name of the foe in question. Most of the time, the health bar above each enemy you face will list the name or a portion of it. You can then recognize the hostile you are about to face.

Loadout

This shows the main weapon that the foe carries. Variants of the same enemy may carry a different weapon and have slightly different survival tactics. This is also the name you'll usually see when you die, and you check what killed you.

Type

This shows an example of a base unit, with a regular health bar.

This shows a Elite unit, with a segmented health bar.

This shows a Boss unit, with a different segmented health bar.

This indicates whether the type of enemy is encountered as a Base, Elite, or Boss.

A **base** enemy is a usual infantry foe, and engaged all the time. Note that you also encounter toughened Base variants, with more orange health bars, from time to time.

An **Elite** enemy heads up a contingent of base foes and has a yellow health bar. This is a stronger foe and poses more of a threat.

A **Sub-Boss** enemy: There is also a type of enemy existing (in strength and power) between an Elite and Boss. Expect it to be weaker than a Boss, and stronger than an Elite.

A **Boss** is the strongest of that enemy type, it can be faced at the culmination of certain Strikes, Campaign Missions, and Patrols. Note the skull in the health bar. Expect an elongated and tough battle.

Role

The Hive Thrall is fodder; it exists to overwhelm you without a care for its own life.

This indicates the general purpose of the enemy unit when it engages you or a rival enemy in combat. These are split into one of the following categories:

Fodder: An expendable grunt with little value to the enemy group, except to slow you down.

Soldier: The main fighting unit of an enemy race.

Commander: The usual leader of a cluster of enemies, which typically is more cunning and has more health.

Artillery: Deliver heavy weapons fire. Vehicles can serve this purpose, too.

Vehicle: Primary mode of transport rather than for combat.

Survival Tactics

Stopping a foe from reaching melee range is a survival tactic known as Melee Pressure.

If you want to know the technique for surviving a particular enemy type while dealing with other foes, or while you get into position to take them down, check the following tactical advice. This also works as you start to remove health from an enemy during the early-to-mid stages of combat with them.

Area Denial: The foe has an attack that takes a few seconds to activate but then becomes extremely damaging, such as a Cabal Incendior's flame attack. You must preempt this attack before it can occur by engaging the foe in ranged combat.

(Grenade): A Fallen Dreg uses this weapon.

(Darkness Cloud): A Hive Wizard uses this weapon.

Close-range Pressure: You must destroy the foe before it reaches close range, as it becomes much more deadly at this point (like an Exploder Shank).

Dodge Enemy Fire: The foe has a predisposition for a barrage of rifle or rocket fire, or constant shooting of other weaponry. Watch the projectiles, and avoid them when they strike. Quick maneuvers are needed because this foe usually fires weaponry with an area-of-effect damage.

Melee Pressure: Do everything you can to stop the foe from reaching your melee range. This means spotting them early and defeating them at range, as they usually have a very damaging melee attack.

(Explode): This foe explodes when they reach you, like a Cursed Thrall.

(Berserking): This foe can be partially destroyed before becoming frenzied and rushing you, like a Vex Goblin.

Stay in Cover: The foe is likely a sharpshooter, and you're encouraged to find and stay in cover to avoid possible damage from the foe's rifle.

Stay Mobile: The foe can easily damage you severely if you remain in one place. Perhaps it emits a stream of damaging energy. The trick is executing sprints, dodges, jumps, and other maneuvers to avoid the attack.

Suppression (Line of Sight): Attempt to engage the foe in continuous combat and ensure that it stays visible to you. Its attack must be suppressed due to the danger it poses (like a Hive Ogre's energy blast).

Takedown Tactics

Concentrating your firepower on a particular part of a foe? A takedown tactic known as Target Practice.

When you've decided to kill a particular enemy, check the preferred technique from the list below.

Flank Target: The enemy has a physical shield. Aside from shooting the shield, you can leap to the side or above the foe, outflanking them so their shield is useless. Then, strike the foe itself.

(Shield): A Cabal shield used by Phalanxes.

(Wall of Darkness): A Hive shield used by Knights.

Line of Sight: You must keep the foe in your line of sight and fire at them, usually from range and while moving in and out of cover.

Maintain Pressure (Shield): The foe has an active Energy Shield. Ensure your attacks are continuous, so the shield is quickly removed. Break off from combat, and the shield recharges, lengthening the fight (which is not desirable). Using Energy weapons depletes shield more quickly. If you match the energy type, a powerful localized explosion occurs when the shield pops.

Priority Target: This foe is particularly troublesome or works as a shield for other enemies. You must take it down first.

Target Practice: The foe can be struck anywhere, though aimed headshots work well.

Targeting Challenge: The foe in question has an area of their body or a special Ability that you must focus all your aiming attention on. While a regular takedown (raking the enemy with gunfire) may still yield effective takedown results, paying special attention to one of the following areas means even quicker dispatching:

(Cloak): The foe uses a cloaking device. Track and fire at the shimmering the enemy gives off.

(Evasion): The foe is particularly adept at dodging; use your own dexterity and impressive aiming to slow down and eventually kill them.

(Jetpack): The foe utilizes a jetpack. Leaping over, flanking, or otherwise enabling yourself to see and aim at the jetpack means the enemy will be defeated more quickly.

(Shield): The foe uses an Energy Shield (Arc = light blue, Void = purple, and Solar = Orange). Use a matching Energy weapon to remove the shield easily.

(Teleport): The foe is capable of teleporting short distances, so keep your gun trained on them, even when they blink in and out of existence.

(Torso): Attempt to target the foe's torso to quicken the takedown process.

Weak Spot: The foe has a particular area (usually the head or lower torso) that is extremely susceptible to precision gunfire (indicated by the yellow damage numbers). Note that most enemies should be targeted in the head; this tactic is employed for even quicker takedowns.

Weaken and Beat Down: The target is likely to be relatively weak. Sprint while firing, and finish the foe with a melee strike.

Cabal: The Red Legion

A Cabal invasion force led by Dominus Ghaul. They favor advancements in technology to aid in their plans for the destruction of humanity. Toughened infantry from this force may have the prefix "Impact." Higher-ranking infantry from this force are known as the Blood Guard.

War Beast

Threat Level: 1 **Weak Spot:** Head

Loadout	Types	Role	Survival Tactics	Takedown Tactics
Bite and claws	Base, Elite, Sub-Boss, Boss	Fodder	Melee Pressure	Target Practice

Notes: Found in packs of around a dozen, they attack three or four at a time. Treat as priority targets (as they don't find cover), even if other foes are causing you difficulty. Defeat by aiming at the head. At melee range, just fire at the heads or melee attack and back up, taking evasive maneuvers or finding higher ground to shoot down from.

Psion

Threat Level: 2 **Weak Spots:** Head and jetpack

Loadout	Types	Role	Survival Tactics	Takedown Tactics
Sniper rifle	Base, Elite	Fodder	Stay in Cover	Weaken and Beat Down
Slug rifle	Base, Elite, Sub-Boss, Boss	Fodder	Dodge Enemy Fire	Weaken and Beat Down
Shotgun	Base, Elite, Sub-Boss, Boss	Fodder	Close-range Pressure	Weaken and Beat Down
Cabal Bronto Cannon	Elite, Sub-Boss, Boss	Fodder	Dodge Enemy Fire	Weaken and Beat Down

Notes: The Psion can launch a projectile ball that causes a rolling distortion along the ground. It eventually knocks you high into the air, allowing them and others to strike you while you're exposed during this unwelcome jump. They also tend to use their jetpacks to maneuver at speed along the ground, though they also head through the air. Fortunately, Psions are only lightly armored, and they don't usually withstand more than a couple of headshots or a melee attack at close range.

Legionary

Threat Level: 2 **Weak Spots:** Helmet and head (front), jetpack (back)

Loadout	Types	Role	Survival Tactics	Takedown Tactics
Shotgun	Base, Elite, Sub-Boss, Boss	Soldier	Close-range Pressure	Target Practice
Slug rifle	Base, Elite, Sub-Boss, Boss	Soldier	Dodge Enemy Fire	Target Practice
Sniper rifle	Elite, Sub-Boss, Boss	Soldier	Stay in Cover	Target Practice
Projection rifle	Elite, Sub-Boss, Boss	Soldier	Stay Mobile	Target Practice

Notes: All Legionary types have a close-combat gauntlet blade, and they charge at their targets to inflict a powerful melee strike. They can also use this blade as a grenade to push you around.. They use jetpacks in open areas to cover distance. Shoot them in the head whenever possible. If that's not possible, aim for their jetpack if you're striking from behind. Softening them up with gunfire and melee striking them is also a viable proposition.

Incendior

Threat Level: 2 **Weak Spots:** Flame launcher backpack and a jetpack

Loadout	Types	Role	Survival Tactics	Takedown Tactics
Flame Launcher	Base, Elite, Sub-Boss, Boss	Soldier	Area Denial	Weak Spot

Notes: Aim for the center of the backpack (behind the head of the foe, between the two tanks), and watch the Incendior explode and topple over. This explosion can also coat you in fire, so back away and attempt ranged takedowns if you're after the explosive dispatch. Time the piercing of the fuel tanks to coincide with the Incendior being close to other foes. This can set off a chain reaction or badly wound nearby Cabal, a little like a grenade does.

Phalanx

Threat Level: 3 **Weak Spots:** Shield, head, and jetpack

Loadout	Types	Role	Survival Tactics	Takedown Tactics
Slug rifle	Base, Elite, Sub-Boss, Boss	Soldier	Dodge Enemy Fire	Flank Target (Shield), Weak Spot
Shotgun	Base, Elite, Sub-Boss, Boss	Soldier	Close-range Pressure	Flank Target (Shield), Weak Spot
Projection rifle	Elite, Sub-Boss, Boss	Soldier	Stay Mobile	Flank Target (Shield), Weak Spot

Notes: The biggest concern is the defensive posture the Phalanx takes, enabling it and other Cabal forces to hide behind a wide shield that expands when the Phalanx anchors himself in place. React by attacking from the flanks (left, right, or above), shooting over the shield. Grenades landing behind the Phalanx are also excellent. If the shield is up and flanking is impossible, shoot the center of the shield so it retracts, and mow with Phalanx down with headshots as it staggers back.

Gladiator

Threat Level: 4 **Weak Spot:** Head and jetpack

Loadout	Types	Role	Survival Tactics	Takedown Tactics
Thermal Cleaver	Base, Elite, Sub-Boss, Boss	Commander	Melee Pressure	Targeting Challenge (Jetpack)

Notes: Arguably the most problematic of Cabal foes to face, Gladiators are extremely aggressive. They can charge in quickly and deliver devastating melee strikes. If you can use your dodges and jumps effectively while pressuring the Gladiator as it rushes you, attempt to strike the enemy's jetpack, which damages it more quickly than headshots or general fire. Gladiators are always priority targets.

Centurion

Threat Level: 5 **Weak Spot:** Head and jetpack

Loadout	Types	Role	Survival Tactics	Takedown Tactics
Rail cannon	Base, Elite, Sub-Boss, Boss	Artillery	Suppression (Line of Sight), Stay Mobile (MIRV missiles)	Line of Sight
Heavy slug thrower	Base, Elite, Sub-Boss, Boss	Artillery	Suppression (Line of Sight), Stay Mobile (MIRV missiles)	Line of Sight

Notes: These walking artillery batteries are of great concern if you're caught in their line of sight. You can be cut down in seconds if you remain an open target. It's better to seek cover or take evasive maneuvers so the Centurion cannot quickly aim and strike you. Move to a ranged cover position, start to whittle down the Centurion' health with a good line of sight, and don't stop until the foe falls. Follow up with grenades to stagger before continuing a rapid-fire assault.

Centurion

Threat Level: 4 **Weak Spot:** Head and jetpack

Loadout	Types	Role	Survival Tactics	Takedown Tactics
Cabal Bronto Cannon	Base, Elite, Sub-Boss, Boss	Commander	Dodge Enemy Fire	Maintain Pressure (Shield), Targeting Challenge (Jetpack)
Projection rifle	Base, Elite, Sub-Boss, Boss	Commander	Stay Mobile	Maintain Pressure (Shield), Targeting Challenge (Jetpack)
Slug rifle	Base, Elite, Sub-Boss, Boss	Commander	Dodge Enemy Fire	Maintain Pressure (Shield), Targeting Challenge (Jetpack)

Notes: Centurions have active shields to remove, which are almost always powered by Solar energy (so have an Energy weapon of this type ready). Kinetic weapons also work, but they take much longer to neutralize the shield defenses. Centurions also like to jet vertically up before firing down on you. Learn to accurately shoot up at them, or find higher ground or cover. Remove the shield, then finish the Centurion with shots to its jetpack if you can navigate to aim at it, or slower takedowns with headshots (from either Kinetic or Energy weaponry).

Scorpius

Threat Level: 3 **Weak Spot:** Top, cube-shaped section

Loadout	Types	Role	Survival Tactics	Takedown Tactics
Machinegun or Flamethrower	Base, Elite, Sub-Boss, Boss	Artillery	Dodge Enemy Fire	Line of Sight

Notes: These sentry guns activate when they receive visual confirmation of your presence, and then fire rapidly. The incoming fire is highly damaging and can shred you to death in seconds. Use cover, range, grenades, and rapid-fire weaponry to destroy these sentries. Make them a priority.

Interceptor

Threat Level: 4 **Weak Spot:** Psion pilot

Loadout	Types	Role	Survival Tactics	Takedown Tactics
Rockets	Vehicle	Soldier	Dodge Enemy Fire	Target Practice

Notes: Slower than a Sparrow or Pike but more durable, the Cabal Interceptor has excellent offensive capabilities (rockets with area-of-effect damage). Hijacking one requires you to aim for the head of the Interceptor pilot until you execute him. The Interceptor is then neutralized, and you can drive it. Otherwise, you can blast the vehicle repeatedly until it catches fire and explodes (which isn't optimal).

Goliath Tank

Threat Level: 5 **Weak Spot:** Corner thrusters

Loadout	Types	Role	Survival Tactics	Takedown Tactics
Missile swarm, slug repeater	Vehicle	Artillery	Suppression (Line of Sight)	Target Practice

Notes: This heavy hover tank can cause havoc with a massive main turret and a secondary cluster missile swarm of (usually) Solar rockets. It can slay you with a direct hit, so remaining mobile is a must. Aim at the corner thrusters until they are set on fire, which damages the tank more quickly than just firing everything you've got at it.

Thresher

Threat Level: 4 **Weak Spot:** None

Loadout	Types	Role	Survival Tactics	Takedown Tactics
Rockets	Vehicle	Artillery	Suppression (Line of Sight)	Line of Sight

Notes: Not usually encountered as a hostile (except on a Strike, or when you're able to easily counter it in a Drake tank), this ship occasionally deposits foes before leaving the theater of battle. You have a slight advantage if you can seek cover and rake the engines of the craft (attached at the end of each wing). However, damaging the hull until the craft flees or explodes is the main way to tackle it.

Fallen

A race of insect-like alien scavengers, once organized into hierarchical houses. The remnants of House of Dusk are still active, mainly on the EDZ. They are hostile but tend to exhibit more lurking tendencies compared to the all-out aggression of the Cabal. Toughened Fallen usually take the prefix "Resilient."

Dreg

Threat Level: 1 **Weak Spot:** Head

Loadout	Types	Role	Survival Tactics	Takedown Tactics
Shock pistol	Base, Elite, Sub-Boss, Boss	Fodder	Dodge Enemy Fire, Area Denial (Grenade)	Weaken and Beat Down
Shrapnel launcher	Elite, Sub-Boss, Boss	Fodder	Close-range Pressure, Area Denial (Grenade)	Weaken and Beat Down
Molten Welder	Elite, Sub-Boss, Boss	Fodder	Dodge Enemy Fire, Area Denial (Grenade)	Weaken and Beat Down

Notes: An aptly named homunculus with base facets of cunning and a sinewy frame. They like to hide, stepping around cover and shooting you at range, lobbing in a shock grenade, or stabbing you at close quarters. In most combat conditions, a fine plan is to simply charge and melee attack them; they usually fall with a single strike from your hands. Soften them up with a few bullets so they're off-balance first, if you want.

Shank

Threat Level: 2 **Weak Spot:** Glowing Eye Slit (Heavy Shank only)

Loadout	Types	Role	Survival Tactics	Takedown Tactics
Shock pistol	Base, Elite, Sub-Boss, Boss	Fodder	Dodge Enemy Fire	Target Practice
Wire rifle	Base, Elite, Sub-Boss, Boss	Fodder	Stay in Cover	Target Practice
Explosives	Base, Elite, Sub-Boss, Boss	Fodder	Close-range Pressure (Explode)	Target Practice
Turret	Base, Elite, Sub-Boss, Boss	Artillery	Suppression (Line of Sight)	Line of Sight

Notes: These floating sentry machines have the largest number of variants of any specific enemy. Most are dealt with as priority targets due to their lack of artificial intelligence; they don't hide but simply head toward you, firing or setting up an explosion to kill you. Pepper their metal hides with your favored weapon, and make Tracer, Exploder, and Heavy Shanks priority targets.

Wretch

Threat Level: 2 **Weak Spot:** Head

Loadout	Types	Role	Survival Tactics	Takedown Tactics
Shock spear	Base, Elite, Sub-Boss, Boss	Fodder	Melee Pressure	Targeting Challenge (Evasion)

Notes: A more acrobatic foe that favors close-combat melee instead of ranged firing. Retaliate with your own melee attack. Wretches like to charge you and are a priority target when faced with them. Because they dash in straight lines, they are easy to shoot and finish with a melee strike.

Vandal

Threat Level: 3 **Weak Spot:** Head

Loadout	Types	Role	Survival Tactics	Takedown Tactics
Shock rifle	Base, Elite, Sub-Boss, Boss	Soldier	Stay Mobile	Targeting Challenge (Evasion)
Wire rifle	Base, Elite, Sub-Boss, Boss	Solider	Stay in Cover	Targeting Challenge (Evasion)
Molten Welder	Elite, Sub-Boss, Boss	Soldier	Dodge Enemy Fire	Targeting Challenge (Evasion)

Notes: There is significant variation among the Vandals regarding the main weapon they carry, and therefore, what offensive maneuvers you need to muster in order to survive. However, the swiftness of this foe means targeted takedowns are a must to kill any Vandal you encounter. Most Vandals like to snipe, so respond with your own long-range attacks accordingly.

Marauder

Threat Level: 3 **Weak Spot:** Head

Loadout	Types	Role	Survival Tactics	Takedown Tactics
Shrapnel launcher	Base, Elite, Sub-Boss, Boss	Soldier	Close-range Pressure	Targeting Challenge (Cloak)
Shock blade	Base, Elite, Sub-Boss, Boss	Soldier	Melee Pressure	Targeting Challenge (Cloak)

Notes: Marauders are more than Vandals with the ability to cloak themselves. They usually take a more proactive role in scurrying up to you and slicing you with a their blades, though they are just as active at range. Your main tactics are to look for the blue shimmering that indicates the Marauder has activated their cloaking device. Aim at this mass until one of you is defeated. A shotgun is more than adequate for this task, as these foes tend to seek out melee combat.

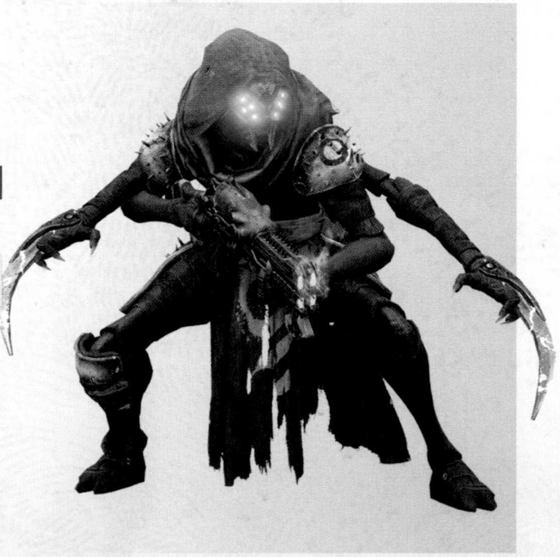

Servitor

Threat Level: 5 **Weak Spot:** Central eye

Loadout	Types	Role	Survival Tactics	Takedown Tactics
Servitor Blast	Base, Elite, Sub-Boss, Boss	Artillery	Dodge Enemy Fire	Priority Target

Notes: These floating globes are always priority targets, as they can link to other Fallen (usually Dregs, Vandals, or Shanks), protecting them in combat. Such enemy invulnerability is a real problem. Blast them anywhere, but focus on the central "eye" to maintain a good aim and constant damage.

Captain

Threat Level: 3-4 **Weak Spot:** Head

Loadout	Types	Role	Survival Tactics	Takedown Tactics
Shrapnel launcher	Base, Elite, Sub-Boss, Boss	Commander	Close-range Pressure	Maintain Pressure (Shield), Targeting Challenge (Teleport)
Shock rifle	Base, Elite, Sub-Boss, Boss	Commander	Stay Mobile	Maintain Pressure (Shield), Targeting Challenge (Teleport)
Molten Welder	Base, Elite, Sub-Boss, Boss	Commander	Dodge Enemy Fire	Maintain Pressure (Shield), Targeting Challenge (Teleport)

Notes: Taller than the fodder and soldiers they fight with, Captains can be found leading troops, as well as encountered alone. Though the survival tactics may change depending on the weapon the Captain is wielding, the takedown plan is always the same. Match the Energy weapon to the Captain's shield type (mainly Arc, but Solar and Void Shields have been seen used by Captains), and maintain hits so the shield is removed. Keep up the pressure, and track the Captain if he teleports a short distance. You don't want to break off combat so the Captain's shields can recharge.

Pike

Threat Level: 4 **Weak Spot:** Dreg pilot

Loadout	Types	Role	Survival Tactics	Takedown Tactics
Shock Cannons	Vehicle	Soldier	Dodge Enemy Fire	Target Practice

Notes: As quick as a Sparrow but with added offensive capabilities, the Fallen Pike is a great vehicle to own temporarily, once you've spotted a Pike Gang roaming a Public Sector and engaged them in combat. Hijack one by aiming at the head of the Dreg pilot until you execute him. The Pike is then neutralized, and you can drive it. Otherwise, you can blast the vehicle repeatedly until it catches fire and explodes (which isn't optimal).

Walker

Threat Level: 5 **Weak Spot:** Engine and legs

Loadout	Types	Role	Survival Tactics	Takedown Tactics
Laser Cannon, Battery, Chain-gun	Vehicle	Artillery	Stay Mobile	Line of Sight, Targeting Practice

Notes: Also known as the spider tank, this large Fallen vehicle provides impressive artillery fire support, and its weaponry can seriously impede your survival chances. Remain active and find cover, and target the vehicle's legs until the machine slumps forward on its knees and the engine compartment is exposed behind the head. Aim at that, then repeat the process.

Playing Ketch Up

The Fallen use the Ketch to bring Skiff dropships to ferry troops into battle. These vehicles appear consistently throughout your exploration but aren't usually engaged in combat, as they flee after depositing their troops.

The Hive

This parasitic alien presence, predominantly encroaching across the methane base of Titan, has a skeletal appearance and a nesting habit. They exist to exterminate all other life forms in an almost religious fervor. They cannot be reasoned with. Toughened Hive foes are usually known by the prefix "Revenant."

Thrall

Threat Level: 1 **Weak Spot:** Head

Loadout	Types	Role	Survival Tactics	Takedown Tactics
Claws	Base	Fodder	Melee Pressure	Target Practice

Notes: These husk-like foes exist to swarm and overwhelm you before savaging you with their claws and bites. Their lack of subtlety means you should employ similarly savage counterattacks; make these priority targets (unless Cursed Thralls are active), and mow them down with a rapid-fire weapon. Push back with melee and gun attacks, and retreat if you're overwhelmed.

Cursed Thrall

Threat Level: 3 **Weak Spot:** Head

Loadout	Types	Role	Survival Tactics	Takedown Tactics
Explosion	Base	Fodder	Melee Pressure (Explode)	Target Practice

Notes: Cursed Thralls move more slowly than their revolting cousins, but they carry a glowing and rancid explosive growth within themselves, detonating it when in melee range. Make these priority targets, not least because the explosion can remove other foes (usually Thralls and Cursed Thralls) in the immediate vicinity. Otherwise, Thrall tactics apply here, although you never want to be at melee range.

Acolyte

Threat Level: 2 **Weak Spot:** Head

Loadout	Types	Role	Survival Tactics	Takedown Tactics
Arc rifle	Base, Elite, Sub-Boss, Boss	Soldier	Dodge Enemy Fire	Weaken and Beat Down
Splinter	Base, Elite, Sub-Boss, Boss	Soldier	Stay Mobile, Area of Denial	Weaken and Beat Down

Notes: Possessing the intelligence and tactical knowledge to hide, flank, use cover, and engage in different ways depending on their main weapon, Acolytes aren't happy when you're making deft maneuvers. Finish up with rapid-fire shots into their skulls and a melee attack flourish to complete the takedown. Acolytes also have a fireball grenade, creating area of denial. Watch for it!

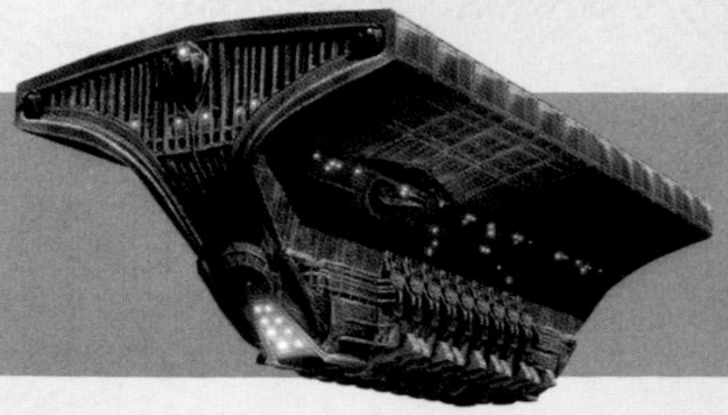

Catching a Cutter

The Hive use the Cutter dropship to ferry troops into battle. These vehicles appear occasionally throughout your exploration but aren't usually engaged in combat, as they flee after depositing their troops.

Knight

Threat Level: 3-4 **Weak Spot:** Head

Loadout	Types	Role	Survival Tactics	Takedown Tactics
Boomer	Base, Elite, Sub-Boss, Boss	Commander	Dodge Enemy Fire	Flank Target (Wall of Darkness)
Splinter	Base, Elite, Sub-Boss, Boss	Commander	Stay Mobile	Flank Target (Wall of Darkness)
Cleaver	Base, Elite, Sub-Boss, Boss	Commander	Melee Pressure	Flank Target (Wall of Darkness)

Notes: The most troublesome of the regularly encountered Hive foes, the Knight is large, fast, and capable of wreaking havoc with a close-range attack if you let him. It's best to take him out at range with well-aimed headshots while remaining active so the Knight can't successfully shoot you. The Knight has a Wall of Darkness Ability, a protective barrier it conjures while it heals after taking damage. You can wait the few seconds it takes for the wall to disappear, and then complete the Knight takedown. Or, if you want to conserve ammunition, you can move to the Knight's flank where the wall isn't active and finish the job.

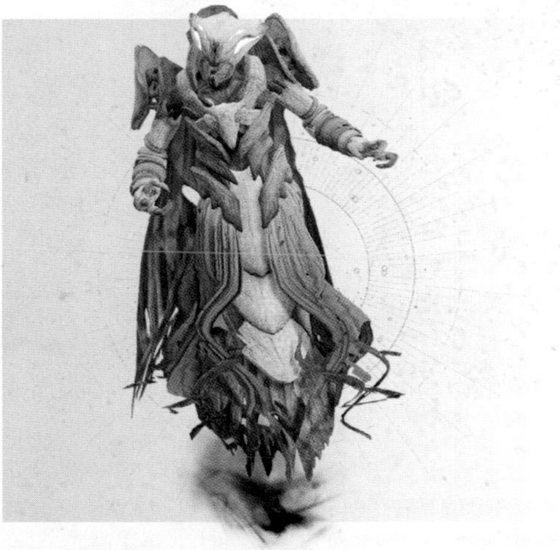

Wizard

Threat Level: 4 **Weak Spot:** Head

Loadout	Types	Role	Survival Tactics	Takedown Tactics
Darkness Blast	Base, Elite, Sub-Boss, Boss	Commander	Suppression (Line of Sight), Area Denial (Darkness Cloud)	Maintain Pressure (Shield)

Notes: These floating fiends are extremely dangerous, and they sometimes come with a Thrall entourage. At all other times, consider them a priority target due to their Darkness Cloud, which inflicts area-of-effect damage and can block your visibility. Retaliate by staying out of their line of sight, and when you're ready, attack their shields. Match the Energy weapon to the Wizard's shield type (mainly Solar have been seen), and keep up the pressure until the shield is removed. The Wizard is then very susceptible to your continued gunfire. Do not break off combat at this point; you don't want the Wizard's shield to recharge.

Ogre

Threat Level: 5 **Weak Spot:** Head

Loadout	Types	Role	Survival Tactics	Takedown Tactics
Eye Blast	Base, Elite, Sub-Boss, Boss	Artillery	Suppression (Line of Sight)	Line of Sight

Notes: Ogres can be terrifying, as their bulk and their Eye Blast attacks are extremely intimidating. Seek cover immediately so you aren't cut down in seconds. Then, train your weaponry at the Ogre's glowing "eye head" (though most of its body can also be struck). Take it down with precise shooting as often as you can, avoiding hits from that stream of energy. Make Ogres a priority target when you (occasionally) encounter them.

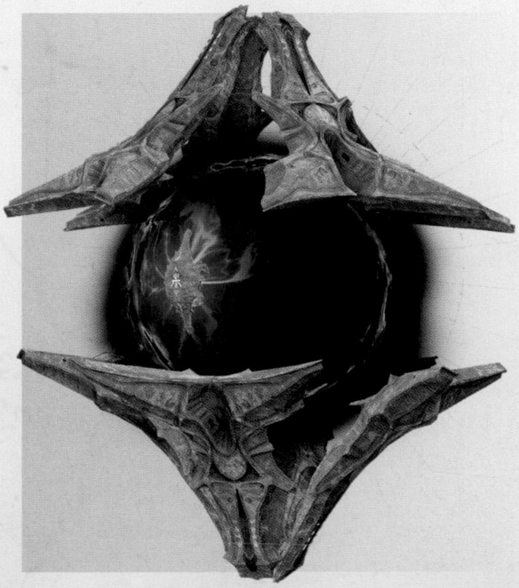

Shrieker

Threat Level: 4 **Weak Spot:** Central "eye"

Loadout	Types	Role	Survival Tactics	Takedown Tactics
Energy bolts	Base, Elite	Artillery	Dodge Enemy Fire, Suppression (Line of Sight)	Target Practice

Notes: A large floating eye with a piercing shriek and (usually) a good number of Hive infantry to provide additional headaches as you try to take this tough foe down. Seek cover, making this a priority target after any hostile that charges you. Continue to stay in cover, peeking out to fire at the central "eye" of the Shrieker to damage it before returning to cover. Its energy bolts are fired in highly damaging, almost continuous streams of projectiles.

The Vex

Constantly finding imperfections and altering worlds anew, Vex are cybernetic hostiles primarily focusing on terraforming Nessus. They seem to have a central intelligence, and they are responsible for almost impossible architecture. Toughened Vex foes are usually known by the prefix "Quantum."

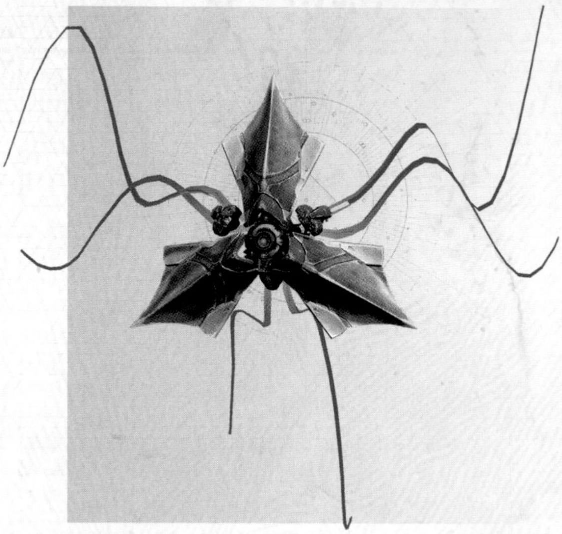

Harpy

Threat Level: 2 **Weak Spot:** Eye

Loadout	Types	Role	Survival Tactics	Takedown Tactics
Laser rifle	Base, Elite, Sub-Boss, Boss	Fodder	Suppression (Line of Sight)	Target Practice
Slap rifle	Base, Elite, Sub-Boss, Boss	Fodder	Suppression (Line of Sight)	Target Practice

Notes: The Harpies are mainly encountered at longer distances, as they prefer to shoot their rifles at you from range. React by aiming and shooting back after stepping out of their line of sight. Harpies are relatively weak, so keeping a consistent targeted pressure on these low-priority foes yields quick takedowns.

Fanatic

Threat Level: 3 **Weak Spot:** Lower torso

Loadout	Types	Role	Survival Tactics	Takedown Tactics
Slap rifle	Base, Elite, Sub-Boss, Boss	Fodder	Melee Pressure, Area Denial	Target Practice

Notes: Fanatics are always priority targets, as they exist to saunter their way toward you before exploding. This can easily kill you, so deft maneuvering and preventing their progress are the keys to victory. Because their explosion can set off a chain reaction and destroy other Fanatics (and damage Goblins), use them as moving explosives when you encounter multiple foes. When killing a Fanatic they also leave behind a dangerous pool of Radiolarian Fluid which can quickly negate large areas of of the combat zone for a short time.

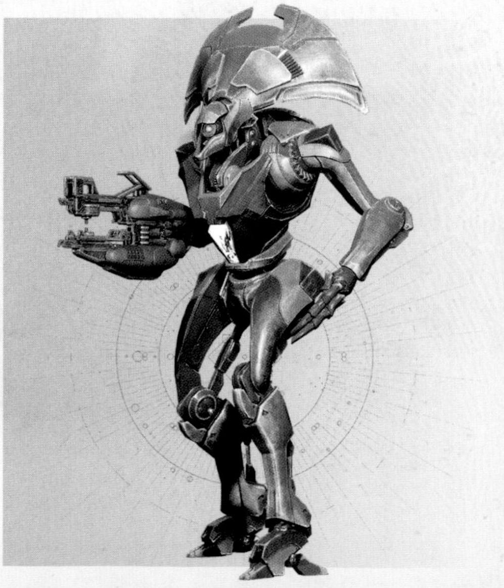

Goblin

Threat Level: 2 **Weak Spot:** Lower torso

Loadout	Types	Role	Survival Tactics	Takedown Tactics
Slap rifle	Base, Elite, Sub-Boss, Boss	Soldier	Dodge Enemy Fire, Melee Pressure (Seizure)	Targeting Challenge (Torso)
Torch Hammer	Elite, Sub-Boss, Boss	Soldier	Dodge Enemy Fire	Targeting Challenge (Torso)

Notes: Goblins are the main infantry threats you encounter when battling the Vex. Initial combat involves remaining mobile or behind cover to dodge their attacks, and executing long or short takedowns to take the Goblin's head off. This provokes a "seizure," after which the Goblin staggers at you like a Fanatic. Drop it with torso shots at this point. Or, aim at the torso consistently, and avoid the seizure entirely.

Hobgoblin

Threat Level: 3 **Weak Spot:** Lower torso

Loadout	Types	Role	Survival Tactics	Takedown Tactics
Line rifle	Base, Elite, Sub-Boss, Boss	Soldier	Stay in Cover, Area Denial	Targeting Challenge (Torso)
Laser rifle	Base, Elite, Sub-Boss, Boss	Soldier	Stay Mobile, Area Denial	Targeting Challenge (Torso)

Notes: The Hobgoblin is primarily a sharpshooter, designed to wound you from distance and finish you off before you have a chance to respond. Prevent this from happening by pressing the attack to this foe. Shoot it in the lower torso, and it crouches in a temporary invulnerable state. Any damage dealt to the Hobgoblin causes him to enter this state. During this time focus on other targets or reload your weapon before reengaging him after the immunity wears off.

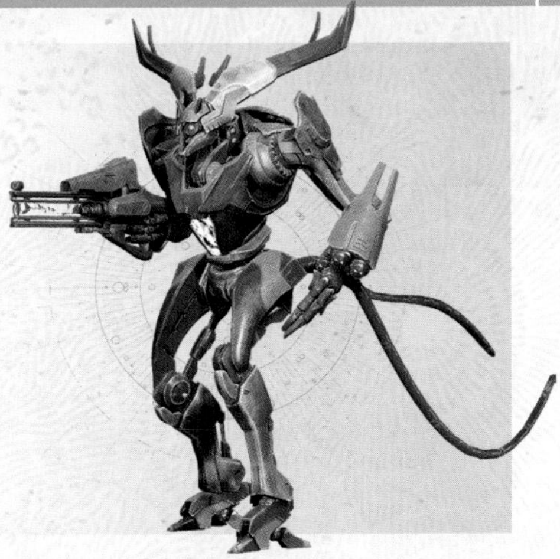

Minotaur

Threat Level: 3-4 **Weak Spot:** Lower torso

Loadout	Types	Role	Survival Tactics	Takedown Tactics
Torch Hammer	Base, Elite, Sub-Boss, Boss	Commander	Dodge Enemy Fire, Melee Pressure (Seizure)	Maintain Pressure (Shield), Targeting Challenge (Teleport)
Laser rifle	Elite, Sub-Boss, Boss	Commander	Stay Mobile, Melee Pressure (Seizure)	Maintain Pressure (Shield), Targeting Challenge (Teleport)

Notes: The largest bipedal Vex foe is the shielded Minotaur, a tough and problematic entity that should be prevented from encroaching into close combat. While you can shoot it in the head and induce a "seizure" where it targets and moves more rapidly toward you, the biggest concern is this foe's shield. Match the Energy weapon to the Minotaur's shield type (mainly Void, but Arc and Solar Shields have been seen), and keep on maintaining hits so the shield is removed. Keep up the pressure, and track the Minotaur if it teleports a short distance. You don't want to break off combat so the Minotaur's shields can replenish.

Hydra

Threat Level: 5 **Weak Spot:** Eye

Loadout	Types	Role	Survival Tactics	Takedown Tactics
Aeon Maul	Base, Elite, Sub-Boss, Boss	Artillery	Suppression (Line of Sight)	Targeting Challenge (Shield)

Notes: This large floating enemy has a pair of dual Torch Hammers that ignore gravity when fired: the Aeon Maul. It uses them to badly damage you in seconds, so seek cover when you're attempting to take one of these foes down. Stay active, and vary your speed, height, and range so the Hydra doesn't easily hit you. Fire at it (usually the central eye, though anywhere is fine) when you have a direct shot through its rotating shield. Otherwise, your offense has no effect. Stay away from a Hydra that has just been destroyed, as its explosion can kill you.

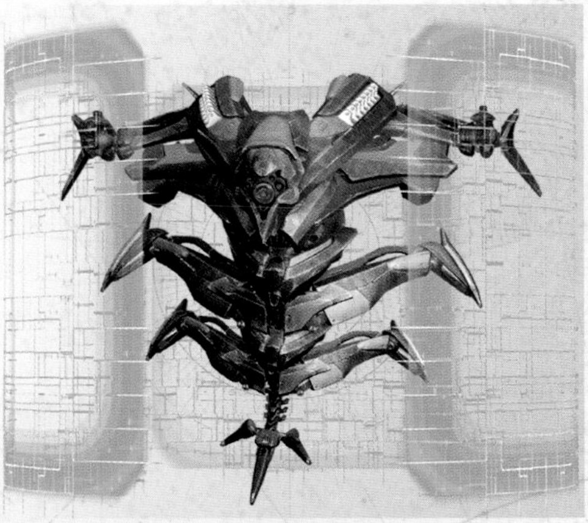

Cyclops

Threat Level: 4 **Weak Spot:** Central "eye"

Loadout	Types	Role	Survival Tactics	Takedown Tactics
Vex turret	Base, Elite, Sub-Boss, Boss	Artillery	Suppression (Line of Sight)	Line of Sight, Target Practice

Notes: Rarely encountered, think of this as a slightly smaller Hydra, with the tendencies of a sentient sentry gun. Use the fact that the Cyclops is stationary to your advantage. Find a way into cover, leap around, and generally stop the Cyclops from lining up its attack on you. Then, shoot its central "eye" intermittently while avoiding this turret's attack.

The Taken

Torn from their own dimension, only to return as the tormented and possessed shell of the darkness, Taken are corrupted forms of enemies you may already be familiar with. Their charred bodies writhe with twisted pain, and a strange glowing light coalesces where their eyes once peered out. Toughened Taken foes are usually known by the prefix "Ravenous."

Taken Psion

Threat Level: 2 **Weak Spot:** Head

Loadout	Types	Role	Survival Tactics	Takedown Tactics
Slug rifle	Base, Elite, Sub-Boss, Boss	Fodder	Dodge Enemy Fire	Weaken and Beat Down

Notes: Aside from an ability to dart around, which can throw off your aim, treat a Taken Psion like their non-possessed Cabal counterpart. They tend to use their slug rifle over any other attack. Attempt headshots and melee strikes. Taken Psions also replicate. If you don't kill all the Psions in an encounter there is a good chance they will split and multiply their count back to a full squad. So sustain your pressure and kill all of them before moving onto other foes.

Taken Phalanx

Threat Level: 3 **Weak Spot:** Head

Loadout	Types	Role	Survival Tactics	Takedown Tactics
Slug rifle	Base, Elite, Sub-Boss, Boss	Soldier	Dodge Enemy Fire	Target Practice

Notes: The Taken Phalanx is distinctly different and deadlier than their Cabal cousins. Their shield is used to power a massive blast of energy that can seriously impede your constitution. You must sidestep, jump over, or hide from it before you step out and rattle off gunfire into the inky blackness of the foe's head and torso, staggering and following up with more firepower.

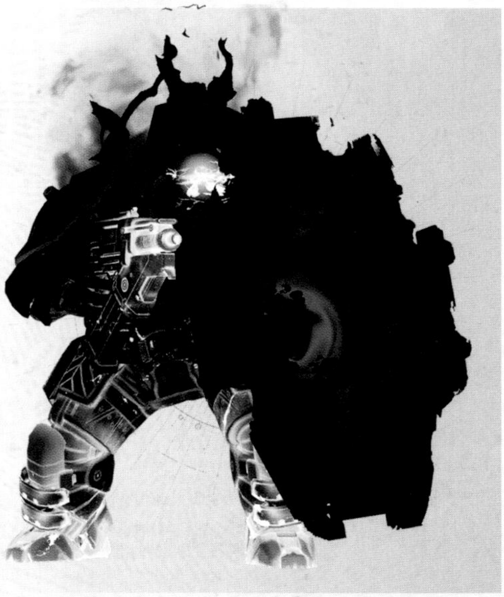

Taken Centurion

Threat Level: 4 **Weak Spot:** Head

Loadout	Types	Role	Survival Tactics	Takedown Tactics
Projection rifle	Base, Elite, Sub-Boss, Boss	Commander	Stay Mobile	Maintain Pressure, Target Practice
Slug rifle	Base, Elite, Sub-Boss, Boss	Commander	Dodge Enemy Fire	Maintain Pressure, Target Practice

Notes: Taken Centurions sometimes conjure a ball of rift energy from their forms that homes in, even moving around corners to strike you. This projectile is slow-moving but devastating, exploding with the force of a grenade. Shoot it out of the sky, then make a Taken Centurion a priority target so you don't have to deal with this attack again.

Taken Vandal

Threat Level: 3 **Weak Spot:** Head

Loadout	Types	Role	Survival Tactics	Takedown Tactics
Wire rifle	Base, Elite, Sub-Boss, Boss	Soldier	Stay in Cover	Targeting Challenge (Evasion)
Shrapnel launcher	Base, Elite, Sub-Boss, Boss	Soldier	Close-range Pressure	Targeting Challenge (Evasion)

Notes: Taken Vandals are just as sharp a shooter as their Fallen counterparts, and they can quickly conjure an additional dome-shaped shield, forcing you to dash in and shoot them so it dissipates. Attempt this as you close in for final combat, usually ending in a melee attack. Otherwise, long-range combat works well, with your targets firmly on what passes for this foe's head. Watch for a Vandal's short teleports, too.

Taken Captain

Threat Level: 4 **Weak Spot:** Head

Loadout	Types	Role	Survival Tactics	Takedown Tactics
Shrapnel launcher	Base, Elite, Sub-Boss, Boss	Commander	Close-range Pressure	Maintain Pressure (Shield), Targeting Challenge (Teleport)
Shock blade	Base, Elite, Sub-Boss, Boss	Commander	Melee Pressure	Maintain Pressure (Shield), Targeting Challenge (Teleport)

Notes: This Captain may be able to teleport short distances, and it also has similar attacks to the Fallen Captain it originated from. Check the weapon carried and vary your survival tactics accordingly, then take out the Captain's shield type (mainly Solar, but Arc and Void are also possible). Press the attack so the Captain's shield never gets a chance to recharge. The most notable aspect of the Taken Captain is his blinding Darkness Bolt. This slow moving projectile will blind any enemy in its path, making it one of the most dangerous abilities the Taken have.

Taken Thrall

Threat Level: 2 **Weak Spot:** Head

Loadout	Types	Role	Survival Tactics	Takedown Tactics
Claws	Base, Elite, Sub-Boss, Boss	Fodder	Melee Pressure	Target Practice

Notes: These Thrall variants are more solid than their shadow brethren, but they have the same dogged determination to charge and claw at you as the Hive Thralls. The only real difference is the quick, blurry teleports they attempt occasionally. Pull back, and mow down.

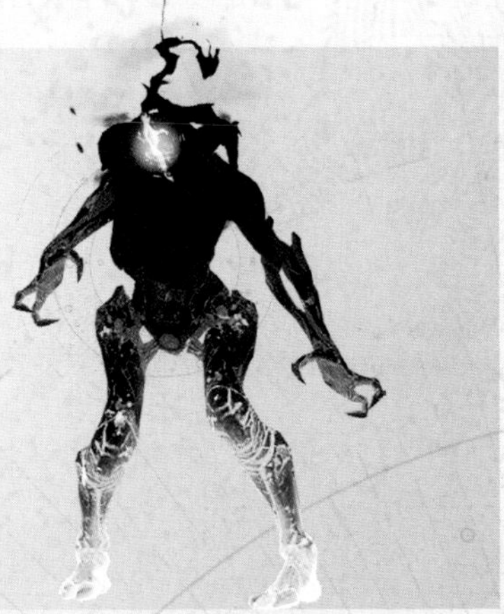

Taken Shadow Thrall

Threat Level: 2 **Weak Spot:** None

Loadout	Types	Role	Survival Tactics	Takedown Tactics
Claws	Base, Elite	Fodder	Melee Pressure	Target Practice

Notes: These minions of a particularly powerful Taken Wizard are not yet fully formed entities. They dash and flit around much more quickly and frequently, and they have no real light within them. You can attack them in the same way as a Taken Thrall, however.

Taken Acolyte

Threat Level: 2 **Weak Spot:** Head

Loadout	Types	Role	Survival Tactics	Takedown Tactics
Arc rifle	Base, Elite, Sub-Boss, Boss	Fodder	Dodge Enemy Fire	Weaken and Beat Down
Boomer	Base, Elite, Sub-Boss, Boss	Fodder	Dodge Enemy Fire	Weaken and Beat Down

Notes: Taken Acolytes are sometimes mistaken for Taken Psions. They share similarities right down to their tendency for ranged fire and their blurred and quick teleportation across short distances. Dispatch them by rushing them while firing, and melee strike them if they're still standing when you get there. Taken Acolytes also have the ability to summon dangerous Taken Eye turrets to provide additional suppressive fire. Cut them down before this opportunity presents itself to your foes.

Taken Knight

Threat Level: 4 **Weak Spot:** Head

Loadout	Types	Role	Survival Tactics	Takedown Tactics
Boomer	Base, Elite, Sub-Boss, Boss	Commander	Dodge Enemy Fire	Target Practice
Arc rifle	Base, Elite, Sub-Boss, Boss	Commander	Dodge Enemy Fire, Area of Denial	Target Practice

Notes: Expect long-range devastation when facing a Taken Knight; it tends to fire off its weapon, as well as shower you with flame from its mouth. Aim for its head, and keep going until it drops.

Taken Wizard

Threat Level: 5 **Weak Spot:** Head

Loadout	Types	Role	Survival Tactics	Takedown Tactics
Solar Blast	Base, Elite, Sub-Boss, Boss	Commander	Suppression (Line of Sight), Area Denial (Shadow Thrall)	Maintain Pressure (Shield)

Notes: Expect a Taken Wizard to act like their Hive counterparts, but with a different type of defensive "spell": the conjuring of Shadow Thralls that quickly flit toward and claw at you. Retaliate by staying out of their line of sight, and when you're ready, attack their shields. Match the Energy weapon to the Wizard's shield type (mainly Void, though Solar and Arc have been seen), and keep up the pressure until the shield is removed. The Wizard is then very susceptible to your continued gunfire. Do not break off combat at this point; you don't want the Wizard's shield to recharge.

Taken Goblin

Threat Level: 3 **Weak Spot:** Head

Loadout	Types	Role	Survival Tactics	Takedown Tactics
Slap rifle	Base, Elite, Sub-Boss, Boss	Soldier	Dodge Enemy Fire	Target Practice
Torch Hammer	Base, Elite, Sub-Boss, Boss	Soldier	Dodge Enemy Fire	Target Practice

Notes: Taken Goblins are always priority targets because of their extremely problematic energy link, similar to that of a Servitor's. It can link to a stronger Taken, effectively making it invincible. If your Taken Goblin or other Taken hostiles are glowing green, this link is occurring. The takedown plan is the same: send rapid-fire shots into the glowing light where the Goblin's head used to be. Lower torso fire isn't necessary, and this Goblin's head does not explode.

Taken Hobgoblin

Threat Level: 3 **Weak Spot:** Head

Loadout	Types	Role	Survival Tactics	Takedown Tactics
Line rifle	Base, Elite, Sub-Boss, Boss	Soldier	Stay in Cover, Area Denial	Target Practice
Slap rifle	Base, Elite, Sub-Boss, Boss	Soldier	Dodge Enemy Fire, Area Denial	Target Practice

Notes: Taken Hobgoblins are perhaps the most like their Vex counterparts, with a predisposition for long-range sharpshooting. Remove them with ranged attacks from a distance, or close the gap and demolish them at close quarters with rapid-fire or high-powered hand cannon accurate strikes. Taken Hobgoblin's most important trait is their retaliation shots. If the Hobgoblin has energy swirling around him, the next time it receives damage from an enemy (usually you), these projectiles will fly towards them.

Taken Minotaur

Threat Level: 4 **Weak Spot:** Head

Loadout	Types	Role	Survival Tactics	Takedown Tactics
Torch Hammer	Base, Elite, Sub-Boss, Boss	Commander	Dodge Enemy Fire	Maintain Pressure, Targeting Challenge (Cloak)
Slap rifle	Base, Elite, Sub-Boss, Boss	Commander	Dodge Enemy Fire	Targeting Challenge (Cloak)

Notes: A Taken Minotaur has all the strengths of its Vex cousin, with the added ability to cloak like a Fallen Marauder. This means it must be tracked via the glow of its head, which is also where you must shoot it.

Weapons

Spend enough time in the field and you'll amass quite a collection of weapons. Choosing the right combination of Kinetic, Energy, and Power weapons can be a bit of a challenge. Luckily, you'll have plenty of opportunities to test out new finds.

Every weapon you encounter features an Intrinsic Perk. Specifics can vary quite a bit, but most intrinsic Perks fall into one of six categories:

ADAPTIVE FRAME: This Perk usually indicates a weapon with balanced stats.

AGGRESSIVE FRAME: This usually indicates that a weapon features High Caliber Rounds as a native Perk.

HIGH-IMPACT FRAME: Weapons with this Perk typically favor Range over other stats, and they almost always offer improved accuracy and recoil when the user is standing still.

LIGHTWEIGHT FRAME: This Perk often indicates better handling or a boost to movement speed.

PRECISION FRAME: This Perk usually indicates a stable weapon with relatively linear recoil pattern.

RAPID-FIRE FRAME: This Perk usually indicates a weapon with a high rate of fire that reloads much faster whenever the magazine is empty.

As you experiment with new weapons, you're likely to find that many of your favorite weapons share a similar Intrinsic Perk.

The following tables list the bulk of the weapons currently in the game, along with what tend to be the most likely methods of acquiring them. While some weapons are simply random drops, many are given out as rewards for missions or activities – and some of the best weapons can be gained by earning Reputation with various vendors.

As you review your options, note that weapons are listed in order of Rarity – and within those categories, they're arranged in the order you're most likely to encounter them.

Remember, you can only equip one weapon of each type (Kinetic, Energy, and Power), and you can never have more than one Exotic weapon equipped, but you can always carry a few useful options with you. If a new weapon combination isn't working for you, duck into cover and adjust your loadout. The more options you have, the better off you'll be.

Kinetic and Energy Weapons

Auto Rifles

Weapon Name	Rarity	Intrinsic Perk	Source
KINETIC AUTO RIFLES			
Pariah	Common	Precision Frame	Drop
Home Again	Uncommon	High-Impact Frame	Drop
Cydonia-AR1	Uncommon	Adaptive Frame	Drop
Suros Throwback	Uncommon	Precision Frame	Drop
Rebuke AX-GL	Rare	Adaptive Frame	Reward
Lionheart	Rare	Adaptive Frame	Reward
Ros Lysis II	Rare	Adaptive Frame	Drop
Cuboid ARU	Rare	Precision Frame	Drop
Origin Story	Legendary	Precision Frame	Zavala Rep
Halfdan-D	Legendary	High-Impact Frame	Banshee-44 Rep
Skathelocke	Legendary	Adaptive Frame	Drop
Sweet Business	Exotic	Unique	Varies
ENERGY AUTO RIFLES			
Jiangshi AR1	Uncommon	Lightweight Frame	Drop
Yellowjacket-3AU	Rare	Rapid-Fire Frame	Reward
Sand Wasp-3AU	Rare	Rapid-Fire Frame	Drop
Refrain-23	Rare	Adaptive Frame	Drop
Martyr's Make	Legendary	Adaptive Frame	Shaxx Rep
Galliard-42	Legendary	Adaptive Frame	Banshee-44 Rep
Jiangshi AR4	Legendary	Precision Frame	Banshee-44 Rep
Deathstalker -4AU	Legendary	Rapid-Fire Frame	Reward
Hymn-34	Legendary	Adaptive Frame	Drop
Uriel AR3	Legendary	Precision Frame	Drop
Valakadyn-3AU	Legendary	Rapid-Fire Frame	Drop
Coldheart	Exotic	Unique	Varies
Hard Light	Exotic	Unique	Varies

Hand Cannons

Weapon Name	Rarity	Intrinsic Perk	Source
KINETIC HAND CANNONS			
Headstrong	Common	Aggressive Frame	Drop
One Earth	Uncommon	Lightweight Frame	Drop
MOS Ultima II	Uncommon	Adaptive Frame	Drop
Picayune MK. 33	Uncommon	Aggressive Frame	Drop
Guseva-C	Rare	Aggressive Frame	Reward
Ballyhoo MK.27	Rare	Adaptive Frame	Drop
Azimuth DSU	Rare	Aggressive Frame	Drop
Better Devils	Legendary	Adaptive Frame	Shaxx Rep
Pribina-D	Legendary	Aggressive Frame	Banshee-44 Rep
Chaos Falcon	Legendary	Aggressive Frame	Reward
Camilla-C	Legendary	Aggressive Frame	Drop
Sturm	Exotic	Unique	Varies
ENERGY HAND CANNONS			
Helios HC1	Common	Lightweight Frame	Drop
Minuet-12	Uncommon	Adaptive Frame	Drop
Presto-48	Rare	Adaptive Frame	Reward
Lamia HC2	Rare	Lightweight Frame	Drop
Allegro-34	Rare	Adaptive Frame	Drop
Deadalus Code	Legendary	Lightweight Frame	Zavala Rep
Minuet-42	Legendary	Adaptive Frame	Banshee-44 Rep
Imset HC4	Legendary	Lightweight Frame	Banshee-44 Rep
Shattered Peace HC3	Legendary	Lightweight Frame	Drop
Baroque-36	Legendary	Adaptive Frame	Drop
Sunshot	Exotic	Unique	Varies

Pulse Rifles

Weapon Name	Rarity	Intrinsic Perk	Source
KINETIC PULSE RIFLES			
Lost and Found	Common	Rapid-Fire Frame	Drop
Standing Tall	Uncommon	High-Impact Frame	Drop
Psi Ferox II	Uncommon	Lightweight Frame	Drop
Psi Termina II	Uncommon	Adaptive Frame	Drop
Triumph DX-PR	Rare	High-Impact Frame	Reward
Nanty Narker	Rare	Rapid-Fire Frame	Reward
Bayesian MSU	Rare	Adaptive Frame	Drop
PSI Cirrus II	Rare	Rapid-Fire Frame	Drop
Nightshade	Legendary	Lightweight Frame	Zavala Rep
Eystein-D	Legendary	High-Impact Frame	Reward
Naimon-C	Legendary	High-Impact Frame	Drop
Lincoln Green	Legendary	Rapid-Fire Frame	Drop
Vigilance Wing	Exotic	Unique	Varies
ENERGY PULSE RIFLES			
Cadenza-11	Uncommon	Adaptive Frame	Drop
Argona PR2	Rare	Lightweight Frame	Drop
Encore-25	Rare	Adaptive Frame	Drop
Last Perdition	Legendary	Adaptive Frame	Shaxx Rep
Cadenza-43	Legendary	Adaptive Frame	Banshee-44 Rep
Nergal PR4	Legendary	Lightweight Frame	Banshee-44 Rep
Quadrille-34	Legendary	Aggressive Frame	Drop
Canobus PR2	Legendary	Lightweight Frame	Drop
Graviton Lance	Exotic	Unique	Varies

Sidearms

Weapon Name	Rarity	Intrinsic Perk	Source
KINETIC SIDEARMS			
Roderic-C	Rare	Precision Frame	Drop
Atehlflad-D	Legendary	Precision Frame	Banshee-44 Rep
Pinabel-C	Legendary	Precision Frame	Drop
Rat King	Exotic	Unique	Varies
ENERGY SIDE ARMS			
Spiderbite-1SI	Common	Lightweight Frame	Drop
Victoire SI2	Uncommon	Adaptive Frame	Drop
Recital-17	Uncommon	Rapid-Fire Frame	Drop
Dissonance-34	Rare	Rapid-Fire Frame	Drop
Requiem SI2	Rare	Adaptive Frame	Drop
Vinegaroon-2SI	Rare	Lightweight Frame	Drop
The Last Dance	Legendary	Adaptive Frame	Zavala Rep
Etana SI4	Legendary	Adaptive Frame	Banshee-44 Rep
Urchin-3SI	Legendary	Lightweight Frame	Banshee-44 Rep
Octave-44	Legendary	Rapid-Fire Frame	Reward
Interlude-33	Legendary	Rapid-Fire Frame	Drop
Last Hope SI3	Legendary	Adaptive Frame	Drop
Boomslang-3SI	Legendary	Lightweight Frame	Drop
Drang	*Legendary	Adaptive Frame	Drop

***Drang** pairs with **Sturm** to create an Exotic weapon set; this weapon is rated as *Legendary* to allow for both set pieces to be equipped at the same time.

Scout Rifles

Weapon Name	Rarity	Intrinsic Perk	Source
KINETIC SCOUT RIFLES			
Thistle and Yew	Common	Precision Frame	Drop
Fare-Thee-Well	Uncommon	Lightweight Frame	Drop
Trax Arda II	Uncommon	High-Impact Frame	Drop
Inverness-SR2	Uncommon	Precision Frame	Drop
Trax Dynia	Rare	Lightweight Frame	Reward
Armillary PSU	Rare	Precision Frame	Drop
Trax Lysis II	Rare	High-Impact Frame	Drop
Does Not Compute	Legendary	High-Impact Frame	Shaxx Rep
Nameless Midnight	Legendary	Precision Frame	Zavala Rep
Carloman-D	Legendary	High-Impact Frame	Reward
Call to Serve	Legendary	Precision Frame	Drop
MIDA Multi-tool	Exotic	Unique	Varies
ENERGY SCOUT RIFLES			
Sea Scorpion-1SR	Uncommon	Rapid-Fire Frame	Drop
Sonata-48	Rare	Precision Frame	Reward
Black Tiger-2SR	Rare	Rapid-Fire Frame	Drop
Madrugada SR2	Rare	Lightweight Frame	Drop
Tango-45	Legendary	Precision Frame	Banshee-44 Rep
Manannan SR4	Legendary	Lightweight Frame	Banshee-44 Rep
Black Scorpion-4SR	Legendary	Rapid-Fire Frame	Banshee-44 Rep
Tonic-37	Legendary	Precision Frame	Drop
Macaria PR3	Legendary	Lightweight Frame	Drop
Skyburner's Oath	Exotic	Unique	Varies

Submachine Guns

Weapon Name	Rarity	Intrinsic Perk	Source
KINETIC SUBMACHINE GUNS			
Rare	Sondok-C	Precision Frame	Reward
Rare	Protostar CSU	Adaptive Frame	Drop
Rare	Philippis-B	Precision Frame	Drop
Legendary	The Showrunner	Lightweight Frame	Zavala Rep
Legendary	Antiope-D	Precision Frame	Banshee-44 Rep
ENERGY SUBMACHINE GUNS			
Common	Etude-12	Adaptive Frame	Drop
Uncommon	Daystar SMG2	Lightweight Frame	Drop
Uncommon	Forte-15	Adaptive Frame	Drop
Rare	Sorrow MG2	Lightweight Frame	Reward
Rare	Whip Scorpion-3MG	Lightweight Frame	Reward
Rare	Furina-2MG	Lightweight Frame	Drop
Rare	Harmony-21	Adaptive Frame	Drop
Legendary	Resonance-42	Adaptive Frame	Banshee-44 Rep
Legendary	Phosphorous MG4	Lightweight Frame	Banshee-44 Rep
Legendary	Death Adder-4SMG	Lightweight Frame	Reward
Legendary	Atropos SB3	Lightweight Frame	Drop
Legendary	Red Mamba-3MG	Lightweight Frame	Drop
Legendary	Symphony-39	Adaptive Frame	Drop
*Legendary	MIDA Mini-Tool	Lightweight Frame	Drop
Exotic	Riskrunner	Unique	Varies

***MIDA Mini-Tool** pairs with **MIDA Multi-Tool** to create an Exotic weapon set; this weapon is rated as *Legendary* to allow for both set pieces to be equipped at the same time.

The Fighting Lion

There's one Energy weapon that stands apart from all others: **Fighting Lion**. This Exotic Grenade Launcher features a selection of unique qualities, but the fact that it serves as an energy weapon is by far the most noteworthy.

Power Weapons

Fusion Rifles and Linear Fusion Rifles

Weapon Name	Rarity	Intrinsic Perk	Source
FUSION RIFLES			
Nox Calyx II	Uncommon	Adaptive Frame	Drop
Nox Reve II	Uncommon	High-Impact Frame	Drop
Equinox TSU	Uncommon	Precision Frame	Drop
Nox Lumen II	Rare	High-Impact Frame	Drop
Nox Cordis II	Rare	Rapid-Fire Frame	Drop
Parsec TSU	Rare	High-Impact Frame	Drop
Critical Sass	Legendary	Rapid-Fire Frame	Shaxx Rep
Main Ingredient	Legendary	Precision Frame	Zavala Rep
Erentil FR4	Legendary	High-Impact Frame	Banshee-44 Rep
Nox Echo III	Legendary	Adaptive Frame	Drop
Cartesian TSM	Legendary	Rapid-Fire Frame	Drop
Keres FR3	Legendary	High-Impact Frame	Drop
Merciless	Exotic	Unique	Varies
LINEAR FUSION RIFLES			
King Cobra-4FR	Rare	Precision Frame	Reward
Man O' War-4FR	Legendary	Precision Frame	Reward
Tarantula-3FR	Legendary	Precision Frame	Drop

Shotguns

Weapon Name	Rarity	Intrinsic Perk	Source
Stubborn Oak	Common	Aggressive Frame	Drop
Hand in Hand	Uncommon	Precision Frame	Drop
DED Acumen II	Uncommon	Lightweight Frame	Drop
DED Nemoris II	Uncommon	Aggressive Frame	Drop
Requiem-43	Rare	Precision Frame	Reward
Botheration MK.28	Rare	Aggressive Frame	Drop
Badlands MK.24	Rare	Lightweight Frame	Drop
Fussed Dark MK.21	Rare	Precision Frame	Drop
Retrofuturist	Legendary	Lightweight Frame	Shaxx Rep
Deadpan Delivery	Legendary	Aggressive Frame	Zavala Rep
Somerled-D	Legendary	Aggressive Frame	Banshee-44 Rep
Opus-46	Legendary	Precision Frame	Reward
Baligant-C	Legendary	Aggressive Frame	Drop
Bolero-39	Legendary	Precision Frame	Drop
Hawthorne's Field-Forged Shotgun	Legendary	Lightweight Frame	Drop
Tractor Cannon	Exotic	Unique	Varies
Legend of Acrius	Exotic	Unique	Varies

Grenade Launchers

Weapon Name	Rarity	Intrinsic Perk	Source
Stay Away	Common	Lightweight Frame	Drop
Resilient People	Uncommon	Lightweight Frame	Drop
Hadrian-A	Uncommon	Aggressive Frame	Drop
Para Torus I	Uncommon	Adaptive Frame	Drop
Penumbra GSM	Rare	Precision Frame	Reward
Gareth-C	Rare	Aggressive Frame	Reward
Harsh Language	Rare	Lightweight Frame	Reward
Plemusa-B	Rare	Adaptive Frame	Drop
Stampede MK.32	Rare	Aggressive Frame	Drop
Last Stand	Legendary	Adaptive Frame	Shaxx Rep
Wicked Sister	Legendary	Adaptive Frame	Zavala Rep
Acantha-D	Legendary	Aggressive Frame	Banshee-44 Rep
Morgenstern GL2	Legendary	Precision Frame	Reward
Sylvanite	Legendary	Lightweight Frame	Drop
Orthrus GL2	Legendary	Precision Frame	Drop
Berenger-C	Legendary	Aggressive Frame	Drop
The Prospector	Exotic	Unique	Varies

Sniper Rifles

Weapon Name	Rarity	Intrinsic Perk	Source
Dead Zone Rifle	Common	Adaptive Frame	Drop
Troubadour	Uncommon	Adaptive Frame	Drop
Luna Nullis II	Uncommon	Rapid-Fire Frame	Drop
Trondheim LR2	Uncommon	Aggressive Frame	Drop
Aachen-LR2	Rare	Adaptive Frame	Drop
Damietta-LR2	Rare	Aggressive Frame	Drop
Tongeren-LR3	Rare	Rapid-Fire Frame	Drop
Gentleman Vagabond	Legendary	Aggressive Frame	Shaxx Rep
Persuader	Legendary	Rapid-Fire Frame	Zavala Rep
Elegy-49	Legendary	Adaptive Frame	Banshee-44 Rep
Veleda-D	Legendary	Aggressive Frame	Banshee-44 Rep
Copperhead-4SN	Legendary	Rapid-Fire Frame	Banshee-44 Rep
Danica RR4	Legendary	Adaptive Frame	Reward
Shepherd's Watch	Legendary	Adaptive Frame	Drop
Virtuoso-38	Legendary	Adaptive Frame	Drop
Widow's Bite-3SN	Legendary	Rapid-Fire Frame	Drop
Olivier-C	Legendary	Aggressive Frame	Drop
D.A.R.C.I.	Exotic	Unique	Varies

Rocket Launchers

Weapon Name	Rarity	Intrinsic Perk	Source
Butler RS/2	Uncommon	High-Impact Frame	Drop
Weaver-C	Rare	Precision Frame	Reward
Cup-Bearer SA/2	Rare	Adaptive Frame	Drop
Reginar-B	Rare	Precision Frame	Drop
Curtain Call	Legendary	Aggressive Frame	Zavala Rep
Pentatonic-48	Legendary	Adaptive Frame	Banshee-44 Rep
Morrigan-D	Legendary	Precision Frame	Banshee-44 Rep
Hoosegow Mk. 32	Legendary	Adaptive Frame	Drop
MOS Epoch III	Legendary	Aggressive Frame	Drop
Blue Shift CSM	Legendary	High-Impact Frame	Drop
The Wardcliff Coil	Exotic	Unique	Varies

Swords

Weapon Name	Rarity	Intrinsic Perk	Source
Nasreddin	Uncommon	Adaptive Frame	Drop
Rest for the Wicked	Rare	Adaptive Frame	Drop
Future Imperfect	Rare	Adaptive Frame	Drop
Steel Sybil Z-14	Legendary	Adaptive Frame	Shaxx Rep
Negative Space	Legendary	Adaptive Frame	Drop
Complex Solution	Legendary	Adaptive Frame	Drop
Unspoken Promise	Legendary	Adaptive Frame	Drop
Quickfang-4BL	Legendary	Lightweight Frame	Reward
Crown-Splitter	Legendary	Aggressive Frame	Reward
Eternity's Edge	Legendary	Adaptive Frame	Reward

Class-Specific Swords

It's important to note that Quickfang-4BL is only usable by Hunters; Crown-Splitter is a Titan-only Sword, and Eternity's Edge is exclusive to Warlocks.

Exotic Weapons

Offering qualities you won't find anywhere else, Exotic weapons can change quite a bit about the way you perform in a firefight. Of course, they do have a few drawbacks: they're extremely scarce, you can only equip one at a time, and (aside from the odd Weapon Ornament) they can't be modified.

Exotic Kinetic Weapons

MIDA Multi-Tool

Weapon Type	Damage Type
Scout Rifle	Kinetic

Perks	
Intrinsic	Mida Multi-Tool: This weapon boosts move speed.
Barrel	Corkscrew Rifling: Balanced Barrel. Slightly increases range and stability. Slightly increases handling speed.
Magazine	High-Caliber Rounds: Shots from this weapon knock the target back farther. Slightly increases range.
Trait	MIDA Radar: Radar stays active while aiming down sights.
Stock	Hand-Laid Stock: This weapon is optimized for recoil control. Increases stability.

MIDA Multi-Tool grants additional benefits when the Legendary Submachine Gun **MIDA Mini-Tool** is equipped in your Energy weapon slot.

Sturm

Weapon Type	Damage Type
Hand Cannon	Kinetic

Perks	
Intrinsic	Accomplice: Kills with this weapon fill the magazine of the equipped Energy weapon from reserves.
Barrel	Extended Barrel: Weighty barrel extension. Increases range. Decreases handling speed.
Magazine	Extended Mag: This weapon has a greatly increased magazine size, but reloads much slower.
Trait	Storm and Stress: Kills with Drang grant bonus precision damage until the next reload.
Grip	Combat Grip: This weapon causes much less vertical recoil.

Sturm grants additional benefits when the Legendary Sidearm **Drang** is equipped in your Energy weapon slot.

Rat King

Weapon Type	Damage Type
Sidearm	Kinetic

Perks	
Intrinsic	Rat Pack: This weapon becomes stronger when nearby fireteam members also have it equipped. Stacks up to 6 times.
Barrel	Smallbore: Dual strength barrel. Increases range. Increases stability.
Magazine	Tactical Mag: This weapon has multiple tactical improvements. Slightly increases stability. Slightly increases reload speed. Slightly increases magazine size.
Trait	Vermin: Reloading immediately after a kill grants a brief period of invisibility.
Grip	Smooth Grip: This weapon is slightly easier to hold and aim. Slightly increases stability. Slightly increases handling speed.

Sweet Business

Weapon Type	Damage Type
Auto Rifle	Kinetic

Perks	
Intrinsic	Payday: Larger magazine. Increased accuracy when firing from the hip.
Barrel	Polygonal Rifling: Barrel optimized for recoil reduction. Increases stability.
Magazine	High-Caliber Rounds: Shots from this weapon knock the target back farther. Slightly increases range.
Trait	Business Time: Holding down the trigger boosts this weapon's range and rate of fire, and automatically loads ammo pickups into the magazine.
Stock	Composite Stock: This weapon has a versatile dual-purpose stock. Slightly increases stability. Slightly increases handling speed.

Vigilance Wing

Weapon Type	Damage Type
Pulse Rifle	Kinetic

Perks	
Intrinsic	Harsh Truths: This weapon fires a 5-round burst. When a nearby ally is killed, gain health regeneration and increased movement speed.
Barrel	Corkscrew Rifling: Balanced Barrel. Slightly increases range and stability. Slightly increases handling speed.
Magazine	Alloy Magazine: Faster reloads when the magazine is empty.
Trait	Last Stand: Improved weapon performance when its wielder is the last living member of a fireteam.
Stock	Composite Stock: This weapon has a versatile dual-purpose stock. Slightly increases stability. Slightly increases handling speed.

Exotic Energy Weapons

Coldheart

Weapon Type	Damage Type
Trace Rifle	Arc

Perks	
Intrinsic	Cold Fusion: This weapon shoots a steady cold fusion-powered laser
Barrel	Extended Barrel: Weighty barrel extension. Increases range. Decreases handling speed.
Battery	Enhanced Battery: Strong battery life. Increases magazine size.
Trait	Longest Winter: Coldheart's laser does exponentially more damage the longer it remains on a target.
Stock	Hand-Laid Stock: This weapon is optimized for recoil control. Increases stability.

Hard Light

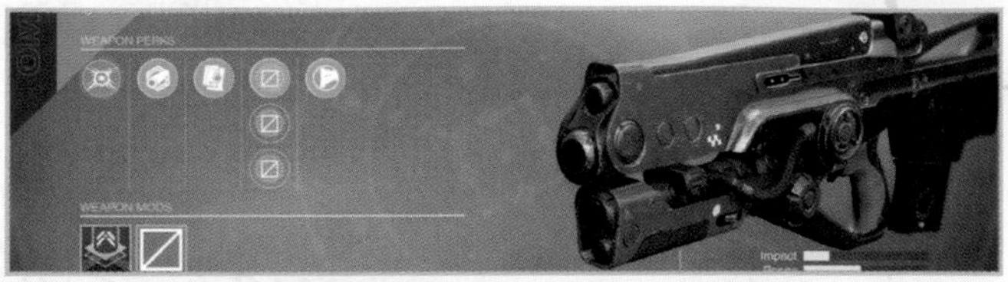

Weapon Type	Damage Type
Auto Rifle	Arc/Solar/Void

Perks	
Intrinsic	Volatile Light: Rounds fired from this weapon have no damage falloff, overpenetrate targets, and richochet off hard surfaces.
Barrel	Polygonal Rifling: Barrel optimized for recoil reduction. Increases stability.
Magazine	Alloy Magazine: Faster reloads when the magazine is empty.
Trait	(Variable) Arc Core/ Solar Core/ Void Core: Modifies this weapon's damage type to Arc/ Solar/ Void.
Stock	Composite Stock: This weapon has a versatile dual-purpose stock. Slightly increases stability. Slightly increases handling speed.

Fighting Lion

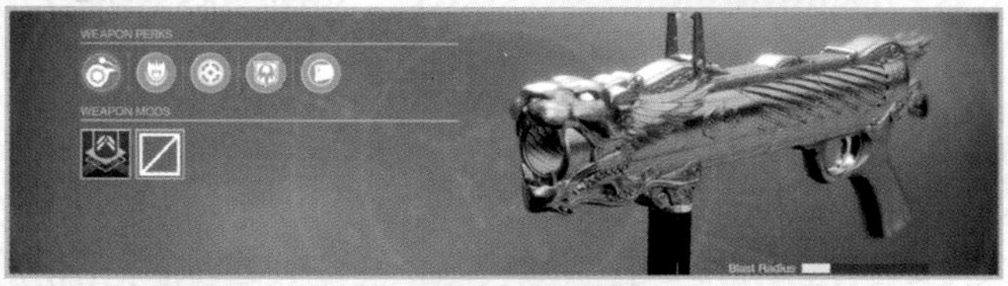

Weapon Type	Damage Type
Grenade Launcher	Void

Perks	
Intrinsic	Delayed Gratification: Grenade projectiles will bounce off surfaces. Hold [Fire] to fire, and release to detonate.
Launcher Barrel	Countermass: This weapon is weighted for vertical recoil. Greatly controls recoil. Increases stability. Increases handling speed.
Magazine	Implosion Rounds: Grenades travel faster and have a controlled explosion. Increases projectile speed. Greatly increases stability. Decreases blast radius.
Trait	Thin the Herd: Direct hits with this weapon do more damage to shielded enemy combatants. Rapid Kills against grenade-damaged enemies will refill the magazine.
Stock	Short-Action Stock: This weapon is especially easy to grip. Greatly increases handling speed.

Although **Fighting Lion** is a Grenade Launcher, it can only be equipped as an Energy weapon.

Riskrunner

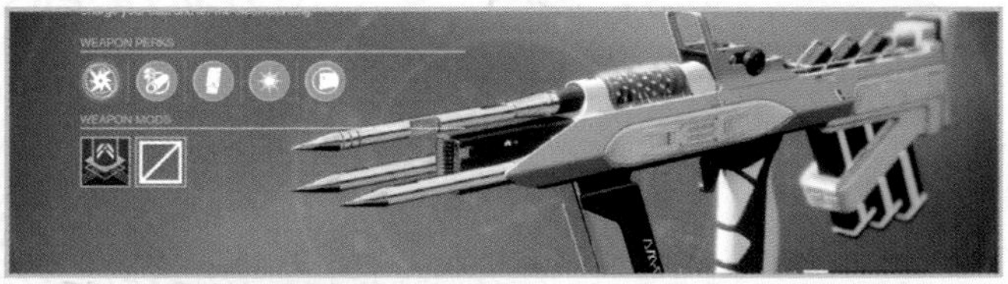

Weapon Type	Damage Type
Submachine Gun	Arc

Perks	
Intrinsic	Arc Conductor: When taking Arc Damage, this weapon becomes more powerful and resists incoming Arc Damage. Kills extend the time in this overcharged state.
Barrel	Arrowhead Break: Lightly vented barrel. Greatly controls recoil. Increases handling speed.
Magazine	Extended Mag: This weapon has a greatly increased magazine size, but reloads much slower.
Trait	Superconductor: When Arc Conductor is active, shots fired have the chance to become chain lightning and return ammo.
Stock	Short-Action Stock: This weapon is especially easy to grip. Greatly increases handling speed.

Graviton Lance

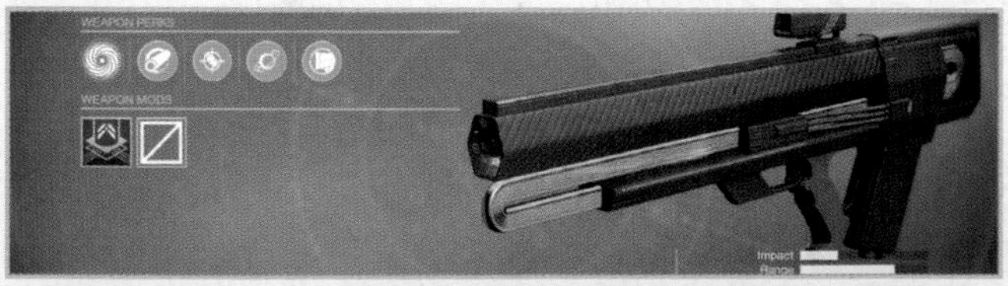

Weapon Type	Damage Type
Pulse Rifle	Void

Perks	
Intrinsic	Black Hole: Third shot of a burst rips a hole through spacetime, doing high damage and recoil with no fall-off.
Barrel	Hammer-Forged Rifling: Durable ranged barrel. Increases range.
Magazine	Accurized Rounds: This weapon can fire longer distances. Increases range.
Trait	Cosmology: Kills with this weapon cause enemy targets to detonate.
Stock	Fitted Stock: This stock makes the weapon stable but heavy. Increases stability. Improves recoil direction. Slightly decreases handling speed.

Skyburner's Oath

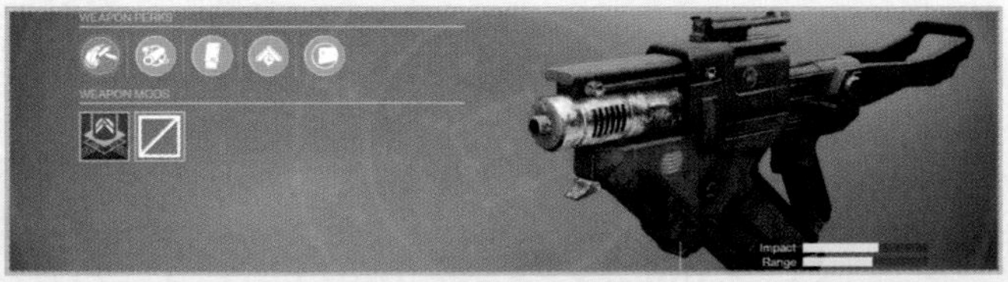

Weapon Type	Damage Type
Scout Rifle	Solar

Perks	
Intrinsic	Slug Rifle: This weapon fires Solar slugs that get stronger when aiming down sights.
Barrel	Extended Barrel: Weighty barrel extension. Increases range. Decreases handling speed.
Magazine	Extended Mag: This weapon has a greatly increased magazine size, but reloads much slower.
Trait	For the Empire: This weapon is Full Auto, does extra damage to Cabal, and penetrates Phalanx Shields.
Stock	Short-Action Stock: This weapon is especially easy to grip. Greatly increases handling speed.

Sunshot

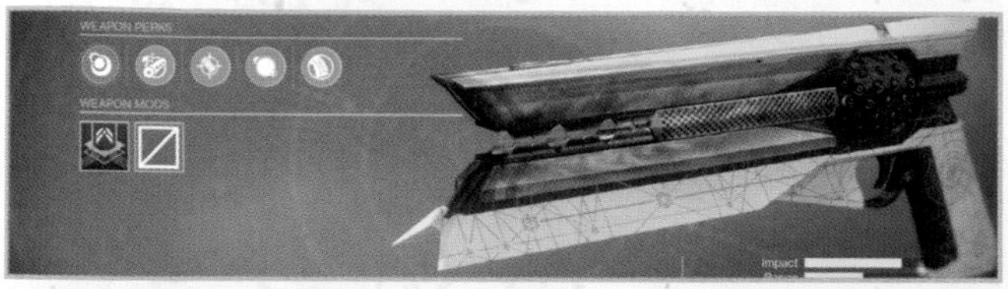

Weapon Type	Damage Type
Hand Cannon	Solar

Perks	
Intrinsic	Sunburn: This weapon fires explosive roungs and highlights targets that take damage from Sunshot.
Barrel	Chambered Compensator: Stable barrel attachment. Increases stability. Improves recoil and direction. Slightly decreases handling speed.
Magazine	Accurized Rounds: This weapon can fire longer distances. Increases range.
Trait	Sun Blast: Targets killed with Sunshot explode in Solar energy.
Grip	Textured Grip:ofriction on this weapon's grip is particularly strong. Greatly increases handling speed. Slightly decreases stability.

Exotic Power Weapons

D.A.R.C.I.

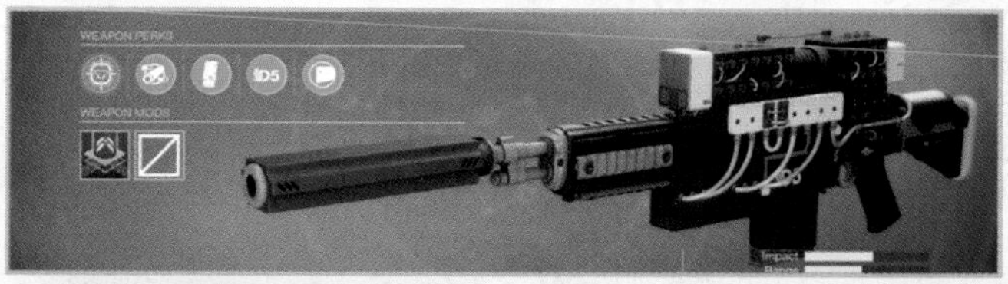

Weapon Type	Damage Type
Sniper Rifle	Arc

Perks	
Intrinsic	Personal Assistant: Aim at an enemy to view its health and other critical information on the scope.
Barrel	Extended Barrel: Weighty barrel extension. Increases range. Decreases handling speed.
Magazine	Extended Mag: This weapon has a greatly increased magazine size, but reloads much slower.
Trait	Target Acquired: When Personal Assistant is active, this weapon has better target acquisition and deals more Precision damage.
Stock	Short-Action Stock: This weapon is especially easy to grip. Greatly increases handling speed.

Merciless

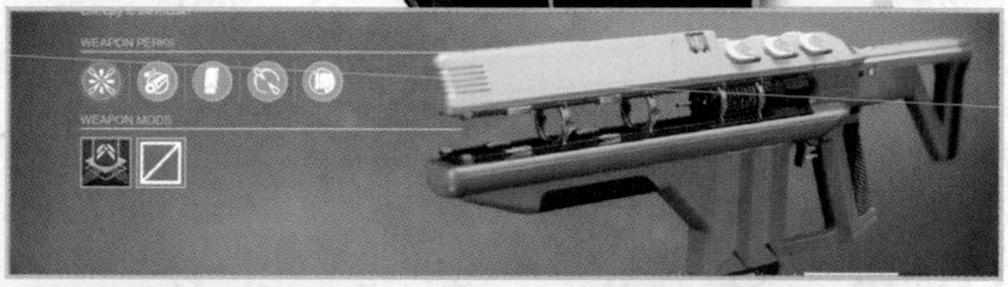

Weapon Type	Damage Type
Fusion Rifle	Solar

Perks	
Intrinsic	Conserve Momentum: Non-lethal hits with projectiles make this weapon charge faster until its wielder gets a kill.
Barrel	Chambered Compensator: Stable barrel attachment. Increases stability. Improves recoil direction. Slightly decreases handling speed.
Magazine	Extended Mag: This weapon has a greatly increased magazine size, but reloads much slower.
Trait	Impetus: Reloading immediately after a kill increases weapon damage for a short time.
Stock	Fitted Stock: This stock makes the weapon stable but heavy. Increases stability. Improves recoil direction. Slightly decreases handling speed.

Legend of Acrius

Weapon Type	Damage Type
Shotgun	Arc

Perks	
Intrinsic	Shock Blast: This weapon fires blasts of high-damage Arc energy that overpenetrates enemies.
Barrel	Full Bore: Barrel optimized for distance. Greatly increases range. Decreases stability. Slightly decreases handling speed.
Magazine	Accurized Rounds: This weapon can fire longer distances. Increases range.
Trait	Long March: Detect enemies on your radar from farther away.
Stock	Fitted Stock: This stock makes the weapon stable but heavy. Increases stability. Improves recoil direction. Slightly decreases handling speed.

The Prospector

Weapon Type	Damage Type
Grenade Launcher	Arc

Perks	
Intrinsic	Excavation: Hold [Fire] to fire grenades. Release to detonate all live grenades simultaneously.
Launcher Barrel	Volatile Launch: This weapon is optimized for an especially explosive payload. Greatly increased blast radius. Slightly decreases handling speed. Slightly decreases projectile speed.
Magazine	Augmented Drum: Heavy, high capacity drum. Greatly increases magazine size. Greatly decreases reload speed.
Trait	Full Auto Trigger System: Holding down the trigger will fire this weapon at full auto.
Stock	Hand-Laid Stock: This weapon is optimized for recoil control. Increases stability.

Tractor Cannon

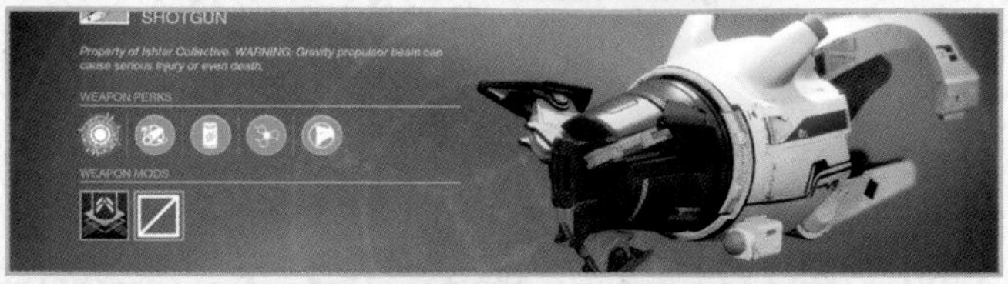

Weapon Type	Damage Type
Shotgun	Void

Perks	
Intrinsic	Repulsor Force: This weapon fires a powerful impulse to push enemies away.
Barrel	Extended Barrel: Weighty barrel extension. Increases range. Decreases handling speed.
Battery	Particle Repeater: Constrains recoil for every bolt. Increases stability.
Trait	The Scientific Method: Damaging an opponent temporarily increases speed and handling.
Stock	Composite Stock: This weapon has a versatile dual-purpose stock. Slightly increases stability. Slightly increases handling speed.

The Wardcliff Coil

Weapon Type	Damage Type
Rocket Launcher	Arc

Perks	
Intrinsic	Mad Scientist: This weapon fires a volley of rockets.
Launcher Barrel	Volatile Launch: This weapon is optimized for an especially explosive payload. Greatly increased blast radius. Slightly decreases handling speed. Slightly decreases projectile speed.
Magazine	Extended Mag: This weapon has a greatly increased magazine size, but reloads much slower.
Trait	Mechanized Autoloader: This weapon automatically reloads on ammo pickup.
Stock	Composite Stock: This weapon has a versatile dual-purpose stock. Slightly increases stability. Slightly increases handling speed.

Armor

Your equipped armor determines how fast you move, how much damage you can survive, and how quickly you recover lost health. Finding the proper balance of Mobility, Resilience, and Recovery isn't always easy, but it's definitely important.

During your adventures, you'll encounter a wide variety of armor pieces. Although you'll find a few one-off pieces, most of the items you collect will belong to various armor sets. At lower levels, your choices are fairly limited.

However, as you gain Experience and Power, you'll come to rely on armor that provides noticeable benefits and a bit of customization.

The armor sets in this section are separated by Class, and arranged in the order you're most likely to encounter them. As with the weapons, likely sources are listed. Make sure you check out the Exotic armor pieces available to your class. They're hard to come by, and you can only equip one Exotic armor piece at a time, but a lucky find can have dramatic effects.

Titan Armor

Titan Armor Sets

Mobile Titan Armor: Additional Mobility at the cost of shield strength
Restorative Titan Armor: Improved Recovery with a balance of Mobility and Resilience
Heavy Titan Armor: Additional Resilience at the cost of Mobility

Set Name	Rarity	Intrinsic Perk	Source
LEVELING SETS			
Refugee	Common	–	Drop
Renegade	Common	–	Drop
Fieldplate Type 10	Uncommon	–	Drop
Firebreak Field	Uncommon	–	Drop
Fortress Field	Uncommon	–	Drop
Atgeir 2T1	Uncommon	–	Drop
Legion-Bane	Rare	Restorative Titan Armor	Drop
Primal Siege	Rare	Restorative Titan Armor	Drop
ENDGAME SETS			
RPC Valiant	Rare	Restorative Titan Armor	Drop
Hardcase	Rare	Restorative Titan Armor	Drop
Wildwood	Legendary	Heavy Titan Armor	Devrim Rep (EDZ)
Lost Pacific	Legendary	Mobile Titan Armor	Sloane Rep (Titan)
Exodus Down	Legendary	Heavy Titan Armor	Failsafe Rep (Nessus)
Gensym Knight	Legendary	Restorative Titan Armor	Asher Rep (Io)
The Shelter in Place	Legendary	Heavy Titan Armor	Zavala Rep (Tower)
Phoenix Strife Type 0	Legendary	Restorative Titan Armor	Shaxx Rep (Tower)
Noble Constant Type 2	Legendary	Heavy Titan Armor	Ikora Rep (Tower)
Retro-Grade TG2	Legendary	Restorative Titan Armor	Drop
Devatation Complex	Legendary	Mobile Titan Armor	Drop
Kerak Type 2	Legendary	Restorative Titan Armor	Drop

Exotic Titan Armor: Head

Insurmountable Skullfort

Intrinsic Perk: Transfusion Matrix

Kills with Arc melee abilities trigger health regeneration and restore Melee energy.

Mask of the Quiet One

Intrinsic Perk: Dreaded Visage

Grants ability energy when damaged, and health regeneration when inflicting Void damage.

Exotic Titan Armor: Arms

ACD/0 Feedback Fence

Intrinsic Perk: Fury Conductors

Melee kills build up explosive energy within the ACD/0 Feedback Fence. Being struck by a melee attack unleashes this energy in a devastating explosion.

Doom Fang Pauldron
Intrinsic Perk: Horns of Doom
Shield Bash melee kills recharge Shield Throw. Melee Ability kills recharge Sentinel Shield Super

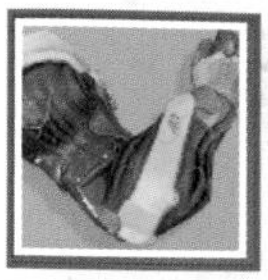

Synthocepts
Intrinsic Perk: Biotic Enhancements
Increased melee lunge range. Improved damage when surrounded.

Exotic Titan Armor: Chest

Actium War Rig
Intrinsic Perk: Auto-Loading Link
Steadily reloads a portion of your equipped Auto Rifle's magazine from reserves.

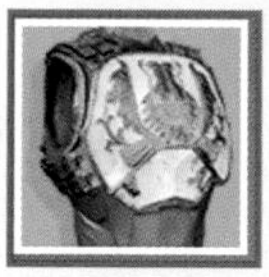

Crest of Alpha Lupi
Intrinsic Perk: Survival Well
Generates and additional Orb of Light from Supers and a healing pulse when Barricade is activated.

Hallowfire Heart
Intrinsic Perk: Sunfire Furnace
Greatly improves the recharge rate of your Solar abilities while Hammer of Sol is charged.

Exotic Titan Armor: Legs

Dunemarchers
Intrinsic Perk: Linear Actuators
Increases sprint speed. Springing builds up a static charge. After melee attacking an enemy, that charge will chain damage to nearby enemies.

Lion Rampant
Intrinsic Perk: Jump Jets
Provides additional aerial maneuverability.

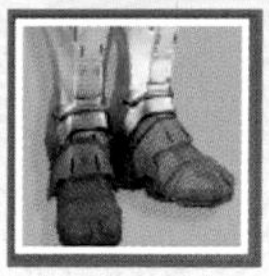

Peacekeepers
Intrinsic Perk: Mecha Holster
Reloads stowed Submachine Guns and allows you to ready them instantly.

Hunter Armor

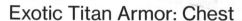

Hunter Armor Sets

Mobile Hunter Armor: Additional Mobility at the cost of Resilience
Survivalist Hunter: Armor Improved Resilience and Recovery
Heavy Hunter Armor: Improved Resilience

Set Name	Rarity	Intrinsic Perk	Source
LEVELING SETS			
Refugee	Common	–	Drop
Wastelander	Common	–	Drop
Makeshift Suit	Uncommon	–	Drop
Scavenger Suit	Uncommon	–	Drop
Kit Fox	Uncommon	–	Drop
Mechanik	Uncommon	–	Drop
War Mantis	Rare	Survivalist Hunter Armor	Drop
Mythos Hack	Rare	Survivalist Hunter Armor	Drop
ENDGAME SETS			
Shadow Specter	Rare	Survivalist Hunter Armor	Drop
The Outlander's	Rare	Survivalist Hunter Armor	Drop
Wildwood	Legendary	Heavy Hunter Armor	Devrim Rep (EDZ)
Lost Pacific	Legendary	Mobile Hunter Armor	Sloane Rep (Titan)
Exodus Down	Legendary	Heavy Hunter Armor	Failsafe Rep (Nessus)
Gensym Knight	Legendary	Survivalist Hunter Armor	Asher Rep (Io)
The Took Offense	Legendary	Heavy Hunter Armor	Zavala Rep (Tower)
Swordfight 4.1	Legendary	Mobile Hunter Armor	Shaxx Rep (Tower)
Frumious	Legendary	Mobile Hunter Armor	Ikora Rep (Tower)
Dead End Cure 2.1	Legendary	Heavy Hunter Armor	Drop
Road Complex AA1	Legendary	Survivalist Hunter Armor	Drop
Errant Knight 1.0	Legendary	Mobile Hunter Armor	Drop

Exotic Hunter Armor: Head

Celestial Nighthawk
Intrinsic Perk: Hawkeye Hack
Modifies Golden Gun to fire a single, high damage shot. Victims killed by the shot explode.

Foetracer
Intrinsic Perk: Relentless Tracker
Visually marks targeted enemies.

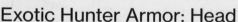

Knucklehead Radar
Intrinsic Perk: Upgraded Sensor Pack
Provides radar while aiming.

Exotic Hunter Armor: Arms

Mechaneer's Tricksleeves
Intrinsic Perk: Spring-Loaded Mounting
Increases Sidearm ready and reload speed.

Young Ahamkara's Spine
Intrinsic Perk: Wish-Dragon Teeth
Increases Tripmine Grenade duration and marks enemies damaged by the blast.

Exotic Hunter Armor: Chest

The Dragon's Shadow
Intrinsic Perk: Quicksilver Mail
Grants increased movement and weapon handling speed for a short time after Dodging.

Lucky Raspberry
Intrinsic Perk: Probability Matrix
Increases the chaining capabilities of Arc Bolt Grenade and has a chance to recharge it each time it deals damage.

Raiden Flux
Intrinsic Perk: Synapse Junctions
Quick successive attacks with Arc Staff increase its damage output and duration.

Exotic Hunter Armor: Legs

Lucky Pants
Intrinsic Perk: Illegally Modded Holster
Increases Hand Cannon ready speed and initial accuracy.

Orpheus Rig
Intrinsic Perk: Uncanny Arrows
Provides ability energy for each enemy tethered by Shadowshot anchors.

STOMP-EE5
Intrinsic Perk: Hydraulic Boosters
Increases sprint speed and slide distance. Improves jump.

Warlock Armor

Warlock Armor Sets
Mobile Warlock Armor: Additional Mobility at the cost of Resilience
Restorative Warlock Armor: Improved Recovery with a balance of Mobility and Resilience
Heavy Warlock Armor: Additional Resilience at the cost of Mobility

Set Name	Rarity	Intrinsic Perk	Source
LEVELING SETS			
Refugee	Common	–	Drop
Aspirant	Common	–	Drop
Cry Defiance	Uncommon	–	Drop
Vector Home	Uncommon	–	Drop
Raven Shard	Uncommon	–	Drop
Cosmic Wind III	Uncommon	–	Drop
Atonement Tau	Rare	Restorative Warlock Armor	Drop
Aurora Snow III	Rare	Restorative Warlock Armor	Drop
ENDGAME SETS			
Chiron's Cure	Rare	Restorative Warlock Armor	Drop
Farseeker's	Rare	Restorative Warlock Armor	Drop
Wildwood	Legendary	Heavy Warlock Armor	Devrim Rep (EDZ)
Lost Pacific	Legendary	Heavy Warlock Armor	Sloane Rep (Titan)
Exodus Down	Legendary	Restorative Warlock Armor	Failsafe Rep (Nessus)
Gensym Knight	Legendary	Restorative Warlock Armor	Asher Rep (Io)
Xenos Vale IV	Legendary	Heavy Warlock Armor	Zavala Rep (Tower)
Ankaa Seeker IV	Legendary	Mobile Warlock Armor	Shaxx Rep (Tower)
Ego Talon IV	Legendary	Mobile Warlock Armor	Ikora Rep (Tower)
Heiro Camo	Legendary	Restorative Warlock Armor	Drop
High-Minded Complex	Legendary	Heavy Warlock Armor	Drop
Philomath	Legendary	Restorative Warlock Armor	Drop

Exotic Warlock Armor: Head

Crown of Tempests
Intrinsic Perk: Conduction Tines
Arc ability kills increase the recharge rate of your Arc abilities.

Eye of another World
Intrinsic Perk: Cerebral Uplink
Highlights priority targets and improves the regeneration speed of your Grenade, Melee, and Rift abilities.

Nezarec's Sin
Intrinsic Perk: Abyssal Extractors
Void Damage kills grant ability energy.

Skull of Dire Ahamkara
Intrinsic Perk: Actual Grandeur
Provides additional damage resistance during Nova Bomb. Nova Bomb kills grant Super energy.

Exotic Warlock Armor: Arms

Karnstein Armlets
Intrinsic Perk: Vampire's Caress
Melee attacks grant health recovery and ability energy.

Sunbracers
Intrinsic Perk: Helium Spirals
Increases the duration of Solar Grenades and grants grenade energy on melee hits.

Winter's Guile
Intrinsic Perk: Warlord's Sigil
Eliminating enemies with melee attacks increases your melee damage.

Exotic Warlock Armor: Chest

Starfire Protocol
Intrinsic Perk: Fusion Harness
Provides an additional Fusion Grenade charge. Fusion Grenade kills grant Rift energy.

Wings of Sacred Dawn
Intrinsic Perk: Dawnstar Tome
When Dawnblade is equipped, aiming weapons while in the air suspends you in midair for a short time. Precision hits extend this effect's duration.

Exotic Warlock Armor: Legs

Lunafaction Boots
Intrinsic Perk: Alchemical Etchings
Your Rifts gain the additional ability to automatically reload allies' weapons.

Transversive Steps
Intrinsic Perk: Strange Protractor
While sprinting, movement speed is increased and energy weapons are automatically reloaded.

Trophies and Achievements

Claiming all of the available Trophies/Achievements requires a great deal of time, effort, and a character belonging to each of the game's three classes.

More tasks are sure to be introduced down the line, but you've got plenty of items to cross off your list before then.

Icon	Name	Description	Score Value	
			PS4	Xbox One
	Long and Winding Road	Reach level 20.	Silver	40
	Zavala's Lieutenant	Acquire each Titan subclass.	Gold	60
	Cayde's Pathfinder	Acquire each Hunter subclass.	Gold	60
	Ikora's Protégé	Acquire each Warlock subclass.	Gold	60
	The People's Hero	Complete a Heroic public event.	Silver	40
	Show Me What You Got	Complete Shaxx's Call to Arms.	Gold	80
	In A Flash	Complete a Flashpoint.	Gold	80
	Heart of Darkness	Complete a Nightfall strike.	Gold	80
	The Life Exotic	Collect 15 exotic weapons or armor.	Gold	120
	Challenge Accepted	Complete 30 challenges.	Gold	80
	Belly Of The Beast	Complete the Leviathan raid.	Gold	100
	The Prestige	Complete the Leviathan raid or a Nightfall strike on Prestige difficulty.	Gold	120
	Lest Ye Be Judged	Encounter an Emissary from beyond.	Gold	80

DESTINY 2

Written by David S. J. Hodgson and Nick Von Esmarch
Maps created by Loren Gilliland

Credits

Book Designers
Brent Gann
Dan Caparo

Production Designer
Wil Cruz

Production
Liz Stenberg

Copy Editor
Angie Griffin

Prima Games Staff

VP & Publisher
Mike Degler

Editorial Manager
Tim Fitzpatrick

Design and Layout Manager
Tracy Wehmeyer

Licensing
Paul Giacomotto

Digital Publishing
Julie Asbury
Shaida Boroumand

Operations Manager
Stacey Ginther

DK/Prima Games, a division of Penguin Random House LLC
6081 East 82nd Street, Suite #400
Indianapolis, IN 46250

ISBN: Collector's Edition 9780744018486
Standard Edition 9780744018479

Printing Code: The rightmost double-digit number is the year of the book's printing; the rightmost single-digit number is the number of the book's printing. For example, 17-1 shows that the first printing of the book occurred in 2017.

20 19 18 17 4 3 2 1

001-308795-Aug/2017

Printed in the USA.

Acknowledgments

David S. J. Hodgson

Cheers to Chris and all at Prima for their patience during this project. Thanks to my loving wife Melanie; Mum, Dad, and Ian; Loki; Cam, Louie and Clara; The Moon Wiring Club, Laibach, Kraftwerk, The Benningtons; and S, for Shuggoths: Shapeless congeries of protoplasmic bubbles, that crush, devour and kill, all for a thrill. Causing, oh, just no end of troubles.

Nick Von Esmarch

Thanks to David and Loren, of course. On-site work is always a challenge, but I think we made the most of it. Thanks to everyone at Prima, but especially Chris, Brent, Wil, and Tim. This was a big project on a tight schedule, and I know it meant a lot of long hours for everyone involved. Thanks to everyone at Bungie for being incredibly gracious hosts, and for all of the work done during and outside of our visits. Special thanks to Lorraine, Katie, Jim, Tristen, and Tucker. Super-massive thanks to Blake for some impressive (and much appreciated) hero moments, along with Tim for what I have to imagine was some really labor-intensive footage-type stuff. And, of course, my deepest thanks go to Dobbs, for being an absolute champion of everything, ever. No foolin', Dobbs; I've never met a single human who's better at what they do. Thanks to all of the Bungie folks who took the time to speak with us and/or assemble much-needed assets. Far too many to list here, but I have to give special thanks to Stephanie, and to Lars, Victor, and everyone who indulged my shamelessly self-serving questions during PVP playtests. Now that the book is wrapped, I intend to put all of your advice to good use in the Crucible. Back home, thanks to all of my family and friends. Special thanks to Kurt and Damien for absorbing my nonsense on a daily basis, and to my beautiful Joy for keeping me alive through the worst of it. I don't know what I'd do without you.

Loren Gilliland

As a Guardian it has been a great pleasure and honor to have been given the opportunity to work with the brilliant, talented, and dedicated members of Bungie. It is obvious when setting foot into the studio that everyone is passionate and driven to provide an exceptional experience. I want to give particular praise to Jonathon Dobbs who has been of incalculable assistance throughout the entirety of our stay at Bungie. Thank you Dobbs! Thank you to Blake Battle for flying our ship, securing meetings, and ensuring productivity. Thank you to Lorraine McLees for the invaluable art direction. Thank you so very much to leaders of our Fireteam, Katie Lennox and Tristen Nelson, for shepherding us through this process. Thank you to the rowdy test team for all the assists. I applaud the engineers and programmers for how well the engine of this game runs. The maps contained within this guide are a testament to how well this engine handles everything that is thrown at it without so much as a hiccup. Thank you to all the various members of the Bungie teams who've provided time and energy in fulfilling our requests. Finally, thank you to my wife D'dee and my little lights for joining me with this obsession. If you appreciate the maps let Prima and Bungie know! I hope to make you many more! See you out there Guardians.

—The Cartographer